THE MOTHER OF GOD

"I love you..
If you knew how much I love you,
you would cry for joy."

Imprimatur

Nicola Rotunno, Archbishop

+ Nicol

Passo Corese, 14.9.1998

Exaltation of the Holy Cross

"PRAY, PRAY, PRAY"

Contributors:
Text: Sister Maria Gabriella of the Annunciation, CMOP
Spiritual Adviser: Father Gianni Sgreva
Translated from the Italian text by: Sr. Maria Thérèsè
dell'Incarnazione CMOP

Copyright © Editrice Shalom
ISBN 8 8 - 8 6 6 1 6 - 1 6 - 3
08.12.2003 Solemnity of the Immaculate Conception
To order this book please quote the code number 8148

SHALOM

For further info:

Editrice Shalom

Via San Giuseppe, 57
60020 Camerata Picena (An)

Tel. 0039 71 74 50 440

Further information may be obtained
and orders may be made by tele-
phoning the following number from
Monday to Friday 9 a.m. to 7 p.m.

Fax 071. 74 50 140

(This line is open 24 hours a day
including Sundays and bank-holidays)

e-mail: ordina@editriceshalom.it
http://www.editriceshalom.it

Dedication

Thank you, Mary, because you continue to call us to conversion and invite us to return to God, guiding us in our journey of faith and prayer with motherly concern. We wish to dedicate this book. To you and to Saint Joseph, your beloved spouse. We would like to offer all those who are already following a path of prayer, and also to those who wish to embark on Such a journey, either individually or in groups.

Help us, Mary, to walk towards Jesus day by day in simplicity and humility, not seeking to satisfy our own desires, but seeking rather to fulfil the will of God the Father, in order to bear witness to Christ in every thought, word and action, without shame or false human respect, trying to please God at all times rather than looking for recognition from other human beings. Help us to be attentive to the needs of our neighbours, to treat them with gentleness and patience, and to accept them, especially those who disturb us most because they do not live up to our expectations, and also those who live with us and with whom we may find it difficult to communicate.

Help us to live a life of love, for love of Jesus, even when this calls for a great effort on our part and does not offer us human gratification. May our life's journey of faith not stop at the first difficulties which we meet, but continue, day by day, thanks to your motherly help, in perseverance and faith, even in moments of trial, until we accomplish all that you desire for each one of us: namely the salvation of our souls and the souls of others, as well as our true happiness in this life and in the next.

We ask you therefore, to bless this book and to use it for the fulfilment of your plans.

Letter

of Monsignor Nicola Rotunno, former Apostolic Nuncio and Bishop

> *"The Lord my God refreshes me,*
> *he leads me in the path of righteousness for*
> *his name's sake" (ref. Ps 22).*

25th of June, 1992

Men and women of today, perhaps more so than in the recent past, feel tired, discouraged and disturbed by the level of material well-being, by their riches, be they great or small, which they have created with enormous sacrifice in the hope that the possession of more and more things, ever bigger and more costly will bring them peace, serenity, joy and love. We discover instead that what the Word of God has always affirmed through out the centuries is true: money is the root of all evil. Today the scandal of bribery gives the impression that public and private morality has degenerated. Organized crime increasingly threatens the possibility of living together democratically. Drugs sow death among young people, and the plague of AIDS creates fear. Honest people (and I believe we are in the majority), that is, those who are conscious of not being holy and immaculate, now find themselves in an arid desert devoid of human values, lost, without strength, and not knowing which road to take. And yet they are certain of having a clear conscience. Believers in Christ, the Son of God and Son of the Blessed Virgin. Mother, Mary, will know how to find the voice of God, in this book Pray, pray, pray which gives us solace and shows us the right path. In the light of the Second Ecumenical Vatican Council (Dogmatic Constitution on the Church, Lumen Gentium, No.67) this book promotes devotion towards the Blessed Virgin, holds in high esteem the practice and exercises of devotion to her, recommended throughout the centuries by the Magistery of the Church, and abstains from fanatical exaggeration as well as from narrow-mindedness. This book succeds in reminding the faithful that true devotion does not consist in sterile and passing sentiments, nor in a vain belief, but arises rather from true faith and encourages us to imitate Mary's virtues. I wish this book *Pray, pray, pray* a renewed and great success, because it describes the "Brave Virgin" (Christi Fidelis Laici, No.64) who, pointing to her Son Jesus, can respond to the fears of his disciples who ask, "Lord, we do not know where you are going, so how can we know the way?" (Jn 14:5). Mary points to the "narrow door" and she urges us to enter through this door (ref. Lk 13:24). [Furthermore], This book helps us to hear the voice of Jesus which assures his disciples whose mind are closed" (Mk 6,52): "Courage! It is I! Do not be afraid!" (Mk 6:30). Our generation is sometimes a "faithless generation" (Mk 9:19). People do not understand the signs of the times and are afraid of questioning Jesus (ref. Mk 9:13). I am certain that the book *Pray, pray, pray* and the wonderful cover (which I hope will not be changed because of its universal enchantment created by the image of Mary) will help many, even unbelievers, to discover that the Bible is the Word of God, the Eucharist is the Bread of the Church, charity is the bond of perfection, even when, because of the weakness of our faith, we have "big quarrels" which cause separations between those, who like Paul and Barnabas, are unable to live in communion with each other in a community and, while continuing to be Church and aspiring to sanctity, sail to their respective shores (ref. Ac 15:36-41). "The Catholic Church encourages the school of perfection; advises everyone to rise higher, and comes to the aid of man and woman [a like], regardless of what sufferings they may have in both of body and soul. In each person the Word becomes flesh and the flesh becomes the Word" (see Juitton, Limpu, Desclee de Brouwer, 1991). Every page of *Pray, pray, pray* acts as an antidote, allowing a certain relaxation of the tension which can arise from the relationships in our lives. Singing together with Mary, we will surely come closer to Jesus, even though the worse part which each of us possesses has us "only the capacity to do evil" (ref. Rm 7:21) so that "the good thing I want to do I never do" (Rm 7:19).

+ Nico Schum

Preface

I gladly accept the invitation to write the preface for this collection of prayers entitled Pray, pray, pray. It is a help offered to those who, called by the maternal invitation of Mary, Mother of the Church, wish to complete their participation in the liturgical prayer of the Church, with the search for continuous prayer which, when said at particular times of the day, will then touch all expressions of Christian life. It is an unpretentious book: it will be loved and welcomed by those simple and humble souls who feel that they are beginners in a life of prayer. In this way, they are sure that, by living the mystery of the relationship with the Father in the secrecy of the inner room, or with other brothers and sisters in prayer groups, they can benefit from the revelation and knowledge of the Son from which the wise and learned of this world are excluded. In this book, one finds no aid for liturgical prayer (the Mass and the Sacraments) but precious help towards popular devotion, the expression of the Christian soul which was the root of culture and tradition, widely experienced by our Christian people before ill-omened winds of secularization attempted to shake the foundations of Christian thoughts and actions. These prayers can be used by everyone, by a cardinal, a bishop, a priest, a fashionable theologian or lay person who has not forgotten how he learnt to pray on his mother's lap when she taught him to say the Hail Mary, the Our Father, the Angel of God, not forgetting the faithful departed with the "Eternal Rest". The Second Vatican Council did not discourage the pious exercises of popular Christian devotion, which are, on the contrary, intended to be in harmony with the ecclesiastical liturgy. The Pastoral Note on Liturgical Renewal in Italy by the Episcopal Commission for the Liturgy echoes this idea. In this document we also read that "the expressions of devotion and faith of popular tradition are the object of a rediscovery everywhere today and this is certainly a providential fact....they express an ardour of faith, a passion of love, an acceptance of dependence, a clinging to religious traditions which alone constitute authentic values and fertile possibilities of evangelization... We are now faced with a whole field of work: that of harmonizing liturgy and popular devotion, inspiring the latter by the former and giving life to the former by the latter without exclusivism and preclusion, but also without merging or confusing the two forms of devotion; Christian people will always need both, and we must leave all the roads which lead to the heart of man open to God" (Pastoral Note, No.18).

These prayers take us back to the pure natural Christian environment of which the director Ermanno Olmi gave us an unforgettable example some years ago in his film The Tree of Wooden Shoes: a sequence of rural images, in which the earth, plants and animals appear to share in genuine expressions of the faith of humanity and the Christian family from within their being.

The theme which characterizes this collection of prayers is the presence of Mary, Queen of Peace, her repeated invitations to prayer, her teaching which leads "those who welcome her call" to transform their life into prayer. It certainly echoes that which the Holy Father John Paul II affirms in the encyclical Dominum et Vivificantem, N.65: "Our difficult era has a special need for prayer... in these years an increasing number of people, in movements and groups, ever more widespread, put prayer in the first place and seek the renewal of their spiritual life in prayer. This is a significant and consoling symptom, as from such an experience a real contribution has been made to the renewal of prayer among the faithful who have been helped to consider the Holy Spirit more as the one who gives rise to a deep yearning for holiness in the heart of man". We hope that this small contribution may also constitute a small learning manual, which will be useful to those who wish to follow the Mother of the Church who, says to us for the sake of the renewal of the same Church: "Pray, pray, pray".

Father Gianni Sgreva

## Part One

Everyday
Prayers

- **PRINCIPAL TRUTHS OF THE CHRISTIAN FAITH**

- **PRAYERS OF THE CHRISTIAN FAITH**

- **MORNING PRAYERS**

- **PRAYERS TO BE SAID THROUGHOUT THE DAY**

- **EVENING PRAYERS**

PRINCIPAL TRUTHS OF THE CHRISTIAN FAITH

THE TEN COMMANDMENTS

"Master, what must I do to obtain eternal life?" Jesus replied to the young man who asked him this question by saying that there is "one alone who is good" (Mt 19:17), who is goodness itself, and the origin of everything that is good. He added, "If you wish to enter into life, keep the commandments," and proceeded to indicate the commandments which concern love of one's neighbour: "You shall not kill, you shall not commit adultery, you shall not steal, you shall not bear false witness, honour your father and your mother" (ref. Mt 19: 16-19). When the following question was put to Jesus: "Master, which is the greatest commandment of the Law?" (Mt 22:36), Jesus answered: "Love the Lord your God with all your heart, with all your soul, and with all your mind. This is the greatest and the first commandment. The second one is similar to the first: love your neighbour as yourself. On these two commandments hang the whole Law, and the Prophets also" (Mt 22:37-40).

I   **I am the Lord your God;**
   you shall not have other gods before me.

II   You shall not take the name of the Lord your God in vain.

III   Remember to keep holy the Sabbath Day.

IV   Honour your father and your mother.

V   You shall not kill.

VI   You shall not commit adultery.

VII You shall not steal.

VIII You shall not bear false witness against your neighbour.

IX   You shall not covet your neighbour's wife.

X   You shall not covet your neighbour's goods.

THE SEVEN SACRAMENTS
OF THE CHURCH

The sacraments are efficacious signs of grace, instituted by Jesus Christ, to sanctify us.

Baptism
Confirmation
The Holy Eucharist
Reconciliation or Penance
Anointing of the sick
Holy Orders
Marriage

THE PRECEPTS OF THE CHURCH

You shall attend Mass on Sundays and holy days of obligation.

You shall confess your sins at least once a year and you shall humbly receive your Creator in Holy Communion at least during the Easter season.

You shall keep holy the holy days of obligation.

You shall observe the prescribed days of fasting and abstinence.

The faithful also have the duty of providing for the material needs of the Church, each according to his abilities.

THE SEVEN GIFTS OF THE HOLY SPIRIT

Wisdom

Understanding

Counsel (Right judgement)

Fortitude (Courage)

Knowledge

Piety (Reverence)

Fear of the Lord (Wonder and awe in God's presence)

THE THREE THEOLOGICAL VIRTUES
Faith

Faith is the theological virtue by which we believe in God and believe all that He has revealed to us and that the Holy Church proposes for our belief because he is truth itself.

Hope

Hope is the theological virtue by which we desire the kingdom of heaven and eternal life as our happiness, placing our trust in Christ's promises and relying not on our own strength, but on the help of the grace of the Holy Spirit.

Charity

Charity is the theological virtue by which we love God above all things for his own sake, and our neighbour as ourselves for the love of God.

Charity is superior to all the virtues and "binds everything together in perfect harmony".

THE FOUR CARDINAL VIRTUES

Prudence

Prudence disposes the practical reason to discern in every circumstance one's true good and to choose the right means for achieving it.

Justice

Justice consists in the firm and constant will to give God and one's neighbour what is due to them.

Fortitude

Fortitude ensures firmness in difficulties and constancy in the pursuit of good.

Temperance

Temperance moderates the attraction of the pleasures of the senses and provides balance in the use of created goods.

BLASPHEMY AGAINST THE HOLY SPIRIT

(Sins against the Holy Spirit ref. CCC, 1864,1866)
Whoever blasphemes against the Holy Spirit never has forgiveness, but is guilty of an eternal sin.
There are no limits to the mercy of God, but anyone who deliberately refuses to accept his mercy by repenting, rejects the forgiveness of his sins and the salvation offered by the Holy Spirit. Such hardness of heart can lead to final impenitence and eternal loss. This sin blocks the person's route to Christ and the sinner puts himself outside the range of God's forgiveness. In this sense, the sins against the Holy Spirit cannot be forgiven.

Despair of salvation.
Presumption of saving oneself without merit.
Contestation of known truth.
Envying another's grace.
Obstinacy in sin.
Final impenitence.

THE SEVEN CORPORAL WORKS OF MERCY

Feeding the hungry.

Giving drink to the thirsty.

Clothing the naked.

Sheltering the homeless.

Visiting the sick.

Visiting the imprisoned.

Burying the dead.

THE SEVEN SPIRITUAL WORKS OF MERCY

Counselling the doubtful.

Instructing the ignorant.

Admonishing sinners.

Comforting the afflicted.

Forgiving offences.

Bearing wrongs patiently.

Praying for the living and the dead.

Sins that cry to heaven

Catechetical tradition recalls that there are "sins that cry to heaven":

Wilful murder (The blood of Abel).
Sin of impurity against nature (The sin of the Sodomites).
Injustice to the wage earner.
Ignoring the cry of the people oppressed in Egypt and that of the foreigner, the widow and the orphan.

The last judgement

Death
Judgement
Hell
Heaven

The seven capital sins and opposed virtues

Capital Sins	Opposed Virtues
•Pride	•Humility
•Covetousness	•Liberality
•Lust	•Chastity
•Anger	•Meekness
•Gluttony	•Temperance
•Envy	•Brotherly love
•Sloth	•Diligence

PRAYERS OF THE CHRISTIAN FAITH

THE SIGN OF THE CROSS

*In the name of the Father, and of the Son,
and of the Holy Spirit. Amen.*

OUR FATHER

Our Father, who art in heaven,
hallowed be thy name.
Thy kingdom come.
Thy will be done on earth, as it is in heaven.
Give us this day our daily bread,
and forgive us our trespasses,
as we forgive those who trespass against us,
and lead us not into temptation,
but deliver us from evil. **Amen.**

*Pater noster, qui es in cælis:
sanctificétur nomen tuum;
advéniat regnum tuum;
fiat volúntas tua, sicut in cælo et in terra.
Panem nostrum cotidiánum da nobis hódie;
et dimítte nobis débita nostra,
sicut et nos dimíttimus debitóribus nostris;
et ne nos indúcas in tentatiónem;
sed líbera nos a malo. **Amen.***

THE HAIL MARY

Traditional version
Hail Mary, full of grace,
the Lord is with thee;
Blessed art thou among women,
and blessed is the fruit of thy womb, Jesus.
Holy Mary, Mother of God,
pray for us sinners,
now and at the hour of our death. **Amen.**

Modern version
Hail Mary, full of grace,
the Lord is with you;
Blessed are you among women,
and blessed is the fruit of your womb, Jesus.
Holy Mary, Mother of God,
pray for us sinners,
now and at the hour of our death. **Amen.**

Ave, María, grátia plena,
Dóminus tecum;
benedicta tu in muliéribus,
et benedíctus fructus ventris tui, Iesus.
Sancta María, Mater Dei,
ora pro nobis peccatóribus
*nunc et in hora mortis nostræ. **Amen.***

THE GLORY BE (THE DOXOLOGY)

Glory be to the Father, and to the Son,
and to the Holy Spirit.
As it was in the beginning, is now,
and ever shall be, world without end. **Amen.**

*Glória Patri et Fílio
et Spíritui Sancto.
Sicut erat in principio, et nunc et semper,
et in sáecula saeculórum. Amen.*

HAIL HOLY QUEEN

Traditional Version
Hail, holy Queen, mother of mercy;
hail, our life, our sweetness and our hope!
To thee do we cry, poor banished children of Eve.
To thee do we send up our sighs, mourning
and weeping in this valley of tears.
Turn then, most gracious Advocate,
thine eyes of mercy towards us, and after this,
our exile, show unto us the blessed fruit
of thy womb, Jesus.
O clement, O loving, O sweet Virgin Mary.

Modern Version

Hail, holy Queen, mother of mercy;
hail, our life, our sweetness and our hope!
To you do we cry, poor banished children of Eve.
To you do we send up our sighs, mourning
and weeping in this valley of tears.
Turn then, most gracious Advocate,
your eyes of mercy towards us, and after this,
our exile, show unto us the blessed fruit
of your womb, Jesus.
O clement, O loving, O sweet Virgin Mary.

V. Pray for us, O holy Mother of God.
**R. That we may be made worthy of the
promises of Christ.**

Salve Regína, mater misericórdiæ:
vita, dulcédo et spes nostra, salve.
Ad te clamámus, éxsules filii Evæ.
Ad te suspirámus, geméntes et flentes
in hac lacrimárum valle.
Eia ergo, advocáta nostra,
illos tuos misericórdes óculos ad nos convérte.
Et Iesum, benedíctum fructum ventris tui,
nobis post hoc exsilium osténde.
O clemens, O pia, O dulcis Virgo Maria.

V. Ora pro nobis sancta Dei Génetrix.
R. Ut digni efficiámur promissiónibus Christi.

PRAYERS TO THE GUARDIAN ANGEL

O Angel of God, my guardian dear,
to whom God's love
commits me here,
ever this day (or night) be at my side,
to light and guard, to rule and guide. **Amen.**

Angel sent by God to guide me,
Be my light and walk beside me;
Be my guardian and protect me;
On the paths of life direct me.

ACT OF FAITH

O my God, I firmly believe that you are one God
in three divine Persons, Father, Son and Holy
Spirit; I believe that your divine Son became man
and died for our sins, and that he shall come to
judge the living and the dead.
I believe these and all the truths that the holy
Catholic Church teaches, because you have
revealed them, who can neither deceive nor be
deceived.
or
O my God, I believe in you and in all that your
Holy Church teaches because you have said it
And your word is true. You are the Christ, the Son
of the living God. You are my Lord and my God.
Lord, I believe, increase my faith.

ACT OF HOPE

O my God, I place my hope in You, because You are all powerful, most merciful, and faithful to Your promises. I hope to obtain the forgiveness of my sins, the grace of living a holy life and of a happy death, and to obtain life everlasting, through the merits of Jesus Christ, my Lord and Redeemer.

or

O my God, I put my hope in you Because I am sure of your promises. Deliver us, Lord, from every evil and grant us peace in our day, as we wait in joyful hope for the coming of our Saviour, Jesus Christ.

ACT OF LOVE

O my God, I love You with all my heart above all things, for You are infinite goodness and our eternal happiness; and for love of You, I will love my neighbour as myself, and forgive all the offences I have received. Lord, grant that I may love You ever more and more!

or

O my God, I love you with all my heart, with all my soul, and with all my strength. Lord, increase our love. Help us to love one another.

THE PROFESSION OF FAITH

1. The Apostles' Creed

I believe in God, the Father Almighty,
creator of heaven and earth.
I believe in Jesus Christ, his only Son, our Lord.
He was conceived by the power of the Holy Spirit
and born of the Virgin Mary.
He suffered under Pontius Pilate,
was crucified, died, and was buried.
He descended into hell.
On the third day he rose again.
He ascended into heaven,
and is seated at the right hand of the Father.
He will come again to judge the living
and the dead.
I believe in the Holy Spirit,
the holy Catholic Church,
the communion of saints,
the forgiveness of sins,
the resurrection of the body,
and the life everlasting.
Amen.

2. The Nicene Creed

The Creed of the Nicene Council (325A.D.) and Constantinople

We believe in one God, the Father, the Almighty, maker of heaven and earth, of all that is, seen and unseen. We believe in one Lord, Jesus Christ, the only Son of God, eternally begotten of the Father, God from God, Light from Light, true God from true God, begotten, not made, of one Being with the Father.

Through him all things were made. For us men and for our salvation he came down from heaven: *(all bow)* by the power of the Holy Spirit, he became incarnate from the Virgin Mary, and was made man. For our sake he was crucified under Pontius Pilate; he suffered death and was buried. On the third day he rose again in accordance with the Scriptures; he ascended into heaven and is seated at the right hand of the Father.

He will come again in glory to judge the living and the dead, and his kingdom will have no end. We believe in the Holy Spirit, the Lord, the giver of life, who proceeds from the Father and the Son. With the Father and the Son he is worshipped and glorified. He has spoken through the Prophets. We believe in one holy catholic and apostolic Church. We acknowledge one baptism for the forgiveness of sins. We look for the resurrection of the dead, and the life of the world to come.
Amen.

Renewal of baptismal promises

I reject Satan and all his works and all his empty promises.

I believe in God the Father Almighty, Creator of heaven and earth.

I believe in Jesus Christ, his only Son, our Lord, who was born of the Virgin Mary, was crucified, died, and was buried, rose from the dead and is now seated at the right hand of the Father.

I believe in the Holy Spirit, the holy Catholic Church, the communion of Saints, the forgiveness of sins, the resurrection of the body, and the life everlasting.

The Gloria

The Gloria is an ancient and venerable hymn which is sung during Mass and in which the Church, assembled by the Holy Spirit, glorifies and prays to God the Father and to the Son, the Lamb of the New Passover.

Glory to God in the highest,
and peace to his people on earth.

Lord God, heavenly King,
almighty God and Father,
we worship you,
we give you thanks,
we praise you for your glory.

Lord Jesus Christ, only Son of the Father,
Lord God, Lamb of God,
you take away the sin of the world:
have mercy on us;
you are seated at the right hand of the Father:
receive our prayer!

For you alone are the Holy One,
you alone are the Lord,
you alone are the Most High,
Jesus Christ,
with the Holy Spirit,
in the glory of God the Father.
Amen.

MORNING PRAYERS

In the name of the Father, and of the Son,
and of the Holy Spirit. Amen.

I ADORE YOU

O my God, I adore You, and I love You
with all my heart. I thank You for having
created me, and for showing me Your love.
Thank You for having kept me safe this night.
I offer You my actions of this day;
grant that they may all be according
to Your holy will and for Your greater glory.
Keep me from sin and all evil.
May Your grace be always with me
and with all those dear to me. **Amen.**

MORNING PRAYER TO GOD THE FATHER

Father in heaven, you love me,
You are with me night and day.
I want to love you always
In all I do and say.
I'll try to please you, Father,
Bless me through the day. **Amen.**

GOD OUR FATHER

O God our Father from whom all good comes, we thank you for the help you give us in our work. We pray to you for all those who work in factories, in mines, in the country, in offices, in schools, in hospitals, on the roads, on the seas, in the sky and at home. Guide our youth in their choice of vocations and professions, and may no one be without work. Grant that each one of us may carry out your will, working with courage and diligence, in joy and fraternal love.
Amen.

MORNING OFFERING TO JESUS

O Jesus, through the Immaculate Heart of Mary, Mother of the Church, I offer you my prayers, works, joys and sufferings of this day for all the intentions of your Sacred Heart, in union with the holy sacrifice of the Mass throughout the world, in thanksgiving for Your favours, in reparation for my sins, for the salvation of all humanity and in particular for the intentions of the Holy Father.
Amen.

MORNING OFFERING TO THE BLESSED VIRGIN MARY

O Mary, Mother of the Word Incarnate, our sweetest Mother we kneel at your feet as a new day dawns, another great gift from the Lord. We place in your hands and Heart all of our being. May we always be yours in will, thought, heart and body. We beseech you this day, in your maternal goodness, to create a new life in us, the life of your Son Jesus. O Queen of Heaven, we ask you to anticipate and to accompany with your motherly inspiration all our actions, even the smallest, so that everything may be pure and acceptable at the moment of the holy and immaculate sacrifice of the Mass. Make us holy, O good Mother, holy as Jesus commanded us to be, and as your Heart asks and ardently desires us to be. **Amen.**

I BLESS YOU, O FATHER

I bless you, o Father, at the beginning of this new day. Accept my praise and thanks for the gift of life and faith. By the strength of your Spirit, guide my plans and actions: grant that they may all be in accordance with your will. Keep me from being discouraged in my difficulties and protect me from all evil. Help me to be attentive to the needs of others. Protect my family with your love. **Amen.**

LORD JESUS

Lord Jesus, Son of the living God,
you who according to your Father's will
and by the works of the Holy Spirit
have given new life to the world by your death,
deliver me from all faults and all evil;
grant that I may always be faithful to your law
and that I may never be separated from you.
Amen.

O JESUS, POUR OUT YOUR BLESSING

O Jesus, pour out your blessing on the Holy Church, our Mother, and on our Holy Father the Pope, on the leaders of the government, on our country and on all her children. Sanctify our priests, comfort the missionaries, increase the fervour of religious orders, fortify the just, convert sinners, enlighten the unfaithful and the heretics, console the afflicted, give work and food to the poor, protect children, give joy to the elderly, defend the widows and orphans, grant peace and prosperity to all families, relieve the sick, assist the dying, free the souls in Purgatory and establish in all our hearts the sweet empire of your love!

THE BEATITUDES
(Mt 5:3-10; Lk 6:20-23)

How blessed are the poor in spirit:
the kingdom of Heaven is theirs.

Blessed are the gentle:
they shall have the earth as their inheritance.

Blessed are those who mourn:
they shall be comforted.

Blessed are those who hunger
and thirst for uprightness:
they shall have their fill.

Blessed are the merciful:
they shall have mercy shown them.

Blessed are the pure in heart:
they shall see God.

Blessed are the peacemakers:
they shall be recognized
as children of God.

Blessed are those who are persecuted
in the cause of uprightness:
the kingdom of heaven is theirs.

Prayer of St. Ignatius

Take, Lord, all my liberty. Receive my memory, my understanding, and my whole will. Whatever I have and possess, you have given me; to you, I restore it wholly and to your will I utterly surrender it for my direction. Give me the love of you only, with your grace, and I am rich enough; nor do I ask anything besides.

Teach us, good Lord, to serve you as you deserve;
to give and not to count the cost;
to fight and not to heed the wounds;
to toil, and not to seek for rest;
to labour and to ask for no reward, save that of knowing that we do your will;
through Jesus Christ our Lord.

THE ANGELUS

For centuries, Christian tradition has recited the Angelus, especially at noon, in honour of the Incarnation of the Son of God and also in honour of the Blessed Virgin, Mother of Christ and of humanity.

V. The Angel of the Lord declared unto Mary;
R. And she conceived by the Holy Spirit.
Hail Mary

V. Behold the handmaid of the Lord.
R. Be it done to me according to your (thy) word.
Hail Mary

V. And the Word was made Flesh,
R. And dwelt among us.
Hail Mary

V. Pray for us, O Holy Mother of God,
R. That we may be made worthy of the promises of Christ.

Let us pray.
Pour forth, we beseech you, O Lord, your grace into our hearts, that we, to whom the incarnation of Christ, your Son, was made known by the message of an angel, may by his passion and

cross, be brought to the glory of His Resurrection, through the same Christ, our Lord.

R. Amen.

or

(To be said by all)
Lord,
Fill our hearts with your love,
And as you revealed to us by an angel
The coming of your Son as man,
So lead us through his suffering and death
To the glory of his resurrection,
For he lives and reigns with you and the Holy Spirit,
One God, for ever an ever.
Amen.

May the Lord bless us, protect us from all evil, and lead us to life everlasting.
Amen.

The angelus (latin version)

V. Angelus Dómini nuntiávit Maríæ.
R. Et concépit de Spíritu Sancto.
Ave Maria

V. Ecce ancílla Dómini.
R. Fiat mihi secúndum verbum tuum.
Ave Maria

V. Et Verbum caro factum est.
R. Et habitavit in nobis.
Ave Maria

V. Ora pro nobis, sancta Dei Génetrix.
R. Ut digni efficiámur promissiónibus Christi.

Orémus.
Grátiam tuam, quáesumus, Dómine, méntibus nostris infúnde; ut qui, ángelo nuntiánte, Christi Fílii tui incarnatiónem cognóvimus, per passionem eius et crucem ad resurrectiónis glóriam perducámur.
Per eúndem Christum Dóminum nostrum.
R. Amen

Gloria Patri

Dóminus nos benedícat, et ab omni malo deféndat, et ad vitam perdúcat ætérnam. **Amen.**

REGINA CAELI

By Gregory V († 998)

The following prayer is said in lieu of the Angelus from noon of Holy Saturday to the eve of Trinity Sunday. It expresses the joy of Mary and of all Christians at the resurrection of the Lord.

V. Queen of heaven, rejoice! Alleluia.
R. For he whom you did merit to bear. Alleluia.

V. Has risen, as he said. Alleluia.
R. Pray for us to God. Alleluia.

V. Rejoice and be glad, O Virgin Mary. Alleluia.
R. For the Lord is truly risen. Alleluia.

Let us pray.
O God, who gave joy to the world through the resurrection of your Son our Lord Jesus Christ, grant, we beseech you, that through the intercession of the Virgin Mary, his Mother, we may obtain the joys of everlasting life, through the same Christ our Lord.
R. Amen.

SPIRITUAL COMMUNION

It is good to repeat this prayer often throughout the day

O my Jesus, I firmly believe that You are truly present in the most Holy Sacrament of the Altar. I love You above all things and I desire that You remain in my soul. Since I cannot receive you sacramentally at this moment, I beseech You most earnestly to come into my heart spiritually. Believing that You have already come, I embrace you and unite myself to You. I beseech You, do not permit that I may ever be separated from you.

(Brief pause)

Eternal Father, I offer you the most precious Blood of Jesus Christ in atonement for my sins, for the holy souls in Purgatory and for the needs of the Church.

THE BLESSING OF MOSES

This blessing contains the words which God Himself said to Moses (ref. 6: 24-26).

May the Lord bless you and keep you.
Amen.

May the Lord let his face shine upon you
and be gracious to you.
Amen.

May the Lord show you his face
and bring you peace.
Amen.

And may the blessing
of God the Father Almighty, Son and Holy Spirit
descend upon you and remain with you forever.
Amen.

GRACE BEFORE AND AFTER MEALS

Any of the proposed formulas may be used.

Grace at Meals
Bless us, O Lord, and these your gifts which we
are about to receive by your goodness, through
Christ our Lord. **Amen.**

or

Bless, Lord, this food you give us. As we eat it,
help us to think of those who are hungry, to be
sparing in satisfying our appetites, and thoughtful
of those who are still hungry, not just in ideas,
but in action for freedom, peace and justice.
Amen.

or

We give you thanks, almighty God, for these and
all your gifts which we have received through
Christ our Lord. **Amen.**

or

Bless us, O God, as we sit together.
Bless the food we eat today.
Bless the hands that made the food.
Bless us, O God. **Amen.**

After meals
After meals, we may recite the following simple prayer, say spontaneous prayers of thanksgiving or recite the Canticle of the Blessed Virgin Mary.

Thank you, God, for the food we have eaten.
Thank you, God, for all our friends.
Thank you, God, for everything.
Thank you, God. **Amen.**

THE MAGNIFICAT

The Canticle of Mary (Lk 1:46-55)

My soul glorifies the Lord,
my spirit rejoices in God, my Saviour.

He looks on his servant in her lowliness;
henceforth all ages will call me blessed.

The Almighty works marvels for me.
Holy is his name!

His mercy is from age to age,
on those who fear him.

He puts forth his arm in strength,
and scatters the proud-hearted.

He casts the mighty from their thrones
and raises the lowly.

He fills the starving with good things,
sends the rich away empty.

He protects Israel, his servant,
remembering his mercy,

The mercy promised to our fathers,
for Abraham and his sons for ever.

Glory be

TRUST IN PROVIDENCE *(Mt 6:24-34)*

"No one can be the slave of two masters: he will either hate the first and love the second, or be attached to the first and despise the second. You cannot be the slave both of God and of money.

That is why I am telling you not to worry about your life and what you are to eat, nor about your body and what you are to wear. Surely life is more than food, and the body more than clothing! Look at the birds in the sky. They do not sow or reap or gather into barns; yet your heavenly Father feeds them. Are you not worth much more than they are? Can any of you, however much you worry, add one single cubit to your span of life? And why worry about clothing?

Think of the flowers growing in the fields; they never have to work or spin; yet I assure you that not even Solomon in all his royal robes was clothed like one of these.

Now if that is how God clothes the wild flowers growing in the field which are there today and thrown into the furnace tomorrow, will he not much more look after you, you who have so little faith? So do not worry; do not say, 'What are we to eat? What are we to drink? What are we to wear?' It is the gentiles who set their hearts on all these things. Your heavenly Father knows you need them all. Set your hearts on his kingdom first, and on God's saving justice, and all these other things will be given you as well.

So do not worry about tomorrow: tomorrow will take care of itself. Each day has enough trouble of its own".

HYMN TO LOVE *(1 Cor 13:1-8,13)*

Though I command languages both human and angelic, if I speak without love, I am no more than a gong booming or a cymbal clashing.

And though I have the power of prophecy, to penetrate all mysteries and knowledge, and though I have all the faith necessary to move mountains - if I am without love, I am nothing.

Though I should give away to the poor all that I possess, and even give up my body to be burned - if I am without love, it will do me no good whatever. Love is always patient and kind; love is never jealous; love is not boastful or conceited, it is never rude and never seeks its own advantage, it does not take offence or store up grievances.

Love does not rejoice at wrongdoing, but finds its joy in the truth. It is always ready to make allowances, to trust, to hope and to endure whatever comes. Love never comes to an end.

But if there are prophecies, they will be done away with; if tongues, they will fall silent; if knowledge, it will be done away with.

As it is, these remain: faith, hope and love, the three of them; and the greatest of them is love.

PRAYER FOR PRIESTS

Lord our God,
you guide your people by the ministry of priests.
Keep them faithful in obedient service to you,
that by their life and ministry
they may bring you glory in Christ. **Amen.**

PRAYER FOR RELIGIOUS VOCATIONS

Jesus, Good Shepherd, you have come to search for and to save what was lost. You have instituted the priesthood of the Church to continue your work for all time. We beseech you earnestly: send labourers into your vineyard. Raise up in your Church holy priests and religious brothers and sisters. Grant that all whom you have chosen from eternity for your service may follow your call, but that nobody may intrude into your sanctuary without being called.

Strengthen all priests in their difficult vocation and bless their efforts and labours. Let them be the salt of the earth that will preserve it from corruption, the light of the world that enlightens all the faithful through word and example. Give them wisdom, patience and strength so that they may promote your glory, spread your kingdom in the hearts of your people and lead the souls entrusted to them to eternal life. **Amen.**

Mary, Queen of Apostles,
pray for us.

BRIEF EVERYDAY FORMULAS AND INVOCATIONS

(These can be repeated often throughout the day).

1. BRIEF INVOCATIONS OF THE HOLY TRINITY

Glory be to the Father, and to the Son, and to the Holy Spirit.

Blessed be the Holy Trinity.

My God and my all.

Blessed be God forever.

"Most Holy Trinity, Father, Son and Holy Spirit, I adore you profoundly, and I offer you the most Precious Body, Blood, Soul and Divinity of Jesus Christ, present in all tabernacles of the world, in reparation for the outrages, sacrileges and indifference with which He himself is offended. And, through the infinite merits of His most Sacred Heart, and the Immaculate Heart of Mary, I beg of you the conversion of poor sinners"

(Prayer of the Angel at Fatima).

2. Brief invocations of God the Father

Blessed be God.

"Father, into your hands I commit my spirit"
(Lk 23:46).
"I bless you, Father, Lord of heaven and of earth"
(Lk 10:21).

Take, Lord, and receive all my liberty, my memory, my intelligence and my will. My Father, render me worthy of doing your Holy Will, because I am all yours.

Eternal Father, I offer You the most precious Blood of Jesus in atonement for my sins, for the holy souls in Purgatory and for the needs of your Holy Church.

"Have mercy on me, O God, in your faithful love, in your great tenderness wipe away my offences"
(Ps 50:1).

"God, be merciful to me, a sinner" *(Lk. 18:4)*.

Heavenly Father, I love You with the Immaculate Heart of Mary.

Save us, O Precious Blood of Christ.

3. BRIEF INVOCATIONS OF JESUS, THE SON OF GOD.

Maran atha. (The Lord comes!)

"Maranà tha. (Come, Lord!)" *(1 Cor 16: 22)*.

"Amen, come, Lord Jesus!" *(Revelation 22:20)*.

"Save us, Lord, we are lost!" *(Mt 8:25)*.

"You are the Christ, the Son of the living God" *(Mt 16: 16)*.

"Lord, increase our faith" *(Lk 17: 5)*.

Stay with us, Lord" *(Lk 24: 29)*.

"My Lord and my God" *(Jn 20: 28)*.

Blessed be the name of Jesus.

Blessed be Jesus in the most Holy Sacrament of the altar.
Jesus, I love You. May Your kingdom come!

Praised be Jesus Christ! May He always be praised!

Jesus, I trust in You.

I am in Jesus, Jesus is in me, and I am at peace.

Deliver us, Jesus, from all evil.

My Lord and my God, may Your mercy save us, may Your merciful love deliver us from all grave sin.

Jesus, meek and humble of heart, make my heart like unto thine.

Sweet Heart of Jesus, make me love you ever more.

Have mercy on me, O God, in your faithful love, in your great tenderness, wipe away my offences.

Heart of Jesus, I trust in You.

Heart of Jesus, you know; Heart of Jesus, you can; Heart of Jesus, you see; Heart of Jesus, provide; Heart of Jesus, decide.

O Jesus, it is for love of You, for the conversion of poor sinners, and for the remission of sins committed against the Immaculate Heart of Mary.

In the morning and evening, when kissing the crucifix, we can pray the words:
We adore You, O Christ, and we bless You because by Your holy cross, You have redeemed the world.

4. BRIEF INVOCATIONS OF THE HOLY SPIRIT

Come, Holy Spirit, come through the powerful intercession of the Immaculate Heart of Mary, your beloved spouse.

Send forth Your Spirit, O Lord, and renew the face of the earth.

Come, Holy Spirit, come, Divine Power of Love, come and fill my poor heart: purify it, sanctify it, make it all yours.

Holy Spirit, I want to do what is right;
Help me.
Holy Spirit, I want to live like Jesus;
Guide me.
Holy Spirit, I want to pray like Jesus;
Teach me.

5. Brief invocations of the
blessed virgin mary

Enlighten, O Mary, all humanity by thy flame of love, now and at the hour of our death. **Amen.**

Remember me, O Mother of God.
O Virgin and Mother, may I always remember you.

O Mary, I give myself entirely to You, accept me and keep me firm in my intentions.

Our Lady, may Jesus never be far from me.

I am all yours, and all that I possess I offer to you, dear Jesus, through Mary, your Holy Mother.

Holy Mary, my advocate, pray for me.

Most Holy Virgin, you are my mother, the Mother of all of us sinners.

6. Invocations (Miscellaneous)

My Lord and my God, remove from me everything which takes me away from you.
My Lord and my God, grant me everything which brings closer me to you.
My Lord and my God, take me away from myself and let me give myself all to you.

Jesus and Mary, I love you!
Save the souls of all priests, save all souls.
This we beseech you imploringly, and grant us to be able to repeat this act of love a thousand times with every breath, with every heartbeat.
O Jesus, ardent with love, I am sorry for having offended You.
O my dear and good Jesus, by thy help of Your grace, I never wish to offend You again.

Jesus, Mary and Joseph, I give you my heart and my soul.
Jesus, Mary and Joseph, assist me in my last agony.
Jesus, Mary and Joseph, may sleep and take my rest in peace with you.

Sweet Heart of Jesus, make me love you ever more.
Sweet Heart of Mary, be the salvation of my soul and of my family.

I can't, you can; please do!

Jesus and Mary, I love You, save all souls.
Saint Joseph, pray for us.

Saint Michael the Archangel, pray for us.
Holy Angels of God, pray for us.

7. THE DIVINE PRAISES

Blessed be God.

Blessed be God.

Blessed be His holy name.

Blessed be God.

Blessed be Jesus Christ, true God and true man.

Blessed be God.

Blessed be the name of Jesus.

Blessed be God.

Blessed be His most Sacred Heart.

Blessed be God.

Blessed be His most Precious Blood.

Blessed be God.

Blessed be Jesus in the Most Holy Sacrament
of the Altar.

Blessed be God.

Blessed be the Holy Spirit the Paraclete.

Blessed be God.

Blessed be the great Mother of God,
    Mary most holy.

Blessed be God.

Blessed be her holy and Immaculate Conception.

Blessed be God.

Blessed be her glorious Assumption.

Blessed be God.

Blessed be the name of Mary, virgin and mother.

Blessed be God.

Blessed be St. Joseph, her most chaste spouse.

Blessed be God.

Blessed be God in His angels and in His saints.

Blessed be God.

EVENING PRAYERS

*In the name of the Father, and of the Son,
and of the Holy Spirit. Amen.*

I ADORE YOU

I adore You, my God,
and I love You with all my heart.
I thank You for having created me,
for having given me my
Christian faith,
and for having kept me safe this day.
Forgive me for the wrong I have done today,
and if I have done some good, accept it.
Watch over me when I am at rest and free me
from all danger.
May Your grace always accompany me
and all my dear ones.
Amen.

**Our Father
Hail Mary
Glory Be
Angel of God**

Examination of conscience

Among the various forms of private prayer, including meditation, it is good pratice to make a daily examination of conscience, as it helps the progressive purification of our hearts. We examine our actions and attitudes, good and bad, and focus our attention on a particular state of mind, renewing each time our sincere repentance, our firm proposal to resist temptation and to avoid occasions of sin.

Act of contrition
(Act of sorrow)

O my God, I am heartily sorry for all my sins because they have offended You, who are infinitely good, and I firmly resolve, by the help of Your grace, never to offend You again.
Amen.

or

O my God, I thank you for loving me.
I am sorry for all my sins:
For not loving others and not loving you.
Help me to live like Jesus and not sin again.
Amen.

or

O my God, because you are so good
I am sorry that I have sinned against you,
And with your help I will not sin again.
Amen.

THE CONFITEOR

I confess to almighty God, and to you, my brothers and sisters that I have sinned through my own fault *(All strike their breast)* In my thoughts and in my words, in what I have done, and in what I have failed to do, and I ask blessed Mary, ever virgin, all the angels and saints, and you, my brothers and sisters, to pray for me to the Lord our God.

O MY FATHER

O my Father, now that the voices are silent and the clamour is over, here at the foot of my bed, my soul rises up to you and says: I believe in you, I trust in you, I love you with all my heart. Glory be to you, O Lord.

I put in thy hands my weariness and my struggles, the happiness and disappointment of the day just gone by.

If I lost my nerve, if my selfishness dominated me, if I allowed space for rancour and sadness, forgive me, Lord. Have mercy on me.

If I was unfaithful, if I spoke useless words, if I allowed myself to be overcome by impatience, if I caused trouble to someone, forgive me, O Lord.

I do not want to fall asleep this night without feeling the security of your mercy in my soul, your sweet mercy, Lord, which is entirely free.

I thank you, O my Father; you have been a fresh shadow which covered me throughout the day.

I thank you because by being invisible, affectionate and embracing me, you helped me like a mother this day.

Lord, I am already surrounded by peace and tranquillity. Send your angel of peace to this house.

Relax my nerves, calm my spirit, free me from all tensions and stress, fill my being with silence and serenity. Watch over me, O beloved Father, while I fall asleep in trustful abandonment, like a child who sleeps happily in his mother's arms. In your name, Lord I will rest peacefully.
Amen.

NIGHT PRAYER TO GOD THE FATHER

God Our Father, I come to say
Thank you for your love today.
Thank you for my family
And all the friends you give to me.
Guard me in the dark of night
And in the morning send your light.
Amen.

PRAYER FOR THE FAITHFUL DEPARTED

1. *Prayers after death*

The following prayers may be recited immediately after the person's death and may be repeated in the hours that follow. Saints of God, come to his (her) aid! Come to meet him (her), angels of the Lord!

R. Receive his (her) soul and present him (her) to God, the Most High.

May Christ, who called you, take you to himself; may angels lead you to Abraham's side. **R.**

Give him (her) eternal rest, O Lord,
and may your light shine on him (her) for ever. **R.**

Let us pray.

All-powerful and merciful God, we commend to you **N.**, your servant. In your mercy and love, blot out the sins he (she) has committed through human weakness. In this world he (she) has died: let him (her) live with you for ever. We ask this through Christ our Lord. **Amen.**

The following verses may also used:

V. Eternal rest grant unto him (her), O Lord.
R. And let perpetual light shine upon him (her).
V. May he (she) rest in peace. **R. Amen.**
V. May his (her) soul and the souls of all the faithful departed, through the mercy of God, rest in peace. **R. Amen.**

2. Eternal rest

Eternal rest grant unto them, O Lord. And let perpetual light shine upon them. May they rest in peace. **Amen.**

Réquiem ætérnam dona eis Dómine, et lux perpétua lúceat eis. Requiéscant in pace. **Amen.**

3. Remember, Lord, those, who have died and have gone before us marked with the sign of faith, especially those for whom we now pray, N. and N. May these, and all who sleep in Christ find in your presence light, happiness and peace. Through Christ our Lord. **Amen.**

The Roman Canon

4. The De Profundis (Psalm 130)

Out of the depths I have cried to you, O Lord,
Lord, hear my voice.
Let your ears be attentive
to the voice of my supplication.
If you, O Lord, shall observe iniquities,
Lord, who shall endure it?
For with you there is merciful forgiveness;
and by reason of your law I have waited for you,
O Lord. My soul has relied on his word;
my soul has hoped in the Lord.
From the morning watch even until night
let Israel hope in the Lord.
Because with the Lord there is mercy,
and with him plentiful redemption.
And he shall redeem Israel from all its iniquities.

## Part Two

The Most Holy Trinity

- **HYMNS**
  - **PRAYERS**
- **NOVENAS**
  - **CHAPLETS**

HYMNS

HYMNS TO THE MOST HOLY TRINITY FROM THE LITURGY

The following hymns are taken from the Liturgy of the Hours (the Daily Prayer of the Church) and are the hymns sung at Evening Prayer I and Morning Prayer respectively on the solemnity of the most Holy Trinity, the first Sunday after Pentecost.

1. Firmly I believe and truly
God is Three, and God in One;
And I next acknowledge duly
Manhood taken by the Son;

And I trust and hope most fully
In that manhood crucified;
And each thought and deed unruly
Do to death, as he has died.

Simply to his grace and wholly
Light and life and strength belong;
And I love supremely, solely,
Him the holy, him the strong.

Adoration aye be given,
With and through the angelic host,
To the God of earth and heaven,
Father, Son and Holy Ghost.

2. Father most holy, gracious and forgiving,
Christ, high exalted, prince of our salvation,
Spirit of counsel, nourishing creation,
God ever-living.

Trinity blessed, Unity unshaken,
Only true Godhead, sea of bounty endless,
Light of the angels,
succour thou the friendless,
Shield the forsaken.

All things thou madest-nothing doth but
preach thee,
Serving thee ever in its course ordained;
We too would hymn thee;
this our prayer unfeigned
Hear, we beseech thee.

Boundless thy praise be,
whom no limit boundeth,
God in three Persons, high in heaven living,
Where adoration, homage and thanksgiving
Ever resoundeth.

HAIL, O ETERNAL SOVEREIGN

Hymn to the most Holy Trinity

*God wants to save all people. Just as he allowed the
Blessed Virgin Mary to speak at Lourdes (1858) and at
Fatima (1917) so too in our times has he permitted Mary to
appear in various places throughout the world, including
Marienfried near Pfaffenhofen (Bavaria, Germany) in
1946. There, the Blessed Virgin introduced herself as the
Great Mediatrix of Graces. The message of Marienfried is
the heartfelt appeal of our Heavenly Mother who wants to
guide her children along the path of salvation.*

*This hymn was sung on the 25th of June, 1946, at Marien-
fried by a great host of angels during the apparition of the
Virgin.*

Hail, O Eternal Sovereign,
the living God who exists from eternity!
O tremendous and just judge,
Father always good and merciful!
To you may new and eternal entreaty be made,
praise, honour and glory be rendered,
through your Daughter adorned with the sun,
our admirable Mother! **Amen.**

**"You, O great Mediatrix of graces,
pray for us!"**

Hail, O Man, God sacrified,
bleeding Lamb, King of Peace,
Tree of life, you, our Head,
Gateway to the Heart of the Father,
eternal Son of the living God,

who with Him reign eternally!
To you be the power, now and for ever,
and glory and greatness,
and adoration and reparation and praise,
through your Immaculate Mother,
our admirable Mother! **Amen.**

**"You, faithful Mediatrix of graces,
pray for us!"**

Hail, O Spirit of Eternity,
endless source of sanctity,
acting with God from eternity!
Stream of fire from the Father to the Son,
impetuous hurricane,
you who breathe strength, light and fire
into the members of the Mystical Body!
You, eternal fire of love,
Spirit of God, who act in the living,
You, red stream of fire
which flows ever alive, among mortals,
to you, be glory, power and beauty,
now and in eternity
through your spouse
crowned with stars,
our admirable Mother! **Amen.**

**"You, Mediatrix of all graces,
pray for us!"**

MY GOD, HOLY TRINITY, WHOM I ADORE

Blessed Elizabeth of the Holy Trinity

O my God, Holy Trinity whom I adore, may I immerse myself at every moment ever more in the depth of your mystery. Give peace to my soul, make it your heaven, the place of your rest.

O eternal Word, Word of my God, Christ my Lord, I want to pass my life listening to you, and in the night of the soul and in my emptiness, I want to contemplate you always and remain before your great light.

O my beloved star, attract me, so that I may never again draw myself away from the radiation of your light.

O my Three persons, my All, my Beatitude, infinite Solitude, Immensity in which I lose myself, I abandon myself to you.

Bury yourself in me so that I may be buried in you, while waiting to contemplate in your light the abyss of your greatness.

MAY MY SOUL BE A LITTLE PARADISE

Blessed Elizabeth of the Holy Trinity

O Lord, grant that I may live with you as with a friend. Help me to keep my faith alive, to unite myself to you in all things.

O Lord, may my soul be a little paradise where you may rest in delight; help me, therefore, to remove from it everything which could spoil your divine gaze. And then, may I live in this little heaven, remaining with you forever. Wherever I am and whatever I do, you never leave me; grant, therefore, that I may always remain with you too; in every hour of the day and night, in every joy and sorrow, in every deed and every action, may you find yourself within me.

My God, Holy Trinity, be my dwelling place, my nest, the father's house that I must never leave. May I be united with you, not only for a few moments or a few hours which soon pass by, but in a permanent habitual way.

Grant that I may always pray, adore, love, suffer, work and act in you. May I remain in you in order to be available for everybody and for everything, to apply myself to any duty, venturing ever further into the depths of your Divinity.

Lord, grant that I may advance further along this path which guides me to you every day, this path which lets me glide along its slope with a trust full of love.

I DESIRE NOTHING ELSE BUT YOU

Saint Thérèse of Lisieux

O my God! Blessed Trinity, I wish to love you and to make everyone love you; I wish to work for the glorification of the Holy Church, saving the souls which are on earth and releasing all those who are suffering in Purgatory.

I wish to fulfil your will perfectly and to enter into the glory which you have prepared for me in your kingdom; in a word, I wish to be holy but I am aware of my weakness and I ask that you yourself, O my God, be my holiness. As you have loved me to the point of giving me your only Son as my Saviour, the infinite treasures of his merits are mine; I offer them to you with joy, beseeching you to look at me only through the face of Jesus and through his heart, ardent with love.

I feel in my heart such an immense desire and a great trust that I ask you to come and take possession of my soul. I do not want to accumulate merits for Heaven, but to work only for love of, with the intention of pleasing only you, of consoling your Sacred Heart and of saving souls which will love you eternally. In the evening of this life, I shall come before you with empty hands, indeed, I do not ask you, Lord, to count my good deeds.

All my good deeds are imperfect in your eyes. I want to clothe myself in your righteousness and to receive from your love the eternal possession of you yourself.

I desire nothing else but you, O my beloved!

MAY YOUR GOSPEL LEAD OUR PEOPLE TO JUSTICE

Pope John Paul II

O God our Father, we praise and thank you.
You who love everyone and guide all people, accompany the steps of our country, which are often difficult but full of hope. Let us see the signs of your presence and feel the strength of your love which never fails.

Lord Jesus, Son of God and Saviour of the world, made man in the womb of the Virgin Mary, we profess our faith to you. May your Gospel be light and strength for our personal and social decisions. May your law of love guide our community to justice and solidarity, to reconciliation and peace.

O Holy Spirit, love of the Father and the Son, with confidence we invoke you; You are our interior master; reveal to us the thoughts and ways of God. Grant that we may look at the circumstances of life with innocent and penetrating eyes; grant that we may conserve the heritage of holiness and culture of our people, and grant us the conversion of our minds and our hearts in order to renew our society.

Glory be to you, O Father, who bring all things into being in all people.

Glory be to you, O Son, who, out of love, became our servant.

Glory be to you, O Holy Spirit, who sow your gifts in our hearts.

Glory be to you, O Holy Trinity, who live and reign forever and ever. **Amen.**

GOD, THE UNFATHOMABLE MYSTERY

O blessed Trinity! You are an unfathomable sea in which the more I immerse myself, the more I find you, and the more I find you, the more I search for you. Of you, nobody can ever say: enough! The soul which satisfies itself in your great depths desires you constantly, because it always hungers for you; it always desires to see the light in your light. Could you give me anything more than the gift of yourself?

You are the fire which burns without consuming itself. You are the fire which consumes by itself all the self-conceit of a soul; you are the light above all lights. You are the clothing which covers our nakedness, the nourishment which satisfies all those who are hungry with its sweetness.

Clothe me, O Blessed Trinity, clothe me with yourself, that I may pass this life in true obedience and in the light of faith with which you have inebriated my soul.

ROSARY

ROSARY OF THE TRINITY

This chaplet, composed by a priest, is a wonderful prayer, especially when meditated profoundly. It brings us closer to the mystery of God, three persons in One, allowing us to think of our eternal destiny. Moreover, this prayer has received the sincere approval of the Holy Father. The chaplet follows the scheme of the Holy Rosary, and can thus be said using the same beads. Before each series of five mysteries, which are referred to Joyful, Sorrowful and Glorious we say or sing the following prayer on the beads of the Our Father:

**"We sing to you, Father, giver of life,
God of immense love, infinite Trinity."**

JOYFUL MYSTERIES
*On the Hail Mary beads
we recite the following words:*

"Praise and glory be to you, O Holy Trinity".

First mystery: The eternal existence of God the Father.

Second mystery: The generation of the Son from eternity.

Third mystery: The eternal love of the Holy Spirit.

Fourth mystery:	The unity of nature in the Three Divine Persons.
Fifth mystery:	The outpouring of divine life upon all people made in the image and likeness of God.

SORROWFUL MYSTERIES

On the Hail Mary beads
we recite the following words:

"O Holy Trinity, forgive me and
have mercy on me".

First mystery:	The loss of friendship with God because of original sin.
Second mystery:	The loss of God's grace because of the mortal sins committed in these times.
Third mystery:	The impending danger of eternal damnation because of the tragedy of habitual sin.
Fourth mystery:	The spiritual tragedy of the soul which is in mortal sin and fails to believe in God's mercy.
Fifth mystery:	The eternal consequences of those who die and are not in a state of grace. Final impenitence.

GLORIOUS MYSTERIES

On the Hail Mary beads
we recite the following words:

"Praise and glory be to you, O Holy Trinity".

First mystery: The great work of the Eternal Father in Creation.

Second mystery: The manifestation of the Wisdom of the Son, Jesus Christ, our Redeemer in the Creation of the world.

Third mystery: The sanctification of our souls with the outpouring of the Holy Spirit: an efficacious fruit of Redemption.

Fourth mystery: The recapitulation of the story of salvation in the Last Judgement.

Fifth mystery: The coronation of our Redemption in eternal glory through our communion with God, Three Persons in One: Paradise!

At the end of the Rosary we say:

O Holy Trinity, Father, the Creator; Son, our Redeemer;
Sanctifying Spirit, our only Source of life,
let us dwell in you!
Alleluia!

NOVENAS

NOVENA TO THE HOLY TRINITY

*In the name of the Father, and of the Son,
and of the Holy Spirit. Amen.*

O God, come to my aid.
O Lord, make haste to help me.

Glory Be

Eternal Father, I thank you for having created me in your love. I beseech you to save me in your infinite mercy by the merits of Jesus Christ.

Glory Be

Eternal Son, I thank you for having redeemed me with your most Precious Blood; I beseech you to save me by your infinite merits.

Glory Be

Eternal Holy Spirit, I thank you for having adopted me by your divine grace; I beseech you to let me grow in holiness through your infinite love.

Glory Be

Novena to Obtain a Grace in the Name of the Father, Son and Holy Spirit

In the name of the Father, and of the Son, and of the Holy Spirit. Amen.

O God, come to my aid.
O Lord, make haste to help me.

Glory Be

Eternal Father, here I am, a poor and powerless creature; I recognize my weakness and your infinite power in which I take recourse for this necessity of mine *(we make our request)* and in which I hope and trust. May you take care of this need of mine.

Glory Be

Eternal Son, here I am a poor and ignorant creature; I know nothing but recognize my great ignorance and your infinite Wisdom in which I take recourse for this necessity of mine *(we make our request)* and in which I trust and to which I abandon myself.

Glory Be

Eternal Holy Spirit, here I am a poor and ungrateful creature; I merit nothing but recognize my great ingratitude and your infinite goodness in which I take recourse and which I embrace; may you take care of this need of mine *(we make our request)*. To you I abandon myself and in you I trust.

## Part Three

The Father

- **REFLECTIONS**
  - **PRAYERS**
- **CHAPLETS**
  - **NOVENAS**
- **ROSARIES**
- **PRAYERS OF THANKSGIVING**

REFLECTIONS

MEDITATION OF THE HOLY CHURCH ON THE OUR FATHER

In the Our Father the first three requests concern the Glory of the Father: the sanctification of His name, the coming of His Kingdom and the accomplishment of his Divine Will.

The other four requests present to him our desires: these questions focus on how our life can be nourished, and how it can be healed from sin, and they are related to our battle for the victory of good over evil.

Praying the words "Hallowed be thy name", we enter into God's design for humanity: the sanctification of His name which was revealed to Moses and then in the person of Jesus, by us and in us, in every nation and in every person. With the words "Thy kingdom come" the Church focuses mainly on the return of Christ and on the final coming of the Kingdom of God.

It is also a plea for the growth of the Kingdom of God in our daily life. In praying, "Thy will be done" we beseech our Father to unite our will to that of His Son, in order to realize His Plan of Salvation for the world. In the fourth request, with the words "Give us", we express, together with our brothers and sisters, our faith in our Father in heaven.

"Our bread" signifies the earthly nourishment necessary to sustain us, but it also indicates the bread of life: the Word of God and the Body of Christ.

It is given to us in the "Today" of God as essential nourishment for our life, in order that we may share in the banquet of the Kingdom, which is anticipated by the Eucharist.

The fifth request, "Forgive us our trespasses", implores God's mercy for our offences; however, if we have not forgiven our enemies, following the example of Christ and with His help, these words cannot reach our heart. In saying, "Lead us not into temptation", we beseech God to help us to avoid the path which leads to sin. This request implores the Spirit of discernment and fortitude and it seeks also the grace of vigilance and perseverance.

In the last request "Deliver us from evil", the Christian, together with the Church, asks God to show the victory which has already been achieved by Christ over the "Prince of this world", over Satan, the angel who opposes both God and His Plan of Salvation. With the final "Amen" we express our "fiat" to the seven requests: "So be it".

REFLECTION ON THE OUR FATHER

FATHER
Who is this Father?
Whose is this Father?
Where is this Father?

OUR
This is your Father. Why are you afraid of Him? Stretch out your hands to Him.

(Brief pause)

OUR FATHER
It means that he gave himself to you as a Father, he has given you everything. You know that your earthly fathers do everything for you; much more so does your heavenly Father.

Our Father

It means: I give you everything, my child.

WHO ART IN HEAVEN
(Brief pause)

FATHER WHO ART IN HEAVEN

It means: your earthly father loves you but your heavenly Father loves you even more. Your father is capable of getting angry; He is not, He offers you only love...

HALLOWED BE THY NAME

In return you must respect Him, because He has given you everything and because He is your Father and you must love Him. You must glorify and praise His name. You must say to sinners: He is the Father; yes, he is my Father and I desire to serve Him and to glorify his name. This is what is meant by "hallowed be thy name".

YOUR KINGDOM COME

In this way we thank Jesus and we want to say: Jesus, we know nothing, without your kingdom we are weak, if You are not present with us. Our kingdom passes, while Yours does not pass.

YOUR WILL BE DONE

O Lord, may our kingdom collapse, may your Kingdom alone be the true one, may we realize that our kingdom is destined to come to an end and may we let your will be done at once, "now".

ON EARTH AS IT IS IN HEAVEN

Here Lord, we are told how the angels obey you, how they respect you; may we also be like them, grant that our hearts may open too, and that we may respect each other as the angels do now. And grant that on earth all may be Holy as it is in heaven.

Give us this day our daily bread

Give us, Lord, bread and food for our soul; give it to us now, give it to us today, give it to us always; may this bread become eternal. O Lord, we pray to you for our bread. O Lord, grant that we may receive it. O Lord, help us to understand what we must do. Grant that we may realize that our daily bread cannot be given to us without prayer.

Forgive us our trespasses

Forgive us our sins, Lord. Forgive us because we are not good and we are not faithful.

As we forgive those who trespass against us

Forgive us our trespasses so that we too may be able to forgive the sins of those whom we have not been able to forgive until now. O Jesus, forgive us our trespasses, we beseech you. You pray that your sins may be forgiven in the same measure as you forgive those who trespass against you, without realizing that if your sins were really forgiven as you forgive others, it would not be much at all. That is what your heavenly Father is telling you with these words.

And lead us not into temptation

Lord, free us from great trials. Lord, we are weak. Grant, O Lord, that trials may not lead us to do evil.

But deliver us from evil

Lord, free us from evil. Grant that in all trials we may suceed in finding something worthwhile, a step forward in our lives.

Amen

So be it, Lord; may your will be done.

Reflection on the Our Father
by Fr. Antonio Zanotti

Our Father

You are by my side on my pilgrimage, O Father; you accompany and help me. You know everything about me. You know my needs and my desire to grow. Your name is full of joy and richness. You know how many years we shall live and you know how to be present in every step of our lives. You know how to accompany my steps with Love and how to help me to reach the destiny of your beauty and sweetness; you are communion and accept me with love; you free my life from every fear and make my journey smooth so that I may remain with you. Come, my Friend and Father. You will always remain with me.

Father who art in heaven

Thank you, Father, for this immense blue sky that looks at me and loves me, home of all dreams of the blessed souls and of the saints, heaven of God Almighty, and of men and women, pilgrims who succeed in finding a place with the Father. You, alone, O Heaven, await us, after our having passed through the narrow door of the Gospel to contemplate you. The heaven of heavens is your glory and our home.

Father, hallowed be Thy name

I kneel before Thy name, as does the whole universe. Thank you, Father, for this name given to all the needs of humanity, those deep, infinite and holy needs. You alone are Holy, and we search for the path to reach the perfection of sanctity, the infinite sweetness of adoring you and of feeling your caresses which allow us to enjoy your name to the full, and live eternally in love. I believe in the greatness of your name which has granted me every wisdom and blessing.

Father, Thy kingdom come

You alone could offer us the opportunity to imitate the earth in being a dwelling place for you and the expression of your peace. May Your Kingdom come within me, Father, so that I may graze in the fields of your beatitudes. Your Kingdom is joy.

Thy will be done

Your light shines on the path of life. You teach me how to attain happiness. The fulfilment of every plan of happiness is the threshold of eternity. Your will is the spirituality that guides our life and everything becomes fresh dew for each step of my climb to the summit of the beauty of life. Bring me with you, Almighty Will, so that I may savour every moment in which your Son obeyed your will in his earthly existence.

On earth as it is in heaven

I will leave this earth enriched with your know-ledge and filled with the power of the Holy Spirit. Heaven is the devotion which palpitates inside me; earth is the ark of blessings and of the victory of good over evil. Lord Jesus, in honour of your Father, I fill the earth with psalms and with heaven, as everything becomes Paradise when I fulfil your will.

Give us this day our daily bread

The earth can provide bread for all people; earth to which you, Lord, give the seeds of strength and of nourishment, for every season of life. May infinite care be the gift which everyone provides for his brother on earth. Do not steal anything, brothers and sisters, from the produce of the earth, because I will buy the field of wheat with my sacrifices in order that we may be able to call Your love our daily bread in all the universe.

And Forgive Us Our Trepasses

Lord, I have seen your palaces in Creation called seasons; I have seen them vibrant with a thousand colours. I leave debts and sins upon this earth. I lack the courage to carry my cross and climb the mountain to my home where Christ forgave the debts of all my days. Leave me a corner of peace, Lord, so that thirsting for you, I may return with joy to that home as a pilgrim, and may touch with my forehead that gift of love which is your Cross.

As We Forgive Those Who Trepass Against Us

Lord, I beg only for your wounds which were touched by Thomas in order to believe that you have forgiven all trespassers. Imprint upon me the memory of your Passion so that I may live on an earth where poems and poetry of one hundred verses of good and perfect words are written. May they fly to heaven in order that reconciliation may be poured out on all the nations of the earth.

And Lead Us Not Into Temptation
But Deliver Us From Evil

I have learnt that harmony within ourselves opens us to the words of the Gospel. Your Word is the water and the life which gives us strength and freedom. Only He, the Friend of our journey, brings back love in our heart and, like the star of every morning, also enlightens us about our trials and temptations. In the midst of this web of trials, I await only you, my Saviour and Holy One; for you alone will I sing sweet songs with the notes of your immortal love. I feel as if I have been moulded by you, like a new person who can sing with a thousand voices his "amen" to life.

I will remember you. You will be like a navigator's compass in the ocean of the earth. And on the banks of the river of humanity, I will place my lamp, lit to illuminate for you the words of the Our Father, the prayer of your "Amen", on every page of your life.

FOOTSTEPS

A reflection on the Father's loving care for us

One night a man had a dream. He dreamed he was walking along the beach with the Lord. Across the sky flashed scenes from his life. For each scene he noticed two sets of footprints in the sand; one belonging to him and the other to the Lord.

When the last scene of his life flashed before him he looked back at the footprints in the sand. He noticed that many times along the path of his life there was only one set of footprints. He also noticed that it happened at the very lowest and saddest times in his life.

This really bothered him and he questioned the Lord about it. "Lord, you said that once I decided to follow you, you'd walk with me all the way. But I have noticed that during the most troublesome times in my life there is only one set of footprints. I don't understand why when I needed you most you would leave me".

The Lord replied, "My son, My precious child, I love you and I would never leave you. During your times of trial and suffering, when you see only one set of footprints, it was then that I carried you".

PRAYER TO THE FATHER

Father, the earth needs you; everyone needs you; we pray to you, Father, because even the heavy and polluted air needs you; come back to walk along the roads of the world, come back to live among your children, come back to rule nations, come back to bring Peace and Justice, come back to enkindle the fire of love so that, redeemed from sorrow, we can become new creatures.

PRAYER OF ABANDONMENT
TO THE FATHER

My Father, I abandon myself to you; do with me whatever you desire. For whatever you do, I thank you. I am ready for everything, I accept everything, as long as your will be done in me and in all your creatures. I do not desire anything else, O my God. I place my soul in your hands; I give it to you, O my Lord, with all the love of my heart because I love you, and out of love, I want to give myself to you, to place myself totally in your hands with infinite trust, because you are my Father.

Prayer to ask God for the Gift of Divine Wisdom

Saint Louis De Montfort

God of our Fathers, merciful Lord, Spirit of truth! I, a poor creature, prostrate before your Divine Majesty, am aware of my deep need of your Divine Wisdom which I have lost because of my sins.

Hopeful that you will be faithful to Your promise to grant wisdom to all those who ask it of you without hesitation, I ask you for it today with lively insistence and deep humility. Send us, Lord, this Wisdom which is always present before your throne and includes all your gifts.

May it sustain our weakness, enlighten our mind, inflame our hearts, teach us to speak and to act, to work and to suffer with you.

May it guide our steps and fill our souls with the virtues of Jesus Christ and the gifts of the Holy Spirit.

Merciful Father, God of all consolation! Through the maternal goodness of Mary, the precious Blood of your beloved Son, and your great desire to communicate your gifts to all creatures, we ask you for the infinite treasure of your Wisdom. Hear and grant this my prayer. **Amen.**

PRAYER OF TOTAL TRUST

My God, my God, not only do I trust in you but I trust in you alone. Give me, therefore, the spirit of abandonment to accept the things I cannot change. Give me also the spirit of strength to change the things I can. Give me, finally, the spirit of wisdom, to discern what truly depends on me, and thus may I do only your holy will!
Amen.

MY GOD AND MY FATHER

My God and my Father! May my sorrowful loneliness glorify you, may my patience and obedience soothe you! Do not vent your righteous anger on all souls. Look at your Son, forgive all souls in the name of his suffering, sustain them, do not let them succumb under the burden of their weakness, be at their side in their hours of "imprisonment" and give them strength to bear the sufferings and trials of life in accordance with your holy adorable will.
Amen.

O GOD OF MERCY

O God of mercy, have mercy on our human fragility. Give strength to all souls, in order that they may not be caught in the snares of the enemy and may return with new strength to the path of virtue.

Join your suffering to mine, your sorrow to mine and present them to the Father through the merits and the sufferings of all righteous souls.

O Most Holy Father, in whose presence not even the angels and saints are worthy to be, forgive our faults, both in thought and in desire. In atonement for these offences, accept the head of your Divine Son pierced with thorns.

O Holy Father, accept the sufferings and the merits of all souls who, united with the merits and sufferings of Jesus, offer themselves to You with Him and for Him in order that you may forgive the world!

O God of Mercy and of Love! Be the strength of the weak, the light of the blind, the object of love of all souls.

Amen.

FATHER, GIVE JESUS TO ME

Father, give me the most beautiful, the greatest
and most precious gift you have: Jesus!
When I am ill, give Jesus to me
because He is Health.
When I feel sad, give Jesus to me
because He is Joy.
When I am weak, give Jesus to me
because He is Strength:
When I feel alone, give Jesus to me
because He is a Friend.
When I feel imprisoned, give Jesus to me
because He is Freedom.
When I feel discouraged, give Jesus to me
because He is Victory.
When I feel I am in darkness, give Jesus to me
because He is Light.
When I feel the weight of my sin, give Jesus to me
because He is our Saviour.
When I need love, give Jesus to me
because He is Love.
When I need food, give Jesus to me
because He is the Bread of Life.
When I need money, give Jesus to me
because He is infinite richness.
Father, to any of my requests,
for any of my needs,
answer me by only one word,
your eternal Word: Jesus!

CONSECRATION TO THE DIVINE WILL

O divine and adorable Will, here I am before the immensity of Your Light, so that Your eternal goodness may open its door to me, and let me enter into it so that I may found my life entirely upon You, O Divine Will. Therefore, O adorable will, I, the smallest of your creatures in the little host of the children of Your Supreme Fiat, come before You, and bow down before Your Light.

Prostrate in my nothingness, I implore and beseech Your unending Light to surround me and leave in the shade all that does not belong to You, so that I may only look, understand and live in You, O Divine Will.

Your Divine Will shall be my life, the centre of my mind, that which steals my heart and all of my being. In this heart of mine, human desires shall live no more except those which conform to Your Will, thus forming a new Garden of Eden where peace, happiness and love shall reign. By living according to the Divine Will, I shall always be content, it shall be my sole source of strength, a source of holiness which is sanctifying and draws everything to God. Here, prostrate, I invoke the help of the most Holy Trinity that it may grant me to live in the cloister of the Divine Will, so that the original order of creation, when life was created, may be re-established in me.

Heavenly Mother, Sovereign Queen of the

Divine Fiat, take me by the hand and keep me always in the light of the Divine Will. You will be my guide, my tender Mother. You shall look at your daughter and shall teach her to live and keep herself in the order and within the enclosure of the Divine Will.

Heavenly Sovereign, my Mother, I entrust all my being to your Heart. I will be one of your little children: you will instruct me at the school of the Divine Will and I will listen to You attentively. You will cover me with your blue mantle, so that the infernal serpent dare not enter into this Sacred Garden of Eden to tempt me and cause me to fall in the labyrinth of earthly desires. Heart of Jesus my Greatest Good, You will give me Your flames so that they may burn, consume and nourish me to create within me the life of the Supreme Will.

Saint Joseph, you shall be my Patron and the Guardian of my heart and you shall keep the keys of my will in your hands. You will guard my heart jealously and will not give it to me ever again so that I may be certain of not fleeing from the Will of God in any way.

O Guardian Angel, be my protection, defend me, help me in everything, so that the flowers in my Garden of Eden may grow and blossom, and may embroider all the world with the will of God. O Heavenly Court, come to my aid and I promise you to live always according to the Divine Will.

My God, come into my soul

My God, come into my soul and sanctify it. My God, come into my heart and purify it. My God, enter into my body, guard it and let it never be separated from your love. Burn, consume all that you see inside of me which is unworthy of your presence, consume everything which may be an obstacle to your grace and love. O manna from Heaven, may I find joy in your presence, so that I may consider all the pleasures of this world to be insipid and inferior to those of the life to come.

Eternal father

Eternal Father, out of love for all people you have given unto death your Only Begotten Son; through His Blood, through His merits, with His Heart, have mercy on all the world and forgive all the sins which we commit. Accept the humble reparation offered to you by the souls you have chosen; unite it to the merits of your Divine Son, so that it may acquire a great efficacy. O Eternal Father, have mercy on all souls, and remember that the time of judgement has not yet come, but it is still the time of Mercy!

Trust in God

My Father,
I abandon myself to you;
do with me whatever you desire.
For whatever you do, I thank you.
I am ready for everything,
I accept everything,
as long as your will be done in me
and in all your creatures.
I do not desire anything else, O my God.

I place my soul in your hands.
I give it to you, O my Lord,
with all the love of my heart,
because I love you, and it is out of love
that I wish to give myself to you,
to place myself totally in your hands
with infinite trust, because you are my Father.

O God of Mercy

God of mercy, giver of all that is good, we thank
you because you chose the Blessed Virgin Mary
from all our human ancestry to be the Mother of
your Son made man.

Hail Mary *(3 times)*

MY ONLY DESIRE

My God, I love You!
My only desire is to love You
until I take my last breath.
My Lord, I love You!
The only grace I ask of You is to love You
unto eternity.
My God,
if my tongue cannot always tell You I love You,
let my heart repeat it with every breath I take...
I love You, Divine Saviour,
because You were crucified for me;
I love You, God,
because You keep me crucified for You.
My God,
as I approch the end of my life,
grant me this grace:
increase my love.

HOLY FATHER, I ABANDON MYSELF TO YOU

Holy Father, I abandon myself to You: do with me as You please. I am poor and weak, but I give You my humble "yes". In my weakness show Your power, uniting my sufferings to that of Your Son, for the salvation of the world.

May my sufferings, permeated by a Christlike spirit of sacrifice, lead the way to the Grace which transforms our hearts and manifests the strength of Redemption in the story of humanity.

I offer You every tear and secret complaint, every fear and feeling of powerlessness, in order that Your Kingdom may come among the little ones of this world. May my stability be a strength to all missionaries who consume themselves in going to the ends of the earth.

I offer You my humble love for every person who lives unjustly in spiritual and material poverty, for every mother who watches helplessly as her child dies of hunger, for every child who is abandoned.

I offer You everything, so that all people may come to know love through the brotherly love of others and may come to know You as the God of Love, Liberation and Consolation. **Amen.**

PRAYER TO ASK GOD THAT ALL ILLNESS MAY BRING FORTH GOOD

Lord, Your Spirit is always so good and so gentle: in all things; give me, therefore, Your grace so that I may not behave in an unchristian manner in the condition in which You have permitted me to find myself.

As a true Christian, may I recognize You as my Father and my God, whatever my physical or mental state may be, because the change in my condition does not change anything in Yours, for You are always the same God, both when you allow me to suffer and when You comfort me.

You gave me health to serve You and I have (often) used it disrespectfully.
Now You permit illness in my life: do not let me use it to irritate You with my impatience!

Lord, keep away from me the sadness which self-centredness may bring because of my own sufferings and because of the love I have for those things of the world which I can no longer enjoy.

May I desire the gifts of health and life only in order that I may use them for You, with You and in You, thus fulfilling Your will in all things.

I ask You neither for health nor for illness, neither for life nor for death; but dispose of my health, of my illness, of my life and of my death as You please, for Your glory, for my salvation and for the good of the Church and all its members.

Lord, may I accept Your will and may I glorify You in my illness with my sufferings. May they bring me closer to You, and even You Yourself, Lord, chose to touch my heart through Your own sufferings.

It is by the very signs of Your suffering that You were recognized by Your disciples; and it is by the crosses which they carry that You recognize those who are Your disciples. Know that I too am Your disciple by the sufferings I bear.

Unite my will to Yours, my pains to those which You suffered. Let my suffering become Yours. Unite me to Yourself. Fill me with Yourself and with Your Holy Spirit.

Enter into my heart and my soul to sustain me in my suffering so that, in my own body, I may make up all the hardships that still have to be undergone by Your Passion so that you may accomplish through the members of your Body, the Church, her perfect consumation and fulfilment; and once filled with Your presence, O Lord my Saviour, grant that it shall be no longer I who live or suffer, but Christ who shall live and suffer in me.

THE UNIVERSAL PRAYER

By Pope Clement XI

Lord, I believe in you: increase my faith.
I trust in you: strengthen my trust.
I love you: let me love you more and more.
I am sorry for my sins: deepen my sorrow.

I worship you as my first beginning,
I long for you as my last end,
I praise you as my constant helper,
and call on you as my loving protector.

Guide me by your wisdom,
correct me with your justice,
comfort me with your mercy,
protect me with your power.

I offer you, Lord, my thoughts:
to be fixed on you;
my words: to have you for their theme;
my actions: to reflect my love for you;
my sufferings:
to be endured for your greater glory.

I want to do what you ask of me:
in the way you ask,
for as long as you ask,
because you ask it.

Lord, enlighten my understanding,
strengthen my will,

purify my heart,
and make me holy.

Help me to repent of my past sins
and to resist temptation in the future.

Help me to rise above my human weakness
and to grow stronger as a Christian.

Let me love you, my Lord and my God,
and see myself as I really am:
a pilgrim in this world,
a Christian called to respect and love
all whose lives I touch,
those in authority over me
or those under my authority,
my friends and my enemies.

Help me to conquer anger by gentleness,
greed by generosity, apathy by fervour.

Help me to forget myself
and reach out towards others.

Make me prudent in planning,
courageous in taking risks.

Make me patient in suffering,
unassuming in prosperity.

Keep me, Lord, attentive in prayer,
temperate in food and drink,

diligent in my work,
firm in my good intentions.

Let my conscience be clear,
my conduct without fault,
my speech blameless,
my life well-ordered.

Put me on guard against my human weaknesses.

Let me cherish your love for me,
keep your law,
and come at last to your salvation.

Teach me to realize that this world is passing,
that my true future is the happiness of heaven,
that life on earth is short,
and the life to come eternal.

Help me to prepare for death
with a proper fear of judgement,
but a greater trust in your goodness.

Lead me safely through death
to the endless joy of heaven.

Grant this through Christ our Lord.
Amen.

Prayer of reparation

This is the prayer which a sister of the Poor Clares used to recite daily until her dying day. After her death she appeared to the Abbess of her convent who was praying for her and said, "I went directly to heaven because, I paid all my debts and was preserved from Purgatory by reciting this prayer every evening":

**Eternal Father, through the hands
of Our Lady of Sorrows,
I offer you the Sacred Heart of Jesus
with all his love, with all his sufferings
and with all his merits:**

*to atone for all the sins I have committed today
and throughout my past life;*
Glory Be

Eternal Father, through the hands...

*to purify the good which I did badly today
and throughout my past life;*
Glory Be

Eternal Father, through the hands...

*to compensate for the good that I failed to do
today and throughout my past life.*
Glory Be

PLEA TO GOD

O God, our heart is in deep darkness,
although it is united to your Heart.
Our heart is struggling between you and Satan;
let it not be so!
And each time our heart is divided between good
and evil,
let it be enlightened by your light and be united
to you.

May there not be two lovers inside us,
may two beliefs not coexist,
do not permit lies and sincerity, love and hate,
honesty and dishonesty, humility and pride to
exist together in us.

Help us rather, to have a heart
lifted up to you like that of a child;
may our heart be full of peace
with a continual desire for you.

Let your holy will and your love
dwell within us, so that at least sometimes
we may truly desire to be your children.

And when, Lord,
we do not desire to be your children,
remember our former desires
and help us to welcome you again into our lives.

We open our hearts to you so that
your holy love may dwell in them.

We open our souls to you
so that they may be touched by your holy mercy,
which shall help us to see all our sins clearly
and make us understand that sin is what renders
us impure!

God, we want to be your children, so humble and
devoted
that we may become true and dear children,
as the Father would like us to be.

Help us, Jesus, our brother,
to obtain forgiveness from the Father
and to be good to him.
Help us, Jesus, to comprehend fully what God
gives us
because, at times, we renounce
doing a good action considering it to be wrong.

Glory Be *(3 times)*

CHAPLETS

THE CHAPLET OF DIVINE TENDERNESS

FIRST MYSTERY

In the first mystery we contemplate the tenderness of the Father in the mystery of predestination: "He decided beforehand who were the ones destined to be moulded to the pattern of his son" *(Rm 8:29)*.

Our Father
Tenderness of the Father,
comfort us! *(10 times)*
Glory Be

SECOND MYSTERY

In the second mystery we contemplate the tenderness of Jesus in the mystery of Salvation: "He offered himself for us" *(Tt 2:14)*.

Our Father
Tenderness of the Father,
comfort us! *(10 times)*
Glory Be

THIRD MYSTERY

In the third mystery we contemplate the tenderness of the Holy Spirit in the mystery of Pentecost: "When the Paraclete comes, whom I shall send to you from the Father, the Spirit of truth who issues from the Father, he will be my witness" *(Jn 15:26)*.

Our Father
Tenderness of the Father,
comfort us! *(10 times)*
Glory Be

FOURTH MYSTERY

In the fourth mystery we contemplate the tenderness of Our Lady, Mother of the Church, Mediatrix of all graces, Mother of Jesus and our Mother.

Our Father
Tenderness of the Father,
comfort us! *(10 times)*
Glory Be

FIFTH MYSTERY

In the fifth mystery we contemplate the tenderness of all the saints in the witness which they bore with their lives and in their intercession with the Father, on our behalf.

Our Father

Tenderness of the Father,
comfort us! *(10 times)*
Glory Be

Invocation
May God's tenderness towards us be acknowledged, praised, loved and receive thanks!

Litany of the Divine Tenderness
(See page 125)

THE CHAPLET OF DIVINE PROVIDENCE
Saint John Calabria

This chaplet is recited using the traditional rosary beads, praying with faith, trust and great abandonment to the Love of the Father.

In the name of the Father, and the Son, and of the Holy Spirit. Amen.

O God, come to my aid.
O Lord, make haste to help me.
Glory Be

On the Our Father beads, we recite the following words:
Most Sacred Heart of Jesus, graciously hear us.
Heart most pure of Mary, graciously hear us.

On the Hail Mary beads, we recite the following words:
Most Holy Providence of God, provide for us.

After the last decade, we pray as follows:
Look upon us, Mary, with your eyes of mercy.
Come to our aid, O Queen, with your love.

Hail Mary

O Father, Son and Holy Spirit: most Holy Trinity; Jesus, Mary, Angels, and all you Saints of heaven, we ask these graces through the Holy Blood of Jesus Christ:

Glory Be

In honour of Saint Joseph:
Glory Be

In honour of Saint John Calabria:
Glory Be

For the holy souls in Purgatory:
Eternal rest...

For our benefactors:

Grant, O Lord, that all those who help us may be rewarded with eternal life, for the glory of your holy Name.
Amen.

NOVENA TO MY FATHER

Introduction

The "Novena to my Father" is a hymn of thanksgiving for the many gifts given to us, but is also a request for further graces.

The Novena is intended to be an act of reparation for those who do not show their gratitude to the Lord for the gifts they have received. Many Christians, even good-living people, do not feel the need to thank Jesus for the numerous benefits and graces which he lavishes upon them.

Too many Christians are negligent in the fundamental duty of thanksgiving to the Giver of all that good.

Ingratitude, while being a source of sorrow for humanity, is much more offensive to the Lord who generously fills every living creature with his great gifts, at every moment of every day.

When we need graces, we pray earnestly to God, to Our Lady, to the saints; but how many people thank them?

Perhaps only one out of ten!...

When Jesus healed the ten lepers, only one of them returned to thank him, and the Divine Master revealed his disappointment in the following words: "Were not all ten, made clean? The other nine, where are they?". (ref.Lk 17:17)

*In the name of the Father, and of the Son,
and of the Holy Spirit. Amen.*

O God, come to my aid.
O Lord, make haste to help me.
Glory Be

O Lord God, Eternal Father, I remind you of the words of your Divine Son Jesus: "Whatever you ask of my Father in my name, he will give it to you". Therefore, it is in the name of Jesus, in memory of his Blood and of his infinite merits, that I come to you today, in humility and like a poor person before someone who is rich, to ask you for a particular grace. But before making my request, I feel the need to repay you, at least in some small way, for my infinite debt of acknowledgement and gratitude towards you, O good and powerful God.

Thus, I am certain to make it easier for you to grant my prayer. Accept, therefore, O merciful God, my most heartfelt thanks, because a sense of gratitude overwhelms me.

Thank you for the benefits of Creation, for its preservation and for your vigilant paternal providence which manifests itself every day without my realizing it. Thank you for the benefits you have given us through the Incarnation of your Son and through his work of Redemption when he most generously offered his life on the cross for the salvation of the world.

Thank you for the Sacraments, source of every good, especially for the Sacrament of the Eucharist and for the holy sacrifice of the Mass by which the sacrifice of the crucifixion, in which the Blood of Christ was shed for us, becomes perpetual.

Thank you for the institution of the Roman Catholic Church, catholic and apostolic, for the Pope, for all the bishops and priests, under whose authority and by whose ministry I navigate with certainty in the sea of this treacherous life.

Thank you for the spirit of faith, of hope and of love, with which you have filled my mind and my heart.

Thank you for the doctrine of the Gospel and of its principles which I have sought to treasure in my life according to the teaching and example of Jesus Christ, and above all for the doctrine of the eight beatitudes which comfort me in the sorrows of life, especially that which says: "Blessed are those who suffer, because they will be comforted". And now that I have fulfilled my duty of thanking you, God the Father, generous author of every good, I dare to ask you in the name and by the merits of Jesus Christ for the grace I hope he will grant in his mercy.

(Here we mention the grace we desire.)
Glory Be

**Eternal Divine Father,
I thank you for all the gifts,
which you have bestowed
on the Church, on all nations,
on all souls and particularly on me,
and in the name of Jesus Christ,
I ask you to grant me more graces.**

Thank you, O God our Father, for your spirit of humility and of charity, of mercy and zeal, of patience and generous forgiveness, and of every good sentiment enkindled in us by listening to your Word, by the guidance of our confessor, by meditation and spiritual reading. I thank you also for the many good inspirations which you give to me.

Thank you for having freed me from many spiritual and material dangers and from many occasions of sin. Thank you for the vocation which you have given to me and for the graces you have granted to me in order to fulfil it. Thank you for the Paradise which you have promised me and for the place you have prepared for me there, where I hope to come both by the merits of Jesus Christ and by my co-operation, avoiding every occasion of sin; thank you that your Son has redeemed me in spite of the wrong that I have done in the past. Thank you for having given me the dear Mother of your Son, the Virgin Mary, as my heavenly mother, ever merciful and loving towards me; thank you for having endowed her with many privileges, above all with that of the Immaculate Conception, her Assumption into Heaven and for having chosen her to be "Mediatrix of all graces".

Thank you for having given me Saint Joseph as patron of a holy death and also many other saints besides as models of holiness and patrons to protect us; thank you for having given me my Guardian Angel who prompts me continuously with good inspirations in order to keep me on the right path.

Thank you for all beautiful and useful devotions which the Church puts at my disposal in order to help me on my road to holiness, especially the devotions to the Sacred Heart of Jesus; to the Blessed Eucharist; to his Passion; to the Immaculate Virgin, venerated by numerous different titles; devotions to Saint Joseph and to many other saints and angels.

Thank you for the good example given me by my neighbour, and for having helped me to understand that, according to the words of the Gospel, whoever does the will of God everywhere and in every moment is the brother, sister and mother of the Lord Jesus.

Thank you for having inflamed a spirit of thanksgiving in me which is the foundation and the orientation of my spiritual life. Thank you for the good which you have been pleased to do through me; I am amazed and humbled that you,

O Lord, have made use of me, a poor creature. I thank you already for seeking to lessen the pains of Purgatory for me through the merits of Jesus Christ, the Virgin Mary, the saints and the intercession of the holy souls. And now that I have thanked you once more, God our Father, generous author of all that is good, I dare to ask you in the name and by the merits of Jesus Christ for the grace I desire that you grant in your mercy.

(We mention the grace we desire)
Glory Be

Eternal Divine Father,
I thank you for the gifts,
which you have bestowed on
the Church, on all nations,
on all souls and particularly on me,
and in the name of Jesus Christ,
I ask you to grant me more graces.

I also thank you, O God our Father, for the troubles, the pains, the humiliations, the illnesses and the sorrowful heritage of sin which you have permitted me to experience, as they have led me to make the sacrifice which is necessary in order to follow your Divine Son who said, "No one who does not carry his cross and come after me can be my disciple" (Lk 14: 27). Thank you for the universe, immense and sparkling with stars, which "declares your glory" in its silent speech; for the sun, fountain of light and heat for us; for the water which takes away our thirst; for the flowers which beautify the earth.

Thank you for the place in society which you have given me, and that I have never lacked the necessities of life, neither honour nor daily bread; thank you for having given me the comfort and the material advantages which many people do not have.

Thank you for the graces I have received and for those, ah! much more numerous which I will come to know about only in Heaven!

Thank you for all the benefits of a natural and supernatural kind which you have given and continue to give to my relatives, friends and benefactors, to all the souls of the earth, to the good and the bad, to those who deserve them and to those who do not; for the benefits which you have given to the Catholic Church and to all its members, to my country and to all the world.

I want to thank you for all the graces which I recognize and for all those I do not recognize, not only in my daily devotions, but also every time I utter a short prayer. And now that I have fulfilled once more my humble duty of thanking you, God our Father, generous author of all that is good, I dare to ask you in the name and by the merits of Jesus Christ for the grace I desire that you grant to me in your mercy.

(We mention the grace we desire)
Glory Be

**Eternal Divine Father,
I thank you for the gifts,
which you have bestowed on
the Church, on all nations,
on all souls and particularly on me,
and in the name of Jesus Christ,
I ask you to grant me more graces.**

NOVENA TO DIVINE TENDERNESS

This novena is made from the 16th to the 24th of August, or at any other suitable time in order to express our love for God the Father.

In the name of the Father, and of the Son, and of the Holy Spirit. Amen.

O God, come to my aid.
O Lord, make haste to help me.
Glory Be

Eternal Father, who, moved by infinite tenderness for all humankind, sent your Divine Son Jesus on earth, grant that I may come to know your tenderness and that I may be clothed in it so that I may live in accordance with your will.

Glory Be

O Jesus, Tenderness of the Father, who came on earth to pour out on all people your merciful tenderness, grant me the grace to be invaded by this tenderness of yours, so that I may live in the hope of eternal salvation.

Glory Be

O Holy Spirit, most tender Love, who proceed from the Father and the Son, and who after the

Ascension of Jesus into heaven, moved by tenderness for all humankind, descended on the Apostles and on all the Church, enkindle in my heart a flame of your Love so that I may be able to taste your ineffable sweetness and be obedient to divine inspirations.

Glory Be

Let us pray.
O Jesus, Tenderness of the Father who has left the splendours of heaven to look down upon us and envelop us in your tenderness, have mercy on us in our weakness and sufferings, so that we may follow you one day to heaven.
Amen.

THE LITANY OF DIVINE TENDERNESS

Lord, have mercy on us.

Lord, have mercy on us.

Christ, have mercy on us.

Christ, have mercy on us.

Lord, have mercy on us.

Lord, have mercy on us.

Christ, hear us.

Christ, graciously hear us.

God, the Father of Heaven,

Have mercy on us.

God the Son, Redeemer of the world,

Have mercy on us.

God the Holy Spirit,

Have mercy on us.

Holy Trinity, one God,

Have mercy on us.

Tenderness of the Father
who has loved us from eternity,

Console us.

Tenderness of the Father
who has chosen us in Christ,

Console us.

Tenderness of the Father
who speaks to us in Creation,

Console us.

Tenderness of the Father
who has called us into existence,

Console us.

Tenderness of the Father
who governs the universe,

Console us.

Tenderness of the Father who sustains us,

Console us.

Tenderness of the Father who feeds us,

Console us.

Tenderness of the Father in the Abraham,
Isaac and Jacob,

Console us.

Tenderness of the Father in Moses
and in the prophets,

Console us.

Tenderness of the Father,
who awaits us in the House of Heaven,

Console us.

Tenderness of the Father
in the design of Redemption,

Console us.

Tenderness of Jesus in the Incarnation,

Save us.

Tenderness of Jesus in his childhood,

Save us.

Tenderness of Jesus
in his humble life at Nazareth,

Save us.

Tenderness of Jesus in his public life,

Save us.

Tenderness of Jesus in his miracles,

Save us.

Tenderness of Jesus in accepting sinners,

Save us.

Tenderness of Jesus in his Word of life,

Save us.

Tenderness of Jesus in the Eucharist,

Save us.

Tenderness of Jesus in his priesthood,

Save us.

Tenderness of Jesus in his Passion,

Save us.

Tenderness of Jesus
in his forgiveness of the repentant thief,

Save us.

Tenderness of Jesus
in giving us his most Holy Mother,

Save us.

Tenderness of Jesus in his death on the cross,

Save us.

Tenderness of Jesus,
gushing forth from the wound in his side,

Save us.

Tenderness of Jesus in his Resurrection,

Save us.

Tenderness of Jesus in his Ascension,

Save us.

Tenderness of Jesus in sending us the Holy Spirit,

Save us.

Tenderness of Jesus in Mary,
Mother of the Church,

Save us.

Tenderness of Jesus in his Vicar on earth,
the Pope,

Save us.

Tenderness of Jesus in the Apostles,

Save us.

Tenderness of Jesus in the Guardian Angels,

Save us.

Tenderness of Jesus in his glory,

Save us.

Tenderness of Jesus in all his trials,

Save us.

Tenderness of Jesus in all the saints,

Save us.

Lamb of God, who take away the sins of the world,
spare us, O Lord.

Lamb of God, who take away the sins of the world,
graciously hear us, O Lord.

Lamb of God, who take away the sins of the world,
have mercy on us.

Let us pray:
O God our Father, who have loved us from eternity with such "infinite tenderness" that you sent your only Son Jesus on earth for our salvation, free us from all evil, console us with your grace in every moment of our present life and at the end of our earthly days, bring us to the splendour of eternal life in your heavenly home, to enjoy forever your paternal tenderness. **Amen.**

ROSARY

THE ROSARY OF THE FATHER

This Rosary is a sign of the times, of these times which are witnessing the return of Jesus on earth "with great power" (Mt 24:30). "Power" is predominantly the characteristic of the Father ("I believe in God, the Father almighty"): it is the Father who comes in Jesus, and we must pray to him with fervour in order that the "new creation" which we await with such eagerness (ref. Rm 8:19), may come into being even sooner.

The Rosary of the Father is composed of five decades. It helps us to reflect on his mercy, which "is more powerful than evil, more powerful than sin and death" (Dives in Misericordia, VIII, 15). and reminds us how people may and indeed, must become the instruments of the triumph of the Father's Love, responding to Him fully with their "Fiat" and in this way, form part of the circle of the Trinitarian Love which renders people the "living glory of God".

This rosary also teaches us to live the mystery of suffering which is a great gift, as it allows us to bear witness to our love for the Father and permits Him to manifest Himself in us, having condescended to live within us.

The Father promises that for every Our Father recited, many souls will be saved from eternal damnation and many shall be freed from the pains of Purgatory. Moreover, God the Father will grant particular graces to the families that recite this rosary and the graces received shall be transmitted from generation to generation. In the lives of all those who recite it with faith and love, and live according to the Gospel, he will perform great miracles.

In the name of the Father, and of the Son,
and of the Holy Spirit. Amen.

PRAYER TO THE FATHER

Father, the earth needs you;
everyone needs you;
we pray to you, Father,
because even the heavy and polluted air needs
you; come back to walk along the
roads of the world,
come back to live among your children,
come back to rule nations,
come back to bring peace and justice,
come back to enkindle the fire of your love,
so that, redeemed from our sorrow,
we can become new creatures.

O God, come to my aid.
O Lord, make haste to help me.
Glory Be

O my Father, good Father,
I offer myself to You, I give myself to You.

Angel of God

FIRST MYSTERY

In the first mystery we contemplate the triumph of the Father in the Garden of Eden when, after the sin of Adam and Eve, he promises that a Saviour will come.

"Then Yahweh God said to the snake, 'Because you have done this, accursed be you of all animals wild and tame! On your belly you will go and on dust you will feed as long as you live. I shall put enmity between you and the woman, and between your offspring and hers; it will bruise your head and you will strike its heel' " *(Gn 3:14-15)*.

Hail Mary
10 Our Fathers
Glory Be
O my Father...
Angel of God...

SECOND MYSTERY

In the second mystery we contemplate the triumph of the Father at the moment of the "Fiat" of Mary during the Annunciation.

"The angel said to her, 'Mary, do not be afraid; you have won God's favour. Look! You are to conceive in your womb and bear a son, and you must name him Jesus. He will be great and will be called Son of the Most High. The Lord God will give him the throne of his ancestor David; he will rule over the House of Jacob for ever and his reign will have no end'... Mary said, 'You see before you the Lord's servant, let it happen to me as you have said' " *(Lk 1: 30-38)*.

Hail Mary
10 Our Fathers
Glory Be
O my Father...
Angel of God...

THIRD MYSTERY

In the third mystery we contemplate the triumph of the Father in the garden of Gethsemane when he gave all his power to his Son.

" 'Father', Jesus said, 'if you are willing, take this cup away from me. Nevertheless, let your will be done, not mine.' Then an angel appeared to him, coming from heaven to give him strength. In his anguish he prayed even more earnestly, and his sweat fell to the ground like great drops of blood" *(Lk 22: 42-44)*. "Then he came back to the disciples and said to them, 'You can sleep on now and have your rest. Look, the hour has come when the Son of man is to be betrayed into the hands of sinners. Get up! Let us go! Look, my betrayer is not far away" *(Mt 26: 45-46)*. "Jesus came forward and said: 'Who are you looking for?' They answered 'Jesus, the Nazarene.' He said 'I am he.' They moved back and fell to the ground" *(Jn 18: 4-6)*.

Hail Mary
10 Our Fathers
Glory Be
O my Father...
Angel of God...

FOURTH MYSTERY

In the fourth mystery we contemplate the triumph of the Father at the moment of individual judgement.

"While he was still a long way off, his father saw him and was moved with pity. He ran to the boy, clasped him in his arms and kissed him. Then the father said to his servants, 'Quick! Bring out the best robe and put it on him; put a ring on his finger and sandals on his feet. Bring the calf we have been fattening, and kill it; we will celebrate by having a feast, because this son of mine was dead and has come back to life; he was lost and is found'" (Lk 15: 20-24).

Hail Mary
10 Our Fathers
Glory Be
O my Father...
Angel of God...

FIFTH MYSTERY

In the fifth mystery we contemplate the triumph of the Father at the Last Judgement.

"Then I saw a new heaven and a new earth; the first heaven and the first earth had disappeared now, and there was no longer any sea. I saw the holy city, the new Jerusalem, coming down out of heaven from God, prepared as a bride dressed for her husband. Then I heard a loud voice call from the throne, 'Look, here God lives among human beings. He will make his home among them; they will be his people, and they will be their God, God-with-them. He will wipe away all tears from their eyes; there will be no more death, and no more mourning or sadness or pain. The world of the past has gone' " *(Rev 21:1-4).*

Hail Mary
10 Our Fathers
Glory Be
O my Father...
Angel of God...

LITANY OF THE FATHER

Father of infinite majesty,

Have mercy on us.

Father of infinite power,

Have mercy on us.

Father of infinite goodness,

Have mercy on us.

Father of infinite tenderness,

Have mercy on us.

Father, well of love,

Have mercy on us.

Father, powerful grace,

Have mercy on us.

Father, light of resurrection,

Have mercy on us.

Father, light of peace,

Have mercy on us.

Father, joy of salvation,

Have mercy on us.

Father, ever more fatherly,

Have mercy on us.

Father of infinite mercy

Have mercy on us.

Father of infinite splendour,

Have mercy on us.

Father, salvation of the hopeless,

Have mercy on us.

Father, hope of those who pray,

Have mercy on us.

Father, compassionate towards everyone
who is in pain,

Have mercy on us.

Father, for the weakest children,

We pray to you.

Father, for the most hopeless children,

We pray to you.

Father, for the less hopeless children,

We pray to you.

Father, for the children who are not greatly loved,

We pray to you.

Father, for the children who have not known you,

We pray to you.

Father, for the most desolate children,

We pray to you.

Father, for the most neglected children,

Have mercy on us.

Father, for the children who combat
for the coming of your Kingdom,

Have mercy on us.

We now recite:
Our Father
Hail Mary
Glory Be
for the Holy Father

Let us pray.

Father, we pray to you for your children, for each child, for all children: give us peace and salvation in the name of the Blood of your Son Jesus and in the name of the Heart of our Mother Mary who has suffered for us. **Amen.**

Trust in God *(See page 99)*

PRAYERS OF THANKSGIVING

To give thanks to the Father we may read or recite the following psalms:
Ps 18; 65; 84; 92; 95; 100; 103; 116; 136; 147;
thus praising the Lord in the Word inspired by His Holy Spirit. We may also use the following hymns in thanksgiving, both of which form part of the Liturgy of the Hours.

CANTICLE OF DANIEL
Canticle of the Three Children
(Dn 3: 57-88,56)

O all you works of the Lord, O bless the Lord.
To him be highest glory and praise for ever.
And you, angels of the Lord, O bless the Lord.
To him be highest glory and praise for ever.

And you, the heavens of the Lord,
O bless the Lord.
And you, clouds of the sky, O bless the Lord.
And you, all armies of the Lord,
O bless the Lord.
To him be highest glory and praise for ever.

And you, sun and moon, O bless the Lord.
And you, the stars of the heav'ns,
O bless the Lord.
And you, showers and rain, O bless the Lord.
To him be highest glory and praise for ever.

And you, all you breezes and winds,
O bless the Lord.
And you, fire and heat, O bless the Lord.
And you, cold and heat, O bless the Lord.
To him be highest glory and praise for ever.

And you, showers and dew, O bless the Lord.
And you, frosts and cold, O bless the Lord.
And you, frost and snow, O bless the Lord.
To him be highest glory and praise for ever.

And you, night-time and day, O bless the Lord.
And you, darkness and light, O bless the Lord.
And you, lightning and clouds, O bless the Lord.
To him be highest glory and praise for ever.

O let the earth bless the Lord.
To him be highest glory and praise for ever.

And you, mountains and hills, O bless the Lord.
And you, all plants of the earth, O bless the Lord
And you, fountains and springs, O bless the Lord.
To him be highest glory and praise for ever.

And you, rivers and seas, O bless the Lord.
And you, creatures of the sea, O bless the Lord.
And you, every bird in the sky, O bless the Lord.
And you, wild beasts and tame, O bless the Lord.
To him be highest glory and praise for ever.

And you, children of men, O bless the Lord.
To him be highest glory and praise for ever.

O Israel, bless the Lord. O bless the Lord.
And you, priests of the Lord, O bless the Lord.
And you, servants of the Lord, O bless the Lord.
To him be highest glory and praise for ever.

And you, spirits and souls of the just,
O bless the Lord.
And you, holy and humble of heart,
O bless the Lord.
Ananias, Azarias, Mizael, O bless the Lord.
To him be highest glory and praise for ever.

Let us praise the Father, the Son, and Holy Spirit:
To you be highest glory and praise for ever.
May you be blessed, O Lord, in the heavens.
To you be highest glory and praise for ever.

THE "TE DEUM"

This hymn from the Liturgy is sung at the end of the Divine Office on Sundays and feast-days.

We praise you, O God,
we acclaim you as the Lord.

Everlasting Father,
all the world bows down before you.

The angels sing your praise
the hosts of heaven and all the angelic powers,

all the cherubim and seraphim
call out to you in unending song:

Holy, Holy, Holy
is the Lord God of angel hosts!

The heavens and the earth are filled
with your majesty and glory.

The glorious band of apostles,
the noble company of prophets,

the white-robed army who shed their blood for
Christ, all sing your praise.

And to the ends of the earth
your Holy Church proclaims her faith to you:

Father, whose majesty is boundless,
your true and only Son, who is to be adored,
the Holy Spirit sent to be our Advocate.

You, Christ, are the king of glory,
Son of the eternal Father.

When you took our nature to save mankind
you did not shrink from birth in the Virgin's
womb.

You overcame the power of death
opening the Father's kingdom to all who believe
in you.

Enthroned at God's right hand in the glory of the
Father,
you will come in judgement according to our
promise.

You redeemed your people by your precious
blood. Come, we implore you, to our aid.

Grant us with the saints
a place in eternal glory.

Lord, save your people
and bless your inheritance.

Rule them and uphold them

for ever and ever.
Day by day we praise you:
we acclaim you now and to all eternity.

In your goodness, Lord, keep us free from sin.
Have mercy on us, Lord, have mercy.

May your mercy always be with us, Lord,
for we have hoped in you.

In you, Lord, we put our trust:
we shall not be put to shame.

## Part Four

The Son

1. THE CHILD JESUS

2. JESUS OUR SAVIOUR

3. THE SACRED HEART OF JESUS

4. JESUS IN THE EUCHARIST

5. THE PRECIOUS BLOOD OF JESUS

6. JESUS CRUCIFIED

7. THE MERCY OF JESUS

1.
THE CHILD JESUS

- **Reflection**
  - **Prayers**
- **Novenas**
  - **Triduum**
- **Chaplets**

THE NARROW DOOR OF BETHLEHEM

A reflection on the mystery of the Incarnation

Those who wish to visit the church on arriving at Bethlehem, which the emperor Constantine built on the site where, according to tradition, Christ was born, will find no trace of the splendid portals which at one time drew attention to the dignity of the house of God. For reasons which we are unable to discern precisely, even the last main entrance to exist was walled up, so that only a secondary entrance remains. The visitor has to stoop if he wishes to enter.

Although this has occurred by pure chance, it expresses something at a much deeper level. In some way, the low and narrow door is more befitting to the Event which is venerated here and to the Person for whom this space was constructed than a magnificent portal. God made himself small and thus every fear of ours in his presence dispelled; we can come close to him; a communion between us and him can be established. He humbled himself to the point of coming down to earth, to this little planet, to the point of penetrating the misery of our humanity.

The Fathers of the Church tell us that he has lowered himself so much that he can release the lost sheep from the bush where it is caught, take it on his shoulders and bring it with him. Those who come to the place where Jesus was born must stoop as God himself stooped: we must give up our presumptions, our suppositions, our arrogance, our prejudices, and become simple once more. Only in this way can we begin again to see and meet God who wished to become a child.

Only in this way can peace be established among us, because what separate us are our pretensions, our wanting to be in the right, our presumptuousness. What unites us is "the return to the heart" to which St. Augustine refers in this context.

Those who enter into the Church of the Nativity experience contrasting feelings. This country has always been the barometer of the history of the world. Here, the three continents Asia, Africa and Europe touch each other. Here, the religions and the powers of the world have come into conflict with one another. And this church has remained standing throughout the centuries; the power of the Child has been stronger than the destructive powers which have been unleashed here. Certainly the church has suffered; often it has been near to total ruin, and even today, the disputes among divided Christians prevent its being restored definitively definitive restoration. The frescoes have been destroyed to a great extent; only for a time was it one of the most beautiful churches in Christendom.

Here, we see both aspects: the decline and the continuity, the weakness and the strength of the faith. We may be struck by a great sadness on seeing the inability to make peace and to renounce one's own demands and interests for the sake of unity in faith, but the inability of humans leads them to humble themselves and thus to reach God and others.

It is also tremendously consoling to see that all the destructive frenzy of humanity has not succeded in quenching the feeble light which had its origin here two thousand years ago.

Accompanied by such thoughts we shall descend the stairway which leads to the cave, the stable where the Saviour of the world was born. Yes, it is necessary to descend once again, to follow, as it were, the descent of God, to lower oneself even more in order to reach the place of the mystery.

There, where - according to a tradition which has its origin in the second century - Mary gave birth to her Son, a silver star has been placed on the stone surrounded by lamps which light up the site with their bright and warm light. We find an inscription which quotes the first sentence of the Gospel according to St. John: "Here the Word was made flesh". In this place we can only remain silent, kneel down and allow ourselves to be penetrated by this mystery.

Among those who kneel down, pray and kiss the ground here, in spite of differences of place of orign, culture and creed, a bond is born that is impregnated with mystery. We are freed from our differences; taken away from the middle wall of separation which was raised up between us. Near to the Child there is no longer any division but like a heart beat we perceive the presence of Something Greater, of God. The silver star and the lamps appear to be a suitable image which signifies the following: heaven has shaken the earth and from that moment the earth shall not be allowed to go to ruin. It was not a destructive blow as when the planets collided with one another; it was rather a good and timely jolt which left behind a fount of light.

Many of the lights which light up the streets and houses at Christmas have little to do with this light. There are glittering lights which are used for business and cannot give heat in any way. They remind me of the fact that the astronomical observatories now have to be moved out of Europe because the lighting of our cities has become so dazzling that it covers the light of the stars, the light which comes from above. Many of the modern Christmas lights are simply human lights which, instead of demonstrating the light of God, hide it.

However, we should not be too pessimistic; we must not dwell on the rejection of the consumerism of Christmas, allowing our hearts to become embittered. A warm and humble light is always enkindled in our hearts from the cave of the Nativity, re-awakening the goodness buried within us which is the flame of God in our souls. Let us *imagine, just for a moment, what would happen if belief in the incarnation of God at Bethlehem were to wane. The places where atheism and hatred of God and of Christ have triumphed permit us to have an inkling of the frightful darkness which would be created if this were to happen.*

If we contemplated such a thing, perhaps we would cease to complain about the futility of Christianity in the history of the world. With his incarnation God has not cast a spell in order to transform the world into an earthly paradise as we may have desired. As the fate of the church of the Nativity shows us, the world is even more filled with worry than before. Nevertheless, God has brought into it a calm light of love and mercy which shall never let itself be extinguished. It is a light which is neither overpowering nor forceful. It invites us to humility, to liberty, to love.

It is to this light that we should open our hearts on Christmas Day.

Cardinal Joseph Ratzinger

PRAYERS

LET US ADORE THE LORD JESUS WHO CAME INTO THE WORLD

O Lord Jesus, eagerly awaited by humanity for centuries, and longed for by our poor hearts, too, we greet and adore you. In the name of all creatures, we express our immense gratitude to you for having come to save us according to the Divine Promise. We want to honour you with as much joy and fervour as we can muster, and together we cry: "Glory, honour and blessing be to you, Word of God, made Flesh". We adore and praise you, Son of God and of Mary. We adore you in your extreme poverty. We adore you, Lamb of God, who came to take away our sins. We adore you, Bread of Life, who came to give us true life.

We adore you because you unite yourself to us in our tears and in our suffering, in order to give us true happiness. We adore you, O God, who became a Child, to you we sing: "Glory be to God in the highest!". We adore and love you with the heart of Mary, your most Holy Mother, and of Joseph, your most chaste Father.

We love you and offer you our hearts with all the power of love that you yourself have given us and we hold you close to our humble hearts with all the strength that you have given us.

We love you, O Divine Victim of love, who came to bring us peace, hope and joy.

O Jesus, Divine Child, all of us here present embrace you and ask that we may we never be separated from you. **Amen.**

PRAYER TO THE CHILD JESUS FOR HOPELESS CASES

Remember, O Holy Child Jesus, the sweet pro-mise which you made to your dear disciple, Venerable Margaret of the most Holy Sacrament of the Altar when you addressed her with those beautiful words which anoint the broken soul with the balsam of heavenly consolation:

"Take recourse to my heart, and every time you wish to obtain a grace, ask for it through the merits of my holy infancy, and I will not refuse to grant it to you".

Full of confidence in your promise, here I am at your feet, O Divine Child; I come to place my needs before you. Help me to live a holy life so that one day I may reach our heavenly home; and through the merits of your infancy, through the intercession of your most lovable Mother, and of the Holy Archangels, Michael and Gabriel, grant me the grace which I now implore. *(Here we mention our specific request)* I ask it of you with lively hope because you know how much I need it. O sweet Child, do not let my hopes be deluded!

I trust in your tenderness and in the mercy of your Divine Heart, certain that you will hear my prayer. **Amen.**

PRAYER TO THE INFANT OF PRAGUE
A prayer revealed by Our Lady to the Venerable Father Cyril, Discalced Carmelite

O Child Jesus, I take recourse to you and I beseech you to assist me, through the intercession of your Holy Mother, in my particular need... *(We express our intention)* because I firmly believe that your divinity can assist me. I hope and trust that I may obtain your Holy Grace. I love you with all my heart and with all the strength of my soul.

I am heartily sorry for all my sins and I beseech you, O good Jesus, to give me the strength to be victorious in my struggle against evil. I resolve never to offend you again. I offer myself to you and would prefer to suffer rather than displease you in any way.

From now on I want to serve you with all my faith, and for love of you, O Divine Child, I will love my neighbour as myself.

All-powerful Child, Lord Jesus, I beseech you once more to help me in this particular situation and to give me the grace of possessing you in eternity, with Mary and Joseph, and of adoring you with the Angels and Saints in the Light of Heaven. **Amen.**

NOVENAS

IN PREPARATION FOR CHRISTMAS
(From the 15th to the 23rd of December)

The Christmas Novena is a path proposed to us in order to prepare for this solemnity. It is based on the most significant episodes of the Gospel which refer to the mystery of the birth and childhood of Jesus. In view of its simplicity, the Novena is particularly suitable for groups in which children take part. In this way they can discover the signs of Jesus' coming into the world, a useful exercise, especially when accompanied by the rest of the family; praying together, each family can renew its interpretation of the meaning of Christmas. It is very important to suggest (after the Our Father each day) an important action or good deed to be done, for example, kissing the Bible or the crucifix, sprinkling ourselves with holy water, exchanging the sign of peace, a small sacrifice, visiting a sick child or an elderly person, greeting one's mother and father in a special way on their return home, putting one's room in order, getting out of bed at the right time, writing Christmas greetings to those who would not otherwise receive them, paying special attention at school, giving money from one's savings to a fund for the children of the Third World, abstaining from every type of bad humour or bad behaviour. Thus the Novena allows us to grow not only in the spirit of prayer but also encourages us to help our neighbour.

In the name of the Father, and of the Son,
and of the Holy Spirit. Amen.

O God, come to my aid.
O Lord, make haste to help me
Glory Be

FIRST DAY: 15th OF DECEMBER
THE FULFILMENT OF THE PROPHECIES

*The waiting of the Old Testament is accomplished
in the virginal birth of Jesus.*

From the Gospel according to Matthew

1:1-2,6, 12,16,22-23.

"Roll of the genealogy of Jesus Christ, son of David, son of Abraham: Abraham fathered Isaac, Isaac fathered Jacob, Jacob fathered Judah and his brothers... David fathered Solomon, whose mother had been Uriah's wife... After the deportation to Babylon: Jechoniah fathered Shealtiel, Shealtiel fathered Zerubbabel... Jacob fathered Joseph, the husband of Mary; of her was born Jesus who is called Christ... Now all this took place to fulfil what the Lord had spoken through the prophet: 'Look! the virgin is with child and will give birth to a son whom they will call Immanuel, a name which means God-is-with-us.' "

Brief pause

O God, ancient prophecies announced your coming on earth: help your people who are waiting for you, to welcome the birth of their Redeemer with joy and to receive his heavenly gifts and the fullness of his blessing.
You who live and reign forever and ever. **Amen.**

Our Father • Hail Mary • Glory Be

SECOND DAY: 16th OF DECEMBER
THE ANNOUNCEMENT MADE TO JOSEPH

What is generated in her comes from the Holy Spirit.

From the Gospel according to Matthew   *1:18-21.*

"This is how Jesus Christ came to be born. His mother Mary was betrothed to Joseph; but before they came to live together she was found to be with child through the Holy Spirit. Her husband Joseph, being an upright man and wanting to spare her disgrace, decided to divorce her informally. He had made up his mind to do this when suddenly the angel of the Lord appeared to him in a dream and said: 'Joseph son of David, do not be afraid to take Mary home as your wife, because she has conceived what is in her by the Holy Spirit. She will give birth to a son and you must name him Jesus, because he is the one who is to save his people from their sins.' "

Brief pause

O Lord God, grant that we may await with great fervour the divine event, in which the Blessed Virgin, by the work of the Holy Spirit, gives birth to a God and Christ who becomes Lord and Saviour for all people.

He lives and reigns forever and ever. **Amen.**

Our Father • Hail Mary • Glory Be

THIRD DAY: 17th OF DECEMBER
THE ANNOUNCEMENT
MADE TO ZECHARIAH

John has been chosen to prepare the way of the Lord.

From the Gospel according to   *Lk 1:8-17.*

"Now it happened that it was the turn of his section to serve, and he was exercising his priestly office before God when it fell to him by lot, as the priestly custom was, to enter the Lord's sanctuary and burn incense there. And at the hour of incense all the people were outside, praying. Then there appeared to him the angel of the Lord, standing on the right of the altar of incense. The sight disturbed Zechariah and he was overcome with fear. But the angel said to him, 'Zechariah, do not be afraid, for your prayer has been heard. Your wife Elizabeth is to bear you a son and you shall name him John. He will be your joy and delight and many will rejoice at his birth, for he will be great in the sight of the Lord; he must drink no wine, no strong drink; even from his mother's womb he will be filled with the Holy Spirit, and he will bring back many of the Israelites to the Lord their God. With the spirit and power of Elijah, he will go before him to reconcile fathers to their children and the disobedient to the good sense of the upright, preparing for the Lord a people fit for him.'"

Brief pause

Lord God, who, at the beginning of time, created the light to free the world from the darkness which surrounded it, we ask you to send us the same Creator of light come, the Spouse of the true wedding prepared by you from eternity, and may all Christians, having been freed from original sin by baptism and purified by doing acts of charity, come ever closer to your Son, who lives and reigns forever and ever. **Amen.**

Our Father
Hail Mary
Glory Be

FOURTH DAY: 18th OF DECEMBER
THE ANNUNCIATION OF MARY

The Virgin, full of grace, is called to divine maternity.

From the Gospel according to   *Lk 1:26-33.*

"In the sixth month the angel Gabriel was sent by God to a town in Galilee called Nazareth, to a virgin betrothed to a man named Joseph, of the House of David; and the virgin's name was Mary. He went in and said to her: 'Rejoice, you who enjoy God's favour! The Lord is with you.' She was deeply disturbed by these words and asked herself what this greeting could mean, but the angel said to her: 'Mary do not be afraid; you have won God's favour. Look! You are to conceive in your womb and bear a son, and you must name him Jesus. He will be great and will be called Son of the most High. The Lord God will give him the throne of his ancestor David; he will rule over the House of Jacob for ever and his reign will have no end.'"

Brief pause

O God, eternal majesty, the Immaculate Virgin accepted your unutterable Word through the annunciation of an angel and became the living temple of God, enlightened by the Holy Spirit: we ask you that she, who was worthy of carrying Christ, God and man, in her holy and pure womb, may protect the faithful through her intecession. Through Christ our Lord. **Amen.**

Our Father • Hail Mary • Glory Be

FIFTH DAY: 19th OF DECEMBER
MARY'S ANSWER

The Holy Spirit will descend upon you...
I am the handmaid of the Lord.

From the Gospel according to   *Lk 1:34-38.*
"Mary said to the angel: 'But how can this come about, since I have no knowledge of man?' The angel answered, 'The Holy Spirit will come upon you, and the power of the Most High will cover you with its shadow. And so the child will be holy and will be called Son of God. And I tell you this too: your cousin Elizabeth also, in her old age, has conceived a son, and she whom people called barren is now in her sixth month, for nothing is impossible to God.' Mary said, 'You see before you the Lord's servant, let it happen to me as you have said.' And the angel left her."

Brief pause

O God, you desired that your Son take on our flesh in a virginal womb; grant, we beseech you, that the joy of knowing him as a man like us may bring us to have a share in the gifts of heaven. Through Jesus Christ, our Lord. **Amen.**

Our Father
Hail Mary
Glory Be

SIXTH DAY: 20th OF DECEMBER
THE VISITATION

Blessed is she who believed.

From the Gospel according to   *Lk 1:39-45.*

"Mary set out at that time and went as quickly as she could into the hill country to a town in Judah. She went into Zechariah's house and greeted Elizabeth. Now it happened that as soon as Elizabeth heard Mary's greeting, the child leapt in her womb and Elizabeth was filled with the Holy Spirit. She gave a loud cry and said: 'Of all women you are the most blessed, and blessed is the fruit of your womb. Why should I be honour-ed with a visit from the mother of my Lord? Look, the moment your greeting reached my ears, the child in my womb leapt for joy. Yes, blessed is she who believed that the promise made her by the Lord would be fulfilled.' "

Brief pause

Father, lover of life, your Church is radiant with joy while awaiting your Child whose coming was announced by the prophets and who now enters into this world like dew on dry soil; may the earth tremble with the new energy from heaven and, clothed with prayer and with song, may it encounter its Redeemer who lives and reigns for ever and ever. **Amen.**

Our Father • Hail Mary • Glory Be

SEVENTH DAY: 21st OF DECEMBER
THE MAGNIFICAT

The spiritual canticle of Mary.

From the Gospel according to   *Lk 1:46-55.*

"And Mary said: My soul proclaims the greatness of the Lord and my spirit rejoices in God my Saviour; because he has looked upon the humiliation of his servant. Yes, from now onwards all generations will call me blessed, for the Almighty has done great things for me. Holy is his name, and his faithful love extends age after age to those who fear him. He has used the power of his arm, he has routed the arrogant of heart. He has pulled down princes from their thrones and raised high the lowly. He has filled the starving with good things, sent the rich away empty. He has come to the help of Israel his servant, mindful of his faithful love - according to the promise he made to our ancestors - of his mercy to Abraham and to his descendants for ever."

Brief pause

Almighty God, fill with your goodness the earth which is waiting anxiously for the coming of its Saviour: may your people, full of the eternal joy which comes from your grace, be always sustained by your heavenly aid.

Through Christ our Lord. **Amen.**

Our Father • Hail Mary • Glory Be

EIGHTH DAY: 22nd OF DECEMBER
THE BIRTH OF JOHN AND THE CANTICLE OF ZECHARIAH

The Lord has visited his people.

From the Gospel according to   Lk 1:56-58,67-70,78-79.
"Mary stayed with her some three months and then went home. The time came for Elizabeth to have her child, and she gave birth to a son; and when her neighbours and relations heard that the Lord had lavished on her his faithful love, they shared her joy. (John's) father Zechariah was filled with the Holy Spirit and spoke this prophecy: Blessed be the Lord, the God of Israel, for he has visited his people, he has set them free, and he has established for us a saving power in the House of his servant David, just as he proclaimed, by the mouth of his holy prophets from ancient times... because of the faithful love of our God in which the rising Sun has come from on high to visit us, to give light to those who live in darkness and the shadow dark as death, and to guide our feet into the way of peace."

Brief pause

O Lord our God, true light, you have expressed from the depth of your heart your saving Word: and as you have allowed it come down from heaven into the uncontaminated womb of the Blessed Virgin Mary, in such a marvellous way, grant that we, your servants, may await his glorious Birth with joyful hearts.
Through Christ, our Lord. **Amen.**

Our Father • Hail Mary • Glory Be

NINTH DAY: 23rd OF DECEMBER
THE CENSUS AND THE
JOURNEY TO BETHLEHEM

The time came for Mary to have her child.

From the Gospel according to   *Lk 2:1-5.*
"Now it happened that at this time Caesar Augustus issued a decree that a census should be made of the whole inhabited world. This census - the first - took place while Quirinius was governor of Syria, and everyone went to his own town to be registered. So Joseph set out from the town of Nazareth in Galilee and travelled up to Judaea, to the town of David called Bethlehem, since he was of David's House and line, in order to be registered together with Mary, his betrothed, who was with child. Now it happened that while they were there the time came for her to have her child, and she gave birth to a son, her first-born. She wrapped him in swaddling clothes, and laid him in a manger because there was no room for them at the inn."

Brief pause

O God, Saviour of the world and Redeemer of all people who lay hidden in the flesh of Mary and, in revealing yourself, left the virginity of your Mother intact, we pray to you now that you have come to life on earth! We shall adore your two natures which shine in you so brightly, and we shall sing hymns to you, our only Lord with ardent faith.

You who live and reign for ever and ever. **Amen.**

Our Father • Hail Mary • Glory Be

Novena to the Infant of Prague

Devotion to the Infant of Prague began in the convent of the Discalced Carmelites, Prague, in the year 1628. The monks had received a beautiful little waxen statue of the child Jesus as a gift from a devoted princess, Polissena. The statue represented the Infant in royal robes with his right hand raised in the gesture of blessing while in his left hand, he held a small globe. It was placed in the internal oratory of the convent so as to be venerated by the faithful, and rapidly became a source of great blessings.

In the name of the Father, and of the Son, and of the Holy Spirit. Amen.

O God, come to my aid.
O Lord, make haste to help me.
Glory Be

FIRST DAY

Child Jesus, here I am at your feet. I turn to you who are my all. I greatly need your help! Look upon me, in your mercy, O Jesus and as you are all-powerful, come to my aid in my time of need.

Our Father • Hail Mary • Glory Be

O Jesus, through your Divine Infancy, O Jesus, grant me the grace I ask of you...
(Here express our desire)
if it be in accordance with your plan for me and for my benefit. Look not on my unworthiness, but on my faith and on your infinite Mercy.

Hymn

The sweet thought of Jesus
gives joy to the heart;
His presence sweeter than honey
and than all other things.

Nothing that can be sung is sweeter,
nothing that can be heard is more delightful,
nothing that can be thought of is sweeter
than Jesus, the Son of God.

Jesus, hope for all those who repent,
how merciful you are to those who pray to you,
how good you are to those who search for you
but what are you for those who find you?

Neither can tongue describe it
nor written words express
the joy one feels on finding the Lord,
it means to love Jesus.

Jesus, who are our future reward,
May you always be our source of happiness;
Let us glorify you
Now and forever. **Amen.**

Let us pray.
O God, who appointed your only Son to be the
Saviour of humankind, and ordered that He
should be called Jesus, grant that we may enjoy
in heaven the vision of the One whose name we
venerate here on earth.
Through the same Christ our Lord. **Amen.**

SECOND DAY

Jesus, splendour of the heavenly Father, in whose face shine the rays of divinity, I adore you while acknowledging you to be the true Son of the living God. I offer you, O Lord, the humble homage of my entire being. May I never be separated from you, who are my greatest possession.

Our Father
Hail Mary
Glory Be
O Jesus, through your Divine Infancy...
Hymn

THIRD DAY

Holy Child Jesus, while contemplating your face upon which appears the sweetest smile, I am inspired with a lively trust. Yes, I hope for everything from your goodness. O Jesus, let your smiles of grace rest upon me and upon all those who are dear to me, and I will exalt your infinite Mercy.

Our Father
Hail Mary
Glory Be
O Jesus, through your Divine Infancy...
Hymn

FOURTH DAY

O Child Jesus, who have a crown upon your foreheard, I acknowledge you as my Divine Sovereign. I wish to give in no more to the devil, my passions and sin. Reign, O Jesus, in this poor heart of mine; may it become all yours forever.

Our Father
Hail Mary
Glory Be
O Jesus, through your Divine Infancy...
Hymn

FIFTH DAY

I contemplate you, O sweetest Redeemer, clothed in a purple mantle. It is your royal uniform. How it speaks to me of blood! That blood which you shed for me. O Child Jesus, may I respond to your sacrifice and may I never refuse to accept any affliction which you may offer me in order to suffer with you and for you.

Our Father
Hail Mary
Glory Be
O Jesus, through your Divine Infancy...
Hymn

SIXTH DAY

Most lovable Child, as I watch you sustain the world, my heart is filled with joy. I am one of the countless beings you sustain. You see me, you support me in every moment, you take care of me as you would of a personal possession. Jesus, watch over me, and help me in my needs.

Our Father
Hail Mary
Glory Be
O Jesus, through your Divine Infancy...
Hymn

SEVENTH DAY

On your breast, Child Jesus, shines a cross. It is the sign of our Redemption. I also have my cross, Divine Saviour, which even if it is light, is often a burden. Help me to carry it, so that it may always bear fruit. You are conscious of my weaknesses. Help me, Jesus!

Our Father
Hail Mary
Glory Be
O Jesus, through your Divine Infancy...
Hymn

EIGHTH DAY

Child Jesus, together with the cross on your breast I see a little heart. It is the image of your Heart, truly golden, because of its infinite tenderness. You are the true friend, who generously gives of himself, and sacrifices himself for the person he loves. Enkindle in me, O Jesus, the fire of your charity, and teach me to respond to your love.

**Our Father
Hail Mary
Glory Be
O Jesus, through your Divine Infancy...
Hymn**

NINTH DAY

Little King, how many blessings your almighty Right Hand has poured out on all those who honour and invoke you. Bless me too, Child Jesus: my soul, my body, my necessities. Bless my needs in order that they may be satisfied, my desires in order that they may be fulfilled... Listen to my vows and I will bless your Holy Name every day.

**Our Father
Hail Mary
Glory Be
O Jesus, through your Divine Infancy...
Hymn**

Triduum

Triduum to the Infant of Prague

To obtain a special grace

*In the name of the Father, and of the Son,
and of the Holy Spirit. Amen.*

O God, come to my aid.
O Lord, make haste to help me.
Glory Be

O Child Jesus, here I am to open my heart to you.
I need your help! You are my all, while I am
nothing. You are the highest power, I am the greatest poverty; you are holiness, I am a sinner; you
are infinite goodness, while I... But do not refuse
to look at my nothingness; have mercy on me. Do
not reject me although I am a miserable creature.
I detest my faults and I humbly ask your forgiveness.

On your childish face shines the most lovable
smile and it tells me that everything is forgiven.
And as you instil me with confidence, let me
show you what has brought me to your feet...

(We express the grace which we desire)

I have told you everything, Jesus; now I await
only your word: "May it be done as you desire."
Say this almighty word: I long for it and will not

leave from here if you do not let me hear it. Only from you do I ask this grace: my faith will not be disappointed.

Glory Be *(3 times)*
Holy Infant Jesus,
hear us.

You are depicted, O my Jesus, in this image of an infant in order to draw us in a special way to your Heart, to make us feel your love more strongly, and to fill us with confidence; you alone are our support. I was wrong in turning to others in the past! Too often I have experienced the incapacity of human help; the earth easily gives rise to delusion and bitterness; but now I ask nothing more from human creatures; I turn to you for everything. Who is more powerful than you? ... Who is more compassionate?... With your promise "I will favour you" you tell us, O Child, that you want to be merciful with us, and the more we love you, the more merciful you will be. I promise to love you more every day; I want to serve you faithfully in future. Answer my request, therefore, in your kindness. Your Most Holy Mother will present it to you. Through her intercession, by the merits of your Divine Infancy, grant me what I ask of you.

Glory Be *(3 times)*
Holy Infant Jesus,
hear us.

LITANY OF THE HOLY INFANT
To be recited on the 25th of every month

Pope Pius VII granted a plenary indulgence to all those who, practise this devotion, dedicated in a particularway to the Infant of Prague on the 5th day of every month, having confessed and received Holy Communion, for the Hly Father's intentions.

Lord,

Have mercy on us.

Jesus Christ,

Have mercy on us.

Lord,

Have mercy on us.

Infant Jesus,

hear us.

Infant Jesus,

graciously hear us.

God, the Father of Heaven,

Have mercy on us.

God the Son, Redeemer of the world,

Have mercy on us.

God the Holy Spirit,

Have mercy on us.

Holy Trinity, one God,

Have mercy on us.

Divine Infant, true Child of the living God,

Have mercy on us.

Divine Infant, true Child of Mary,

Have mercy on us.

Divine Infant, Word made flesh,

Have mercy on us.

Divine Infant, Wisdom of the Heavenly Father,

Have mercy on us.

Divine Infant, object of eternal delight,

Have mercy on us.

Divine Infant, Whose coming was
awaited by the upright,

Have mercy on us.

Divine Infant, desired by all nations,

Have mercy on us.

Divine Infant, greeted by the prophets,

Have mercy on us.

Divine Infant, king of the angels,

Have mercy on us.

Divine Infant, our Saviour,

Have mercy on us.

Divine Infant, our brother,

Have mercy on us.

Divine Infant, who chose a stable for your
dwelling place, a manger for your cradle,
and shepherds to adore you,

Have mercy on us.

Divine Infant, whom the Magi recognised
as the light and salvation of all people,

Have mercy on us.

Divine Infant, treasure of graces,

Have mercy on us.

Divine Infant, treasure of pure love,

Have mercy on us.

Look on us with favour,

Forgive us, O Infant Jesus.

Look on us with favour,

Hear us, O Infant Jesus.

Look on us with favour,

Free us, O Infant Jesus.

From the evil of the world,

Free us, O Infant Jesus.

From the passion of the flesh,

Free us, O Infant Jesus.

From the pride of life,

Free us, O Infant Jesus.

Through your most noble birth,

Free us, O Infant Jesus.

Through your painful circumcision,

Free us, O Infant Jesus.

Through your glorious manifestation,

Free us, O Infant Jesus.

Through your presentation in the temple,

Free us, O Infant Jesus.

Through your innocence,

Free us, O Infant Jesus.

Through your simplicity,

Free us, O Infant Jesus.

Through your obedience,

Free us, O Infant Jesus.

Through your sweetness,

Free us, O Infant Jesus.

Through your humility,

Free us, O Infant Jesus.

Through your love,

Free us, O Infant Jesus.

Lamb of God, you take away the sins of the world,
spare us, O Infant Jesus.

Lamb of God, you take away the sins of the world,
graciously hear us, O Infant Jesus.

Lamb of God, you take away the sins of the world,
have mercy on us, O Infant Jesus.

I will rejoice in God,
And I will exult in the Infant Jesus, my Saviour.

CHAPLETS

CHAPLET OF THE HOLY INFANT

This chaplet was revealed to Venerable Margaret of the Most Holy Sacrament of the Altar who was. Ardently devoted to the Holy Child Jesus One day she received a special grace from the Divine Child who appeared to her, showing her a chaplet shining with heavenly light and said , "Go and spread this devotion among all souls and assure them that I will give special graces of innocence and of purity to those who keep this little chaplet with them and recite it with devotion in memory of my holy infancy".

It consists of:
3 Our Fathers

to honour the three members of the Holy Family
12 Hail Marys

*in memory of the 12 years of
our divine Saviour's childhood*
1 introductory prayer and a final prayer.

*In the name of the Father, and of the Son
and of the Holy Spirit. Amen.*

INTRODUCTORY PRAYER

Holy Child Jesus, I unite my heart to the devoted shepherds who adored you in the manger and to the angels who glorified you in heaven. Divine Infant Jesus, I adore your cross and accept what you are pleased to send me. Adorable Family, I offer you all the adoration of the Most Holy Heart of the Child Jesus, of the Immaculate Heart of Mary and of the Heart of Saint Joseph.

In honour of the Infant Jesus:
Our Father
The Word was made flesh and dwelt among us.

In memory of the first four years of the childhood of Jesus:
Hail Mary *(4 times)*

In honour of the Most Holy Virgin Mary:
Our Father
The Word was made flesh and dwelt among us.

In memory of the next four years of the childhood of Jesus:
Hail Mary *(4 times)*

In honour of Saint Joseph:
Our Father
The Word was made flesh and dwelt among us.

In memory of the last four years of the childhood of Jesus:
Hail Mary *(4 times)*

FINAL PRAYER

Lord Jesus, who were conceived by the Holy Spirit, you wanted to be born of the Blessed Virgin Mary, to be circumcised, to be made known to the gentiles and presented in the temple, to be taken to Egypt and to spend part of your infancy there, to return to Nazareth and to appear in Jerusalem as a prodigy of wisdom among the doctors of the temple. We contemplate the first twelve years of your earthly life and we ask you to grant us the grace of honouring the mysteries of your holy infancy with great devotion so as to become humble of heart and spirit and to conform to you in all ways, O Divine Child, you who live and reign with God the Father, in the unity of the Holy Spirit for ever and ever.
Amen.

Chaplet of the Child Jesus

*In the name of the Father, and of the Son,
and of the Holy Spirit. Amen.*

O God, come to my aid.
O Lord, make haste to help me.
Glory be

Hymn to the Child Jesus e.g.: *Away in a Manger*

O Jesus, most tender Child, who from the heart of
the Father came down from heaven for our salvation to enter the womb of the Virgin Mary where,
conceived by the Holy Spirit, you became the
Word Incarnate, grant that we, humble of heart,
may enjoy the fruits of your redemption.

Hail Mary
Come, Lord Jesus, Saviour of the world!

O Jesus, most tender Child, who through the Virgin Mary, visited Saint Elisabeth and sanctified
your precursor John the Baptist from his time in
the womb of his mother, sanctify our souls with
the most precious treasure of your holy grace.

Hail Mary
Come, Lord Jesus, Saviour of the world!

O Jesus, most tender child who, born of the Virgin Mary in Bethlehem, were wrapped in humble swaddling clothes, were laid in the manger, glorified by the angels and visited by the shepherds, grant that our heart may be worthy of welcoming you as a child and of adoring you as our Redeemer.

Hail Mary
Come, Lord Jesus, Saviour of the world!

O Jesus, most tender child, who were revealed by a star to the Magi and received gifts of gold, incense and myrrh from them, guide us also along the path of humble service that leads to you.

Hail Mary
Come, Lord Jesus, Saviour of the world!

O Jesus, most tender child, who were circumcised eight days after your birth and were called by the glorious name of Jesus, and in name and in blood, were prophesied as being Saviour of the world, free our minds from every impure desire and from every vice.

Hail Mary
Come, Lord Jesus, Saviour of the world!

O Jesus, most tender child, whom Herod sought to put to death, and were taken with your mother to Egypt by Saint Joseph, saved from death by your flight and glorified by the Holy Innocents, deliver us from the snares of our chief enemies: the world, the flesh and the devil.

**Hail Mary
Come, Lord Jesus, Saviour of the world!**

O Jesus, most tender child, who were taken to Jerusalem at twelve years of age, and were separated from Mary and Joseph, searched for with sorrow and found with great joy after three days among the doctors in the temple, fill us with true wisdom so that we never stray away from our mother the Church.

**Hail Mary
Come, Lord Jesus, Saviour of the world!**

O Jesus, most tender child who, living in holiness in the house of Nazareth, led your life in obedience, poverty and labour and, growing in age and grace revealed to us your divine wisdom, keep ever alive in our mind the memory of you, of Joseph and of your most holy Mother.

**Hail Mary
Come, Lord Jesus, Saviour of the world!**

2.

JESUS OUR SAVIOUR

- Reflection
  - Rosaries

REFLECTION

CHRIST, OUR ONLY SAVIOUR
A reflection by Pope John Paul II

Christ reveals himself in all the events that happened to him on earth as the Saviour sent by the Father for the salvation of the world. His very name "Jesus" manifests this mission. In fact it means "God saves".

It is a name which was conferred on him following indications from heaven: both Mary and Joseph (Lk 1:31; Mt 1:21) were given the order to call him this name. In the message to Joseph the name is clarified: "He is the one who is to save his people from their sins".

Christ defines his mission of Saviour as a service, the greatest manifestation of which consists in the sacrifice of his life in the favour of all people: "The Son of man came not to be served but to serve, and to give his life as a ransom for many" (Mk 10:45,; Mt 20:28). These words, spoken to oppose the tendency of the disciples to seek the first place in the Kingdom, are intended in particular to arouse a new mentality in them, more in conformity with that of the Master.

In the book of Daniel the character described "as a son of man" is presented as being surrounded with the glory befitting to leaders, to whom universal homage is paid: "All peoples, nations and languages became his servants." (Dn 7:14). Jesus, in contrast to this figure, presents himself as the Son of man who places himself at the service of everyone. Insofar as he is a person of the Divinity, he has every right to be served. However, having said that he has "come to serve", he manifests an overwhelming aspect of the behaviour of God who, although having the right and the power to have others serve him, he puts himself "at the service" of his creatures.

Jesus expresses in an eloquent and moving way this will to serve in the gesture of the Last Supper, when he washes the feet of the disciples: a symbolic gesture which will be impressed definitively upon their memory as a rule of life: "You too must wash each other's feet" (Jn 13:14).

In saying that the Son of man came to give his life as a ransom for many, (Jesus) refers to the prophecy of the Suffering Servant, who "gives his life as an offering for sin" (Is 53:10). It is a personal offering, very different from the offerings of animals, used in ancient cult. It is the gift of life "as a ransom for many", that is for the immense multitude of human beings, for "all people".

Thus Jesus appears as the universal Saviour: all human beings, according to the divine plan, are redeemed.

St. Paul says, "All have sinned and lack God's glory, and all are justified by the free gift of his grace through being set free in Christ Jesus" (Rm 3:23-24). Salvation is a gift which can be received by everyone according to the extent of a person's free consent and voluntary co-operation.

Being a universal Saviour, Christ is the only Saviour. Peter affirms this clearly: "Only in him is there salvation, for of all the names in the world given to men, this is the only one by which we can be saved." (Ac 4:11-12).

At the same time, He is also proclaimed as being the only mediator between God and humankind, as stated by the First Letter to Timothy: "For there is only one God, and there is only one mediator between God and humanity, himself a human being, Christ Jesus, who offered himself as a ransom for all." (1Tm 2:5-6).

Insofar as God is man, Jesus is the perfect mediator, who bring together God and humanity, obtaining for it the benefits of salvation and of divine life. This is a matter of a unique mediation, which excludes any concurrent parallel mediation, in spite of being compatible with shared or dependent mediations (ref. Redemptoris missio, 5).

Therefore other autonomous founts or ways of salvation cannot be accepted be-sides Christ? Thus in the main great religions, which the Church regards with respect, and esteems along the lines indicated by the Second Vatican Council, Christians recognize the presence of salvific ele-ments, which are dependent, however, on the influence of the grace of Christ for their operation. Such religions can in this way contribute, by virtue of the mysterious action of the Holy Spirit who "blows where it pleases" (Jn 3:8), to helping people in their journey towards eternal happiness, but this rôle is also the fruit of the redemptive action of Christ. Therefore Christ the Saviour acts also in relation to the main religions, uniting the Church to himself in this work, which has been appointed "as a sacrament of the intimate union with God and of the unity of all humankind" (Lumen Gentium, 1).

I like to conclude with a marvellous page of the True Devotion to Mary of St. Louis de Montfort, which proclaims the Christological faith of the Church: "Jesus, our Saviour... is the Alpha and the Omega, the beginning and end of everything. (...) He is the only teacher from whom we must learn; the only Lord on whom we should depend; the only Head to whom we should be united and the only model that we should imitate. He is the only Physician that can heal us; the only Shepherd that can feed us; the only Life that can animate us. He alone is everything to us and he alone can satisfy our desires. (...)

Every one of the faithful who is not united to him is like a branch broken from the stem of the vine. It falls and withers and is fit only to be burnt. If we live in Jesus and Jesus lives in us, we need not fear damnation.

Neither angels in heaven nor men on earth, nor devils in hell, no creature whatever can harm us, for no creature can separate us from the love of God which is in Christ Jesus.

Through him, with him and in him, we can do all things and render all honour and glory to the Father in the unity of the Holy Spirit, we can make ourselves perfect and be for our neighbour a fragrance of eternal life." (True Devotion to the Blessed Virgin, No. 61).

Pope John Paul II

ROSARIES

THE ROSARY OF JESUS

In the Rosary of Jesus, we remember the 33 years of his life.

It should always be recited but it acquires a special meaning when prayed during Lent.

You should pray only with your lips. You must pray with your heart, your whole being must descend into the depth of your heart. Sit down.

The body must be still, with the eyes turned towards Jesus. Put aside any other worry and desire.

The Rosary of Jesus is an effective way of being introduced to contemplative prayer when it is said calmly as Mary desires, alternated with moments of silence for reflection and when the mysteries of the life of Jesus are applied to oneself and to others in this way it fulfils the promise of Mary.

The Rosary is made up of:
33 Our Fathers
The Creed
7 Glory Bes
7 mysteries

HOW TO RECITE THE ROSARY OF JESUS

a. *We contemplate the mysteries of the life of Jesus with the help of a brief introduction. The Virgin Mary exhorts us to pause in silence and to reflect on every single mystery. The mystery of the life of Jesus must speak to our hearts...*

b. *It is suggested to express a particular intention for each mystery.*

c. *After having expressed the particular intention, the Virgin Mary recommends that we should open our hearts together in spontaneous prayer while we contemplate.*

d. *At each mystery, after this spontaneous prayer, it is recommended to sing a suitable hymn.*

e. *After the hymn, we recite 5 Our Fathers (apart from the seventh mystery which we conclude with 3 Our Fathers);*

f. *And we exclaim:*

O Jesus, be our strength and protection!

In the name of the Father, and of the Son,
and of the Holy Spirit. Amen.

O God, come to my aid.
O Lord, make haste to help me.
Glory be

INTRODUCTORY PRAYER

My Jesus, in this moment I want to be with you. You are my brother and my Saviour. You have remained with me and for me. Thank you! In gratitude for your life, here I am, O Jesus, to entrust my life to you at the beginning of my prayer: I leave behind all my worries, all my troubles, everything which attracts me and distracts me from you. I renounce all sin, with which I have destroyed my friendship with you; I renounce all evil, which has made our friendship difficult. I place at your feet, O Jesus, everything I possess; I want to be all yours and to belong to the Father in union with you. O Mary, nobody has ever known how to spend time with Jesus as you have, because He grew and developed by your side. Please be close to me now, so that I may know how to remain with Jesus. O Mary, pray with me, so that the Spirit of Jesus may be poured forth on me and may pray inside me, repeating, "Abba, Father!".
Amen.

The Creed *(See page 26)*

FIRST MYSTERY
Jesus is born in a cave at Bethlehem.

"Joseph set out from the town of Nazareth in Galilee for Judaea, to David's town called Bethlehem, since he was of David's House and line, in order to be registered together with Mary, his betrothed, who was with child. Now it happened that, while they were there, the time came for her to have a child, and she gave birth to a son, her first-born. She wrapped him in swaddling clothes and laid him in a manger because there was no room for them in the living-space... The angel said 'Do not be afraid. Look, I bring you news of great joy, a joy to be shared by the whole people. Today in the town of David a Saviour has been born to you; he is Christ the Lord. And here is a sign for you: you will find a baby wrapped in swaddling clothes and lying in a manger.' And all at once with the angel there was a great throng of the hosts of heaven, praising God with the words: Glory to God in the highest heaven, and on earth peace for those he favours." *(Lk 2: 4-7,10-14).*

Intention:
Let us pray for peace.

Spontaneous prayers

Hymn
Let us pray slowly and meditatively:
5 Our Fathers

O Jesus, be our protection and strength!

SECOND MYSTERY
Jesus helped them and gave everything to them.

"It was late afternoon when the Twelve came up to him and said: 'Send the people away, and they can go to the villages and farms round about to find lodging and food; for we are in a lonely place here.' He replied, 'Give them something to eat yourselves.' But they said: 'We have no more than five loaves and two fish, unless we are to go ourselves and buy food for all these people.'.... Then he took the five loaves and the two fish, raised his eyes to heaven, and said the blessing over them; then he broke them and handed them to his disciples to distribute among the crowd." *(Lk 9: 12-13.16-17).*

Intention:
**Let us pray for the Holy Father
and for all those responsible
for the Church and for all nations.**

Spontaneous Prayers

Hymn

5 Our Fathers

O Jesus, be our protection and strength!

THIRD MYSTERY

*Jesus entrusted himself totally to the Father
and accomplished his Will.*

"Then Jesus came with them to a plot of land called Gethsemane; and he said to his disciples, 'Stay here while I go there to pray.' He took Peter and the two sons of Zebedee with him. And he began to feel sadness and anguish. Then he said to them, 'My soul is sorrowful to the point of death. Wait here and stay awake with me.' And going on a little further he fell on his face and prayed. 'My Father', he said, 'if it is possible, let this cup pass me by. Nevertheless, let it be as you, not I, would have it.'.... Again, a second time, he went away and prayed: 'My Father' he said 'if this cup cannot pass by, but I must drink it, your will be done!' And he came back again and found them sleeping, their eyes were so heavy. Leaving them there, he went away again and prayed for the third time, repeating the same words." *(Mt 26:36-39,42-44).*

Intention:

**Let us pray for priests and for
all those who are called to serve Jesus in a
special way throughout their entire life .**

Spontaneous Prayers

Hymn

5 Our Fathers

O Jesus, be our protection and strength!

FOURTH MYSTERY

Jesus was aware of giving his life for us and he did so without objection, because he loves us.

"After saying this, Jesus raised his eyes to heaven and said: Father, the hour has come: glorify your Son so that your Son may glorify you; so that, just as you have given him power over all humanity, he may give eternal life to all those you have entrusted to him... And for their sake I consecrate myself so that they too may be consecrated in truth." *(Jn 17:1-2,19)*.

Intention:
Let us pray for all families.

O Jesus, you loved us, and because of your love you return to the Father in peace and in complete abandonment. For you nothing was too much, because you were sustained by love for us. Open the heart of each member of our families so that everyone strives to make others happy. Grant that all fathers and mothers may sanctify their life in love, in order to be able to grow in holiness together with their children.

Spontaneous Prayers

Hymn

5 Our Fathers

O Jesus, be our protection and strength!

FIFTH MYSTERY
Jesus made his life a sacrifice for us.

" 'This is my commandment: love one another, as I have loved you. No-one can have greater love than to lay down his life for his friends. You are my friends, if you do what I command you.' " *(Jn 15:12-14).*

Intention:
Let us pray that each of us may be able to offer our life for our neighbour.

Spontaneous Prayers

Hymn

5 Our Fathers

O Jesus, be our protection and strength!

SIXTH MYSTERY

*The victory of Jesus: with his resurrection
he defeated Satan.*

"As they stood there puzzled about this, two men in brilliant clothes suddenly appeared at their side. Terrified, the women bowed their heads to the ground. But the two said to them, 'Why look among the dead for someone who is alive? He is not here; he has risen. Remember what he told you when he was still in Galilee: that the Son of man was destined to be handed over into power of sinful men and be crucified, and rise again on the third day.' *(Lk 24:4-7)*. "The seventy-two came back rejoicing. 'Lord,' " they said, 'even the devils submit to us when we use your name.' He said to them, 'I watched Satan fall like lightning from heaven. Look, I have given you power to tread down serpents and scorpions and the whole strength of the enemy; nothing shall ever hurt you. Yet do not rejoice that the spirits submit to you; rejoice instead that your names are written in heaven.'." *(Lk 10, 17-20)*

Intention:

**Let us pray that we may sin no more
and that Jesus may rise inside us**

Spontaneous Prayers

Hymn • 5 Our Fathers

O Jesus, be our protection and strength!

SEVENTH MYSTERY
The Ascension of Jesus into Heaven

"Then he took them out as far as the outskirts of Bethany, and raising his hands he blessed them. Now as he blessed them, he withdrew from them and was carried up to heaven. They worshipped him and then went back to Jerusalem full of joy; and they were continually in the Temple praising God." *(Lk 24:50-53)*.

Intention:

Let us pray that the will of God may be fulfilled and obeyed.

Spontaneous Prayers

Hymn

5 Our Fathers

O Jesus, be our protection and strength!

After this we contemplate Jesus who sends the Holy Spirit on the apostles, united in prayer with Mary.

"When Pentecost day came round, they had all met together, when suddenly there came from heaven a sound of a violent wind which filled the entire house in which they were sitting; and there appeared to them tongues as of fire; these separated and came to rest on the head of each of them. They were all filled with the Holy Spirit and began to speak different languages as the Spirit gave them power to express themselves". *(Act 2:1-4)*

Intention:
**Let us pray that
the Holy Spirit may be poured out
in his fullness upon us, on our families,
on the Church, on religious communities,
on all who are baptized, on all people,
particularly on those who decide the fate of
the world, so that the Holy Spirit
may inspire in them thoughts of justice and
wise decisions, and guide their steps towards
peace.**

7 Glory Be

FINAL PRAYER

O Jesus, it is good for us to stay with you. Thank you! Thank you for your life, for your love of the Father and for your obedience to the will of the Father. Thank you for having opened to us the way of salvation. O Mary, help us to remain faithful on the way of salvation and to reach eternal glory. **Amen.**

THE ROSARY OF THE LOVE OF JESUS
*In the name of the Father, and of the Son,
and of the Holy Spirit. Amen.*

O God, come to my aid.
O Lord, make haste to help me.
Glory Be

INTRODUCTORY PRAYER

God, our Father, I believe in your eternal and infinite love. You are love. Your Son Jesus Christ is your Word of Love and your Holy Spirit is the bond of love which unites you.

I believe that you have created everything out of love and that you govern everything wisely. I believe that your love has no end, not even when humans, your beloved creatures, turn their backs to you, in sin, and refuse your love.

I believe that out of love, you sent us messages which invite people to conversion. I believe that you have sent your Son to save the world with his love and to show your paternal love towards everybody, above all to sinners. Father, I believe that you, love all people because they are your children: you know no boundaries and love everybody infinitely.

I believe that you love all creatures and that your love gives them the strength to live and imparts meaning to all things.

I believe that you love the Church, the Body of

your Son. I believe that you love me and that my life is a gift of your love.

I believe that you loved me even before my birth and that because of this very love I have come into the world.

I believe that through baptism, you showed me your love and accepted me in the community of the Church.

I believe that you love me even when I sin and that you, out of love, forgive my sins. I believe in your love even when I know I am not worthy of it.

I believe that you love also those who, at this moment, cannot love you. I believe that your love is the guarantee that I can reach eternal life and live together with you, enjoying your boundless love.

I believe that, many of your children will be welcomed into your kingdom.

I believe that you are listening to my prayer now because I wish to pray to you with love.

I believe that you will hear my prayer because I pray to you in union with Mary, Mother of Love, as she is fully open to your love. Mary, my Mother, pray with me, for me and for all your children, to whom you gave birth with love and sorrow at the foot of the cross.

Hear my prayer, you who love, live and reign forever and ever. **Amen.**

FIRST MYSTERY

Lord, you ask us to love God, above all things. Thank you for having invited me to love you. I can love you only if you give me your love. For this reason, I now pray to you: pour into my heart so much love that I may love you infinitely and unconditionally, at every moment of my life. Give me your love so that I may love you in all people and in all creatures.

Forgive me for all the times that I did not respond with love to your love and when you were not in the first place in my everyday life. Purify me, so that from now on I may truly love you above all other things.

Make me love you as your Son Jesus Christ and your humble and faithful servant Mary loved you.

Our Father
10 Hail Marys
Glory Be
O my Jesus, forgive us our sins... *(see page 635)*

SECOND MYSTERY

Lord, you ask me to love myself. Make me understand that life is one of your gifts; that you wanted me for what I am and that your love wants to make me perfect. Grant that I may understand that the love of oneself is the first response to your love. Grant that I may understand that to love oneself means to co-operate constantly with your grace and to grow in your image and likeness. Grant that I may understand that to love oneself means to accept the truth as regards each one of us being in spiritual need of spiritual bread which can be obtained by prayer, by assisting at Mass, by proclaiming and reading your Word.

Forgive my selfishness, my arrogance, my jealousy, heal me of every fear and of every lack of trust in you, free me from everything which frightens me so that I may love you above all things and my neighbour as myself, according to your commandments.

Our Father
10 Hail Marys
Glory Be
O my Jesus, forgive us our sins... *(see page 635)*

THIRD MYSTERY

Lord, you ask that I may love everyone as I love you. Give me the grace to recognise your Son in every one of your creatures, who are your gift to me and to the world. Grant that my heart may be filled with your love and that I may love my brothers and sisters and do for them what I would like to be done to me. Forgive me for every shortcoming of love towards my neighbour, which reveals itself in rejection and in condemnation, in speaking unkindly about others, in exploitation, in abuse, and in seduction. Forgive me because many times I have not acted wisely, courageously and promptly, when my neighbour was suffering or needed my love. To my brothers and sisters give the grace they need to love and forgive me, so that I may forgive them more easily.

May your love unite all hearts and all people. May the love among all people guide us along the road to true peace.

Our Father
10 Hail Marys
Glory Be
O my Jesus, forgive us our sins... *(see page 635)*

FOURTH MYSTERY

Lord, you ask us to love our enemies and all those who have offended us. Father, although you love all people, there is a lot of hate and conflict in the world. Your Fatherly Heart must suffer in seeing how your children hate each other and persecute one another, reject love and harm one another. I beseech you, give love to me and to all people, so that we may love each other. Help us so that our love may overcome all boundaries and obstacles. Give us the strength, by means of your love, to overcome the hate in our hearts, so that there may be no more conflict. Where love is put aside, where it is lacerated by sin, heal it; where hate threatens love, may love forgive; where there is injustice, let love heal the relationships among people; where we raise our hands against our neighbour, let your love transform everything into forgiveness and fraternity. Teach us that those who love their enemies are greater than those who take revenge, so that we may love even those who do not love us.

Our Father
10 Hail Marys
Glory Be
O my Jesus, forgive us our sins... *(see page 635)*

FIFTH MYSTERY

Father, you ask me now to love everyone. Here, praying to you with love, I offer you all those in my family (community, prayer group) whom I find difficult to love and who would like to be loved by me. Renew my heart, as you have promised to do so by means of your prophecy. Remove my heart of stone and give me a heart capable of loving, suffering and accepting everything with love.

*Now I pause and offer to the Lord
those to whom my love must extend...*

I pray also for those who do not love me, who do not forgive me, so that their hearts may open to me, because it is not good that those who surround me do not love me.

In silence I name all those who do not love me and I pray:
**Our Father • 10 Hail Marys • Glory Be
O my Jesus, forgive us our sins...** *(see page 635)*

CONCLUDING PRAYER

Mary, mother of love, goodness, mercy and reconciliation, I know you are with me and that you invite me to grow in love and to live loving God, myself and my neighbour. Through your intercession, may the Lord God hear my prayer. **Amen.**

3.

THE SACRED HEART OF JESUS

- Prayers
  - Acts of Consecration
- Novenas
  - Chaplets
- Other Devotions

THE GREAT PROMISES OF THE SACRED HEART OF JESUS

The nine First Fridays

In the prayer of the Church the Sacred Heart of Jesus is venerated and honoured.

The Church adores the Incarnate Word and his Heart which, for love of humankind, let itself be pierced by our sins.

Jesus knew and loved each and every one of us during his life, his agony and his Passion, and he offered himself for the sake each one of us: as St. Paul says, "The Son of God has loved me and has given himself for me" (Gal 2: 20).

He loved all of us with a human heart. For this reason, the Sacred Heart of Jesus, transfixed because of our sins and for our salvation, is considered the sign and the principal symbol of that infinite love with which the Divine Redeemer loves the Eternal Father and all people unceasingly.

The Heart of Jesus is the symbol of that infinite and impenetrable love which made the Son of God become our brother, die for us on the Cross and remain forever in the Holy Sacrament of the Altar.

One day, in revealing his Heart to Saint Margaret Mary Alacoque (1647-1690), Jesus said:

"Behold the Heart which has loved people so much and receives from them only ingratitude and contempt...".

In various apparitions to St. Margaret Mary, Jesus made the following promises to those who honoured his Heart which we find in her letters:

1. "I will give them all the graces which are necessary to them in their present state" (Lett. 141).

2. "I will come to the aid of families that are in difficulty

and I will give peace to the families who are divided"
(Lett. 35 and 131).

3. "I will console them in their affliction" (Lett. 141).

4. "I will be their secure refuge in life and above all at the
moment of death" (Lett. 141).

5. "I will shower abundant blessings on all their works"
(Lett. 141).

6. "Sinners will find in my heart the source and the ocean
of mercy" (Lett. 131).

7. I will restore religious communities and all the faithful to
their original fervour" (Lett. 141 and 132).

8. "Fervent souls will reach perfection in a short time"
(Lett. 35).

9. I will bless the places where the image of my Sacred
Heart will be exposed and honoured" (Lett. 35).

10. "To all those who work for the salvation of souls, I will
give the gift of moving the hardest hearts" (Lett. 141).

11. "The name of those who propagate the devotion to my
Sacred Heart will be written in my heart and will never
be erased" (Lett. 39, 41 and 89).

12. "I promise you, in the excess of the Mercy of my Heart,
that my Almighty Love will give the grace of final peni-
tence to all those who receive Holy Communion on the
first Friday of each month for nine months consecuti-
vely. They will not die without being in a state of grace,
nor without receiving the Sacraments and my heart will
be a safe haven in their last hour."

With "the Great promise" (12) Jesus puts the omnipotence of his love at our disposal to ensure our salvation. let
us therefore trust in his infinite love. he desires only to see
us enter one day into heaven to enjoy eternal happiness.

Let us propagate this devotion by advising others to follow the message of the First Fridays because: "Who saves
a soul ensures his own salvation".

The importance of the devotion of the First Fridays is

revealed to us also by the apparition at the "Three Fountains" of Rome, where the Virgin Mary appeared for the first time on the 12th of April, 1947, as we are told by Bruno Cornacchiola and his three sons.

At the time of the apparition, Bruno, who was a bus conductor, dedicated his time off from work to consulting the Bible in order to gather fuel for argument with the clergy.

At the grotto of the Three Fountains he was preparing arguments against the Immaculate Conception, when he saw the Virgin Mary who spoke to him in these words:

"I am the One who is in the Divine Trinity. I am the Virgin of Revelation. You persecute me: stop now! Enter the holy sheep-fold, the heavenly court on earth. The nine Fridays of the Sacred Heart which you fulfilled before entering the way of falsehood, have saved you..."

PRAYERS

PRAYER TO THE HEARTS
OF JESUS AND MARY

Hearts most holy, we greet you.
Hearts most sweet, we greet you.
Hearts most humble, we greet you.
Hearts most pure, we greet you.
Hearts given without reserve,
Heart most wise, we greet you.
Hearts of patience, Hearts of obedience,
Hearts of vigilance, Hearts of faithfulness,
we greet you.
Hearts most joyful, Hearts full of mercy,
we greet you.
Most beloved Hearts of Jesus and of Mary,
we greet you.
We adore you, we praise you, we glorify you,
we give you thanks.
We love you with all our heart, with all our soul,
with all our strength. We offer you our hearts.
We give them to you; we consecrate them to you;
we offer them in sacrifice to you.
Receive them and possess them completely.
Purify them, enlighten them, sanctify them.
In them may you live and reign now and forever.
Amen.

Saint John Eudes

O SWEET HEART OF JESUS

O sweet heart of my beloved Jesus, were you not my Saviour, I would not dare to come to you! But you are my Saviour and my Lord, and your Heart loves me with a tender and ardent love, as no other heart is capable of loving.

I would like to respond to this love which you have for me and I would like to have for you, who are my only love, all the ardour of the seraphims, the purity of the angels and the virgins, the holiness of the saints who possess you and glorify you in heaven. And if I could offer you all of this, it would still not be enough to praise your Goodness and your Mercy.

Therefore I present to you my poor heart as it is, with all its poverty, weakness and good will. Deign to purify it with the Blood of your Heart. May you transform it and inflame it with a pure and ardent love. In this way, poor creature that I am, incapable of doing any good by myself, will love and glorify you like the most ardent seraphims of heaven!

Finally I beseech you, sweet Heart of Jesus, to impart the holiness of your own Heart to my soul, or even better, to let my soul enter into your Divine Heart, so that in it I may love, serve and glorify you, and dwell in it forever! I ask this grace for all those I love. May they render you the glory and honour of which my offences have deprived you!

Amen.

O ADORABLE HEART OF JESUS

O adorable Heart of Jesus, I come to you, because you are my refuge, my one sure hope.

You are the remedy for all my ills, the relief in all my misery, the reparation for all my faults, the substitute for all that is missing in me, the certainty for all requests, the infallible and endless spring of light, strength, peace and blessing for me.

I am sure that you will never become tired of me, and you will not cease to love, help and protect me, because you love me with an infinite love.

Therefore have mercy on me, Lord, in to your great compassion and do with me, in me and for me, all that you want, as I abandon myself to you with the utmost trust that you will never abandon me.

ETERNAL FATHER,
HAVE MERCY ON ALL SOULS

Eternal Father, who for love of humankind, gave your only Son to die for us, through his Blood, through his merits, through his Heart, have mercy on the whole world and forgive all the sins which are committed.

Receive the humble reparation which your chosen souls offer you; unite them to the merits of your Divine Son so that they may acquire a great efficacy.

O Eternal Father! Have mercy on all souls and remember that the time of justice has not yet come, but it is still the time of Mercy!

Amen.

ACTS OF CONSECRATION

PRAYER OF CONSECRATION TO THE SACRED HEART OF JESUS

Jesus, we know that you are Kind and that You gave Your Heart for us. It is crowned with the crown of thorns and with our sins.

We know that even today You pray for us us so that we will not be led into temptation.

Stand by us, Jesus, so we will not fall and sin.

Through Your Sacred Heart, grant us the grace to love each other always.

There must be no more hatred among us.

Show us Your Love!

We all love You and want You with your Shepherd's Heart to protect us from all sin.

Enter every heart! O Jesus Knock, at their closed doors. Be patient and untiring with us.

We have not understood Your Will and thus remain closed to You.

Knock steadfastly and grant us the grace to open our hearts to you at least when we remember the suffering You endured for us.

Amen.

ACT OF CONSECRATION TO THE MOST SACRED HEART OF JESUS

Most Sacred Heart of Jesus, most amiable Heart of our Redeemer, Heart of a father, of a brother, of a friend of our souls, how much we are in debt to you for your love of us! From your adorable Heart we have received many benefits and favours, and we have obtained the most wonderful graces for the sanctification of our souls.

Sweetest Heart of Jesus, you have been consumed by love for us, you have given yourself totally to us for our salvation. Today we want to consecrate ourselves to your Divine Heart. We are entirely yours by grace and nature, and we want to be yours in time and in eternity. We give ourselves totally to you: we give you all our being, our body, our soul and our heart.

Sweetest Heart of Jesus, we give you our memory to remember forever the sweetness of your love, our mind to learn above all the beauty of your Divine Heart, our will to love above all your amiable Heart, our freedom to live only in obedience to your holy Will.

Most Sacred Heart of Jesus, delight of the Eternal Father, comfort of all afflicted hearts, accept and appreciate the irrevocable offering of

our hearts. Take everyone forever into your most
Sacred Heart, so that remaining united to you on
earth, we may come to be together with you in
Heaven. **Amen.**

CONSECRATION TO THE
MERCIFUL HEART OF JESUS

O Merciful Heart of Jesus,
inexhaustible well of love,
I offer myself,
give myself and consecrate myself this day
to your Divine Heart,
which burns with love for us.
Through your merciful Love
make hate and pride disappear,
and love and humility reign.
I beseech you, Divine Heart of Jesus,
remember us, poor sinners, when we fall into sin.
And may we always love you more and more.
O dear Jesus, knock at our hearts,
the doors are open, and if you so desire,
may our hearts be your dwelling-place.

The Creed
Confiteor
Act of Contrition
Our Father
Hail Mary
Glory Be

CONSECRATION OF THE PARISH TO THE SACRED HEART OF JESUS

Prostrate before your Sacrament of love, O Jesus, we adore, praise and love your most Sacred Heart, substantially united to the Word of God. We bless and give thanks to your Heart, from whose fullness we have received all that is good.

O Heart of the Son of God, Heart worthy of adoration, Heart wounded by our sins, to you we want to consecrate ourselves and our parish community.

In particular we consecrate to you the families of our parish, so that they may become true domestic churches, of which you are the centre and the source of unity.

We consecrate our children and our youth to you, so that they may not stray away from you, but rather grow in faith and Christian virtue.

To you we consecrate the sick, so that they may neither become discouraged nor lose hope, but know how to offer their suffering as a sacrifice of expiation and salvation for themselves and for all souls.

To you we consecrate the elderly and those who are lonely, so that they may find relief and comfort in your love and open their hearts to the joyful hope which awaits them.

To you we consecrate our associations, groups

and all our activities, so that they may blossom and bear fruits of Christian witness.

For our part, we promise you to do all we can to render our heart similar to yours, in purity and in love, raising ourselves above earthly matters.

Pour out your blessing upon us, O Lord, so that we may have light in moments of doubt, perseverance in trials and comfort at the moment of our death.

Amen.

ACT OF CONSECRATION TO THE
SACRED HEART OF JESUS

Saint Margaret Mary Alacoque

I *(name and surname)*,
give and consecrate myself and my life, my actions, sorrows and sufferings to the adorable Heart of our Lord Jesus, in order that I may use every part of my being only to honour, love and glorify him. This is my irrevocable will: to belong totally to him and to do everything for love of him, truly abstaining from all that might displease him.

I choose you, Sacred Heart, as the only object of my love, as the custodian of my life, as the token of my salvation, remedy for my weakness and inconsistency, mender of all faults of my life, and sure refuge at the hour of my death.
Be, O Heart of goodness, my justice before God, your Father, and keep far from me his just indignation. O loving Heart, I put all my trust in you, because I am afraid of my malice and weakness, therefore I put all my hope in your goodness.

Consume in me, then, all that displeases or resists you; may your pure love be impressed deeply upon my heart, so that I may never forget or be separated from you.

I ask you, through your mercy, that my name may be written in you, because I want to realize all my happiness and glory by living and dying as your servant.

Loving Heart, I put all my confidence in you, because I fear everything in my weakness, but I hope for everything from your goodness.

CONSECRATION OF HUMANITY TO THE MOST SACRED HEART OF JESUS

Sweet Heart of Jesus, Redeemer of humankind, look upon us, humbly prostrate before your altar. We are yours and we want to be yours and to live closely united to you, so that each one of us today may willingly consecrate himself or herself to your most Sacred Heart.

Unfortunately many people have never known you. Many have despised your commandments and rejected you.

Jesus, have mercy upon us all, and draw us closer to your most Sacred Heart.

Lord, be the king of the faithful who have never left you, but also to the prodigal children who have abandoned you; may they return to the Father's house as soon as possible.

Be the king of those who live in deceit and error or who live in conflict with you, separated from you; call them back to the refuge of truth and to the unity of beliefs, in order that we may soon be one flock under one shepherd.

Give, O Lord, safety and unerring liberty to your Church, give all people the tranquillity of order; from one end of the world to the other, let this one voice resound: may the Divine Heart, from whom our salvation comes, be praised; may glory and honour be sung to him forever.

Amen.

CONSECRATION OF THE FAMILY TO THE SACRED HEART OF JESUS

The act of consecration of the family is one of the most beautiful prayers of consecration to the Sacred Heart of Jesus, and those who live by it with love and faith, soon experience the truth of the divine promises made by Jesus to St. Margaret Mary: "I will bless the house where the image of my Sacred Heart is exposed and venerated; I will put peace in their families; I will pour forth great blessings on their work; I will be their secure refuge in life and especially before their death".

SUGGESTION FOR A PRACTICAL WAY
OF MAKING THE CONSECRATION:
Let the family gather together in a spirit of contemplation Before a beautiful and blessed image of the Sacred Heart, embellished by flowers and lit up by some candles. Then, after a moment of silence, either the father or mother recites this act of consecration.

Sweet Heart of Jesus, who made a great promise to your devoted Saint Margaret Mary: "I will bless the houses in which the image of my Heart is exposed", accept the consecration of our family, by which we intend to recognise you as the King of our souls and to proclaim the dominion which you have over all creatures and over us.

Your enemies, O Jesus, do not want to recognise your sovereign rights and repeat the satanic cry, "We do not want him to reign over us!", lacerating in a most cruel way your most amiable Heart.

We, however, will repeat to you with greater ardour and greater love, "Reign, O Jesus, over our families and over each member; reign in our souls, so that we may always believe the truths which you have taught us; reign in our hearts, so that we may always follow your Divine Commandments".

Divine Heart, may you be the only sweet Sovereign of our souls; of these souls which you have acquired by means of your Precious Blood and which you want to save.

And now, Lord, according to your promise, let your blessing be poured out upon us. Bless our works, our undertakings, our health, our interests; be with us in joy and in sorrow, in prosperity and in adversity, now and forever.

Make peace, unity, respect, mutual love and good example reign among us.

Defend us from danger, illness, misfortunes and, above all, from sin. Finally, deign to write our name in the most Holy Wound of your Heart and do not let it ever be erased, so that having been united as a family here on earth, we may find ourselves united in heaven in order to sing the glory and the triumphs of your mercy. **Amen.**

Our Father
Hail Mary
Glory Be
Hail Holy Queen

NOVENA FOR THE FIRST FRIDAY
OF EACH MONTH

*In the name of the Father, and of the Son,
and of the Holy Spirit. Amen.*

O God, come to my aid.
O Lord, make haste to help me.
Glory Be

The Creed *(see page 26)*

O Jesus, whose Divine Heart is the living symbol of infinite love, draw our souls close to you who consumed yourself for the glory of the Father and for the salvation of all people. May our lives be a continuous witness to our love for you. We offer you our senses, so quick to turn to impurity; our heart, so inconstant; our flesh, so fragile. We offer you all that we possess and all that we are, in order to become an acceptable sacrifice of love.

Glory Be
Sweet Heart of Jesus,
may I love you ever more.

O Jesus, whose Divine Heart has felt the burden and the gravity of sin to the point of agony, let our hearts be sensitive to the tragedy of humanity which resists your love. For our sins and for all sins committed in the world, we want to offer you our generous reparation, uniting it to your redemptive sacrifice. Accept it as an act of faith and love in the hands of the Virgin Mary who makes amends for our sins.

Glory Be
**Sweet Heart of Jesus,
may I love you ever more.**

O Jesus, whose Divine Heart burns with the de-sire to bring all people to love the Father, enkindle in us too the flame of apostolate. May our life become a witness to the Gospel, with the fervour of our words and the efficacy of our example. May your grace help us to draw souls into the kingdom of your love, where humanity, united in your name may become a single family in the eternal embrace of the Father.

Glory Be
**Sweet Heart of Jesus,
may I love you ever more.**

LITANY OF THE FIRST FRIDAY

Heart of Jesus, to your profound adoration,
I unite my heart.
Heart of Jesus, to your ardent love,
I unite my heart.
Heart of Jesus, to your fervent zeal,
I unite my heart.
Heart of Jesus, to your acts of reparation,
I unite my heart.
Heart of Jesus, to your thanksgiving,
I unite my heart.
Heart of Jesus, to your deep trust,
I unite my heart.
Heart of Jesus, to your fervent prayers,
I unite my heart.
Heart of Jesus, to your eloquent silence,
I unite my heart.
Heart of Jesus, to your humility,
I unite my heart.
Heart of Jesus, to your obedience,
I unite my heart.
Heart of Jesus, to your sweetness and peace,
I unite my heart.
Heart of Jesus, to your ineffable goodness,
I unite my heart.
Heart of Jesus, to your universal charity,
I unite my heart.
Heart of Jesus, to your spirit of contemplation,
I unite my heart.

Heart of Jesus, to your deep desire for
the conversion of sinners,

I unite my heart.

Heart of Jesus, to your intimate union
with the heavenly Father,

I unite my heart.

Heart of Jesus, to your intentions,
to your desires and to your will,

I unite my heart.

Love of the Heart of Jesus,

Inflame my heart.

Charity of the Heart of Jesus,

Fill my heart.

Strength of the Heart of Jesus,

Sustain my heart.

Mercy of the Heart of Jesus,

Forgive my heart.

Patience of the Heart of Jesus,

Be patient with my heart.

Kingdom of the Heart of Jesus,

Reign in my heart.

Wisdom of the Heart of Jesus,

Enlighten my heart.

Will of the Heart of Jesus,

Mould my heart.

Zeal of the Heart of Jesus,

Consume my heart.

Immaculate Virgin,

Pray for us to the Sacred Heart of Jesus.

Adorable Trinity, we thank you for all the favours granted to your faithful servants Saint Margaret Mary and Saint Magdalene Sophie and we ask you, to grant through their intercession, the graces which we hope to obtain in this novena. **Amen.**

NOVENA TO THE SACRED HEART OF JESUS

In the name of the Father, and of the Son, and of the Holy Spirit. Amen.

O God, come to my aid.
O Lord, make haste to help me.
Glory Be

The Creed *(see page 26)*

Adorable Heart of Jesus, sweetness of my life, in my present needs I come to you and commend all the suffering of my heart to your power, knowledge and goodness, repeating a thousand times: O Most Holy Heart, source of love, take care of my present needs!

Glory Be

Heart of Jesus, I unite myself to your intimate union with the Heavenly Father.

Most beloved Heart of Jesus, ocean of mercy, I come to you in my present needs, and with complete abandonment I commend to your power, knowledge and goodness the tribulations which oppress me, repeating a thousand times: O Most Tender Heart, my only treasure, take care of my present needs.

Glory Be

Heart of Jesus, I unite myself to your intimate union with the Heavenly Father.

Most loving Heart of Jesus, delight of those who call on you! In my weakness I come to you, sweet solace of those who suffer, and commend to your power, knowledge, and goodness all my sorrows and I repeat a thousand times: O Most generous Heart, only refuge of those who hope in you, take care of my present needs!

Glory Be

Heart of Jesus, I unite myself to your intimate union with the Heavenly Father.

O Mary, Mediatrix of all graces, a single word from you will help me in my present sorrows. Say this word, O Mother of Mercy, and obtain for me the grace I need from the Heart of Jesus.

Hail Mary

CHAPLETS

CHAPLET OF THE
SACRED HEART OF JESUS

The following chaplet was recited every day by Blessed Padre Pio for all those who asked him to remember them in his prayers. Likewise, all the faithful are invited to recite it daily.

*In the name of the Father, and of the Son,
and of the Holy Spirit. Amen.*

O God, come to my aid.
**O Lord, make haste to help me.
Glory Be**

The Creed *(see page 26)*

O my Jesus, who said, **"Truly I say to you, ask and you will receive, search and you will find, knock and the door will be opened to you!"** I come to you knocking, searching and asking for the grace of...

(We mention our special needs).

Our Father • Hail Mary • Glory Be

**Sacred Heart of Jesus,
I hope and trust in you.**

O my Jesus who said, **"Truly I say to you, whate-ver you ask of the Father in my name, He will grant you!"** I come to you asking the Father, in your name, for the grace of...

(We mention our special needs).
Our Father • Hail Mary • Glory Be

**Sacred Heart of Jesus,
I hope and trust in you.**

O my Jesus who said, **"Truly I say to you, heaven and earth will pass away, but my words will never pass away!"** I come to you relying on the infallibility of your holy words asking for the grace of...

(We mention our special needs)
Our Father • Hail Mary • Glory Be

**Sacred Heart of Jesus,
I hope and trust in you.**

O Sacred Heart of Jesus, who cannot fail to have compassion on the afflicted, have mercy on us, miserable sinners, and grant us the graces we implore through the Immaculate Heart of Mary, our tender Mother.

**Saint Joseph, Adoptive Father
of the Sacred Heart of Jesus,
pray for us.**

Hail Holy Queen

CHAPLET OF THE SACRED HEART

(by the Servant of God, Father James Alberione)

In the name of the Father, and of the Son, and of the Holy Spirit. Amen.

O God, come to my aid.
O Lord, make haste to help me.
Glory Be

The Creed *(see page 26)*

O Jesus, my Master, prostrate before you, I adore your Heart, which loved humankind so much that it spared nothing for us. I believe in your infinite love for us. I thank you for the great gifts which, out of love, you have given to all people: the Gospel, the Eucharist, the Church, the priesthood, religious orders, Mary as our Mother and your life itself.

O Jesus, Divine Master, I thank and bless your most generous heart for the great gift of the Gospel. You said, "I have been sent to bring the good news to the poor". Your words bring eternal life. In the Gospel, you revealed the divine mysteries, taught the way of God with truth, offered the means of salvation. Grant me the grace of treating your Gospel with veneration, of listening to it and reading it in the spirit of the Church and spreading it with the love with which you preached it. May it be known, honoured and wel-comed by everyone! May the life, laws, customs and doctrines of the world be modelled upon it! May the fire which you brought to the earth inflame, enlighten and warm all hearts.

**Sweet Heart of Jesus,
may I love you ever more.**

O Jesus, Divine Master, I thank and bless your most loving Heart for the great gift of the Eucha-rist. Your love permits you to dwell in the holy tabernacle, to renew your Passion during the Mass, to give yourself as food for our souls in Holy Communion! Let me know you, o hidden God! Let me drink the water of health from the well of your heart! Grant that I may visit you every day in this sacrament, that I may under-stand and participate actively in the Mass, and with faith and love may I often receive Holy Communion.

**Sweet Heart of Jesus,
may I love you ever more.**

O Jesus, Divine Master, I bless and thank your tender Heart for the great gift of the Church. She is the Mother who teaches us the truth, guides us to heaven, and tells us about heavenly life. Being your mystical body, she continues your saving mission on earth. She is the ark of salvation; infallible, unfailing and catholic. Grant that I may love the Church, as you loved her and sanctified her with your blood. May the world come to know her, so that every sheep may enter your fold and everyone may humbly co-operate in bringing about the coming of your Kingdom.

Sweet Heart of Jesus,
may I love you ever more.

O Jesus, Divine Master, I thank and bless your most loving Heart for the institution of the priesthood. Priests are sent by you, as you were sent by the Father. You have entrusted to them the treasures of your doctrine, your law and your grace, and have commended to them our very souls. Grant me the grace to love them, to listen to them, to let myself be guided by them in your ways. O Jesus, send good labourers into your harvest and may priests be the salt of the earth which purifies and preserves; may they be the light of the world, the city on the hilltop; may they behave according to your desires, and may they be surrounded one day in heaven by a multitude of souls as their crown and joy.

**Sweet Heart of Jesus,
may I love you ever more.**

O Jesus, Divine Master, I thank and bless your most Sacred Heart for the call to consecration in religious life. Just as in heaven, so too on earth there is much to be done. You have chosen your beloved children and called them to the perfection of the Gospel; you have made of yourself an example for them, their help; their reward. O Divine Heart, inerease the number of religious vocations: keep them faithful in their observance of the evangelical counsels; may they be the most perfumed flowers of the Church; may they may be the souls which console you; may they praise you and proclaim your glory in every apostolate.

**Sweet Heart of Jesus,
may I love you ever more.**

O Jesus, Divine Master, I thank and bless your most merciful Heart for having given us Our Lady as Mother, Teacher and Queen. From your Cross, you have put all of us into her hands; you have given her a great heart, great knowledge, and great power. May all humankind come to know her, love her and pray to her! May all people let themselves be led to you, Saviour of humankind, through her! I put myself into her hands, as you yourself did. May this mother be with me now, at the hour of my death and for eternity.

**Sweet Heart of Jesus,
may I love you ever more.**

O Jesus, Divine Master, I thank and bless your meekness of Heart which led you to give your life for me. Your blood, your wounds, the scourging, the crown of thorns, the cross, your reclining head; all tell my heart, "No one loves more than the one who gives his life for the beloved". The shepherd died to give life to his sheep. I too want to give my life for you; may you always use me for your greater glory in all things and in all situations, and let me always repeat: "Thy will be done". Inflame my heart with a divine love for you and for all souls.

**Sweet Heart of my Jesus,
may I love you ever more.**

LITANY OF THE SACRED HEART OF JESUS

In 1900, Pope Leo XIII consecrated all the people of the world to the Sacred Heart of Jesus, explaining his doctrine in an encyclical (Annum Sacrum, 1899) which was elaborated by Pope Pius XII (Haurietis Aquas). The litany of the Sacred Heart, rich in contents and reflecting the words of the Bible, is written in the same theological spirit. It was approved in 1899 for public recitation and, according to tradition, originated at Marseilles, France.

Lord, have mercy, **Lord, have mercy.**

Christ, have mercy, **Christ, have mercy.**

Lord, have mercy, **Lord, have mercy.**

God the Father of Heaven, **Have mercy on us.**

God the Son, Redeemer of the world,

Have mercy on us.

God, the Holy Spirit, **Have mercy on us.**

Holy Trinity, one God, **Have mercy on us.**

We exalt the great riches of the Heart of Jesus:

Heart of Jesus, Son of the eternal Father,

Have mercy on us.

Heart of Jesus, formed by the Holy Spirit
in the womb of the Virgin Mary,

Have mercy on us.

Heart of Jesus, one with the eternal Word,
Have mercy on us.
Heart of Jesus, infinite in majesty,
Have mercy on us.
Heart of Jesus, holy temple of God,
Have mercy on us.
Heart of Jesus, tabernacle of the Most High,
Have mercy on us.
Heart of Jesus, house of God and gate of heaven,
Have mercy on us.
Heart of Jesus, aflame with love for us,
Have mercy on us.
Heart of Jesus, source of justice and love,
Have mercy on us.
Heart of Jesus, full of goodness and love,
Have mercy on us.
Heart of Jesus, wellspring of all virtue,
Have mercy on us.
Heart of Jesus, worthy of all praise,
Have mercy on us.
Heart of Jesus, king and centre of all hearts,
Have mercy on us.

Heart of Jesus, treasure house of wisdom
and knowledge, **Have mercy on us.**

Heart of Jesus, dwelling place of the fullness
of God, **Have mercy on us.**

Heart of Jesus, in whom the Father
is well pleased, **Have mercy on us.**

Heart of Jesus, from whose fullness
we have all received, **Have mercy on us.**

Heart of Jesus, desire of the eternal hills,
Have mercy on us.

Heart of Jesus, patient and full of mercy,
Have mercy on us.

Heart of Jesus, generous to all who turn to you,
Have mercy on us.

Heart of Jesus, fount of life and holiness,
Have mercy on us.

**From the Heart of Jesus we seek forgiveness
and salvation:**

Heart of Jesus, atonement for our sins,
Have mercy on us.

Heart of Jesus, overwhelmed with insults,
Have mercy on us.

Heart of Jesus, broken for our sins,
Have mercy on us.

Heart of Jesus, obedient even unto death,
Have mercy on us.

Heart of Jesus, pierced by a lance,
Have mercy on us.

Heart of Jesus, source of all consolation,
Have mercy on us.

Heart of Jesus, our life and resurrection,
Have mercy on us.

Heart of Jesus, our peace and reconciliation,
Have mercy on us.

Heart of Jesus, victim for our sins,

Have mercy on us.

Heart of Jesus, salvation of all who trust in you,

Have mercy on us.

Heart of Jesus, hope of all who die in you,

Have mercy on us.

Heart of Jesus, delight of all saints,

Have mercy on us.

Lamb of God, who take away the sins of the world,
Spare us, O Lord

Lamb of God, who take away the sins of the world.
Graciously hear us, O Lord

Lamb of God, who take away the sins of the world,
Have mercy on us

V. Jesus, meek and humble of heart,
R. Make our hearts like unto thine (yours).

Let us pray.
Father, we rejoice in the gifts of love we have received from the heart of Jesus, your Son. Open our hearts to share his life, and continue to bless us with his love. We ask this in the name of Jesus the Lord.
Amen.

ACTS OF REPARATION TO THE SACRED HEART

ACT OF REPARATION TO THE SACRED HEART

Prostrate humbly before you, O Sacred Heart of Jesus, we renew our consecration to you in order to atone with increased faith and love for all the offences committed against that same Heart.

The more blasphemies are uttered against your holy mysteries the more we shall believe in the same mysteries.

The more evil tries to rob us of our hope of immortality the more we shall trust in you who are one sure hope of humanity.

The more ungrateful hearts resist your divine attractions the more we shall adore you, O Sweet Heart of Jesus.

The more outrages are committed against your Divine Majesty the more we shall worship it.

The more divine laws are forgotten or broken the more scrupulously we shall observe them.

The more your adorable virtues are ignored the

more we shall strive to practise them, O Sacred Heart, model of all virtues.

The more the Sacraments are despised and abandoned the more we shall receive them with love and respect.

The more hell works for the ruin of souls the more we shall be inflamed with the desire for their salvation.

The more sensuality and pride seek to destroy self-denial and the spirit of duty the more we shall grow in the spirit of mortification and sacrifice.

The more blasphemies are uttered against our Mother Mary for the singular privileges which you bestowed on her the more we shall honour her, invoking her as our Mother and Immaculate Virgin.

The more the Church and the Holy Father are persecuted and humiliated the more we shall respect them, offering them our faithful obedience.

O Heart of Jesus, grant that we may become your true disciples and apostles during this life and that we may share in your glory and joy in eternity. **Amen.**

ANOTHER ACT OF REPARATION
TO THE SACRED HEART

The following prayer is to be recited on the solemnity of the Sacred Heart, on the first Friday of the month and on any other suitable occasion.

O sweet Jesus, your immense love for humankind is repaid by us only with ingratitude, indifference, scorn and sin. Here we are, prostrate before you, as we seek to make suitable amends in reparation for our unworthy behaviour and for the many offences by which your most amiable Heart is wounded by your ungrateful children.

Remembering that we too have been guilty of these sins in the past, and feeling deep sorrow for them, we implore your mercy, especially for ourselves, and are ready to make amends with adequate expiation, not only for our sins, but also for the misdeeds of those who have not kept the promises of baptism and have thus have rejected the light yoke of your law and, as lost sheep, refuse to follow you, shepherd and guide.

While seeking to free ourselves from the slavery of passions and vices, we resolve to make amends for all our sins: for the offences committed against you and your Divine Father, for the sins committed against your commandments and your Gospel, for the injustice and suffering which we have caused to our neighbour, for the immoral practices committed, for the traps set for innocent souls, for the public faults of nations which do not respect human rights and do not allow your Church to exercise its saving ministry, for the negligence and offences of the Church herself.

It is in atonement for these offences that we present to you, O merciful Heart of Jesus, the supreme act of expiation which you yourself offered on the cross to your Father and renew every day on our altars in the holy Sacrifice of the Mass, uniting it to the sacrifices of your holy Mother, of all the saints and of many holy souls.

We intend to make amends for our sins and for those of our brothers and sisters, in offering you our sincere repentance, the detachment of our heart from every disordered affection, the conversion of our lives, the steadfastness of our faith, our faithfulness to your commandments, integrity of life and fervent charity.

O kind Jesus, accept this voluntary act of reparation of ours through the intercession of the Blessed Virgin Mary. Grant us the grace to remain faithful to our duties, in obedience to you and in order to serve our neighbours.

We ask you again for the gift of perseverance until the end of our lives, in order that one day all of us may enter into that blessed Kingdom, where you live and reign with the Father and the Holy Spirit, one God forever and ever. **Amen.**

PRAYER TO THE SACRED HEART OF JESUS PIERCED BY A LANCE

To be recited on the first Friday of the month

O Jesus, so lovable and yet not loved enough! We humbly prostrate ourselves at the foot of your cross, to offer your Divine Heart, pierced by a lance and consumed by love, the homage of our profound adoration. O most beloved Saviour, I thank you for having let the soldier pierce your divine side and for having opened in this way a source of salvation in the mysterious ark of your Sacred Heart. Allow us to seek consolation from it during these difficult times, in order to save ourselves from the excess of immorality which contaminates humankind.

**Our Father
Hail Mary
Glory Be**

We bless a thousand times the hour and moment at which your most Precious Blood and Water coming from the open wound of your Divine Heart gushed forth upon the iron of the lance. Grant that it may save and cleanse this guilty and unhappy world. Wash, purify and regenerate all souls in the waters coming from this fountain of graces. Let us, O Lord, cast into it all our iniquities and those of all humankind, as we beseech you to save us with the immense love which consumes your Sacred Heart.

Our Father
Hail Mary
Glory Be

O sweet Heart of Jesus, help us to spend our life in holiness, making our home in your adorable Heart forever, and remaining there in peace until we take our final breath.

Our Father
Hail Mary
Glory Be

ACT OF OBLATION

For the suffering souls

Ecce venio! Here I am, ready! O my Jesus, meek and sweet Divine Lamb, immolated forever on our altars for the salvation of humankind, I want to be united to you, to suffer with you, to offer myself as a sacrifice with you.

For this purpose I offer you all the pain, hardship, humiliations and crosses which your Providence permits me to ancounter on my path.

To you I present all the intentions for which you offered and sacrificed your sweet Heart. May my humble offering obtain your blessing for the Church, the priesthood, poor sinners, and for all society. And you, dear Jesus, deign to accept it from the hands of the Blessed Virgin Mary, in union with her Immaculate Heart. **Amen.**

Our Father
Hail Mary
Glory Be

4.

JESUS IN THE EUCHARIST

- Benediction
  - Adoration
- Prayers of Consecration
  - Rosary
- Invocations
- Prayers for Holy Communion

INTRODUCTION

Jesus said, "I am the living bread which has come down from Heaven. Anyone who eats this bread will live forever... Anyone who eats my flesh and drinks my blood has eternal life, and I shall raise that person up on the last day... Whoever eats my flesh and drinks my blood lives in me and I live in that person" (Jn 6: 51, 54, 56).

The Eucharist is the heart and culmination of the life of the Church because in the Eucharist Jesus unites his Church and all her members to his own sacrifice of praise and thanksgiving offered to the Father on the cross; through the same sacrifice he pours out graces of salvation on his Body, the Church. The celebration of the Eucharist is always accompanied by the proclamation of the Word of God, by thanksgiving to God the Father for all his gifts, above all for the gift of his Son, by consecration of the bread and wine and by participation in the banquet of the liturgy. The Eucharist is the memorial of the paschal mystery of Christ: his death and resurrection in the plan of salvation. It is Christ himself, eternal high priest of the New Covenant who, acting through the ministry of his priests, offers the sacrifice of the Eucharist.

Furthermore, Christ, who is truly present under the species of bread and wine, continues to be the offering in the sacrifice of the Eucharist. By means of the Consecration, the bread and wine become the Body and Blood of Christ. Within the consecrated species Christ himself is present in a true, real and substantial manner.

Receiving the Body and Blood of Christ in Holy Communion strengthens the communicant's union with the Lord, grants him or her the remission of venial sins and preserves him or her from sin. The Church recommends that the faithful receive Holy Communion every time they participate in the celebration of the Holy Eucharist and makes it an obligation to receive at least once a year (during the Easter season). Since Christ himself is present in the Sacrament of the altar, he is to be honoured in a spirit of adoration.

Visits to the Blessed Sacrament are "an expression of thanksgiving, a sign of love and a debt of gratitude to Christ the Lord".

PRAYERS

This is a beautiful service which can be lengthened or shortened acording to the occasion. For a long time it was the normal evening service, especially on a Sunday, and wa often preceded by the Rosary and a homily. A simple form of Benediction is given below. This may be adapted in many ways, for example by adding or varying the hymns, or including a meditation on a mystery of the Rosary (especially in May and October) or on one of the stations of the Cross (in Lent). Benediction may also follow Evening Prayer or Compline.

As the priest opens the tabernacle Pange Lingua *(or another suitable Eucharistic hymn, is sung:*

PANGE, LINGUA, GLORIOSI

English version

Sing, My tongue, the Saviour's glory,
Of his flesh the mystery sing,
Of the blood, all price exceeding,
Shed by our immortal King;
Destined for the world's redemption,
From a noble womb to spring.

Of a pure and spotless Virgin
Born for us on earth below,
He, as man with man conversing,
Stayed, the seeds of truth to sow;
Then he closed in solemn order

Wondrously his life of woe.
On the night of that last supper,
Seated with his chosen band,
He, the paschal victim eating,
First fulfills the law's command;
Then as food to all his brethren,
Gives himself with his own hand.

Word made flesh, the bread of nature
By his word to flesh he turns;
Wine into his blood he changes:
What though sense no change discerns?
Only be the heart in earnest,
Faith her lesson quickly learns.

Latin version

Pange, lingua, gloriósi
córporis mystérium,
sanguinísque pretiósi,
quem in mundi prétium
fructus ventris generósi
Rex effúdit géntium.

Nobis datus, nobis natus
ex intácta Vírgine,
et in mundo conversátus,
sparso verbi sémine,
sui moras incolátus
miro clausit órdine.

In suprémæ nocte coenæ,
recumbens cum frátribus,
observata lege plene
cibis in legálibus,
cibum turbae duodénæ
se dat suis mánibus.

Verbum caro, panem verum
verbo carnem éfficit,
fitque sanguis Christi
merum; et si sensus déficit,
ad firmándum cor
sincérum sola fides súfficit.

Tantum ergo

There now follows a time of prayer, spoken or silent, with scripture readings and hymns if desired. The prayers and readings are directed to focusing our attention on the person of Jesus Christ, true God and true Man, who died for us and rose again, and sits at the right hand of the Father. Then everybody sings the following hymn:

English version

Down in adoration falling,
Lo, the sacred Host we hail;
Lo, o'er ancient
forms departing
Newer rites of grace prevail;
Faith for all defects supplying
Where the feeble senses fail.
To the everlasting Father,
And the Son who
reigns on high,
With the Holy Spirit
proceeding
Forth from each eternally
Be salvation, honour, blessing,
Might, and endless majesty.
Amen.

Latin version

Tantum ergo Sacraméntum
venerémur cernui:
et antiquum
documéntum
novo cedat rítui:
praestet fides
suppleméntum
sensuum deféctui.

Genitóri Genitóque
laus et iubilátio,
salus, honor,
virtus quoque
sit et benedictio:
procedénti ab utróque
compar sit laudatio.
Amen.

An alternative version of the Tantum Ergo
in English is as follows:

Therefore we, before him bending
this great Sacrament revere;
types and shadows have their ending

for the newer rite is here;
faith, our outward sense befriending,
makes the inward vision clear.

Glory let us give, and blessing
to the Father and the Son;
honour, might and praise addressing,
while eternal ages run;
ever too his love confessing
who from both, with both is one.
Amen.

Celebrant: You have given your people bread
from heaven (*Easter Time* **Alleluia**).
Assembly: The bread which is full of goodness.
(*Easter Time* **Alleluia**).

Latin version

Celebrant: Panem caelo praestitisti eis.
(*Easter Time* **Alleluia**).
Assembly: Omne delectamentum in se haben-
tem. (*Easter Time* **Alleluia**).

Let us pray.
O God, who in this wonderful Sacrament have
left us a memorial of your passion; help us to
revere the sacred mysteries of your Body and
Blood, so that we may always experience in our
lives the effects of your redemption: you who live
and reign for ever and ever. **Amen.**

Now, the assembly bows down in adoration to receive the benediction of the most Holy Sacrament.
The celebrant then recites the Divine Praises which are repeated by the assembly.

The divine praises *(see page 54)*

At this moment, the pious custom of reciting the Prayer of Reparation to the Eucharistic Heart of Jesus may be observed:

May the Heart of Jesus in the most Blessed Sacrament be praised, adored, and loved with grateful affection at every moment in all the tabernacles of the world, now and until the end of time. **Amen.**

While the priest replaces the Blessed Sacrament in the tabernacle, the people may sing one of the following hymns. (A hymn to the Blessed Virgin Mary is equally suitable).

O Sacrament most holy,
O Sacrament divine,
All praise and all thanksgiving
Be every moment Thine.
or
Holy God, we praise thy name!
Lord of all, we bow before thee;
All on earth thy sceptre claim,
All in heav'n above adore thee;
Infinite thy vast domain,
Everlasting is thy reign.

or

Adorémus aetérnum sanctíssimum Sacraméntum.

Laudáte Dóminum omnes gentes;
Laudáte eum omnes populi.
Quóniam confirmáta est super nos misericórdia eius;
Et véritas Dómini manet in aetérnum.

Gloria Patri et Filio, et Spiritui Sancto.
Sicut erat in principio, et nunc, et semper,
et in saecula saeculorum. **Amen.**

Adorémus aetérnum sanctíssimum Sacraméntum.

PRAYER BEFORE THE BLESSED SACRAMENT
Saint M. Faustina (Diary, 1692)

I adore you, Lord and Creator, hidden in the Blessed Sacrament. I adore you for all the works of Your hands, that reveal to me so much wisdom, goodness and mercy, O Lord. You have spread so much beauty over the earth, and it tells me about Your beauty, even though these beautiful things are but a faint reflection of You, Incomprehensible Beauty. And although You have hidden Yourself and concealed, Your beauty, my eye enlightened by faith, reaches You, and my soul recognizes its Creator, its Highest Good; and my heart is completely immersed in prayer of adoration.

My Lord and Creator, Your goodness encourages me to converse with You. Your mercy abolishes the chasm which separates the Creator from the creatures. To converse with You, O Lord, is the delight of my heart. In You I find everything that my heart could desire. Here Your light illumines my mind, enabling it to know You more and more deeply. Here streams of graces flow down upon my heart. Here my soul draws eternal life. O my Lord and Crerator, You alone, beyond all these gifts, give Your own self to me and unite Yourself intimately with Your miserable creature. Here, without searching for words, our hearts understand each other. Here, no one is able to interrupt our conversation. What I talk to You about, Jesus, is our secret, which creatures shall not know and Angels dare not ask about. These are secret acts of forgiveness, known only to Jesus and me; this is the mystery of His mercy, which embraces each soul separately. For this incomprehensible goodness of Yours, I adore You, O Lord and Creator, with all my heart and all my soul. And, although my worship is so little and poor, I am at peace because I know that You know it is sincere, however inadequate...

PRAYER OF CONTEMPLATION

"Come to me, all of you who labour and are overburdened, and I will give you rest" *(Mt 11:28).*

When I am deep in meditation before you, O Jesus, I hear interiorly the echo of your words. I would like this silent moment to be prolonged in the contemplation of your mercy which gives solace and strength.

Lord, you are here with me and you want to free me from my worries, anxieties and trials of everyday.

The things which surround me and the thoughts I carry inside me, beset and sometimes oppress me, as if the meaning of my life depended on them. Lord Jesus, you visit me. And with your presence you bring me the good news of the Kingdom of God.

You are the proof that your Kingdom is close at hand, that it is here with us. You assure me that God is the Sovereign of everything and of everyone; that God is great and almighty, good and merciful, just and compassionate, and that his love for us is strong. God governs the circumstances in which humankind finds itself, and in their evolution, he attracts us to himself, as he seeks to be everything in everyone.

Lord Jesus, when you were crucified, the wonderful plan of salvation was accomplished, because full reconciliation came about between heaven and earth through your death and resurrection. Now you, O bread of life, are here as a memorial of your offering on the cross and, perpetuating your sacrifice, you want to embrace me, to associate me with your act of immolation. You want to be in communion with me, and in this way you give me solace, strength and joy. Lord Jesus, enter my life, my thoughts, my everyday events, and stay with me forever. **Amen.**

PRAYER FOR PRIESTS
by Cardinal Mundelein

Almighty and Eternal God, look upon the face of your Christ, Eternal and High Priest, and for love of him, have mercy on our ministers. O merciful God, remember that they are weak and fragile creatures. Keep alive in them the fire of your Love. Keep them united to you, so that the enemy may not prevail against them and they may never be unworthy of their sublime calling.

O Jesus! I pray to you for your faithful and devout pastors, for your tepid and unfaithful pastors, for your pastors working nearby, and for those far away on the missions, for your pastors suffering from solitude and desolation, for your young pastors, for your old pastors, for your pastors who are ill, for your dying pastors, for the souls of your pastors who suffer in Purgatory.

I recommend to you in particular the pastors who are dearest to me: the priest who baptized me, the priests who have absolved me from my sins, the priests at whose Masses I have assisted and who have given me your Body and Blood in Holy Communion, the priests who have guided me and all the pastors to whom I owe a debt of gratitude.

Jesus, look upon them and keep them all close to your heart and give them great graces both in this life and in eternity.

Prayer of saint alphonsus

My Lord Jesus Christ who, because of your immense love for humanity, remain day and night in this Sacrament, awaiting, calling, and welcoming all those who come to visit you, I believe that you are present here, I adore you in the abyss of my nothingness, and I thank you for all the graces you have given me; I thank you for having given yourself to me in this Sacrament, for having given me your Most Holy Mother Mary, as my advocate, and for having called me to visit you in this church.

Today greet your beloved heart, and I intend to greet it for three reasons. Firstly, in thanksgiving for this great gift. Secondly, to make amends for all the offences which you receive in this Sacrament. Thirdly, I intend in this visit to adore you in all the places of the earth where you are most abandoned.

My Jesus, I love you with all my heart. I repent for having so often offended your infinite goodness. With your grace, I resolve never to offend you again in the future; and at present, unworthy as I am, I consecrate myself entirely to you, I give you my affections and everything I possess. From this day on, do with me all that you please. I ask only for your holy love, for perseverance to the end of my life and for the perfect fulfilment of your will. I commend to you the souls of Purgatory, especially all those most devoted to the Blessed Sacrament and to Mary Most Holy I commend to you all poor sinners.

I unite all my feelings to those of your most beloved heart, and thus united, I offer them to your eternal Father and I pray to him to accept them and to satisfy them out of love for you.

Amen.

If this prayer is recited before the Blessed Sacrament, an indulgence of five years is granted. A plenary indulgence is obtained if the prayer is recited once a month for the Pope's intentions, after having confessed one's sins and received Holy Communion.

PRAYER OF ST. BERNARD TO JESUS, OUR JOY AND GLORY

Jesus, your memory is sweetness and true joy for my heart, but sweeter than honey and all other things is your presence. There is no song more delightful, no sound more joyful, no thought sweeter than you, Jesus, Son of God. O Jesus, who are hope for those who repent, how merciful you are to those who invoke you, how good you are to those who search for you! But what are you for those who find you? No tongue can say it, no writing can express it; only those who have found you can know what it is to love Jesus.

Jesus, admirable king, noble victor, indescribable sweetness, all that is desirable: when you visit our heart, the truth shines forth, vain things of the world appear vile, and your love inflames us. Jesus, sweetness of our hearts, source of light for our souls, you overcome every joy and desire.

Jesus, splendour of the angels, sweet canticle to the ear, delicious honey to the lips, heavenly nectar to the heart. Those who taste you hunger for more; those who are inebriated with you thirst for more, they desire nothing else but Jesus, their love. O sweet Jesus, hope of the soul that sighs, our tears and the intimate cry of our hearts search for you.

Remain with us, O Lord, and enlighten us with your light, remove the mists of sin which encumber our soul, fill the world with your sweetness. Jesus, flower of the Virgin Mary, our most tender love, be our joy, you who shall be our reward: one day may you be our glory, always, forever and ever.

Amen.

PRAYER TO JESUS MOST LOVABLE

O most amiable, beloved Jesus. You who are our life, our hope, our treasure, the only love of our souls; how much it cost you to remain with us in this Sacrament!

You wanted to die in order to remain on our altars. You bore every offence in order to console us with your presence! Your love, your desire to be loved by us in return, overcame all things.

Lord, come into my heart, let no other creature take away the love which I have for you.

Therefore, O Jesus, grant that I may be entirely yours. If I do not obey your commandments fully, may I feel rebuked, so that in the future I may seek to carry out your will in all things.

Grant that my greatest desire may be to please you, to visit you in the Blessed Sacrament of the Altar, to remain in your presence, to receive you into my body. Even if others seek pleausures elsewhere, I love nothing and desire nothing other than your precious love at the feet of the altar.

Grant that I may forget myself in order to remember only your will. I do not envy the blessed seraphims for their glory, but for the love that they have for my God and their God: may they teach me how to love and please him.

PRAISE OF GOD MOST HIGH
(St. Francis of Assisi)

You are holy, the one Lord God,
who do wonderful things.
You are strong. You are great.
You are the most High.
You are the almighty King.
You are the holy Father,
the King of heaven and of earth.
You are three in one, Lord God of gods.
You are goodness, all that is good,
the greatest good,
Lord God, living and true.
You are love, charity. You are wisdom.
You are humility. You are patience.
You are beauty. You are security.
You are peace. You are joy and happiness.
You are our hope. You are justice.
You are temperance. You are our richness.
You are beauty. You are meekness.
You are the protector.
You are our guardian and defender.
You are strength. You are refuge.
You are our hope. You are our faith.
You are our charity. You are our sweetness.
You are our eternal life,
great and venerable Lord,
almighty God,
merciful Saviour.

CONVERSATION WITH JESUS IN THE TABERNACLE

(St. Thérèse of Lisieux)

O God, hidden in the tabernacle! In delight I return to you every evening to thank you for the graces which you have given me and to implore your pardon for my failings committed during this day which is slipping away like a dream.

O Jesus! how happy I would be if I had been faithful, but alas! I am often sad in the evening because I feel I could have responded better to your grace.

And yet, O my God, far from being discouraged at the sight of my unworthiness, I come to you with trust, reminding myself that "it is not the healthy who need the doctor, but the sick".

I beseech you to heal me, to forgive me, and I will remember, Lord, "that the soul whom you have forgiven more must love you more than the others!...".

I offer you all of my heartbeats, together with many other acts of love and reparation and I unite them to your infinite merits.

I ask you earnestly, O my Divine Spouse, that you yourself may be the Doctor of my soul, to work in me without paying attention to my resistance, because I wish to have no will other than yours. And tomorrow, by the help of your grace, I will begin again a new life of which every moment shall be an act of love and renunciation.

ADORATION BEFORE THE
MOST BLESSED SACRAMENT

After Holy Mass, adoration of Jesus in the Blessed Sacrament is the form of prayer that is most pleasing to Our Lord. Our repentance is most sincere when experienced before the Blessed Sacrament, either in a church or in a chapel, looking at the tabernacle. Adoration re-awakens our faith in Him who is present with us and allows us to feel His presence in silence and tranquillity.

O Jesus, you are here present at this very moment! You see and know everything! You love me immensely from eternity and, with the strength of your grace, you guide me towards you. I bow before you, Lord Jesus, and bless you. I believe that you are here, before me now and that you are alive, hidden in this most holy bread, true God and true man. I bow before you with all my being, my body, my soul, my heart and with all my capacities. I trust in you and give myself to you completely and I dedicate every moment of my existence to you.

Jesus, you are aware of all that weighs upon my soul, all that oppresses and saddens me, all that causes me to suffer. I bow before you, Jesus, and beg you to remove from me every distraction, tiredness, heaviness of spirit, difficulty, sorrow, pain and suffering.

I thank you because you always have time for me and you wait for me. I bow before you for all those who seek you and prostrate themselves to adore you. I now commend to you all the men and women of the earth and I place them in your hands. As for me, do with me as you please.

I am ready for everything, I accept everything so that your will may be fulfilled in me and in all your creatures.

I desire nothing else, O Father; I give you my soul with all the love that I possess, because I love you and desire to give myself to you and place myself in your hands.

You are the Lord most holy.

You are the fountain of holiness! You are holy for what you are and for what you do; you are holy because you are the one who creates all things and gives rise to all holiness; you are holy because you desire that all of us recognise and love you, thus finding the path to salvation.

You are worthy of praise, honour and blessing. You have known me and called me from all eternity and you thought of me before I was conceived. What have you not done for me?

Therefore I have easily found the way to follow you. I adore you, Jesus, and I beg you: let me truly understand and sincerely accept your constant call, so that with you and in you I may find the strength to reinforce my will.

May I seek and fulfil your will everywhere. O Jesus in the Blessed Sacrament, you have said:

What benefit is it to anyone to win the whole world and forfeit or lose his very self?

Thank you for admonishing and stimulating me so that living my everyday life and living on this earth, with all the joys and sorrows that accompany it, I may forget neither you, my God, nor the final destiny which you have prepared for me. O my good Jesus, help me to understand and accept in my life that only with you can I be truly happy. Teach me to love God sincerely and to love my neighbour even when he or she does not love me.

Jesus, you are the way, the truth and the life!

Teach me to live honestly, to love sincerely and thus to remain faithful to my God. Let me never forget you! Grant that I may always live, work, make decisions, rejoice and be happy together with you! I wish to render honour, glory, praise, thanksgiving and love to the heavenly Father and to be happy for all eternity. I adore you, Jesus, and I thank you above all at this moment for the great mystery in which I discover your all-embracing love. You have given yourself to me and you have given all that you are and possess. You shed your blood for me and paid for my salvation with your life.

I thank you for everything!

You give of yourself constantly, you always

think of me and rejoice in me; the Blessed Sacrament assures me of this: it speaks to me of the blessed bread which becomes your body. Thank you for remaining with us in this Sacrament, so that today we can experience your living, eternal and all-embracing love.

At this moment I give myself to you and I put myself into your hands. Some time ago, in baptism, the gift of my existence was proclaimed, but this was said by others who wished that I would belong only to you!

Now I give myself and consecrate myself to you; all of my life, my failures and my weaknesses. I give you my work and my rest, my undertakings and my desires, my daily routine and my duties. I give you myself fully and entirely. Accept me, Lord! Accept me for what I am, accept me I ask you again, because I ardently desire to be accepted by you.

I am happy only in you and with you!

Thank you Jesus for accepting me. Grant me the graces I require, so that it may be no longer I who live, but you who live in me. I adore you Jesus and I thank you, because I am happy when I am speaking to you, I receive a special grace when I am with you, and everything in me and around me tells me that you love me deeply.

You love each one of us more than we love our father or mother and your doors are always open to everyone. In your eyes no-one has sinned so much that he or she cannot be loved, taken by the hand and protected from those who judge him or her. You suffer together with those who suffer and you rejoice with those who rejoice, you are close to those who are sad and desolate, you take upon yourself our needs and ailments.

"I am the living bread come down from heaven! Who eats this Bread will have Eternal Life! The Bread which I give you is my body, for the life of the world! Whoever eats of this bread will have Eternal Life!" (ref. Jn 6)

You rejoice in forgiving us and in our reconciliation with you and with others.

I adore you, Jesus, and I beg you: forgive me for my ingratitude for all your gifts and for all that you do for me. You are great in all your works but especially dear to me because of the infinite love that you have shown and continue to show me, that love which draws me closer to you. I adore you, Jesus, and I bless you!

I thank you too for all that you have given me up to now; thank you for the gift of life. Thank you for my eyes, my ears, my hands, my feet, my heart and for all my body.

I thank you for each heart beat, for the air I breathe, for the warmth of the sun... for everything.

I adore you, Jesus, and I thank you and I render you glory and honour because, for love of me, you made yourself man and brother of all people.

Thank you for having lived in conditions similar to mine. You did not come down to this valley of tears only to pass through it and then to go away. You have remained with us and in our midst in a real way, hidden under the form of bread in the most Blessed Sacrament.

We thank you so much!

Divine Saviour, I know well that you wished to transform this valley of tears into Paradise, all humanity into the family of God, each person into a child of God. Grant that the flame of your great love may warm the hearts of all people and give peace to each heart and to each soul. I give myself to you, O Jesus, with living faith and devotion.

I adore you in the Blessed Sacrament together with the saints and your chosen people. In this Host you are now looking at me, you re-cognize me and call me by my name. I adore you, O mysterious God, unfathomable and immense. Even though I neither see your face nor hear you, my soul yearns for you; my heart senses your presence and longs for you!

Good God, I believe that you have created and continue to create everything out of love and that you loved us and all this world to the point of sending your Son down to earth. Through him and in him, your reality becomes accessible and your greatness comes nearer to us. Thank you, good God, because you live in us and you are close to us, you take care of us and gather us into one family.

I adore you, Jesus, Son of God, true God and true man. You are the same Jesus who came into this world, became man, suffered for us and died for our salvation. Now you are here in the form of bread, you have loved us so much that you decided to remain with us always and in a tangible way. You have remained in a sacramental way, in order to testify your love. You allow us to become children of God.

May your grace penetrate us fully and may your love inspire us. You are here to bless, restore and heal us, to dry our tears and forgive our sins. You are here to be our most faithful friend. Forgive me Jesus because I forget that you are the source of our faith and the instrument of our salvation.

Here I am, Jesus! I place myself before you. I gaze at the eternal light, this little piece of consecrated bread and realize that you are near to me: I feel you in the depth of my soul, I see you with the eyes of faith, I experience you in your love, richness and mercy. I hear your voice: "Come to me, all you who are weary and overburdened, and I will give you rest!".

I adore you, Jesus, and I thank you because

you grant me the grace of an ardent desire to become like you. Dear Jesus, sometimes I am overcome by my longing to come close to you, to look into your eyes and to embrace you.

You have a great heart, you performed miracles, but you have always retained your simplicity and serenity. You know the mysteries of the universe, of the earth and of humanity, you possess all that anyone could desire, yet you have sought out the poor and despised members of society. You passed through the world doing good, comforting the afflicted, healing the sick, forgiving sinners. You helped and saved everyone and today you are here with us; you have not abandoned us.

Create in us a new heart and give us your Spirit! Jesus, without you we would be blind; we would not have understood why we live; we would not have discovered the meaning of life. Thank you, Jesus!

ACT OF CONSECRATION TO
JESUS IN THE BLESSED SACRAMENT

O Jesus, I believe that you are really present in the Eucharist in which your death and resurrection are present, so that all people may experience the Father's love, and in believing, they may come to love Him with your own love. You desire that all believers become one in you, and, by means of your Spirit, enter into communion with the Father as a single offering with you. In this plan of love of yours, you have reserved a place also for me.

You have already incorporated me into your body in baptism and now you come to meet me in your Eucharistic presence. I cannot refuse your invitation. With this aim and with this purpose today **I consecrate myself** to your love here present and at work in this adorable Sacrament.

In making this act of adoration, I express my intention to live out my baptismal promises and those made in the Universal Association of Eucharistic Reparation, by means of your sacrifice. In particular I resolve to assist at Mass with the spirit of the little host, which seeks to offer itself, sacrifice itself, and give itself together with you. My desire is to extend this life-giving meeting with you to all aspects of my life, incorporating my actions into your uninterrupted sacrifice, continuing your offering and sacrifice in the various circumstances of my daily life.

O Jesus, I want to live in union with your Eucharistic mystery in order to compensate for the lack of charity in your mystical body. I wish to make up for the lack of love of indifferent brothers and sisters, making reparation for all unfaithfulness and betrayals, all negligence and coldness.

I would like all my life to become an echo of the Eucharistic message of your saving love. I re-solve to bring to this tabernacle the souls of others, prepared to allow themselves to be used by you and to be consumed by an ardent desire for the Father's glory and for the salvation of their brothers and sisters, so that the requests of your Heart may find a greater acceptance and a more generous response.

O Virgin Mary, you who are present at the altar as you were present on the hill of Calvary, accept my consecration and make it worthy of your Son's love. I ask you for the grace to be able to imitate you; to re-live in my life the desires of your Immaculate Heart, and to be consecrated totally to your Son and to his work of redemption. I put myself in your hands; make use of me so that Jesus, who is always present and at work in our churches, may be known, loved and glorified.

ROSARY

EUCHARISTIC ROSARY

*In the name of the Father, and of the Son,
and of the Holy Spirit. Amen.*

O God, come to my aid.
O Lord, make haste to help me.
Glory Be

FIRST MYSTERY

In the first mystery, we contemplate how Jesus
instituted the Blessed Sacrament, to remind us of
his passion and death.

Our Father

Then the following prayer is recited or sung 10 times:

May you be praised in every moment,
O my Jesus in the Blessed Sacrament.
May you be praised now and forever,
O my Consecrated Jesus.

SECOND MYSTERY

In the second mystery we contemplate how Jesus instituted the Blessed Sacrament in order to remain with each one of us throughout our lives.

Our Father

**May you be praised in every moment,
O my Jesus in the Blessed Sacrament.
May you be praised now and forever,
O my Consecrated Jesus.**

(10 times)

THIRD MYSTERY

In the third mystery, we contemplate how Jesus instituted the Blessed Sacrament in order to perpetuate his sacrifice on the altar, unto the end of this world.

Our Father

**May you be praised in every moment,
O my Jesus in the Blessed Sacrament.
May you be praised now and forever,
O my Consecrated Jesus.**

(10 times)

FOURTH MYSTERY

In the fourth mystery we contemplate how Jesus instituted the Blessed Sacrament in order to make himself food and drink for our souls.

Our Father

**May you be praised in every moment,
O my Jesus in the Blessed Sacrament.
May you be praised now and forever,
O my Consecrated Jesus.**

(10 times)

FIFTH MYSTERY

In the fifth mystery we contemplate how Jesus instituted the most Blessed Sacrament so that he would be able to visit us at the hour of our death and bring us to Paradise.

Our Father

**May you be praised in every moment,
O my Jesus in the Blessed Sacrament.
May you be praised now and forever,
O my Consecrated Jesus.**

(10 times)

LITANY OF THE HOLY EUCHARIST

Lord, have mercy.

Lord, have mercy.

Christ, have mercy.

Christ, have mercy.

Lord, have mercy.

Lord, have mercy.

Christ, hear us.

Christ, graciously hear us.

God the Father of Heaven,

Have mercy on us.

God the Son, Redeemer of the world,

Have mercy on us.

God the Holy Spirit,

Have mercy on us.

Holy Trinity, one God,

Have mercy on us.

Most Holy Eucharist,

We adore you.

Ineffable gift of the Father,

We adore you.

Sign of the supreme love of the Son,

We adore you.

Prodigy of the love of the Holy Spirit,

We adore you.

Blessed Fruit of the Virgin Mary,

We adore you.

Sacrament of the Body and of Blood of Christ,

We adore you.

Sacrament which perpetuates the sacrifice of the Cross,

We adore you.

Sacrament of the new and eternal covenant,

We adore you.

Memorial of the death and resurrection
of Our Lord,

We adore you.

Memorial of our salvation,

We adore you.

Sacrifice of praise and thanksgiving,

We adore you.

Sacrifice of expiation and reconciliation,

We adore you.

Dwelling place of God with all people,

We adore you.

Wedding Feast of the Lamb,

We adore you.

Bread of life come down from Heaven,

We adore you.

Manna full of hidden sweetness,

We adore you.

True Paschal Lamb,

We adore you.

Crown of priests,

We adore you.

Treasure of the faithful,

We adore you.

Viaticum of the pilgrim Church,

We adore you.

Remedy for our daily infirmities,

We adore you.

Medicine of immortality,

We adore you.

Mystery of our faith,

We adore you.

Sustenance of our hope,

We adore you.

Bond of charity,

We adore you.

Sign of unity and peace,

We adore you.

Source of pure joy,

We adore you.

Sacrament that gives birth to virgins,

We adore you.

Sacrament that gives strength and vigour,

We adore you.

Foretaste of the heavenly banquet,

We adore you.

Promise of our resurrection,

We adore you.

Promise of future joy,

We adore you.

Lamb of God, who take away the sins of the world,
Spare us, O Lord.

Lamb of God, who take away the sins of the world,
Graciously hear us, O Lord.

Lamb of God, who take away the sins of the world,
Have mercy on us.

You have given your people bread from Heaven.
The bread which is full of all goodness.

Let us pray.
O God, who in this wonderful sacrament have left us a memorial of your passion; help us to reverence the sacred mysteries of your Body and Blood, so that we may always experience in our lives the effects of your Redemption, you who live and reign for ever and ever.
Amen.

INVOCATIONS

INVOCATIONS OF THE HOLY EUCHARIST

FIRST INVOCATION
MAY YOU BE BLESSED, O LORD.

For the world you have created and for
humanity which you have redeemed,
May you be blessed, O Lord.

For the sun which warms us and for
your love which comforts us,
May you be blessed, O Lord.

For the water which purifies us and for
your forgiveness which consoles us,
May you be blessed, O Lord.

For the bread which nourishes us and for
your body which fortifies us,
May you be blessed, O Lord.

For the air we breathe and for
the prayer which raises us up to you,
May you be blessed, O Lord.

For all creatures of the earth and for
all the saints and angels of heaven,
May you be blessed, O Lord.

Second Invocation
MAY YOUR WILL BE DONE, O LORD.

Should our future path continue to be
     strewn with crosses,
          May your will be done, O Lord.

Whether our life be long or short,
          May your will be done, O Lord.

When we are hurt by others,
          May your will be done, O Lord.

When our life is not as we would like it to be,
          May your will be done, O Lord.

When the good we do is misinterpreted,
          May your will be done, O Lord.

When misfortunes make our crosses heavier,
          May your will be done, O Lord.

When our sacrifices are not acknowledged,
          May your will be done, O Lord.

Should illness takes away joy from our homes,
          May your will be done, O Lord.

Should we find no consolation,
     not even in prayer,
          May your will be done, O Lord.

In the saddest hours of our life,
May your will be done, O Lord.

On the day when death shall call us to you,
May your will be done, O Lord.

Third Invocation
WE BELIEVE IN YOU, O LORD.

Blessed are the poor in spirit, the kingdom
of Heaven is theirs.
We believe in you, O Lord.

Blessed are the gentle, they shall have the
earth as their inheritance.
We believe in you, O Lord.

Blessed are those who mourn, they shall
be comforted.
We believe in you, O Lord.

Blessed are those who hunger and thirst for
righteousness, they shall have their fill.
We believe in you, O Lord.

Blessed are the merciful, they shall have
mercy shown them.
We believe in you, O Lord.

Blessed are the pure of heart, they shall see God.
We believe in you, O Lord.

Blessed are the peacemakers, they shall be
called children of God.
We believe in you, O Lord.

Blessed are those who are persecuted in the
cause of righteousness.
We believe in you, O Lord.

Anyone who wants to become great among
you must be your servant.
We believe in you, O Lord.

It is not anyone who says to me, "Lord, Lord!"
who will enter the Kingdom of Heaven,
but the person who does the will of God.
We believe in you, O Lord.

Whoever loves me, will keep my commandments.
We believe in you, O Lord.

Beware of false prophets who come to you
dressed as lambs.
We believe in you, O Lord.

Love your enemies and pray for those who
persecute you.
We believe in you, O Lord.
Do not judge, so that you will not be judged.
We believe in you, O Lord.

Do not store up treasures on earth, but in heaven.
We believe in you, O Lord.

No one can serve two masters, God and money.
We believe in you, O Lord.

It is hard for someone rich to enter
  the kingdom of Heaven.
     We believe in you, O Lord.

Seek first the kingdom of God, and all
  these things shall be added unto you.
     We believe in you, O Lord.

You have only one Master, Christ, and you are
  all brothers.
     We believe in you, O Lord.

Fourth Invocation
WE OFFER YOU, O LORD.

The bread which becomes your Body and
    the wine which becomes your Blood,
        We offer you, O Lord.

The worries of our families, our sufferings
    and our pain,
        We offer you, O Lord.

Our joys, our home, our children's smiles,
        We offer you, O Lord.

The work of our neighbour in the office,
    in the workshop, in the laboratory,
        We offer you, O Lord.

The labour of all people and the prayer of the
    cloisters and monasteries,
        We offer you, O Lord.

Our life and the life of all people,
        We offer you, O Lord.

Our family of origin and our colleagues at work,
        We offer you, O Lord.

FIFTH INVOCATION
STAY WITH US, O LORD

When doubts regarding our faith assail us,
Stay with us, O Lord.

When doubt causes our hope to waver,
Stay with us, O Lord.

When our love for you diminishes,
Stay with us, O Lord.

When our days are filled with distractions,
Stay with us, O Lord.

When temptation seems too strong for us,
Stay with us, O Lord.

When we are discouraged by our failures,
Stay with us, O Lord.

When we find ourselves alone and abandoned
by everyone,
Stay with us, O Lord.

When sorrow makes us despair,
Stay with us, O Lord.

When the hour comes for our return to you,
Stay with us, O Lord.

In joy and sorrow, in life and death,
Stay with us, O Lord.

INVOCATIONS OF REPARATION
TO THE HOLY EUCHARIST

For all sacrileges committed against the Eucharist
Forgive us, O Lord.

For the times Holy Communion is received
in mortal sin, **Forgive us, O Lord.**

For all profanity committed against of the
Eucharist, **Forgive us, O Lord.**

For irreverence in churches,
Forgive us, O Lord.

For outrages committed against the tabernacle,
Forgive us, O Lord.

For contempt of sacred things,
Forgive us, O Lord.

For neglect of churches,
Forgive us, O Lord.

For sins of immorality,
Forgive us, O Lord.

For the separation of souls from God,
Forgive us, O Lord.

For blasphemy against your most Holy Name,
Forgive us, O Lord.

For indifference to your love,
Forgive us, O Lord.

For outrages committed against the Pope,
Forgive us, O Lord.

For derision of bishops and priests,
Forgive us, O Lord.

For blasphemy against the name of Mary,
Forgive us, O Lord.
For mockery of her Immaculate Conception,
Forgive us, O Lord.
For lack of veneration towards Mary,
Forgive us, O Lord.
For offences committed against the
images of Mary, **Forgive us, O Lord.**

For neglect of the Holy Rosary,
Forgive us, O Lord.
For indifference to the motherly love of Mary,
Forgive us, O Lord.

Soul of Mary,

Enlighten me.

Ardent Heart burning with love,

Inflame me.

Body of Mary without stain,

Purify me.

Motherly hands of Mary,

Sustain me.

Immaculate feet of Mary,

Direct me.

Merciful eyes of Mary,

Look upon me.

Tears of Blessed Mary,

Wash me.

Sinless tongue of Mary,

Speak in my favour.

Sorrowful passion of Mary,

Fortify me.

O Mary, Mother of graces,

Hear my prayer.

O Mary, from being tepid,

Preserve me.

O Mary, into your lap,

Take me.

O Mary, do not allow,

That I may ever be separated from you.

O Mary, in the Heart of Jesus,

Hide me.

O Mary, from the enemies of my health,

Defend me.

O Mary, in my last agony,

Assist me.

O Mary, at the hour of my death,

Call me.

To Jesus and to you, O Mary,

Bring me.

So that, with him and with all your chosen,

I may praise you for ever and ever.

Amen.

# PRAYERS FOR HOLY COMMUNION

PRAYER BEFORE HOLY COMMUNION

We come to Your banquet with joy, dear Father; and may the effusion of Your Spirit transform us into the image of your glory. The body of Christ, offered in sacrifice for us is the food which gives us strength; His blood poured out for us is the drink which washes away our guilt.

Lord Jesus, Son of the living God, by the will of the Father and the work of the Holy Spirit, Your death brought life to the world. By Your Holy Body and Blood free me from all evil. Keep me faithful to your teaching and never let me be parted from you.

Lord Jesus Christ, with faith in Your love and mercy, I eat Your Body and drink Your Blood. Let it not bring me condemnation but health in mind and body.

Almighty, everlasting God, behold, I approach the Sacrament of your only-begotten Son, our Lord Jesus Christ; I approach this Sacrament as a sich person who goes to the to physician who will save his life, as a thirsty person who goes to the fountain of mercy, as a poor person who goes towards the light of heaven and earth. Therefore, I invoke Your boundless generosity: in Your mercy, cure my sickness, enlighten my blindness, enrich my poverty so that I may receive the bread of angels for my salvation.

PRAYER AT HOLY COMMUNION

O Jesus, hear my prayer; Lord, be it done unto me according to Your word! Jesus, You came to save each one of us, therefore, I commend everyone to You: my family, my parents, brothers, sisters and friends, my community and the whole world.

Many do not even know You and yet You also came for them too, O Jesus! The hearts of many are empty; they serve other gods, they destroy their own lives and those of others. I beseech You, with Mary and with all those who serve You, to give them the grace of faith. Many worship the evil one and they serve him with all their lives, causing harm to themselves and to others in mercy, Jesus, restore them to freedom, so that they may adore You. Send Your Spirit into the world and enlighten every heart so that it may abandon the darkness of unbelief and the slavery of sin to enter into the freedom of being a child of God.

Jesus, I adore You, because You renew the world! Jesus, I love You, because You are the Saviour of the world. Jesus, I believe in You, because You are the Redeemer of the world.

Jesus, I adore You with Mary who was preserved from original sin and from all sin sin from the moment of her conception. You are the Redeemer of the world. I honour and glorify You, Jesus, because in Mary You manifested the fruits of full redemption. I glorify You, Jesus, because the marvellous light of Your love shone in the heart of Mary from the beginning of her life. Oh, how beautiful was Her soul, always full of grace! In her the friendship between God and humanity was re-established and renewed. I bless You, Jesus, because Your Mother has become the dawn of every new day, a light which has shone in its fullness since your coming down to earth. I bless You because in the heart of Mary You found a worthy home.

Jesus, I honour and exalt You together with Mary, conceived without sin.

Prayer after Holy Communion

Stay with me, Lord, because I need Your presence in order not to forget You. You know how easily I abandon You... Stay with me, Lord, because I am weak and I need Your strength in order not to fall many times! Stay with me, Lord, because You are my life and without You my fervour wanes. Stay with me, Lord, because You are my light and without You I am in darkness. Stay with me, Lord, so that I may hear Your voice and follow you...

Stay with me Lord because I want to love You ardently and to be always in Your company. Stay with me, Lord, if You want me to be faithful to you. Stay with me, Jesus, because although my poor soul is most unworthy, it desires to be a refuge of consolation for You, a nest of love. Stay with me, Jesus, because it is getting late and the day is drawing to a close... life is passing... I need more courage so that I will not fail to reach the end of my journey of faith and therefore I need You...

At times darkness, temptations, aridity, crosses and sufferings oppress me, and oh! how much I need You, my Jesus in such a night of exile! Stay with me, Lord, because in these dark moments of life and in times of danger I need You most. Let me recognise You as Your disciples did at the breaking of the bread... may the Eucharist be the light which dispels my darkness, may it give me strength and vigour to sustain me and let it be the joy of my heart.

Stay with me, Lord, so that when death draws near, I shall want to remain united to You, and if it be impossible for me to receive Holy Communion, may I be united to You at least by grace and love. Jesus, stay with me; I do not ask You for divine consolation, because I do not deserve it, but for the gift of Your most holy presence; oh, yes, that I do ask!

Stay with me, Lord. I seek only You, Your love, Your grace, Your will, Your heart, Your Spirit, because I love You and ask for no reward other than an increase in my love, that it may become steadfast love that speaks through actions. May I love You with all my heart while on earth, in order to be able to continue loving You to perfection for all eternity.

Amen.

The daily prayer in honour of the Holy Wounds of Jesus may also be recited.

(See page 343)

5.
THE MOST PRECIOUS BLOOD OF JESUS

- **Prayers**
- **Prayers of Consecration**
- **Chaplets Litany**
- **Offerings**
- **Novenas**

THE IMPORTANCE OF THE BLOOD

The Church is holy, even though her members are sinners, because she has no life other than that of grace. Living within the Church, her members grow in sanctity; drawing away from her life, they fall into sin and disorder, thus preventing her sanctity from being diffused throughout the world. Thus the Church suffers and does penance for these sins, penance which also has the power to heal her children with the Blood of Christ and with the gift of the Holy Spirit. St. Thomas said, "We cannot learn with our intellect that the true Body and Blood of Christ are present in this Sacrament but only through faith, which is based on the authority of God". Similarly, St. Cyril, when commenting on the following verse from the Gospel of Luke: "This is my body given up for you." (Lk 22:19), said, "Do not doubt that this is true, but rather accept with faith the words of the Saviour: because, being the truth, he does not lie."

Adoro te devote, latens Deitas... I adore you with devotion, O hidden God, who truly conceal yourself under the appearance (of bread and wine): to you my heart submits itself entirely, as in contemplating you, it becomes weaker.

Fresh light and inspiration was shed upon the Precious Blood of Jesus during the Pontificate of Pope John XXIII, especially through his apostolic letter "Inde a primis", the first papal document having the sole aim of promoting devotion to the most Precious Blood. In our own times, devotion to the Precious Blood has been greatly enriched by the Second Vatican Council. The fervour of study which characterized the council brought a welcome return to the Bible and to the Liturgy which gave origin to this devotion and have nourished it throughout the ages. Indeed, the key declarations of the Council documents explicitly mention the mystery of the Precious Blood; for example, the Constitution of the Church refers to it eleven times, thus emphasizing the importance of this devotion and the high regard of the Church for the same.

PRAYER OF ST. CASPAR TO THE MOST PRECIOUS BLOOD

O Wounds, O Precious Blood of my Lord, may I bless you in eternity.

O love of my Lord transformed into a wound! How far we are from conforming to your life.

O Blood of Jesus Christ, balsam for our souls, source of all mercy, grant that my tongue, reddened by blood in the daily celebration of the Mass, may bless you now and always.

O Lord, who would not love you? Who would not burn with affection for you? Your wounds, your Blood, the thorns, the Cross, and especially the Divine Blood shed unto the last drop; with what an eloquent voice, they cry out to my poor heart! As you suffered and died for me to save me, I will give, if necessary, my very life, so that I may attain the blessed possession of heaven.

O Jesus, you have become our redemption.

From your open side, ark of salvation, furnace of love, gushed forth blood and water as a sign of the benefits of the Sacraments and of the tenderness of your love, O Christ, who loved us and washed us in your Blood!

PRAYER FOR AN OBSTINATE SINNER
By St. Catherine of Siena

My Lord, I know that if you look at our iniquities, there is no one who can escape eternal damnation. But remember that you suffered the most cruel tortures, shed your most precious Blood and died with the single aim of forgiving us.

I have no other consolation on earth, save that of seeing sinners returning to your feet. Grant me the conversion of this obstinate sinner: his soul is in your hands.

PRAYER FOR ENEMIES

O Jesus, who commanded us to forgive and love those who do us wrong, I beg you for the sake of your Precious Blood: grant me the strength to observe this commandment of yours.

Jesus, who from the Cross prayed, "Father, forgive them, for they do not know what they are doing", for the sake of your Precious Blood, grant that I may carry out this heroic act towards my enemies.

Jesus, for the sake of your Precious Blood, I beg you that they may repent and sing your praises one day with me in heaven.

Jesus, Divine Lamb, sacrificed for peace, love and salvation of the world, graciously hear and grant this prayer of mine. **Amen.**

PRAYER TO THE
MOST PRECIOUS BLOOD

Precious Blood of Jesus, infinite price paid in ransom for the universe, drink and cleansing water for our souls, and defence of humanity before the throne of supreme mercy, we adore you profoundly.

We desire, insofar as we can, to make reparation to you for the ingratitude, for the outrages that you receive continuously from so many sinners, especially from the hardened sinners who blaspheme against you.

May you always be blessed, O Blood of infinite value, and may Jesus be blessed a thousand times, he who shed you for our salvation. It was his immense love for us that caused you to flow from his veins unto the last drop!

O Blood of redemption and of life, of unity and peace, source of grace and pledge of eternal life, grant that all hearts and tongues may praise, bless and thank you, both now and for ever.
Amen.

PRAYER TO OUR LORD JESUS CHRIST

Lord Jesus Christ, who have redeemed us with your Precious Blood, we adore you!

Infinite price paid to ransom the universe, mystical purification of our souls, your Divine Blood is the pledge of our salvation before our merciful Father.

May you always be blessed and praised, O Jesus, for the gift of your Blood, which with the Spirit of love you offered unto the last drop, to allow us to participate in the divine life. May the Blood, which you poured out for our redemption, purify us from sin and save us from the temptations of the devil.

O Blood of the new and eternal convenant, our drink in the sacrifice of the Eucharist, unite us to God and to each other in love, peace and mutual respect, especially for the poor.

O Blood of life, unity and peace, mystery of love and source of grace, inebriate our hearts with the Holy Spirit. Lord Jesus, we would like to atone for the ingratitudes and the outrages with which your creatures continually offend you.

Accept our life in union with the offering of your Blood, so that in our own body we can make up for all the hardships that still have to be undergone by Christ for the benefit of the Church and the redemption of the world.

Lord Jesus Christ, may all people and all tongues bless and thank you here on earth and in the glory of heaven, with the hymn of praise: "You have redeemed us, O Lord, with your Precious Blood and have made of us a kingdom for our God".
Amen.

ANIMA CHRISTI (SOUL OF CHRIST)

A prayer of St. Ignatius of Loyola

Soul of Christ, sanctify me.
Body of Christ, heal me.
Blood of God, drench me.
Water from the side of Christ, wash me.
Passion of Christ, strengthen me.
Good Jesus, hear me.
In Your wounds shelter me.
From turning away keep me.
From the evil one protect me.
At the hour of my death call me.
Into your presence lead me,
to praise you with all your saints
for ever and ever. **Amen.**

 **PRAYER OF CONSECRATION**

CONSECRATION TO THE
BLOOD OF JESUS

Lord Jesus, you who love us and have freed us from our sins with your Blood, I adore you, I bless you and I consecrate myself to you with living faith.

By the help of your Spirit, I desire to make all my existence, animated by the memory of your Precious Blood, into a faithful service of the will of God, for the coming of your Kingdom.

Through the Blood which you shed for the remission of sins, purify me of all sin and renew my heart, so that the image of a new person, created in justice and holiness may become ever more evident in me.

By your Blood, which is the sign of reconciliation with God and reconciliation with each other, make me a malleable instrument of brotherly love and communion.

By the power of your Blood, supreme proof of your mercy, give me the courage to love you and to love my brothers and sisters, even to the point of offering my life.

Jesus, my Redeemer, help me to carry your cross everyday, in order that a drop of my blood, united with yours, may contribute to the redemption of the world. O Divine Blood, which together with your grace gives life to the Mystical Body, make me a living stone in the Church.

Give me an ardent desire for Christian unity. Infuse my heart with a great zeal for the salvation of my brothers and sisters. Raise up in the Church numerous missionary vocations, so that all people may know, love and serve the true God.

Most Precious Blood, sign of liberation and of new life, grant that I may persevere in faith, in hope and in love, so that, having been chosen by you, I may leave this exile and enter the promised land of Paradise, to sing my praise to you with all those whom you have chosen.

Amen.

CHAPLET

CHAPLET TO THE
MOST PRECIOUS BLOOD

*A special red chaplet may be used to recite this prayer.
First the mystery is announced, then on each bead a Glory
Be is recited. At the seventh mystery, the Glory Be is recited
three times on the three beads near the Crucifix.*

*In the name of the Father, and of the Son,
and of the Holy Spirit. Amen.*

O God, come to my aid.
O Lord, make haste to help me.
Glory Be

FIRST MYSTERY

Jesus sheds his Blood at the circumcision (ref. Lk 1:59).
O Jesus, Son of God, through the first drops of
Blood which you shed for our salvation, you
reveal to us the value of life and the duty of con-
fronting it with faith and courage, in the light of
your name and in the joy of grace.

Our Father
Glory Be *(5 times)*

We beseech you, O Lord, to come to the aid of your children, whom you have redeemed by your Precious Blood.

SECOND MYSTERY

Jesus sweats Blood in the Garden of Olives (ref. Lk 22:39-54).

O Son of God, may the Blood which you sweated in Gethsemane help us to hate sin, because offending you is the only true evil which spoils your love and makes our life sorrowful.

Our Father
Glory Be *(5 times)*

We beseech...

THIRD MYSTERY

Jesus sheds his Blood in the scourging at the pillar (ref. Jn 19:1).

O Divine Master, may your Blood shed in the scourging at the pillar encourage us to love purity, so that we may live in the intimacy of your friendship and contemplate with pure eyes the wonders of creation.

Our Father
Glory Be *(5 times)*

We beseech...

FOURTH MYSTERY

Jesus sheds his Blood in the crowning with thorns (ref. Jn 19:2-5).

O King of the universe, may your Blood shedin the crowning of thorns, destroy our selfishness and our pride, so that we may grow in love and serve all our brothers and sisters who are in need with humility.

Our Father
Glory Be *(5 times)*

We beseech... *(see page 313)*

FIFTH MYSTERY

Jesus sheds his Blood on the road to Calvary (ref. Jn 19:18).

O Saviour of the world, may your Blood shed on the way to Calvary light up our path and may it help us to carry the cross with you, to complete your Passion in our flesh.

Our Father
Glory Be *(5 times)*

We beseech... *(see page 313)*

SIXTH MYSTERY

Jesus sheds his Blood in the Crucifixion (ref.Lk 23:33-34).

O Lamb of God, sacrificed for us, teach us to forgive those who offend us and to love our enemies. And you, Mother of the Lord and our Mother, reveal to us all the power and richness of the Precious Blood of Jesus.

Our Father
Glory Be *(5 times)*

We beseech... *(see page 313)*

We beseech... *(see page 313)*

SEVENTH MYSTERY

Jesus, sheds his Blood as his side is pierced by a lance (ref. Jn 19:31-34).

O adorable Heart, pierced for us, accept our prayers for the needs of the poor, the tears of those who suffer, the hopes of all people, in order that humanity may one day become one body, united in your kingdom of love, justice and peace.

Our Father
Glory Be *(5 times)*

We beseech... *(see page 313)*

LITANY OF THE
MOST PRECIOUS BLOOD

Lord, have mercy.

Lord, have mercy.

Christ, have mercy.

Christ, have mercy.

Lord, have mercy.

Lord, have mercy.

Christ, hear us.

Christ, graciously hear us.

God the Father of Heaven,

Have mercy on us.

God the Son, Redeemer of the world,

Have mercy on us.

God the Holy Spirit,

Have mercy on us.

Holy Trinity, one God,

Save us.

Blood of Christ, Only Son of the Eternal Father,

Save us.

Blood of Christ, Incarnate Word of God,

Save us.

Blood of Christ of the new and eternal convenant,

Save us.

Blood of Christ, flowing down upon the
earth in your agony,

Save us.

Blood of Christ, shed profusely in the
scourging at the pillar,

Save us.

Blood of Christ, poured out in the crowning
of thorns,

Save us.

Blood of Christ, shed upon the cross,

Save us.

Blood of Christ, price of our salvation,

Save us.

Blood of Christ, without which there is no
forgiveness,

Save us.

Blood of Christ, drink and purification for
our souls in the Eucharist,

Save us.

Blood of Christ, stream of mercy,

Save us.

Blood of Christ, victorious over demons,

Save us.

Blood of Christ, strength of martyrs,

Save us.

Blood of Christ, strength of confessors,

Save us.

Blood of Christ, which gives birth to virgins,

Save us.

Blood of Christ, which sustains those who doubt,

Save us.

Blood of Christ, solace for the suffering,

Save us.

Blood of Christ, consolation in grief,

Save us.

Blood of Christ, hope for those who repent,

Save us.

Blood of Christ, comfort of the dying,

Save us.

Blood of Christ, peace and sweetness
of our hearts,

Save us.

Blood of Christ, token of eternal life,

Save us.

Blood of Christ, which frees the souls
of Purgatory,

Save us.

Blood of Christ, worthy of all praise and honour,

Save us.

Lamb of God, who take away the sins of the world,
Spare us, O Lord.

Lamb of God, who take away the sins of the world,
Graciously hear us O Lord

Lamb of God, who take away the sins of the world,
Have mercy on us.

You have redeemed us, Lord, with your Blood,
**and you have made of us a kingdom
for our God.**

Let us pray.
Father, who, through the Precious Blood of your Only Begotten Son have redeemed all people, continue to show your mercy to us, so that we, by celebrating these holy mysteries, may obtain the fruits of our redemption. Through Christ our Lord.
Amen.

OFFERINGS

PRAYERS OF OFFERING OF THE MOST PRECIOUS BLOOD TO THE ETERNAL FATHER

Eternal Father, we offer you the most Precious Blood which Jesus shed on the cross and offers every day on the altar, for the glory of his holy name, for the coming of his Kingdom and for the salvation of all souls.

Glory Be
May Jesus be always blessed and thanked because he has saved us by his Precious Blood.

Eternal Father, we offer you the most Precious Blood which Jesus shed on the cross and offers every day on the altar, for the Holy Church, for our Holy Father the Pope, for bishops, priests, missionaries, religious and for all the faithful.

Glory Be
May Jesus be always blessed and thanked because he has saved us by his Precious Blood.

Eternal Father, we offer you the most precious Blood which Jesus shed on the cross and offers every day on the altar, for the conversion of sinners, for Christian unity, and so that your word may be obeyed out of love.

Glory Be
May Jesus be always blessed and thanked because he has saved us by his Precious Blood.

Eternal Father, we offer you the most Precious Blood which Jesus shed on the cross and offers every day on the altar, for civil authorities, for an increase in morality, and for peace and justice among all people.

Glory Be
May Jesus *(See above)*

Eternal Father, we offer you the most Precious Blood which Jesus shed on the cross and offers every day on the altar, so that work and pain may be consecrated to you, and we offer it to you also for the poor, the sick, those who suffer and for all those who have asked our prayers.

Glory Be
May Jesus *(See above)*

Eternal Father, we offer you the most Precious Blood which Jesus shed on the cross and offers every day on the altar, for our spiritual and temporal necessities, as well as for those of our relatives, benefactors and enemies.

Glory Be
May Jesus *(See above)*

Eternal Father, we offer you the most Precious Blood which Jesus shed on the cross and offers every day on the altar, for those who will pass into the next life on this day, for the holy souls of Purgatory and for their union in eternity with Christ in his glory.

Glory Be
May Jesus *(See above)*
May the Blood of Jesus be praised,
now and forever.
Amen.

Let us pray.
Almighty and eternal God, who sacrificed your only-begotten Son, the Redeemer of the world, and desired to be placated by his Blood, grant, we beseech you, that we may venerate the price of our salvation, in order that, by its power, we may be defended here on earth from the evils of everyday life, so that we my enjoy the fruits of heaven in eternity. Through Christ our Lord.
Amen.

OFFERING OF THE MOST PRECIOUS BLOOD OF JESUS FOR THE DEAD

Eternal Father, I offer you the Blood which Jesus, your beloved Son, shed during the painful agony in the Garden of Olives, in order to obtain the liberation of the holy souls of Purgatory, especially for the soul of...

Eternal rest...

Eternal Father, I offer you the Blood which Jesus, your beloved Son, shed during the cruel scourging at the pillar and the crowning with thorns, in order to obtain the liberation of the holy souls of Purgatory, especially for the soul of...

Eternal rest...

Eternal Father, I offer you the Blood which Jesus, your beloved Son, shed on his way to Calvary, in order to obtain the liberation of the holy souls of Purgatory, especially for the soul of...

Eternal rest...

Eternal Father, I offer you the Blood which Jesus, your beloved Son, shed in the crucifixion and in the three hours of agony on the cross, in order to obtain the liberation of the holy souls of Purgatory, especially for the soul of...

Eternal rest...

Eternal Father, I offer you the Blood which Jesus, your beloved Son, shed from the wound of his most Sacred Heart, in order to obtain the liberation of the holy souls of Purgatory, especially for the soul of...

Eternal rest...

Let us pray.
Most lovable Jesus, I humbly implore you to offer to the eternal Father, for the sake of the holy souls of Purgatory, your most Precious Blood, shed from the wounds of your adorable Body in your agony and in your death. And we ask you, Our Lady of Sorrows to present to the Father the sorrowful Passion of your beloved Son and all the sorrow which your heart suffered, so that the holy souls of Purgatory may obtain relief and once freed from their torments, may sing of your Divine Mercy forever in heaven.
Amen.

OFFERING OF THE MOST PRECIOUS BLOOD FOR THE SICK

Jesus, our Saviour, Divine Physician who heals the wounds of the soul and those of the body, we commend to you... *(name of the ill person)*. By the merits of your most precious Blood, grant him (her) the grace of good health.

Glory Be

Jesus, our Saviour, you who were ever merciful when faced with the miserable conditions of humanity, and healed all types of infirmity, have compassion on... *(name of the ill person)*. By the merits of your most precious Blood, we beseech you to free him (her) from his (her) illness.

Glory Be

Jesus, our Saviour, who said, "Come to me, all of you who are weary and overburdened and I will give you rest" say again for... *(name of the ill person)* the words heard by many sick people: "Get up and walk!", so that through the merits of your most precious Blood, he (she) may run immediately to the foot of your altar and thank you.

Glory Be
Mary, Health of the sick,
pray for... *(name of the ill person)*

Hail Mary

OFFERING OF THE
BLOOD OF CHRIST FOR THE DYING

Eternal Father, I offer You the merits of the most Precious Blood of Jesus, your beloved Son and my Divine Redeemer, for all those who shall die this day; preserve them from the pains of hell and lead them into Paradise where they may live forever in union with you.
Amen.

Glory Be

DAILY OFFERING OF THE
PRECIOUS BLOOD OF JESUS
TO THE ETERNAL FATHER

Eternal Father, I offer you, through the most pure hands of Mary, Mother of our Redeemer, the most Precious Blood of Jesus, generously shed in his passion and every day upon the altar; I unite my prayers, actions and sufferings of this day, for the divine intentions of the Holy Victim, in reparation for my sins, for the conversion of sinners and for the needs of the Holy Church.
In particular I offer to you...

(Here we express our private intentions).

OFFERING OF THE PRECIOUS BLOOD OF JESUS TO THE FATHER

Eternal Father, by the most Precious Blood of Jesus Christ, I glorify his most Holy Name, in accordance with the desire of his most beloved Heart.

OFFERING OF THE PRECIOUS BLOOD TO THE FATHER, SON AND HOLY SPIRIT

I offer to you the Blood of the Incarnate Word: I offer it to you, Father, I offer it to you, Holy Spirit, and I offer it to you, Mary, so that you may offer it to the Holy Trinity in atonement for all the faults which may be found in my soul and for all the failings which may be found in my heart.

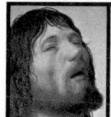
NOVENA TO THE
MOST PRECIOUS BLOOD
To be recited for nine days.

*In the name of the Father, and of the Son,
and of the Holy Spirit. Amen.*

O God, come to my aid.
O Lord, make haste to help me.

Blood of Jesus,
save us.

Glory Be
The Creed *(see page 26)*

Eternal Father, we offer you the merits of the most Precious Blood shed by your beloved Son during his circumcision, for the sanctification of the Church, of the Pope and of the bishops and for the liberation of the holy souls of Purgatory, especially the soul that has been most forgotten.

Glory Be

Eternal Father, I offer you the most Precious Blood of Jesus in reparation for my sins, for the needs of the Holy Church, and for the holy souls of Purgatory.

Glory Be
Blood of Jesus,
save us.

Eternal Father, we offer you the merits of the most Precious Blood shed by your beloved Son during his agony in the garden and we ask you that there may be peace among nations and that the Jewish people may be ever more enlightened by your truth. We pray also for the conversion of the enemies of the Church, for the grace of which we have most need and for the liberation of the holy souls of Purgatory, especially the souls nearest to the threshold of your glory.

Glory Be

Eternal Father, I offer you the most Precious Blood of Jesus in reparation for my sins, for the needs of the Holy Church, and for the holy souls of Purgatory.

Glory Be
Blood of Jesus,
save us.

Eternal Father, we offer you the merits of the most Precious Blood shed by your beloved Son during his scourging at the pillar and we ask you to enlighten the heretics and all those who do not believe in you. We also pray to you for the conversion of sinners and for the liberation of the holy souls of Purgatory, especially those who must spend most time there.

Glory Be

Eternal Father, I offer you the most Precious Blood of Jesus in reparation for my sins, for the needs of the Holy Church, and for the holy souls of Purgatory.

Glory Be
Blood of Jesus,
save us.

Eternal Father, we offer you the merits of the most Precious Blood shed by your beloved Son during his crowning with thorns and we ask you for all the graces which we need, along with those needed by our relatives, friends and ene-mies, and we ask for the liberation of the holy souls of Purgatory, especially that soul who is most deserving in your eyes.

Glory Be

Eternal Father, I offer you the most Precious Blood of Jesus in reparation for my sins, for the needs of the Holy Church, and in suffrage for the holy souls of Purgatory.

Glory Be
Blood of Jesus,
save us

Eternal Father, we offer you the merits of the most Precious Blood shed by your beloved Son on his journey to Calvary and we ask you for the salvation of those who on this day are about to appear before your judgement. We ask you also for the liberation of the holy souls of Purgatory, especially that soul which was most devoted to your Precious Blood.

Glory Be

Eternal Father, I offer you the most Precious Blood of Jesus in reparation for my sins, for the needs of the Holy Church, and for the holy souls of purgatory.

Glory Be
Blood of Jesus,
save us.

Eternal Father, we offer you the merits of the most Precious Blood shed by your beloved Son during his crucifixion for all priests who are ministers of this Blood and we ask you for the liberation of the holy souls of Purgatory, especially that soul to whom we are most indebted.

Glory Be

Eternal Father, I offer you the most Precious Blood of Jesus in reparation for my sins, for the needs of the Holy Church, and for the holy souls of Purgatory.

Glory Be
Blood of Jesus,
save us.

Eternal Father, we offer you the merits of the most Precious Blood shed by your beloved Son when a cruel lance opened his side and we ask that you may come to the salvation of all those for whom it was shed and liberate the holy souls of Purgatory, especially that soul which was most devoted to the Virgin Mary.

Glory Be

Immaculate Virgin, I beseech you to offer to the Eternal Father the Holy Passion and the most Precious Blood of our Lord Jesus Christ in order that in some part of the earth this day *(or this night)* at least one mortal sin may be avoided.

Glory Be
Blood of Jesus,
save us.

NOVENA OF THE BLOOD
SHED BY JESUS

This novena was composed by the Venerable Father Bartholomew of Saluzzo, Italy (1588-1617),and is to be prayed for nine consecutive days.
If you add the following prayer when invoking God's help: "O Father, O Son, O Holy Spirit, O Most Holy Trinity, O Jesus, O Mary, O Saints of Paradise, I ask this grace through the Blood of Christ", you may be sure that if you have faith and persevere in prayer, you will receive the grace for which you humbly ask, if it be in accordance with God's holy will.

In the name of the Father, and of the Son, and of the Holy Spirit. Amen.

O God, come to my aid.
O Lord, make haste to help me.
Glory Be
The Creed *(see page 26)*

O Mary, you are all beautiful and original sin is not found in you. You are all pure, O Virgin Mary, Queen of heaven and earth, Mother of God. I greet you, I venerate you and bless you for ever and ever.

O Mary, I turn to you and invoke you. Help me, sweetest Mother of God; help me Queen of heaven; help me, most merciful Mother and Refuge of sinners; help me, Mother of my sweet Jesus. And as there is nothing that we ask of you in virtue of the Passion of Jesus Christ which you, with living faith I beg you to grant me the grace I carry in my heart; I ask for it through the Divine Blood of Jesus, shed for our salvation.

O Mother of mercy, I am hoping to obtain this grace; I ask for it through the infinite merits of the most precious Blood of your Beloved Son. O sweetest Mother, by the merits of the most Precious Blood of your Divine Son, grant that I may...

Here we ask for the grace we wish to obtain; then we continue to pray as follows:

I ask you for this grace, most Holy Mother, for the sake of that pure, innocent and blessed Blood which Jesus shed in the circumcision at the tender age of only eight days.

Hail Mary

O Virgin Mary, through the merits of the Precious Blood of your Divine Son, intercede for me before the heavenly Father.

I ask it of you, most Holy Mother, for the sake of that pure, innocent and blessed Blood which Jesus shed profusely in the agony of the Garden.

Hail Mary

O Virgin Mary, through the merits of the Precious Blood of your Divine Son, intercede for me before the heavenly Father.

I beg you for it, O most Holy Mary, for the sake of that pure, innocent and blessed Blood which Jesus shed copiously when, having been stripped and tied to the columnn, he was cruelly scourged.

Hail Mary

O Virgin Mary, through the merits of the Precious Blood of your Divine Son, intercede for me before the heavenly Father.

I ask it of you, O most Holy Mother, for the sake of that pure, innocent and blessed Blood, which Jesus shed from his head when he was crowned with thorns.

Hail Mary

O Virgin Mary, through the merits of the Precious Blood of your Divine Son, intercede for me before the heavenly Father.

I ask it of you, O most Holy Mary, for the sake of that pure, innocent and blessed Blood, which Jesus shed while carrying the Cross on the way to

Calvary, and above all for that Living Blood mixed with tears which you shed when accompanying him to the extreme sacrifice.

Hail Mary

O Virgin Mary, through the merits of the Precious Blood of your Divine Son, intercede for me before the heavenly Father.

I beg of you to hear my prayer, most Holy Mary, for the sake of that pure, innocent and blessed Blood, which Jesus shed from his body when he was stripped of his clothes and the Blood shed from his hands when he was crucified with the hardest and most piercing nails. I ask you for this favour in particular for the sake of the Blood which he shed during his bitter agony and torments on the Cross.

Hail Mary

O Virgin Mary, through the merits of the Precious Blood of your Divine Son, intercede for me before the heavenly Father.

Grant my prayer, most pure Virgin and Mother Mary, for the sake of that most sweet and mystical Blood and Water, which flowed from the side of Jesus, when his Heart was pierced by a lance.

Through the merits of that Blood so pure, grant me the grace which I ask of you. For the sake of that most Precious Blood which I adore and which becomes my drink at the table of the Lord, graciously hear me, O merciful and sweet Virgin Mary. **Amen.**

Hail Mary

O Virgin Mary, through the merits of the Precious Blood of your Divine Son, intercede for me before the heavenly Father.

Now we address our invocation to all the angels and saints in heaven, so that they may unite their intercession to that of the Virgin Mary in order to implore the grace which we desire to obtain:

O holy angels of Paradise, who contemplate the glory of God, unite your prayer to that of our dear Mother and Queen, Mary Most Holy, and grant that I may obtain this grace from the heavenly Father through the merits of the Precious Blood of our Divine Redeemer.

I invoke you too, holy souls of Purgatory, so that you may pray for me and ask the heavenly Father for the grace I implore through that most Precious Blood which our Saviour shed from his most sacred wounds.

It is also for you that I offer the most Precious Blood of Jesus, to the Eternal Father so that you may enjoy its merits to the full and exalt it for ever in the glory of heaven, singing: "You have redeemed us, O Lord, with your Blood and have made of us a kingdom for our God".

Amen.

To conclude our prayer, we recite the following simple but effective invocation:

O dear and amiable Jesus, sweet and merciful, have compassion on me and on all souls, both living and deceased, which you have redeemed by your precious Blood.

Amen.

Blessed be the Blood of Jesus.
now and for ever.

6.
JESUS CRUCIFIED

- **Prayers**
  - **Chaplets**
- **Rosary**
- **The Stations of the Cross**
  - **A Holy Hour**
    - **Devotions**

The way of the Cross is the only way to heaven.

When he allows us to suffer for him,
let us thank him and consider ourselves blessed
for such an honour.

Suffering borne with love
is the mystery of life.
For this reason the Cross of Jesus
has become the means of universal salvation.

My Jesus, today, as my soul is in great pain,
the only way to be happy
in this place of exile
is to love the cross,
because it is the cross which renders us similar to
you.

In this great sadness
I do not always feel the sweetness of your love,
my Jesus:
and as you can see,
I can only ask that your Divine Will may be
accomplished in me,
even if I do not understand it,
even if I cannot see it.

 # PRAYERS

PRAYER TO JESUS CRUCIFIED

Behold, O kind and most sweet Jesus,
I cast myself on my knees in your sight,
and with the most fervent desire of my soul,
I pray and beseech you
to impress upon my heart
lively sentiments of faith, hope and charity,
with a true repentance for my sins
and a firm desire of amendment,
while with deep affection and grief of soul
I ponder within myself and mentally contemplate
your five most precious wounds
having before my eyes that which David
spoke in prophecy of you,
O good Jesus:
"They have pierced my hands and my feet, they have numbered all my bones". **Amen.**

**Our Father
Hail Mary
Glory Be**

*To receive a plenary indulgence,
we add the following words:*

My Jesus, have mercy on me!
Through the merits of your Holy Wounds.

Pope Pius IX granted a plenary indulgence on Good Friday and on every Friday during Easter time to all those who recited this prayer after receiving Holy Communion before an image of Jesus Crucified; he granted a partial indulgence for the recitation of the prayer on all other days of the year.

I ADORE YOU, O HOLY CROSS

Pope Adrian VI, Pope Gregory XIII and Pope Paul VI all confirmed that if this prayer was recited thirty-three times on Good Friday, it freed 33 souls from Purgatory; if recited fifty times every Friday, it frees five souls.

I worship you, O Holy Cross, which was adorned with the most Holy Body of my Lord, covered and stained by his most precious Blood. I worship you, my God, crucified for me. I worship you, O Holy Cross, for love of the one who was my Lord. **Amen.**

DAILY PRAYER IN HONOUR OF THE HOLY WOUNDS

To be recited at each invocation:
Our Father
Hail Mary
Glory Be

For the Holy Wound of his right hand.

For the Holy Wound of his left hand.

For the Holy Wound of his right foot.

For the Holy Wound of his left foot.

For the Holy Wound of his Sacred Side.

For our Holy Father the Pope.

For the outpouring of the Holy Spirit.

ADORATION OF JESUS CRUCIFIED

*In the name of the Father, and of the Son,
and of the Holy Spirit. Amen.*

O God, come to my aid.
O Lord, make haste to help me.

Glory be
The Creed *(see page 26)*

IN HONOUR OF THE WOUND OF HIS RIGHT HAND

My most beloved Lord Jesus Crucified, prostrate before you and in union with Mary most Holy, and all the angels and saints in heaven, I adore profoundly the most Holy Wound of your right hand. I thank you for the infinite love with which you wanted to bear so many and such cruel pains in order to atone for my sins which I detest with all my heart. I ask you the grace of granting the Church victory over its enemies and of letting all its children walk along the holy path of your commandments.

Our Father
Hail Mary
Glory Be

IN HONOUR OF THE WOUND OF HIS LEFT HAND

My most beloved Lord Jesus Crucified, prostrate before you and in union with Mary, most Holy, and all the angels and saints in heaven, I adore profoundly the most Holy Wound of your left hand. I implore your grace for poor sinners and for the dying, especially for those who do not wish be reconciled with you.

Our Father
Hail Mary
Glory Be

IN HONOUR OF THE WOUND OF HIS RIGHT FOOT

My most beloved Lord Jesus Crucified, prostrate before you and in union with Mary most Holy, and all the angels and saints in heaven, I adore profoundly the most Holy Wound of your right foot. I ask you, to make many saints blossom among the clergy and among those consecrated to you.

Our Father
Hail Mary
Glory Be

In honour of the wound of his left foot

My most beloved Lord Jesus Crucified, prostrate before you and in union with Mary most Holy, and all the angels and saints in heaven, I adore profoundly the most Holy Wound of your left foot. I beg you to free all the holy souls from Purgatory, especially those who were most devoted to your Holy Wounds throughout their lives.

Our Father
Hail Mary
Glory Be

In honour of the wound of his sacred side

My most beloved Lord Jesus Crucified, prostrate before you and in union with Mary most Holy, and all the angels and saints in heaven I adore profoundly the most Holy Wound of your Sacred Side. I beg you to bless and to hear the prayer of all those who have asked me to pray for them.

Our Father
Hail Mary
Glory Be

We then repeat 3 times:
O Virgin most sorrowful,
pray for us.

O Jesus Crucified, hear these prayers of mine through the merits of your passion. May I live in holiness, and devote myself entirely to the establishment of your Kingdom and grant that I may receive your Sacraments at the moment of death, and thus remain with you forever in the glory of heaven. **Amen.**

Prayer to the Holy Wounds of Jesus for the Church

O Jesus, together with the Immaculate Heart of Mary, I greet and worship the Holy Wound of your right hand, and place in this wound all the priests of your Holy Church. Enkindle in them the fire of your Divine Love every time they celebrate the holy sacrifice of the Mass , so that they may communicate the same love to the souls who are commended to their care. **Amen.**

Glory Be

I greet and worship the Holy Wound of your left hand, and place in it all those who are living in error or who do not believe in you, and also those poor souls who do not know you. For love of these souls, Jesus, send many labourers to work in your vineyard, so that they may find the way to your most Sacred Heart. **Amen.**

Glory Be

I greet and worship the most Holy Wounds of your sacred feet, and I place in them the hardened sinners who prefer to live for the pleasures of this world; I commend to you in a special way those who are going to die today. Do not allow, Jesus, that your most Precious Blood be shed in vain for them. **Amen.**

Glory Be

I greet and worship the Holy Wounds of your Sacred Head, and I place in them the enemies of the Holy Church, all those who continue to scourge you in our times unto the shedding of your blood and who persecute you in your mystical Body. I beg you, Jesus, to convert them: call them as you called Saul to become Saint Paul, so that there may soon be only one fold and one Shepherd. **Amen.**

Glory Be

I greet and worship the Holy Wound of your most Sacred Heart and to this same wound, O Jesus, I entrust my own soul and all those for whom you would like me to pray, especially those who suffer and are afflicted and those who are persecuted and abandoned. O most Sacred Heart of Jesus, give them your light and your grace. Fill every-one with your love and your true peace. **Amen.**

Glory Be

Heavenly Father, I offer you myself, by means of the Immaculate Heart of Mary, together with your most beloved Son: with him, in him, through him, and also all his intentions in the name of all creatures. **Amen.**

IF YOU ARE UNHAPPY, DO NOT BLAME ME!

I am the Light,
and you do not see me.

I am the Way,
and you do not follow me.

I am the Truth,
and you do not believe me.

I am the Life,
and you do not search for me.

I am the Master,
and you do not listen to me.

I am the Leader,
and you do not obey me.

I am your God,
and you do not pray to me.

I am your great friend,
and you do not love me.

O Jesus, you are right, we neither think of you nor love you enough, and so we are unhappy. But your open arms invite us to take refuge in your heart and assure us of your forgiveness. In your heart, source of light, we shall find once more the strength to follow you - the Way, the Truth and the Life; the grace to hear you, Leader and Master; the joy of loving you, God of Love and Friend of all those who trust in you.

PRAYER TO HELP US TO SUFFER

Lord, I do not ask you that I may not suffer, but that you may help me in my suffering.

I do not ask you not to be afraid, but to make suffering one of my friends.

I do not ask you to protect me, but to give me the courage to face both this life and death itself.

I do not implore your pity, but ask you to give me patience and hope in your Light.

I do not implore you to give me wisdom, but ask you to give me faith in you.

I do not ask you to grant me strength for the fu-ture, but desire with all my heart to be united to you, in order to affront, together with you, the present and the future.

I do not want you ever to be far from me, rather I beg of you: remain within me for ever. **Amen.**

The Creed *(see page 26)*
Our Father • Hail Mary • Glory Be

STEPS OF THE PASSION

O sweet Jesus, who were filled with anguish while praying to the Father in the Garden of Gethsemane and sweated blood in your agony, have mercy on us.

Lord, have mercy.

O sweet Jesus, who by the kiss of the traitor were handed over to the wicked, arrested and bound like a thief, and abandoned by the disciples, have mercy on us.

Lord, have mercy.

O sweet Jesus, who were pronounced worthy of death by the unjust council of chief priests and elders, were led like a criminal before Pilate and were mocked and treated with contempt by Herod, have mercy on us.

Lord, have mercy.

O sweet Jesus, who were stripped of your clothes and scourged most cruelly at the pillar, have mercy on us.

Lord, have mercy.

O sweet Jesus, who were crowned with thorns, beaten, struck with a reed, blindfolded, dressed in a purple cloak in order that you be mocked, treated with scorn and became an object of derision in many ways, have mercy on us.

Lord, have mercy.

O sweet Jesus, whose release was deferred for that of Barabbas, who were condemned by the

Jews and sentenced unjustly to death on a cross, have mercy on us.

Lord, have mercy.

O sweet Jesus, who, weighed down by the wood of the cross, were led to the place of your execution like a lamb to its slaughter, have mercy on us.

Lord, have mercy.

O sweet Jesus, who were counted among the thieves, cursed and derided, given bitter wine mixed with gall to drink, and were racked with excruciating pains on the cross from the sixth to the ninth hour, have mercy on us.

Lord, have mercy.

O sweet Jesus, who died on the scaffold of the cross and were pierced by a lance in the presence of your Holy Mother, and who let blood and water gush forth from your wound, have mercy on us.

Lord, have mercy.

O sweet Jesus, who, having been taken down from the Cross, were bathed in tears by your most sorrowful Mother, have mercy on us.

Lord, have mercy.

O sweet Jesus, who, covered in sores and marked by wounds, were anointed with perfumed ointments and laid in the tomb, have mercy on us.

Lord, have mercy.

PRAYER IN TIME OF TEMPTATION

St. Albert the Great

Christ continues to warn his disciples against the seduction of evil and the evil one, as he did in the last night of his earthly existence: "Pray not to be put to the test!" (ref. Lk 22:40-46).

Lord Jesus Christ, who have led me into the desert of penance, protect me, so that I do not succumb to the Tempter. May pride neither obliterate my dignity of being a child of God, nor keep me away from the rigours of penance.

With your word of truth, change the rigours of penance, which the Tempter calls stones, so that they may become bread, and turn into stones the pleasures which the Tempter calls bread.

May the Tempter not set me on the pinnacle of the Temple to make me believe I am superior to others. May he not throw me down to the ground with false humility, testing the Lord with imprudent acts of penance which exhaust my physical strength and expose me to danger.

May the Tempter not take me to the mountain of ambition where, incited by greed, I would pay him homage bending the knees of the heart, the will, the mind.

Drive far away from me all things that are in opposition to you so that I may adore and serve you alone, my Lord. May the Tempter let go so that your angels may surround me to guard me from evil and sustain me in doing good.

PRAYER FOR THE SICK

When the following prayer is said, Jesus wishes that the sick person and also those who intercede for him or her be commended to God.

O my God, this sick person comes before you to ask you what he (she) desires and considers to be the most important thing for him.

God, allow these words to enter into his (her) heart: "It is important to be healthy in soul!"

Lord, may your holy will be done in him (her), in everything!

If you want him (her) to be healed, may health be given to him (her).

But if this is not your will, may he (she) continue to carry his (her) cross.

I pray also for us who intercede for him (her); purify our hearts to make us worthy of manifesting in ourselves, your holy mercy.

Protect him (her) and relieve his (her) pains, let your holy will be done in him (her).

May your holy Name be revealed through him (her), help him (her) to carry his (her) cross with courage.

Glory Be

PRAYER IN ILLNESS

O Jesus, you said, *"Come to me, all of you who are weary and overburdened, and I will give you rest"*; I come to you, broken-hearted by suffering, because I feel the need of your comfort.

O Lord, be close to me, at all times, especially when pain torments my body and soul.

When desperation threatens to take possession of me; when I consider myself to be a useless and bothersome burden to others; when everything becomes dark all around me; when I am at the limits of my strength, do not abandon me, O Lord, but come to my aid with your grace!

You who have suffered so much, and were prophesied to become "a man of sorrows", let me take your merciful hand and offer my sacrifice together with your immolation which is repeated continuously on the altar.

Bless those who assist me in my illness, and give acceptance and courage to all those who suffer in this world.

Our Lady of Sorrows, who participated with heroic strength in the passion of our Saviour and your Child, stay by my side as a mother; do not permit that my faith and hope fail in the hour of trial.

I turn also to you, St. Anthony, my heavenly friend and protector: accompany me on the difficult road to Calvary; fill me with sentiments of

filial abandonment to the will of God so that I may never lose my inner serenity. I have always trusted in you: do not let the offering of my pain be given in vain.
Amen.

MY GOD, DO NOT FORGET ME

My God, do not forget me when I forget you.

Do not abandon me, O Lord, when I abandon you. Do not go far from me when I go far from you. Call me if I flee from you, draw me to yourself if I resist, pick me up if I fall.

Give me, O Lord my God, a vigilant heart, so that no vain thought may take me away from you, a just heart, so that no perverted intention may lead me astray, a strong and courageous heart that resists every adversity, a free heart which no disordered passion can dominate.

Grant me, I beg you, the will to seek you, the wisdom to find you, a life that pleases you, a perseverance that awaits you trustfully, and grant me to trust that at the end of my life I shall be united to you.

REQUEST FOR HELP IN ILLNESS

To you, Lord, who passed through this world, "healing all evil and infirmity", I, a poor tree struck by pain, raise my cry and weeping. Son of David, have mercy on me.

My God, every morning I wake up feeling tired. I feel the bites of pain. And most of all, Lord, I am full of fears. What will become of me? Will my health ever improve? Will I be able to sing one day the "alleluia" of someone who has been healed? Will you visit me sometimes, my God? Did you not say on one occasion: "Get up and walk!"? Did you not say to Lazarus, "Come out!" when he lay buried in the tomb? Were not the lepers healed and did not the lame walk at the command of your voice? Did you not command them to throw away their crutches; did you not invite your apostle Peter to walk on the water?

When shall my hour come? When shall I be able to recount your wonders? Son of David, have pity on me; You are my only hope.

However, I know there is something worse than illness; anguish. Health is good, but peace is better. What good is health without peace? What I miss above all is peace, Lord Jesus Christ. Anguish assails me at times, and sometimes it dominates me completely. I often feel oppressed by sadness, and sometimes the sadness of death. I need peace, Lord Jesus, the peace that only you can give me.

Give me the peace that comes from your consolation, the peace which is the result of a trustful abandonment. Give me health and long life... but not my will be done, Lord, but yours. I know that you will comfort me this night. Fill me with your serenity; that is all I ask.

Amen.

I LOVE YOU, MY LORD

I love you, my God; my only wish is to love you until my last breath.

I love you, O Lord, who are infinitely lovable, and I would prefer to die loving you than to live one instant without loving you.

I love you, Lord, and the only grace I ask of you is to love you in eternity.

I love you, my God, and I desire heaven, only for the joy of loving you perfectly.

My God, if my tongue cannot say at every instant: "I love you", I want my heart to repeat it to you every time take a breath.

I love you, my Divine Saviour, because you were crucified for me, and you keep me here on earth to be crucified with you.

My God, grant that I may die loving you, and knowing that I love you.

LOVE ME AS YOU ARE

"I know your misery, the battles and the tribulations of your soul, the deficiencies and the infirmities of your body; I know your misery and your sins, and I say to you in spite of them, 'Give me your heart, love me as you are...'

"If you wait to be an angel before abandoning yourself to love, you will never love. Even though you have failings in the practice of duty and virtue, if you fall again into those ways in which you would like to sin no more, I forbid you not to love me. Love me as you are.

"In every instant and in whatever situation you may find yourself, in times of fervour or aridity, in times of faithfulness or unfaithfulness, love me... as you are... I want the love of your poor heart; if you wait to be perfect, you will never love me.

"Would I not be able to turn every grain of sand into a seraphim, radiant with purity, nobility and love? Am I not the Almighty? And if I prefer to leave those marvellous creatures in darkness and prefer the poor love of your heart, am I not free to do with my love as I want?

"My child, let me love you; I want your heart.

I certainly want to change you in time, but for now, I love you as you are... and I want you to do the same; I want to see your love arising from the dregs of your misery.

"I also love your weakness; I love the love of the poor and of the miserable; I want a great cry to rise continuously from poor people: "Jesus, I love you". I want only the song of your heart, I need neither your knowledge nor your talent. Only one thing is important to me, and that is to see you work with love.

"I do not desire your virtues; if I granted you some virtue, you are so weak that your self-conceit would ibecome greater; do not let this worry you. I could have destined you to great things; but instead, you shall be the useless servant; I will take you, even the little you have...
because I created you only for love...Today I am at the door of your heart as a beggar, I the King of Kings! I knock and wait; make haste and open up to me.

"Do not let your misery grow greater; if you truly understood the degree of your poverty, you would die of sorrow. What would injure my heart would be to see you mistrust me and not confide in me.

"I want you to think of me every hour of the day

and of the night; I want you to do even the most insignificant actions for the sake of love alone. I count on you to give me joy...

"Do not be afraid if you have no virtues; I will give you mine. When you have to suffer, I will give you strength. You have given me love; I will give you the knowledge to love above and beyond all that you could ever dream of ...

"But remember, love me as you are...
I gave you my Mother: let everything pass through her pure Heart.

"Whatever happens, do not wait to be holy before abandoning yourself to love, for you would never love me... Go in peace."

Mons. Lebrun

THE PRAYERS OF
ST. BRIDGET OF SWEDEN

The promises of Jesus to St. Bridget

As St. Bridget, for a long time, had wished to know the number of blows Jesus had received during His Passion, one day He appeared to her, saying: "On my body I received 5480 blows. If you desire in some way to honour them, you should say fifteen Our Fathers and fifteen Hail Marys together with the following prayers (which He taught her) for a whole year; at the end of the year you will have honoured each of the wounds". He added that to whoever would recite these prayers for a year:

• *I will free 15 souls of his relatives from Purgatory.*

• *15 righteous relatives of his would be confirmed and maintained in Grace.*

• *15 sinners of his milieu would be converted.*

• *The person who recites them will thus reach the first grade of perfection and fifteen days before his death, he will receive the precious body of Jesus which will appease him of eternal hunger, and His precious Blood which will quench his thirst for ever.*

• *15 days before his death he will have full knowledge of all his sins and will experience a bitter repentance.*

• *I will place the sign of my victorious Cross in front of him, in order to succour and defend him against the attacks of his enemies.*

• *Before his death, I will appear together with my most beloved and dear Mother.*

- *I will kindheartedly receive his soul and I will lead it to eternal joys.*

- *By leading it there, I will give it a singular gift: to drink from the source of my Divinity, which I will not give to those who have not said these Prayers.*

- *It is necessary to know that whoever had lived in mortal sin for 30 years and who will either devoutly say these Prayers or intended to say them, the Lord will forgive all his sins.*

- *I will defend him from temptations.*

- *I will protect his 5 senses.*

- *I will preserve him from sudden death.*

- *I will save his soul from eternel punishment.*

- *If he had always lived according to his will and should have had to die tomorrow, his life will be lengthened.*

- *He will receive all that he asks from God and from the Blessed Virgin Mary.*

- *Every time he says these prayers he will gain 100 days of indulgence*

- *He will be sure of being added to the choir of angels.*

- *Whoever teaches them to someone else will have everlasting joy and merit.*

- *Wherever these prayers are said God is present with His grace.*

PRAYER I

O Lord Jesus Christ, eternal sweetness to those who love you, joy surpassing all happiness and all desires, salvation and love to those who repent, to whom you said: *"My delight is to be with the children of man"*, having been made man for their salvation; remember the Love that urged you to take our human nature and all that you had to endure from the begining of your incarnation right up to your redeeming passion planned by God from eternity.

Remember the anguish you experienced in your soul when you said: *"My soul is sorrowful to the point of death"*, when at the Last Supper which you shared with your disciples, giving them for food your Body and your Blood, washing their feet and lovingly consoling them, you foretold your coming passion.

Remember the fear, the anguish and pain that you suffered in your most Holy Body before your crucifixion; when after having prayed to the Father 3 times and sweating blood, you were betrayed by one of your disciples, accused by false witnesses and unjustly condemned to death by three Judges; at the most solemn time of Easter you were betrayed, mocked, stripped of your clothes, blindfolded and smitten with blows, bound to the Pillar and crowned with thorns.

In memory of all these pains, give me O sweet

Jesus, I beseech you, before I die, true contrition, a sincere confession and the remission of all my sins. **Amen.**

Hail, O most sweet Jesus, have mercy on me a sinner.
O Jesus, Son of God, born of the Virgin Mary, have mercy on us.

Our Father
Hail Mary
Glory be to the Father

Prayer II

O Jesus, true joy of angels and Paradise of delights, remember the horrible torments that you endured when your enemies surrounded you like fierce lions, and tortured you by slapping you, spitting upon you, scraping you and inflicting upon you other unheard of suffering. In virtue of the offending words, the harsh blows, and the severe torments inflicted on you by your enemies, I beseech you to free me from all my enemies both visible and invisible, and grant me to find again under the shadow of your wings the path to eternal salvation.
Amen.

Hail, O most...

Prayer III

O incarnate Word, Omnipotent creator of the world, you who are infinite and incomprehensible, remember the most bitter pain that you endured when your hands and your feet were pierced with sharp nails and nailed to the wood of the cross. How much suffering you endured O Jesus, when your cruel crucifiers wrentched and distended you the length and the breadth of your Cross, so that the joints of your limbs were loosened. I beseech you, by the memory of such great suffering you endured on the cross, grant me to love you more and more. **Amen.**

Hail, O most... *(see above)*

Prayer IV

Jesus, heavenly Healer, remember the suffering and pain you endured in your lacerated body, when the cross was being erected. From the soles of your feet to the top of your head, no part of your body was free from pain; however, you forgot so much suffering and prayed to the Father for your enemies, saying: *"Father forgive them for they know not what they do"*. In virtue of your infinite love and mercy and in memory of your suffering, may I remember your dearest Passion so that it may grant me the full remission of all my sins. **Amen.**

Hail, O most... *(see above)*

Prayer V

O Jesus, mirror of eternal brightness, remember the grief you endured when, despite the salvation you offered to souls through your Passion, you foresaw that still many souls would not accept it.

I therefore ask that, through the infinite mercy you showed, not only in suffering for the lost and destitute souls, but also for the benefit of the thief, when you said to him: *"This day you will be with me in Paradise,"* you may show mercy on me at the hour of my death. **Amen.**

Hail, O most... *(see page 366)*

Prayer VI

O Jesus, beloved King, remember the sorrow you experienced when you hung naked and despised on the cross, without having, among so many friends who were around you, anyone to console you except your beloved Mother whom you entrusted to your favourite disciple, saying: *"Woman, this is your son".* Then to the disciple you said, *"This is your mother".*

With great trust, I beseech you, most merciful Jesus, that, by the sword which pierced her soul, you may have compassion on me in all my corporal and spiritual afflictions and tribulations, and that you may grant me comfort and joy in every trial and adversity. **Amen.**

Hail, O most... *(see page 366)*

Prayer VII

O Lord Jesus Christ, inexhaustible source of compassion, who lovingly said on the Cross: "I am thirsty", meaning "I deeply desire the salvation of the world," inspire us, with the desire to live a saintly life, by queuching completely our thirst of all concupiscences and the seeking of worldly pleasures. **Amen.**

Hail, O most... *(see page 366)*

Prayer VIII

O Lord Jesus Christ, sweetness of hearts and delight of the spirit, by the bitterness of vinegar and gall which you tasted in the hour of your death, grant us, at all times, and especially at the hour of our death, that we may worthily receive your Body and Blood, as remedy and consolation of our souls. **Amen.**

Hail, O most... *(see page 366)*

Prayer IX

O Lord Jesus Christ, joy of our spirit, remember the anguish and sorrow you endured when, for the biterness of your death and
the insults of the Jews, you cried out to your Father: "Eli, Eli, lama sabachthani", that is: "My God, my God, why have you forsaken me?" By this anguish, I beseech you my Lord and my God, not to abandon me in the hour of my death.
Amen.

Hail, O most... *(see page 366)*

Prayer X

O Lord Jesus Christ, Alpha and Omega, of our love, who from the soles of your feet to the crown of your head, were plunged into a sea of suffering, and I beeseech you by your long and profoundly deep wounds to teach me to keep through pure love, your law and teachings.
Amen.

Hail, O most... *(see page 366)*

Prayer XI

O Lord Jesus Christ, most profound abyss of mercy and compassion I beseech Thee, on account of the depths of your wounds which penetrated to the very marrow of your bones and your being, raise me from the depth of my sins and hide me in the hollow of your wounds.
Amen.

Hail, O most... *(see page 366)*

Prayer XII

O Jesus Christ, mirror of truth, symbol of unity, remember the innumerable wounds which covered your Body, from head to foot, crimsoned with your most precious Blood.
O Lord, I beg you inscribe with that same blood your wounds in my heart, so that by meditating on your suffering and your love, your pain and your suffering may be renewed in me every day, that love may increase, and that I may persevere in thanking you till the end of my days, when I will come to you filled with all the goodness and merits which you gave me from the treasure of your Passion. **Amen.**

Hail, O most... *(see page 366)*

Prayer XIII

O Lord Jesus Christ, invincible and immortal King, remember the pain you endured when, all the strength of your Body and Heart having failed, you bowed your head and exclaimed *"It is fulfilled"*.

I, therefore beg you, have mercy on me at the hour of my death, when my soul will be in anguish and my spirit troubled. **Amen.**

Hail, O most... *(see page 366)*

Prayer XIV

O Jesus Christ, Only-begotten Son of the Father most high, splendour and figure of His substance, remember the humble prayer by which you commended your spirit, saying: *"Father, into your hands I commend my spirit"*, and after having bowed your head and having freed from your heart your mercy for us, you passed away.

By this most precious blood, I beseech you, King of Saints, strengthen me in order to resist the temptations of the devil, of the world and of the flesh, so that being dead to the world, I may live in you alone and in the hour of my death, you may receive my spirit, which after a long exile and pilgrimage is longing to return to its homeland. **Amen.**

Hail, O most... *(see page 366)*

Prayer XV

O Lord Jesus Christ, true and fruitful vine, remember the abundant outpouring of your Blood, when, after having bowed your head on the Cross, the soldier pierced your side with a lance and the last drops of blood and water issued forth.

In virtue of your most bitter Passion, pierce, I beg you, most sweet Jesus my heart, so that I may shed tears of love and contrition. May I be totally converted to you so that my heart may become your eternal home. May my conversion delight you and be accepted by you, and the end of my life be so commendable that I may be worthy to contemplate you with all the saints in eternity. **Amen.**

Hail, O most... *(see page 366)*

Let us pray:
O Lord Jesus Christ, Son of the living God, accept this prayer with the same love with which you sustained all the wounds of your Most Holy Body; grant your mercy, your grace, the forgiveness of all our sins and punishments, and eternal life,to us and to all the faithful whether living or dead. **Amen.**

THE PRAYERS OF SAINT BRIDGET
To be recited for 12 years

The Lord Jesus revealed to Saint Bridget to have received more than sixthousand blows during His Passion and to have shed for us more than thirtythousand drops of his holy blood, and further promising her: *"May it also be known that I will grant the following graces to the person who will have honoured my most precious Blood for 12 years with seven Our Father and seven Hail Mary:*

• *He will not be sent to Purgatory.*

• *He will be numbered amongst the martyrs as if he had shed his blood for the faith.*

• *I will keep the souls of three of his relatives of his choice, in a state of sanctifying Grace.*

• *The souls of his relatives up to the fourth kinship will avoid being sent to hell.*

• *He will come to know of his death a month beforehand.*
If he should die before the end of the twelve years of prayer I will consider his prayers valid, as if he had completed them".

HOW TO RECITE THE PRAYERS
The following prayers have to be recited every day for twelve consecutive years. As for the Fifteen Prayers, they have to be recited every day; but if, for a very serious reason, on one particular day, one should not manage to recite them, the following day they must be recited twice. It is, however, necessary not to underestimate the importance of being faithful to the daily recital of the Prayers, since, if

prayer is truly the sole centre of the day, what reason could be sufficient to make us avoid saying them?

Further, it is not enough to read them without paying attention to them, as they have to be said devotedly and meditating on the words which are said.

BEGINNING OF THE PRAYERS

In the name of the Father, of the Son,
and of the Holy Spirit. Amen.

O God, come to our aid.
O Lord, make haste to help us.

Glory be
The Creed *(see page 26)*

INITIAL PRAYER

O Jesus, I wish to recite your prayer to the Father, seven times, uniting myself to the Love with which you sanctified it in your Heart and you uttered it with Your lips.

Bring it from my lips to your divine Heart, improve it and complete it in such a perfect way so as to offer to the Most Holy Trinity, the same honour and joy that You showed reciting it when on earth.

May the honour and joy flow on Your Sacred Humanity for the glorification of Your Holy Wounds and of Your Most Precious Blood, which gushed forth from them.

1. THE CIRCUMCISION

Eternal Father, through the immaculate hands of Mary and the divine Heart of Jesus, I offer you the first wounds, the first pains and the first drops of blood of Jesus, to pardon the sins of my youth and of those of all men as protection against the first mortal sins, especially those of my relatives.

Our Father
Hail Mary
Glory be

2. THE SWEATING OF BLOOD

Eternal Father, through the immaculate hands of Mary and the divine Heart of Jesus I offer you the terrible sufferings of the Heart of Jesus experienced on the Mount of Olives, and every drop of his blood, to pardon the the sins of my heart and those of all men, as protection against such sins and for the propagation of the love towards God and towards our neighbours.

Our Father
Hail Mary
Glory be

3. THE SCOURGING

Eternal Father, through the immaculate hands of Mary and the Divine Heart of Jesus, I offer you all the thousands of strokes, the suffering and the Most Precious Blood of Jesus, shed during the scourging in atonement of my sins of the flesh and those of all men, as protection against such sins and as a safeguard of innocence, in particular among my relatives.

Our Father
Hail Mary
Glory be

4. THE CROWNING WITH THORNS

Eternal Father, through the immaculate hands of Mary and through the Divine Heart of Jesus, I offer you the wounds and the Most Precious Blood which flowed from the Head of Jesus when he was crowned with thorns, in amends of my sins of the spirit and of those of all men, as protection against such sins and for the propagation of the Kingdom of God on earth.

Our Father
Hail Mary
Glory be

5. THE PATH TO CALVARY OF JESUS UNDER THE WEIGHT OF CROSS

Eternal Father through the immaculate hands of Mary and through the divine Heart of Jesus, I offer you the suffering endured by Jesus on the Way to Calvary, and in particular the Holy Wounds of his Shoulder and from which his Most Precious Blood poured forth, in amends of my sins of rebellion against the Cross and of those of all men, of the murmering against your holy plan and of all those sins of the tongue and, as protection against such sins and for a true love of your Holy Cross.

Our Father • Hail Mary • Glory be

6. THE CRUCIFIXION

Eternal Father, through the immaculate hands of Mary and the divine Heart of Jesus, I offer you your divine Son, nailed and mounted on the cross the cross, the wounds and the Most Precious Blood of his hands and of his feet poured out for us, his extreme poverty and his perfect obedience. I also offer you all the terrible torments of His mind and of His soul, His precious death and the peaceful renewal of it in all the Holy Masses celebrated on Earth, in amends for all the offences committed against the Holy evangelical vows and the rules of all religious Orders; in amends for all my sins and those of the whole world, for the sick and the dying, for priests and lay people, for the intentions of the Holy Father concerning the renewal of Christian families, for the unity of the faith, for our homeland, for the unity of all people in Christ and in His Church and for the Diaspora. (of the Jews)

Our Father • Hail Mary
Glory be

7. THE WOUND OF THE SACRED SIDE

Eternal Father, be so kind as to accept the precious Blood and water which gushed forth from the wounds of the Heart of Jesus for the needs of the Holy Church and for the forgiveness of the sins of all men. We beg you to be compassionate and merciful to all men!

Last precious drops of the Blood of the Sacred Heart of Jesus Christ, wash away all my sins and purify all my brothers of all sins!

Water from the side of Christ cleanse me from the punishments for all my sins and quench the flames of Purgatory for me and for all the poor souls of the dead. **Amen.**

Our Father • Hail Mary
Glory be
Prayer to the Guardian Angel

GIVE ME, LORD, A WING IN RESERVE

Mons. Tonino Bello

I want to thank you, Lord, for the gift of life.
I read somewhere that men are angels with only
one wing: they can fly only if in the arms of
someone.
Sometimes, in moments of trust, I dare to think,
Lord, that even you have only one wing.
The other you have kept hidden: perhaps to make
me understand that you do not want to fly
without me.
For this reason you gave me life so that I could be
your companion in flight.

Teach me, then, to fly with you.
Because living is not "dragging through life", it
is not "struggling through life", it is not "nibbling
at life".
To live is to let oneself go, as a sea-gull on the
breeze.
To live is to experience the adventure of life.
To live is to spread the wing, the only wing, with
the faith of the one who is aware of having a
flying partner as great as you are!

I ask your forgiveness for each sin against life.
Above all for the lives killed before their birth.
They are broken wings. They are flights you had
planned to make and have been impeded. Flights
annulled for ever. Dreams cut down at dawn.

But I ask you forgiveness, Lord, also for the

wings which I did not help to spread. For the flights I did not know how to encourage. For the indifference with which I left an unhappy brother alone to roam around the courtyard with a wing hanging off; one whom you had destined to fly to heaven. And you waited for him in vain, for the crossing which will never be done.

Help me to glide down now, Lord. In reality, abortion is, so to speak, a serious injury to your feelings. It is a crime against your genious. It is the sinking of the dawn into the depth of the ocean. It is the most cruel of all crimes. It is the most devastating form of destruction. But help me also to say that giving birth is not everything.

It is necessary to give life. Abortion is not the only form of antichristianism; so too is every failure to accept life: every refusal to give bread, housing, work, education, or to grant basic human rights.

War, every war, is unchristian. It is unchristian to leave our neighbour in the melancholy doorway of life where "people struggle to live", where people vegetate. it is unchristian to pass by our neighbour with indifference, the neighbour with only one wing, inextricably caught in the net of misery and solitude, when he has already convinced you that he is no longer worthy of flying with you.

Give me an extra wing, Lord, above all for that unfortunate neighbour.

CHAPLETS

CHAPLET OF THE HOLY WOUNDS OF OUR LORD JESUS CHRIST
Chaplet of Mercy

Origin of the devotion
The humble Sister Mary Martha Chambon of the Convent of the Visitation, at Chambery, France (who died a holy death on the 21st of March, 1907), claimed to have been taught two invocations as well as the following prayers and promises by our Lord Jesus Christ himself in a private revelation.

Promises of our Lord
- *"I will grant all that is asked of me through the invocation of my Holy Wounds. It is necessary to spread this devotion."*
- *"In truth this prayer is not of the earth but of heaven... and it may obtain everything."*
- *"My wounds sustain the world... ask that you may love them constantly, because they are the source of every grace. You must invoke them often, attract your neighbour to this devotion and impress it on their souls."*
- *"When you have pains to suffer, bring them immediately to my Wounds and they will be eased."*
- *"It is necessary to repeat this invocation often near the sick: 'My Jesus, forgiveness and mercy through the merits of your Holy Wounds.' This prayer will relieve both body and soul."*
- *"And the sinner who says, 'Eternal Father, I offer you the Wounds of our Lord Jesus Christ, to heal the sins of our souls' will obtain conversion."*
- *"My Wounds will heal yours."*

- *"There will no death for the soul which dies in my Wounds: they give true life."*
- *"For every word you say in the Chaplet of Mercy, I will let a drop of my Blood fall on the soul of a sinner."*
- *"The soul which has honoured my Holy Wounds and has offered them to the Eternal Father for the souls of purgatory shall be accompanied at the hour of death by the most Holy Virgin and by the angels, and I shall receive and crown it in shining glory."*
- *"The Holy Wounds are the treasure of all treasures for the souls of Purgatory."*
- *"Devotion to my Wounds is the remedy for this time of iniquity."*
- *"From my wounds come the fruits of Sanctity; by meditating on them you shall always be able to mature in love."*
- *"My daughter, if you immerse your actions in my Wounds, they will acquire value; even your smallest actions covered with my Blood will satisfy my Heart..."*

RECITATION OF THE CHAPLET

This chaplet is recited using an ordinary rosary beads and begins with the following prayers:

1. O Jesus, Divine Redeemer, have mercy on us and on the whole world. **Amen.**

2. Holy God, Holy Mighty One, Holy Immortal One, have mercy on us and on the whole world. **Amen.**

3. Grace and mercy, my God, in present dangers; cover us with your most Precious Blood. **Amen.**

4. O Eternal Father, have mercy on us for the sake of the Blood of your only Son Jesus Christ; have mercy on us, we implore you. **Amen, Amen, Amen.**

On the beads of the Hail Mary,
the following invocation is recited:
O my Jesus, forgiveness and mercy,
through the merits of your Holy Wounds.

On the beads of the Our Father we recite the following:
Eternal Father, I offer you the Wounds of our
Lord Jesus Christ, to heal those of our souls.

At the end we recite 3 times:
Eternal Father, I offer you the Wounds of our
Lord Jesus Christ, to heal those of our souls.

CHAPLET OF THE WOUND OF THE SHOULDER OF JESUS

While at prayer, St. Bernard, Abbot of Clairveaux asked Our Lord which was His greatest unrecorded suffering, and the Lord answered, "I had on My Shoulders, while I bore My Cross on the Way of Sorrow, a grievous Wound which was more painful than the others, and which is not recorded by men. Honour this wound with your devotion, and I will grant you whatever you ask through its virtue and merit, and in regard to all those who shall venerate this Wound I will remit to them all their venials sins, and will

*no longer remember their mortal sins, and they will not die
a sudden death, and before dying they will be visited by the
Blessed Virgin and will also obtain grace and mercy". Pope
Eugene III, at the request of St. Bernard, granted indulgences to those who propagated the following prayer and
always carried it with them, and also to those who recited
five Our Fathers, five Hail Marys and five Glory Bes,
received the Sacraments and prayed for the Holy Father.*

Most Holy Trinity, Father, Son and Holy Spirit, by means of the Immaculate Heart of Mary, I
offer you the most precious Wound of the shoulder of our Lord Jesus Christ. Jesus Christ, you
who revealed to Saint Bernard that whatever
grace is asked of you in virtue of the sacred
Wound of your shoulder, will be granted, I ask
you...

(Here we express our intentions)

5 Our Fathers
5 Hail Marys
5 Glory Bes

Most Holy Trinity, Father, Son and Holy Spirit,
Praise and glory be to the Holy Wound of the
shoulder of our Lord Jesus Christ *(10 times).*

5 Glory Bes
The Creed

THE LITANY OF HUMILITY

Cardinl Merry del Val, who composed this litany, often recited it after the celebration of the Eucharist.

O Jesus, meek and humble of heart,

Hear me.

From the desire of being esteemed,

Deliver me, Jesus.

From the desire of being loved,

Deliver me, Jesus.

From the desire of being extolled,

Deliver me, Jesus.

From the desire of being honoured,

Deliver me, Jesus.

From the desire of being praised,

Deliver me, Jesus.

From the desire of being preferred to others,

Deliver me, Jesus.

From the desire of being consulted,

Deliver me, Jesus.

From the desire of being approved,

Deliver me, Jesus.

From the fear of being humiliated,

Deliver me, Jesus.

From the fear of being despised,

Deliver me, Jesus.

From the fear of suffering rebukes,

Deliver me, Jesus.

From the fear of being calumniated,

Deliver me, Jesus.

From the fear of being forgotten,

Deliver me, Jesus.

From the fear of being ridiculed,

Deliver me, Jesus.

From the fear of being wronged,

Deliver me, Jesus.

From the fear of being suspected,

Deliver me, Jesus.

That others may be loved more than I,

Jesus, grant me the grace to desire it.

That others may be esteemed more than I,

Jesus, grant me the grace to desire it.

That in the opinion of the world others
may increase and I may decrease,

Jesus, grant me the grace to desire it.

That others may be chosen and I set aside,

Jesus, grant me the grace to desire it.

That others may be praised and I unnoticed,

Jesus, grant me the grace to desire it.

That others may be preferred to me in everything,

Jesus, grant me the grace to desire it.

That others become holier than I, provided that
   I may become as holy as I should,

  Jesus, grant me the grace to desire it.

An awareness and love of my nothingness,

     Grant me, O Jesus

The perpetual memory of my sinfulness,

     Grant me, O Jesus.

The conviction of my weakness,

     Grant me, O Jesus.

The abhorrence of every vanity,

     Grant me, O Jesus.

The pure intention of serving God,

     Grant me, O Jesus.

Perfect submission to the will of God,

     Grant me, O Jesus.

The true spirit of repentance,

     Grant me, O Jesus.

Obedience without reserve to my superiors,

     Grant me, O Jesus.

A holy hate of all envy and jealousy,

     Grant me, O Jesus.

A readiness to forgive the offences I receive,

     Grant me, O Jesus.

The prudence to say nothing about the affairs
   of others,

     Grant me, O Jesus.

Peace and love towards everyone,

Grant me, O Jesus.

An ardent longing for scorn and humiliation
and to be treated like you and the grace
to accept this in a holy manner,

Grant me, O Jesus.

O Mary, my Queen and Mother, teacher
of the humble,

Pray for me.

O all you righteous souls, sanctified
particularly for your spirit of humility,

Pray for me.

Let us pray.
O God, who resist the proud and give grace to the humble, grant us the virtue of true humility, which your only Son exemplified to the faithful by his very life; so that your indignation may never be provoked by our exalting ourselves with pride, but rather grant that by living in humble obedience to you, we may receive the gifts of your grace.
Amen.

THE LAST SEVEN WORDS
OF JESUS CHRIST

Devotion to the seven precious words of Jesus on the Cross is not well known, although recently, Pope John Paul II has strongly recommended that the faithful meditate upon these very words. Indeed many souls have obtained graces by practising this devotion. In the following section we draw on the words of Our Lord to Sr. Josepha Menéndez (1890-1923), a humble sister of the congregation of the Religious of the Sacred Heart in Spain who was asked by the Lord in a private revelation to be the Apostle of his Mercy Jesus encouraged Sr. Josepha to meditate upon his passion and communicated to her the feelings which he experienced therein, saying to her on one occasion,

"In my most holy wounds sinners will find forgiveness and life!... My Blood will wash away and remove the stain of their sins."

The following is a reflection upon the last words of Our Lord before he commended his Spirit to the Father:

"Father, forgive them for they do not know what they are doing!"

They have not truly known Him who is their life. And they heaped upon Him all the rage of their iniquities!... But I beg you, my Father!... pour out on them all the strength of your mercy.

**Our Father
Hail Mary
Glory Be**

"Today you will be with me in paradise."

Your faith in the mercy of your Saviour has cancelled your sins, and it will lead you to eternal life...

Our Father • Hail Mary • Glory Be

"Woman, this is your Son!

My Mother, these are my Brothers and Sisters! Protect them, love them. You are not alone, all of you, for whom I have given my life. Now you have a Mother in whom you can take refuge for all your necessities... I have united all of you to me with a very tight bond in giving you my own Mother!...

Our Father • Hail Mary • Glory Be

**"My God! My God!
Why have you abandoned me?"**

Yes, the soul has already the right to say to his God, "Why have you abandoned me?" In fact, when the mystery of Redemption was accomplished, men and women became children of God once more, brothers and sisters of Jesus Christ, heirs to eternal life...

Our Father • Hail Mary • Glory Be

"I am thirsty."

O my Father!... I am thirsty for your glory!... and now at last the time has come... from this day on, having seen that all my words have been fulfilled, the world will know that you have sent me and you will be glorified. I am thirsty for your glory! Thirsty for souls!... and in order to find relief for this thirst, I shed my blood to the last drop.

Our Father • Hail Mary • Glory Be

"Therefore I can say, 'It is fulfilled'."

The great Mystery of Love, in which God gave his own Son unto death, is brought to fulfillment, in order to restore life to humanity... I came into the world to obey your will. My Father! It is accomplished.

Our Father • Hail Mary • Glory Be

"Into your hands I commit my Spirit."

To you I offer my soul! Thus the souls who fulfil my will can truly say, "All has been consumed!" My Lord and my God! Receive my soul; I place it in your hands.

Our Father • Hail Mary • Glory Be

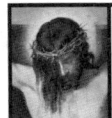
ROSARY OF THE SEVEN WORDS

The Rosary of the seven words is recited on the same beads as used for the Chaplet of the seven sorrows of Mary: these two devotions are closely linked, as the passion of Our Lord is inseparable from that of Our Lady of Sorrows.

In the name of the Father, and of the Son, and of the Holy Spirit. Amen.

O God, come to my aid.
O Lord, make haste to help me.
Glory Be

The Creed *(see page 26)*

FIRST MYSTERY

In the first mystery we meditate on how Jesus Christ, while looking from the Cross, at those who had crucified him took pity on them and thus prayed to his Eternal Father saying the first (of the last) words: **"Father, forgive them they do not know what they are doing!"**

Our Father • 7 Hail Marys • Glory Be

Through the power of your seven admirable words, **Save us, O Lord!**
Through the Seven Sorrows of the Immaculate Heart of Mary, **Have mercy on us!**

SECOND MYSTERY

In the second mystery we meditate on how Jesus Christ took pity on the good thief, promising him Paradise, and pronounced the following words: **"Today you will be with me in Paradise."**

Our Father • 7 Hail Marys • Glory Be

Through the power of your seven admirable words, **Save us, O Lord!**
Through the Seven Sorrows of the Immaculate Heart of Mary, **Have mercy on us!**

THIRD MYSTERY

In the third mystery we meditate on how Jesus, while looking from the Cross at his Holy Mother and at the disciple whom he loved, said: **"Woman, this is your Son!". "This is your Mother."**

Our Father • 7 Hail Marys • Glory Be

Through the power of your seven admirable words, **Save us, O Lord!**
Through the Seven Sorrows of the Immaculate Heart of Mary, **Have mercy on us!**

FOURTH MYSTERY

In the fourth mystery we meditate on how Jesus, in the depths of desolation, spoke to the Father and said: **"My God! My God! Why have you abandoned me?"**

Our Father • 7 Hail Marys • Glory Be

Through the power of your seven admirable words,   **Save us, O Lord!**
Through the Seven Sorrows of the Immaculate Heart of Mary,   **Have mercy on us!**

FIFTH MYSTERY

In the fifth mystery we meditate on how Jesus Christ, burning with fever and thirsty for the salvation of Souls, asked for a drink, and said: **"I am thirsty."**

Our Father • 7 Hail Marys • Glory Be

Through the power of your seven admirable words,   **Save us, O Lord!**
Through the Seven Sorrows of the Immaculate Heart of Mary,   **Have mercy on us!**

SIXTH MYSTERY

In the sixth mystery we meditate on how Jesus, seeing that the Scriptures had been accomplished, exclaimed: **"It is fulfilled."**

Our Father • 7 Hail Marys • Glory Be

Through the power of your seven admirable words, **Save us, O Lord!**
Through the Seven Sorrows of the Immaculate Heart of Mary, **Have mercy on us!**

SEVENTH MYSTERY

In the seventh mystery we meditate on how Jesus, commended his Soul to God, accepting death in obedience to his Father, and said: **"Father into your hands I commit my Spirit".**

Our Father • 7 Hail Marys • Glory Be

Through the power of your seven admirable words, **Save us, O Lord!**
Through the Seven Sorrows of the Immaculate Heart of Mary, **Have mercy on us!**

Hail Holy Queen

(This is said in memory of the Seven Swords of Sorrow which pierced the Immaculate Heart of Our Lady of Sorrows at the foot of the Cross).
The Rosary is concluded by reciting:

The Litany of the most Precious Blood

(see page 316)

PRAYER OF CONSECRATION

O most Holy Divine Crucified one, who, when lifted up from the earth, drew all people to yourself through the merits of your agony on the Cross, and through the power of your seven admirable words spoken from the same cross, we ask for the grace to practise your life's teachings, to remember your Holy Passion, and to live in gratitude for your Love. Trusting in the infinite value of your Divine Blood, we beg you to protect us and to defend us from the snares of Satan, to free us from sin and from all evil.

Therefore we place our trust in you, and we consecrate ourselves to the devotion of your seven words, and, through the intercession of the Immaculate and Sorrowful Heart of Mary, pierced with many swords of pain, we beg you for the grace of... (*We express the grace which we need in a special way*) in the hope that our desire may be fulfilled.

Amen.

THE STATIONS OF THE CROSS

STATIONS OF THE CROSS
(FIRST SCHEME)

*In the name of the Father, and of the Son,
and of the Holy Spirit. Amen.*

*Before meditating on the passion of Jesus, let us humbly
acknowledge that we are sinners before God and let us
purify ourselves of our sins.*

(We pause for a moment of silence).

FIRST STATION
JESUS IS CONDEMNED TO DEATH

V. We adore you, O Christ, and we bless you.
**R. Because, by your holy cross,
you have redeemed the world.**

"*Pilate then summoned the chief priests and
the leading men and the people and said to them,
'You brought this man before me as a popular
agitator. Now I have gone into the matter myself
in your presence and found no grounds in the
man for any of the charges you bring against
him. Nor has Herod either, since he has sent him*

back to us. As you can see, the man has done nothing that deserves death, so I shall have him flogged and then let him go. But as one man they howled, 'Away with him! Give us Barabbas!'

This man had been thrown into prison because of a riot in the city and murder. In his desire to set Jesus free, Pilate adressed them again, but they shouted back, 'Crucify him! Crucify him!' and for the third time he spoke to them, 'But what harm has this man done? I have found no case against him that deserves death, so I shall have him flogged and then let him go.' But they kept on shouting at the top of their voices, demanding that he should be crucified. And their shouts kept growing louder. Pilate then gave his verdict: their demand was to be granted. He released the man they asked for, who had been imprisoned because of rioting and murder, and handed Jesus over to them to deal with as they pleased". (Lk 23: 13-2)

Hear how the people pronounce the sentence of my death. Consider with what silence, with what patience and meekness my Heart receives it. O Souls, that seek to imitate my behaviour, learn to keep silent and to be serene before what humiliates you and is against your will.

Our Father • Hail Mary • Glory Be

*One or more of the following prayers
may be said after each station:*

I love you, Jesus, my Love, above all things, I repent with my whole heart for having offended you. Never permit me to separate myself from you again. Grant that I may love you always, Then do with me what you will.

Have mercy on us, Lord,
have mercy on us.

O Holy Mother! Let the wounds of Our Lord be impressed upon my heart

Eternal Father, we offer you through the Immaculate and Sorrowful Heart of Mary, the Divine Blood which Jesus Christ, our Lord, shed during his Passion: through his wounds, through his Head pierced with thorns, through his Heart, through all his Divine Merits, forgive all souls and save them.

Divine Blood of my Redeemer, I adore you with deep respect and great love, in reparation for the insults which you are made to suffer by souls.

Jesus and Mary I love you! Save all souls that are consecrated to you, and save all souls.

At public recitations a verse of the hymn "Stabat Mater Dolorosa" is traditionally sung at each station as follows:
At the cross her station keeping, stood the mournful mother weeping, close to Jesus at the last.

SECOND STATION
JESUS TAKES UP HIS CROSS

V. We adore you, O Christ, and we bless you.
**R. Because, by your holy cross,
you have redeemed the world.**

"Then, speaking to all, he said, 'If anyone wants to be a follower of mine, let him renounce himself and take up his cross every day and follow me. Anyone who wants to save his life will lose it; but anyone who loses his life for my sake, will save it'" (Lk 9: 23-24).

**Look at the Cross which they put on my shoulders. Its weight is great, but the love I feel towards all souls is much greater.
O Souls that love me, compare the depth of my suffering to the depth of love which you show me and do not let disheartenment quench the flame of this love.**

Prayers as for the first station...

**Through her heart, his sorrow sharing,
all his bitter anguish bearing,
now at length the sword had passed.**

THIRD STATION
JESUS FALLS THE FIRST TIME

V. We adore you, O Christ, and we bless you.
**R. Because, by your holy cross,
you have redeemed the world.**

"All of you who pass this way, look and see: is any sorrow like the sorrow inflicted on me, with which Yahweh struck me on the day of his burning anger?" (Lm 1: 12).

**The weight of the Cross makes me fall to the ground, but zeal for saving souls makes me rise again, take heart once more and follow the way.
Souls that I have invited to share the weight of the Cross, see if your zeal for saving souls infuses you with new energy to go forward on the path of self-denial and renouncement of your own will, or if self-centredness prostrates your strength and does not allow you to bear the weight of the Cross.**

Prayers as for the first station...

**Oh, how sad and sore distressed
was that mother highly blest,
of the sole-begotten One.**

FOURTH STATION
JESUS MEETS HIS BLESSED MOTHER

V. We adore you, O Christ, and we bless you.
**R. Because, by your holy cross,
you have redeemed the world.**

"Simeon blessed them and said to Mary his mother, 'Look, he is destined for the fall and the rise of many in Israel, destined to be a sign that is opposed and a sword will pierce your soul too - so that the secret thoughts of many may be laid bar.' ... As for Mary, she treasured all these things and pondered them in her heart" (Lk 2:34-35;1:19).

Here I meet my most holy and beloved Mother. Consider the martyrdom that our two Hearts suffered! Yet we unite the pain which each one of us experiences; it becomes mutual, and love, however painful it may be, triumphs over all. O Souls, walking along the same path, and seeking the same God, may the sight of your mutual suffering encourage and fortify you so that love may triumph. May your unity in sorrow sustain you and make you embrace lovingly the thorns along your way.

Prayers as for the first station...

**Christ above in torment hangs;
she beneath beholds the pangs
of her dying glorious Son.**

FIFTH STATION
SIMON OF CYRENE HELPS JESUS TO CARRY THE CROSS

V. We adore you, O Christ, and we bless you.
**R. Because, by your holy cross,
you have redeemed the world.**

"As they were leading him away they seized on a man, Simon from Cyrene, who was coming in from the country, and made him shoulder the cross and carry it behind Jesus" (Lk 23:26).

Consider how Simon of Cyrene accepted this cruel and painful weight under constraint, and reflect upon how my body is losing its strength. O Souls, if your strength wanes because of the continual struggle against your own nature, contemplate the carrying of my Cross, not merely to receive a small reward or a fleeting earthly consolation, but in order to bring about the same happiness to other souls.

Prayers as for the first station...

**Is there one who would not weep,
whelmed in miseries so deep,
Christ's dear mother to behold?**

SIXTH STATION
VERONICA WIPES THE FACE OF JESUS

V. We adore you, O Christ, and we bless you.
**R. Because, by your holy cross,
you have redeemed the world.**

"He had no form or charm to attract us, nor beauty to win our hearts; he was despised, the lowest of men, a man of sorrows, familiar with suffering, one from whom, as it were, we averted our gaze, despised, for whom we had no regard" (Is 3:2-3).

Consider the charity with which this woman (Veronica) comes and wipes my face, and how her love conquers every regard for human respect. Ah! do not let a trifling fear of losing your reputation or your good name prevent you from wiping my face with acts of generosity and of love! See how it is covered in blood!

Prayers as for the first station...

**Can the human heart refrain
from partaking in her pain,
in that mother's pain untold?**

SEVENTH STATION
JESUS FALLS FOR THE SECOND TIME

V. We adore you, O Christ, and we bless you.
**R. Because, by your holy cross,
you have redeemed the world.**

"We had all gone astray like sheep, each taking his own way, and Yahweh brought the acts of rebellion of all of us to bear on him. Ill-treated and afflicted, he never opened his mouth, like a lamb led to the slaughter-house, like a sheep dumb before its shearers he never opened his mouth" (Is 53:6-7).

The Cross is exhausting my strength. The path is long and painful; nobody is near to help me, and my pain is such that I fall a second time. Souls that walk along my way, do not be discour-aged if, during your lifetime, you experience periods of aridity and are deprived of spiritual and human consolation. Take heart at the vision of your Model on the way to Calvary. As you see, it is the second time that I fall, but I rise and follow my path till the end. If you need strength, come and kiss my feet.

Prayers as for the first station...

**Bruised, derided, cursed, defiled,
she beheld her tender child,
all with bloody scourges rent.**

EIGHTH STATION
JESUS CONSOLES THE WOMEN OF JERUSALEM

V. We adore you, O Christ, and we bless you.
**R. Because, by your holy cross,
you have redeemed the world.**

"Large numbers of people followed him, and women too, who mourned and lamented for him. But Jesus turned to them and said, 'Daughters of Jerusalem, do not weep for me; weep rather for yourselves and for your children. For look, the days are surely coming when people will say, "Blessed are those who are barren, the wombs that have never borne children, the breasts that have never sucked!" Then they will begin to say to the mountains, "Fall on us!"; to the hills, "Cover us!". For if this is what is done to green wood, what will be done when the wood is dry?' " (Lk 23:27-31).

The women of Jerusalem weep at seeing me in such a shameful state. The world weeps in front of suffering; but I say to you, O Souls who follow me along the same narrow path, may the world one day see you walking through wide fields carpeted with flowers.

Prayers as for the first station...

**For the sins of his own nation,
saw him hang in desolation,
till his spirit forth he sent.**

NINTH STATION
JESUS FALLS THE THIRD TIME

V. We adore you, O Christ, and we bless you.
**R. Because, by your holy cross,
you have redeemed the world.**

"It is for us who are strong to bear with the susceptibilities of the weaker ones, and not please ourselves. Each of us must consider his neighbour's good, so that we support one another. Christ did not indulge his own feelings, either; indeed, as scripture says: The insults of those who insult you fall on me" (Rm 15:1-3).

Contemplate me as I approach Calvary and fall for the third time. In this way I give strength to those souls who, when in danger of eternal death, mend their ways through the blood of the wounds produced by this third fall: I will give them the grace to get up once more and obtain eternal life. O Souls that wish to imitate me, never refuse to do even the smallest act of charity, even if it causes you new wounds. It does not matter! This blood will give life to a soul! Imitate your Lord Jesus who proceeds towards Calvary.

Prayers as for the first station...

**O thou mother! fount of love!
touch my spirit from above,
make my heart with thine accord.**

TENTH STATION
JESUS IS STRIPPED OF HIS GARMENTS

V. We adore you, O Christ, and we bless you.
**R. Because, by your holy cross,
you have redeemed the world.**

"When the soldiers had finished crucifying Jesus they took his clothing and divided it into four shares, one for each soldier. His undergarment was seamless, woven in one piece from neck to hem; so they said to one another, 'Instead of tearing it, let's throw dice to decide who is to have it. 'In this way the words of scripture were fulfilled: They divide my garments among them and cast lots for my clothes. That is what the soldiers did" (Jn 19:23-24).

Consider with what cruelty they take away my clothes! Contemplate how I remain in silence and in total isolation! Let yourselves be deprived of all you have, both of possessions and of your own will. In return I will dress you with the tunic of purity and with the treasures of my Heart.

Prayers as for the first station...

**Make me feel as thou hast felt,
make my soul to glow and mel
with the love of Christ my Lord.**

ELEVENTH STATION
JESUS IS NAILED TO THE CROSS

V. We adore you, O Christ, and we bless you.
**R. Because, by your holy cross,
you have redeemed the world.**

"When they reached the place called The Skull, there they crucified him and the two criminals, one on his right, the other on his left. Jesus said, 'Father, forgive them; they do not know what they are doing'. Then they cast lots to share out his clothing" (Lk 23:33-34).

I have already come to the summit of the hill where they will crucify me. They are already stretching out my arms and nailing me to the cross! I have nothing left, not even the liberty to move a hand or a foot. It is not the nails which hold me down, but love! ...so that neither a cry nor a sigh is uttered from my lips. Are you nailed to the cross; are you kept there by nails? Do not complain, do not moan when those blessed nails lacerate your hands and your feet. Come and kiss mine, and you will find strength!

Prayers as for the first station...

**Holy Mother, pierce me through,
in my heart each wound renew
of my Saviour crucified.**

TWELFTH STATION
JESUS DIES ON THE CROSS AFTER THREE HOURS OF AGONY

V. We adore you, O Christ, and we bless you.
**R. Because, by your holy cross,
you have redeemed the world.**

"When the sixth hour came there was darkness over the whole land until the ninth hour. And at the ninth hour Jesus cried out in a loud voice, 'Eloi, eloi, lama sabachthani?', which means, 'My God, my God, why have you forsaken me?' When some of those who stood by heard this, they said, 'Listen, he is calling on Elijah.' Someone ran and soaked a sponge of vinegar and putting it on a reed, gave it to him to drink saying, 'Wait! And see if Elijah will come to take him down.' But Jesus gave a loud cry and breathed his last. And the veil of the Sanctuary was torn in two from top to bottom. The centurion, who was standing in front of him, had seen how he had died, and said, 'In truth this man was Son of God' " (Mk 15:33-37).

**The Cross is my companion on the way to Calvary, and on the Cross I take my last breath.
O Souls that have had the cross as an inseparable companion during your lives, be sure that you shall take your last breath upon it,**

but it will also be the door through which you will enter life. Kiss this sacred and blessed token constantly: embrace it tenderly and love it as the greatest of your treasures.

Prayers as for the first station...

Let me share with thee his pain
who for all my sins was slain
who for me in torments died.

THIRTEENTH STATION
JESUS IS TAKEN DOWN FROM THE CROSS AND LAID IN THE ARMS OF HIS BLESSED MOTHER

V. We adore you, O Christ, and we bless you.
R. Because, by your holy cross, you have redeemed the world.

"And now a member of the Council arrived, a good and upright man named Joseph. He had not consented to what the others had planned and carried out. He came from Arimathaea, a Jewish town, and he lived in the hope of seeing the kingdom of God. This man went to Pilate and asked for the body of Jesus. He then took it down, wrapped it in a shroud and put it in a tomb which was hewn in stone and which had never held a body. It was Preparation day and the Sabbath was beginning to grow light" (Lk 23: 50-53).

Consider the love of Joseph of Arimathaea who takes it upon himself to remove my body from the Cross. He puts it into the arms of my Mother.
She adores my body and kisses it; she lets her tears fall upon my face and over all of my body. Then she gives it to those who will embalm it and place it in the tomb.
Come, all Souls! Take my body, embalm it with

the spices of your virtues! Adore my wounds! Kiss them and let your tears fall on my face! And then place me in the sepulchre of your heart.

And say also a word of comfort to my dear Mother, who is your dear Mother.

Prayers as for the first station...

Let me mingle tears with thee mourning him who mourned for me, all the days that I may live.

FOURTEENTH STATION
JESUS IS LAID IN THE TOMB

V. We adore you, O Christ, and we bless you.
**R. Because, by your holy cross,
you have redeemed the world.**

"So Joseph took the body, wrapped it in a clean shroud and put it in his own new tomb which he had hewn out of the rock. He then rolled a large stone across the entrance of the tomb and went away. Now Mary of Magdala and the other Mary were there, sitting opposite the sepulchre" (Mt 27: 59-60).

Consider with what tenderness they place me in the tomb. It is new and therefore pure without the slightest stain. O Souls that are united to me, seek to carry out all the acts of kindness and tenderness which your love inspires you to do, until your heart becomes pure and well prepared to bury me in tender, strong, constant and generous love.

Prayers as for the first station...

By the cross with thee to stay there with thee to weep and pray, is all I ask of thee to give.

Now kiss and adore my Wounds and recite the "Miserere".

PSALM 51 (THE "MISERERE")

Have mercy on me, O God, in your faithful love,
in your great tenderness wipe away my offences;
wash me clean from my guilt,
purify me from my sin.

For I am well aware of my offences,
my sin is constantly in mind.
Against you, you alone, I have sinned,
I have done what you see to be wrong,

that you may show your saving justice when you
pass sentence,
and your victory may appear when you give
judgement,
remembe, I was born guilty,
a sinner from the moment of conception.

But you delight in sincerity of heart,
and in secret you teach me wisdom.
Purify me with hyssop till I am clean,
wash me till I am whiter than snow.

Let me hear the sound of joy and gladness,
and the bones you have crushed will dance.
Turn away your face from my sins,
and wipe away all my guilt.

God, create in me a clean heart,
renew within me a resolute spirit,

do not thrust me away from your presence,
do not take away from me your spirit of holiness.

Give me back the joy of your salvation,
sustain in me a generous spirit.
I shall teach the wicked your paths,
and sinners will return to you.

Deliver me from bloodshed, God, God of my salvation,
and my tongue will acclaim your saving justice.
Lord, open my lips,
and my mouth will speak out your praise.

Sacrifice gives you no pleasure,
burnt offering you do not desire.
Sacrifice to God is a broken spirit,
a broken, contrite heart you never scorn.

In your graciousness do good to Zion,
rebuild the walls of Jerusalem.
Then you will delight in upright sacrifices,
- burnt offerings and whole oblations -
and young bulls will be offered on your altar.

*We now pray the following for the intentions
of our Holy Father the Pope:*

Our Father
Hail Mary
Glory Be

A further station is suggested below:

FIFTEENTH STATION
THE RISING OF JESUS FROM THE TOMB

**V. We adore you, O Christ, and we bless you.
R. Because, by your holy cross,
you have redeemed the world.**

"After the Sabbath, and towards dawn on the first day of the week, Mary of Magdala and the other Mary went to visit the sepulchre. And suddenly there was a violent earthquake, for an angel of the Lord, descending from heaven, came and rolled away the stone and sat on it. His face was like lightning, his robe white as snow.

The guards were so shaken by fear of him that they were like dead men. But the angel spoke; and he said to the women, 'There is no need for you to be afraid. I know you are looking for Jesus, who was crucified. He is not here, for he has risen, as he said he would.

Come and see the place where he lay, then go quickly and tell his disciples, "He has risen from the dead and now he is going ahead of you to Galilee; that is where you will see him." Look I have told you.' Filled with awe and great joy the women came quickly away from the tomb and ran to tell his disciples" (Mt 28:1-7).

Thank you, thank you, thank you, O Mary! I have been able to meditate the Passion by

which he redeemed the world, and in which you shared, united in love to your Son, thank you for the experience of life which the resurrection has given to me: the belief that everything can be transformed into good. Thank you, because with new trust, new joy and with renewed love, I can set out on the road to meet others, and seek to alleviate the suffering and anguish of humanity. Do not let me forget this experience. Amen. Alleluia!

Prayers as for the first station...

STATIONS OF THE CROSS WITH OUR HOLY FATHER THE POPE
(Second Scheme)

THE FIRST STATION
JESUS IN THE GARDEN OF OLIVES

"They came to a plot of land called Gethsemane, and he said to his disciples, 'Stay here while I pray.' Then he took Peter and James and John with him. And he began to feel terror and an-guish. And he said to them, 'My soul is sorrowful to the point of death. Wait here, and stay awake.' And going on a little further he threw himself on the ground and prayed that, if it were possible, this hour might pass him by. 'Abba, Father!' he said, 'For you everything is possible. Take this cup away from me. But let it be as you, not I would have it'.". (Mk 14: 32-36)

"Abba, Father!". Words of trustful abandonment, which reveal the abyss of love in which Jesus lives, being Son of the Father. He can confide everything to the Father: his fears, necessities and desires. For the Father, everything is possible. But Jesus does not impose himself on the Father: "My food is to do the will of the one who sent me, and to complete his work" *(Jn 4:34)*. And immersed in extreme anguish, he now reaffirms this. Only one thing is good: the will of the Father. Stripped of himself, emptied, Jesus gives everything, a response without reserve to the depth of being love of his Father. This is also our destiny as human: to live as children, abandoned in total faith to the Father, letting Jesus live in us and pervade all our activity, so that we may become, in the hands of Providence, instruments of peace and of unity in the world.

Prayers as for the previous Stations of the Cross
(See page 398)

SECOND STATION
JESUS IS ARRESTED, HAVING BEEN BETRAYED BY JUDAS

"And at once, while he was still speaking, Judas, one of the twelve, came up and with him a number of men armed with swords and clubs, sent by the chief priests and the scribes and the elders. Now the traitor had arranged a signal with them saying, 'The one I kiss, he is the man. Arrest him, and see he is well guarded when you lead him away.' So when the traitor came, he went up to Jesus at once and said, 'Rabbi!' and kissed him. The others seized him and arrested him". (Mk 14:43-46)

A crowd with swords and clubs: innumerable scenes of history come to mind in which human beings have fought each other. The kiss of the betrayer is a symbol of the deceit which has always corrupted relationships among people. It is the result of a free will which does not open itself to giving, this is the result when humans become prisoners of themselves, slaves of their own selfishness. And yet Judas had always been immensely loved and Jesus had chosen him as his disciple with fondness.

Judas, what a tragic figure! He does not understand God's plan of salvation: it is a scandal for him. Turned in on himself, in the arrogant certainty of his own haughty presumptuousness, he perverts his freedom and loses it for ever. How different is the freedom of Jesus! For love of the Father and of humankind, he gives himself. He does not use the sword. He does not lie. He gives himself. And giving himself he wins over evil and frees men and women, forever.

Prayers as for first station...

THIRD STATION
JESUS IS CONDEMNED BY THE SANHEDRIN

"The chief priests and the whole Sanhedrin were looking for evidence against Jesus in order to have him executed. But they could not find any.... The high priest put a (second) question to him, saying, 'Are you the Christ, the Son of the Blessed One?.' 'I am,' said Jesus... Their verdict was unanimous: he deserved to die". (Mk 14:55.61.64)

The chief priests and the Sanhedrin: a dramatic image of those who are slaves of their own convictions, prisoners of politics and of their own system; unmerciful mirror of those who, rigid in their own opinions, do not know how to receive the manifestation of God; a violent sign of those, who clinging to power, are incapable of recognising and serving the Truth.

Jesus said, "No-one can serve two masters" *(Mt 6:24)*. This is the challenge flung at men and women of all ages: the challenge of oneself forgetting, letting go of one's advantages and security, opening oneself unconditionally to the Truth which alone sets us free.

Those who make an idol of their customs and institutions feel that Truth is a threat: they do not accept it but rather renounce it. People and nations, open the doors to Christ! Open your minds to the Truth which saves us! Open your hearts to the Truth of Love!

Prayers as for first station...

FOURTH STATION
JESUS IS DENIED BY PETER

"About an hour later another man insisted, saying, 'This fellow was certainly with him. Why, he is a Galilean.' Peter said, 'My friend I do not know what you are talking about'. At that instant, while he was still speaking, the cock crowed, and the Lord turned and looked straight at Peter, and Peter remembered the Lord's words when he had said to him: 'Before the cock crows today, you will have disowned me three times' And he went outside and wept bitterly".
(Lk 22:59-62)

It is not enough to have known Jesus and to have heard the Word of Life; it is not enough to have heard extraordinary promises and to have witnessed great miracles; it is not enough to have seen Jesus transfigured in order to remain faithful and to be saved.

Having been elevated to the highest dignity, Peter now fails dismally, he who declared to be ready to face death with Jesus! In a bitter cry, all of Peter's security vanishes. But Peter does not fall into darkness. From the depth of love and mercy of God, he is born again: "Lord, you know everything; you know I love you" *(Jn 21:17)*. "Recreated by Him who has chosen that which is weakest in the world" *(ref. 1Cor 1,27)*, he will be leader of a new people. And with a heart finally free, he will follow his Lord to the end and like Him, sacrifice his life.

Prayers as for first station...

FIFTH STATION
JESUS IS SCOURGED AT THE PILLAR

*"Pilate then summoned the chief priests and the lea-
ding men and the people. In his desire to set Jesus free,
Pilate addressed them again, but they shouted back, 'Crucify him! Crucify him!' And for the third time he spoke to
them, 'But what harm has this man done? I have found no
case against him that deserves death, so I shall have him
flogged and then let him go.' But they kept on shouting at
the top of their voices, demanding that he should be crucified. And their shouts kept growing louder. Pilate then gave
his verdict: their demand was to be granted. He released
the man they asked for, who had been imprisoned because
of rioting and murder, and handed Jesus over to them to
deal with as they pleased". (Lk 23:13.20-25)*

Pilate: once again man is a slave to false
values. As a guardian of justice, Pilate does not
want to hand over Jesus, but the weakness of his
will crumbles under the pressure of the crowd.
His heart is not anchored to the only One who
saves; it wavers between the duty of saving the
innocent and the desire to save himself. In the
end fear and human respect prevail. Political
compromise wins. It was an encounter which
Pilate wasted, having come so near to meeting the
Truth in Jesus. The divine offering is choked by
"thorns": the cares of the world, the deception of
richness *(ref. Mt. 13:22)*. How much freedom is
needed to meet Jesus, to discover his love and to
respond to it: freedom from all ties and from

human conditioning, freedom from all compromises, freedom from oneself!

Prayers as for first station...

SIXTH STATION
JESUS IS CROWNED WITH THORNS

*"They dressed him up in purple, twisted some thorns
into a crown and put it on him. And they began saluting
him, 'Hail, King of the Jews!' They struck his head with a
reed and spat on him; and they went down on their knees to
do him homage. And when they had finished making fun of
him, they took off the purple robe and dressed him in his
own clothes". (Mk 15:17-19)*

Humiliated, despised, struck: the Son of man
is led along the path of suffering. In him, the
prophetic words of Isaiah are realized: "Man of
sorrows... yet ours were the sufferings he bore,
ours the sorrows he was carried." (Is 53: 3-4).

Jesus, man of sorrows, he who takes on himself the sufferings of all humankind: betrayed
with the betrayers, persecuted with those who
perse-cute, a failure, rejected, tormented, tortured, bartered, condemned to death, he became a
curse, was treated like a sinner, and identified
himself with all people to save all people. There
is no sorrow which he did not make his own... for

us... in order to bear it together with us. Jesus, man of sorrows, you are near to us, even in the greatest sorrow. In your infinite love, you always wanted to be united to every person. Grant that we may recognise your face in every suffering person; teach us to welcome you when you come towards us, in order to consummate your passion with us.

Prayers as for first station...

SEVENTH STATION
JESUS CARRIES THE CROSS

*"And when they had finished making fun of him, they took off the purple robe and dressed him in his own clothes. They led him out to crucify hi*m". *(Mk 15:20)*

The Way of the Cross is the way against the trend. We flee from difficulties, dangers, and sorrows. Jesus takes them upon himself, for love of his Father, for love of us: "Father, let your will be done, not mine" *(Lk 22:42)*.
He made a free choice, abandoning himself completely into the loving hands of the Father.
The Way of the Cross is the way of Divine Wisdom. How different are the decisions of God from the decisions of humanity! By sending his

Son into the world, God chose for him the way of sorrow. In this way he defied humanity to look far ahead: in times of trial, to leap forward, freeing ourselves from the narrow horizons of our ego rather than dwelling on our sense of defeat; to give all of one's self after experiencing the night of suffering, and thus find the fullness of life: "The one who tries to save his own life will lose it, who instead loses his life will save it" *(Lk 17:32)*.

The Way of the Cross is the way of love: a new way of life; a new way of seeking salvation, success, and happiness; a new way of resolving, in a radical way, the enormous problems of humankind.

Prayers as for first station...

EIGHTH STATION
JESUS IS HELPED BY SIMON OF CYRENE TO CARRY THE CROSS

"As they were leading him away they seized on a man, Simon from Cyrene, who was coming in from the country, and made him shoulder the cross and carry it behind Jesus". (Lk 23:26)

The cross of Jesus and our crosses: without that first cross, the sorrow of a thousand people would have no significance. However through that cross, each suffering is an invitation to unite ourselves to Jesus, each sorrow is a chance to tell him: "Here I am, Lord, I have chosen you, I want to follow you."

Simon from Cyrene and Jesus: on the way of the cross, they carry the same cross. Hosts of martyrs did the same, not under obligation, but in complete freedom. What a mystery! Jesus shares his cross with us. How can we not embrace it then, every day, in our sufferings, in the burden of our daily life? Let us say with Paul, "It makes me happy to be suffering for you now, and in my own body to make up all the hardships that still have to be undergone by Christ for the sake of his body, the Church" *(Col 1:24)*.

Jesus, you kept nothing for youself. You share everything with us, to the point of raising us up to your dignity, of making us share in your work of redemption. Help each one of us to carry your cross when carrying our neighbour's cross!

Prayers as for first station...

NINTH STATION
JESUS MEETS THE WOMEN OF JERUSALEM

"Large numbers of people followed him, and women too, who mourned and lamented for him. But Jesus turned to them and said, 'Daughters of Jerusalem, do not weep for me; weep rather for yourselves and for your children'.". (Lk 23:27-28)

Again we see the absolute freedom of Jesus! On the way to Calvary, he meets the daughters of Jerusalem, who mourn for him: "Do not weep for me, but weep for yourselves and for your children". Jesus does not think of himself, nor is his heart closed in his sorrow: he weeps for the destiny which awaits his people.

Jesus, you gave your life so that we could have life. What an annihilation, what a great depth of love!

Jesus, free our bodies from selfishness, from arrogance, from presumption of self-sufficiency. Open the hearts of all people, men and women of all countries, so that they may love their brothers and sisters; make us ready to meet you, together with the Father, and the Holy Spirit. Give us a mind similar to your heart, which embraces all humanity!

Prayers as for first station...

TENTH STATION
JESUS IS CRUCIFIED

"Then they crucified him, and shared out his clothing, castings lots to decide what each should get". (Mk 15:24)

God in his human form is dying. The soldiers share his clothes and cast lots to decide who will get his tunic: the logic of "getting" makes clothes more important than a living man. But on the gloomy background of human selfishness shines the light of Divine Love; love which gives everything: clothes and every material good, freedom and every spiritual good.

Jesus takes nothing for himself: on the cross his arms are open to receive, his hands are open to give. He offers everything for us, to reconcile us to God. His body is nailed to the cross, His spirit is nailed to his Father's will. People, when they take, divide; Jesus, in his giving, unites heaven and earth.

Jesus, only your love can heal us from our greediness, only your grace can uproot from our hearts the culture of "getting and possessing", which divides men and women of all countries.

Establish, Lord, on earth the culture of "giving and sharing". Establish a new era, in which a society of solidarity and love shall flourish among all people.

Prayers as for first station...

ELEVENTH STATION
JESUS PROMISES HIS KINGDOM TO THE GOOD THIEF

"One of the two criminals hanging there abused him: 'Are you not the Christ? Save yourself and us as well.' But the other spoke up and rebuked him. 'Have you no fear of God at all?' he said. Then he said, 'Jesus, remember me when you come into your kingdom'.". (Lk 23:39-40.42)

In Jesus, every person, whatever his condition may be, finds reason to hope: in his infinite love he promises salvation to everyone. But how easy it is to fail to believe in the promise of Jesus, who appears disarmed and crucified between two crucified criminals! How easy it is to fail to accept his love!

Who has not been tempted to lock himself stubbornly into the ways of sin, like the impenitent thief? Who among us has never reacted with an impulsive refusal of forgiveness at a time of trial? Blessed be the good thief!

Although he has many faults, he is touched by the love of Jesus and recognises in him the God who saves. Like the publican in the temple, all the thief has to offer to Jesus is a heart open to forgiveness and a humble request for friendship: "Jesus, remember me when you come into your kingdom" *(Lk 23:42)*.

Such is the miracle of the love of God: the one who opens himself to the gift received: "Today you will be with me in Heaven" *(Lk 23:43)*. Jesus, give us the courage to commend our past to your mercy, teach us to become simple, free us from theories and useless mental schemes. And lead us all to your kingdom of unconditional love.

Prayers as for first station...

TWELFTH STATION
JESUS BEHOLDS, HIS MOTHER AND DISCIPLE FROM THE CROSS

"Seeing his mother and the disciple whom he loved standing near her, Jesus said to his mother, 'Woman, this is your son.' Then to the disciple he said, 'This is your mother'. And from that hour the disciple took her into his home". (Jn 19:26-27)

"Now the hour has come" *(Jn 12:23)*, the hour of the new creation, the hour in which, as if from the pains of labour, the Church is born. John is commended to Mary, Mary is commended to John: it is the beginning of the new people born from the Cross of Christ and marked forever by his commandment: "Love one another, as I have loved you. No one can have greater love than to lay down his life for his friends" *(Jn 15:12-13)*. Mary and John are the beginning of the Church. But what a price there is to be paid! After having given everything, Jesus also gives his Mother. From that moment, Jesus is alone on the cross. His mother is also alone, deprived of her Son. But Jesus wants his place to be taken by one of us; and once again Mary proclaims her "fiat" and becomes a mother: mother not only of Jesus, but of his entire body: Mother of the Church. We too have been commended to his Mother, and his Mother has been commended to us; following the example of John, we too must bring Mary into our home, in order to learn her way of thinking and acting, of serving and loving, by living close to her.

Prayers as for first station...

THIRTEENTH STATION
JESUS DIES ON THE CROSS

"And at the ninth hour Jesus cried out in a loud voice, 'My God, my God, why have you forsaken me?'. Someone ran and soaked a sponge in vinegar and, putting it on a reed, gave it to him to drink saying, 'Wait! And see if Elijah will come to take him down. But Jesus gave a loud cry and breathed his last". (Mk 15:34,36-37)

Jesus, the world rejected you. Now, having lifted you up on the cross, it seems to wish that you would return to heaven. You who were rejected and annihilated, pray for all people: "Father, forgive them; they do not know what they are doing" *(Lk 23:34)*. Your only refuge is the Father; but here the unheard-of - the inconceivable - takes place: even heaven seems to be closed. The Father remains silent. An abyss opens, from which the most agonizing cry of all time is heard: "My God, my God, why have you forsaken me?" *(Mk 15:34)*.

It is a cry of anguish, and yet a cry of love, like the cry of a woman in childbirth *(ref. Jn 16:21)*. Jesus allows the arid desert of the heart of all people to enter into his own heart; he takes into his own heart all men and women throughout history who have invoked the grace of God, sometimes without even being aware of it. Jesus, you experienced the silence of God, in the darkness of this trial and yet, with a supreme act of love you commended yourself into his hands: "Father, into your hands I commit my spirit" *(Lk 23:46)*. And as you died, your sacrifice became a gift for us, the gift of the Holy Spirit who enables us to cry out, with the freedom of children, "Abba, Father!" *(ref.Rm 8:15)*.

Prayers as for first station...

FOURTEENTH STATION
JESUS IS PLACED IN THE SEPULCHRE

"Joseph from Arimathaea bought a shroud, took Jesus down from the cross, wrapped him in the shroud and laid him in a tomb which had been hewn out of the rock". (Mk 15:46)

The sepulchre: it is the end of all hope based only on human thinking. A lifeless body: here is all that remains of Jesus in the eyes of the world. How limited are the views of humankind; how much greater are the horizons opened by God.

The tomb of Jesus is also the place of resurrection. His body is "a grain of wheat" which "falling to earth, produces much of fruit" *(ref. Jn 2:24)*.

Jesus, who died on the cross, you alone have risen from the dead, the "eldest of many brothers" *(Rm 8:29)*. By offering yourself for us, you formed your Body, the Church, from us *(ref. Col 1:18)*. Your mortal flesh was buried in the earth; your resurrected flesh awaits "a new heaven and a new earth" *(ref. Is 65:17; Rev 21:1)*.

Your sepulchre is the sacred seal of your life, the seal of true love. Only the one who is able to die out of love brings life: life which does not create delusion, life which conquers death.

Prayers as for first station...

LITANY OF THE SACRED PASSION OF CHRIST

Lord, have mercy on us.

Lord, have mercy on us.

Christ, have mercy on us.

Christ, have mercy on us.

Lord, have mercy on us.

Lord, have mercy on us.

Christ, hear us.

Christ, graciously hear us.

God the Father of Heaven,

Have mercy on us.

God the Son, Redeemer of the world,

Have mercy on us.

God the Holy Spirit,

Have mercy on us.

Holy Trinity, one God,

Have mercy on us.

O Mary, Mother of our Redeemer and
Mediatrix of graces,

Have mercy on us.

Jesus, King of glory, who went to Jerusalem
in order to complete the work of our
redemption,

Have mercy on us.

Jesus, prostrate before the Father in the
Garden of Olives, and oppressed by
the iniquity of all the world,

Have mercy on us.

Jesus, struck by fear, overcome by sadness,
reduced to agony, covered in a sweat of
blood and abandoned by everyone,

Have mercy on us.

Jesus, betrayed by one of your nearest friends
and sold at a low price as if you were a slave,

Have mercy on us.

Jesus, bound, beaten, insulted, brought
before Annas and Caiaphas, and treated as
an evildoer and blasphemer,

Have mercy on us.

Jesus, taken before Pilate and accused of
being an agitator and a dangerous rebel,

Have mercy on us.

Jesus, brought before Herod, treated like a
madman and mocked by being dressed up
in a rich purple cloak

Have mercy on us.

Jesus, cruelly scourged by thirty-nine lashes of
a triple Roman whip with leaden
endings which tore your flesh off the bone
in more than one part of your body,

Have mercy on us.

Jesus, crowned with thorns, dressed up in a
purple robe, insulted and mocked in many
different ways, and finally exposed to
the crowd,

Have mercy on us.

Jesus, compared to a violent criminal who
was set free instead of you,

Have mercy on us.

Jesus, condemned by Pilate and abandoned
to the anger of your enemies,

Have mercy on us.

Jesus, exhausted by your suffering, and,
burdened by the great weight of the cross
on the road to Calvary,

Have mercy on us.

Jesus, stripped of your clothes, laid on the
ground and nailed to the cross,

Have mercy on us.

Jesus, nailed without pity to the infamous
wood and ranked among of the worst sinners,

Have mercy on us.

Jesus, who tenderly forgive those who want
you to drink wine mixed with gall,

Have mercy on us.

Jesus, who pray to the Father and ask
forgiveness for those who persecute
you and cruelly torment you,

Have mercy on us.

Jesus, who reveal yourself as being obedient
to the Father unto death and who
commend your spirit into his hands,

Have mercy on us.

Jesus, who bow your head and die out of
ardent love for us,

Have mercy on us.

Jesus, who died for us and let your Heart be
pierced by a lance to reveal your eternal
mercy even more clearly to us,

Have mercy on us.

From every evil,

Deliver us, O Lord.

From rage, hatred and from all ill will,

Deliver us, O Lord.

From pride in possession,

Deliver us, O Lord.

From disordered bodily desires and
disordered desires of the eyes,

Deliver us, O Lord.

From all hardness of heart,

Deliver us, O Lord.

From sudden death,

Deliver us, O Lord.

From eternal damnation,

Deliver us, O Lord.

For the sake of your sweat of blood,

Have mercy on us.

For the sake of your painful scourging,

Have mercy on us.

For the sake of your crowning with thorns,

Have mercy on us.

For the sake of your exhaustion under the
weight of the cross,

Have mercy on us.

For the sake of your painful crucifixion,

Have mercy on us.

For the sake of your sacred wounds,

Have mercy on us.

For the sake of your death,

Have mercy on us.

At the hour of our death,

Have mercy on us.

On the day of judgement,

Have mercy on us.

We adore you, O Christ, and we bless you,
**Because, by your holy cross,
you have redeemed the world**

Lamb of God, who take away the sins of the world,
Spare us, O Lord.

Lamb of God, who take away the sins of the world,
Graciously hear us, O Lord.

Lamb of God, who take away the sins of the world,
Have mercy on us.

Let us pray.
O Jesus, who redeemed us by your death on the cross out of love for us, pour out on us the merits of your holy passion and death, and, grant, in your mercy, that by these merits, we may obtain the special grace which we desire...

(Here we express our intention)

We earnestly ask you for this grace, while entreating you to consider the sorrow and the prayers of your Holy Mother at the foot of the cross. **Amen.**

HOLY HOUR

AN HOUR OF ADORATION WITH JESUS IN HIS AGONY AT GETHSEMANE

To be done if possible on Thursday night from 11 o'clock to 12 midnight, or at least on the first Thursday of the month.

This devotion consists in spending an entire hour in prayer on Thursday evening (either praying out loud or silently) while contemplating the agony of Our Lord in the Garden of Olives.

The devotion of the Holy Hour originates from the recommendation which Jesus himself gave to Saint Margaret Mary Alacoque (1647-1690) during his second apparition to her on the 2nd of July, 1674.

On that occasion Jesus said to her: "You will receive Holy Communion on the first Friday of each month and on all nights between Thursday and Friday, I will let you share in that mortal sadness which I felt in the Garden of Olives. It shall be a bitter experience which will bring you, without your being able to understand it, to a kind of agony even harsher than death itself. In order to keep me company in the humble prayer which at that time, in the midst of my agonies, you will present to the Father, you shall rise between eleven o'clock and twelve midnight to prostrate yourself together with me with your face to the ground for one hour. And this is in order to placate divine anger, to ask for mercy for sinners, to sweeten in some way the bitterness which I felt at being abandoned by the apostles, which obliged me to reproach them for not being able to keep watch with me for one hour."

From the Autobiography of
St. Margaret Mary Alacoque

In her commantary on the request of Our Lord, Saint
Margaret Mary Alacoque says:

*"Put yourself, O pious soul, in the presence of your
most beloved Saviour, and reflect on that night when the
good Lord, having instituted the Holy Eucharist in order to
become food for you, went out with his Apostles from the
supper-room to go to the Garden of Olives and began that
most cruel Passion through which he had to save the world.
A mortal sadness is shown on his forehead and is understood by the words of Jesus who is distressed. The pallor of
death overshadows that face upon which, until now, all the
graces of Paradise have shone. Meanwhile, the breathless
Saviour lays his eyes upon you, as if to say, 'Dear soul,
who cause me so much pain, stay with me for at least an
hour, and see if there is a sorrow to compare with mine...
But know that, in the night of my agony, I looked in vain for
consolation: Consolantem me quaesivi et non inveni?'.*

*Adorable Jesus, could there ever exist a creature so
ungrateful and so hard of heart that would refuse to spend
an hour in your company, remembering those mysteries of
supreme pain and sorrow and of supreme love which took
place in the darkness of the night of your Passion on the
sacred soil of Gethsemane? Good Jesus, here I am before
you: deign to reveal to me the atrocity of your pain and
that excess of love which led you to make yourself the victim of my sins and of the sins of all people."*

FIRST QUARTER OF AN HOUR
The sadness of Jesus

In truth, there is no greater pain than the pains of death.

Now our Saviour, who is infallible truth, in order to make us understand the tremendous pain which overwhelmed Him when entering Gethsemane, says that His soul is filled with mortal sadness: that is to say, the sorrow which He suffers is sufficiently great to cause His death. And after saying this, he enters the Garden of Olives and goes to the place where He used to spend hours in adoration; He then urges his disciples (whom He had taken with him into the Garden in order to make them witnesses of his suffering) to watch and pray with him. Going a stone's throw away, He then kneels before the majesty of the Father to begin the most sorrowful and yet most generous prayer which has ever been prayed on earth.

The first reason for the sadness of Jesus in Gethsemane was the horrific accumulation of torment and shame which, as stormy waves of the sea in all its fury was to befall him in a short time. In fact, as soon as He moved away from his beloved disciples, the horrible scene of pain and blood of his imminent Passion appeared in his mind: betrayals, embarrassments, sneers, slander and even more, an atrocious scourging with such a fury of blows that it would lacerate Him and send pieces of His flesh flying, exposing His bones. But it is not enough.

The sacred head must be tor-mented by many large thorns, which remain in place until his death. And furthermore He suffers slaps, spits and sneers. But it is not enough. He must swallow the shame of a legal condemnation and find Himself rejected by the leaders of his country and by His people. Dying from the many pains He has received, he must drag himself to the mountain of sacrifice with the cross on His lacerated shoulders, and fall many times, half dead, under that enormous weight.

He must drink the bitter gall and be stripped in the middle of a violent crowd. He lets his hands and feet be nailed to the cross. He must hang for three hours from hooks of iron and remain suspended there between heaven and earth in order to atone for the iniquity of humankind in an abyss of pain.

But it is still not enough. To His atrocious spasms of pain must be added the most piercing of insults and provocations; there follows a most acute thirst, which is made even more tormenting by vinegar; then the abandonment of the Father, the infinite sorrow of His most beloved Mother, and a horrible and desolate death.

Redeemed soul, child born from the terrible pains of Jesus, consider your Saviour, overwhelmed by extreme sorrow out of His love for you, in order to save you and lead you to heaven together with Him. Oppressed by so much anguish, Jesus approaches the three disciples whom He has asked to watch and pray, but He finds them asleep. In his agony Jesus receives no words of sympathy.

In the bitterness of His abandonment, He looks at you with the gaze of a dying man to see if he can find in your heart some feeling of pity and of gratitude. And have you not got a word to say to dear Jesus? What would you have said if you were near Him in his night of agony? Alas! Open your heart, and do now what you would have done at that time, as He always accepts with the same joy the expressions of tenderness which come from the hearts of His faithful.

Pause

OFFERINGS

Holy Father, who loved the world so much that You sacrificed your Son made man, I thank You, in the name of all those who have been redeemed, for this act of infinite mercy and offer you the most perfect sanctity and all the merits of Your only-begotten Son.

Our Father • Hail Mary • Glory Be

Holy Father, who, in order to free us from eternal damnation, put upon the adorable humanity, Your only-begotten Son the abominable burden of all our iniquity, I offer You the agony of Jesus in Gethsemane and beg You to grant that I may enjoy the fruits of His awful suffering in eternity.

Our Father • Hail Mary • Glory Be

Holy Father, who, in order to reconcile sinful humankind to your wounded majesty, allowed Your innocent only-begotten Son to be submitted to a rigorous trial so that He could expiate the punishments merited by our iniquity, I offer You the loving obedience of Jesus in the garden of Gethsemane and implore You to grant the conversion and the salvation of all sinners.

Our Father • Hail Mary • Glory Be

Litany of the Sacred Passion *(see page 437)*

SECOND QUARTER OF AN HOUR
Jesus groans under the weight
of human iniquity.

Already, Jesus has passed a long hour of anguish, having experienced the darkness of night and having been abandoned by His disciples. Great dread of the atrocious torments awaiting Him has filled His blessed soul with terror and anxiety. He feels ever more the great weight of his mission as Saviour of the world. The time for Him to sacrifice Himself has come. Heaven, earth and hell are already armed against Him and He has to face a great fight where all blows are aimed at Him. And what does Jesus do? Pale and trembling, He turns to the Father and humbly prays: **"Father, if it is possible let this cup pass me by!"**

What will be the answer to the humble prayer of the Son of God? Heaven is closed. For Jesus there is no answer. He wants to suffer this affliction in order to obtain for us humble perseverance in prayer, and patience, when heaven seems to be closed to our pleas. Ah, good Jesus, there is no pain you refused to suffer in order that we be consoled and edified by your example!

Therefore, follow your Lord, O pious soul, who, driven by love, goes even further along the way of sorrow. The horrible series of crimes and iniquities of the children of Adam comes to his mind and lacerates His heart. Meanwhile, He sees that he must take upon Himself that terrible burden and come before the eyes of the Father, laiden down with a thousand loads.

It is impossible for us to comprehend, or even to imagine the horrible pain that the blessed and most innocent soul of Jesus suffered at that moment. He had already lamented pitifully about this hour, saying through the mouth of the prophet; **"Supra dorsum meum fabricaverunt peccatores!"** *"Sinners have worked on my back!". (ref. Ps 128)*

Oh, how oppressed is our dear Saviour under the weight of so many sins! And yet the Divine Lamb is going to offer Himself to Divine Justice, which has been so greatly offended by humankind, having expiated our human iniquities with the sacrifice of His precious life on the scaffold in order to remove sin from the world.

Can he hope at least that humanity will be grateful for such a great gift, will sin no more and remain always faithful to Him, who has saved them from eternal damnation by all the pain that he suffered? Ah, poor Jesus, may it be so. Meanwhile an image more horrible than the previous one appears before Him: after redeeming humankind through His Passion and washing the earth with his Blood, after filling His followers with the Holy Spirit and making the earth a paradise of grace with the adorable Eucharist, after lavishing His mercy on the world, He sees that sin continues to reign on the earth. He sees sacred laws trampled upon, His Church and his ministers persecuted, His graces rejected, his love despised and, He exclaims, weeping: **"Of what use is my blood?"**

"Why shed all my blood? Why die in acute pain on a scaffold, if humans, ungrateful for so many benefits want to place themselves in the devil's hands and condemn themselves to eternal damnation? When will the reign of sin end in the world?". Jesus gets a glimpse of future centuries, and in each century He sees sins, in each year He sees sins. Sins every day, sins at every moment. And the burden of all these sins oppresses Him ever more and makes him repeat: **"Supra dorsum meum fabricaverunt peccatores; prolongaverunt iniquitatem sua"** *"Sinners have worked on my back; they have prolonged his iniquity."*

Soul of mine, would you ever be among those who provoke that cry, so full of justified sorrow, from the heart of the agonizing Jesus, by making the chain of sin longer, and postponing ever more the promised time of conversion.

How horrible is sin after God had shed all His blood in order to destroy it! How terrible is sin in souls already washed by that Divine Blood, in souls united in Holy Communion to the Heart of Jesus! Most afflicted Saviour, how right You are to lament and cry! But if Jesus justly complains about the sins of all his redeemed people, will He not then suffer in foreseeing the sins of his most dear friends, namely of the souls consecrated to him?

Beloved souls: He exclaims, "Souls of my peace, who are so intimately familiar with my heart, who live in my house, who eat my bread and feed at my table, why do you afflict my Heart by sin? People of my Heart, what have I ever done to you? How have I caused you sorrow? I have quenched your thirst with the heavenly waters of my grace, and you give me vinegar and gall... I have satisfied your hunger with the precious manna of my Flesh and you injure me with slaps and scourges!...

My people, what have I ever done to you? How have I caused you sorrow? I have prepared you a place in heaven, and you offer me the scaffold!... Dear soul, what could I have ever done for you that I did not do? And in exchange for so much love, you give me sorrow and thorns!".

Pause

OFFERINGS

O my afflicted Saviour, why cannot I offer you my heart and the hearts of all people, enkindled by the flames of perfect mercy in order to return in some way Your infinite love? Sorry for my coldness and that of other people, I offer you, O good Jesus, the holy ardour with which the ancient patriarchs and prophets longed for Your coming, and that sacred zeal with which your apostles brought Your Name over all the earth.

Our Father • Hail Mary • Glory Be

I offer you, O my Beloved Good, that perfect and most tender compassion with which your Immaculate Mother, whose soul was pierced by a sword of sorrow, shared Your pain, and furthermore, I offer You that most perfect gratitude with which, on behalf of all humankind, she thanked, praised and blessed You for the never-ending benefits of Redemption.

Our Father • Hail Mary • Glory Be

My agonizing Jesus, as I, a miserable creature, cannot comfort you in Your great pain as I would like to do, I offer You that feeling of joy with which the Adorable Trinity in union with all the angels of heaven, wel-comed the great act of Redemption accomplished by You with great sorrow and with great love; and together with them, I beseech You to help all those who have been redeemed to comprehend that mystery of infinite mercy.

Our Father • Hail Mary • Glory Be

Miserere *(Psalm 51; see page 416)*
Litany of the Sacred Passion *(see page 437)*

THIRD QUARTER OF AN HOUR
The great Fiat

O redeemed soul, contemplate your Saviour who, having had His Heart pierced by human ingratitude, has fallen in agony on the hard soil of Gethsemane. He is alone, abandoned, with no-one to help Him. He never ceased to help the weak and the suffering, and He even comforted the disciple who, in his tiredness, laid his head upon His Heart. Come, faithful soul, the moment has arrived to return the love of Jesus who is suffering.

What would you have done if you had found yourself in Gethsemane near to Jesus in his agony on the night of his Passion? O my suffering Lord, I want to raise You from the ground. I want to offer you my heart to sustain Your drooping head and then I want to say to You a word to console You. O sweetest Saviour, I love You, I love You, I love You!

I want to seek love for You, I want to procure love for You, I want everybody to love You. I want to consume my very life so that You may be loved; yes, much loved, always loved, loved by all those who have been redeemed. My sweet Jesus, I have said that I would even consume my life so that You may be loved, that is, I would make whatever sacrifice necessary no matter how great, but then, when I encounter some minor difficulties, some little humiliation, a refusal, a reproach, rude behaviour, am I able to bear it? Do I really love sacrifice? Am I happy to offer you the self-denial of one of my desires?

O good Jesus, I am ashamed of the reply. But here, close to you, here at the school of sorrow and of love, I want to learn how to mortify myself, to sacrifice myself in all things for love of you, O my sweet master. Meanwhile the hours of the mortal agony pass by slowly for Jesus. He, the God of heaven and earth, lies languishing upon the ground, and nobody cares for Him. But what are His disciples doing? They are asleep!

In the night of his Passion, Jesus had to bear also the sorrow of being abandoned by His dear ones and this caused Him to feel a deep sadness in his heart. At that moment Jesus accepted it, He had wanted that sorrow, but now He wants it no more. On the contrary He desires that all those redeemed by Him keep watch with him, meditating upon his passion. And yet most of them have fallen into the sleep of the ungrateful, which consists in forgetting the one who loves us and provides for us. What terrible ingratitude and hardness of heart! O good Jesus, we do not know You, because if we knew You, we would think of You of all times and our heart would beat only for You. While my good Jesus languishes alone in agony on the ground, an angel of heaven comes to comfort him.

With the humility of an obedient son, Jesus welcomes the messenger of the Father, and is ready to obey his commands. The angel comes to comfort Jesus, but not to lessen His agony, nor to take the bitter cup away from Him. In fact he urges Jesus to sustain the great battle that he is about to encounter and to receive heroically all the blows with which heaven, the world and hell will strike Him; heaven, as the eternal justice of the Father was to punish in the person of Jesus all the iniquities of humankind; the world, which, unable to bear the holiness of the Son of God, prepares the scaffold for Him, and hell, which, out of hate for the Holy of Holies incites a greater cruelty in the enemies of Jesus so that the angel exhorts Him to drink the abominable cup of all human iniquity to the last drop and to bear the whole burden of divine vengeance.

Meanwhile, justice and mercy await the"Fiat" of Jesus, by which they are to be united for ever. Heaven awaits it, in order to become populated by saints; the earth awaits it as it yearns to see the curse merited by the first sin cancelled by the Blood of the Divine Redeemer; the righteous imprisoned in the breast of Abraham await it in order to be able to fly into the embrace of the Creator; the poor mortal beings await it in order to become once more children of God and to see the doors of Paradise opening for them. But how much that Fiat costs my Jesus; He who is most innocent, he who is holy and immaculate, must take upon Himself the rejection of the sinner and of the wicked: he has to make himself guilty, and take upon Himself our iniquities. This causes Him immense sorrow and makes Him repeat the words: **"Transeat, Transeat a me calix iste!"** *"Let this cup pass me by!"*

But at the same time, He understands that if He does not render himself guilty for our sins, if He does not agree to take upon Himself all the scourges of the penalties of Justice and wash our iniquities in His Blood, we will be lost. Then with a powerful effort of heroic love, Jesus pronounces His great: **"Fiat"**.

In this way He accepts to take upon Himself all our sins and, as if He were to blame for them, He accepts, or rather, invokes upon Himself horrible punishments. Thus he says **"Fiat"** to the thorns in order to expiate our bad thoughts; **"Fiat"** to the scourging in order to punish himself for our sins of sensuality; **"Fiat"** to insults, to being spat upon and to slaps in order to expiate our pride; **"Fiat"** to the vinegar and to the gall in order to expiate our sins of the tongue and of gluttony; **"Fiat"** to the cross and to the nails as reparation for our disobedience; **"Fiat"** to those three hours of atrocious sufferings on the scaffold in order to heal all our wounds and to expiate all our sins; **"Fiat"** to death in order to give us eternal life! O precious **"Fiat"** which gladdens Heaven, saves the Earth, defeats hell! **"Fiat"** which breaks many chains, and wipes away many tears! Thank You, O good Jesus, thank you for Your generous obedience to the plan of the Father. I bless You and thank You in the name of all humankind.

Pause

OFFERINGS

Holy Father, You who in reparation for our rebellious behaviour and disobedience wanted to be honoured by the generous "Fiat" of Jesus in Gethsemane, I offer You that "Fiat" in expiation for all the offences that Your adorable Majesty has received from my rebellious will, imploring You to grant me, by the merits of that same Fiat, perfect meekness and obedience.

Our Father • Hail Mary • Glory Be

Holy Father, for the sake of the glory that the generous "Fiat" of Jesus in Gethsemane caused You, I implore You to forgive all of my rebellious behaviour and dis-obedience, and to grant me to live always in complete submission to Your will and to that of my superiors for love of You.

Our Father • Hail Mary • Glory Be

Holy Father, for the sake of those generous efforts and for those pains which cost Jesus that "Fiat" pronounced in Gethsemane, I implore You to give to me, to all the souls consecrated to You and to all Christians, a spirit of holy fortitude and constancy, united to a generosity which accepts with joy every sacrifice for Your glory.

Our Father • Hail Mary • Glory Be

Chaplet of the Sacred Heart *(See page 233)*

LAST QUARTER OF AN HOUR
The Blood of Jesus and its fruits

My Jesus has thus pronounced the great "Fiat", but the enormous strain of this "Fiat" causes Him to fall once more to the ground in His agony under the enormous weight He has taken upon Himself. On one hand, He feels the pressure of Divine Justice which considers Him to be the universal victim in whom all sins and all punishments are accumulated and on the other hand, He feels the pressure of His infinite desire to fulfil His great mission as Redeemer of the world, which shall follow that painful baptism of blood which He so much desires.

The infinite sorrow which wrings His Heart causes Blood to begin to trickle from all parts of His body and it is shed so copiously that it flows over the earth of Gethsemane. How much that great "Fiat" cost Jesus! How much He had to suffer in order to pay our debts! And how shameful it is that I refuse to make even the smallest sacrifice, while I witness my God who willingly makes Himself a victim for love of me! **Oblatus es quia ipse voluit!** *He is an offering because He wanted to be so!*

But why, sweet Jesus, why consume Yourself with infinite grief? You who with a single prayer, with a sigh, with one beat of your heart, could have saved the whole world. And yet a prophet had already said that the Redemption of Jesus would be generous. And the redemption accomplished by Him is truly generous, as it not only frees us from eternal death but it restores to us the honour of the innocent, of the righteous and of the saints.

Only God could accomplish a work so great! But Jesus is not yet satisfied: His incomprehensible love desires that, through his sorrows, the treasure of His merits may be put into our hands, as something that is entirely ours, and through which we may obtain every blessing from the Most High. What more could we desire? There are blessings so great that no-one would ever dare to ask for them; indeed no-one would ever imagine that they could be obtained. But the infinite mercy of our Blessed Saviour grants us these blessings through the gift of the Eucharist. And as if this would not be sufficient to satisfy His mercy which knows no boundaries, he wants His Spirit, the Divine Paraclete, to fill us and dwell for ever in our souls. "I will pray to the Father," He said that same evening to his disciples, "and He will give you the Holy Spirit."

And now here in Gethsemane, in agony and dripping with blood, He fulfils this promise, thus obtaining for us the pouring out of the Divine Paraclete and raising up humanity in this way to the highest degree of happiness, grace and glory. At this point Jesus can do no more for us, although He still desires to do so. He remembers that his Father said to Him, "Ask me and I shall give you all nations as your inheritance." And raising His forehead dripping with Blood to heaven, He asks his Father that, among the many nations promised to Him as His inheritance, He may have a small group of "spouse souls" who are the beloved of His heart, faithful disciples who imitate His example, and those on whom he can pour out abundantly the graces earned by Him through His great suffering. **"Da mihi animas, da mihi animas, cetera tolle tibi."** *(Father,) give me souls, give me souls, and I shall give you all the rest... ... even my life which shall be consummated on the scaffold for all souls."*

"Da mihi animas." *"Give me souls."*

And among many souls Jesus chose also yours, He desires it ardently, He wants it, He begs the Father for it and renews the offering of His whole being and of His infinite sufferings especially for your soul. O soul, O soul, how much you are loved by that God who, sweating blood, chose you, wanted you, embraced you as His bride! And as Jesus shall soon say to His Mother from the cross, "Here is your son" and thus commend to her all redeemed souls represented by John, in the same way Jesus adresses His Father in the Garden of Gethsemane and says, "Here are your children; I, your natural Son, take the place of the sinner, so that the sinner may take my place and become your child through grace. O Father, chastise *me* and grant peace and forgiveness to the sinner: give *me* death, and give life to the sinner; abandon *me*, O Father, and grant to the sinner perfect, blessed and eternal union with you. Look, here are your children. Embrace them. My blood makes them pure, beautiful and worthy of you.Father, I want (Jesus never said, 'I want' but now He says it) the souls You have given to me become one with us, melted into us, as I am one with You. Remember, O Father, that I humbled myself to become man in order that humankind be raised up to God, and so that it could share Your glory in the Kingdom for all eternity." Here are the unknown mysteries of love which work in the heart of a God who sweats blood for humankind! Here are the marvellous fruits of the Blood of Jesus! Silence, admiration and generous love: these are the only gifts, O redeemed soul, O "spouse soul" of God made man, which you can offer to that Great, to that Holy, to that Infinite Love who sacrifices Himself for you!

Pause

OFFERINGS

Holy Father, with my heart full of sincere gratitude, I thank You in the name of all humanity, for you have given us a Redeemer so good and generous through whom we have regained, along with infinite benefits, the blessings lost with original sin. I offer you the Blood that He shed for the salvation of all those who have been redeemed. Grant that the fruits of Redemption may be as generous as the act of Redemption itself and that Jesus may be known, blessed, loved and thanked by all the children of Adam for all eternity.

Our Father • Hail Mary • Glory Be

Holy Father, I offer you the Precious Blood of Jesus so that I may implore You to grant, in your mercy, the sanctification of the Catholic Church, the conversion of all sinners, the perseverance of the righteous and the liberation of the holy souls of Purgatory. I offer it to You for the greater well-being of all my superiors and of all the persons dearest to me. Futhermore, I offer it to You for the sanctification of my own soul and so that I may obtain the grace of.....

(Here we express our needs and desires)

Our Father • Hail Mary • Glory Be

Holy Father, who loved the world so much that You gave to us your only-begotten Son and offered Him as a sacrifice which was accompained by much suffering, now we ask You to let the world love Jesus ardently, to be grateful to Him, to bless and exalt Him, and we ask You furthermore that many souls may become united to Him in a perfect way and be constantly faithful to him. Grant, Father, that my poor soul may be among such souls. Holy Father, I offer you the pleas, prayers, and anguish of Jesus in Gethsemane, so that you may awake in the heart of all Christians a lively devotion to the wonderful mysteries of Redemption accompanied by that true and generous spirit of sacrifice which renders souls similar to Jesus.

Our Father • Hail Mary • Glory Be

THE HOLY CROSS AND MEDAL OF ST. BENEDICT

BRIEF EXPLANATION OF THE CROSS AND MEDAL OF ST. BENEDICT

An ancient tradition tells us that the medal of St. Benedict was already in use in the seventh century. The devotion became widespread and popular around the year 1050 as a result of the miraculous recovery of a young man who, with ardent faith, touched the medal which had been offered to him. The young man, Brunone by name, subsequently became a Benedictine monk. In later years he was appointed Pope and took the name of Leo IX. Finally, some time after his death, he was canonized, thus bearing witness to the fruits of his faith in the medal.

On one face of the medal there is a simple cross with the following letters between the four arms:

C. S. P. B. - CRUX SANCTI PATRIS BENEDICTI
The Cross of the holy Father Benedict.

Along the vertical arm of the same Cross the following words are found:
C. S. M. L. - CRUX SANCTA SIT MIHI LUX
May the holy Cross be my light.

*On the horizontal arm the following words
are written:*
N. D. S. M. D. - NON DRAGE SIT MIHI DUX
May the devil not be my leader.

Around the cross are the following words:
**V. R. S. N. S. M. V. S. M. Q. L. I. V. B. - VADE
RETRO SATANA, NUMQUAM SUADE MIHI
VANA, SUNT MALA QUAE LIBAS: IPSE
VENENA BIBAS**
*Get behind me, Satan: do not attract me to
vanities, your drinks are evil: drink your
poison yourself.*

On the other face of the medal we find the image
of St. Benedict while standing before the altar at
which he died after receiving the Holy Eucharist;
surrounding the image are the words:

**EJUS. IN. OBITU. NRO. PRAESENTIA
MUNIAMUR.**
May he help us with his presence at our death.

Uses, graces and indulgences associated with the medal

The blessed medal is to be carried on our person in whatever way we desire. Numerous and supernatural favours are obtained for those who use it with great faith in cases of sickness, epidemics and poisoning and also in moments of temptation or danger. The Holy See has enriched it with special indulgences, which benefit the holy souls of Purgatory:

1. A plenary indulgence is granted to those who put into practice one of the following at least once a week:

* *recitation of the Rosary, the Divine Office or the Little Office of the Virgin Mary;*
* *recitation of the Penitential or Gradual Psalms (Psalm 120 - Psalm 134);*
* *a visit to the sick or those in prison, almsgiving to the poor or teaching the first principles of the Faith;*

A plenary indulgence is also granted to those who, having made a good confession, assist at or celebrate Mass, and pray for the Holy Father's intentions (the recitation of five Our fathers is sufficient) on the following feast days:

Christmas Day, Feast of the Epiphany, Feast of the Ascension, Pentecost Sunday, Trinity Sunday, Corpus Christi, Feasts of the Immaculate Conception, Birth, Annunciation, Presentation at the Temple (1st of November) and Assumption of the Blessed Virgin Mary, the feast day of St. Benedict (1st of March) and on All Saints Day.

2. A plenary indulgence is granted once a year to all those who fast every Friday in honour of the passion and death of Our Lord, or fast every Saturday in honour of the Blessed Virgin Mary, fulfilling the usual conditions for the indulgence.

3. A plenary indulgence is granted at the hour of death to those who, even if they are no longer able to receive the Sacraments, invoke verbally or mentally, with true contrition, the Holy Names of Jesus and Mary.

4. *Those who pray for the exaltation of the Holy Church and the preservation of the Holy Father on Holy Thursday or Easter Sunday, having received the Sacrament of Confession and Holy Communion, receive a plenary indulgence which the Pope grants on that day with his solemn apostolic blessing.*

5. *Those who pray to God for the propagation of the order of St. Benedict (the Benedictines) share the spiritual fruits of all prayers and good deeds which are carried out by members of the Order.*

6. *Many partial indulgences are granted, as can be seen in the books which describe the medal in more detail. Besides these indulgence, granted in association with the ancient medal by Pope Benedict XIV on the 23rd of December, 1741, and confirmed by him and by the Papal Brief of the 12th of December, 1742, Pope Pius IX, granted many indulgences, described in the Brief of the 31st of August, 1877, to all those who carried on their person the Jubilee Medal of St. Benedict which the Abbot of Monte Cassino had struck. These indulgences, already given by all Popes to the Cathedral of Montecassino and to the Sanctuary of the Tower inhabited by Saint Benedict, are granted to those who wear the medal, providing that they visit any church or public oratory and pray there for the Pope's intentions, in particular for the conversion of sinners.*

THE MEDAL OF THE HOLY FACE OF OUR LORD JESUS CHRIST

The Medal of the Holy Face was struck in the city of Milan, Italy, at the request of Mother Maria Pierini De Micheli (1890 - 1945), a religious sister of the Daughters of the Immaculate Conception of Buenos Aires. The Blessed Virgin Mary appeared to Sister Maria Pierini one day in the early years of her religious life while she was praying before the Blessed Sacrament. The Virgin was surrounded by a globe of light and held in her hand a scapular made of two pieces of white flannel joined by a little cord: on one face of the scapular was the image of the Holy Face of Our Lord with the following words around it:

"Illumina, Domine, vultum tuum super nos"
Let your face shine upon us.

On the other face, there was a Host, surrounded by rays of light, and the following quotation was inscribed around it:

"Mane nobiscum, Domine."
Stay with us, O Lord.

The Blessed Virgin Mary approached the privileged Sister and said to her, "This scapular, or the medal which repla-

ces it, is a pledge of love and mercy, which Jesus wants to give to the world in these times of sensuality and of hatred of God and the Church. Diabolical nets are being thrown to tear the faith from the hearts of people... A divine remedy is needed. And this remedy is the Holy Face of Jesus. All those who carry on their person a scapular like this, or a medal similar to it, and who visit the Blessed Sacrament every Thursday in reparation for all offences received by the Holy Face of my Son Jesus during his Passion and received by Him everyday in the Sacrament of the Eucharist:

• *Shall be strengthened in their faith.*

• *Shall be ready to defend it.*

• *Shall have the grace to overcome internal or external spiritual difficulties.*

• *Shall be helped in dangers to the body.*

• *Shall die in serenity under the smiling gaze of my Divine Son".*

*The message, entrusted to the privileged sister, could not have been more gentle nor more precious; gentle because it concerns the face of the Redeemer and the Sacred Host, **precious because it ensures perseverance** in faith and a happy death.*
Mother Maria Pierini encountered strong opposition to the fulfilment of the message: permission was not given to strike medals of the Holy Face and moreover, the financial means were lacking. Both difficulties were admirably over-come: the permission which had been refused to everyone,

was eventually given; and an envelope containing the exact sum of money required was found one morning on the table in the room of Mother Maria Pierina.

The medal was struck and it was presented first to Pope Pius XII. Its distribution then began. The medal was immediately acknowledged to be miraculous; everyone felt a great power from it: men, women, children, the healthy, the wealthy, the sick, prisoners, soldiers, Christians and Jews alike. On earth, at sea, in aeroplanes and even in submarines, numerous miracles have occurred and continue to happen in association with this medal, and countless graces have been granted. No-one who has received a death sentence has been killed after having been given the medal. Indeed, our soul is prompted to exclaim: What do you want, O Lord, through the medal of your Holy Face?

We are invited to carry it on our person and it is recommended to recite five Glory Bes every day in honour of the Holy Face of Our Lord Jesus. It can be said with absolute certainty that, sooner or later, the devotion allows us to feel that we are carrying a powerful means of protection on our person. Therefore we invite the reader to wear it and thus experience its wonderful benefits.

"Lord, at the hour of our death, look upon us with the merciful gaze with which you looked upon the repentant thief."

DAILY PRAYER OF OFFERING
TO THE HOLY FACE OF JESUS

Holy Face of my sweet Jesus, living and eternal expression of love and of Divine Martyrdom, suffered for the Redemption of humanity, I adore and love you.

I consecrate myself to you, today and always.

I offer you, through the most pure hands of the Immaculate Queen, the prayers, actions and sufferings of this day, in expiation and in reparation for the sins of all poor creat-ures.

Make me one of your disciples.

May I always contemplate your gentle gaze, and may it light up with mercy at the hour of my death.

Amen.

NOVENA TO THE HOLY FACE OF OUR LORD JESUS CHRIST

In the name of the Father, and of the Son, and of the Holy Spirit. Amen.

O God, come to my aid.
O Lord, make haste to help me.
Glory Be
The Creed *(see page 26)*

Most sweet Face of Jesus, who, with infinite gentleness, looked at the shepherds and the three holy Magi who came to adore you in the stable at Bethlehem, look with tenderness at my soul too, which, prostrate before you, praises and blesses you, and graciously hear my prayer.

Glory Be

Most sweet Face of Jesus, who, moved to compassion when confronted by human affliction, wiped away tears of suffering and healed the bodies of those in pain, look with kindness at the miseries of my soul and at the physical infirmities which make me suffer. For the sake of the tears you shed, strengthen what is good in me, deliver me from evil, and grant me what I ask you.

Glory Be

Most compassionate Face of Jesus, who, having come to this valley of tears, were moved so much by our affliction that you called yourself doctor for the sick and Good Shepherd of those who had gone astray, do not let Satan prevail over me but keep me always under your gaze, together with all the souls who comfort you.

Glory Be

Most holy Face of Jesus, worthy only of praise and love, and yet struck and spat upon in the most bitter tragedy of our Redemption, turn towards me with that gaze of merciful love with which you looked at the good thief. Grant me to understand the heavenly wisdom of humility and charity.

Glory Be

O Divine Face of Jesus, who, with eyes wet with blood, lips sprinkled with gall, your forehead wounded, and your cheeks bleeding, sent a most precious cry from the wood of the cross in your unsatisfied thirst, I ask you to keep that blessed thirst for me and for those dear to me. And now, in your kidness, hear my prayer for this urgent need of mine.

(Here we express our intention)
Glory Be

DEVOTION TO THE
HOLY NAME OF JESUS

JESUS AND THOSE WHO BLASPHEME

In 1843, Jesus revealed the following to the Servant of God, Sr. Marie of St. Peter, a Carmelite nun of Tours (France), and Apostle of Reparation: "Blasphemy against 'my name' is committed by everyone: even children swear and this horrible sin openly wounds my Heart. The sinner with his blasphemies curses God, challenges him openly, crushes Redemption, pronounces his own condemnation.

Blasphemy is a poisoned lance which penetrates my heart. I will give you a golden lance in order to heal the wound of sinners, and it is this:

'May the most holy, most sacred, most adorable, most incomprehensive and ineffable Name of God be forever praised, blessed, loved, adored and glorified in Heaven, on earth, and under the earth, by all the creatures of God and by the Sacred Heart of Our Lord Jesus Christ, in the Most Holy Sacrament of the Altar. Amen.'

Every time you repeat these words you will wound my Heart with love. You cannot understand the malice and the horror of blasphemy... Oh, if only you knew the degree of glory that heaven would give you if you only said:

'O admirable Name of God!'
*in a spirit of reparation
for the blasphemies committed."*

ROSARY OF REPARATION IN HONOUR OF THE HOLY NAME OF JESUS

In 1846, the Virgin Mary appeared at La Salette, France, crying and complaining that she could no longer hold off the arm of Divine Justice provoked by blasphemers. The Virgin said that grave chastisements would occur if people did not cease to insult the Holy Name of God.

On the beads of the Our Father we recite the Glory Be and the following powerful prayer suggested by Jesus himself:

"May the most holy, most sacred, most adorable, most incomprehensive and ineffable Name of God be forever praised, blessed, loved, adored and glorified in Heaven, on earth, and under the earth, by all the creatures of God and by the Sacred Heart of Our Lord Jesus Christ, in the Most Holy Sacrament of the Altar. Amen."

*On the beads of the Hail Mary
we recite the following invocation ten times:*
"Divine Heart of Jesus, convert sinners, save the dying, free the holy souls of Purgatory."

We conclude the Rosary with the following prayers:

**Glory Be
Hail Holy Queen
Eternal rest...**

LITANY TO THE MOST HOLY NAME OF JESUS

Lord, have mercy on us.

Christ, have mercy on us.

Lord, have mercy on us.

Jesus, graciously hear us.

God the Father of heaven,

Have mercy on us.

God the Son, Redeemer of the world,

Have mercy on us.

God the Holy Spirit,

Have mercy on us.

Holy Trinity, one God,

Have mercy on us.

Jesus, Son of the living God,

Have mercy on us.

Jesus, splendour of the Father,

Have mercy on us.

Jesus, brightness of eternal light,

Have mercy on us.

Jesus, King of glory,

Have mercy on us.

Jesus, sun of justice,

Have mercy on us.

Jesus, Son of the Virgin Mary,

Have mercy on us.

Jesus, most amiable,

Have mercy on us.

Jesus, most admirable,

Have mercy on us.

Jesus, mighty God,

Have mercy on us.

Jesus, Father of the world to come,

Have mercy on us.

Jesus, angel of the great council,

Have mercy on us.

Jesus, most powerful,

Have mercy on us.

Jesus, most patient,

Have mercy on us.

Jesus, most obedient,

Have mercy on us.

Jesus, meek and humble of heart

Have mercy on us.

Jesus, lover of chastity,

Have mercy on us.

Jesus, lover of us,

Have mercy on us.

Jesus, God of peace,

Have mercy on us.

Jesus, author of life

Have mercy on us.

Jesus, model of virtues,

Have mercy on us.

Jesus, lover of souls,

Have mercy on us.

Jesus, our God,

Have mercy on us.

Jesus, our refuge,

Have mercy on us.

Jesus, treasure of the faithful,

Have mercy on us.

Jesus, Good Shepherd,

Have mercy on us.

Jesus, true light,

Have mercy on us.

Jesus, eternal wisdom,

Have mercy on us.

Jesus, infinite goodness,

Have mercy on us.

Jesus, our way and our life,

Have mercy on us.

Jesus, joy of angels,

Have mercy on us.

Jesus, King of patriarchs,

Have mercy on us.

Jesus, master of apostles,

Have mercy on us.

Jesus, teacher of evangelists,

Have mercy on us.

Jesus, strength of martyrs,

Have mercy on us.

Jesus, light of confessors,

Have mercy on us.

Jesus, purity of virgins,

Have mercy on us.

Jesus, crown of all saints,

Have mercy on us.

Be merciful,

Spare us, O Jesus.

Be merciful,

Graciously hear us, O Jesus.

From all evil,

Jesus, deliver us.

From all sin,

Jesus, deliver us.

From the snares of the devil,

Jesus, deliver us.

From impurity of spirit,

Jesus, deliver us.

From everlasting death,

Jesus, deliver us.

From the neglect of your inspirations,

Jesus, deliver us.

Through the mystery of Your holy incarnation,

Jesus, deliver us.

Through Your nativity,

Jesus, deliver us.

Through Your infancy,

Jesus, deliver us.

Through Your most divine life,

Jesus, deliver us.

Through Your labours,

Jesus, deliver us.

Through Your agony and Passion,

Jesus, deliver us.

Through Your cross and dereliction,

Jesus, deliver us.

Through Your sufferings,

Jesus, deliver us.

Through Your death and burial,

Jesus, deliver us.

Through Your Resurrection,

Jesus, deliver us.

Through Your Ascension,

Jesus, deliver us.

Through Your institution of the most
Holy Eucharist,

Jesus, deliver us.

Through Your joys,

Jesus, deliver us.

Through Your glory,

Jesus, deliver us.

.

Let us pray:

Yahweh our Lord, how majestic is your name throughout the world!

Whoever keeps singing of your majesty higher than the heavens, even through the mouths of children, or of babes in arms, you make him a fortress, firm against your foes, to subdue the enemy and the rebel.

I look up at your heavens, shaped by your fingers, at the moon and the stars you set firm what are human beings that you spare a thought for them, or the child of Adam that you care for him? Yet you have made him little less than a god, you have crowned him with glory and beauty, made him lord of the works of your hands, put all things under his feet, sheep and cattle, all of them, and even the wild beasts, birds in the sky, fish in the sea, when he makes his way across the ocean.

Yahweh our Lord,
how majestic your name throughout the world!

(Psalm 8)

LITANY OF THE SACRED HEAD OF JESUS

"It is God's will that his Sacred Head be adored as the Sanctuary of Divine Wisdom, as the Temple of the powers of the soul and of the faculties of the spirit, and within these the Wisdom which guided every affection of the Sacred Heart and all the movements of the entire Being of Jesus, our Lord and our God."   *Teresa Higginson*

Teresa Higginson (1844-1905) is buried at Neston (Cheshire, England). Her experience as a Catholic teacher was exemplary. She bore her heavy crosses patiently and received the heavenly favours of the stigmata and a mystical marriage. She was chosen to convey to the world the great desire of Jesus to see his Sacred Head be adored as a Sanctuary of Divine Wisdom, and as an act of reparation for intellectual pride, one of the great evils of our times. Jesus said to Teresa Higginson in a private revelation, "I desire that the first Friday after the feast of my Sacred Heart be reserved as a feast in honour of my Sacred Head which is the Temple of Divine Wisdom, and that public adoration be offered to me in order to repair for all outrages and sins which are continuously committed against me!". He also promised, "Whoever helps you to spread this devotion will be blessed a thousand times... To all those who honour me, I will give my power. I will be their God and they will be my children. I will put my sign on their foreheads and my seal on their lips". (In this context, "seal" signifies Wisdom). Teresa tells us, "He made me understand that he will crown and cover with particular glory all those who have striven to make progress in this devotion. He will clothe them in glory before the angels and before humankind."
Thus devotion to the Sacred Head shall receive its crown.

Lord,

Have mercy on us.

Jesus Christ,

Have mercy on us.

Lord,

Have mercy on us.

Jesus Christ,

Hear us.

Jesus Christ,

Hear my prayer.

God the Father of heaven,

Have mercy on us.

God the Son, Redeemer of the world,

Have mercy on us.

God the Holy Spirit,

Have mercy on us.

Holy Trinity, one God,

Have mercy on us.

Sacred Head of Jesus, formed by the
    Holy Spirit in the womb of Mary,

Have mercy on us.

Sacred Head of Jesus, united substantially
    to the Word of God,

Have mercy on us.

Sacred Head of Jesus, Temple of Divine Wisdom,
Have mercy on us.

Sacred Head of Jesus, Heart of eternal light,

Have mercy on us.

Sacred Head of Jesus, Sanctuary of
  infinite intelligence,

Have mercy on us.

Sacred Head of Jesus, Providence against error,

Have mercy on us.

Sacred Head of Jesus, Sun of heaven and earth,

Have mercy on us.

Sacred Head of Jesus, Treasure of Science
  and token of the Faith,

Have mercy on us.

Sacred Head of Jesus, radiant with beauty,
  justice and love,

Have mercy on us.

Sacred Head of Jesus, full of grace and of truth,

Have mercy on us.

Sacred Head of Jesus, living Lesson of humility,

Have mercy on us.

Sacred Head of Jesus, Reflection of the
  infinite Majesty of God,

Have mercy on us.

Sacred Head of Jesus, centre of the Universe,

Have mercy on us.

Sacred Head of Jesus, in whom the
  Heavenly Father is well pleased,

Have mercy on us.

Sacred Head of Jesus, caressed by
  the Virgin Mary,

Have mercy on us.

Sacred Head of Jesus, upon which the
　　Holy Spirit rested,

Have mercy on us.

Sacred Head of Jesus, who allowed a reflection
　　of Your Glory to shine on Mount Tabor,

Have mercy on us.

Sacred Head of Jesus, who had no place
　　to rest on earth,

Have mercy on us.

Sacred Head of Jesus, who welcomed the
　　anointing with nard by Mary,

Have mercy on us.

Sacred Head of Jesus, who on entering the
　　house of Simon, graciously reminded
　　him that he had not oiled your Head,

Have mercy on us.

Sacred Head of Jesus, flooded with a sweat
　　of blood in the Garden of Gethsemane,

Have mercy on us.

Sacred Head of Jesus, who wept for our sins,

Have mercy on us.

Sacred Head of Jesus, crowned with thorns,

Have mercy on us.

Sacred Head of Jesus, offended with
　　abuse during your Passion,

Have mercy on us.

Sacred Head of Jesus, comforted by the
　　loving action of Veronica,

Have mercy on us.

Sacred Head of Jesus which inclined towards
the earth at the moment at which you
saved it on the cross through the
separation of your Soul from your Body,

Have mercy on us.

Sacred Head of Jesus, Light of everyone
who is born into this world,

Have mercy on us.

Sacred Head of Jesus, our Guide and our Hope,

Have mercy on us.

Sacred Head of Jesus, who knows all our needs,

Have mercy on us.

Sacred Head of Jesus, who grants all graces,

Have mercy on us.

Sacred Head of Jesus, which guides the
movements of the Divine Heart,

Have mercy on us.

Sacred Head of Jesus, who governs the world,

Have mercy on us.

Sacred Head of Jesus, who judges all our actions,

Have mercy on us.

Sacred Head of Jesus, who knows the
depths of our hearts,

Have mercy on us.

Sacred Head of Jesus which we want to
make known and adored throughout
all the earth,

Have mercy on us.

Sacred Head of Jesus, which entraptures
    all Angels and Saints,

Have mercy on us.

Sacred Head of Jesus, which we hope one
    day to contemplate,

Have mercy on us.

We adore your Sacred Head, O Jesus,
**And we submit ourselves to all the decrees
of your Infinite Wisdom.**

Let us pray.
O Jesus, who deigned to reveal to your servant
Teresa Higginson your immense desire to see
your Sacred Head adored, grant us the joy of
spreading devotion to it so that it may become
known and honoured. Let a ray of your light
descend upon our souls so that we may go
forward, from light to light, led by your Adorable
Wisdom, towards the reward promised to your
chosen ones. **Amen.**

7.

THE MERCY OF JESUS

- **Words from Scripture**

- **Devotion to The Divine Mercy**

- **The Sanctuary of Merciful Love**

WORDS FROM SCRIPTURE

WORDS OF INCARNATE WISDOM ABOUT MERCY

In the following quotations from scripture, St. Louis De Montfort gathers from the living voice of Jesus the essential ideas and teachings which must be followed by those who desire to live a life which conforms to that of Christ who is Wisdom Incarnate and Eternal!

1. "If anyone wants to be a follower of mine, let him renounce himself and take up his cross every day and follow me" *(Lk 9: 23)*.

2. "Anyone who loves me will keep my word, and my Father will love him, and we shall come to him and make a home in him" *(Jn 14:23)*.

3. "So then, if you are bringing your offering to the altar and there remember that your brother has something against you, leave your offering there before the altar, go and be reconciled with your brother first, and then come back and present your offering" *(Mt 5:23-24)*.

4. "Anyone who comes to me without hating his father, mother, wife, children, brothers, sisters, yes and his own life too, cannot be my disciple" *(Lk 14:26)*.

5. "Everyone who has left houses, brothers, sisters, father, mother, children or land for the sake of my name will receive a hundred times as much, and also inherit eternal life" *(Mt 19:29)*.

6. "If you wish to be perfect, go and sell your possessions and give the money to the poor, and you will have treasure in heaven; then come and follow me" *(Mt 19:21)*.

7. "It is not anyone who says to me, 'Lord, Lord', who will enter the kingdom of Heaven, but the person who does the will of my Father in heaven" *(Mt 7:21)*.

8. "Therefore, everyone who listens to these words of mine and acts on them will be like a sensible man who built his house on rock" *(Mt 7:24)*.

9. "In truth I tell you, unless you change and become like little children you will never enter the kingdom of Heaven" *(Mt 18:3)*.

10. "Shoulder my yoke and learn from me, for I am gentle and humble in heart, and you will find rest for your souls" *(Mt 11:29)*.

11. "And when you pray, do not imitate the hypocrites: they love to say their prayers standing up in synagogues and at the streets corners for people to see them" *(Mt 6:5)*.

12. "In your prayers do not babble... as your Father knows what you need before you ask him" *(Mt 6:7-8)*.

13. "And when you stand in prayer, forgive whatever you have against anybody, so that your Father in Heaven may forgive your failings too" *(Mk 11:25)*.

14. "I tell you, therefore, everything you ask and pray for, believe that you have it already, and it will be yours" *(Mk 11:24)*.

15. "When you are fasting, do not put on a gloomy look as the hypocrites do: they go about looking unsightly to let people know they are fasting. In truth I tell you, they have had their reward" *(Mt 6:16)*.

16. "There will be more rejoicing in heaven over one sinner repenting than over ninety-nine upright people who have no need of repentance" *(Lk 15:7)*.

17. "I have come to call not the upright but sinners to repentance" (Lk 5: 32).

18. "Blessed are those who are persecuted in the cause of uprightness: the kingdom of Heaven is theirs" *(Mt 5:10)*.

19. "Blessed are you when people hate you, drive you out, abuse you... on account of the Son of man. Rejoice... because look! your reward will be great in heaven" *(Lk 6:22-23)*.

20. "If the world hates you, you must realise that it hated me before it hated you. If you belonged to the world, the world would love you as its own; but because you do not belong to the world... that is why the world hates you" *(Jn 15:18-19)*.

21. "Come to me, all you who labour and are overburdened, and I will give you rest".   *(Mt 11:28)*.

22. "I am the living bread which has come down from heaven. Anyone who eats this bread will live for ever; and the bread that I shall give is my flesh, for the life of the world" *(Jn 6:51)*.

23. "For my flesh is real food and my blood is real drink. Whoever eats my flesh and drinks my blood lives in me and I live in that person" *(Jn 6:55-56)*.

24. "You will be hated universally on account of my name, but not a hair of your head will be lost" *(Lk 21:17-18)*.

25. "No one can be the slave of two masters, he will either hate the first and love the second, or be attached to the first and despise the second" *(Mt 6:24)*.

26. "For from the heart come evil intentions... These are the things that make a person unclean. But eating with unwashed hands does not make anyone unclean" *(Mt 15:19-20)*.

27. "Good people draw good things from their store of goodness; bad people draw bad things from their store of badness" *(Mt 12:35)*.

28. "Once the hand is laid on the plough, no one who looks back is fit for the kingdom of God" *(Lk 9:62)*.

29. "Why, every hair on your head has been counted. There is no need to be afraid: you are worth more than many sparrows" *(Lk 12:7)*.

30. "For God has sent him into the world not to judge the world, but that through him the world will be saved" *(Jn 3:17)*.

31. "Everybody who does wrong hates the light and avoids it, to prevent his actions from being shown up" *(Jn 3:20)*.

32. "God is spirit, and those who worship must worship in spirit and truth" *(Jn 4:24)*.

33. "It is the spirit that gives life, the flesh has nothing to offer. The words I have spoken to you are spirit and they are life" *(Jn 6:63)*.

34. "Everyone who commits sin is a slave. Now a slave has not permanent standing in the household, but a son belongs to it for ever" *(Jn 8:34-35)*.

35. "Anyone who is trustworthy in little things is trustworthy in great; anyone who is dishonest in little things is dishonest in great" *(Lk 16:10)*.

36. "It is easier for heaven and earth to disappear than for one little stroke to drop out of the Law" *(Lk 16:17)*.

37. "Your light must shine in people's sight, so that, seeing your good works, they may give praise to your Father in heaven" *(Mt 5:16)*.

38. "If your uprightness does not surpass that of the scribes and Pharisees, you will never get into the Kingdom of Heaven" *(Mt 5:20)*.

39. "If your right eye should be your downfall, tear it out and throw it away; for it will do you less harm to lose one part of yourself than to have your whole body thrown into hell" *(Mt 5:29)*.

40. "The kingdom of heaven has been subjected to violence and the violent are taking it by storm" *(Mt 11:12)*.

41. "Do not store up treasures for yourselves on earth, where moth and woodworm destroy them and thieves can break in and steal. But store up treasures for yourselves in heaven... where thieves cannot break in and steal" *(Mt 6:19-20)*.

42. "Do not judge, and you will not be judged; because the judgements you give are the judgements you will get" *(Mt 7:1-2)*.

43. "Beware of false prophets who come to you disguised as sheep but underneath are ravenous wolves. You will able to tell them by their fruits" *(Mt 7:15-16)*.

44. "See that you never despise any of these little ones, for I tell you that their angels in heaven are continually in the presence of my Father in heaven" *(Mt 18:10)*.

45. "So stay awake because you do not know either the day or the hour" *(Mt 25:13)*.

46. "Do not be afraid of those who kill the body and after that can do no more... Fear him who, after he has killed, has the power to cast into hell" *(Lk 12:4-5)*.

47. "That is why I am telling you not to worry about your life and what you are to eat, nor about your body and how you are to clothe it... Your Father well knows you need (these things)" *(Lk 12:22-30)*.

48. "For nothing is hidden but it will be made clear, nothing secret but it will be made known and brought to light" *(Lk 8:17)*.

49. "Anyone who wants to become great among you must be your servant, and anyone who wants to be first among you must be your slave" *(Mt 20:26-27)*.

50. "How hard it is for those who have riches to enter the kingdom of God!" *(Mk 10:23)*.

51. "It is easier for a camel to pass through the eye of a needle than for someone rich to enter the kingdom of God" *(Lk 18:25)*.

52. "But I say to you: love your enemies and pray for those who persecute you" *(Mt 5:44)*.

53. "But alas for you who are rich: you are having your consolation now" *(Lk 6:24)*.

54. "Enter by the narrow gate, since the road that leads to destruction is wide and spacious, and many take it; but it is a narrow gate and a hard road that leads to life, and only a few find it" *(Mt 7:13-14)*.

55. "The last will be first, and the first, last" *(Mt 20:16)*. "For many are invited but not all are chosen". *(Mt 22:14)*. "There is more happiness in giving than in receiving!" *(Ac 20:35)*.

56. "If anyone hits you on the right cheek, offer him the other as well; if someone wishes to go to law with you to get your tunic, let him have your cloak as well" *(Mt 5:39-40)*.

57. "He told them a parable about the need to pray continually and never to lose heart" *(Lk 18:1)*. "Stay awake and pray not to be put to the test" *(Mt 26:41)*.

58. "For anyone who raises himself up will be humbled, and the one who humbles himself will be raised up" *(Lk 14:11)*.

59. "Give alms from what you have and, look, everything will be clean for you" *(Lk 11:41)*.

60. "If your hand or your foot should be your downfall, cut it off and throw it away: it is better for you to enter into life crippled or lame, than to have two hands or two feet and be thrown into eternal fire. And if your eye should be your downfall, tear it out and throw it away: it is better for you to enter into life with one eye, than to have two eyes and be thrown into the hell of fire" *(Mt 18:8-9)*.

61. " 'Lord, how often must I forgive my brother if he wrongs me? As often as seven times?'. Jesus answered, 'Not seven, I tell you, but seventy-seven times' " *(Mt 18:21-22)*.

62. The eight Beatitudes:
- Blessed are the poor in spirit: the kingdom of Heaven is theirs.
- Blessed are the gentle: they shall have the earth as inheritance.
- Blessed are those who mourn: they shall be comforted.
- Blessed are those who hunger and thirst for uprightness: they shall have their fill.
- Blessed are the merciful: they shall have mercy shown them.
- Blessed are the pure in heart: they shall see God.
- Blessed are the peacemakers: they shall be recognised as children of God.
- Blessed are those who are persecuted in the cause of uprightness: the kingdom of Heaven is theirs" *(Mt 5,3-10)*.

63. "I bless you, Father, Lord of Heaven and of earth, for hiding these things from the learned and the clever and revealing them to little children. Yes, Father, for that is what it pleased you to do" *(Mt 11:25-26)*.

These are the great and important truths that Divine Wisdom came on earth to teach us, after having put them into practice, in order to heal us of our blindness and dispel the confusion caused by our sins. Happy are those who comprehend these eternal truths! Even happier are those who believe in them!

Even happier therefore, are those, who believe in them, put them into practice and teach them to others.

**They shall shine like stars in heaven
for all eternity.**

# DEVOTION TO DIVINE MERCY
(FROM THE WRITINGS OF SAINT FAUSTINA KOWALSKA)

INTRODUCTION

1. Trust characterizes our attitude towards God and expresses not only hope, but also a lively faith, humility, perseverance and repentance for the sins we have committed. Thus, it is a childlike attitude with which we trust without reserve in every situation, in the merciful love and omnipotence of the Heavenly Father.

Trust is an essential element of devotion to The Divine Mercy, without which this devotion could not exist. In fact, there is an act of trust at its very origin. Indeed the attitude of trust alone (even without the practice of other forms of this devotion) is sufficient to obtain graces from the mercy of God.

"I desire to grant unimaginable graces," *said the Lord,* "to those souls who trust in my Mercy" *(Diary, 687)* "I have opened My Heart as a living fountain of mercy. Let all souls draw life from it Let them approach this sea of mercy with great trust. Sinners will attain justification, and the just will be confirmed in good. Whoever places his trust in My mercy will be filled with My divine peace at the hour of death" *(Diary, 1520).*

Trust is not only the essence and the founda-

tion of devotion to The Divine Mercy, but it is also a condition to receive graces. "The graces of my Mercy," - *explained Jesus to Sister Faustina,* "are drawn by means of only one vessel, and that is - trust. The more a soul trusts, the more it will receive. Souls that trust boundlessly are a great comfort to Me, because I pour all the treasures of My graces into them. I rejoice that they ask for much, because it is My desire to give much, very much. On the other hand, I am sad when souls ask for little, when the narrow their hearts" *(Diary, 1578).* On one occasion Jesus said to Saint Faustina, "No soul that has called upon My mercy has been disappointed or brought to shame. I delight particularly in a soul which has placed its trust in my goodness" *(Diary, 1541)* Indeed the benefits of the soul that trusts in God's mercy are manifold, for Jesus said, "The soul which will trust in My mercy is most fortunate, because I myself take care of it" *(Diary, 1273).*

2. Mercy *characterizes our attitude towards everyone. Jesus said to Saint Faustina,* "My daughter ... I demand from you deeds of mercy, which are to arise out of love for Me. You are to show mercy to your neighbours always and everywhere. You must not shrink from this or try to excuse or absolve yourself from it.

I am giving you three ways of exercising mercy toward your neighbour: the first - by deed, the second - by work, the third - by prayer. In these three degrees is contained the fullness of mercy, and it is an unquestionable proof of love for Me. By this means a soul glorifies and pays reverence to My mercy" *(Diary, 742). Acts of mercy towards one's neighbour are a necessary condition to receive graces. Jesus said,* "If a soul does not exercise mercy in somehow or other, it will not obtain My mercy on the day of judgement. Oh, if only souls knew how to gather eternal treasure for themselves, they would not be judged, for they would forestall My judgement with their mercy" *(Diary, 1317).* Furthermore, to encourage those who feel limited in their capacities to do good works, He said, "Write this for the many souls who are often worried because they do not have the material means with which to carry out an act of mercy. Yet spiritual mercy, which requires neither permissions nor storehouses, is much more meritorious and is within the grasp of every soul" *(Diary, 1317).*

Jesus desires that his faithful do at least one act of mercy every day. In this way they help their neighbour and remind others of the infinite Mercy of God. "My daughter," He said to Saint Faustina, "Know that My Heart is mercy itself. From this sea of mercy, graces flow out upon the whole world. No soul that has ever approached me has ever gone away unconsoled. All misery gets buried in the depths of My mercy, and every saving and sanctifying grace comes from this fountain... I desire that this mercy flow out upon the whole world through your heart. Let no-one who approaches you go away without that trust in My mercy which I so ardently desire for souls.

Pray as much as you can for the dying.

By your entreaties, obtain for them trust in My mercy, because they have most need of trust, and have it the least. Be assured that the grace of eternal salvation for certain souls in their final moment depends on your prayer.

You know the whole abyss of My mercy, so draw upon it for yourself and especially for poor sinners.

Sooner would heaven and earth turn into nothingness than would My mercy not embrace a trusting soul" *(Diary, 1777)*.

ACT OF FAITH IN THE DIVINE MERCY

O most merciful Jesus, your goodness is infinite and the riches of your graces are inexhaustible. I trust completely in your mercy which exceeds all of your works. I give myself to you without reserve, in order to live and reach Christian perfection.

I desire to adore and to exalt your mercy, putting into practice works of mercy both corporal and spiritual, in order to obtain above all the conversion of sinners and to give consolation to those who need it, to the sick and to the afflicted.

Protect me, O Jesus, as I belong only to you and to your glory. The fear which seizes me as soon as I become aware of my weakness is conquered by my immense faith in your mercy. May all people come to know in time the infinite depth of your mercy, may they trust in it and may they praise it for ever.
Amen.

GESU CONFIDO IN TE

The image of the vision which Saint Faustina had in Plock
on the 22nd of February, 1931.

THE IMAGE OF THE MERCIFUL JESUS

The picture of the Merciful Jesus is an iconographic representation of the vision which Saint Faustina Kowalska had on the 22nd of February, 1931, in which Christ ordered that he be painted in the same way as he revealed himself. "In the evening, when I was in my cell," the sister tells us, "I saw the Lord Jesus clothed in a white garment. One hand (was) raised in the gesture of blessing, the other was touching the garment at the breast. From beneath the garment, slightly drawn aside at the breast, there were emanating two large rays, one red, the other pale. (...) After a while, Jesus said to me, 'Paint an image according to the pattern you see, with the signature: Jesus, I trust in You!' *"* (Diary, 47).

Three years later, with the help of her confessor Father Sopocko, Sister Kowalska witnessed the fulfilment of the order Jesus had given: an artist from Vilnius, E. Kazimiowski, had painted the Divine Mercy according to the directions of Sister Faustina. Although many other painters have been inspired by this first picture, it must be emphasized that the "original", the model, remains the most faithful to the vision described by the mystic. The Christ of the picture is the living Christ who is walking, the Resurrected Christ who goes towards all people. The background is dark with no element of landscape, while the light around the head of our Saviour has the form of a halo.

While the image represents the risen Christ, it is noteworthy that He bears the signs of the crucifixion in his hands and feet. From his pierced heart, which is not visible in the picture, issue forth two rays - one red and the other pale. Christ himself explained the deep symbolical meaning of the two rays: "The two rays denote Blood and Water. The pale ray stands for the Water which makes souls righteous.The red ray stands for the Blood which is the life of souls... These two rays issued forth from the very depths of My tender mercy when My agonized Heart was opened by a lance on the Cross" *(Diary, 299).*

In other words, these two rays represent both the Sacraments of the Church to which the pierced Heart of Christ gave birth, and the gifts of the Holy Spirit whose biblical symbol is water. In reference to the same rays, Jesus said, "Happy is the one who will dwell in their shelter, for the just hand of God shall not lay hold of him" (Diary, 299).

The image itself, according to the words of Jesus, "is to be a reminder of the demands of My mercy, because even the strongest faith is of no avail without works" (Diary, 742). Devotion to this image involves prayer with trust united to works of mercy. Jesus has associated the following promises to such devotion: the grace of salvation, great progress along the road of Christian perfection, the grace of a holy death, as well as all the other graces and earthly benefits requested with confidence by the faithful. The Lord said, "I am offering people a vessel with which they are to keep coming for graces to the fountain of mercy. That vessel is this image with the signature: 'Jesus, I trust in you' " (Diary, 327).

"By means of this Image I shall be granting many graces to souls; so let every soul have access to it" (Diary, 570).

"I promise that the soul that will venerate this image will not perish. I also promise victory over (its) enemies already here on earth, especially at the hour of death. I Myself will defend it as My own glory" (Diary, 48).

"The flames of mercy are burning Me. I desire to pour them out upon human souls. Oh, what pain they cause Me when they do not want to accept them!...Tell aching mankind to snuggle close to My merciful Heart, and I will fill it with peace" (Diary, 1074).

"Mankind will not have peace until it turns with trust to

My mercy" (Diary, 50)

"Write down these words, my daughter. Speak to the world about My mercy; let all mankind recognize My unfathomable mercy. It is a sign for the end times; after it will come the day of justice. While there is still time, let them have recourse to the fount of My mercy; let them profit from the Blood and Water which gushed forth for them" (Diary, 848).

"Before I come as a just Judge, I first open wide the door of My mercy. He who refuses to pass through the door of My mercy must pass through the door of My justice..." (Diary, 1146).

The first public exhibition of the picture painted by Kazimirowski took place at Vilnius in April of the year 1935 at the closure of the Jubilee Year of Redemption.

During the celebration Saint Faustina saw how many of the faithful received graces. "When I was at Ostra Brama to attend the ceremony during which the image was displayed, I heard a sermon given by my confessor (Father Sopocko). This sermon about Divine Mercy was the first of the things that Jesus had asked for so very long ago. When he began to speak about the great mercy of the Lord, the image came alive and the rays pierced the hearts of the people gathered there, but not all to the same degree. Some received more, some less. Great joy filled my soul to see the grace of God" (Diary, 417).

This vision illustrates the boundless generosity of God who lavishes his mercy upon humanity. It depends only on us when and how much we receive; prayer and trust in God determine the measure of this generous gift from God.

The picture is a physical sign of the great mystery of the Merciful Love of God, which is no less before a great sinner, but rather welcomes the latter's plea for mercy with infinite patience.

THE CHAPLET OF THE DIVINE MERCY

The Chaplet of The Divine Mercy was dictated by Our Lord to Saint Faustina Kowalska at Vilnius in the year 1935. In the revelations which followed, Jesus explained the value and efficacy of this prayer together with the promises associated with it.

In this prayer we offer to God the Father "the Body and Blood, Soul and Divinity" of Jesus Christ and we unite ourselves to His sacrifice on the cross for the salvation of the whole world. By offering to God the Father his Beloved Son, we use the most powerful means of having a prayer granted. We implore mercy for ourselves and for the entire world. The word "us" in this prayer indicates both the person who is reciting the Chaplet and all those for whom he or she wishes to pray. On the other hand the expression "entire world" signifies all people living on the earth and also the holy souls of Purgatory. By praying with the words of the Chaplet, we are carrying out an act of fraternal love which, associated with trust in God, constitutes an indispensable condition for obtaining the graces associated with this devotion.

The Chaplet originates from the mystical vision seen by Saint Faustina Kowalska in which she saw an angel who was punishing the world for its sins.

Wanting to calm the wrath of God, she felt at first the strength of grace in her heart, then she began to implore Him with the following words heard interiorly:

"Eternal Father, I offer you the Body and Blood, Soul and Divinity of your dearly beloved Son, our Lord Jesus Christ, in atonement for our sins and those of the whole world; for the sake of His sorrowful Passion, have mercy on us"(Diary, 475). As she was praying in this manner, she sas the Angel's helplessness: "He could not carry out the just punishment which was rightly due for sins"(Diary, 474).

Subsequently, Jesus himself recommended the recitation of the Chaplet, saying to Sister Faustina, "My daughter, encourage souls to say the chaplet which I have given to you. It pleases Me to grant everything they ask of Me by saying the chaplet. When hardened sinners say it, I will fill their souls with peace, and the hour of their death will be a happy one" (Diary, 1541).

The promises associated with the Chaplet refer to the hour of death, and in particular to the grace of dying in serenity and peace. This grace may be granted not only to those who have recited the chaplet with trust and perseverance, but also to the dying at whose bedside the chaplet is recited (ref. Diary, 811).

Jesus recommended that priests encourage sinners to recite the chaplet as their last hope of salvation: "Even if there were a sinner most hardened, if he were to recite this chaplet only once, he would receive grace from My infinite mercy" (Diary, 687).

To be effective the Chaplet must be recited with great trust - a requisite characteristic of all other forms of devotion to the Mercy of God - but even more so than with regard to other forms of this devotion, the Chaplet must be recited with an extraordinary constancy. Only in the case of a prayer which asks the grace of a holy death has Christ promised to grant this grace after a single recitation, while in all other cases He has repeated insistently the importance of perseverance in the devotion. The latter is moreover a sign of trust because we continue to pray only when we have great confidence that our prayer will be heard. Certainty of being heard, however, is not synonymous with being answered immediately, nor with receiving precisely what we anticipate.

The Chaplet of Divine Mercy is a powerful prayer and a prayer for a good intention, namely the conversion and the salvation of entire humanity: Jesus said to Saint Faustina:

"By saying the chaplet you are bringing humankind closer to Me" (Diary, 929).

The text of the Chaplet, along with the attitude of abandonment to the will of God and of trust in His Mercy with which it should be recited, make this act of devotion become one of the ways of imitating the prayer of Christ. It is also a way of participation in the mission of salvation of the Son of God who was sent "not to judge the world, but so that through him the world might be saved"(Jn 3:17).

Ideally, the chaplet is recited every day at 3 o'clock in the afternoon, however it may be recited at any time throughout the day.

*The Chaplet is recited as follows,
using the beads of the Holy Rosary:*

*In the name of the Father, and of the Son,
and of the Holy Spirit. Amen.*

O God, come to my aid.
O Lord, make haste to help me.

**Our Father
Hail Mary
The Creed** *(see page 26)*

*On the beads of the Our Father
the following prayer is recited:*
Eternal Father, I offer you the Body and Blood, Soul and Divinity of Your dearly beloved Son, Our Lord Jesus Christ.
**In atonement for our sins
and those of the whole world.**

On the beads of the Hail Mary,
the following invocation is recited ten times:

For the sake of His sorrowful Passion.
Have mercy on us and on the whole world

In conclusion the following invocation
is recited three times:

Holy God, Holy Mighty One,
Holy Immortal One.
have mercy on us and on the whole world.

THE HOUR OF MERCY

*On one occasion Jesus said to Saint Faustina "I remind you, My daughter, that as often as you hear the clock strike the third hour, immerse yourself completely in My mercy, adoring and glorifying it; invoke its omnipotence for the whole world, and particularly for poor sinners; for at that moment mercy was opened wide for every soul. In this hour you can obtain everything for yourself and for others for the asking" (*Diary, 1572*).*

Christ desires that the moment of his agony on the Cross be honoured every day at three o'clock in the afternoon when, as he said, *"It was the hour of grace for the whole world - mercy triumphed over justice"* (Diary, 1572*). He desires that his sorrowful Passion be meditated at that hour because it was then that the love of God for humankind was made manifest.

Jesus desires that the mercy of God be adored and exalted and that those who recite the chaplet implore graces for themselves, for the entire world and especially for sinners, through the merits of his Passion. *"My daughter, try your best to make the Stations of the Cross in this hour, provided that your duties permit it"* Jesus recommended to Sister Faustina, *"and if you are not able to make the Stations of the Cross, then at least step into the chapel for a moment and adore, in the Blessed Sacrament, My Heart, which is full of mercy; and should you be unable to step into the chapel, immerse yourself in prayer there where you happen to be, if only for a very brief instant"* (Diary, 1572*). On another occasion Jesus said to Saint Faustina, *"In this hour, I will refuse nothing to the soul that makes a request of Me in virtue of My Passion..."* (Diary, 1320*).

The prayer at the Hour of Mercy is strictly linked to the third hour in the afternoon and we should address our petitions to Jesus himself. It is also necessary to refer to the virtues and merits of his sorrowful Passion.

Prayer at the Hour of Mercy

"O Blood and Water, that gushed forth from the Heart of Jesus, as a fount of mercy for us, I trust in you" *(Diary, 187).*

Jesus said to Saint Faustina, "When you say this prayer, with a contrite heart and with faith on behalf of some sinner, I will give him the grace of conversion" *(Diary, 186).*

Extracts from the Diary of Saint Faustina for Meditation

1. "God, You could have saved thousands of worlds with one word; a single sigh from Jesus would have satisfied Your justice. But You Yourself, Jesus, purely out of love for us, underwent such a terrible Passion. Your Father's justice would have been propitiated with a single sigh from You, and all Your self-abasement is solely the work of Your mercy and Your inconceivable love.

On leaving the earth, O Lord, You wanted to stay with us, and so You left us Yourself in the Sacrament of the Altar, and You opened wide Your mercy to us. There is no misery that could exhaust You; You have called us all to this fountain of love, to this spring of God's compassion.

Here is the tabernacle of Your mercy, here is the remedy for all our ills. To You, O living spring of mercy, all souls are drawn; some like deer, thirsting for Your love, others to wash the wound of their sins, and still others, exhausted by life, to draw strength.

At the moment of Your death on the Cross, You bestowed upon us eternal life; allowing Your most holy side to be opened, You opened an inexhaustible spring of mercy for us, giving us Your dearest possession, the Blood and Water from Your Heart. Such is the omnipotence of Your mercy. From it all grace flows to us" *(Diary, 1747)*.

2. "O Jesus, eternal Truth, our Life, I call upon you and I beg Your mercy for poor sinners. O sweetest Heart of my Lord, full of pity and unfathomable mercy, I plead with You for poor sinners.

O Most Sacred Heart, Fount of Mercy from which gush forth rays of inconceivable graces upon the entire human race, I beg of You light for poor sinners. O Jesus, be mindful of Your own bitter Passion and do not permit the loss of souls redeemed at so dear a price of Your most precious Blood.

O Jesus, when I consider the great price of Your Blood, I rejoice at its immensity, for one drop alone would have been enough for the salvation of all sinners. Although sin is an abyss of wickedness and ingratitude, the price paid for us can never be equalled. Therefore, let every soul trust in the Passion of the Lord, and place its hope in His mercy. God will not deny His mercy to anyone. Heaven and earth may change, but God's mercy will never be exhausted. Oh, what immense joy burns in my heart when I contemplate Your incomprehensible goodness, O Jesus! I desire to bring all sinners to Your feet that they may glorify Your mercy throughout endless ages" *(Diary, 72)*.

3. "O Jesus, stretched out upon the cross, I implore You, give me the grace of doing faithfully the most holy will of Your Father, in all things, always and everywhere. And when this will of God will seem to me very harsh and difficult to fulfil, it is then I beg You, Jesus, may power and strength flow upon me from Your wounds, and may my lips keep repeating, 'Your will be done, O Lord.' O Saviour of the world, Lover of man's salvation, who in such terrrible torment and pain forget Yourself to think only of the salvation of souls, O most compassionate Jesus, grant me the grace to forget myself that I may live totally for souls, helping You in the work of salvation, according to the most holy will of Your Father..." *(Diary, 1265)*.

THE FEAST OF THE DIVINE MERCY

In accordance with Christ's desire, the Feast of The Divine Mercy must be celebrated on the first Sunday after Easter. This is in order to emphasize the strict unity which exists between the Paschal mystery of Salvation and this feast. Indeed the Liturgy of that day praises God in particular for the mystery of his mercy. The Feast of Mercy must also be a day of grace for all people, because Christ has associated great promises with this feast, and the greatest refers to Holy Communion: receiving it, one obtains the total remission of sins and of temporal punishment, that is one receives the same grace as that of Baptism.

The importance of this Feast lies in the fact that everyone, even those who are converted on that very day, can ask for all the graces which are in accordance with God's Will. Jesus said to Saint Faustina, "I want this image to be blessed solemnly on the first Sunday after Easter; this Sunday is to be the Feast of Mercy" (Diary, 49). "I desire that the Feast of Mercy be a shelter and refuge for all souls and especially for poor sinners. On that day the very depths of My tender mercy are open, I pour out a whole ocean of graces upon those souls who approach the fount of My mercy. The soul that will go to Confession and receive Holy Communion, shall obtain complete forgiveness of sins and punishment. On that day all the divine floodgates through which graces flow are open. Let no soul fear to draw near to Me, even though its sins be as scarlet. My mercy is so great that no mind, be it of man or of angel, will be able to fathom it throughout all eternity" (Diary, 699). "The Feast of My Mercy has issued forth from My very depths for the consolation of the whole world" (Diary, 1517). "By means of this (my) image I shall grant many graces to souls" (Diary, 742).

The Feast of Divine Mercy is to be preceded by a nove-

na, which consists in reciting the Chaplet of Divine Mercy, starting on Good Friday. In the Diary of Saint Faustina there is also a Novena which Our Lord dictated to her and it may be used as a suitable accompaniment to the recitation of the Chaplet.

THE CELEBRATION OF THE FEAST OF DIVINE MERCY

Jesus desires that on the Feast of Divine Mercy, the image of the Merciful Jesus be blessed and venerated in public and that priests speak about the great and unfathomable Mercy of God.

The faithful, to obtain the great gifts that Jesus desires to offer to every person and to all humanity, must be in a state of grace, having made a good confession, must fulfil the conditions requested for devotion to The Divine Mercy (namely, have trust in God and do acts of charity towards their neighbour) and approach on that day approach the "Fount of life" which is Holy Communion.

On the 13th of June 2003, Pope John Paul II officialised the application of indulgence for the aforementioned Sunday that will be referred to as the "Sunday of Divine Mercy" from now on. "Plenary indulenece is granted to the faithful according to the usual conditions (sacramental confession, Eucharistic Communion and prayer for the intentions of the Pope). Such indulgence is granted to the faithful who participate in practices of piety carried out in honour of Divine Mercy on the Sunday after Easter, or the Sunday of "Divine Mercy" in any church or oratory, with their soul completely removed from attachment to any sin, even venial ones, alternatively, in the presence of the Most Blessed Sacrament of the Eurcharist exposed publically or housed in the tabernacle, they should recite the Our Father and the Apostles Creed, with the addition of a pious invoca-

tion to the Merciful Lord Jesus. Partial indulgence is also granted to the faithful who, with a contrite heart, offer one of the legitimately approved inovcations to the Most Merciful Heart of the Lord Jesus.

NOVENA TO THE DIVINE MERCY

The following novena is that which we find in the Diary of Saint Faustina, *(Diary, 1209-1229)*. Our Lord dictated it to her and instructed her to make it before the Feast of Mercy, beginning on Good Friday. However, the novena may also be recited by all the faithful who wish to do so, at any time of the year.

*Jesus said to Saint Faustina, "I desire that during these nine days you bring souls to the fount of My mercy, that they may draw therefrom strength, and refreshment and whatever graces, they need in the hardships of life and, especially at the hour of death. On each day you will bring to My heart a different group of souls and you will immerse them in the ocean of My mercy, and I will bring all these souls into the house of My Father. You will do it in this life and in the next I will deny nothing to any soul whom will you bring to the fount of My mercy. On each day you will beg of My Father, on the strength of My bitter Passion, graces for these souls" (*Diary, 1209*).*

In the name of the Father, and of the Son, and of the Holy Spirit. Amen.

O God, come to my aid.
O Lord, make haste to help me.

Our Father
Hail Mary
The Creed *(see page 26)*

THE FIRST DAY

"Today, bring me all of mankind, especially all sinners, and immerse them in the ocean of My mercy."

"And in this way you will console me in the bitter grief into which the loss of souls plunges me."

Most merciful Jesus, whose very nature is to have compassion on us and pardon us, look not upon our sins, but on the trust which we place in your infinite goodness and welcome us into your Most Compassionate Heart, and allow us to remain there for all eternity.

We beg this of you by the love which unites you with the Father and the Holy Spirit.

Oh omnipotence of divine mercy, refuge of sinners, You who are a sea of mercy and compassion, come to the aid of those who humbly invoke you.

Eternal Father, turn your merciful gaze upon all mankind and especially poor sinners, who are all enclosed within the Most Compassionate Heart of Jesus, and by His painful passion show us your mercy, so that we may praise its omnipotence for all eternity. Amen.

The Chaplet of Divine Mercy is now to be recited (see page 508)

THE SECOND DAY

"Today bring me the souls of priests and religious people, and immerse them in my unfathomable mercy."
"It was they who gave me the strength to endure My bitter passion. By means of them, as if by means of canals, by mercy flows out upon humankind".

Most merciful Jesus, from whom all good things come, increase Your grace in us, so that we may perform works of mercy, so that all who see us may glorify the Father of Mercy in Heaven.

The fountain of God's love dwells in pure hearts, purified in the sea of mercy, radiant as stars, bright as the dawn.

Eternal Father, turn your merciful gaze upon the ones who were chosen for your vineyard, the souls of priests and religious people; endow them with the strength of your blessing. For the love of the Heart of Your Son, in which they are enclosed, give them the gift of your power and your light, so that they may be able to guide others on the road to salvation, and so that they may sing together the praises of your infinite mercy for all eternity.
Amen.

The Chaplet of Divine Mercy is now to be recited (see page 508)

THE THIRD DAY

"Today bring me all the faithful and devout souls, and immerse them in the sea of my mercy".

"These souls comforted me on the road to Calvary, they were a drop of consolation in the midst of a sea of bitterness".

Oh most merciful Jesus, from the treasury of Your mercy, You impart Your graces in great abundance to each of us, welcome us into your most compassionate heart and let us remain there for all eternity. We beg this of you by that most wonderful love for the heavenly father with which your heart burns so fiercely.

The marvels of Your mercy are impenetrable, neither the sinner nor the just one can fathom them. You cast a gaze of compassion upon all of us, drawing us ever closer to Your love.

Eternal Father, look with mercy on the souls of the faithful, as upon the inheritance of Your own son and, by his sorrowful passion, grant them your blessing and surround them with your constant protection, so that they may not loose the love nor the holy faith, but with all the hosts of angels and saints, they may glorify Your boundless mercy for ever and ever. Amen.

The Chaplet of Divine Mercy is now to be recited (see page 508)

THE FOURTH DAY

"Today bring me the pagans and those who do not yet know me".
"I also thought of them during my bitter Passion, and their future zeal comforted my heart. Immerse them in the sea of my mercy".

Oh most merciful Jesus, You who are the light of the whole world. Welcome into Your Most Compassionate Heart the souls of pagans who do not yet know you. Let the rays of Your grace illuminate them, so that they too, together with us, may glorify the merits of Your mercy, and do not let them ever leave Your most Compassionate heart.

May the light of Your love illuminate the shadows of the souls, grant that these souls may know you and, together with us, praise Your mercy.

Eternal Father, look with mercy upon the souls of the pagans and those who do not yet know you, but who are enclosed in the Most Compassionate Heart of Jesus. Draw them towards the light of the Gospel. These souls do not know what great happiness it is to love You. Grant that they too may glorify the generosity of Your mercy for all eternity. Amen.

The Chaplet of Divine Mercy is now to be recited (see page 508)

THE FIFTH DAY

"Today bring me the souls of heretics and schismatics and immerse them in the sea of My mercy".

"During My passion they lacerated My body and My heart, that is, My church.

When they shall return to be united with the Church, My wounds will be healed and in this way My passion will be alleviated."

Most Merciful Jesus, the embodiment of Goodness, You do not refuse light to those who ask it of You. Welcome into Your most Compassionate Heart the souls of heretics and schismatics. Draw them, by means of Your light, into the unity of the Church and do not let them leave Your Most Compassionate Heart, but let them come to glorify the generosity of Your mercy.

Even for those who have torn the garment of Your unity, let a fountain of mercy flow from Your heart. The omnipotence of Your mercy, Oh God, can also lead these souls out of error.

Eternal Father, look mercifully upon the souls of heretics and schismatics, who have squandered Your blessings and misused Your graces by obstinately persisting in their errors. Look not upon their errors but on the love of Your Son and upon his bitter Passion which he

took upon himself for their sake, seen as they too are enclosed within the Most Compassionate Heart of Jesus. Let them also glorify Your great mercy for all eternity.
Amen.

The Chaplet of Divine Mercy is now to be recited (see page 508)

THE SIXTH DAY

"Today bring me the meek and humble souls and the souls of little children and immerse them in My mercy."
"These souls most closely resemble My Heart, They strengthened Me during My bitter agony.
"I saw them as earthly angels, who would keep vigil at My alters.
"I pour graces in great torrents upon them. Only a humble soul is capable of receiving My grace, I give my complete trust to humble souls".

Oh, Most Merciful Jesus, You who have said: *"Learn from me for I am meek and humble of heart"*, welcome into Your Most Compassionate Heart all the meek and humble souls and the souls of little children.

These souls are worthy of the admiration of all of Heaven and they are the heavenly Father's favourites. They form a sweet smelling bouquet of flowers before the throne of God and God himself delights in their fragrance.

These souls are permanently present in Your Most Compassionate Heart, Oh Jesus, and there they sing endless hymns of love and mercy for all eternity.

A truly gentle and humble soul, already here on earth breaths the air of Paradise, and the Creator himself delights in the fragrance of its humble heart.

Eternal Father, look with mercy on the meek and humble souls and upon the souls of little children, who are enclosed within the Most Compassionate Heart of Jesus.

These souls are those who most resemble Your Son. Their fragrance rises from the earth and reaches Your very throne. Father of mercy and of every goodness, I beg You by the love You have for these souls and by the delight You take in them: bless the whole world, that all souls together may sing out the praises of Your mercy for ever and ever.
Amen.

The Chaplet of Divine Mercy is now to be recited (see page 508)

THE SEVENTH DAY

"Today bring Me the souls who venerate and exalt in My mercy in a particular way and immerse them in my mercy.

"These souls sorrowed most over My passion and they penetrated deep into My Spirit. They are living images of My Compassionate Heart.

"These souls shall shine with a special brightness in the next life. Not one of them shall perish in the fires of Hell; I will particularly defend each one of them at the hour of their death".

Most merciful Jesus, whose Heart is Love itself, welcome into Your Most Merciful Heart the souls of those who in a particular way venerate and exalt in Your mercy.

These souls are mighty, with the very power of God himself, in the midst of all afflictions and adversities they remain confidant in Your Mercy. These souls are united with Jesus and they carry all of mankind on their shoulders. These souls shall not be judged severely, but Your Mercy will embrace them at the hour of their death.

A soul who exalts the goodness of his Lord, is especially loved by Him, and shall always be close to the living fountain, and draws grace from Divine Mercy.

Eternal Father, look with mercy upon the souls of those who exalt and venerate Your greatest attribute, which is Your fathomless mercy, those who are already enclosed within the Most Compassionate Heart of Jesus. These souls are a living Gospel; their hands are full of works of mercy and their spirit, which is full of joy, sings a hymn of mercy to the Most High!

I beseech You, Oh God: show them Your mercy according to the hope and trust that they have placed in You. Let the promise of Jesus be accomplished in them, Jesus who said to them: "The souls who honour my unfathomable mercy, I myself will defend them as My own glory, during their lifetime, and especially at the hour of their death."
Amen.

The Chaplet of Divine Mercy is now to be recited (see page 508)

THE EIGHTH DAY

"Today, bring me the souls who find themselves in the prison of Purgatory and immerse them in the abyss of My mercy. Let the torrents of My Blood cool down the scorching flames.".

"All of these souls are much loved by me; They are making retribution to My justice. It is in your power to bring them relief. Take all the indulgences from the treasury of the Church and offer them up for them... Oh, if only you knew their torment, you would continually offer up the alms of the spirit for their sake in order to pay off their debt to My justice."

Oh Most Merciful Jesus, You who have said that You desire Mercy, I lead the souls of Purgatory into Your Most Compassionate Heart, these souls who are so dear to You, and who despite this, must satisfy Your justice.

The torrents of Blood and Water which gush forth from Your Heart quench the flames of Purgatory, so that the power of Your mercy may be praised there too.

From the tremendous heat of the fire of Purgatory, a plaint to Your mercy rises, and the souls receive comfort, relief and refreshment in the torrent which is a mix of Blood and Water.

Eternal Father, look with mercy upon the suffering souls of Purgatory, who are enclosed within the Most Compassionate Heart of Jesus. I beseech You, by the agonising passion of Jesus, Your Son, and by all the bitterness with which His most sacred Soul was flooded, show Your mercy to the souls who are under the gaze of Your justice, look upon them only through the wounds of Your dearly beloved Son; so that we may believe that Your goodness and Your mercy are limitless. Amen.

The Chaplet of Divine Mercy is now to be recited (see page 508)

THE NINTH DAY

"Today, bring me those souls who have become lukewarm, and immerse them in the abyss of my mercy. These souls wound My heart in the most painful of ways".
"In the Garden of Olives, my soul suffered the most dreadful loathing because of lukewarm souls. They were the reason for which I cried out: "Father, take this chalice away from Me, if it be Your will". For them, the last hope for salvation, is to flee to My Mercy".

Most Merciful Jesus, You who are Compassion itself, I welcome lukewarm souls into Your Most Compassionate Heart. Let these icy souls who are similar to corpses and who filled You with such deep loathing, be warmed by Your pure Love. Oh Most Compassionate Jesus, exercise the omnipotence of Your Mercy, draw them into the very ardour of Your Love and grant them the gift of holy love, for nothing is beyond Your power.

Fire and ice cannot be joined, either the fire shall be quenched or the ice be melted, but by Your Mercy, oh God, You can make up for all that is lacking.

Eternal Father, look with mercy upon the lukewarm souls, who are enclosed within the

Most Compassionate Heart of Jesus. Father of mercy, I beseech You, by the bitter Passion of Your son and by His three-hour agony on the cross, let them too praise the abyss of Your Mercy. Amen.

The Chaplet of Divine Mercy is now to be recited (see page 508)

THE LITANY OF DIVINE MERCY
(ref. Diary, 949)

The love of God is the flower of which his mercy is the fruit. Let the doubtful soul read these considerations on Divine Mercy and become trusting. (ref. Diary, 948-949*)*

Lord, have mercy.

Lord, have mercy.

Christ, have mercy.

Christ, have mercy.

Lord, have mercy.

Lord, have mercy.

Christ, hear us.

Christ, graciously hear us.

God, the Father of Heaven,

Have mercy on us.

God the Son, Redeemer of the World,

Have mercy on us.

God the Holy Spirit,

Have mercy on us.

Holy Trinity, one God,

Have mercy on us.

Divine Mercy, gushing forth from
the bosom of the Father,

We trust in You.

Divine Mercy, greatest attribute of God,

We trust in You.

Divine Mercy, incomprehensible mystery,

We trust in You.

Divine Mercy, fount gushing forth from
the mystery of the Most Blessed Trinity,

We trust in You.

Divine Mercy, unfathomed by
any intellect, human or angelic,

We trust in You.

Divine Mercy, from which wells forth
all life and happiness,

We trust in You.

Divine Mercy, better than the heavens,

We trust in You.

Divine Mercy of God, source of
miracles and wonders,

We trust in You.

Divine Mercy, encompassing the whole universe,

We trust in You.

Divine Mercy, descending to the earth
in the Person of the Incarnate Word,

We trust in You.

Divine Mercy, which flowed out from
the open wound of the Heart of Jesus,

We trust in You.

Divine Mercy, enclosed in the Heart
of Jesus for us and especially for sinners,

We trust in You.

Divine Mercy, unfathomed in the institution
of the Sacred Host,

We trust in You.

Divine Mercy, in the founding of
the Holy Church,

We trust in You.

Divine Mercy, in the Sacrament of Holy Baptism,
We trust in You.

Divine Mercy, in our justification through
Jesus Christ,
We trust in You.

Divine Mercy, accompanying us through
our whole life,
We trust in You.

Divine Mercy, embracing us especially
at the hour of death,
We trust in You.

Divine Mercy, endowing us with immortal life,
We trust in You.

Divine Mercy, accompanying us every
moment of our life,
We trust in You.

Divine Mercy, shielding us from the fire of hell,
We trust in You.

Divine Mercy, in the conversion of hardened
sinners,
We trust in You.

Divine Mercy, astonishment for Angels,
incomprehensible to Saints,
We trust in You.

Divine Mercy, unfathomed in all the mysteries
of God,
We trust in You.

Divine Mercy, lifting us out of every misery,
We trust in You.

Divine Mercy, source of our happiness and joy,
>**We trust in You.**

Divine Mercy, in calling us forth from
nothingness to existence,
>**We trust in You.**

Divine Mercy, embracing all the works
of His hands,
>**We trust in You.**

Divine Mercy, crown of all God's handiwork,
>**We trust in You.**

Divine Mercy, in which we are all immersed,
>**We trust in You.**

Divine Mercy, sweet relief for anguished hearts,
>**We trust in You.**

Divine Mercy, only hope of despairing souls,
>**We trust in You.**

Divine Mercy, repose of hearts,
peace amidst fear,
>**We trust in You.**

Divine Mercy, delight and ecstasy of holy souls,
>**We trust in You.**

Divine Mercy, inspiring hope against all hope,
>**We trust in You.**

**Lamb of God, you take away
the sins of the world,**
spare us, O Lord.

**Lamb of God, you take away
the sins of the world,**
graciously hear us, O Lord.

**Lamb of God, you take away
the sins of the world,**
have mercy on us.

O Eternal Father, whose mercy is infinite and in whom the treasure of compassion is inexhaustible, turn Your merciful gaze upon us with kindness and inerease Your Mercy towards us, so that in times of hardship we may not despair nor lose heart but, with great confidence, submit ourselves to Your holy will, which is Love and Mercy. **Amen.**

PRAYER TO OBTAIN MERCY FROM
GOD FOR ALL THE WORLD

O Greatly Merciful God, Infinite Goodness, today all humankind calls out from the abyss of its misery to Your mercy - to Your compassion, O God; and it is with its mighty voice of misery that it cries out. Gracious God, do not reject the prayer of this earth's exiles!

O Lord, Goodness beyond our understanding, Who are acquainted with our misery through and through, and know that by our own power we cannot ascend to You, we implore You: anticipate us with Your grace and keep on increasing

Your mercy in us, that we may faithfully do Your holy will all through our life and at death's hour. Let the omnipotence of Your mercy shield us from the darts of our salvation's enemies, that we may with confidence, as Your children, await Your final coming - that day known to You alone. And we expect to obtain everything promised us by Jesus in spite of all our wretchedness. For Jesus is our Hope: Through His merciful Heart, as through an open gate, we pass through to heaven.

PRAYER FOR SINNERS

God of great mercy, who deigned to send us Your Only Begotten Son as the greatest proof of Your fathomless love and mercy, You do not reject sinners; but in Your boundless mercy You have opened for them also Your treasures, treasures from which they can draw abundantly, not only justification, but also all the sanctity that a soul can attain. Father of great mercy, I desire that all hearts turn with confidence to Your infinite mercy. No one will be justified before You if he is not accompanied by Your unfathomable mercy. When You reveal the mystery of Your mercy to us, there will not be enough of eternity to properly thank You for it.

O Jesus, how sorry I feel for poor sinners. Jesus, grant them contrition and repentance. Remember Your own sorrowful Passion. I know Your infinite mercy and cannot bear it that a soul that has cost You so much should perish. Jesus, give me the souls (267) of sinners; let Your mercy rest upon them. Take everything away from me, but give me souls. I want to become a sacrificial host for sinners. Let the shell of my body conceal my offering, for Your Most Sacred Heart is also hidden in a Host, and certainly You are a living sacrifice.

Transform me into Yourself, O Jesus, that I may be a living sacrifice and pleasing to You. I desire to atone at each moment for poor sinners. The sacrifice of my spirit is hidden under the veil of the body; the human eye does not perceive it, and for that reason it is pure and pleasing to You. O my Creator and Father of great mercy, I trust in You, for You are Goodness Itself. Souls, do not be afraid of God, but trust in Him, for He is good, and His mercy is everlasting.

PRAYER FOR THE GRACE TO DO WORKS OF MERCY TOWARDS OUR NEIGHBOUR

O Most Holy Trinity! As many times as I breathe, as many times as my heart beats, as many times as my blood pulsates through my body, so many thousand times do I want to glorify Your mercy.

I want to be completely transformed into Your mercy and to be Your living reflection, O Lord. May the greatest of all divine attributes, that of Your unfathomable mercy, pass through my heart and soul to my neighbour.

Help me, O Lord, that my eyes may be merciful, so that I may never suspect or judge from appearances, but look for what is beautiful in my neighbours' souls and come to their rescue.

Help me, that my ears may be merciful, so that I may give heed to my neighbours' needs and not be indifferent to their pains and moanings.

Help me, O Lord, that my tongue may be merciful, so that I should never speak negatively of my neighbour, but have a word of comfort and forgiveness for all.

Help me, O Lord, that my hands may be merciful and filled with good deeds, so that I may do only good to my neighbours and take upon myself the more difficult and toilsome tasks.

Help me, that my feet may be merciful, so that I may hurry to assist my neighbour, overcoming my own fatigue and weariness. My true rest is in the service of my neighbour.

Help me, O Lord, that my heart may be merciful so that I myself may feel all the sufferings of my neighbour. I will refuse my heart to no one. I will be sincere even with those who, I know, will abuse my kindness. And I will lock myself up in yhe most merciful Heart of Jesus. I will bear my own suffering in silence. May Your mercy, O Lord, rest upon me.

You yourself command me to exercise the three degrees of mercy. The first: the act of mercy, of whatever kind. The second: the word of mercy - if I cannot carry out a work of mercy, I will assist by my words. The third: prayer - if I cannot show mercy by deeds or words, I can always do so by prayer. My prayer reaches out even there where I cannot reach out physically.

O my Jesus, transform me into Yourself, for you can do all things. *(Diary, 163)*.

PRAYER FOR THE CHURCH AND FOR PRIESTS

O my Jesus, I beg You on behalf of the whole Church: Grant it love and the light of Your Spirit, and give power to the words of priests so that hardened hearts might be brought to repentance and return to You, O Lord. Lord, give us holy priests; You yourself maintain them in holiness. O Divine and Great High Priest, may the power of Your mercy accompany them everywhere and protect them from the devil's traps and snares which are continually being set for the souls of priests. May the power of Your mercy, O Lord, shatter and bring to naught all that might tarnish the sanctity of priests, for You can do all things. *(Diary, 1052)*

Jesus, my most beloved Spouse, I beg you for the triumph of the Church... for a blessing on the Holy Father... and on all the clergy; (I ask You) for the grace of conversion for impenitent sinners. And I ask You for a special blessing and for light, O Jesus, for the priests before whom I will make my confessions throughout my lifetime.

For further information write to:
Congregation of Sisters of Our Lady of Mercy
Via Penitenzieri, 12 - 00193 Roma Italy
Tel. 0039 06 68 80 50 94

THE CROSS OF MERCIFUL LOVE OF COLLEVALENZA; THE DEVOTION OF VENERABLE MOTHER SPERANZA

As regards the doctrine of Merciful Love, Mother Speranza was not called to tell us anything new; the teachings about the Mercy of God are as old as God is eternal. Indeed, devotion to Merciful Love was present and widespread before Mother Speranza was born: St. Margaret Mary Alacocque enlightened humankind about devotion to the Sacred Heart in the 1600s; St. Thérèse of the Child Jesus offered herself to Merciful Love at the end of the 1800s; in more recent times Saint Faustina conveyed the mercy of the Lord Jesus to the world.

Mother Speranza was called by God to translate devotion to Merciful Love into a **way of life** *founded on Merciful Love.*

First, let us consider the image of Merciful Love revealed to Mother Speranza.

- *We find the following written in her diary: "Jesus helped me to understand how to create the image of his Merciful Love and the symbols which must complete it."*

The Spanish sculptor Cullot Valera was subsequently commissioned in 1930 to sculpture a Crucifix which portrayed the love that brought Jesus to the cross in order to expiate our sins with his blood more so than the agony of the Cross.

According to Mother Speranza's instructions, the image was to have an expression and appearance which would bring us to exclaim, as did the centurion on the hill of Calvary:

"Truly this man was the Son of God!"

In order to express the love of Jesus, the image has the following characteristic:

- *Jesus is depicted as being still alive;*
- *His body is neither torn nor crushed, but upright, in the position of a voluntary victim;*
- *His face instils and transmits much serenity to those who behold it, even in the midst of sorrows and suffering;*
- *Jesus' gaze is turned towards heaven while he says to his Father on behalf of us, who have crucified him, "Forgive them, because they do not know what they are doing.";*
- *The word "Charitas" (Love) is written on the heart painted upon his breast;*

The host *behind the crucifix is the Blessed Eucharist of our altars, on which the Lord renews the sacrifice of the Cross everyday and gives himself to us as food, a sign of his infinite love for us,*

The globe *at the base of the cross, symbolizes the universality of the saving love of God, for he died in order to save the world.*

The crown *on the globe reminds us that Christ is a King who reigns from the cross; by drawing all of us to himself through his death and resurrection, he allowed us become children of God, members of a kingdom of love and immortality.*

The book *on the left side of the Cross is the Gospel, and is opened at the page where we read: "Love one another, as I have loved you" (Jn 15:12). The practice of this new commandement is the sign of our belonging to the kingdom of God: "It is by your love for one another, that everyone will recognise you as my disciples" (Jn 13:35).*

NOVENA TO MERCIFUL LOVE
Written by Venerable Mother Speranza of Jesus
INTRODUCTION

The Bible and the history of the Church tell us that the Holy Spirit gives charisms or extraordinary gifts continuously and freely to men and women in order that they may do good for all humanity, according to the necessities of a particular period in time. One of the people endowed with such gifts was MOTHER SPERANZA ALHAMA, who was responsible for the construction of the Sanctuary dedicated to the Merciful Love of Jesus.

Mother Speranza was born on the 30th of September, 1893, in Santomera (Murcia) in the south of Spain. At the age of 22, she entered the religious institute known as the "Sisters of Calvary". She left this congregation in 1930, having been called by the Lord to form a new religious family.

Over the years one could perceive ever more in Mother Speranza the gift of a particular knowledge and experience of the mercy of God, a knowledge that came to her neither from books nor from teachers, but from her intimacy with "The Good Jesus", as she used to call him.

The more Mother Speranza came to know the merciful attitude of God towards the sinner the more she desired to announce to everyone that God does not want to be considered as a father who is offended by the ingratitude of his children, nor as a severe judge ready to condemn and chastise them, but rather as a good father who loves and forgives them, forgets their offences and does not bear grudges; a father who awaits his prodigal son to embrace him and have a feast for him; the Good Shepherd who seeks the lost sheep and on finding it, puts it on his shoulders, and then, full of joy, brings it back to the sheepfold.

In 1930, in obedience to the will of God, she established a congregation of sisters in Madrid, the Handmaids of

Merciful Love, which she herself later strengthened with a new group of handmaids in secular dress. Together with these daughters of hers Mother Speranza made known the merciful goodness of Jesus by the token of their lives and their care of the most miserable members of society: homeless children, abandoned elderly people, ostracized handicapped people, sick people and others who found themselves in difficulty because of their limitations or physical and moral fragility.

In April of 1936, she came to Rome, Italy, During the Second World War, she did her very best to help the wounded and persecuted, and to feed hundreds of starving people.

In 1951, Mother Speranza established the congregation of the Children of Merciful Love, whose primary purpose is to promote fraternal union with priests who are called to be touched by the mercy of God and then to become ministers of the same, that is ministers of the mercy of God. Some years later, moved by her maternal love for priests, she established a most original form of union between her sisters and the secular clergy, allowing diocesan priests to become members of her religious family, while remaining attached to and serving their diocese.

On the 18th of August, 1951, through the disposition of Divine Providence, she moved with some members of her congregation to Collevalenza, a little town in the province of Perugia, Italy. In 1955, the construction of the Sanctuary dedicated to the Merciful Love of Jesus was begun.

Within a few years, the Sanctuary and its works had become a centre of spirituality with the purpose of announcing the love and mercy of God.

It was here in Collevalenza that Mother Speranza died at the age of 90 on the 8th of Febraury, 1983.

For further information write to:
Santuario Amore Misericordioso
06050 Collevalenza (PG)-Italy Tel 0039. 075. 89581

FIRST DAY

In the name of the Father, and of the Son,
and of the Holy Spirit. Amen.

O God, come to my aid.
O Lord, make haste to help me.

Our Father
Hail Mary
The Creed *(see page 26)*

INTRODUCTORY PRAYER

My Jesus, my sorrow is great, considering the disgrace I have had of offending you many times.
And yet you, with the heart of a father, have not
only forgiven me but, with your words: "Ask and
you will receive", you invite me to ask for what I
need. Full of confidence, I turn to your Merciful
Love, so that it may grant me what I implore in
this novena, especially the grace to transform my
behaviour and from now on, to bear witness to my
faith with my works, while living according to
your precepts, and to burn in the fire of your love.

MEDITATION

on the words of the Our Father:
"Our" because God, having only one natural Son,
in his infinite love wanted to have many adopted
children on whom he could lavish his riches and
so that, as we all have the same Father and are
brothers and sisters, we may love each other.

"Father" is the title which befits God because we owe to him all that is in us according to the order of nature and all that is in us by the supernatural grace which makes us his adopted children. He wants us to call him Father, so that we, as his children may love him, so that we may obey and venerate him, and to awaken in us the feelings of love and trust through which we shall obtain all that we ask him.

REQUEST

My Jesus, I turn to you in this time of tribulation. If you wish to show your clemency towards this poor creature, may your goodness triumph. In your love and mercy, forgive my faults; and even if I am unworthy of obtaining what I ask of you, graciously hear and grant my desires, if they serve for your glory and for the good of my soul. I put myself into your hands: do with me as you please.

We ask the grace which we desire to obtain in the novena.

PRAYER

My Jesus, be for me a Father, a guardian and a guide in my pilgrimage, so that nothing may disturb me and I may not stray from the path which leads to you. And you, my Mother, who, with great tenderness and thoughtfulness, took care of Good Jesus, educate me and help me to fulfil my duties, leading me along the path of the commandments. Say to Jesus for me: "Receive this child; I commend him (her) to you with all the insistence of my maternal Heart".

3 Our Fathers • Hail Mary • Glory Be

SECOND DAY

In the name of the Father, and of the Son, and of the Holy Spirit. Amen.

(Introductory prayers see page 547)

INTRODUCTORY PRAYER

My Jesus, my sorrow is great, considering the disgrace I have had of offending you many times. And yet you, with the heart of a father, have not only forgiven me but, with your words: "Ask and you will receive", invite me to ask for what I need. Full of confidence, I turn to your Merciful Love, so that it may grant me what I implore in this novena, especially the grace to transform my behaviour and from now on, to bear witness to my faith with my works, while living according to your precepts, and to burn in the fire of your love.

MEDITATION
on the words of the Our Father:
"Who art in heaven"
We say that "you are in heaven" even if God is everywhere, being the Lord of heaven and earth,

so that the contemplation of heaven may move us to love him with more ardour, living this life as pilgrims, while letting our thoughts be on the things of heaven.

REQUEST

My Jesus, I turn to you in this time of tribulation. If you wish to show your clemency towards this poor creature, may your goodness triumph. In your love and mercy, forgive my faults; and even if I am unworthy of obtaining what I ask of you, graciously hear and grant my desires, if they serve for your glory and for the good of my soul. I put myself into your hands: do with me as you please.

We ask the grace which we desire to obtain in the novena.

PRAYER

My Jesus, I know that you help the fallen to rise again, and make prisoners free; you do not reject anyone who is afflicted, and look with love and mercy on all those who are in need. Therefore, listen to me, I beseech you, because I need to speak to you about the salvation of my soul and to accept your good counsel. My Jesus, my sins frighten me; I am ashamed of my ingratitude and my lack of trust. I fear that I have misspent the time which you gave me in order to do good, and what is worse, I have offended you. I turn to you, Lord, who have the words of eternal life.

3 Our Fathers • Hail Mary • Glory Be

THIRD DAY

*In the name of the Father, and of the Son,
and of the Holy Spirit. Amen.*

(Introductory prayers see page 547)

INTRODUCTORY PRAYER

My Jesus, my sorrow is great, considering the disgrace I have had of offending you many times. And yet you, with the heart of a father, have not only forgiven me but, with your words: "Ask and you will receive", invite me to ask for what I need. Full of confidence, I turn to your Merciful Love, so that it may grant me what I implore in this novena, especially the grace to change my behaviour and from now on, to bear witness to my faith with my works, while living according to your precepts, and to burn in the fire of your love.

MEDITATION
on the words of the Our Father:
"Hallowed be thy name"

This is the first thing we must desire, the first thing which we must ask for in prayer; this is the intention which must guide all our works and actions: that God may be known, loved, served and adored, and that every creature may submit to his power.

REQUEST

My Jesus, I turn to you in this time of tribulation. If you wish to show your clemency towards this poor creature, may your goodness triumph. In your love and mercy, forgive my faults; and even if I am unworthy of obtaining what I ask of you, graciously hear and grant my desires, if they serve for your glory and for the good of my soul. I put myself into your hands: do with me as you please.

We ask the grace which we desire to obtain in thie novena.

PRAYER

My Jesus, open to me the doors of your mercy; mark me with the seal of your wisdom, grant that I may be free from every disordered affection, and that I may serve you with love, joy and sincerity. Comforted by the sweet perfume of your Divine Word and your Commandments, may I always grow in virtue.

3 Our Fathers
Hail Mary
Glory be

FOURTH DAY

In the name of the Father, and of the Son,
and of the Holy Spirit. Amen.

(Introductory prayers see page 547)

INTRODUCTORY PRAYER

My Jesus, my sorrow is great, considering the disgrace I have had of offending you many times. And yet you, with the heart of a father, have not only forgiven me but, with your words: "Ask and you will receive", invite me to ask for what I need. Full of confidence, I turn to your Merciful Love, so that it may grant me what I implore in this novena, especially the grace to change my behaviour and from now on, to bear witness to my faith with my works, while living according to your precepts, and to burn in the fire of your love.

MEDITATION
on the words of the Our Father:
"Thy kingdom come".
In this request we ask that the kingdom of his grace and of the favours from heaven may come and reign within us; the kingdom of the righteous and the kingdom of glory where He reigns in perfect communion with the Blessed. Therefore we ask too, for an end to the kingdom of sin, of the evil one and of darkness.

REQUEST

My Jesus, I turn to you in this time of tribulation. If you wish to show your clemency towards this poor creature, may your goodness triumph. In your love and mercy, forgive my faults; and even if I am unworthy of obtaining what I ask of you, graciously hear and grant my desires, if they serve for your glory and for the good of my soul. I put myself into your hands: do with me as you please.

We ask the grace which we desire to obtain in the novena.

PRAYER

Lord, have mercy on me, and do what your heart inspires you to do. Have mercy on me, my God, and free me of all that impedes me from coming close to you and grant that, at the hour of my death, my soul may not hear a terrible sentence, but rather hear your voice speak the kind words, "Come, you whom my father has blessed", so that my soul may rejoice at the sight of your Face.

3 Our Fathers
Hail Mary
Glory be

FIFTH DAY

*In the name of the Father, and of the Son,
and of the Holy Spirit. Amen.*

(Introductory prayers see page 547)

INTRODUCTORY PRAYER

My Jesus, my sorrow is great, considering the disgrace I have had of offending you many times. And yet you, with the heart of a father, have not only forgiven me but, with your words: "Ask and you will receive", invite me to ask for what I need. Full of confidence, I turn to your Merciful Love, so that it may grant me what I implore in this novena, especially the grace to change my behaviour and from now on, to bear witness to my faith with my works, while living according to your precepts, and to burn in the fire of your love.

MEDITATION
on the words of the Our Father:
"Thy will be done on earth, as it is in heaven".
Here we ask that the will of God may be done in all creatures; we ask that it may be accomplished with fortitude and perseverance, with purity and perfection; and we ask that we ourselves may fulfil the will of God, in what ever manner or in whatever way it may be made known to us.

REQUEST

My Jesus, I turn to you in this time of tribulation. If you wish to show your clemency towards this poor creature, may your goodness triumph. In your love and mercy, forgive my faults; and even if I am unworthy of obtaining what I ask of you, graciously hear and grant my desires, if they serve for your glory and for the good of my soul. I put myself into your hands: do with me as you please.

We ask the grace which we desire to obtain in the novena.

PRAYER

My Jesus, give me a lively faith, grant that I may observe your Divine Commandments faithfully and that, with a heart full of your love and charity, I may run along the path of your precepts: Grant that I may taste the sweetness of your Spirit and may hunger to do your holy will, so that my humble service may always be acceptable and pleasing to you. My Jesus, may the Omnipotence of the Father bless me. May your Wisdom bless me. May the kind Love of the Holy Spirit give me its blessing and guard me for life everlasting.

3 Our Fathers
Hail Mary
Glory Be

SIXTH DAY

In the name of the Father, and of the Son,
and of the Holy Spirit. Amen.

(Introductory prayers see page 547)

INTRODUCTORY PRAYER

My Jesus, my sorrow is great, considering the
disgrace I have had of offending you many times.
And yet you, with the heart of a father, have not
only forgiven me but, with your words: "Ask and
you will receive", invite me to ask for what I
need. Full of confidence, I turn to your Merciful
Love, so that it may grant me what I implore in
this novena, especially the grace to change my
behaviour and from now on, to bear witness to
my faith with my works, while living according
to your precepts, and to burn in the fire of your
love.

MEDITATION
on the words of the Our Father:
"Give us this day our daily bread".
Here we ask for the bread that is most precious,
the Blessed Sacrament; and for the daily food of
our soul which is grace, the Sacraments and the
inspirations from heaven. We also ask for the
food which is necessary in order to preserve the
life of the body, and is to be taken in moderation.
We call the Eucharistic bread "ours" because it

was instituted to respond to **our** needs and because our Redeemer gives himself to **us** in Holy Communion.

We call it "daily" in order to express the daily dependence that we have on God for all things, those concerning both body and soul, at every moment and at every hour of our lives.

In saying "Give **us**", we accomplish an act of mercy, requesting it for all people so that they need not worry about "tomorrow".

REQUEST

My Jesus, I turn to you in this time of tribulation. If you wish to show your clemency towards this poor creature, may your goodness triumph. In your love and mercy, forgive my faults; and even if I am unworthy of obtaining what I ask of you, graciously hear and grant my desires, if they serve for your glory and for the good of my soul. I put myself into your hands: do with me as you please.

We ask the grace which we desire to obtain in the novena.

PRAYER

My Jesus, you who are the fount of life, grant that I may drink of the living waters that flow from you so that, in tasting you, I may no longer thirst for you; drown me in the abyss of your love and mercy, and renew me with your most precious Blood, by which you redeemed me.

Cleanse me with the water from your most sacred Side of all the stains with which I have contaminated the beautiful vestment of innocence which you gave to me in baptism. My Jesus, fill me with your Holy Spirit and render me pure in body and soul.

3 Our Fathers • Hail Mary • Glory Be

SEVENTH DAY

In the name of the Father, and of the Son, and of the Holy Spirit. Amen.

(Introductory prayers see page 547)

INTRODUCTORY PRAYER

My Jesus, my sorrow is great, considering the disgrace I have had of offending you many times. And yet you, with the heart of a father, have not only forgiven me but, with your words: "Ask and you will receive", invite me to ask for what I need. Full of confidence, I turn to your Merciful Love, so that it may grant me what I implore in this novena, especially the grace to change my behaviour and from now on, to bear witness to my faith with my works, while living according to your precepts, and to burn in the fire of your love.

MEDITATION
on the words of the Our Father:
"And forgive us our trespasses, as we forgive those who trespass against us"

We ask God to forgive us our debts, that is our sins and the punishment merited by them, an enormous debt which we could never pay, with the gifts of grace and nature that we have received from God, and with all that we are and all that we possess, if not for the Blood of Good Jesus. In this request, we commit ourselves to forgiving our neighbour for the trespasses he has committed against us, without seeking to avenge ourselves but on the contrary, forgetting the injuries and offences which he has done.

Thus God puts the judgement that shall be passed upon us into our hands, as if we forgive others, He will forgive us, but if we do not forgive others, He will not forgive us.

REQUEST

My Jesus, I turn to you in this time of tribulation. If you wish to show your clemency towards this poor creature, may your goodness triumph. In your love and mercy, forgive my faults; and even if I am unworthy of obtaining what I ask of you, graciously hear and grant my desires, if they serve for your glory and for the good of my soul. I put myself into your hands: do with me as you please.

We ask the grace which we desire to obtain in the novena.

PRAYER

My Jesus, I know that you call everyone, without exception; I know that you live in those who are humble, that you love those who love you, that you support the cause of the poor, that you have mercy on everyone and that you dismiss nothing that your power created; that you conceal the misdeeds of men and women and await their repentance, you accept the sinner with love and mercy. Open to me, too, Lord, the source of life, grant me forgiveness and destroy everything in me that opposes your Divine Law.

3 Our Fathers
Hail Mary
Glory Be

EIGHTH DAY

*In the name of the Father, and of the Son,
and of the Holy Spirit. Amen.*

(Introductory prayers see page 547)

INTRODUCTORY PRAYER

My Jesus, my sorrow is great, considering the
disgrace I have had of offending you many times.
And yet you, with the heart of a father, have not
only forgiven me, but with your words: "Ask and
you will receive", invite me to ask for what I
need. Full of confidence, I turn to your Merciful
Love, so that it may grant me what I implore in
this novena, especially the grace to change my
behaviour and from now on, to bear witness to
my faith with my works, while living according
to your precepts, and to burn in the fire of your
love.

MEDITATION
on the words of the Our Father:
"And lead us not into temptation"

When asking the Lord to grant that we may not
fall into temptation, we acknowledge that he
allows temptation for our own good; he permits
our weaknesses so that we may conquer them; he
gives us divine strength so that we may have the
victory. We realize that the Lord does not deny
his grace to those who, for their part, do all that

is necessary to defeat our powerful enemies.
In asking that we may not fall into temptation, we are also asking that we may not incur new debts besides those which we already have.

REQUEST

My Jesus, I turn to you in this time of tribulation. If you wish to show your clemency towards this poor creature, may your goodness triumph. In your love and mercy, forgive my faults; and even if I am unworthy of obtaining what I ask of you, graciously hear and grant my desires, if they serve for your glory and for the good of my soul. I put myself into your hands: do with me as you please.

We ask the grace which we desire to obtain in the novena.

PRAYER

My Jesus, be protection and consolation for my soul, be my defence against every temptation and cover me with the shield of your truth. Be my companion and my hope; my defence and refuge against all dangers of the body and soul. Guide me in the vast sea of this world and, in your mercy, comfort me in this trial. May the depths of your love and mercy depth be a safe haven for me, so that I may be saved from the snares of devil.

3 Our Fathers • Hail Mary • Glory Be

NINTH DAY

*In the name of the Father, and of the Son,
and of the Holy Spirit. Amen.*

(Introductory prayers see page 547)

INTRODUCTORY PRAYER

My Jesus, my sorrow is great, considering the disgrace I have had of offending you many times. And yet you, with the heart of a father, have not only forgiven me but, with your words: "Ask and you will receive", invite me to ask for what I need. Full of confidence, I turn to your Merciful Love, so that it may grant me what I implore in this novena, especially the grace to change my behaviour and from now on, to bear witness to my faith with my works, while living according to your precepts, and to burn in the fire of your love.

MEDITATION
on the words of the Our Father:
"But deliver us from evil"

We ask God to deliver us from all evil, that is from the evils of body, and the soul from those that are temporal and those that are eternal; from those present and from those of the future; from sins, from vices and from uncontrolled passions; from inclinations towards evil, from the spirit of anger and from pride.

And this we ask, saying "Amen" with intensity, affection and trust, because God wishes and commands that we ask in this way.

REQUEST

My Jesus, I turn to you in this time of tribulation. If you wish to show your clemency towards this poor creature, may your goodness triumph. In your love and mercy, forgive my faults; and even if I am unworthy of obtaining what I ask of you, graciously hear and grant my desires, if they serve for your glory and for the good of my soul. I put myself into your hands: do with me as you please.

We ask the grace which we desire to obtain in the novena.

PRAYER

My Jesus, wash me with the blood from your Divine Side, so that, by your grace, I may return to live a pure life. Enter, Lord, into my room and rest with me: accompany me along the dangerous path upon which I walk so that I may not lose my way. Lord, strengthen the weakness of my spirit, and comfort me in my anguish of heart, by telling me that, in your mercy, you will never cease to love me at any moment of my life and that you will always remain with me.

3 Our Fathers • Hail Mary • Glory Be

## Part Five

The Holy Spirit

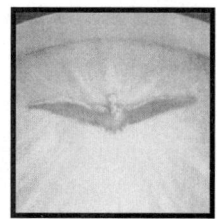

- **PRAYERS**

  - **ACTS OF CONSECRATION**

- **NOVENAS**

  - **CHAPLETS**

INTRODUCTION

"The Holy Spirit" is the name of the person whom we adore and glorify together with the Father and the Son; a name which the Church learnt from the Lord Himself and which she professes in the baptism of her new children. The Sacrament of Baptism grants us the grace of having a new birth in God the Father, through his Son in the Holy Spirit. Indeed all those who have been touched by the Spirit of God are led to the Word, that is to the Son, and the Son presents them to the Father, and the Father grants them immortality. Therefore, without the Spirit, it is not possible to see the Son of God and, without the Son, no-one can approach the Father, because the knowledge of the Father is the Son, and the knowledge of the Son of God comes through the Holy Spirit.

The word *"Spirit"* comes from the Hebrew word *"Ruah"*, which means breath, air, wind. Jesus uses the evocative image of the wind to suggest to Nicodemus the particular characteristics of the One who is the Breath of God, the person of the Spirit of God (ref. Jn 3:8) Moreover, *"Holy"* and *"Spirit"* are divine attributes common to the Three Divine Persons. However, by joining the two words, the Scriptures, the Liturgy and theological language describe the Person of the Holy Spirit, so that the term may not be confused with other uses of the words *"holy"* and *"spirit"*. When announcing the coming of the Holy Spirit, Jesus refers to Him as the *"Paraclete"*, literally *"the one who is called to be at our side"*, *"ad-vocatus"* (Jn 14:16,26; 15:26; 16:7).

"Paraclete" is usually traslated as *"Comforter"*. The Lord himself calls the Holy Spirit the *"Spirit of truth"* (Jn 16:13). As well as finding references to the *"Holy Spirit"*, which is the term most used in the Acts of the Apostles and in the Epistles, we find other names to describe Him in the Letters of St. Paul: *"Spirit of the promise"* (ref. Ep 1:13), *"Spirit of adoption"* (Rm 8:15), *"Spirit of Christ"* (Rm 8:9), *"Spirit*

of the Lord" (2Cor 3:17), "Spirit of God"(Rm 8: 9,14; 1Cor 6:11; 1Cor 7:40), and also in the letters of St. Peter where He is referred to as the"Spirit of glory" (1 Pt 4:14). "Nobody is able to say 'Jesus is Lord' except in the Holy Spirit" (1Cor 12:3). Each time we begin to pray to Jesus, it is the Holy Spirit who, with his grace, draws us along a path of prayer. If it is the Spirit who teaches us to pray, why do we not pray to him? That is why the Church invites us to ask for the gift of the Holy Spirit everyday, especially before and after any important activity.

"God is Love" (1Jn 4:8,16) and Love is the first gift of the Spirit, that which includes all the others, and this love of God has been poured "into our hearts by the Holy Spirit which has been given to us" (Rm 5:5).

As we have been wounded by sin, the first effect of the gift of Love is the remission of our sins, and in the Church, it is the "communion of the Holy Spirit" (ref. 2Cor 13:13) which restores to the baptized the divine likeness which had been lost by sin. It is only when the Hour came for him to be glorified that Jesus promised the coming of the Holy Spirit, as his Death and Resurrection were to be the fulfilment of the Promise made to the Fathers of the Old Testament; the Spirit of Truth, the other Paraclete (Jesus having been the first "Comforter") was sent by the Father through the prayer of Jesus; he was given by the Father in Jesus' name; Jesus sent forth his Spirit when seated at the right hand of the Father, because the Spirit comes from the Father.

The Holy Spirit came; the disciples knew him; he will remain with us forever; he will dwell within us; he will teach us everything, just as he reminded the disciples of all that Jesus had said to them, and we will bear witness to him; he will lead us to the whole truth so that we may glorify Christ; he has shown the world how wrong it was about sin, about who was in the right and about judgement (ref Jn 14:16).

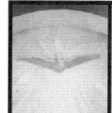
SEQUENCE OF THE HOLY SPIRIT

Come, Holy Spirit, come,
And from Your celestial home
Shed a ray of light divine.

Come, Father of the poor!
Come, source of all our store!
Come, within our bosom shine!

You, of comforters the best,
You, the soul's most welcome guest,
sweet refreshment here below.

In our labour rest most sweet,
Grateful coolness in the heat,
solace in the midst of woe.

O most blessed Light divine,
shine within these hearts of thine
of our inmost being fill!

Where You art not, man has naught;
nothing good in deed or thought,
nothing free from taint or ill.

Heal our wounds; our strength renew,
on our dryness pour Your dew;
wash the stains of guilt away.

Bend the stubborn heart and will;
melt the frozen,
warm the chill;
guide the steps that go astray.

On the faithful, who adore
and confess you, evermore
in your sev'nfold gifts descend.

**Give them virtue's sure reward;
give them our salvation, Lord;
give them joys that never end.
Amen.**

V. Send forth Thy Spirit and they shall be created.
R. And Thou shalt renew the face of the earth.

(Send forth your Spirit and there
shall be a new creation.
And you shall renew the face of the earth)

Let us pray.
O God, who taught the hearts of the faithful by
the light of the Holy Spirit, grant that by the gift
of the same Spirit, we may always desire what is
good, and ever rejoice in his consolation.
Through Jesus Christ our Lord.
Amen.

HYMN TO THE HOLY SPIRIT
(THE VENI CREATOR)

Come, O Creator, Spirit blest
and in our souls take up thy rest;
come, with thy grace and heavenly aid,
to fill the hearts which thou hast made.

Great Paraclete, to thee we cry,
O highest gift of God most high,
O Fount of Life, O Fire of Love,
And sweet anointing from above.

Thou in thy sevenfold gifts art known;
The finger of God's hand we own;
the promise of the Father thou,
Who dost the tongue with pow'r endow.

Our senses kindle from above,
and make our hearts o'erflow with love,
with patience firm and virtue high,
the weakness of our flesh supply.

Drive far from us the foe we dread;
and grant us thy true peace instead;
so shall we not, with thee for Guide,
turn from the path of life aside.

O may thy grace on us bestow,
the Father and the Son to know,

**and thee, through endless times confess'd,
of both th'eternal Spirit blest.**

All glory while the ages run,
Be to the Father and the Son,
who rose from death; the same to thee,
O Holy Ghost, eternally! **Amen.**

Veni Creátor Spíritus,
Mentes tuórum visita,
Imple supérna grátia,
Quae tu creásti péctora.

Qui díceris Páraclitus,
Altíssimi donum Dei,
Fons vivus, ignis, cáritas
Et spiritális únctio.

Tu septifórmis múnere
Dígitus paternae dexterae
Tu rite promíssum Patris,
Sermóne ditans gúttura.

Accénde lumen sénsibus
Infúnde amórem córdibus;
Infírma nostri córporis
Virtúte firmans pérpeti.

Hostem repéllas lóngius,
Pacémque dones prótinus:
Ductóre sic te praévio
Vitémus omne nóxium

Per te sciámus da patrem,
Noscámus atque Fílium,
Teque utriúsque Spíritum
Credámus omni témpore.

Deo Patri sit glória,
Et Fílio, qui a mórtuis
Surréxit, ac Paráclito,
In saeculórum saécula.
Amen.

HYMNS FROM THE LITURGY FOR THE HOUR OF THE HOLY SPIRIT

The Holy Spirit manifested himself at Pentecost at the hour corresponding to "Terce" in the monastic liturgy: nine o'clock in the morning. This is the hour of the Holy Spirit! Given below are some hymns from the Prayer of the Church which may be sung or recited at that hour, or at any time when we feel the need to invoke the Holy Spirit.

1. Come, Holy Spirit, live in us
With God the Father and the Son,
And grant us your abundant grace
To sanctify and make us one.
May mind and tongue made strong in love,
Your praise throughout the world proclaim,
And may that love within our hearts
Set fire to others with its flame.
Most blessed Trinity of love
For whom the heart of man was made,
To you be praise in timeless song,
And everlasting homage paid.

2. Spirit of God, on the waste and the darkness
hov'ring in power as creation began,
drawing forth beauty from clay and from chaos,
breathing God's life in the nostrils of man.
Come and sow life in the waste of our being,
pray in us, from us as sons in the Son.
Open our hearts to yourself, mighty Spirit,
bear us to life in the Three who are One.

Come down, O love divine,
Seek thou this soul of mine,
And visit it with thine own ardour glowing;
O Comforter draw near,
Within my heart appear,
And kindle it, thy holy flame bestowing.

O let it freely burn,
Till earthly passions turn
To dust and ashes in its heat consuming;
And let thy glorious light
Shine ever on my sight,
And clothe me round, the while my path illuming.

Let holy charity
Mine outward vesture be,
And lowliness become mine inner clothing.
True lowliness of heart,
Which takes the humble part,
And o'er its own shortcoming weeps with loathing.
And so the yearning strong,
With which the soul will long,
Shall far outpass the power of human telling;
For none can guess its grace,
Till he become the place
Wherein the Holy Spirit makes his dwelling.

Bianco da Siena d 1434
Tr R. F. Littledale 1833-90

Love of the Father, Love of God the Son,
From whom all came, in whom was all begun;
Who formest heavenly beauty out of strife.
Creation's whole desire and breath of life:

Thou the All-holy, thou supreme in might.
Thou dost give peace, thy presence maketh right.
Thou with thy favour all things dost enfold,
With thine all-kindness free from harm wilt hold.

Purest and highest, wisest and most just,
There is no truth save only in thy trust;
Thou dost the mind from earthly dreams recall,
And bring, through Christ, to him for whom are all.

Eternal Glory, all men thee adore,
Who are and shalt be worshipped evermore:
Us whom thou madest, comfort with thy might,
And lead us to enjoy thy heavenly light.

Robert Bridges 1844-1930
Based on Amor Patris et Filii 12th century

PRAYER TO THE HOLY TRINITY

This prayer came from the heart of St. Francis of Assisi. It is noteworthy that the saint emphasizes the three interior actions of the Holy Spirit who purifies and enlightens us, and enkindles in us the fire of divine love.

Almighty, eternal righteous and merciful God, grant, by your grace that we, poor creatures, may do what we know you want us to do and may always want what pleases you.

And thus, purified in soul, interiorly enlightened and enkindled by the fire of the Holy Spirit, may we follow in the footsteps of Your Son, our Lord Jesus Christ, and reach you, O Most High, with the help of your grace alone.

You who live and reign in glory, in perfect Trinity and in simple unity, O Almighty God, forever and ever. **Amen.**

PRAYER TO THE HOLY SPIRIT
THAT HE MAY RAISE UP HOLY
AND WISE PRIESTS IN THE CHURCH

O Holy Spirit, You who in scripture are called Spirit of Truth, Sanctity and the Field which produces good fruits, raise up in your Church holy and wise priests, so that, through the ministry of the Word, accompanied by their good example, and through the administration of the Sacraments instituted by Christ, they may produce many abundant and eternal fruits of eternal life in souls, in order to bring about soon the religious renewal of the world which our Holy Father the Pope desires.

Our Father
Hail Mary
Glory Be

PRAYER TO THE HOLY SPIRIT TO GROW IN TRUST AND ABANDONMENT

O Holy Spirit,
Spirit of Knowledge,
Spirit of Wisdom,
Spirit of Love,
You alone know the Truth,
You alone can examine the essence
and the true meaning of all reality.
You alone know exactly what is good and what is
bad for me.
Spirit of God, I abandon myself to You.
I do not want to know
more than what I must know.
I do not want to say
more than what I must say.
I want nothing more
than that which You have decided for me.
You love me and know what is good for me.
Spirit of Love, pour out on me
all the gifts that You now wish to give me.
Praise be to You.
Amen.

PRAYER FOR THE COMING OF THE HOLY SPIRIT

Come, O true light. Come, hidden mystery.
Come, treasure without a name.
Come, everlasting happiness.
Come, light without dusk.
Come, expectancy of all those
who are to be saved.
Come, awakening of those
who have gone to sleep.
Come you, O powerful one,
who always do and re-do
and transform by your will alone.
Come, O invisible One.
Come, you who are above the heavens,
you who are always still,
and yet at every moment,
move your entire self to come to us,
who lie in the depths of Sheol.
Come, O beloved Name
that is repeated everywhere; but whose nature
and being we can neither
comprehend nor express.
Come, eternal joy.
Come, purple robe of the great King, our God.
Come, you who have desired
and desire my miserable soul.
Come, O Sun, for as you see, I am alone.
Come, you who have separated me from every-

thing and have given me solitude in this world.
Come, you who have become what I long for,
you who have enkindled in me a desire for you.
Come, my breath and my life.
Come, comforter of my poor soul.
Come, my everlasting joy and glory.

PRAYER TO THE HOLY SPIRIT FOR SOMEONE WHO BLASPHEMES

O Holy Spirit, you know how much I suffer because of blasphemy. You know how many punishments it causes on earth; so I pray to you, with all my heart, that you, like a mighty wind, may shatter the vices which are most deeply rooted in human hearts, so that this person may renounce the habit of offending divine things and, instead of blaspheming, become devout, serene and persevering in adversity.

**Our Father
Hail Mary
Glory Be**

PRAYER FOR THE GIFT
OF THE HOLY SPIRIT

O Jesus, we are your brothers and sisters who suffer in our bodies which have been redeemed by you.

But our spirit calls on you, O God, and invokes your Spirit: pour out on us your Holy Spirit, so that he may increase our love. Send us your Holy Spirit, which is Love, to heal our wounds. We desire to learn from You, to give You all our life and all that we possess. Life is born in our hearts by means of the Spirit, the same life that you lived, O Jesus, the same life that you gave through your Spirit to the Virgin Mary, who conceived You in her womb. Give us your Spirit which is Life. O Jesus, give us and send us the Spirit to free us from our fear of beginning a new life. Free us from every temptation, from the evil spirit who is active everyday, who wants to rush us, who desires to put temptations of intolerance into our hearts: "I haven't the time, I don't understand a thing", who desires to put tension and stress into our heart. O Jesus, we do not fear; we are joyful because your Spirit is capable of changing us. The times in which we live are dangerous. You want to save us; You have no time to lose. You desire to change us immediately, to put your plan into our heart. Yes, we know we are weak. Put your word in our heart, take us by the hand, and on those difficult days, take each one of us, bring us before the Lord, before the Holy Spirit, so that we may become simple, obedient and humble. Help us, O Mother! In the name of your Son and our God, let us pray for the gift of the Holy Spirit.

Glory Be *(3 times)*

PRAYER OF SAINT CATHERINE OF SIENA
to the Holy Spirit

Biographers say that St. Catherine of Siena asked one day in the year 1377 for some cinnabar (the red ink used in that time) although she did not know how to write, and wrote this prayer in her own hand:

O Holy Spirit, come into my heart, through your power draw it to yourself who are the true God, grant me charity and fear of the Lord, deliver me from every evil thought, warm me and inflame me with your love so that every burden may seem light to me. My Holy Father, my sweet Lord, help me in all of my duties; love of Christ, love of Christ. **Amen.**

PRAYERS TO THE HOLY SPIRIT

by Sr. Carmel of the Holy Spirit

1. O Holy Spirit, substance of the love between the Father and the Son, incarnate Love which dwells in the souls of the righteous, come upon me with a new Pentecost, bringing me the abundance of your gifts, your fruits, and your grace, and unite yourself to me to become the sweet spouse of my soul. I consecrate myself entirely to you: invade me, take all of me, possess me entirely. O Spirit who give life, come upon this poor society, and renew the face of the earth. Assist your impoverished Church, give her holy priests and fervent apostles. Enkindle gentle inspirations in good souls, be a sweet torment to sinful souls, a comforting refreshment to suffering and afflicted souls, strength and help to those in temptation, light to those who are in darkness and in the shadow of death.

2. O Holy Spirit, I place myself before you, as a little unripe fruit which must ripen under the sun, as a blade of straw to be burnt by the fire, as a drop of dew which must be absorbed by the sun, as an ignorant child who needs to be instructed... O Holy Spirit, you pour yourself out on the small, poor and humble souls. I want to present myself to you in this attitude,

and with these desires I invoke you: Come, Holy Spirit, sanctify me! I have a great desire for sanctity! Sanctify me, make a saint of me, a great saint, make me a saint quickly, without my becoming aware of it.

PRAYER FROM THE
SACRAMENT OF CONFIRMATION

In this prayer, taken from the Rite of Confirmation, we ask for the gifts of the Holy Spirit which we always need to strengthen our "interior being" in order that we may be healed of our vices.

All powerful God,
Father of our Lord Jesus Christ,
by water and the Holy Spirit
you freed your sons and daughters from sin and gave them new life.
Send your Holy Spirit upon them to be their helper and guide.
Give them the spirit of
wisdom and understanding,
the spirit of right judgement and courage,
the spirit of knowledge and reverence.
Fill them with the spirit of wonder and awe in your presence.
We ask this through Christ our Lord.
Amen.

Prayer to the Holy Spirit for Those Who Speak Ill of the Pope

O Holy Spirit, you who are the heart and soul of the mystical body of the Church and who, in a special way, assist its leader so that he may not err, we ask you to enlighten all those who speak ill of the Pope, so that, after the darkness caused by ignorance and slander has been dissipated, they may understand and acknowledge that the Vicar of Christ speaks in the name of God, in order to spread the Gospel Truth, virtue and peace in the world; may they understand the supreme and divine gift which Jesus Christ has given to his Church in establishing the Papacy; thus, may they join the multitude of true Christians who treat the Pope with great devotion and veneration, and feel the need to pray for him, so that the Lord may grant him life, grant him happiness and blessings on earth and do not abandon him to the mercy of his enemies.

**Our Father
Hail Mary
Glory Be**

PRAYER TO THE HOLY SPIRIT FOR DISCERNMENT OF THE TRUTH

O Spirit of God, who through your light, can distinguish between truth and error, help us to know the truth.

Dispel our illusions and show us reality.
Grant that we may recognise the true language of God in the depth of our soul, and help us to distinguish it from every other voice.
Show us your Divine Will in every circumstance of our life, so that we may make the right decisions.

Help us to discern the signs of God in all events, the proposals which he makes to us, the teachings which he wants to inculcate in us.
Grant that we may discern your suggestions, so that we may not miss any of your inspirations.

Give us that supernatural perception which allows us to discover what love demands, and grant us to understand all that generosity asks of us.

And above all, lift our gaze to you, O Holy Spirit, to wherever your activity reaches us and touches us.
Through Jesus Christ our Lord. **Amen.**

"ADSUMUS"

An ancient prayer to the Holy Spirit

We are here before you, O Holy Spirit: we feel the burden of our weaknesses, but come together in your name; come to us, assist us, come down into our hearts: teach us what we must do, show us the path to follow, may you yourself accomplish what you ask of us.

May you alone be the one to inspire and guide our decisions, because only you, together with God the Father and his Son, have a holy and glorious name: you who love order and peace, do not let righteousness be harmed by us; may ignorance not cause us to stray from the right path, may affection for others not give rise to favouritism on our part, may neither titles nor people influence us; keep us close to you through the gift of your grace, so that we may be one in you and that we may not draw away from the truth in any matter.

Grant that, gathered together in your holy name, we may be able to combine goodness with firmness, so as to do all things in harmony with you, in the hope that we shall earn, through the faithful fulfilment of our duties, eternal happiness in the future.
Amen.

Glory Be *(3 times)*

COME, SPIRIT OF LIFE

Come, Spirit of life, and renew the work of creation, in order to give birth to a more human and righteous society.

Come, Spirit of knowledge, and render your Church wholly obedient to the words of the Gospel.

Come, Spirit of grace, and transform the Church with your holiness, so that she may become ever more the family of the children of God.

Come, Spirit of counsel, and guide your Church along the way of history.

Come, Spirit of mercy, and free your Church with merciful love from the slavery of evil.

Come, Spirit of praise, and impart to your Church wisdom about all matters concerning God.

Come, Spirit of fortitude, and give to your Church the courage to announce the Gospel of salvation to all people.

Come, Spirit of service, build your Church upon the foundations of unity and peace, so that she may dwell in harmony with the joys and sufferings of all humanity.

Come, Spirit of resurrection; as you have raised Jesus from death, bring all people to eternal life and glory.

PRAYER TO OBTAIN THE SEVEN GIFTS OF THE HOLY SPIRIT

O Lord Jesus Christ, before ascending into heaven, you promised to send us the Holy Spirit in order to complete your work in the souls of the apostles and disciples:

Grant that I may receive the same **Holy Spirit** so that he may bring to perfection the work of your grace and love in my soul.

Grant me the **Spirit of Wisdom,** so that I may not become attached to the transient things of this world and desire only those things that last unto eternity.

Grant me the **Spirit of Understanding**, to enlighten my mind with the light of your divine truth.

Grant me the **Spirit of Right Judgement**, so that I may always choose the way that is most likely to please God, by fulfilling his will.

Grant me the **Spirit of Courage**, so that I may carry my cross with you and may overcome with fortitude all the obstacles which oppose my salvation.

Grant me the **Spirit of Knowledge**, so that I may come to know God and myself, and my knowledge may grow to become like that of the saints.

Grant me the **Spirit of Reverence**, so that, with the love of a child, I may consider my service of God to be sweet and amiable.

Grant me the **Spirit of Wonder and awe in God's presence**, so that I may be filled with a loving respect towards God and I may always be wary of displeasing him in any way.

Therefore, I beseech you, O Lord, mark me with the seal of true discipleship and grant that your Spirit may inspire me in all that I do.
Amen.

PRAYER FOR THE GIFT
OF THE HOLY SPIRIT

Eternal Father, in the name of Jesus Christ and through the intercession of the Immaculate Virgin Mary, send me the Holy Spirit.

Come into my heart, O Holy Spirit, and sanctify it. Come, Father of the poor, and give me relief. Come, Author of all that is good, and refresh me. Come, Light of all minds, and enlighten me. Come, Comforter of souls, and console me. Come, sweet Guest of hearts, and do not leave me. Come, true solace of my life, and restore me.

Glory Be *(3 times)*

Holy Spirit, eternal Love.
Come to us with your zeal,
Come, inflame our hearts.

Eternal Father, in the name of Jesus Christ and through the intercession of the Immaculate Virgin Mary, send me the Holy Spirit.

Holy Spirit, God of infinite mercy, give me your holy love. Holy Spirit, God of virtues, convert me. Holy Spirit, Source of heavenly light, dissipate my ignorance. Holy Spirit, God of infinite purity, sanctify my soul. Holy Spirit, God of all happiness, enter into my heart. Holy Spirit, you who live in my soul, transform it and make it all yours. Holy Spirit, substance of the Love of the Father and the Son, make my heart your dwelling place forever.

Glory Be *(see above)*

Eternal Father, in the name of Jesus Christ and through the intercession of the Immaculate Virgin Mary, send me the Holy Spirit.

Come, Holy Spirit, give me the gift of Wisdom. Come, Holy Spirit, give me the gift of Understanding. Come, Holy Spirit, give me the gift of Counsel. Come, Holy Spirit, give me the gift of Fortitude. Come, Holy Spirit, give me the gift of Know-ledge. Come, Holy Spirit, give me the gift of Reverence. Come, Holy Spirit, give me the gift of Wonder and Awe in God's presence.

Glory Be *(see above)*

Let us pray.
O Holy Spirit, soul of my soul, I adore you: enlighten me, guide me, fortify me, comfort me, teach me what I must do, command me. I promise to submit myself to all that you desire of me and to accept all that you may allow to happen to me: grant that I may know Your will.
Amen.

PRAYER OF SUPPLICATION
TO THE HOLY SPIRIT

This prayer has been trnslated from the Croatian language and bears the imprimatur of the Archbishop of Zagabria (dated the 30th of June, 1989). It is a very beautiful and inspired prayer which asks for a new Pentecost for all the Church "through the intecession and under the guidance and protection of Mary, the Spouse of the Holy Spirit, the Queen of Peace".

Come Holy Spirit, pour forth on us the source of Your grace and enkindle a new Pentecost in Your Church!

Come down upon Your bishops, Your priests, Your religious, upon Your faithful and upon those who do not believe, upon the most hardened of sinners, and finally, upon each one of us! Come down upon all the people of the world, upon all races, and upon every class and category of people!

Stir us with Your divine breath, purify us of all our sins, and free us from all deceit and evil! Inflame us with Your fire; grant that we may burn and be consumed in Your love!

Teach us to understand that God is everything - all our happiness and joy, our present, our future and our eternity are in his hands. Come Holy Spirit and transform us, save us, reconcile us, unite us and consecrate us to yourself!

Teach us to belong completely to Christ, to be

totally Yours, to belong totally to God! This we ask you through the intercession and under the guidance and protection of the Blessed Virgin Mary, Your Immaculate Spouse, Mother of Jesus and our Mother, the Queen of Peace!
Amen.

Hymn:
SPIRIT OF THE LIVING GOD

Spirit of the living God, fall afresh on me
Spirit of the living God, fall afresh on me
Melt me, mould me, fill me, use me,
Spirit of the living God, fall afresh on me.

Spirit of the living God, fall afresh on all
Spirit of the living God, fall afresh on all
Melt us, mould us, fill us, use us,
Spirit of the living God, fall afresh on all.

Invocation of the Spirit of Love

Come, O Spirit of Love, and renew the face of the earth; grant that all things may become a new garden of graces and holiness, of justice and love, of communion and peace, so that the Most Holy Trinity may once again be loved and glorified.

Come, O Spirit of Love, and renew the whole Church: bring her to perfection in love, unity and holiness, so that she may become this day a great light to illumine all people in the darkness which envelops the world.

Come, O Spirit of Wisdom and Understanding, and open our hearts so that we may comprehend the whole truth. With the ardent strength of your divine fire, root out every error, sweep away all heresies, so that the light of truth, which Jesus has revealed, may shine on everyone in its fullness.

Come, O Spirit of Counsel and Courage, and grant that we may be courageous witnesses of the Gospel which we have heard. Sustain those who are persecuted; give courage to those who suffer discrimination in society; give strength to those who are imprisoned; grant perseverance to those who are crushed or tortured; give the palm of victory to those who are led to martyrdom in these times.

Come, O Spirit of Knowledge, Reverence, and Wonder and Awe in God's presence, and with the sap of your Divine Love, renew the lives of all those who have been consecrated through Baptism and marked by your seal in Confirmation, of those who have offered themselves to the service of God, of bishops, priests, and deacons, so that they may all co-operate in the plan which you seek to fulfil in these times for the renewed Pentecost invoked and awaited for so long.

SEND FORTH YOUR SPIRIT

Send me, your Spirit O Jesus; pour forth your Spirit upon me, may he penetrate, enlighten and sanctify my soul.

Grant that from now on I may live only according to the will of your Holy Spirit, so that I may be like you, who from the crib to the cross, worked and suffered, inspired by Love alone.

Therefore, I repeat my plea to you: Send me your Spirit, pour forth your Spirit upon me: to be the light which illumines my path, to be the teacher who instructs me, to be the guide who directs me, to be the source which quenches my thirst, purifies and enriches me, to be a companion in my travels and my comforter, to be the bond which confirms me in your friendship, for ever and ever. **Amen.**

COME, HOLY SPIRIT

Come, Holy Spirit: unify all the elements of my being; help me to love myself and to appreciate my human and Christian dignity.

Come, Holy Spirit, and destroy my selfishness with the fire of your light.

Come, Holy Spirit, and grant that my "old self" which leads me to sin may die.

Come, Holy Spirit, and renew me so that I may become a new creature.

Come, Holy Spirit and enkindle in me the fire of your love so that I may love all men and women, especially the poor and those most in need of help.

Come, Holy Spirit, and make me humble, so that I may glorify God.

Come, Holy Spirit, and lead me to the complete truth, renouncing falsity and deceit.

Come, Holy Spirit and enlighten me, so that I may be able to discern what is false, especially when Satan disguises himself as an angel of light.

Come, Holy Spirit and grant that I may open my heart fully to your inspirations.

Do with me as you please; I submit myself to *your* plans rather than mine; I want my life to be only what you want to make of it.

Come, Holy Spirit, and give me understanding and love of the Word of God. Open my ears so that I may hear your Word, and give me a strong will in order that I may follow and obey it.

Come, Spirit of the risen Christ, and render me a member of his Mystical Body.

Come, Spirit of the glorified Christ, and create unity among us, demolish the barriers of hate and discord which we have built up with our selfishness.

Come, Spirit of communion between the Father and the Son, and gather the people of God into one heart, one soul, one faith and one Father.

Come, Spirit of health, and heal our wounded relationships.

Come, Spirit of truth, so that we may act with truth, justice and peace towards each other.

Come, Spirit of unity, and gather all those who call themselves Christians into a single flock guided by a single Shepherd.

Come, Spirit of Creation, and renew the face of the earth; create the new heaven and the new earth of which we are in need and await.

Come, Spirit of renewal, and establish justice in the world.

Come, Spirit of hope, grant that we may believe that good shall have victory over evil; grant that we may sow the seeds of goodness.
Amen.

THREE INVOCATIONS OF MARY TO OBTAIN THE HOLY SPIRIT

O most pure Virgin Mary, who, in the Immaculate Conception became the chosen tabernacle of Divinity by the power of the Holy Spirit, pray for us.

May the Divine Paraclete come soon
and renew the face of the earth.

Hail Mary

O most pure Virgin Mary, who, in the mystery of the Incarnation, became the true Mother of God by the power of the Holy Spirit, pray for us.
May the Divine...

O most pure Virgin Mary, who, while praying together with the Apostles in the Cenacle, were filled with the Holy Spirit, pray for us.
May the Divine...

Send forth thy Spirit, and they shall be created.
And thou shalt renew the face of the earth.

Let us pray.
May your Spirit come, O Lord, and may he transform us interiorly with his gifts: may he create in us a new heart, so that, in all things, we may please you and accomplish your will. Through Christ our Lord. **Amen.**

ACTS OF CONSECRATION

ACT OF CONSECRATION
TO THE HOLY SPIRIT

O Holy Spirit,
Love that proceeds from the Father and the Son,
Endless source of grace and life,
I wish to consecrate myself to you:
my past, my present, my future,
my desires, my choices,
my decisions, my thoughts, my feelings,
all that belongs to me
and all that I am.
Let all those whom I meet, whom I think of,
whom I know, whom I love,
and all things that I will encounter in my life
be glorified by the power
of your Light, your Warmth, and your Peace.
You are the Lord, the giver of live,
and without your strength, nothing is free from
taint or ill.
O Spirit of Eternal Love,
come into my heart, renew it
and make it ever more similar to the Heart of
Mary, so that I may be now and forever
a temple and tabernacle of your Divine Presence.

Glory Be *(3 times)*

CONSECRATION TO THE HOLY SPIRIT

O Holy Spirit, soul of souls, I consecrate myself totally to you. Guide me to Jesus, by the hand of Mary, so that I may become a little song of praise and glory before the Heavenly Father.

Give me a love that is patient and kind, that is never envious, that is not boastful or conceited, a well-balanced love that has no fear, that never seeks its own advantage, that does not become angry or take offence, that neither stores up grievances nor rejoices at wrongdoing but finds its joy in the truth and in discovering the goodness, truth and beauty in others, a love that is always ready to make allowances, to trust, to hope and to endure whatever comes.

(ref. 1 Cor 13:4-6).

Furthermore, grant that I may have an attitude of humility like that of our Lord Jesus Christ, who, being in the form of God, did not count equality with God something to be grasped. But he emptied himself, taking the form of a slave, becoming as human beings are; and being in every way like a human being, he was humbler yet, even to accepting death, death on a cross.

(ref. Phil 2:6-8).

Novena to the Holy Spirit

To be recited for nine consecutive days without interruption (if you forget to recite it one day you must start over), beginning from the friday before the solemnity of the Ascension, or each time you wish to express your devotion to the Holy Spirit or that you wish to request a grace from the Lord by means of his intercession.

*In the name of the Father, the Son,
and the Holy Spirit. Amen.*

O God come to my aid.
O Lord, make haste to help me.

Glory be
The Creed *(see page 26)*

Holy Spirit, **gift of God to my soul,** I am overcome with emotion and admiration when I think of You. I find no words which can express the deep happiness which I feel, knowing that You are my most sweet and divine guest. Contemplation of You fills my soul with peace and love, like water that floods the land.

I am awed at so much condescension on Your part; I think of your beauty, greater than all works and beyond all powers of imagination; I think of

Your infinite wealth of grace, gifts, virtues, fruits and beatitudes.

I think of Your tender goodness, which prompts You to make your dwelling place in me. You have everything, You can do everything, You want to give me everything.

I find myself in a state of wondrous admiration in spite of my wretchedness which makes me the last, the smallest, on the earth.

I bless You, I adore You, I thank You, I ask everything of You. Give me everything, O Holy Spirit.

Glory Be

Spirit of the Lord and Heavenly Giver, I ask You in all humility but also with all the strength of my ardent desires I to give me Your holy gifts, in particular wisdom and reverence. Make these gifts grow in me until they become fully nature, so that **my soul may be meek and obedient to you, Master of my interior life** so that I may always live by Your gifts, and in joyous and intimate contemplation of You and of the Blessed Trinity.

Glory Be

Holy Spirit, Master of holiness and interior life, I beseech You, with untiring insistence, to instruct my mind in Your truth and to speak to my heart; I ask you to make me holy, taking care of my soul as You took care of **Our Lady Your Immaculate Spouse, and of the martyrs and the saint.**

I am thirsty for holiness; not for my own glory, but in order to give glory to You, Master of masters, and in order to render glory to the Holy Trinity and splendour to the Church, and to give a good example to souls. There is no better way of being a true apostle than to be holy because without holiness, very little is achieved. Holy Spirit, hear my prayer and grant all my ardent desires.

Glory Be

Holy Spirit, **most blessed truth and light,** I feel a deep sadness in recognising that You are completely unknown or forgotten by most of us. We never think of you, distracted as we are by so many worries, absorbed by the spirit of the world, careless and heedless of Your cares and thoughtfulness. What ingratitude on our part! The fault is largerly ours, because those of us who know You hardly ever speak to other souls about You. Accept, Divine Spirit, these humble feelings of mine, in reparation for such deplorable forgetfulness, and consider them a request for enlightenment; this I ask for myself, for priests and for all the faithful.

Glory Be

Holy Spirit, **love and gentleness of the Father and of the Son, flower and perfume of the holiness of God,** divine fire enkindled within me, renew my heart; wipe away every stain and all darkness, burn every impurity and grant that I may resemble the image of Your Divine Son.

Spirit of fire, You who deign to live within me in order to sanctify me, enkindle in me the fire of your love, penetrate and surround my soul with your flame; drive away every disordered bodily desire, encourage me to take up apostolic missions; give me the grace of becoming a flame that burns with pure and eternal love.

Glory Be

Spirit of Courage, **who have given the strength to martyrs to die joyfully for the sake of Lord Jesus Christ,** fill me with this divine gift in all its intensity. Shake off my torpor and laziness, make me courageous in undertaking all that the Lord asks of me, willing to make sacrifices and not being discouraged by fatigue, for the sake of Your glory and for the spiritual and material benefit of my brothers and sisters. Give me the strength to go on with burning zeal, without becoming weary or leaving unfinished what I have begun.

Give me courage and energy to defend the Church without fear, to profess before all people the integrity of faith, and grant that I may be truly obedient to the Pope and to the Bishops. Give me heavenly inspirations to carry out my apostolate; may I persevere to the end, even to the point of martyrdom of the body or soul, if that is Your will Divine Spirit, surround me with Your omnipotence, sustain me with Your vigour, and clothe me with Your invincible strength.

Glory Be

Spirit of light and truth, flame and heat coming from the light, that most blessed light, **dissipate and disperse the shadows of error and doubt from my mind.** Irradiate and enlighten with perfect clarity the depths of my soul, so that I may always reject every error and may adhere strongly to the truth in accordance with the teachings of the Church; may my path in life be always illuminated by Your brightness. Clothed with Your holy light, may I always remain faithful to Your truth and radiant purity.

Glory Be

Purifying Spirit, cleanse me of every stain. Sanctify me and give me the virtues of Jesus, His very intentions and interior dispositions. **May You be the same Spirit of Christ within me.** Inspire my soul with the same love towards Jesus that the Father gives to His Divine Son, and give me the same affection that the Father feels for His dearly beloved Son Jesus.

Glory Be

Holy Spirit, **I beseech you to enlighten my mind** with your clarity, so much needed by me and by those who question me; I beg You to sustain my weak will with your gifts of love and courage. **Divine sanctifying Spirit, lead me to the peak of sanctity,** through continuous, patient work on my part, submitting myself to Your inspirations and care. **You are holiness and I must allow you to live in me, co-operating with Your work of perfection.** O Divine Renewing Spirit, renew everything, take away from me all evil, all danger, and everything that does me no good; make me new, pure, and holy. Life-giving Divine Spirit, soul of my soul, give me the strength to bear witness to the Divine Son at all times, and to glorify Him, together with You, and to live for His glory and die in His love. Divine Giver, bestow on me your gifts in order that I may contemplate God in the light of His mysteries, comprehend the true value of life and of all things, and may love everyone with pure love, as if I were already in paradise. Thank you! **Amen.**

LITANY OF THE HOLY SPIRIT

Lord, have mercy on us,	**Have mercy on us.**
Christ, have mercy on us,	**Have mercy on us.**
Lord, have mercy on us,	**Have mercy on us.**
Father all power,	**Have mercy on us.**
Jesus, Eternal Son of the Father, Redeemer of the world,	**Save us.**
Spirit of the Father and the Son, boundless life of both,	**Sanctify us.**
Holy Trinity,	**Hear us.**
Holy Spirit, who proceed from the Father and the Son,	**Enter our hearts.**
Holy Spirit, who are equal to the Father and to the Son	**Have mercy on us.**
Promise of God the Father,	**Have mercy on us.**
Ray of heavenly light,	**Have mercy on us.**
Author of all good,	**Have mercy on us.**
Source of heavenly water,	**Have mercy on us.**
Consuming fire,	**Have mercy on us.**
Ardent charity,	**Have mercy on us.**
Spiritual unction,	**Have mercy on us.**
Spirit of love and truth,	**Have mercy on us.**
Spirit of wisdom and understanding,	
	Have mercy on us.

Spirit of counsel and fortitude,

Have mercy on us.

Spirit of wonder and awe in God's presence,

Have mercy on us.

Spirit of grace and prayer,

Have mercy on us.

Spirit of peace and meekness,

Have mercy on us.

Spirit of modesty and innocence,

Have mercy on us.

Holy Spirit, the Comforter,

Have mercy on us.

Holy Spirit, the Sanctifier,

Have mercy on us.

Holy Spirit, Who govern the Church,

Have mercy on us.

Gift of God, the Most High,

Have mercy on us.

Spirit Who fill the universe,

Have mercy on us.

Spirit of the adoption of the children of God,

Have mercy on us.

Holy Spirit,

Inspire us with horror of sin.

Holy Spirit,

Come and renew the face of the earth.

Holy Spirit,

Shed Your light in our souls.

Holy Spirit,

Engrave Your law in our hearts.

Holy Spirit,

Inflame us with the flame of Your love.

Holy Spirit,

Open to us the treasures of Your graces.

Holy Spirit,

Teach us to pray well.

Holy Spirit,

Enlighten us with Your heavenly inspirations.

Holy Spirit,

Lead us in the way of salvation.

Holy Spirit,

Grant us the only necessary knowledge.

Holy Spirit,

Inspire in us the practice of good.

Holy Spirit,

Grant us the merits of all virtues.

Holy Spirit,

Make us persevere in doing Your will.

Holy Spirit,

Be our everlasting reward.

**Lamb of God, you take away
the sins of the world,**
send us Your Holy Spirit.

**Lamb of God, you take away
the sins of the world,**
pour down into our souls the gifts
of the Holy Spirit.

**Lamb of God, you take away
the sins of the world,**
grant us the Spirit of wisdom and reverence.

Come, Holy Spirit! Fill the hearts of Your faithful.
And enkindle in them the fire of Your Love.

Let us pray.
Grant, O merciful Father, that Your Divine Spirit
may enlighten, inflame and purify us, that He
may penetrate us with His heavenly dew and
make us fruitful in good works; through our Lord
Jesus Christ, Your Son, Who lives and reigns with
You in the unity of the same Spirit, forever and
ever. **Amen.**

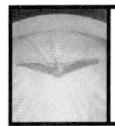

CHAPLET OF THE HOLY SPIRIT

Written by Blessed Elena Guerra following the exhortation of Pope Leo XIII on the 5th of May, 1895.

In the name of the Father, the Son, and the Holy Spirit. Amen.

O God come to my aid.
O Lord, make haste to help me.

Glory be
The Creed *(see page 26)*

Come, O Spirit of Wisdom, may we be detached from the things of this world, and fill us with love and attraction for the things of heaven.

Holy Father, in the name of Jesus,
send your Spirit to renew the world.
(To be said 7 times)

Come, O Spirit of Understanding, enlighten our mind with the light of eternal truth and enrich it with holy thoughts.

Holy Father...

Come, O Spirit of Counsel, render us obedient to your inspirations and guide us on the way of salvation.

Holy Father...

Come, O Spirit of Courage, and give us strength, constancy and victory in the battles against our spiritual enemies.

Holy Father...

Come, O Spirit of Knowledge, be the master of our souls and help us to put your teachings into practice.

Holy Father...

Come, O Spirit of Reverence, come and dwell in our hearts so that you may possess and sanctify all our affections.

Holy Father...

Come, O Spirit of Wonder and Awe in God's presence, reign over our will and grant that we may always be disposed to suffer rather than fall into sin.

Holy Father...

Rosary of the Holy Spirit

*In the name of the Father, the Son,
and the Holy Spirit. Amen.*

O God come to my aid.
O Lord, make haste to help me.

Glory be
The Creed *(see page 26)*

*On the beads of the Our Father,
we recite the following prayer:*

O Holy Spirit, soul of my soul, I adore you: enlighten me, guide me, strengthen me, comfort me, teach me what I must do, give me your commands. I promise to submit myself to all that you desire from me and to accept all that you allow to happen to me: grant that I may only know your will.

*On the beads of the Hail Mary,
we recite the following invocations:*

Come, Holy Spirit,
Come, Divine Power of Love,
Come and fill my poor heart:
Purify it, sanctify it, make it all yours

The Mother of God

1.

THE HOLY ROSARY

INTRODUCTION TO THE HOLY ROSARY

Many people are skeptical about recent Marian apparitions, as they consider Divine Revelation to have ended with the Book of Revelation, maintaining that God has entrusted all the truth and means of grace to the Church, and that these are sufficient.

All of this is true, but it can also be said that the truths of faith need to be renewed continually in our memory. Here-in lies the providential nature of the apparitions of Our Lady: the Virgin Mary comes to remind us of the truth of the Gospel, of the tradition of the Church and of the means necessary to be healed of the ills which we ourselves have caused by our carelessness and by having drawn away from God.

Mary comes to open our hearts to conversion and thus to the grace of the Lord.

*Among the apparitions of the last two centuries, we recall that which occurred at **Rue du Bac, Paris, in 1830** when the Virgin Mary appeared to **St. Catherine Labouré,** inviting her to have the Miraculous Medal struck, a devotion which has spread rapidly throughout the world; through the same medal, many cures and conversions have come about and continue to occur.*

*In 1846, the **Virgin Mary appeared at La Salette in France to two little shepherds, Maximin and Melanie,** and she invited us with insistence and with tears in her eyes to prayer and conversion.*

*In 1858, **Mary appeared to Bernadette Soubirous** seventeen times at Lourdes, inviting us to repentance and to pray for sinners, presenting herself as the Immaculate Conception.*

At Fatima in 1917, the Virgin Mary appeared to three little shepherds (Lucia, Blessed Francisco and Blessed Jacinta) *revealing a secret in three parts to them and* *renewing her invitation to prayer, especially to the Holy Rosary, as well as calling us to repent, to return to God and to make sacrifices. Here she proclaimed herself to be the Virgin of the Holy Rosary.*

*Some years after the Second World War, the presumed **apparitions in Medjugorje** began to take place and remind us of the message of Fatima in all its purity, while inserting it into an educational path of conversion and spiritual growth. This phenomenon takes place in a world which is moving ever further away from God in the name of presumed progress and false freedom.*

Whether or not these facts are authentic, the visionaries have declared that they will adhere scrupulously to the final judgement of the Church. The events began on the 24th of June, 1981: the Virgin Mary appeared to four young girls and two young boys, at Medjugorje (under the municipality of Citluck near Mostar in Croatia) The apparitions, which continue to this day, recur on a daily basis.

The visionaries have been entrusted with many messages, which can be summarized in five simple words: peace, faith, conversion, prayer and fasting.

"Peace, peace, peace! Be reconciled". This is the first message of the Virgin Mary, who pronounced these words on the third day that She appeared. Indeed, at Medjugorje, she appears as the Queen of Peace.

Only God can give us true peace, and for this reason Mary invites us to reconciliation with God, with humankind and with ourselves, so that peace may reign in our hearts.

*The second message of the Virgin Mary concerns **faith.***

Since the first days of the apparitions the Blessed Virgin has spoken about faith, insisting on the importance and necessity of this gift in order to attain peace. Mary also points out that trust in God and abandonment to Him are the primary conditions for the fulfillment of every prayer, desire and request, and for the acceptance of all suffering according to the will of God.

*Mary also indicates **conversion** as being a condition for peace. Conversion of the heart, that is renewal of the heart, creates and nourishes serene and stable social relationships and brings justice to laws, structures, environments and ways of life on a human scale.*

To help us on our road of conversion, the Virgin Mary invites us to go frequently to Confession.

*From the fifth day on, Mary has recommended **prayer** nearly every day in her messages. She invites everyone to pray ceaselessly and to pray with the heart. Prayer in this way strengthens and deepens the bond between people and God, which is necessary for peace.*

- *At the beginning, she asked for 7 Our Fathers, 7 Hail Marys, 7 Glory Bes and the Creed;*
- *Then she asked for at least one Rosary;*
- *Later (in 1984) she asked for the recitation of the whole Rosary (Joyful, Sorrowful and Glorious mysteries);*
- *Mary has also asked that we read the Bible daily and has invited us to attend Mass every day, as well as to live a deeper sacramental life.*

It is obvious that the above is a path of spiritual instruction that Mary follows with all of her children who are ready to live her messages and to work together with her in order to experience peace and to offer it to others.

In many of her messages, the Virgin Mary also recommends the practice of fasting, (except for those who are seriously ill), the best fast being on bread and water. In particular, Our Lady invites us to fast on Wednesdays and Fridays. Apart from being a valuable instrument which God uses to save souls and to bring about other spiritual and material good in the world, fasting greatly benefits those who practise it: by fasting we learn to exercise our self-control, free ourselves from our attachments and disordered bodily desires, and render ourselves capable of giv-

ing ourselves to God and to our neighbour. Fasting is moreover a means of sustaining our prayer, of strengthening our faith and of leading us to abandon ourselves into God's hands; thus it becomes a path towards conversion and peace.

In her messages, Mary also warns against temptations and the plans of Satan which would like to destroy God's plan of salvation. She tells us, however, not to be afraid because she is with us.

The Virgin has declared herself to be a mother, our mother who loves us.

COMMENTARIES OF THE SAINTS AND HOLY FATHERS ON THE "HAIL MARY"

Saint Louis Marie Grignon De Montfort (1673-1716) left us these words: **"I fervently beg you, for the love I have for you in Jesus and Mary, to recite the Holy Rosary every day, because at the moment of your death, you will bless the day and the hour in which you have believed in my message, and after having sown the blessings of Jesus and Mary, you will reap eternal blessings in heaven".**

The Holy Rosary should be preceded by the Creed and by three Hail Marys while meditating on the relationship of Mary with the Holy Trinity: Mary is the Daughter of the Father, Mother of the Son and Spouse of the Holy Spirit.

To make known the importance of the Hail Mary, it was necessary for the Virgin Mary to appear many times to great and enlightened saints, such as St. Dominic, St. John of Capestrano, Blessed Alan of Rupe. The saints have written books on the effectiveness of the Hail Mary to obtain the conversion of souls, and have preached openly about it as follows:

• *The salvation of the world began with the words contained in the Hail Mary, and thus the salvation of all peo-*

ple depends on such a prayer;

- This prayer produced the fruit of life from the sterile and arid earth, and therefore, if recited well, it will allow the Word of God and the fruit of life, Jesus Christ, to germinate within us;
- The Hail Mary is dew from heaven which is sprinkled on the earth of our soul so that, in time, it may bear fruit;
- There is no better secret than this to know if a person is of God: if he or she loves to recite the Hail Mary and the Rosary.
- After the Our Father, the Hail Mary is the most beautiful prayer of all. It is the most perfect compliment we can pay to Mary, a compliment which an archangel paid to her with the permission of God the Most High and indeed, the angel's words were so effective in touching Mary's heart, that she gave her consent to the Incarnation of the Word, in spite of her deep humility. Therefore, surely the faithful will also touch her heart with the same words recited with fervour.

MARIALIS CULTUS
by Pope Paul VI (from the pontifical documents)

"The evangelical nature of the Rosary has appeared in a (more) vivid light, as it takes the names of the mysteries and the principal formulas from the Gospel; it takes inspiration from the Gospel, by beginning with the joyful greeting of the Angel and the religious assent of the Virgin Mary, to suggest the attitude with which the faithful must recite it; and proposes in the harmonious succession of Hail Marys, a fundamental mystery of the Gospel: the "Incarnation of the Word", contemplated at the decisive moment of the Annunciation to Mary. The Rosary is thus an evangelical prayer, as priests and learned people like to call it now, *perhaps more so than in the past.*

Moreover, we now have a better understanding of how the ordered and gradual development of the Rosary reflects the same way in which the Word of God accomplished the work of Redemption, inserting itself with merciful decision into the events of humanity. Indeed the Rosary considers the orderly succession of the principal events of salvation which were brought to fulfilment in Christ: from his virginal conception and the mysteries of his infancy to the culminating moments of the Paschal Feast, the blessed Passion and glorious Resurrection, and the effects which the latter had on the Virgin Mary on the day in which, after her earthly exile, she was assumed in body and soul into the heavenly kingdom.

It has been observed that the triple division of the mysteries of the Rosary not only adheres strictly to the chronological order of the events but, in particular, reflects the scheme of the primitive announcements of faith and represents the mystery of Christ in the same way in which it was viewed by St. Paul in the famous "hymn" of the Letter to the Philippians: humiliation, death, exaltation (Phil 2: 6-11).

The repetition of the Hail Mary is the web upon which the contemplation of the mysteries develops: Jesus, recalled in every Hail Mary, is the same person presented to us step by step by the series of mysteries, Son of God and of the Virgin, born in a stable at Bethlehem; presented by his Mother in the Temple; a young boy full of zeal for the business of his Father; agonizing Redeemer in the garden; scourged and crowned with thorns; weighed down by the cross and dying on Calvary; rising after death and ascending to the glory of the Father, in order to pour forth the gift of the Spirit."

MY FAVOURITE PRAYER
by Pope John Paul II (2nd of October, 1988)

"*Praying the Rosary means to follow the example of Mary, Mother and Disciple of Christ, and to learn from her how to live the demands of the Christian faith, deeply and fully. She was the first believer, the source of ecclesiastical life; in the cenacle She was the centre of unity and charity among the first disciples of her Son.*

In praying the Holy Rosary, it is not so much a question of repeating formulas, but rather a question of entering into a confidential conversation with Mary, speaking to Her, manifesting our hopes to Her, confiding our troubles to Her, opening our hearts to Her, declaring to Her our willingness to accept the plans of God, promising Her our faithfulness in all circumstances, especially in those more difficult and painful times, resting assured of her protection, and being convinced that She will obtain from her Son all the graces necessary for our salvation.

In fact, by praying the Rosary, we contemplate Christ from a privileged point of view, that of Mary herself, His Mother; that is, we meditate upon the mysteries of the life, passion and resurrection of the Lord through with the eyes and heart of the One who was closest to her Son.

Let us be faithful in praying the Rosary, both in our ecclesiastical community and in the intimate life of our families; it shall unite our hearts as we follow the steps of the repeated invocations, it will rekindle the heart of our homes, it will strengthen our hopes and obtain for all people the peace and joy of Christ, who was born, died and rose from the dead for us".

Pope John Paul II

In the fresco of the Last Judgement, the artist Michelangelo depicted a soul that had been saved and draws into

Paradise a host of other souls with the very slender link of the Rosary. It is more than a symbol: it is the image of a reality; the reality of salvation through the intervention of the Virgin Mary. Let us remember the words of the Virgin Mary at Fatima: "Many souls go to hell because there is no one to pray and sacrifice himself for them."

MESSAGE OF OUR HOLY FATHER THE POPE TO THE BISHOP OF LEIRIA-FATIMA FOR THE 80TH ANNIVERSARY OF THE APPARITIONS

Fatima helps us to see the hand of God, our merciful Father, in the twentwieth century and in our own times.

To the Venerable Brother Seraphim de Scousa Ferreira e Silva, Bishop of Leira- Fatima.

"Brotherly greetings in Christ the Lord! The eightieth anniversary of that 13th of October in 1917, when the prodigious 'dance of the sun' took place in the sky, is a suitable occasion to turn to this Sanctuary, in spirit, given that I am unable to be present physically, with a prayer to the Mother of God for the preparation of the Christian people and, in a sense, for humanity as a whole, for the Great Jubilee of the Year 2000, and with an appeal to families and ecclesiastical communities to recite the Rosary daily.

At the threshold of the Third Millenium, considering the signs of the times in this the twentwieth century, (the sign of) Fatima appears to be one of the greatest because it announced in its message many of the signs which were to *follow and invited us to live according to their messages; signs such as the two World Wars, but also great meetings of nations and peoples gathered under the sign of dialogue and peace; the oppression and unrest experienced by various countries and peoples, but also the voice and the opportunities given to groups of people and to individuals who, in the meantime, arose in the international arena; the crises, the desertion and the many sufferings of members of the Church, but also a renewed and intense sense of solidarity and of reciprocal dependence in the Mystical Body of Christ, which is becoming established among all those who are baptized, in accordance with their vocation and mission, the moving away from God and His being abandoned by individuals and society, but also the intervention of the Spirit of Truth in many hearts and communities to the point of their self-sacrifice and martyrdom in order to save the image and likeness of God in humanity (ref. Jn 1: 27), in order to save human beings from other human beings.*

As I said, among these and other signs of the times, Fatima stands out, and helps us to see the hand of God, providential Guide and patient, merciful Father even in this the twentieth century. Looking at how humanity has moved away from God, from (the time of the apparitions at) Fatima, we should recall that this is not the first time that God, feeling rejected and dismissed by humanity, (and yet) respecting the liberty of human beings, gives the impression of moving away, from which results an overshadowing of life, which causes night to fall over history, but only after having provided a shelter.

It happened in the same way on Calvary, when God made man was crucified and died at the hands of human beings. What did Christ do? After having invoked the clemency of heaven with the words, 'Father, forgive them, they do not know what they are doing' (Lk 23:34), He entrusted humanity to Mary, His Mother: 'Woman, this is your Son!' (Jn 19:26).

A symbolical reading of this image from the Gospel permits us to see reflected in it the final scenes, well-known and frequent, of the experience of the child who leaves his home to enter into the night, feeling misunderstood, confused or indignant...

It is the shawl of the mother who covers him in a frozen sleep, as a remedy for the despair and solitude. Beneath the maternal mantle which extends from Fatima over all of the earth, humanity feels nostalgia once again for the House of the Father and for His Bread (ref. Lk 15:17). Beloved pilgrims, as if you were able to embrace all humanity, I ask you to say, in the name of and for humanity, 'We trust in your protection, Holy Mother of God. Do not despise our petitions in our necessities, but free us from all dangers, O glorious and blessed Virgin'.

"Woman, here is your son!'. In these words Jesus spoke to his Mother with regard to John, the beloved disciple, who also found himself at the foot of the Cross. Who does not have a cross? To carry it every day, following the steps of the Master, is a condition which the Gospel lays down for us (ref. Lk 9:23), while it is also without doubt a blessing for our salvation (ref. 1Cor 1: 23-24); the secret lies in not losing sight of the First one who was Crucified, of Him to whom the Father responded with the glory of the resurrection, and who inaugurated this pilgrimage of the blessed.

"This reflection has assumed the simple and efficacious form of the meditation on the mysteries of the Rosary, consecrated by the people (of the Church) and recommended by the Magistery of the Church. Dear brothers and sisters, recite the Rosary every day! I ask the Pastors with all my heart to recite and to teach the recitation of the Rosary in their Christian Communities.

Through the faithful and courageous fulfilment of

human and Christian duties proper to each person's state of life, help the people of God to return to the daily recitation of the Rosary, this sweet conversation between children and their Mother whom they have welcomed into their home (ref. Jn 19:27).

Uniting myself to this conversation and making my own the joys and hopes, the sorrows and afflictions of everyone, I greet fraternally all those who take part, physically or spiritually, in this pilgrimage of October, invoking for all, but in a particular way for the sick, the comfort and strength of God, so that they may agree to make up in their own body all the hardships that still have to be undergone by Christ (ref. Col 1:24), remembering that 'truly tremendous mystery, never meditated upon sufficiently: that is, that the salvation of many depends on prayers and voluntary sacrifices, interpreted by the Mystical Body of Jesus Christ and by the co-operation of Pastors and the faithful for this purpose, especially fathers and mothers of a family, in collaboration with the Divine Saviour' (Pope Pius XII, Mistici Corporis, First Part II §22). May my Apostolic Blessing serve as encouragement to everyone, Pastors and faithful".

Joannes Paulus n. II

SCHEME FOR THE RECITATION
OF THE HOLY ROSARY

In the name of the Father, and of the Son, and of the Holy Spirit. Amen.

O God, come to my aid.
O Lord, make haste to help me.
Glory Be

- *We pause for a moment of reflection, calling to mind our sins, asking the Lord for forgiveness, and reciting a prayer such as the "Confiteor".*
- *Let us free our heart from all that burdens us and present to the Virgin Mary, before beginning this prayer, all problems, troubles and worries which oppress us at this moment;*
Let us say to Mary with our heart:
"Our Lady, I place these worries in your hands."
- *Now let us pray for an outpouring of the Holy Spirit into our hearts, and ask help in order that we recite the Rosary with our hearts.*

We now recite the
The Creed *(see page 26)*

Blessed be you, God our Father, who have called us to meditate and celebrate in faith the mysteries of your Son. Grant that your faithful, diligent in praying the Rosary, may cherish in their hearts, together with Mary, Virgin and Mother, by the grace of the Holy Spirit, the joy, the passion and the glory of our Lord Jesus Christ, who lives and reigns for ever and ever. **Amen.**

On the five beads between the cross and the centre of the Rosary, we recite the following:

1st bead: Our Father
2nd bead: A Hail Mary for the gift of Faith
3rd bead: A Hail Mary for the gift of Hope
4th bead: A Hail Mary for the gift of Love
5th bead: The Glory Be

The Joyful Mysteries are recited on Mondays, Saturdays and on Sundays of Advent; the Luminous mysteries are recited on Thusdays; the Sorrowful Mysteries on Tuesdays, Fridays and on Sundays of Lent; the Glorious Mysteries on Wednesday, Saturdays and Sundays from Christmas until Lent and from Easter until Advent.

For each of the five mysteries, we announce the mystery with an appropriate verse from the Bible. We pause for a moment, according to the time available, in order to meditate upon the mystery which we are about to pray, and ask, through the intercession of the Virgin Mary, for one of the virtues most enhanced by that particular mystery and of which we are in most need. In special circumstances, we can substitute the proposed mysteries with others useful for meditation, taken directly from the Gospel.

Our Father
Hail Mary *(10 times)*
Glory Be

An invocation may follow according to the local custom, for example:

1. O my Jesus, forgive us our sins,
   save us from the fires of hell
   and lead all souls to heaven, especially those
   most in need of Your mercy.

(Our Lady at Fatima, 13th of July, 1917).

2. We may add the words: Give us holy priests and holy families, and grant that we may recognize you in every person and in every circumstance.

3. My God, I believe, I adore, I hope, and I love You. I ask forgiveness for those who do not believe, nor adore, nor hope, nor love You.

Most Holy Trinity, Father, Son and Holy Spirit: I adore You profoundly, and I offer You the most Precious Body, Blood, Soul and Divinity of Jesus Christ, present in all the tabernacles of the world, in reparation for the outrages, sacrileges, and indifference with which He Himself is offended.

And, through the infinite merits of His most Sacred Heart, and the Immaculate Heart of Mary, I beg of you the conversion of poor sinners.

(Words of the Angel of Peace to the three children at Fatima, 1916).

4. Mary, mother of grace, mother of mercy, shield me from the enemy and receive me at the hour of my deat. **Amen.**

5. Come Holy Spirit,
come through the powerful intercession
of the Immaculate Heart of Mary,
your most beloved Spouse.

6. Come Holy Spirit,
Come Divine Power of Love
Come and fill my poor heart:
purify it, sanctify it, make it all yours.

7. O Sacrament most holy,
O Sacrament divine,
All praise and thanksgiving
be every moment Thine.

8. Eternal rest grant unto them, O Lord. And let perpetual light shine upon them. May they rest in peace. **Amen.**

9. Angel of God, my guardian dear, to whom God's love commits me here; ever this day be at my side, to light and guard, to rule and guide. **Amen.**

10. Holy Holy Holy, Lord,
God of power and might,
heaven and earth are full of your glory.
Hosanna in the Highest.
Blessed is He who comes
in the name of the Lord.
Hosanna in the Highest.

11. Queen of Peace,
Pray for us

When the Rosary is recited in a family or prayer group, the beauty of the prayer can be enhanced by alternating the mysteries with suitable hymns.

At the conclusion of the five mysteries we recite:

THE HAIL HOLY QUEEN

Hail, Holy Queen, Mother of Mercy;
Hail our life, our sweetness and our hope!
To you do we cry, poor banished children of Eve.
To you do we send up our sighs; mourning and weeping in this valley of tears.
Turn then, most gracious Advocate,
your eyes of mercy toward us;
and after this, our exile, show unto us the blessed fruit of your womb, Jesus.
O clement, O loving, O sweet Virgin Mary.

V. Pray for us, O holy Mother of God.
R. That we may be made worthy of the promises of Christ.

Let us pray.
O God, whose only-begotten Son, by his life, death and resurrection, has purchased for us the rewards of eternal life; grant, we beseech you, that meditating on these Mysteries in the most Holy Rosary of the Blessed Virgin Mary, we may both imitate what they contain, and obtain what they promise, through the same Christ our Lord. **Amen.**

or

Let us pray.
Almighty and everlasting God, by the coopera-
tion of the Holy Spirit you prepared the body and
soul of Mary, glorious Virgin and Mother, to
become the worthy habitation of your Son; grant
that by her gracious intercession, in whose commemoration we rejoice, we may be delivered
from present evils and from everlasting death.
Through the same Christ our Lord. **Amen.**

V. May the divine assistance remain always with
   us (and may the souls of the faithful departed
   through the mercy of God rest in peace).
R. Amen.

Prayer to St. Joseph

Unto you, O blessed Joseph, do we fly in our tribulation and, having implored the help of your holy spouse, we now also confidently seek your protection. By that affection which united you to the Immaculate Virgin Mother of God, and by your fatherly love for the Child Jesus, we humbly beg you to look down with compassion on the inheritance which Jesus Christ purchased with his blood, and in our need to help us by your powerful intercession.

Do you, O prudent guardian of the Holy Family, watch over the chosen people of Jesus Christ. Keep us, O loving father, safe from all error and corruption. O great protector, from your safe place in heaven, graciously help us in our contest against the power of darkness. And as of old you did rescue the Child Jesus from the danger of death, so now defend God's holy Church from the snares of the enemy and from all adversity. Extend to each one of us your continual protection, that led on by your example and strengthened by your aid, we may live and die in holiness, and obtain everlasting happiness in heaven. **Amen.**

PRAYER TO ST. MICHAEL
THE ARCHANGEL

Saint Michael the Archangel,
defend us in the hour of conflict;
be our safeguard against the wickedness
and snares of the devil;
may God restrain him,
we humbly pray;
and do thou, O Prince of the heavenly host,
by the power of God,
thrust Satan down to hell
and with him all the other wicked spirits
that wander through the world
for the ruin of souls.
Amen.

*At the end of the Rosary, the Litany of the
Blessed Virgin Mary may be recited.*
(See page 723)

THE ROSARY: FIRST SCHEME
(Meditations taken from scripture)

THE JOYFUL MYSTERIES
OF THE HOLY ROSARY

1. THE ANNUNCIATION
From the Gospel according to Luke. (Lk 1: 26-38).

"In the sixth month the angel Gabriel was sent by God to a town in Galilee called Nazareth, to a virgin betrothed to a man named Joseph, of the House of David; and the virgin's name was Mary. He went in and said to her, 'Rejoice, you who enjoy God's favour! The Lord is with you.' She was deeply disturbed by these words and asked herself what this greeting could mean, but the angel said to her, 'Mary, do not be afraid; you have won God's favour. Look! You are to conceive in your womb and bear a son, and you must name him Jesus. He will be great and will be called Son of the Most High. The Lord God will give him the throne of his ancestor David; he will rule over the House of Jacob forever and his reign will have no end.' Mary said to the angel, 'But how can this come about, since I have no knowledge of man?' 'The Holy Spirit will come upon you,' the angel answered, 'and the power of the Most High will cover you with its shadow. And so the child will be holy and will be called Son of God. And I tell you this too: your cousin

Elizabeth also has, in her old age, conceived a son, and she whom people called barren is now in her sixth month, for nothing is impossible to God.' Mary said, 'You see before you the Lord's servant, let it happen to me as you have said.' And the angel left her."

2. THE VISITATION
From the Gospel according to Luke. (Lk 1: 39-45).

"Mary set out at that time and went as quickly as she could to a town in the hill country of Judah. She went into Zechariah's house and greeted Elizabeth. Now it happened that as soon as Elizabeth heard Mary's greeting, the child leapt in her womb and Elizabeth was filled with the Holy Spirit. She gave a loud cry and said, 'Of all women you are the most blessed, and blessed is the fruit of your womb. Why should I be honoured with a visit from the mother of my Lord? Look, the moment your greeting reached my ears, the child in my womb leapt for joy. Yes, blessed is she who believed that the promise made her by the Lord would be fulfilled.' "

3. THE NATIVITY
From the Gospel according to Luke. (Lk 2: 1-7).

"Now it happened that at this time Caesar Augustus issued a decree that a census should be made of the whole inhabited world. This census - the first - took place while Quirinius was governor of Syria, and everyone went to his own town to be registered. So Joseph set out from the town of Nazareth in Galilee and travelled up to Judaea, to the town of David called Bethlehem, since he was of David's House and line, in order to be registered together with Mary, his betrothed, who was with child. Now it happened that while they were there the time came for her to have her child, and she gave birth to a son, her first-born. She wrapped him in swaddling clothes, and laid him in a manger because there was no room for them at the inn."

4. THE PRESENTATION IN THE TEMPLE
From the Gospel according to Luke. (Lk 2: 21-35).

"When the eighth day came and the child was to be circumcised, they gave him the name of Jesus, the name the angel had given him before his conception. And when the day came for them to be purified in keeping with the Law of Moses, they took him up to Jerusalem to present him to the

Lord - observing what is written in the Law of the Lord: Every first-born male must be consecrated to the Lord, and also, to offer in sacrifice in accordance with what is prescribed in the Law of the Lord, a pair of turtledoves or two young pigeons. Now in Jerusalem there was a man named Simeon.

He was an upright and devout man; he looked forward to the restoration of Israel and the Holy Spirit rested on him. It had been revealed to him by the Holy Spirit that he would not see death until he had set eyes on the Christ of the Lord. Prompted by the Spirit he came to the Temple; and when the parents brought in the child Jesus to do for him what the Law required, he took him into his arms and blessed God; and he said: 'Now, Master, you are letting your servant go in peace, as you promised; because my eyes have seen the salvation which you have prepared for all the nations to see, a light of revelation for the gentiles and glory for your people Israel.' As the child's father and mother stood there wondering at the things that were being said about him, Simeon blessed them and said to Mary his mother, 'You see this child: He is destined for the fall and for the rise of many in Israel, destined to be a sign that is opposed - and a sword will pierce your own soul too - so that the secret thoughts of many may be laid bare.' "

5. THE FINDING OF JESUS IN THE TEMPLE
From the Gospel according to Luke. (Lk 2: 41-52).

"Every year his parents used to go to Jerusalem for the feast of the Passover.

When he was twelve years old, they went up for the feast as usual. When the days of the feast were over and they set off home, the boy Jesus stayed behind in Jerusalem without his parents knowing it. They assumed he was somewhere in the party, and it was only after a day's journey that they went to look for him among their relations and acquaintances. When they failed to find him they went back to Jerusalem looking for him everywhere. Three days later, they found him in the Temple, sitting among the doctors, listening to them, and asking them questions; and all those who heard him were astounded at his intelligence and his replies. They were overcome when they saw him, and his mother said to him, 'My child, why have you done this to us? See how worried your father and I have been, looking for you.' He replied, 'Why were you looking for me? Did you not know that I must be in my Father's house?' But they did not understand what he meant.

He then went down with them and came to Nazareth and lived under their authority. His mother stored up all these things in her heart. And Jesus increased in wisdom, in stature, and in favour with God and people."

THE LUMINOUS MYSTERIES
OF THE HOLY ROSARY

1. THE BAPTISM OF JESUS IN THE WATERS
OF THE RIVER JORDAN
Matthew 3:13-17

Then cometh Jesus from Galilee to Jordan unto John, to be baptized of him. But John forbade him, saying, I have need to be baptized of thee, and comest thou to me? And Jesus answering said unto him, Suffer it to be so now: for thus it becometh us to fulfil all righteousness. Then he suffered him.

And Jesus, when he was baptized, went up straightway out of the water: and, lo, the heavens were opened unto him, and he saw the Spirit of God descending like a dove, and lighting upon him: and lo a voice from heaven, saying, This is my beloved Son, in whom I am well pleased.

2. THE WEDDING AT CANA
John 2:1-12

And the third day there was a marriage in Cana of Galilee; and the mother of Jesus was there: and both Jesus was called, and his disciples, to the marriage. And when they wanted wine, the mother of Jesus saith unto him, They have no wine.

Jesus saith unto her, Woman, what have I to do with thee? mine hour is not yet come.

His mother saith unto the servants, Whatsoever he saith unto you, do it.

And there were set there six waterpots of stone, after the manner of the purifying of the Jews, containing two or three firkins apiece.

Jesus saith unto them, Fill the waterpots with water. And they filled them up to the brim. And he saith unto them, Draw out now, and bear unto the governor of the feast. And they bare it.

When the ruler of the feast had tasted the water that was made wine, and knew not whence it was, (but the servants which drew the water knew,) the governor of the feast called the bridegroom, and saith unto him, Every man at the beginning doth set forth good wine; and when men have well drunk, then that which is worse: but thou hast kept the good wine until now.

This beginning of miracles did Jesus in Cana of Galilee, and manifested forth his glory; and his disciples believed on him.

After this he went down to Caper'na-um, he, and his mother, and his brethren, and his disciples; and they continued there not many days.

3. JESUS ANNOUNCES THAT THE KINGDOM
OF GOD IS NEAR AND HE INVITES US
TO CONVERT OUR HEARTS
Matthew 4:12-17

Now when Jesus had heard that John was cast into prison, he departed into Galilee; and leaving Nazareth, he came and dwelt in Caper'na-um, which is upon the seacoast, in the borders of Zeb'ulun and Naph'tali: that it might be fulfilled which was spoken by Isaiah the prophet, saying, The land of Zeb'ulun, and the land of Naph'tali, by the way of the sea, beyond Jordan, Galilee of the Gentiles; the people which sat in darkness saw great light; and to them which sat in the region and shadow of death light is sprung up.

From that time Jesus began to preach, and to say, Repent: for the kingdom of heaven is at hand.

4. JESUS ON MOUNT TABOR, SHOWS HIMSELF TO
THE APOSTLES IN THE SPLENDOUR OF DIVINITY
Matthew 17:1-9

And after six days Jesus taketh Peter, James, and John his brother, and bringeth them up into a high mountain apart, and was transfigured before them: and his face did shine as the sun, and his raiment was white as the light.

And, behold, there appeared unto them Moses and Eli'jah talking with him.

Then answered Peter, and said unto Jesus, Lord, it is good for us to be here: if thou wilt, let us make here three tabernacles; one for thee, and one for Moses, and one for Eli'jah.

While he yet spake, behold, a bright cloud overshadowed them: and behold a voice out of the cloud, which said, This is my beloved Son, in whom I am well pleased; hear ye him.

And when the disciples heard it, they fell on their face, and were sore afraid.

And Jesus came and touched them, and said, Arise, and be not afraid.

And when they had lifted up their eyes, they saw no man, save Jesus only.

And as they came down from the mountain, Jesus charged them, saying, Tell the vision to no man, until the Son of man be risen again from the dead.

5. AND WHEN THE HOUR WAS COME, HE SAT DOWN, AND THE TWELVE APOSTLES WITH HIM
Luke 22:7.14-20

And he said unto them, With desire I have desired to eat this passover with you before I suffer for I say unto you, I will not any more eat thereof, until it be fulfilled in the kingdom of God. And he took the cup, and gave thanks, and said, Take this, and divide it among yourselves: for I say unto you, I will not drink of the fruit of the vine, until the kingdom of God shall come. And he took bread, and gave thanks, and brake it, and gave unto them, saying, This is my body which is given for you: this do in remembrance of me.

Likewise also the cup after supper, saying, This cup is the new testament in my blood, which is shed for you.

THE SORROWFUL MYSTERIES
OF THE HOLY ROSARY

1. THE AGONY IN THE GARDEN
From the Gospel according to Matthew. (Mt 26: 36-46).

"Then Jesus came with them to a plot of land called Gethsemane; and he said to his disciples, 'Stay here while I go over there to pray.' He took Peter and the two sons of Zebedee with him. And he began to feel sadness and anguish. Then he said to them, 'My soul is sorrowful to the point of death. Wait here and keep awake with me.' And going on a little further he fell on his face and prayed. 'My Father,' he said, 'if it is possible, let this cup pass me by. Nevertheless, let it be as you, not I, would have it.'

He came back to the disciples and found them sleeping, and he said to Peter, 'So you had not the strength to keep awake with me one hour? Stay awake, and pray not to be put to the test. The spirit is willing enough, but the flesh is weak.' Again, a second time, he went away and prayed: 'My Father,' he said, 'if this cup cannot pass by without my drinking it, your will be done!' And he came back again and found them sleeping, their eyes were so heavy.

Leaving them there, he went away again and prayed for the third time, repeating the same words. Then he came back to the disciples and said to them, 'You can sleep on now and have your rest. Now the hour has come when the Son of Man is to be betrayed into the hands of sinners. Get up! Let us go! Look! My betrayer is not far away.'"

2. THE SCOURGING AT THE PILLAR
From the Gospel according to Matthew. (Mt 27: 11-26).

"*Jesus, then, was brought before the governor, and the governor put to him this question, 'Are you the king of the Jews?' Jesus replied, 'It is you who say it.' But when he was accused by the chief priests and the elders he refused to answer at all. Pilate then said to him, 'Do you not hear how many charges they have made against you?' But to the governor's complete amazement, he offered not a word in answer to any of the charges.*

At festival time it was the governor's practice to release a prisoner for the people, any one they chose. Now there was at that time a notorious prisoner whose name was Barabbas. So when the crowd gathered, Pilate said to them, 'Which do you want me to release for you: Barabbas, or Jesus who is called Christ?'

For Pilate knew it was out of jealousy that they had handed him over. Now as he was seated in the chair of judgment, his wife sent him a message, 'Have nothing to do with that upright man; I have been upset all day by a dream I had about him.' The chief priests and elders, however, had persuaded the crowd to demand the release of Barabbas and the execution of Jesus. So when the governor spoke and asked them, 'Which of the two do you want me to release for you?' they said, 'Barabbas.' Pilate said to them, 'But in that case, what am I to do with Jesus who is called Christ?' They all said, 'Let him be crucified!' 'Why?' he asked.

'What harm has he done?' But they shouted all the louder, 'Let him be crucified!' Then Pilate saw that he was making no impression, that in fact a riot was imminent. So he took some water, washed his hands in front of the crowd and said, 'I am innocent of this man's blood. It is your concern.' And the people, everyone of them, shouted back, 'Let his blood be on us and on our children!' Then he released Barabbas for them. After having Jesus scourged he handed him over to be crucified."

3. THE CROWNING WITH THORNS
From the Gospel according to Matthew. (Mt 27: 27-31).

"The governor's soldiers took Jesus with them into the Praetorium and collected the whole cohort around him. Then they stripped him and put a scarlet cloak round him, and having twisted some thorns into a crown they put this on his head and placed a reed in his right hand. To *make fun of him they knelt to him saying, 'Hail, king of the Jews!' And they spat on him and took the reed and struck him on the head with it. And when they had finished making fun of him, they took off the cloak and dressed him in his own clothes and led him away to crucify him."*

4. THE CARRYING OF THE CROSS BY JESUS
From the Gospel according to Luke.
(Lk 23: 26 - 27).

"As they were leading him away they seized on a man, Simon from Cyrene, who was coming in from the country, and made him shoulder the cross and carry it behind Jesus. Large numbers of people followed him, and women too, who mourned and lamented for him."

5. THE CRUCIFIXION AND DEATH OF JESUS
From the Gospel according to Luke.
(Lk 23: 33-46).

"When they reached the place called The Skull, they crucified him there and the two criminals, one on his right, the other on his left. Jesus said, 'Father, forgive them; they do not know what they are doing.' Then they cast lots to share out his clothing. The people stayed there watching. As for the leaders, they jeered at him with the words. 'He saved others,' they said, 'let him save himself if he is the Christ of God, the Chosen One.' The soldiers

mocked him too, coming up to him offering him vinegar and saying, 'If you are the king of the Jews, save yourself.'

Above him there was an inscription: 'This is the King of the Jews.' One of the criminals hanging there abused him. 'Are you not the Christ?' he said. 'Save yourself and us as well.' But the other spoke up and rebuked him. 'Have you no fear of God at all?' he said. 'You got the same sentence as he did, but in our case we deserved it: we are paying for what we did. But this man has done nothing wrong. Then he said, 'Jesus remember me when you come into your kingdom.' He answered him, 'In truth, I tell you today you will be with with me in paradise.'

It was now about the sixth hour and, the sun's light failed, so that darkness came over the whole land until the ninth hour. The veil of the Sanctuary was torn right down the middle; and when Jesus had cried out in a loud voice, he said, 'Father, into your hands I commit my spirit.' With these words he breathed his last. Everything has come to pass....!".

"It is fulfilled" (Jn 19:30).

(We pause for a moment of silence).

THE GLORIOUS MYSTERIES
OF THE HOLY ROSARY

1. THE RESURRECTION

From the Gospel according to Luke. (Lk 24: 1-12).

"On the first day of the week, at the first sign of dawn, they went to the tomb with the spices they had prepared. They found that the stone had been rolled away from the tomb, but on entering they could not find the body of the Lord Jesus. As they stood there puzzled about this, two men in brilliant clothes suddenly appeared at their side. Terrified, the women bowed their heads to the ground. But the two men said to them, 'Why look among the dead for someone who is alive?

He is not here; he has risen. Remember what he told you when he was still in Galilee: that the Son of Man was destined to be handed over into the power of sinful men and be crucified, and rise again on the third day.' And they remembered his words. When they returned from the tomb they told all this to the Eleven and to all the others.

The women were Mary of Magdala, Joanna, and Mary the mother of James. The other women with them also told the apostles, but this story of theirs seemed pure nonsense, and they did not believe them. Peter, however, went off to the tomb running. He bent down and looked in and saw the linen cloths but nothing else; he then went back home, amazed at what had happened."

2. THE ASCENSION
From the Gospel according to Luke. (Lk 24:36-51).

"They were still talking about all this when he himself stood among them and said to them, 'Peace be with you!' In a state of alarm and fright, they thought they were seeing a ghost. But he said, 'Why are you so agitated, and why are these doubts stirring in your hearts? Look at my hands and feet; yes, it is I indeed. Touch me and see for yourselves; a ghost has no flesh and bones as you can see I have.' And as he said this he showed them his hands and feet.

Their joy was so great that they still could not believe it, and they stood there dumfounded; so he said to them, 'Have you anything here to eat?' And they offered him a piece of grilled fish, which he took and ate before their eyes. Then he told them, 'This is what I meant when I said, while I was still with you, that everything written about me in the Law of Moses, in the Prophets and in the Psalms, was destined to be fulfilled.'

He then opened their minds to understand the scriptures, and he said to them, So you see how it is written that the Christ would suffer and on the third day rise from the dead, and that, in his name, repentance for the forgiveness of sins would be preached to all the nations, beginning from Jerusalem. You are witnesses to this. 'And now I am sending upon *you what the Father has*

*promised. Stay in the city then, until you are
clothed with the power from on high.' Then he
took them out as far as the outskirts of Bethany,
and lifting up his hands blessed them. As he
blessed them, he withdrew from them and was
carried up to heaven."*

3. THE COMING OF THE HOLY SPIRIT ON
OUR LADY AND THE APOSTLES
From the Acts of the Apostles. (Ac 2: 1-13).

*"When Pentecost day came round, they had all
met together, when suddenly there came from
heaven a sound of a violent wind which filled the
entire house in which they were sitting; and there
appeared to them tongues of fire; these separated
and came to rest on the head of each of them.*

*They were all filled with the Holy Spirit, and
began to speak foreign languages as the Spirit
gave them the power to express themselves. Now
there were devout men living in Jerusalem from
every nation under heaven, and at this sound they
all assembled, and each one was bewildered to
hear these men speaking his own language.*

*They were amazed and astonished. 'Surely,'
they said, 'all these men speaking are Galileans?
How does it happen that each of us hears them in
his own native language? Parthians, Medes and
Elamites; people from Mesopotamia, Judaea and
Cappadocia, Pontus and Asia, Phrygia and Pam-*

phylia, Egypt and the parts of Libya round Cyrene; residents in Rome - Jews and proselytes alike - Cretans and Arabs; we hear them preaching in our own language about the marvels of God.' Everyone was amazed and perplexed; they asked one another what it all meant. Some, however, laughed it off. 'They have been drinking too much new wine,' they said."

4. THE ASSUMPTION

From the Book of Revelation. (Rev 12:1-6;13-17).

"Now a great sign appeared in heaven: a woman, adorned with the sun, standing on the moon, and with the twelve stars on her head for a crown. She was pregnant, and in labour, crying aloud in the pangs of childbirth. Then a second sign appeared in the sky. There was a huge red dragon which had seven heads and ten horns, and each of the seven heads crowned with a coronet. Its tail dragged a third of the stars from the sky and hurled them to the ground, and the dragon stopped in front of the woman as she was having the child, so that he could eat it as soon as it was born from its mother.

The woman brought a male child into the world, the son who was to rule all the nations with an iron sceptre, and the child was taken straight up to God and to his throne, while the woman escaped into the desert, where God had prepared a place of safety ready, for her to be looked after for twelve hundred and sixty days. [...] As soon as the devil found himself thrown down to the earth, he sprang in pursuit of the woman, the mother of the male child, but she was given a huge pair of eagle's wings to fly away from the serpent into the desert, to the place where she was to be looked after for a time, and two times and half a time.

So the serpent vomited water from his mouth, like a river, after the woman, to sweep her away in the current, but the earth came to her rescue; it opened its mouth and swallowed the river spewed from the dragon's mouth. Then the dragon was enraged with the woman and went away to make war on the rest of her children, that is, all who obey God's commandments and have in themselves the witness of Jesus."

5. THE CROWNING OF OUR LADY AS
QUEEN OF HEAVEN
From the Book of Revelation. (Rev 21: 1-8).

"Then I saw a new heaven and a new earth; the first heaven and the first earth had disappeared now, and there was no longer any sea. I saw the holy city, and the new Jerusalem, coming down from God out of heaven, as beautiful as a bride all dressed for her groom. Then I heard a loud voice call from the throne, 'You see this city?

Here God lives among human beings. He will make his home among them; they shall be his people, and he will be their God; his name is God-with-them. He will wipe away all tears from their eyes; there will be no more death, and no more mourning or sadness. The world of the past has gone.' Then the One sitting on the throne spoke: 'Now I am making the whole of creation new,' he said.

'Write this: What I am saying is trustworthy and will come true.' Then he said, 'It is already done, I am the Alpha and the Omega, the Beginning and the End. I will give water from the well of life free to anybody who is thirsty; it is the rightful inheritance of the one who proves victorious; and I will be his God and he will be my son. But the legacy for cowards, for those who break their word, or worship obscenities, for murderers and the sexually immoral, and for sorcerers, worshippers of false Gods, or any other sort of liars, is the second death in the burning lake of sulphur.' "

Hail Mary Queen

For concluding prayers, see pages 638-641

THE ROSARY: SECOND SCHEME

Biblical Rosary

MEDITATION ON THE JOYFUL MYSTERIES

In the name of the Father, and of the Son, and of the Holy Spirit. Amen.

O God, come to my aid.
O Lord, make haste to help me.

1. THE ANNUNCIATION

First we express an intention.

Our Father

The angel Gabriel was sent by God... to a virgin...
The virgin's name was Mary. *(Lk 1:26-27)*

Hail Mary

"Rejoice, you who enjoy God's favour!
The Lord is with you". *(Lk 1:28)*

Hail Mary

She was deeply disturbed by these words
and asked herself what this greeting could mean. *(Lk 1:29)*

Hail Mary

The angel said to her, "Mary, do not be afraid;
you have won God's favour". *(Lk 1:30)*

Hail Mary

"Look! You are to conceive in your womb and bear a son,
and you must name him Jesus". *(Lk 1:32-33)*

Hail Mary

"He will be great and will be called Son of the Most High...
and his reign will have no end". *(Lk 1:32-33)*

Hail Mary

Mary said to the angel, "But how can this come about,
since I have no knowledge of man?". *(Lk 1:34)*

Hail Mary

"The Holy Spirit will come upon you,'
and the power of the Most High will cover you with its shadow". *(Lk 1:35)*

Hail Mary

"And so the child will be holy
and will be called Son of God". *(Lk 1:35)*

Hail Mary

Mary said, "You see before you the Lord's servant,
let it happen to me as you have said". *(Lk 1:38)*

Hail Mary
Glory Be

O my Jesus, forgive us our sins, save us from the fires of hell and lead all souls to heaven, especially those most in need of Your mercy.

(Our Lady at Fatima, 13th of July, 1917).

My God, I believe, I adore, I hope, and I love You.
I ask forgiveness for those who do not believe, nor adore, nor hope, nor love You.

(Words of the Angel of Peace to the three children of Fatima, Spring, 1916).

Eternal rest...
**Queen of Peace,
pray for us**

Hymn: Ave, Ave, Ave Maria
(twice) or another appropriate hymn or chorus.

2. THE VISITATION

We express an intention.

Our Father

Mary set out at that time and went as quickly as she could to a town in the hill country of Judah. **She went into Zechariah's house and greeted Elizabeth**. *(Lk 1:39-40)*

Hail Mary

Now it happened that as soon as Elizabeth heard Mary's greeting, the child leapt in her womb **and Elizabeth was filled with the Holy Spirit**.

(Lk 1:41)

Hail Mary

She gave a loud cry and said, "Of all women you are the most blessed, **and blessed is the fruit of your womb."**

(Lk 1:42)

Hail Mary

"Blessed is she who believed **that the promise made her by the Lord would be fulfilled."** *(Lk 1:45)*

Hail Mary

And Mary said: "My soul proclaims the greatness of the Lord...
because he has looked upon the humiliation of his servant." *(Lk 1:46-48)*

Hail Mary

"Yes, from now onwards all generations will call me blessed,
for the Almighty has done great things for me." (Lk 1: 48-49)

Hail Mary

"Holy is his name,
and his faithful love extends age after age to those who fear him."*(Lk 1,49-50)*

Hail Mary

"He has pulled down princes from their thrones
and raised high the lowly." *(Lk 1:52)*

Hail Mary

"He has filled the starving with good things,
he sent the rich away empty." *(Lk 1:53)*

Hail Mary

"According to the promise he had made to our ancestors -
of his mercy to Abraham and to his descendants for ever." *(Lk 1:55)*

**Hail Mary • Glory Be
O my Jesus...** *(See page 635)*

3. THE NATIVITY
We express an intention.

Our Father

Now it happened that while they were there
the time came for her to have her child. *(Lk 2:6)*

Hail Mary

She gave birth to a son, her first-born.
She wrapped him in swaddling clothes. *(Lk 2:7)*

Hail Mary

And she laid him in a manger
because there was no room for them at the inn.
(Lk 2:7)

Hail Mary

In the coutryside close by there were shep-herds,...
An angel of the Lord stood over them and the glory of the Lord shone round them. *(Lk 2:8-9)*

Hail Mary

"Do not be afraid. Look I bring you news of great joy,
a joy to be shared by the whole people." *(Lk 2:10)*
Hail Mary

"Today in the town of David a Saviour has been born to you;
he is Christ the Lord." *(Lk 2:11)*

Hail Mary

"Glory to God in the Highest heaven,
and on earth peace for those he favours."
(Lk 2:14)

Hail Mary

Some Magi came from East...
and going into the house they saw the child with his mother, and falling to their knees they did him homage. *(Mt 2:1-11)*

Hail Mary

Then, opening their treasures,
they offered him gifts of gold and frankincense and myrrh. *(Mt 2:11)*

Hail Mary
As for Mary, she treasured all these things
and pondered them in her heart *(Lk 2:19)*

Hail Mary • Glory Be
O my Jesus... *(See page 635)*

4. THE PRESENTATION
We express an intention.

Our Father

In keeping with the Law of Moses, they took him up to Jerusalem
to present him to the Lord. *(Lk 2:22)*

Hail Mary

Now in Jerusalem there was a man named Simeon.
He was an upright and devout man. *(Lk 2:25)*

Hail Mary

It had been revealed to him by the Holy Spirit that

he would not see death
until he had set eyes on the Christ of the Lord.

(Lk 2:26)

Hail Mary

When the parents brought in the child Jesus to do
for him what the Law required,
he took him into his arms and blessed God.

(Lk 2:27-28)

Hail Mary

"Now, Master, you are letting your servant go in
peace,
as you promised." *(Lk 2:29)*

Hail Mary

"Because my eyes have seen the salvation
**which you have prepared for all the nations to
see**." *(Lk 2:30-31)*

Hail Mary

"A light of revelation for the gentiles
and glory for your people Israel." *(Lk 2:32)*

Hail Mary

Simeon... said to Mary, 'You see this child: he is

destined for the fall and for the rise of many in Israel,
destined to be a sign that is opposed." *(Lk 2:34-35)*

Hail Mary

"And a sword will pierce your own soul too
that the thoughts of many heart may be revealed." *(Lk 2:35)*

Hail Mary

They went back... to Nazareth. And as the child grew to maturity, he was filled with wisdom;
and God's favour was with him. *(Lk 2:39-40)*

Hail Mary • Glory Be
O my Jesus... *(See page 635)*

5. THE FINDING OF JESUS IN THE TEMPLE
We express an intention.

Our Father

Every year his parents used to go to Jerusalem
for the feast of the Passover. *(Lk 2:42)*

Hail Mary

When the days of the feast were over and they set off home, the boy Jesus stayed behind in Jerusalem
without his parents knowing it. *(Lk 2:43)*

Hail Mary

They went back to Jerusalem looking for him everywhere.
Three days later, they found him in the Temple. *(Lk 2:45-46)*

Hail Mary

He was sitting among the doctors,
listening to them, and asking them questions.
(Lk 2:46)

Hail Mary

And all those who heard him were astounded
at his intelligence and his replies. *(Lk 2:47)*
Hail Mary

"My child, why have you done this to us?
See how worried your father and I have been, looking for you." *(Lk 2:48)*

Hail Mary

"Why were you looking for me?" he replied. **"Did you not know that I must be in my Father's house?."**.*(Lk 2:49)*

Hail Mary

But they did not understand **what he meant**. *(Lk 2:50)*

Hail Mary

He then went down with them and came to Nazareth and lived under their authority. **His mother stored up all these things in her heart**. *(Lk 2:51)*

Hail Mary

And Jesus increased in wisdom, in stature, and in favour **with God and people**. *(Lk 2:52)*

Hail Mary • Glory Be
O my Jesus... *(See page 635)*

If the Rosary is concluded at this point,
the Hail Holy Queen is recited (see pages 638-641)

MEDITATION ON THE
LUMINOUS MYSTERIES

*In the name of the Father, and of the Son,
and of the Holy Spirit. Amen.*

O God, come to my aid.
O Lord, make haste to help me.

1. THE BAPTISM OF JESUS IN THE WATERS OF THE RIVER JORDAN

We express an intention.

Our Father

Then Jesus came from Galilee to the Jordan
to be baptized by John *(Mt 3:13)*

Hail Mary

But John tried to deter him, saying,
**"I need to be baptized by you,
and do you come to me?"** *(Mt 3:14)*

Hail Mary

Jesus replied, "Let it be so now;
it is proper for us to do this to fulfill all righteousness." *(Mt 3:15)*

Hail Mary

As soon as Jesus was baptized, he went up out of the water. At that moment heaven was opened, **and he saw the Spirit of God descending like a dove and lighting on him.** *(Mt 3:16)*

Hail Mary

And a voice from heaven said, "This is my Son, whom I love;
with him I am well pleased." *(Mt 3:17)*

Hail Mary

The true light that gives light to every man **was coming into the world.** *(Jh 1:9)*

Hail Mary

We have seen his glory,
the glory of the One and Only, who came from the Father. *(Jh 1:14)*

Hail Mary

John testifies concerning him. He cries out, saying, "This was he of whom I said, '
He who comes after me has surpassed me because he was before me.' *(Jh 1:15)*

Hail Mary

In him was life,
and that life was the light of men. *(Jh 1:4)*

Hail Mary

The light shines in the darkness,
but the darkness has not understood it. *(Jh 1:5)*

Hail Mary • Glory Be
O my Jesus... *(See page 635)*

2. THE WEDDING AT CANA
We express an intention.

Our Father

On the third day a wedding took place at Cana in Galilee.
Jesus' mother was there. *(Jh 2:1)*

Hail Mary

When the wine was gone,
Jesus' mother said to him, "They have no more wine." *(Jh 2:3)*

Hail Mary

"Dear woman, why do you involve me?"
Jesus replied, "My time has not yet come." *(Jh 2:4)*

Hail Mary

His mother said to the servants,
"Do whatever he tells you." *(Jh 2:5)*

Hail Mary

Jesus said to the servants, "Fill the jars with water";
so they filled them to the brim. *(Jh 2:7)*

Hail Mary

"Now draw some out and take it to the master of the banquet."
They did so. *(Jh 2:9)*

Hail Mary

When the master of the banquet tasted the water that had been turned into wine, he said,
you have saved the best till now." *(Jh 2:9-10)*

Hail Mary

Jesus thus revealed his glory,
and his disciples put their faith in him. *(Jh 2:11)*

Hail Mary

You prepare a table before me
You anoint my head with oil; my cup over-flows. *(Ps 23:5)*

Hail Mary

On this mountain the Lord Almighty will prepare a feast of rich food for all peoples,
a banquet of the best of meats and the finest of wines. *(Is 25:6)*

Hail Mary

**Hail Mary • Glory Be
O my Jesus...** *(See page 635)*

3. THE ANNUNCIATION OF THE KINGDOM
We express an intention.

Our Father

After John was put in prison, Jesus went into Galilee, proclaiming the good news of God.
"The time has come," he said. "The kingdom of God is near. Repent and believe the good news!". *(Mk 1:14-15)*

Hail Mary

When the Sabbath came, Jesus went into the synagogue
he began to teach. and he taught them as one who had authority. *(Mk 1:21-22)*

Hail Mary

The people were all so amazed that they asked each other, "What is this?
He even gives orders to evil spirits and they obey him." *(Mk 1:27)*

Hail Mary

Jesus healed many who had various diseases.
He also drove out many demons. *(Mk 1:34)*

Hail Mary

Jesus could no longer enter a town openly but stayed outside in lonely places.
Yet the people still came to him from everywhere. *(Mk 1:45)*

Hail Mary

While Jesus was having dinner at Levi's house,
many tax collectors and sinners were eating with him *(Mk 2:15)*

Hail Mary

On hearing this, Jesus said to them, "It is not the healthy who need a doctor,
but the sick." *(Mk 2:17)*

Hail Mary

Jesus went up on a mountainside and called to him those he wanted,
He appointed twelve designating them apostles that they might be with him. *(Mk 3:13-14)*

Hail Mary

Then he looked at those seated in a circle around him and said,
Here are my mother and my brothers!
Whoever does God's will is my brother and sister and mother. *(Mk 3:34-35)*

Hail Mary

Again Jesus began to teach by the lake.
He taught them many things by parables.*(Mk 4:1-2)*

Hail Mary

Hail Mary • Glory Be
O my Jesus... *(See page 635)*

4. The Transfiguration

We express an intention.

Our Father

Jesus said "I tell you the truth, some who are standing here will not taste death
before they see the kingdom of God. *(Lk 9:27)*

Hail Mary

Jesus took Peter, John and James with him
and went up onto a mountain to pray. *(Lk 9:28)*

Hail Mary

As he was praying, the appearance of his face changed,
and his clothes became as bright as a flash of lightning. *(Lk 9:29)*

Hail Mary

Two men, Moses and Elijah, appeared in glorious splendour, talking with Jesus.
They spoke about his departure, which he was about to bring to fulfilment at Jerusalem. *(Lk 9:30-31)*

Hail Mary

Peter and his companions were very sleepy,
but when they became fully awake, they saw his glory. *(Lk 9:32)*

Hail Mary

Peter said to Jesus,
"Master, it is good for us to be here." *(Lk 9:33)*

Hail Mary

A cloud appeared and enveloped them,
and they were afraid *(Lk 9:34)*

Hail Mary

A voice came from the cloud, saying,
"This is my Son, whom I have chosen; listen to him." *(Lk 9:35)*

Hail Mary

Then he turned to his disciples and said privately,
Blessed are the eyes that see what you see. *(Lk 10:23)*

Hail Mary

Jesus replied, "Blessed rather are those who hear the word of God
and obey it. *(Lk 11:27)*

Hail Mary

Hail Mary • Glory Be
O my Jesus... *(See page 635)*

5. THE LAST SUPPER

We express an intention.

Our Father

It was just before the Passover Feast. Jesus knew that the time had come for him to leave this world and go to the Father.
Loved his own who were in the world, he now showed them the full extent of his love. *(Jh 13:1)*

Hail Mary

Jesus knew that the Father had put all things under his power
so he got up from the meal, took off his outer clothing, and wrapped a towel round his waist.
(Jh 13:3-4)

Hail Mary

After that, he poured water into a basin and began to wash his disciples' feet, drying them with the towel that was wrapped round him.
I have set you an example that you should do as I have done for you. *(Jh 13:5.15)*

Hail Mary

Jesus himself came up and walked along with them;
but they were kept from recognising him. *(Lk 24:15-16)*

Hail Mary

He said to them, "How foolish you are, and how slow of heart to believe all that the prophets have spoken!"
"Stay with us, for it is nearly evening; the day is almost over." *(Lk 24:25.29)*

Hail Mary

When he was at the table with them, he took bread, gave thanks, broke it and began to give it to them.
Then their eyes were opened and they recognised him. *(Lk 24:30-31)*

Hail Mary

"Were not our hearts burning within us while he talked with us on the road and opened the Scriptures to us?"
They got up and returned at once to Jerusalem... and saying, It is true! The Lord has risen and has appeared to Simon. *(Lk 24:32-34)*

Hail Mary

A new command I give you: **Love one another. As I have loved you, so you must love one another.** *(Jh 13:34)*

Hail Mary

He who loves me will be loved by my Father, **and I too will love him and show myself to him.** *(Jh 14:21)*

Hail Mary

Put your trust in the light while you have it, **so that you may become sons of light.** *(Jh 12:36)*

Hail Mary
Hail Mary
Glory Be
O my Jesus... *(See page 635)*

If the Rosary is concluded at this point,
the Hail Holy Queen is recited (see pages 638-641)

MEDITATION ON THE
SORROWFUL MYSTERIES

1. THE AGONY IN THE GARDEN
We express an intention.

Our Father

Then Jesus came with them to a plot of land called Gethsemane...
and he began to feel sadness and anguish. *(Mt 26:36-37)*

Hail Mary

My soul is sorrowful to the point of death.
Wait here and keep awake with me. *(Mt 26:38)*

Hail Mary

Then he withdrew from them,
about a stone's throw away, and knelt down and prayed. *(Lk 22:41)*

Hail Mary

Father if you are willing, take this cup away from me.
Nevertheless, let your will be done, not mine. *(Lk 22:42)*

Hail Mary

Then an angel appeared to him, coming from heaven
to give him strength. *(Lk 22:43)*

Hail Mary

In his anguish
he prayed even more earnestly. *(Lk 22:44)*

Hail Mary

And his sweat like great drops of blood
fell to the ground. *(Lk 22:44)*

Hail Mary

He came back to the disciples and found them sleeping,
and he said to Peter, "So you had not the strength to keep awake with me one hour." *(Mt 26:40)*

Hail Mary

Stay awake, and pray
not to be put to the test. *(Mt 26:41)*

Hail Mary

The spirit is willing enough,
but the flesh is weak. *(Mt 26:41)*

Hail Mary • Glory Be
O my Jesus... *(See page 635)*

2. The scourging at the pillar
We express an intention.

Our Father

They had Jesus bound and took him away and handed him over to Pilate.
Pilate put to him this question: "Are you the King of the Jews?". *(Mk 15:1-2)*

Hail Mary

Jesus replied: "Mine is not the kingdom of this world;...
It is you who say that I am a king." *(Jn 18:36-37)*

Hail Mary

I was born for this, I came into the world for this, to bear witness to the truth,
and all who are on the side of truth listen to my voice. *(Jn 18:37)*

Hail Mary

"Truth," said Pilate, "What is that?".
And so saying he went out again to the Jews and said, "I find no case against him." *(Jn 18:38)*

Hail Mary

Pilate then had Jesus taken away
and scourged. *(Jn 19:1)*

Hail Mary

He was despised, the lowest of men,
a man of sorrows, familiar with suffering. *(Is 53:3)*

Hail Mary

Ill-treated and afficted,
he never opened his mouth, like a lamb led to the slaughter-house. *(Is 53:7)*

Hail Mary

He was being wounded for our rebellions,
crushed because of our guilt. *(Is 53:5)*

Hail Mary

Yet ours were the sufferings he was bearing,
ours the sorrows he was carrying. *(Is 53:4)*

Hail Mary

The punishment reconciling us fell on him,
and we have been healed by his bruises. *(Is 53:5)*

**Hail Mary • Glory Be
O my Jesus...** *(See page 635)*

3. THE CROWNING WITH THORNS

We express an intention.

Our Father

The governor's soldiers took Jesus with them into
the Praetorium...
**they stripped him and put a scarlet cloak
round him.** *(Mt 27:27-28)*

Hail Mary

And having twisted some thorns into a crown
they put this on his head
and placed a reed in his right hand. *(Mt 27:27-29)*

Hail Mary

To make fun of him they knelt to him
saying, "Hail, king of the Jews!.." *(Mt 27:29)*

Hail Mary

And they spat on him
and took the reed and struck him on the head with it. *(Mt 27:30)*

Hail Mary

Jesus then came out
wearing the crown of thorns and the purple robe. *(Jn 19:5)*

Hail Mary

Pilate said: "Here is the man!'
When they saw him, the chief priests and the guards shouted, "Crucify him! Crucify him!"
(Jn 19:6)

Hail Mary

Pilate said to the Jews: "Here is your king!"
But they shouted "Away with him, away with him, crucify him." *(Jn 19:14-15)*

Hail Mary

Pilate said: "Shall I crucify your king?"
The chief priests answered, "We have no king except Caesar." *(Jn 19:15)*

Hail Mary

So Pilate took some water, washed his hands in front of the crowds
and said: "I am innocent for this man's blood. It is your concern." *(Mt 27:24)*

Hail Mary
So Pilate handed him over to them
to be crucified. *(Jn 19:16)*

Hail Mary
Glory Be
O my Jesus... *(See page 635)*

4. The Carrying of the Cross by Jesus

We express an intention.

Our Father

If anyone wants to be a follower of mine,
let him renounce himself. *(Lk 9:23)*

Hail Mary

Let him take up his cross every day
and follow me. *(Lk 9:23)*

Hail Mary

And carrying his own cross
**he went out to the Place of the Skull or, as it
called in Hebrew, Golgotha**. *(Jn 19:17)*

Hail Mary

They enlisted a passer-by, Simon of Cyrene...
to carry his cross. *(Mk 15:21)*

Hail Mary

Shoulder my yoke
and learn from me. *(Mt 11:29)*

Hail Mary

Learn from me, for I am gentle and humble in heart,
and you will find rest for your souls. *(Mt 11:29)*

Hail Mary

Yes, my yoke is easy
and my burden light. *(Mt 11:30)*
Hail Mary

Large numbers of people followed him,
and women too, who mourned and lamented for him. *(Lk 23:27)*

Hail Mary

But Jesus turned to them and said, "Daughters of Jerusalem, do not weep for me;
weep rather for yourselves and for your children." *(Lk 23:28)*

Hail Mary

They were also leading out two others, criminals
to be executed with him. *(Lk 23:32)*

Hail Mary
Glory Be
O my Jesus... *(See page 635)*

5. THE CRUCIFIXION AND DEATH OF JESUS
We express an intention.

Our Father

When they reached the place called The Skull,
**they crucified him there and the two criminals,
one on his right, the other on his left.** *(Lk 23:33)*

Hail Mary

Jesus said, "Father, forgive them;
they do not know what they are doing.". *(Lk 23:34)*

Hail Mary

One of the criminals... said, "Jesus, remember me
when you come into your kingdom."
**He answered him "In truth, I tell you today you
will be with with me in Paradise."**

(Lk 23:39;42-43)

Hail Mary

Near the cross of Jesus stood his mother...
and the disciple whom he loved. *(Jn 19:26-27)*

Hail Mary

So he said to his mother "he is your son". Then he **said to the disciple "She is your mother".**

Hail Mary

Jesus cried in a loud voice...
"My God, my God, why have you forsaken me?." *(Mt 15:34)*

Hail Mary

Jesus... said: "I am thirsty".
Putting a sponge soaked in the wine on hyssop stick, they held it up to his mouth. (Jn 19:28-29)

Hail Mary

Jesus cried out in a loud voice,
saying, "Father, into your hands I commit my spirit." *(Lk 23:46)*

Hail Mary

Jesus said, "It is fulfilled!"
and bowing his head he gave up his spirit.

(Jn 19:30)

Hail Mary

He laid down his life for us;
and we too ought to lay down our lives for our brothers. *(1Jn 3:16)*

Hail Mary
Glory Be
O my Jesus... *(See page 635)*

If the Rosary is concluded at this point,
the Hail Holy Queen is recited (see pages 638-641)

MEDITATION ON THE
GLORIOUS MYSTERIES

1. THE RESURRECTION
We express an intention.

Our Father

You will be sorrowful,
but your sorrow will turn to joy. *(Jn 16:20)*

Hail Mary

You are sad now, but I shall see you again, and your hearts will be full of joy,
and that joy no one shall take from you. *(Jn 16:22)*

Hail Mary

On the first day of the week, at the first sign of dawn, they went to the tomb
with the spices they had prepared. *(Lk 24:1)*

Hail Mary

And suddenly... an angel of the Lord, descending from heaven,
came and rolled away the stone and sat on it.

(Mt 28:2)

Hail Mary

The angel spoke; and he said to the women, ...
"There is no need for you to be afraid.
I know you are looking for Jesus, who was crucified. He is not here." *(Mt 28:5)*

Hail Mary

"He has risen, as he said he would.
Come and see the place where he lay." *(Mt 28:6)*

Hail Mary

"Then go quickly and tell his disciples: *He has risen from the dead and now he is going ahead of you to Galilee;*
that is where you will see him." *(Mt 28:7)*

Hail Mary

If you declare with your mouth that Jesus is Lord,
and if you believe with your heart that God raised him from the dead then you will be saved. *(Rm 10:9)*

Hail Mary

I am the resurrection.
Anyone who believes in me, even though that person dies, will live. *(Jn 11:25)*

Hail Mary

In that way you must see yourselves as being dead to sin
but alive for God in Christ Jesus. *(Rm 6:11)*

**Hail Mary • Glory Be
O my Jesus...** *(See page 635)*

2. THE ASCENSION

We express an intention.

Our Father

Then he took them out as far as the outskirts of Bethany,
and lifting up his hands blessed them". *(Lk 24:50)*
Hail Mary

(Jesus) said, "All authority in heaven and on earth
has been given to me." *(Mt 28:18)*
Hail Mary

"Go, therefore,
make disciples of all nations". *(Mt 28:19)*
Hail Mary

"Baptize them
in the name of the Father and of the Son and of the Holy Spirit". *(Mt 28:19)*

Hail Mary

"Teach them to observe
all the commands I gave you". *(Mt 28:20)*

Hail Mary

"Whoever believes and is baptized will be saved;
whoever does not believe will be condemned"

(Mk 16:16)

Hail Mary

"And look, I am with you always;
yes, to the end of time". *(Mt 28:20)*

Hail Mary

"As he said this he was lifted up while they looked on,
and a cloud took him from their sight". *(Ac 1:9)*

Hail Mary

"Since you have been raised up to be with Christ,
you must look for the things that are above,
where Christ is, sitting at God's right hand".

(Col 3:1)

Hail Mary

"But when Christ is revealed - and he is your life
you, too, will be revealed with him in glory"
(Col 3:4)

Hail Mary
Glory Be
O my Jesus... *(See page 635)*

3. THE COMING OF THE HOLY SPIRIT
ON OUR LADY AND THE APOSTLES
We express an intention.

Our Father

With one heart all these joined constantly in prayer,
together with some women, including Mary, the Mother of Jesus, and with his brothers.

(Ac 1:14)

Hail Mary

Suddenly there came from heaven a sound as of a violent wind
which filled the entire house in which they were sitting. *(Ac 2:2)*

Hail Mary

And there appeared to them tongues of fire;
these separated and came to rest on the head of each of them. *(Act 2:3)*

Hail Mary

They were all filled with the Holy Spirit,
and began to speak different languages as the Spirit gave them the power to express themselves. *(Ac 2:4)*

Hail Mary

Now there were devout men living in Jerusalem **from every nation under heaven**. *(Ac 2:5)*

Hail Mary

Then Peter stood up with the Eleven **and addressed them in a loud voice...** *(Ac 2:14)*

Hail Mary

You must repent, and everyone of you must be baptized in the name of Jesus Christ for the forgiveness of your sins, **and you will receive the gift of the Holy Spirit.** *(Ac 2:38)*

Hail Mary

They accepted what he said and were baptized. **That very day about three thousand were added to their number**. *(Ac 2:41)*

Hail Mary

Perseverance develops a tested character, something that gives us a hope which will not let us down, **because the love of God has been poured into our hearts by the Holy Spirit which has been given to us**. *(Rm 5:4-5)*

Hail Mary

Do you not realize that your body is the temple of the Holy Spirit,
who is in you and whom you received from God?" *(1Cor 6:19)*

Hail Mary • Glory Be
O my Jesus... *(See page 635)*

4. THE ASSUMPTION
We express an intention.

Our Father

"The reign of the Lord our God Almighty
has begun." *(Rev 19:6)*

Hail Mary

"Let us be glad and joyful...
because this is the time for the marriage of the Lamb." *(Rev 19:7)*

Hail Mary

"I saw the holy city, the new Jerusalem,
coming down from God out of heaven, prepared as a bride dressed for her husband" *(Rev 21:2)*

Hail Mary

"(The Angel) showed me Jerusalem, the holy city, **coming down out of heaven from God.**"*(Rev 21:10)*

Hail Mary

"It had all the glory of God and glittered like **some precious jewel of crystal-clear diamond.**"
(Rev 21:11)

Hail Mary

"The nations will come to its light, **and the kings of the earth will bring it their treasures and wealth.**" *(Rev 21:24-26)*

Hail Mary

"The sanctuary of God in heaven opened, **and the ark of the convenant could be seen inside.**" *(Rev 11:19)*

Hail Mary

"(God) will make his home among them... **He will wipe away all the tears from their eyes; there will be no more death**." *(Rev 21:3-4)*

Hail Mary

"There will be no more mourning or sadness. The world of the past has gone...

Now I am making the whole of creation new."

(Rev 21:4-5)

Hail Mary

(The one sitting on the throne said): "Write this,
What I am saying is trustworthy
and will come true... it has already happened".

(Rev 21:5-6)

Hail Mary
Glory Be
O my Jesus... *(See page 635)*

5. THE CROWNING OF OUR LADY
QUEEN OF HEAVEN
We express an intention.

Our Father

"Now a great sign appeared in heaven:
a woman, adorned with the sun." *(Rev 12:1)*

Hail Mary

"(She was) standing on the moon,
and on her head (there was) a crown of twelve stars." *(Rev 12:1)*

Hail Mary

"I heard a voice shout from heaven, 'Salvation and power and empire for ever have been won by our God,
and all authority for his Christ'.". *(Rev 1:10)*

Hail Mary

"And now children, listen to me:
happy are those who keep my ways." *(Pr 8:32)*

Hail Mary

"Blessed whoever listens to me,
who day after day keeps watch at my gates to guard my portals". *(Pr 8:34)*

Hail Mary

"For whoever finds me finds life,
and obtains the favour of Yahweh". *(Pr 8:35)*

Hail Mary

"I love those who love me;
whoever searches eagerly for me finds me".
(Pr 8:17)

Hail Mary

"Blessed be God, the Father of our Lord Jesus Christ,
who has blessed us with all the spiritual blessings of heaven in Christ". *(Ep 1:3)*

Hail Mary

"God raised (his Son) high, and gave him the name which is above all other names; so that all beings in the heavens,
on earth and in the underworld, should bend the knee at the name of Jesus". *(Ph 2:9-10)*

Hail Mary

"And... every tongue should acknowledge Jesus Christ as Lord,
to the glory of God the Father". *(Ph 2:11)*

Hail Mary
Glory Be
O my Jesus... *(See page 635)*

Hail Mary Queen

For concluding prayers, see pages 638-641

HOLY ROSARY: THIRD SCHEME

The Missionary Rosary

We quote from the Pontifical Missionary Works:

"Eternal God, deign to receive the sacrifice of my life, for the benefit of the mystical body of the Holy Church. I have nothing to offer you other than that which you yourself gave to me. Take my heart and press it against the face of this spouse".

The purpose of the Missionary Rosary is to encourage us to pray for peace in the world and for the salvation of all people. The five different colours mentioned below represent the five continents and remind us of the intention for which we must pray:

- The **green** decade is for Africa. It evokes the green forests of the African continent as well as the colour sacred to the Muslims;
- The **red** decade is for the American continent whose original inhabitants were the Red (North American) Indians;
- The **white** decade is for Europe and for our Holy Father the Pope;
- The **blue** decade recalls Oceania and the numerous islands scattered in the blue waters of the ocean;
- The **yellow** decade is for Asia, the land of the Rising Sun, the cradle of civilization.

It is good to recite the final three Hail Marys for all the missionaries scattered throughout the world. Our Lady said at Fatima, "Recite the Holy Rosary every day. Ask for peace in the world." We encourage the reader to pray for this intention, to pray with openess of heart to all the world, commending its problems and sufferings to Our Lady, so that She, in turn, may present humanity's needs to God the Father.

Finally, let us recall that a world that prays remains united.
In the name of the Father, and of the Son,
and of the Holy Spirit. Amen.

O God, come to my aid.
O Lord, make haste to help us.
Glory Be

The Creed *(see page 26)*

On the five beads between the cross and the centre of the Rosary, we recite the following:

1st bead: Our Father
2nd bead: A Hail Mary for the gift of Faith
3rd bead: A Hail Mary for the gift of Hope
4th bead: A Hail Mary for the gift of Love
5th bead: The Glory Be

Blessed be you, God our Father, who have called us to meditate and celebrate in faith the mysteries of your Son. Grant that your faithful, diligent in praying the Rosary, may cherish in their hearts, together with Mary, Virgin and Mother, by the grace of the Holy Spirit, the joy, the passion and the glory of our Lord Jesus Christ, who lives and reigns for ever and ever. **Amen.**

JOYFUL MYSTERIES

1. The Annunciation
On the Missionary Rosary Beads, this mystery corresponds to the green colour for Africa.

Passage suggested for meditation: Lk 1:26-36
Christ came into the world in order to do the will of the Father showing his humble obedience. In him everyone is called to announce salvation to the world.

2. The Visitation
This mystery corresponds to the red decade for America.

Passage suggested for meditation: Lk 1:35-39
Only the one who makes himself servant of all is the first of all and the greatest in the kingdom of heaven. For every Christian, to live is to make oneself an echo of the hymn of joy of the Virgin Mary.

3. The Nativity
This mystery corresponds to the white decade for Europe and the Pope.

Passage suggested for meditation: Lk 2:22-35
Mary gave birth to a son whom she called Jesus. Those who believe in Christ are called to share the joy of Christmas with the whole world.

4. The Presentation in the Temple
This mystery corresponds to the blue colour for Oceania.

Passage suggested for meditation: Lk 2:22-35

Jesus made himself similar to humankind in all things, in order to share its lot. The joy of life is offering oneself to the Father for the salvation of the world, as Jesus did.

5. The Finding of Jesus in the Temple
This mystery corresponds to the yellow decade for Asia.

Passage suggested for meditation: Lk 2:41-51

Having taken the road back to Jerusalem, Mary and Joseph found their Son Jesus in the Temple. Every human existence is a journey in which we search for Jesus, a journey in which we seek the Lord with humility... and then we must go out into the world and proclaim with joy that we have found Him.

LUMINOUS MYSTERIES

1. The baptism of Jesus in the waters of the river Jordan

On the Missionary Rosary Beads, this mystery corresponds to the green colour for Africa.

Passage suggested for meditation: Mk 1:9-11

Contemplation of Mary is a form of recollection above all else. We must understand this word in the biblical sense of the memory (zakar), which actualised the works carried out by God in the history of Salvation. These events are not only a "yesterday", they are also the "today" of salvation. "Remembering them", in a spirit of faith and love, means opening oneself up to the grace that Christ obtained for us with his Mysteries of life, death and resurrection.

2. Jesus manifests his glory at the wedding feast of Cana by answering Mary's prayer

This mystery corresponds to the red decade for America.

Passage suggested for meditation: Jn 2:5.11

Christ is the master par excellence, he who reveals and the revelation. It is not only a question of learning the things that he taught, but of "learning him". But what teacher is more of an expert than Mary in this subject? If, spiritually speaking, the Holy Spirit is the inner Teacher who leads us to the full truth of Christ *(ref. Jn.*

14:26, 15:26, 16:13), among humans, nobody knows Christ better than her, nobody like His Mother can introduce us to a profound consciousness of his Mystery.

3. Jesus announces that the kingdom of God is near and he invites us to convert our hearts
This mystery corresponds to the white decade for Europe and the Pope.

Passage suggested for meditation: Mk 1:14-15
The qualifying characteristic of Christian Spirituality is the willingness of the disciple to conform ever more fully to his Teacher.
In the spiritual pathway of the Rosary, which is based on incessant contemplation, in the company of Mary, the face of Christ, this exigent ideal to conform to Him is obtained by means of what we could refer to as the pathway of a "friendly" relationship. This leads us naturally into the life of Christ and lets us "breathe in" his feelings.

4. Jesus on mount tabor, shows himself to the apostles in the splendour of divinity
This mystery corresponds to the blue colour for Oceania.

Passage suggested for meditation: Lk 9:28-29
"Ask and it will be given to you, seek and you will find, knock and the door shall be opened onto you" (*Mt 7:7*). The foundation of this effec-

tiveness of the prayer is the goodness of the Father, but also the meditation by Christ himself and the action of the Holy Spirit. We in fact "do not even know what we should ask for" (*Ro 8:26*) and sometimes our prayers are not answered because "we do not ask correctly". As a form of support for the prayer that Christ and the Holy Spirit cause to burst forth from our heart, Mary intervenes with her maternal intercession.

5. Jesus gives the Eucharist to the Church as a testament of love

This mystery corresponds to the yellow decade for Asia.

Passage suggested for meditation: Mt 26:26-28
The Rosary is also a *pathway to an announcement and a development,* in which the Mystery of Christ is continually represented on various different levels of the Christian experience. The Virgin of the Rosary also continues her work of the annunciation of Christ in this way. Today we are before new challenges. Why not take the Crown into our hands with the faith of those who preceded us? The Rosary conserves all the force and it remains an undeniable resource in the pastoral baggage of a good evangelist.

SORROWFUL MYSTERIES

1. The Agony in the Garden
This mystery corresponds to the green colour for Africa.

Passage suggested for meditation: Lk 22:39-46
The Son of God suffered pain in His own body in order to save us, and to grant peace and justice to all people who carry the burden of injustice in the world, in imitation of Christ.

2. The Scourging at the Pillar
This mystery corrsponds to the red colour for America.

Passage suggested for mediatation: Mt 27:22-26
The servant of God bore our sufferings and the punishment reconciling us fell on him. In order to follow the road of salvation, we must accept trials, abandoning ourselves totally to God and trusting in him.

3. The Crowning with Thorns
This mystery corresponds to the white colour for Europe.

Passage suggested for meditation: Jn 19:1-7
Ill treated and afflicted he let himself be humiliated and never opened his mouth, like a lamb led to the slaughter-house; the King of the Universe wore on his head a crown of thorns.

4. The Carrying of the Cross
This mystery corresponds to the blue colour for Oceania.

Passage suggested for meditation: Lk 23:26-31
Let us keep our eyes fixed on Jesus; who has shown us the way of the cross. Let us renounce ourselves every day and follow him, as in losing our life for his sake, we will save it.

5. The Crucifixion and Death of Jesus
This mystery corresponds to the yellow colour for Asia.

Passage suggested for meditation: Jn 19:25-30
The son of God accepted the supreme humiliation from the hands of the Father: that of dying on the cross. The world will be saved by staying, as Mary did, at the foot of the cross.

GLORIOUS MYSTERIES

1. The Resurrection
This mystery corresponds to the green colour for Africa.

Passage suggested for meditation: Mk 16:1-7
Christ is risen. The joy of Easter is not only that of knowing that we too may rise one day, but we rejoice in the new presence of the risen Christ who gives us his Spirit.

2. The Ascension
This mystery corresponds to the red colour for America.

Passage suggested for meditation: Ac 1:2-3,9-14
In heaven Christ enjoys being seated at the right hand of the Father. However, before ascending into heaven, Jesus promised that he would be with us always, even to the end of time, and invited us to go out to the whole world, and proclaim the Gospel to all creation.

3.The Coming of the Holy Spirit on Our Lady and the Apostles
This mystery corresponds to the white colour for Europe.

Passage suggested for meditation: Ac 2:1-4
Those who let themselves be guided by the Spirit of God are children of God. We have not received a spirit of slavery to bring us back into fear, but

rather the Spirit of God who allows us to become children of God and enables us to cry out, "Abba, Father!".

4. The Assumption
This mystery corresponds to the blue colour for Oceania.

Passage suggested for meditation: Lk 1:46-52
In the mystery of the assumption we rejoice in the glorification of the Mother of Jesus: let us say with Mary, "I want to praise the Lord for the great things he has done for me. God is my Saviour: I am full of joy."

5. The Crowning of Our Lady as Queen of Heaven
This mystery corresponds to the yellow colour for Asia.

Passage suggested for meditation: Rev 21:1-5
Mary is Queen of heaven and earth. Having been given Christ, She gave him to the world. "May you be blessed by God Almighty, you who are above all women of the earth."

Litany of the Blessed Virgin Mary *(See page 723)*

2.
LITANIES

LITANY OF THE BLESSED VIRGIN MARY
(commonly called the LITANY OF LORETO)

The Litany of the Blessed Virgin Mary has been defined as being a "masterpiece of popular Marian Devotion". Having been approved by Pope Sextus V in 1587, it was the only litany recognized and authorized to be recited and sung in the whole Church by the Decree of the Holy Office in 1601. The litany consists of 51 invocations: the first three come from the Litany of the Saints, twelve are based on the title "Mother", six on the title "Virgin", while thirteen invoke Mary with biblical and patristic symbols, four invoke her as "helper" and thirteen as "Queen".

Lord, have mercy
Christ, have mercy
Lord, have mercy
Christ, hear us
Christ, answer our prayers
Father in Heaven, you who are God
Have mercy on us
Son, redeemer of the world, you who are God
Have mercy on us
Holy Spirit, only God
Have mercy on us
Holy Trinity, one God
Pray for us
Holy Mary
Holy Mother of God
Holy Virgin of virgins
Mother of Christ
Mother of the Church

Kyrie, eléison.
Kyrie, eléison.
Christe, eléison.
Christe, eléison.
Kyrie, eléison.
Kyrie, eléison.
Christe, audis nos.
Christe, audis nos.
Christe, exáudis nos.
Christe, exáudis nos.
Pater de caelis Deus,
Miserére nobis.
Fili, Redémptor mundi Deus,
Miserére nobis.
Spíritus Sancte Deus,
Miserére nobis.
Sancta Trínitas, unus Deus,
Miserére nobis.

Mother of divine grace	Sancta María,
Pray for us	**ora pro nobis**
Mother most pure	Sancta Dei Génetrix,
Mother most chaste	Sancta Virgo vírginum,
Mother ever virgin	Mater Christi,
Mother undefiled	Mater Ecclésiae,
Mother most amiable	Mater divínae grátiae,
Mother most admirable	Mater puríssima,
Mother of good counsel	Mater castíssima,
Mother of our Creator	Mater invioláta,
Mother of our Savour	Mater intemeráta,
Virgin most prudent	(Mater immaculáta,)
Virgin most venerable	Mater amábilis,
Virgin most renowned	Mater admirábilis,
Virgin most powerful	Mater boni consílii,
Virgin most clement	Mater Creatóris,
Virgin most faithful	Mater Salvatóris,
Mirror of perfection	Virgo prudentíssima,
Seat of wisdom	Virgo veneránda,
Source of our joy	Virgo praedicánda,
Temple of the Holy Spirit	Virgo potens,
Tabernacle of eternal glory	Virgo clemens,
Consecrated dwelling place of God	Virgo fidélis,
Mystical rose	Spéculum iustítiae,
Tower of the holy city of David	Sedes sapiéntiae,
Impregnable fortress	Causa nostrae laetítiae,
Sanctuary of the divine presence	Vas spirituále,
Ark of the covenant	Vas honorábile,
Gate of Heaven	Vas insígne devotiónis,
Morning star	Rosa mystica,
Health of the sick	Turris Davídica,
Refuge of sinners	Turris ebúrnea,
	Domus áurea,
	Foéderis arca,
	Iánua coeli,
	Stella matutína,
	Salus infirmórum,
	Refúgium peccatórum,

Comforter of the afflicted
Pray for us
Help of Christians
Queen of angels
Queen of patriarchs
Queen of prophets
Queen of apostles
Queen of martyrs
Queen of confessors
of the faith
Queen of virgins
Queen of all saints
Queen conceived without
original sin
Queen assumed into Heaven
Queen of the most holy
Rosary
Queen of families
Queen of peace

Lamb of God, you take away the sins of the world
Have mercy on us

Lamb of God, you take away the sins of the world
Have mercy on us

Lamb of God you take away the sins of the world
Grant us peace

Pray for us, oh holy Mother of God.
That we may be made worthy of the promises of Christ.

Consolátrix afflictórum,
ora pro nobis.
Auxílium Christianórum,
Regína Angelórum,
Regína Patriarchárum,
Regína Prophetárum,
Regína Apostolórum,
Regína Mártyrum,
Regína Confessórum,
Regína Vírginum,
Regína Sanctórum ómnius,
Regína sine labe origináli
concépta,
Regína in caelum assúmpta,
Regína Sacratíssimi
Rosárii,
Regína familiae,
Regína pacis,

Agnus Dei, qui tollis peccáta mundi,
Parce nobis, Dómine.

Agnus Dei, qui tollis peccáta mundi,
Exáudi nos, Dómine.

Agnus Dei, qui tollis peccáta mundi,
Miserére nobis.

Ora pro nobis, Sancta Dei Génetrix,
Ut digni efficiámur
promissiónibus Christi.

Let us pray.
Grant that we your servants, Lord, may enjoy unfailing health of mind and body, and through the glorious intentions of the ever blessed Virgin Mary in her glory, free us from our present adversities and give us unending joy. Through Christ our Lord. **Amen.**

or

Oh God, whose only begotten Son, by his life, death and resurrection has purchased for us the rewards of eternal life, grant, we beseech thee that meditating on these Mysteries in the most holy Rosary of the Blessed Virgin Mary, we may both imitate what they contain, and obtain what they promise, through the same Christ our Lord. **Amen.**

or

Let us pray.
Almighty and everlasting God, by the co-operation of the Holy Spirit you prepared the body and soul of Mary, glorious Virgin and Mother, to become the worthy habitation of your Son; grant that by her gracious intercession, in whose commemoration we rejoice, we may be delivered from present evils and from everlasting death. Through the same Christ our Lord. **Amen.**

A pious custom suggests the addition of the following intercessional prayers after the litany:

For the needs of the Church and of our country:

Our Father
Hail Mary
Glory Be

For the (arch)bishop of this diocese and his intentions:

Our Father
Hail Mary
Glory Be

For the holy souls in Purgatory:

Our Father
Hail Mary

May they rest in peace.
Amen.

DOMINICAN LITANY

This litany, quite different from the ordinary ones, has been used since the birth of the Dominican Order, and has proven to be very very effective in obtaining Our Lady's protection and prompt assistance in great times of trial of the Order and of the faith. The persecution of the Order in 1300 by a certain "Willam of Holy Love" is well known. Blessed Humbert, who was Superior General of the Order at that time, asked all the convents to recite this litany. Subsequently, not only did the persecution stop, but the Dominican Order also grew in honour and favour.

(To be said in times of trial)

Lord,	**have mercy on us.**
Christ,	**have mercy on us.**
Lord,	**Have mercy on us.**
Christ,	**Hear us.**
Christ,	**Graciously hear us.**

God the Father of heaven,

Have mercy on us.

God the Son, Redeemer of the world,   ”
God the Holy Spirit,   ”
Holy Trinity, one God,   ”

Holy Mary, hope in all mysteries
   and sweet consolation of those who suffer,

Pray for us.

Holy Mary, most holy Mother of Christ,   ”

Holy Mary, Virgin Mother of God, **Pray for us.**

Holy Mary, Mother undefiled, "

Holy Mary, Mother inviolate, "

Holy Mary, Virgin of Virgins, "

Holy Mary, ever Virgin, "

Holy Mary, full of the grace of God, "

Holy Mary, Daughter of the eternal King, "

Holy Mary, Mother and Spouse of Christ, "

Holy Mary, Temple of the Holy Spirit, "

Holy Mary, Queen of heaven, "

Holy Mary, Mistress of Angels, "

Holy Mary, new Mother, "

Holy Mary, stairway to God, "

Holy Mary, gate of Paradise, "

Holy Mary, our Mother and Our Lady, "

Holy Mary, our true hope, "

Holy Mary, object of faith of all believers, "

Holy Mary, perfect charity towards God, "

Holy Mary, our Sovereign Queen, "

Holy Mary, source of sweetness, "

Holy Mary, Mother of mercy, "

Holy Mary, Mother of the eternal Prince, "

Holy Mary, Mother of Good Counsel, "

Holy Mary, Mother of the true faith, "

Holy Mary, our resurrection, **Pray for us.**

Holy Mary, through whom every
creature is renewed, "

Holy Mary, who gave birth to the eternal Light, "

Holy Mary, who sustain Him who
sustains all things, "

Holy Mary, gem of Divine Incarnation, "

Holy Mary, depositary of heavenly treasure, "

Holy Mary, who begot the Creator of all things, "

Holy Mary, mystery of heavenly counsel, "

Holy Mary, our true salvation, "

Holy Mary, treasure of the faithful, "

Holy Mary, most beautiful Lady, "

Holy Mary, iris full of joy, "

Holy Mary, Mother of true joy, "

Holy Mary, our way to the Lord, "

Holy Mary, our advocate, "

Holy Mary, most resplendent star of heaven, "

Holy Mary, more brilliant than the moon, "

Holy Mary, who shine more brightly
than the sun, "

Holy Mary, Mother of the eternal God, "
Holy Mary, who dissipate the darkness
of eternal night, "

Holy Mary, who wipe away the sentence
of our punishment, **Pray for us.**

Holy Mary, source of true wisdom, "

Holy Mary, Light of true science, "

Holy Mary, our inestimable joy, "

Holy Mary, our reward, "

Holy Mary, desire of our heavenly homeland, "

Holy Mary, mirror of divine contemplation, "

Holy Mary, most blessed among all the Blessed, "

Holy Mary, most worthy of all praise, "

Holy Mary, most merciful Lady, "

Holy Mary, comforter of those who have
recourse to you, "

Holy Mary, full of tenderness, "

Holy Mary, abounding in every sweetness, "

Holy Mary, beauty of the angels, "

Holy Mary, flower of the patriarchs, "

Holy Mary, humility of the prophets, "

Holy Mary, treasure of the apostles, "

Holy Mary, praised by the martyrs, "

Holy Mary, glory of priests, "

Holy Mary, honoured by the virgins, "

Holy Mary, lily of chastity, "

Holy Mary, blessed among all women, "

Holy Mary, redemption of all who are lost,

Pray for us.

Holy Mary, praised by all the just,   "

Holy Mary, who know the secrets of God,   "

Holy Mary, most holy of all women,   "

Holy Mary, Lady most noble,   "

Holy Mary, gem of the heavenly Spouse,   "

Holy Mary, dwelling place of Christ,   "

Holy Mary, Immaculate Virgin,   "

Holy Mary, temple of the Lord,   "

Holy Mary, glory of Jerusalem,   "

Holy Mary, joy of Israel,   "

Holy Mary, daughter of God,   "

Holy Mary, most beloved Spouse of Christ, "

Holy Mary, star of the sea,   "

Holy Mary, who stretch out your hand and
touch our hearts in order to enlighten us
and free us sinners,   "

Holy Mary, crown on the head of the
Most High king,   "

Holy Mary, most worthy of every honour, "

Holy Mary, filled with every sweetness,   "

Holy Mary, reward of the heavenly Kingdom, "

Holy Mary, gate to heavenly life,   "

Holy Mary, door locked and opened,

Pray for us.

Holy Mary, by whom we are introduced
to the Lord, "

Holy Mary, rose which never fades, "

Holy Mary, more precious than all things
that are pure, "

Holy Mary, more desirable than any treasure, "

Holy Mary, more sublime than the sky, "

Holy Mary, whose brightness is more
dazzling than the angels, "

Holy Mary, joy of the archangels, "

Holy Mary, exultation of all saints, "

Holy Mary, our honour, praise, glory and trust, "

Mary, Daughter of God,

Look upon us.

Mary, Daughter of Joachim,

Love us.

Mary, Daughter of Anna,

Draw us to yourself.

**Lamb who are the Daughter of God
and the gate of hope,**
lead us to your Son.

**Lamb, who are the Daughter of God
and the virginal lily,**
unite us to Him.

Lamb, who are the Daughter of God,
grant us a kingdom of repose after this our exile.

Pray for us, O holy Mother of God.
That we may be made worthy of the promises
of Christ.

Let us pray.
O Lord Jesus, who, to attain your glory, wanted
first to live a human existence interwoven with
joys and sorrows like our own, grant that your
Church may never lack fervent priests, religious
and lay people who, through the Rosary of Mary,
may teach others the mysteries of our Redemption. You who live and reign for ever and ever.
Amen.

Litany of "lumen gentium"

As regards "Marian phenomena", rich in theme and varied in their expression, the Church of our time has had extraordinary historical, theological and mystical experience: after meditating at length, the bishops wrote a document, chapter VIII of Lumen Gentium, in which they propose, with new language and new perspectives, the perennial doctrine of the Church on the Mother of Christ. However, as the Council itself pointed out, not all Marian themes were considered, nor were all the theological and cultural ways of approaching the figure of the Virgin Mary explored.
The following litany is taken from their document.

Lord, have mercy.

Lord, have mercy.

Christ, have mercy.

Christ, have mercy.

Lord, have mercy.

Lord, have mercy.

Christ, hear us.

Christ, graciously hear us.

Holy Mother of God,

Pray for us.

Beloved Daughter of the Father,   "

Mother of the Word Incarnate,   "

Temple of the Holy Spirit,   "

Virgin chosen from all eternity,   "

New Eve,

Pray for us.

Daughter of Adam,	,,
Daughter of Zion,	,,
Virgin Immaculate,	,,
Virgin of Nazareth,	,,
Virgin overshadowed by the Spirit,	,,
Mother of Our Lord,	,,
Mother of Emmanuel,	,,
Mother of Christ,	,,
Mother of Jesus,	,,
Mother of our Saviour,	,,
Partner of our Redeemer,	,,
You who accepted the Word,	,,
You who gave Life to the world,	,,
You who presented Jesus in the Temple,	,,
You who showed Jesus to the Magi,	,,
You who gladdened those at the table of Cana,	,,
You who co-operated in the work of salvation,	,,
You who suffered at the Cross,	,,
You who implored the gift of the Spirit,	,,
Mother of the living,	,,
Mother of all the faithful,	,,
Mother of all people,	,,

Chosen from among the poor of the Lord,

Pray for us.

Humble handmaid of the Lord,	,,
Servant of Redemption,	,,
Pilgrim in the walk of faith,	,,
Virgin of obedience,	,,
Virgin of hope,	,,
Virgin of love,	,,
Model of sanctity,	,,
Eminent member of the Church,	,,
Image of the Church,	,,
Mother of the Church,	,,
Advocate for us,	,,
Help of Christians,	,,
Succour of the poor,	,,
Mediatrix of grace,	,,
Assumed into heavenly glory,	,,
Glorified in body and soul,	,,
Exalted above the angels and saints,	,,
Queen of the universe,	,,
Sign of consolation,	,,
Sign of sure hope,	,,
Sign of future glory,	,,

**Lamb of God, who take away
the sins of the world,**
Spare us, O Lord.

**Lamb of God, who take away
the sins of the world,**
Graciously hear us, O Lord.

**Lamb of God, who take away
the sins of the world,**
Have mercy on us.

Pray for us, O holy Mother of God.
That we may be made worthy of the promises of
Christ.

Let us pray.
Grant that we your servants, Lord, may enjoy
unfailing health of mind and body and through
the prayers of the ever blessed Virgin Mary in her
glory, free us from our sorrows in this world, and
give us eternal happiness in the next.
Through Christ our Lord. **Amen.**

Litany of Mary our Queen

The following invocations express the journey which brought Mary to queenship. Our Lady was an obedient servant and a perfect disciple, and thus shares in the sovereignty of Christ, her Son, because of the radicality of her service and her unlimited love. Nonetheless these invocations do not ring of worldly triumph but, on the contrary, are warm, affectionate and appealing; as children of Mary, we exalt our Mother, not to keep our distance from her, but rather to brighten with hope both our daily toil and our future as disciples of the Lord.

Lord, have mercy.

Lord, have mercy.

Christ, have mercy.

Christ, have mercy.

Lord, have mercy.

Lord, have mercy.

Christ, hear us.

Christ, graciously hear us.

God, the Father of heaven,

Have mercy on us.

God the Son, Redeemer of the world,　　　　"

God the Holy Spirit,　　　　"

Holy Trinity, one God,　　　　"

Holy Mary,　　　　　　　　**Pray for us.**

Holy Mother of God,　　　　"

Holy Virgin of virgins,　　　　"

Beloved Daughter of the Father,

Pray for us.

Mother of Christ, king of the centuries, "

Glory of the Holy Spirit, "

Virgin daughter of Zion, "

Virgin, poor and humble, "

Virgin, mild and meek, "

Obedient servant of the faith, "

Mother of our Lord, "

Collaborator with our Redeemer, "

Full of grace, "

Fount of beauty, "

Treasure of virtue and wisdom, "

First fruit of Redemption, "

Perfect disciple of Christ, "

Purest image of the Church, "

Woman of the new covenant, "

Woman robed with the sun, "

Woman crowned with stars, "

Our Lady of infinite goodness, "

Our Lady of forgiveness, "

Mistress of our families, "

Joy of the new Israel, "

Splendour of the Holy Church, "

Honour of humankind,

Pray for us.

Advocate of grace,   "

Minister of mercy,   "

Help of the people of God,   "

Queen of love,   "

Queen of mercy,   "

Queen of peace,   "

Queen of angels,   "

Queen of patriarchs,   "

Queen of prophets,   "

Queen of apostles,   "

Queen of martyrs,   "

Queen of confessors,   "

Queen of virgins,   "

Queen of all saints,   "

Queen conceived without original sin,   "

Queen assumed into heaven,   "

Queen of the earth,   "

Queen of heaven,   "

Queen of the universe,   "

**Lamb of God, who take away
the sins of the world,**
Spare us, O Lord.

**Lamb of God, who take away
the sins of the world,**
Graciously hear us, O Lord.

**Lamb of God, who take away
the sins of the world,**
Have mercy on us.

Pray for us, O holy Mother of God.
That we may be made worthy
of the promises of Christ.

Let us pray.
O God, our most clement Father, hear the prayer
of your people who venerate the Blessed Virgin
Mary, your servant, and who acknowledge her as
Mother of grace and Queen of mercy: may we
serve you with love in our brothers and sisters so
that one day, together with them, we may have a
share in the glory of your kingdom.
Through Christ our Lord. **Amen.**

BIBLICAL LITANIES

A most pure form of praising Our Lady is to draw from Scripture itself, as is done in the Biblical Litanies below. These formulas have been meditated on and recommended by the Church throughout the centuries. The First Biblical Litany draws on the Old Testament in its first part, corresponding to the "first covenant" between God and his people; in its second part the invocations concern the New Testament, in particular Divine Revelation through Jesus Christ. The Second and Third Biblical Litanies are both based on the New Testament.

FIRST BIBLICAL LITANY

Lord, have mercy.

Lord, have mercy.

Christ, have mercy.

Christ, have mercy.

Lord, have mercy.

Lord, have mercy.

Christ, hear us.

Christ, graciously hear us.

God, the Father of heaven,

Have mercy on us.

God the Son, Redeemer of the world,

Have mercy on us.

God the Holy Spirit, "

Holy Trinity, one God, "

Holy Mary, Mother of God,

Pray for us.

New Eve,	**Pray for us.**
Mother of the living,	"
Descendent of Abraham,	"
Heiress of the promise,	"
Shoot of Jesus,	"
Daughter of Zion,	"
Virginal earth,	"
Ladder of Jacob,	"
Burning Bush,	"
Tabernacle of the Most High,	"
Ark of the Covenant,	"
Seat of wisdom,	"
City of God,	"
Eastern gate,	"
Font of living water,	"
Dawn of salvation,	"
Joy of Israel,	"
Glory of Jerusalem,	"
Honour of our people,	"
Virgin of Nazareth,	"
Virgin full of grace,	"
Virgin overshadowed by the Spirit,	"
Virgin in labour,	"
Servant of the Lord,	"
Servant of the Word,	"
Servant, humble and poor,	"

Spouse of Joseph,	**Pray for us.**
Blessed among all women,	,,
Mother of Jesus,	,,
Mother of Emmanuel,	,,
Mother of the Son of David,	,,
Mother of our Lord,	,,
Mother of the disciples,	,,
Mother, sollicitous in the Visitation,	,,
Mother, joyful in Bethlehem,	,,
Mother, suffering in the Temple,	,,
Mother, exiled in Egypt,	,,
Mother, anxious in Jerusalem,	,,
Mother, provident at Cana,	,,
Mother, strong at Calvary,	,,
Mother, prayerful in the Cenacle,	,,
Woman of the New Covenant,	,,
Woman robed with the sun,	,,
Woman crowned with stars,	,,
Queen at the right hand of the King,	,,
Blessed because you believed,	,,
Blessed because you kept the Word,	,,
Blessed because you accomplished the will of the Father,	,,

**Lamb of God, who take away
the sins of the world,**
Spare us, O Lord.

**Lamb of God, who take away
the sins of the world,**
Graciously hear us, O Lord.

**Lamb of God, who take away
the sins of the world,**
Have mercy on us.

Pray for us, O holy Mother of God.
That we may be made worthy of the promises
of Christ.

Let us pray.
O God, Father of Christ our Saviour, who, in
Mary, a holy virgin and attentive mother, gave us
an image of the Church, send us your Spirit to
help us in our weakness so that, persevering in
faith, we may grow in love and walk together
unto the destination of blessed hope.
Through Christ our Lord. **Amen.**

SECOND BIBLICAL LITANY

Mary of Nazareth,	**Pray for us.**
Mother of the Son of the Most High,	"
Mother by the power of the Holy Spirit,	"
Mother of the Lord and Messiah,	"
Mother of the beloved disciple,	"
Virgin, spouse of Joseph,	"
Virgin, humble and poor,	"
Blessed among all women,	"
You, who accepted Christ in faith,	"
You, who said "yes" to the angel,	"
You, who gave birth to the Son of God,	"
You, exultant in God your Saviour,	"
You, pierced by a sword of sorrow,	"
You, who did not understand the words of your Son,	"
You, who stored up all things in your heart,	"
You, who prompted the miracle of Cana,	"
You, who were by the Cross,	"
Blessed for the great things that God did for you,	"
Blessed for all ages,	"

For concluding prayer, see page above

THIRD BIBLICAL LITANY

Mary, sweet flower of Nazareth, **Pray for us.**

Mary, one of the Lord's poor, "

Mary, full of grace, "

Mary, humble servant of the Lord, "

Mary, spouse of Joseph, an upright man, "

Mary, Ark of the New Covenant, "

Mary, temple of the Holy Spirit, "

Mary, Mother of the Son of the Most High, "

Mary, blessed among all women, "

Virgin who store up all things in your heart, "

Mother, presence of peace and love, "

Mother, who presented Jesus in the Temple, "

Mother whom the Magi found
with the Child Jesus, "

Mother whom Joseph led into Egypt, "

Mother who looked for Jesus for three days, "

Mother who found Jesus in the Temple, "

Mother under whose authority Jesus lived, "

Mother, silent disciple of the Master, "

Blessed are you who listened
to the Word of the Lord, "

Blessed are you who lived according
    to the Word of God,   **Pray for us.**

Mother beneath the Cross,   "

Mother entrusted by the Son
    to the virgin Disciple,   "

Mother who rejoiced at the dawn
    of the Resurrection,   "

Mother who persevered in prayer
    with the apostles,   "

Mother filled with the Holy Spirit
    in the Cenacle,   "

Mary, Mother of the Body of Christ
    which is the Church,   "

Woman robed with the sun,   "

Woman crowned with twelve stars,   "

Mary, image of the heavenly Jerusalem,   "

For concluding prayer, see page 746

LITANY OF OUR LADY OF HOPE

The Litany of Our Lady of Hope was composed by the International Liturgical Commission of the Order of the Servants of Mary, and is based on the text of the Latin American Episcopal Conference of Puebla. A choir or soloist intones and the assembly responds. After each group of seven petitions the whole assembly responds with the antiphon: "Our Lady of Hope, light up our path."

Lord, have mercy.

Lord, have mercy.

Christ, have mercy.

Christ, have mercy.

Lord, have mercy.

Lord, have mercy.

Our Lady of Hope,   **Pray for us.**
Our Lady of the Way,   ”
Our Lady of Light,   ”
Fullness of Israel,   ”
Prophecy of new times,   ”
Dawn of the new world,   ”
Mother of God,   ”

Mother of the Messiah
    who brought freedom,   ”

Mother of the redeemed,   ”
Mother of all people,   ”

Our Lady of Hope, light up our path.

Virgin of silence,	**Pray for us.**
Virgin who listen,	"
Virgin of song,	"
Servant of the Lord,	"
Servant of the Word,	"
Servant of Redemption,	"
Servant of the Kingdom,	"

Our Lady of Hope, light up our path.

Disciple of Christ,	**Pray for us.**
Witness to the Gospel,	"
Sister of humankind,	"
Initiation of the Church,	"
Mother of the Church,	"
Model of the Church,	"
Image of the Church,	"

Our Lady of Hope, light up our path.

Mary, blessed among women,	**Pray for us.**
Mary, dignity of all women,	"
Mary, greatness of all women,	"
Woman faithful in your waiting,	"
Woman faithful to your commitment,	"
Woman faithful in prayer,	"
Woman faithful by the Cross,	"

Our Lady of Hope, light up our path.

First fruits of Easter,	**Pray for us.**
Splendour of Pentecost,	,,
Star of Evangelization,	,,
Shining presence,	,,
Prayerful presence,	,,
Welcoming presence,	,,
Working presence,	,,

Our Lady of Hope, light up our path.

Hope of the poor,	**Pray for us.**
Confidence of the humble,	,,
Support of the isolated,	,,
Relief of the oppressed,	,,
Defence of the innocent,	,,
Courage of the persecuted,	,,
Comfort of exiles,	,,

Our Lady of Hope, light up our path.

Voice of freedom,	**Pray for us.**
Voice of communion,	,,
Voice of peace,	,,
Sign of the maternal face of God,	,,
Sign of the nearness of the Father,	,,
Sign of mercy,	,,
Sign of fertility of the Spirit,	,,

Our Lady of Hope, light up our path.

Litany from "Marialis Cultus"

(by Pope Paul VI)

Lord, have mercy.

> **Lord, have mercy.**

Christ, have mercy.

> **Christ, have mercy.**

Lord, have mercy.

> **Lord, have mercy.**

Christ, hear us.

> **Christ, graciously hear us.**

God the Father, our Creator,	**Pray for us.**
God the Son, our Redeemer,	"
God the Holy Spirit, our Sanctifier,	"
Holy Trinity, one God,	"
Mother of God,	"
Mother of our Lord,	"
Mother of Jesus,	"
Mother of the Son of God,	"
Mother of the Word Incarnate,	"
Mother of the Author of life,	"
Mother of the Suffering Servant of Yahweh,	"
Mother who co-operated with the Saviour,	"
Mother who took part in the Passion of the Son,"	

Mother of the King,	**Pray for us.**
Mother of the Head of the Church and her members,	,,
Mother of the Church,	,,
Mother of the living,	,,
Mother of mercy,	,,
Mother of grace,	,,
Mother who leads her children to conquer sin,	,,
Holy Mother,	,,
Most loving Mother,	,,
Glorious Mother,	,,
Virgin Mary,	,,
Holy Virgin,	,,
Obedient and faithful Virgin,	,,
Virgin of Nazareth,	,,
Virgin who listen,	,,
Virgin in prayer,	,,
Virgin mother,	,,
Virgin who offer,	,,
Virgin of sorrows,	,,
Virgi united closely to your Son,	,,
True seat of wisdom,	,,
Way which leads to Christ,	,,
True temple of God,	,,

Victory of hope over anguish,	**Pray for us.**
Victory of solidarity over solitude,	,,
Victory of peace over anxiety,	,,
Our Lady assumed into heaven,	,,
Our Help and Advocate,	,,
Glorious and ever Virgin Mary,	,,
Ark of the Covenant,	,,
Blessed by the Most High,	,,
Blessed Mary,	,,
Comforter of the afflicted,	,,
Co-redemptrix,	,,
New Woman,	,,
Woman of strengh,	,,
Woman, humble and poor,	,,
Dwelling place of the Spirit of God,	,,
Teacher of spiritual life,	,,
Model of evangelical life,	,,
Model of virtue for the entire	,,
population of the chosen ones,	,,
First and perfect follower of Christ,	,,
Queen of mercy,	,,
Refuge of sinners,	,,
Health of the sick,	,,
Sanctuary of the Holy Spirit,	,,

Hope of Christians,	**Pray for us.**
Our true sister,	"
Victory of life over death,	"

**Lamb of God, who take away
the sins of the world,**
Spare us, O Lord.

**Lamb of God, who take away
the sins of the world,**
Graciously hear us, O Lord.

**Lamb of God, who take away
the sins of the world,**
Have mercy on us;

Pray for us, O holy Mother of God.
That we may be made worthy
of the promises of Christ.

Let us pray.
O merciful God, who gave us in the Virgin Mary
a sublime example of faith and adherence to your
Word, grant that, through her intercession, we
may continue our pilgrimage with our hearts
turned towards the light of your truth.
Through Christ our Lord. **Amen.**

LITANY TO OUR LADY OF THE ROSARY

This litany was composed recently and is based on invocations suggested by contemplation of the mysteries of the Holy Rosary. It is made up of fifteen units, each one consisting of five invocations to Our Lady who was the first to accept and experience humanity in her life in a singular way. These invocations may also be recited at the end of each corresponding mystery.

Lord, have mercy.

> **Lord, have mercy.**

Christ, have mercy.

> **Christ, have mercy.**

Lord, have mercy.

> **Lord, have mercy.**

Virgin of silence in the face of mystery,	"
Soil in which love grows,	"
Virgin who listen,	"
Virgin who meet us,	"
Model of charity,	"
Bearer of Christ,	"
Virgin who sing the praises of the Lamb,	"
Woman ever new,	"
Virgin of dawn,	"
Vessel chosen by God,	"
Mother who give your Son to everyone,	"

Virgin who are an example for all motherhood,
Lord, have mercy.

Virgin who offer,   "

Mother of all people,   "

Virgin who accept the difficulties of faith,   "

Image of the Church,   "

Virgin who give joy to the simple,   "

Woman who never belonged to yourself,   "

Blessed among all women,   "

Mother of Christ's priesthood,   "

Virgin who are humble in your
   observance of life,   "

Model of those who search for your Son,   "

Virgin always in prayer,   "

Mother who have known sorrow,   "

Woman who fulfilled the will of the Father,   "

Refuge of those who are far from God,   "

Mother of the suffering servant,   "

Virgin preserved from sin,   "

Woman of living hope,   "

Virgin of patience,   "

Mother of compassion,   "

Woman who have always believed,   "

Humble servant of the Almighty,   "

Woman of a pierced heart,

Lord, have mercy.

Mother who know suffering,   ,,

Sister of all people,   ,,

Queen of the one who is faithful unto death,   ,,

Virginal gratuitous offering to the Father,   ,,

Model for every disciple of your Son,   ,,

Woman who accompany all holiness to Calvary, ,,

Silent and compassionate presence,   ,,

Succour of the faithful,   ,,

Mother who do not abandon your
    children in their suffering,   ,,

Queen of the witnesses to the faith,   ,,

Sure hope of salvation for every pierced heart,   ,,

Mother, Covenant of Christ with the Church,   ,,

Woman who keep watch by the cross
    of every person,   ,,

Model of faith for the pilgrim,   ,,

Woman who are a prophecy
    of victory over evil,   ,,

Mother of hope and joy,   ,,

Temple of the Spirit of life,   ,,

Mother who take part in the development
    of the world,   ,,

Virgin who proclaim that the name
of God is holy, **Lord, have mercy.**

Woman in whom the Almighty has done
great things, ,,

Virgin moulded by the newness of the Spirit, ,,

Mother of those who are enlightened by God, ,,

Virgin, model of unity among Christians, ,,

Mary, unique fulfilment of every creature, ,,

Woman robed with the sun, ,,

Mother intimately united to the Son, ,,

Humble woman exalted by God, ,,

Virginal announcement of life
and resurrection, ,,

Woman glowing with the resurrection, ,,

Star that appears before the rising of dawn, ,,

Prodigy of the Holy Spirit, ,,

Mother of the primitive Church, ,,

Humble woman crowned with
incorruptible glory, ,,

For concluding prayer, see page 746

LITANY OF THE CHURCH OF AQUILEIA

This litany is also referred to as the Venetian Litany. It used to be recited in the Church of Aquileia, and later became popular in Venice. It is perhaps one of the oldest litanies, having emerged from a manuscript written at the end of the twelfth century. One of its peculiarities is the response to the invocations: "Come to our aid."

Lord, have mercy.

Lord, have mercy.

Christ, have mercy.

Christ, have mercy.

Lord, have mercy.

Lord, have mercy.

Father who art in heaven,

Pray for us.

Son, Redeemer of the world, "

Holy Spirit, the Paraclete, "

Holy Trinity, one God, **Come to our aid.**

Holy Mary, Mother of God, "

Holy Mary, Mother of Light, "

Holy Mary, Mother of Christ, "

Holy Mary, Temple of the Spirit, "

Holy Mary, full of grace, "

Holy Mary, filled with joy, "

Holy Mary, Woman of eternal beauty, "

Holy Mary, Woman robed with the sun, "

Holy Mary, radiant Woman, "

Holy Mary, shining star of the morning, "

Holy Mary, brighter than the moon,

Come to our aid.

Holy Mary, more resplendent than the sun,   ,,
Holy Mary, fount of wisdom,   ,,
Holy Mary, light of knowledge,   ,,
Holy Mary, source of meekness,   ,,
Holy Mary, sure way to Christ,   ,,
Holy Mary, ladder to heaven,   ,,
Holy Mary, gate of Paradise,   ,,
Holy Mary, Mother of true joy,   ,,
Holy Mary, Mother of Mercy,   ,,
Holy Mary, Our Lady,   ,,
Holy Mary, our Advocate,   ,,
Holy Mary, our Mother,   ,,
Holy Mary, Mother of the abandoned,   ,,
Holy Mary, comfort of the downcast,   ,,
Holy Mary, confidence of the oppressed,   ,,
Holy Mary, help of sinners,   ,,
Holy Mary, health of the sick,   ,,
Holy Mary, hope of the faithful,   ,,
Holy Mary, Mistress of the angels,   ,,
Holy Mary, Joy of the patriarchs,   ,,
Holy Mary, intuition of the prophets,   ,,
Holy Mary, glory of the apostles,   ,,
Holy Mary, strength of martyrs,   ,,
Holy Mary, honour of virgins,   ,,
Holy Mary, splendour of the blessed,   ,,

Holy Mary, living praise of God,
Come to our aid.
Holy Mary, glory of the Christian people, **"**

**Lamb of God, who take away
the sins of the world,**
Spare us, O Lord.

**Lamb of God, who take away
the sins of the world,**
Graciously hear us, O Lord.

**Lamb of God, who take away
the sins of the world,**
Have mercy on us.

Pray for us, O holy Mother of God.
That we may be made worthy
of the promises of Christ.

Let us pray.
Father, we bless you because in Christ your Son
you have revealed the splendour of your glory,
and in the Virgin Mary you have given us a sign
of your grace and beauty; grant that, by our obedience to the voice of the Spirit, we may follow
the shining path of truth in order that we may we
reach you, life and salvation of all people.
Through Christ our Lord. **Amen.**

LITANY OF OUR LADY OF LOURDES

On the 8th of December, 1854, Pope Pius IX solemnly proclaimed the dogma of the Immaculate Conception of Mary. Since that day the Church has universally and officially declared that the Mother of our Redeemer was miracolously preserved from every stain of original sin and from every inclination to evil from the moment of her conception "in view of the merits of Jesus Christ". Less than four years later, on the 25th of March, 1858, the Virgin Mary appeared to the humble Bernadette of Lourdes, and said to her, "I am the Immaculate Conception!".

Lord, have mercy.

Lord, have mercy.

Christ, have mercy.

Christ, have mercy.

Lord, have mercy.

Lord, have mercy.

Our Lady of Lourdes, Immaculate Virgin,

Pray for us.

Our Lady of Lourdes, Mother
of the Divine Saviour,

Pray for us.

Our Lady of Lourdes, who chose a
poor and humble girl to be your interpreter,

Pray for us.

Our Lady of Lourdes, who made a spring
flow from the earth in order to give
comfort to many pilgrims,

Pray for us.

Our Lady of Lourdes, dispenser
of gifts from heaven,

Pray for us.

Our Lady of Lourdes, to whom Jesus
can refuse nothing,

Pray for us.

Our Lady of Lourdes, whom no one
has ever invoked in vain,

Pray for us.

Our Lady of Lourdes, Comforter of the afflicted,
Pray for us.

Our Lady of Lourdes, who heal every sickness,
Pray for us.

Our Lady of Lourdes, hope of pilgrims,
Pray for us.

Our Lady of Lourdes, who invite us to penance,
Pray for us.

Our Lady of Lourdes, support
of the Holy Church,

Pray for us.

Our Lady of Lourdes, advocate
of the souls of Purgatory,

Pray for us.

Our Lady of Lourdes, Virgin of the Holy Rosary,
Pray for us.

**Lamb of God, who take away
the sins of the world,**
Spare us, O Lord.

**Lamb of God, who take away
the sins of the world,**
Graciously hear us, O Lord.

**Lamb of God, who take away
the sins of the world,**
Have mercy on us.

Pray for us, O holy Mother of God.
That we may be made worthy of the promises
of Christ.

Let us pray.
Lord Jesus, we bless and thank you for all the
graces which, through your Mother in Lourdes,
you have poured forth on your people who pray
and suffer. Grant that we, too, through the intercession of Our Lady of Lourdes, may have a
share in these gifts, may love you more and serve
you better. **Amen.**

LITANY OF THE IMMACULATE HEART OF MARY

On the 13th of June, 1917, the Virgin Mary appeared to the young visionary of Fatima, Lucia, saying to her, "Jesus wants to establish devotion to my Immaculate Heart in this world. I promise salvation to those who shall adopt this devotion, and those souls who practise it will be dear to God. They will be like flowers put in place by me to adorn his Throne."

These solemn promises recall those already expressed by the Virgin Mary 87 years previously to St. Catherine Labouré in the Chapel of Rue du Bac, Paris.

Sorrowful and Immaculate Heart of Mary,

Have mercy on us.

Sorrowful and Immaculate Heart of Mary,

Intercede for us.

Sorrowful and Immaculate Heart of Mary,

Help us.

Sorrowful and Immaculate Heart of Mary,

Come to our assistance.

Sorrowful and Immaculate Heart of Mary,

Protect us.

For concluding prayer see page above

LITANY OF THE MOTHER OF MERCY

Lord,

Have mercy on us.

Jesus Christ,

Have mercy on us.

Lord,

Have mercy on us.

Mother of humanity,

Pray for us.

Mother of Divine Love,

Pray for us.

Mother of Consolation,   "

Mother and Teacher of all peoples,   "

Mother and Queen of families,   "

Mother of Faith,   "

Mother of Hope,   "

Mother of Grace,   "

Mother of Joy,   "

Mother of Divine Mercy,   "

Mother of the Incarnation,   "

Mother of Redemption,   "

Joyful Mother of the Resurrection,   "

Mother of Adoration,   "

Mother of priests,   "

Mother sweet and merciful,   "

Mother of holy gladness,

Pray for us.

Mother of all sorrows,   "

Mother of the New Evangelization,   "

Mother of trust,   "

Mother of purity,   "

Mother of all that is beautiful,   "

Glorious mother,   "

Victorious mother,   "

Mother of the poor,   "

Mother of the redeemed,   "

Mother of intercession,   "

Mother of reparation,   "

Mother of Sorrows,   "

Mother of Jesus as Priest,   "

Mother of the Eucharist,   "

Mother of the Blessed Sacrament, "

Medicine of Paradise,   "

Splendour of Heaven,   "

Heavenly Leader,   "

Divine masterpiece,   "

Rainbow of the New Covenant,   "

Mother of Suffering,   "

Mother of Wisdom,   "

Gate of Divine Mercy,

Pray for us.

Ark of the New Covenant, "

Immaculate Conception, "

Woman robed with the sun, "

Prophetess of the last times, "

Virgin of Revelation, "

Spouse of the Holy Spirit, "

Dawn of the new day of the Lord, "

Fount of Mercy, "

Way of Peace, "

For concluding prayer see page 746

3.
PRAYERS

O MARY, MOTHER OF DIVINE GRACE

by Pope John Paul II

I entrust the new spring of vocations to Mary, Mother of Divine Grace.

We turn to you, Mother of the Church; You who, with Your Fiat, have opened the door to the presence of Christ in the world, in history and in souls, accepting in humble silence and with perfect willingness, the call of the Most High.

Grant that once again in our times many men and women may perceive the inviting voice of Your Son: "Follow me".

Grant that they may have the courage to leave their families, their occupations, their wordly hopes to follow Christ, along the path indicated by Him.

Stretch out Your maternal hand to all Missionaries working throughout the world, to the Religious brothers and sisters who are taking care of the elderly, the sick, the handicapped, the orphans; stretch out Your hand to those who commit themselves to teaching, to members of secular institutes which are the silent leaven of good deeds; to those who, in enclosed orders, live by faith and love, and intercede for the salvation of the world.

Amen.

PRAYER TO MARY, MOTHER OF MERCY
by Pope John Paul II

O Mary, Mother of mercy, watch over us all so that the cross of Christ may not have been borne in vain, so that we may not wander astray from the path of goodness, nor lose our awareness of sin, but rather grow in the hope of God "rich in faithful love" *(Ep 2:4)*, accomplish with freedom "the good works which God has already designated" for us *(Ep 2:10)*, and therefore become with all our life "the praise of his glory" *(Ep 1:12)*. **Amen.**

PRAYER TO THE MOTHER
OF DIVINE (BEAUTIFUL) LOVE
by Pope John Paul II

Hail, O Mother, Queen of the world! You are the Mother of Divine Love, You are the Mother of Jesus, fount of every grace, the perfume of every virtue, the mirror of every purity. You are joy in our weeping, victory in battle, hope in death. What a sweet taste Your name has in our mouth, what gentle harmony it is to our ears, what elation it gives to our heart.

You are the happiness of those who suffer, the crown of martyrs, the beauty of virgins.

Lead us, we beseech, after this our exile to the possession of Your Son Jesus. **Amen.**

O MARY, STAY WITH US YOUR CHILDREN

by Pope John Paul II

O Mary, you who crush the head of the evil one, do not allow us to give in. Do not allow that we may be defeated by evil, but rather grant that we may defeat evil with good. God the Eternal Father bows down to You, who are victorious in your Immaculate Conception, and victorious by the power of God himself, by the power of grace.

Here, the Son, who is of the same substance of the Father and your Son, crucified and risen from the dead, bows down to you. Here the power of the Most High embraces you: the Holy Spirit, the advocate of sanctity.

The inheritance of sin is foreign to you. You are "full of grace". In you the very kingdom of God is established. In you the "new future" of humanity, of redeemed humanity, free from sin, is established. May this future penetrate the darkness which covers the earth, which overshadows human hearts and consciences.

Mary, you who know us, stay with us your children! We know that the annunciation of the Angel is in your ears, the canticle of praise is on your tongue, God made child is in your arms, the cross of Golgotha is in your heart, the light and fire of the Holy Spirit are resting on your head, and beneath your feet is the Evil One who has been defeated.

Pray for us to the Redeemer of humanity, that he may ransom us from sin and from all that renders us slaves, and may unite us with the bond of faithfulness to the Church and to the pastors who guide her.

Show your motherly love to the poor, to those who suffer and to all those who seek the kingdom of your Son. We thank you with all our heart for the gift of faith and we glorify with you the Father of Mercy, through your Son, Jesus Christ, in the Holy Spirit. **Amen.**

PRAYER TO THE VIRGIN OF BEGINNINGS
by Pope John Paul II at the end of the Marian Year

O Holy Mary, Virgin of Beginnings, we invoke you with trust at the troubled threshold of the third Millenium of life of the Holy Church of Christ: a Church which you are already, you the humble curtain of the Word, moved only by the wind of the Spirit.

Accompany with your mercy our steps towards the frontiers of a humanity that is redeemed and pacified and render our heart joyful and secure with the certainty that the Dragon is not stronger than your Beauty, O fragile and eternal woman, the first to be saved and the friend of every creature that continues to suffer and hope in the world. **Amen.**

MOTHER OF OUR REDEEMER

by Pope John Paul II

In this prayer the Pope draws attention to the relationship of Mary with each person of the Holy Trinity. Following the example of Mary, we, too, encounter the Father, the Son and the Holy Spirit and learn how to pray to them with the heart.

Mother of our Redeemer, in this time dedicated to You, we proclaim with joy that You are Blessed.

God the Father chose You before the creation of the world to realize His providential design of salvation. You believed in His love and obeyed His Word. The Son of God wanted You to be His Mother when He became Man to save all people.

You welcomed Him with prompt obedience and an undivided heart. The Holy Spirit loved You as His Mystical Spouse and filled You with singular gifts. You meekly allowed Yourself to be moulded by His hidden and powerful action. To You, on the threshold of the Third Millenium of Christianity, we entrust the Church, who acknowledges and invokes You as Mother. To You, Mother of all people and nations, with confidence we entrust all humanity with its fears and hopes.

Grant that everyone may encounter Christ, the Way, the Truth and the Life. Sustain us, O Virgin Mary, on our journey of faith, and obtain for us the grace of eternal salvation.

O clement, O loving, O sweet Mother of God and our Mother, Mary.

PRAYER TO OUR LADY OF LORETO

by Pope John Paul II

O Mary, we turn to you in your Holy House of Loreto, recalling the mystery of God made man in your most pure womb by the power of the Holy Spirit.

We adore this most prodigious event, a stupendous sign of the love of God for us: your example encourages us to trust in your beloved Son so that we may construct our lives on the words of the Gospel.

Mother of Mercy, obtain for us from Jesus forgiveness of our sins and deliverance from evil; obtain salvation and peace for all humanity - still governed by hate and selfishness.

In the footsteps of numerous pilgrims, who, for seven centuries, have come to this house, we too come and place in your hands our commitment to a true and deep conversion.

May your House of Nazareth become for our homes a model of living faith and unwavering hope, so that the Holy Church may grow in the domestic churches of our homes, and the love of Christ may spread everywhere.

O clement, O loving, O sweet Virgin Mary.

PRAYER TO MARY, OUR MOTHER
by Pope Paul VI

Look, O Mary, upon all humanity, this modern world in which the divine plan has called us to live and to work; it is a world which turns its back on the light of Christ; and then it fears and groans in the fearful shadows which it has created for itself by acting in this way.

Your most human voice, O most beautiful among virgins, O most worthy among mothers, O blessed among all women, invites the world to turn its gaze towards life, towards you who are the light of all people, towards you who are the heralding lamp of Christ, the one supreme light of the world; and implore for the world the joy of living as the creation of God, and thus the desire and capacity to converse, in prayer, with its Maker, of whom it reflects the mysterious and blessed image; implore for the world the capacity to regard everything as a gift from God, and the virtue to act, therefore with goodness and to use such gifts with wisdom and providence.
Implore peace for the world.

Grant that all people, who continue to be so divided among themselves, may become brothers and sisters; lead us to a more orderly and united society. Grant comfort to the suffering and eternal rest to the deceased.

Show yourself to be a Mother to us.

This is our prayer: O clement, O loving, O sweet Virgin Mary. **Amen.**

O MARY, MOTHER OF THE CHURCH
by Pope Paul VI

O Virgin Mary, Mother of the Church, to you we entrust the whole Church.

You, who were given as mother to the beloved disciple by your Divine Son at the moment of his redemptive death, remember the Christian people who commend themselves to you.

Remember all your children; sustain us in our prayers to God; keep our faith steadfast; strengthen our hope; increase our love. Remember all those who suffer.

Unite all Christians into a single family.

Temple of light without shadow or stain, intercede for us before your only-begotten Son, mediator of our reconciliation with the Father, so that he may grant us mercy in our shortcomings, and keep far from us every discord, filling our hearts with the joy of loving.

And grant that the whole Church may always raise a hymn of praise and thanksgiving to the God of Mercy, a hymn of joy and exultation, because the Lord has done great things by means of you, O clement, O loving, O sweet Virgin Mary.

PRAYER TO OUR LADY
OF GOOD JOURNEYS
by Pope Paul VI

To you, O Holy Virgin and our most sweet Mother, whom we invoke by the name of "Our Lady of Good Journeys", we commend ourselves at the moment of our departure. You know the perils which we are going to face, our worries about the journey and the comfort of our coming home.

May You be, therefore, our guide, our support, our consolation.

You, too, in the days of Your earthly life, made journeys which were long and full of difficulties, in the territories of Palestine and the hot lands of Egypt, prompted only by the will of God, confidently abandoned to him with Your faith and love.

Grant that we may follow Your shining example, so that our journey may be accomplished in serenity and in an orderly manner, and may be safe and peaceful; grant that we may be preserved from all dangers of the body and soul.

And hold us by Your hand, as a mother does with her children; help those whose hard work keeps them on the streets in a service that is tiring and monotonous; guide us also when we are on vacation, so that it may become for us a time of enrichment of human qualities, comfort for the spirit, encouragment and renewal of our strength. Mary, mother of mercy, guide our steps along the path of peace, so that our life may be a jouney towards heaven and bring us one day to our final and much desired destination where, united with You, we may rejoice in the joy of God.

O, Mother most sweet and Our Lady of Good Journeys we commend ourselves into Your hands and take refuge under your mantle. **Amen.**

I AM YOUR MOTHER

O tender loving Mother Virgin, most prudent, who are the Mother of my Redeemer, I greet you today with the greatest love with which a daughter's heart can love You as a Mother.

Yes, I am Your daughter and as I am so helpless, I will draw ardour from the passion of the Heart of Your Divine Son: with Him I will greet You as the purest of creatures, for You were formed in accordance with the desires and preferences of God three times Holy!

Conceived without stain of original sin, free from corruption, You have always been faithful to the promptings of grace and Your soul has been enriched in this way with such merits so as to be raised above all creatures.

Chosen to be the Mother of Jesus Christ, You guarded Him as in a sanctuary of the utmost purity and He, who came to give life to souls, began His own human life in You, and from You received His nourishment.

O incomparable Virgin! Immaculate Virgin! Delight of the most Holy Trinity! Admired by the Angels and Saints, You are the delight of Heaven! Morning star, Rosary that has blossomed in spring, whitest Lily, delicate and graceful Iris, scented Violet, Garden tended and reserved to give delight to the King of Heaven! You are my Mother, O Virgin most prudent. Precious Ark in which all virtues are enclosed!.

You are my Mother, O most powerful Virgin, O merciful Virgin, O faithful Virgin! You are my Mother, refuge of sinners! I greet you and rejoice at the sight of so many gifts which the Almighty has granted You and of so many privileges with which He has crowned You.

May You be blessed and praised, Mother of my Redeemer, Mother of poor sinners! Have mercy on us and clothe us with Your maternal protection. I greet You in the name of all men and women, of all the saints and of all the angels.

I would like to love You with the love and the ardour of the most zealous seraphims, and as this would still be too little to satisfy my desires, I greet You and love You through the Father and through Your Son, who is my Redeemer, my Saviour and my Bridegroom!

I greet you with the purity of the Holy Spirit and with the holiness of the adorable Trinity.

And through these Divine Persons, I bless You, and desire to give You always the constant and pure praise of a child of Yours: a filial, constant and most pure praise.

O incomparable Virgin, bless me because I am Your daughter. Bless all men and women!

Protect them, pray for them to Him who is Almighty, who can refuse nothing to You.

Farewell, tender and most beloved Mother! I greet you night and day, in time and in eternity!

A SEQUENCE OF PRAYERS TO
THE BLESSED VIRGIN MARY

My Mother, You who always remain with open arms, imploring Your Divine Son for mercy and compassion for the poor and needy, ask Him to give me His holy love, His holy fear and His holy grace, and grant that I may never commit a mortal sin. Grant me the grace, O my Mother, to have for my good Jesus the love and trust that the saintly souls have, and that my Faith, Hope and Love may grow, and I ask You, my Mother, to teach me to accomplish His divine will at all times.

Holy Virgin, bless my family and deliver it from all evil. Help all dying sinners and ask Your divine Son to forgive them and to free them from the torments of hell. Intercede for us, my Mother, before your Divine Son so that the whole world may be saved. Pray, Mother of mine, for our beloved country, and free it from the evils which threaten it. Finally, I ask You to pour forth on our souls the shining rays of mercy of the Good Lord Jesus, and to be close to me in all the dangers I shall encounter in life. **Amen.**

Hail Mary *(3 times)*
Glory Be

O Mary, blessed by the Most High, mother of grace: the praise of the Church ascends to You.

Beloved Daughter of the Father, by accepting the annunciation of the Angel, you co-operated in the salvation of humanity: in You, the creature began to obey the Creator once again. Mother of Jesus, Son of God, by keeping the Word in Your heart, you have shown us the way of wisdom:

in You the Good News is revealed to humanity. Beloved Spouse of the Spirit, by welcoming the Word of God into Your womb, You gave life to the world. In You humanity became the dwelling place of the Eternal one. The image of Your singular dignity and maternal intercession has been devoutly remembered for centuries. Merciful Mother, prayerful Virgin, we turn to you: may Your intercession sustain our plea; may Your mercy obtain peace and salvation for us and for our families, our communities, all our brothers and sisters in the faith, and for all men and women.

Implore for us from the Father a true knowledge of Christ, the gifts of the Holy Spirit, protection and deliverance from evil.

Grant that, with You we may establish the kingdom of the Lord, a kingdom of perennial praise, a kingdom of justice and peace, for all people and for ever. **Amen.**

Hail Mary *(3 times)*
Glory Be

Dear Jesus, when You were about to accomplish the ultimate sacrifice by which, redeeming me, You would bring about my rebirth, You turned to the apostle John, who represented all humanity, and indicating Mary, said to him: "This is your mother" *(Jn 19:27)*.

With that announcement You wished say to him: She whom I entrust to you is the One who acts as and is a Mother to you for your rebirth in the order of supernatural life, just as your mother acts and is a mother to you in the natural and physical life. O Jesus, I ask You to repeat to me, too, the words: "This is your mother", and to impress upon my heart the consoling truth that Mary is truly my Mother.

You, who, by becoming her Son, gave Yourself totally to her, grant that I, too, following Your example, may give myself entirely to this most tender Mother, without reserve and forever, as her beloved son (daughter).

You who loved and continue to love this Mother of wonderful beauty and holiness, who lived only for You, and accepted generously, for Your sake, the most terrible martyrdom that any creature has ever suffered, impart also to me the living flame of a child's love towards Her.

You, who have always trusted in Her, give me the grace to cultivate that same unshakable trust in this same mother, Whom you made all-powerful so that She could grant all the graces which

She desires to grant, to whomsoever She wants and whenever She wishes to do so.

Teach me and persuade me that, here on earth, loving is not so much enjoying things and exulting, but rather working and suffering; therefore I must consecrate to Her my activity, my labour, my time, but above all, I must not refuse to suffer for Her, trying to accept with as much love as possible the chain of little efforts and sacrifices that I meet in my daily life.

Impress indelibly upon my mind the conviction that the most beautiful act of devotion to Mary and that most preferred by her is the imitation of Her virtues.

Enkindle in me, therefore, the desire to imitate the humility, poverty, obedience and purity of this dear Mother, so that I may become truly similar to Her, so that She may render me similar to You.

Hail Mary *(3 times)*
Glory Be

O Mother of Mercy, as You are so merciful, You have a great desire to provide for the needs of us miserable creatures, and to satisfy our requests. Today, I, the most wretched of all people, appeal to Your mercy, so that you may grant me what I ask of You. I will let others make requests to You such as health of body, worldly gains or earthly benefits, while I ask You, Mother, to grant me those things that You desire for me and that conform and are pleasing to your Most Holy Heart. You were so humble; grant me therefore, the humility and the joy of being despised.

You were so patient in the difficulties of life; grant me, therefore, patience in adversity. You were so filled with love towards God; grant me the gift of holy and pure love.

You were perfect charity towards your neighbour; grant that I may be charitable to all people and in particular towards those who are my enemies. You were perfect humility before the will of God; grant that I may conform totally to whatever God wishes of me. You are the most Holy among all creatures; I beg You, Mary, to make me holy. You are not lacking in love; already You wish to grant me all that I have asked of You. Therefore, only my failure to take recourse in You or my lack of confidence in Your intercession can hinder me from receiving Your graces. You Yourself can obtain for me the desire to pray to you and the certainty of haing my prayer answered.

I ask You for these two great graces; I desire to obtain them from you and await with the certainty of being heard, O Mary, my Mother, my Hope, my Love, my Life, my Refuge, my Help and my Consolation. **Amen.**

Hail Mary *(3 times)*
Glory Be

Most Holy Immaculate Virgin and my Mother Mary, who are the Mother of my Lord, the Queen of the world and the advocate, hope and refuge of sinners, I, a miserable creature on earth, turn to You today; I venerate You, O great Queen, and thank you for all the graces which You have given me until now; above all for having saved me from being lost. I love You, most lovable Lady; and for the love I have for You, I promise to want to serve You always, and to do all I can, so that You may be loved by others too. I have placed all my hopes and health in the hands of Jesus, and now wish to place them in Your hands too. Accept me as your servant, and take me under your mantle, O Mother of Mercy. And as Your intercession is so powerful before God, I ask You to deliver me from all temptations; or at least give me the strength to overcome them until my death.

Hail Mary *(3 times)*
Glory Be

O sublime Virgin, I know that You, besides being Queen of the universe, are also my Queen, I wish to dedicate myself totally and in a special way to Your service, so that You can dispose of me as You please: therefore, together with St. Bonaventure, I say to You, "O Lady, I want to trust in Your discreet power, so that you may sustain me and govern me completely. Do not abandon me." Guide me, my Queen, and do not leave me alone. Command me, use me as it pleases You to do so, correct me when I do not obey You, as the reproaches which come from Your hands are healthy for me. I consider it more important to be your servant than to be lord of all the earth. "I am Yours: save me!". O Mary, accept me as yours and take it upon yourself to save me. I do not want to belong to myself any more, I give myself to You.

If I served you poorly in the past and missed many good occasions in which to honour You, in the future I wish to unite myself to Your more loving and faithful servants. From now on, I wish to honour and love you with all my heart, my beloved Queen. I promise and hope to persevere in this intention of mine, with Your help. **Amen.**

Hail Mary *(3 times)*
Glory Be

O great Mother of God, together with St. Bernard I say to You, "Pray, O Mother, that Your Son may hear You and that whatever You ask for You will obtain. Your Son hears you and will grant You all that You ask of Him".

Speak, therefore, O Mary, our Advocate, speak in favour of us, miserable creatures. Remember that you received so much power and dignity for our benefit also, and that God wanted to become Your debtor, becoming incarnate in You, so that You could dispense, according to your will, the treasures of Divine Mercy to the poor.

We are Your servants, assigned in a special way to Your service, and I, too, hope to be among these. We are proud of living under Your protection. If You do good to everyone, even to those who neither know nor honour You, but rather insult You and blaspheme against You, how much more must we, who honour, love and trust in You, hope in Your goodness which searches for the needy in order to comfort them!

We are great sinners, but God has enriched you with mercy and with a power superior to all our sinfulness. You can and want to save us, and the more unworthy we are, the more we hope that You will do so, in order that we may glorify Your name more in heaven when we reach it through your intercession. O Mother of Mercy, we offer our souls to You. They were once beautiful and cleansed by the Blood of Jesus Christ but they then became stained by sin. We present them to you; may You take it upon Yourself to purify them. Obtain for us true sorrow for our sins, obtain for us a true love of God, the grace of perseverance, Paradise. We ask great things of You, but surely You can grant us everything?

Surely it is not too much to ask, considering the love that God has for You? It is suffcent that You speak to Your Son in order that You may have what You ask of Him. He does not refuse anything to You! Pray then, pray for us, O Mary! Pray; You will surely be heard and we shall surely be saved.

Hail Mary *(3 times)*
Glory Be

I greet you, Mary, most beloved Daughter of the Eternal Father, admirable Mother of the Son, faithful Spouse of the Holy Spirit, living Temple of the Most Holy Trinity.

I greet You, royal Lady!

Everything in heaven and on earth is under the authority of Your Son. I greet You, sure refuge of sinners and merciful Queen!

You reject no one, therefore I, a sinner, throw myself at Your feet and beg you to obtain for me from Your beloved Son Jesus, the grace of sincere repentance together with forgiveness for all my sins and the gift of Divine Wisdom.

I give myself totally to You with all that I possess, and I choose You today as my Mother and Queen. Treat me, therefore, as the last of Your children and the most lowly of Your servants.

Hear, O my Sovereign, the sighs of a heart which desires to love You and serve You faithfully. May it never be said that, among all those who turn to You, I am the first not to be heard!

O my hope! O my life!

O faithful and immaculate Virgin Mary!

Graciously hear me, defend me, nourish me, instruct me, save me. **Amen.**

O Sacrament most holy,
O Sacrament divine,
all praise and all thanksgiving
Be every moment thine.

O Jesus, beloved Jesus!
O Mary, Mother of Jesus and our Mother!
Give us the grace of Your holy blessing.
Amen.

bear with us in our weaknesses,
graciously hear our prayers,
and defend us from the world
and from the evil one.
Amen.

O Most Holy Virgin, who called yourself the humble handmaid of the Lord, You were chosen by the Most High to become the Mother of His only-begotten Son, our Saviour Jesus Christ. We admire Your greatness and invoke Your maternal goodness. We know that You look upon us with the tenderness of a mother, because we, too, by the grace of God, have become Your children. Therefore, we lift up our hearts to you; we consecrate ourselves to You with filial trust; we commend ourselves to Your heavenly protection so that You may watch over our path with love. Gather us into your maternal embrace, O Mary, as you embraced Jesus, Your Divine Son.

Hail Mary *(3 times)*
Glory Be

O Most Holy Lady, through the grace that God granted You, exalting you to the point of giving Himself to You and rendering everything possible for You, we beseech You to allow us to have a share in Your glory through the fullness of the grace which You merited.

O most merciful Lady, do not tire of striving to obtain for us the benefits which God desired to grant us by making Himself flesh in Your most pure body. Do not delay in granting our prayer. If You deign to pray to Your Son, He will hear your prayer immediately. With Your help, we cannot fail to be saved. Who can confine the bounds of Your Mercy?

If You, who are the Mother of Mercy, had no compassion, what would become of us? Son? Therefore, look not on our sins but come to our help, O most merciful Lady.

Consider that our Creator took human flesh from you not to condemn sinners, but to save them.

If You had been made Mother of God only for Your own advantage, one may mistakenly think that you did not care much about our destiny, but God took Your flesh upon Himself not only for Your salvation but for the salvation of all men and women.

What use would Your power and glory be to us if You did not let us share in your happiness? Help and protect us: You know how much we need Your help. We commend ourselves to You: grant that we may not be lost but may serve and love our God now and in eternity. **Amen.**

Hail Mary *(3 times)*
Glory Be

Holy Mary, Mother of God, keep within me the heart of a child, pure and limpid like the water of a spring. Give me a simple heart, which neither dwells on nor wallows in its own sadness; a heart generous in giving itself, easily moved to compassion, a faithful and generous heart, which neither forgets any good deed nor bears any grudges. Create in me a sweet and humble heart which loves without demanding to be loved in return, which is content to disappear in other hearts, sacrificing itself for Your divine Son; a good heart that cannot be subdued so that no form of ingratitude may ever be able to close it; that it may never be; a heart tormented by the glory of Christ, wounded by His love, with a wound that can only be healed in heaven.

Hail Mary *(3 times)*
Glory Be

Mary, Mother of Jesus and of the Church, we need You. We long for the light which shines from Your goodness, the comfort which comes to us from Your Immaculate Heart, the charity and peace of which You are Queen. With confidence, we commend our needs to You so that You may attend to them; to You we commend our sorrows so that You may make them more bearable, our illnesses so that You may heal them, our bodies so that You may render them pure, our hearts so that they may be filled with love and true repentance, and our souls so that they may be saved with Your help. Remember, Mother of goodness, that Jesus refuses nothing that You ask of Him in prayer.

Grant comfort to the souls of the dead, healing to the sick, purity to young people, faith and harmony to families and peace to humanity. Remember those who go astray from the right path. Grant us many vocations and holy priests; protect the Pope, the bishops and the Holy Church of God.

Mary, hear us and have mercy on us. Turn Your eyes of mercy towards us. After this our exile, show unto us the blessed fruit of Your womb, Jesus. O clement, O loving, O sweet Virgin Mary. **Amen.**

Hail Mary *(3 times)*
Glory Be

Holy Mother, help and guide us in this time of great contrasts and grant that, under Your guidance, we may obtain that peace, joy and serenity longed for by all Christians.

Holy Mother, You are our joy and our love and we would like all our dear ones, and all our brothers and sisters of this poor world to have the same feelings of affection towards You as we have.

With the help of Your goodness, Your immense love and signs which You continually give us, grant that humanity may walk along the right path, the path of light. You who are a true light for us, illuminate our hearts so that we may, as beacons, bring the light of the Lord to all our brothers and sisters.

Continue, we beseech You, and never cease, to speak to us; continue to walk among us.

Our Mother, Heavenly Mother, Mother of us all, with Your cry of sorrow bring unity to the the world and spare us from darkness.

Grant that we, with Your help and merciful Love, may keep far from evil, be sustained by the Holy Spirit, and come to know the great and merciful Father ever more intimately through Your Son, Jesus. **Amen.**

Hail Mary
Queen of Peace,
pray for us.

O Holy Mother, teach us to keep silence; teach us to enter into the silence of the great plains, the silence of the extensive and dense forests, the silence of starry and serene nights.

Teach us to keep silence in church, where Jesus awaits us perpetually and where, through the intimacy of His love, we can perceive His voice, meek and friendly, His discrete and affectionate words, so that our souls become strengthened and we can take courage once more.

O Holy Virgin Mary, teach us to love silence as You loved it, and to keep it as You kept it.

Teach us the art of staying silent and the art of speaking; teach us in particular to speak words that inspire enthusiasm and wise decisions in other souls.

Fill our life with silence, O Mother; fill our silence with love for You, for our brothers and sisters and for our God.

Queen of the Universe, our most beloved Lady, You are the hope of the Father, You are above all saints and represent their joy. Through you, we have been reconciled with our God; You are the advocate of sinners, the sure haven of those whose life seems to be ruined. You are the comfort of the world, the ransom of the wicked, the joy of the sick, the solace of the afflicted, the refuge and salvation of all the world. O great princess, Mother of God, cover us with wings of mercy; have mercy on us for we trust in You!

O most pure Virgin, You are our hope. We have consecrated ourselves to You and to Your service: we call ourselves "Your servants". Do not allow us to fall into sin. O Immaculate Virgin, we are under Your protection, so we turn to You and beg You to allow that Jesus, wounded by our sins, give us the strength to resist temptation.

O Fullness of Grace, enlighten our minds, and loosen our tongues so that we may sing Your praises, especially the angelic Canticle which You proclaimed so worthily. I greet You, Peace, Joy, Salvation and Comfort of all the world. I greet You, the most wonderful mir-acle, ever performed on earth, Paradise of joys, sure haven of those who are in danger, fountain of graces, Mediatrix between God and humankind.

Hail Mary *(3 times)*
Glory Be

O Mary, Queen of heaven and earth, who are Mother of the Lord of the world, and the greatest, the most magnificent and most lovable of all creatures; it is true that many on this earth neither know nor love You but there are also countless angels and saints in heaven who love and praise You continuously. On earth, too, many happy souls burn with love for You and are enamoured of your goodness! O most lovable Lady, grant that I, too, may love You. I would like to serve, praise and honour You always, and make sure that everyone loves You! You allowed God to love You and with Your beauty plucked Him from the heart of the Eternal Father, drawing Him to earth in order to become man and Your Son: how can I, therefore, miserable worm that I am, fail to fall in love with You? No, my sweetest Mother, I too want to love You greatly, and desire to do all that I can in order to see that you are loved by others.

Accept, therefore, O Mary, my desire to love You, and help me to put it into practice. I know that those who love You are very pleasing to God. Besides His own glory, he desires no other than Yours; He wishes to see You honoured and loved by all people.

From You, Blessed Mother, I hope to receive all my joys; You will obtain for me the forgiveness of all my sins and the grace of perseverance: You will assist me at the hour of my death; You will save me from Purgatory and finally, it shall be You who will lead me to Paradise. These are the graces that those who love You hope to obtain from You; I, too, hope to obtain them from You because I love You with all my heart and above all things after God. Thank you, Mary.

Hail Mary *(3 times)*

O Queen of Paradise, who are seated above all the choirs of angels and are closed to God, I, a poor sinner, greet You from this valley of tears and beseech You to turn your eyes of mercy towards me.

Look, O Mary, at how many dangers now surround me and will surround me while on this earth, especially the danger of offending God. In you, my Queen I put all my hope; I love you and long to come and see you soon in Paradise.

O Mary, when will the day come when I shall finally find myself at Your feet? When will I kiss that hand that has given me so many graces?

It is true, my Mother, that in my life I have been very ungrateful, but if I reach heaven, I will love You in every moment for ever and ever, and will make up for my ingratitude by blessing and thanking You forever. I thank God for having granted me such a great trust in the Blood of Jesus Christ and in your powerful intercession.

Your devoted children have placed great hope in You and none of them has ever been disappointed. Surely, then, I will not be disappointed either. O Mary, ask Your Son Jesus, as I, too, ask Him through the merits of his Passion, to grant that these hopes of mine may be strengthened and fulfilled. **Amen.**

Hail Mary *(3 times)*

O Immaculate Virgin, Mother of God and Mother of all people, we believe in Your assumption into heaven, body and soul, where Your name is proclaimed by all the choirs of angels and hosts of saints. We unite ourselves with them in praising and blessing the Lord who has exalted You above all creatures and in offering You our desire to love and to devote ourselves to You.

We trust that Your eyes of mercy will turn towards us in our troubles and sufferings; that your lips will smile on our joys and victories; that you will hear the voice of Jesus repeating for each one of us "Here is your Son". We invoke You as our Mother and accept You, as John did, as the one who shall guide us and be our strength and comfort in this mortal life.

We believe that in Your glory in heaven, where You reign, robed with the sun and crowned with stars, You are the joy and happiness of all the angels and saints. And from this earth, where we live as pilgrims, we look towards You, our hope; appeal to us with the sweetness of Your voice in order to show unto us, after this our exile, the blessed fruit of Your womb, Jesus. O clement, O loving, O sweet Virgin Mary. **Amen.**

Hail Mary *(3 times)*
Glory Be

Remember and remind Yourself, sweetest Virgin, that You are my Mother and I am Your child; that You are all powerful and I am poor, timid and weak.

I beseech You, sweetest Mother, to guide me in all my paths and actions. Do not say to me, wonderful Mother, that you cannot do so because Your most beloved Son has given You every power both in heaven and on earth. Do not say to me that You are not obliged to do so, for You are the Mother of all humanity and my Mother.

If You were unable to help me, I would make excuses for You, saying, "It is true that She is my Mother and that She loves me as Her child, but She has neither the means nor the capacity to guide me. "If you were not my Mother, I would be patient and say, "She would be capable of helping me, but alas, She is not my Mother and does not love me." But no, most sweet Virgin, You are my Mother and moreover, You are most powerful: how could I make excuses for You if You did not help me and come to my aid? As You can see, O Mother, You are obliged to hear all my prayers. For the honour and glory of Your Son Jesus, accept me as Your child, in spite of my misery and my sins. Free my soul and body from every evil, give me all virtues, especially that of humility and grant me all gifts, blessings and graces that are pleasing to the Most Holy Trinity, Father, Son and Holy Spirit. **Amen.**

Prayer to the Virgin Mary, Health of the Sick

Most Holy Virgin, who are honoured by the sweet name of Health of the Sick, because throughout the ages You have given relief in human illness, I beseech you to grant me and all my dear ones health of body, or at least the strength to unite our sufferings to the afflictions of Christ our Redeemer.

Hail Mary

Most Holy Virgin, who know not only how to heal the illnesses of the body, but also of the soul, I beseech you to free my soul and those of my dear ones from every sin, in order to be always worthy of the friendship and grace of God.

Hail Mary

Most Holy Virgin, who grant to your devoted the joy of obtaining eternal salvation, I entrust You with the care of my soul and the souls of all my dear ones, and grant that we may attain with you the joy and light of heaven.

Hail Mary

PRAYER TO THE MOTHER OF GOODNESS, LOVE AND MERCY

O my Mother,
Mother of goodness, love and mercy,
I love you infinitely
and I offer myself to you.
Through your goodness, your love
and your grace, save me.

I desire to be yours.
I love you infinitely,
and desire that you guard me.
From the depth of my heart I beseech you,
Mother of Goodness,
give me your goodness.
Grant that through it I may attain Paradise.

I beseech you through your infinite love,
to give me grace,
so that I may love all people,
as you loved Jesus Christ.
Grant me the grace to love
your Will which is different from mine.

I offer myself totally to you and desire
that you follow every step of mine.
Because you are full of grace.
And I desire that I may never forget it.
And if by chance I should fall from grace,
I beg you to restore it to me. **Amen.**

THE MARIAN CREED

Adopted from the booklet of CEM

I believe in the Virgin Mary, and I firmly believe in her with all my heart!

I believe in her divine maternity, and in her perpetual virginity, in her Immaculate Conception, in her mission of Co-redemptrix by the side of her Son, our Redeemer.

I believe in her Assumption and heavenly glorification in body and soul, for Mary is the image of the Church which shall have her fulfilment in the age to come.

I believe in her spiritual maternity, in her ecclesiastical maternity, in her true queenship.

I believe in her intercession of grace for the growth of the divine life of souls.

I believe, therefore, in her loving presence at the side of all creatures as Mother, help of Christians, Our Lady of perpetual succour.

I believe in the universal triumph of the Immaculate Heart of Mary... because this is her hour!

**I give my heart to you,
Mother of my Jesus, Mother of love.**

AUGUST QUEEN OF ANGELS

On the 13th of January, 1863, a soul accustomed to receiving favours from the Virgin Mary was suddenly struck by a ray of divine light. She believed that she saw demons, throwing themselves upon the earth, causing ruins and incredible massacres. At the same time the Holy Virgin appeared, saying that demons had indeed broken loose in the world and the time had come to invoke her as Queen of Angels and to ask her to send Legions of Angels to combat and annihilate the powers of hell. The soul addressed the Virgin with the following words: "O my Mother, You who are so good, could you not send your Angels without us having to ask you?" "No," the Virgin replied, "prayer is a condition established by God himself to obtain graces". "Then, Mother," said the soul, "would you like to teach us how we should pray to you?". And the Most Holy Virgin dictated this prayer to her: "O august Queen ...".

O august Queen of Heaven and Our Lady of Angels, who received from God the power and mission of crushing the head of Satan, we humbly beg You to send us heavenly Legions, with St. Michael the Archangel as head so that under your orders they may chase the demons, combat them everywhere, repress their boldness and drive them back into the abyss.

"Who is like God?" O good and tender Mother, you shall always be our love and our hope.

O Divine Mother, send your Holy Angels to defend us, and to drive away from us the cruel enemy. Holy Angels and Archangels, defend us and guard us.

Hail Mary *(3 times)*

PRAYER TO OUR LADY
OF GUADALUPE

In January 1979, Pope John Paul II, in the first year of his pontificate, made a pastoral visit to Mexico. He visited the shrine of Our Lady of Guadalupe, Mother of the Americas, and there, in the presence of all the bishops of America, he addressed this prayer to the Blessed Virgin.

O Immaculate Virgin, mother of the true God and mother of the Church!

You, who from this place revealed your clemency and your pity to all those who ask for your protection, hear the prayer that we address to you with filial trust, and present it to your Son Jesus, our sole Redeemer.

Mother of mercy, teacher of hidden and silent sacrifice, to you, who come to meet us sinners, we dedicate on this day all our being and all our love.

We also dedicate to you our life, our work, our joys, our infirmities, and our sorrows.

Grant peace, justice, and prosperity to our peoples, for we entrust to your care all that we have and all that we are, our lady and mother.

We wish to be entirely yours and to walk with you along the way of complete faithfulness to Jesus Christ in his Church: hold us always with your loving hand.

Virgin of Guadalupe, Mother of the Americas, we pray to you for all the bishops, that they may lead the faithful along paths of intense Christian life, of love and humble service of God and souls.

Contemplate this immense harvest, and intercede with the Lord that he may instil a hunger for holiness in the whole People of God and grant abundant vocations of priests and religious, strong in the faith and zealous dispensers of God's mysteries.

Gain for our homes the grace of loving and respecting life in its beginnings with the same love with which you conceived in your womb the life of the Son of God.

Blessed Virgin Mary, Mother of Fair Love, protect our families, so that they may always be united, and bless the upbringing of our children.

Our hope, look upon us with compassion, teach us to go continually to Jesus, and if we fall, help us to rise again, to return to him, by means of the confession of our faults and sins in the sacrament of Penance, which gives peace to the soul.

We beg you to grant us a great love for all the holy sacraments, which are, as it were, the signs that your Son left us on earth.

Thus, most holy mother, with the peace of God in our conscience, with our hearts free from evil and hatred, we will be able to bring to all true joy and true peace, which come to us from your Son, our Lord Jesus Christ, who, with God the Father and the Holy Spirit, lives and reigns for ever and ever.

Amen.

4.
ANTHEMS TO THE
BLESSED VIRGIN MARY

Prayer of Saint Bernard
(The Memorare)

Remember O most compassionate Virgin Mary that never was it known that anyone who fled to your protection, implored your assistance, or sought your intercession was left unaided.

Inspired with this confidence, we fly unto you, O Virgin of Virgins our Mother. To you we come, before you we kneel (stand), sinful and sorrowful. O Mother of the Word Incarnate, despise not our petitions, but in your clemency hear and answer them.

Hail, O Queen of Heaven

The author of this anthem is unknown. It probably dates back to the twelfth or thirteenth century. It is an exaltation of the relationship of Mary with heaven and earth. She is greeted as Queen of heaven, Mistress of Angels, root of Jesse, gate through which the light of the world, the Redeemer, has come to us. It concludes with a request for the intercession of the Blessed Virgin Mary on behalf of her children.

Hail, Queen of Heaven, beyond compare, to whom the angels homage pay; Hail, Root of Jesse, Gate of Light, that opened for the world's new Day. Rejoice, O Virgin unsurpassed, in whom our ransom was begun, for all your loving children pray to Christ, our Saviour, and your Son.

Stanbrook Abbey

or

Hail, O Queen of Heaven enthroned!
Hail, by angels mistress owned,
Root of Jesse! Gate of morn!
Whence the world's true light was born:
Glorious Virgin, joy to thee,
Loveliest whom in heaven they see.
Fairest thou where all are fair!
Plead with Christ our sins to spare.

AVE REGINA CŒLÓRUM

Ave, Regína cœlórum!
Ave, Dómina angelórum;
Salve, radix, salve, porta,
ex qua mundo lux est orta.

Gaude, Virgo gloriósa,
super omnes speciósa;
vale, o valde decóra,
et pro nobis Christum exóra.

LOVING MOTHER OF THE REDEEMER

*In the following anthem, the author Hermann the Lame
o.b.s. (†1054) has recapitulated the wonderful attributes of
Mary: her divine maternity, her co-operation in the redemti-
ve work of Christ, her universal mediation and her perpetual virginity. Contractus wrote this highly poetical anthem,
according to the laws of artistic expression. The last line is
the most moving one: "Peccatorum miserere" ("Have
mercy on sinners"). Only Mary, conceived without sin, the
"all holy one", can understand the seriousness of sin, and
therefore, the misfortune of poor sinners.*

Mother of Christ! hear thou thy people's cry,
Star of the deep, and portal of the sky!
Mother of Him who thee from nothing made,
sinking we strive, and call to thee for aid:
Oh, by that joy which Gabriel brought to thee,
Thou Virgin first and last, let us thy mercy see.

or

Loving mother of the Redeemer,
gate of heaven, star of the sea,
assist your people who have fallen,
as we strive to rise again.
To the wonderment of nature,
you bore your Creator,
yet remained a virgin after as before.
You who received Gabriel's joyful greeting,
have pity on us poor sinners.

ALMA REDEMPTÓRIS MATER

Alma Redemptóris Mater, quæ pérvia cœli porta manes, et stella maris, succúrre cadénti, surgere qui curat, pópulo: tu quæ genuísti, natúra miránte, tuum sanctum Genitórem, Virgo prius ac postérius, Gabriélis ab ore sumens illud Ave, peccatórum miserére.

"ALL FAIR"

Thou art all fair, O Mary: and the original stain is not in thee. Thou art the glory of Jerusalem; thou art the joy of Israel; thou art the honour of our people. Blessed art thou, O Virgin Mary, by the Lord the Most High God above all women upon the earth. Draw us, O immaculate Virgin: we will run after thee in the odour of thy ointments.

TOTA PULCHRA

Tota pulchra es Maria et macula originalis non est in te. Tu gloria Ierusalem, Tu lætitia Israel, tu honorificentia populi nostri. Tu advocata peccatorum. O Maria! O Maria!

Virgo prudentissima, mater clementissima, ora pro nobis, intercede pro nobis ad Dominum Iesu Christum.

WE FLY TO YOUR PATRONAGE

This is the oldest known prayer to Mary. It was probably composed in the fourth century. It is a cry of trust to the Mother of God, comforter of the afflicted, help of Christians, provider for our needs. The Church has enriched it with many indulgences. It is simple and evokes peace, and yet has great power of persuasion.

This sublime prayer demonstrates filial trust that could even be considered defiant, stead fast faith as revealed in the fearless plea for help, and ardent love which knows no pettiness. It is a profession of boundless faith in the maternal goodness of Mary who cannot fail to listen to the cries of her children when they are unhappy. Finally the anthem is a wonderful epic to the mercy of the Virgin Mary which she has always shown towards those who have sought her help.

We fly to your patronage, O Holy Mother of God. Despise not our petitions in our necessities, but deliver us from all dangers, O ever-glorious and blessed Virgin.

SUB TUUM PRÆSIDIUM

Sub tuum præsídium confúgimus, sancta Dei Génitrix; nostras deprecatiónes ne despícias in necessitátibus sed a perículis cunctis líbera nos semper, Virgo gloriósa et benedícta.

ANTHEM TO MARY, INVIOLATE PURE AND CHASTE

Inviolate flower, most pure Virgin,
shining door of heaven, beloved mother of Christ,
most holy lady, hear this our hymn of praise.
May our life be chaste,
may our souls be pure
and may our hearts thus beseech you.
Holy Virgin Mary, most wonderful queen,
inviolate flower,
may the forgiveness of God descend upon us who
have sinned
through your sweet intercession.

INVIOLATA INTEGRA ET CASTA

*Inviolata, integra, et casta es María: Quæ es
effécta fulgida cœli porta. O Mater alma Christi
caríssima: Súscipe pia laudum prœcónia. Te nunc
flagitant devóta corda et ora: Nostra ut pura péctora sint ed córpora. Tua per precáta dulcísona:
Nobis concédas véniam per sœcula.*
*O benígna! O Regína! O María! Quæ sola invio-
lata permansísti.*

HAILL STAR OF THE SEA

The following anthem was composed in the tenth century. The author is unknown. In this hymn, the Virgin Mary is called: "Gate of heavenly rest and is invoked as the One who preserves our peace, helps to redeem sinners and intercedes for our needs". It is the hymn that is sung at vespers on most feasts of the Virgin Maryand may be considered the hymn of the "mediatrix".

Hail, bright star of ocean, God's own Mother blest, Ever sinless Virgin, Gate of heavenly rest.

Taking that sweet Ave Which from Gabriel came, Peace confirm within us, Changing Eva's name.

Break the captives' fetters, Light on blindness pour, All our ills expelling, Every bliss implore.

Show thyself a Mother; May the Word Divine, Born for us thy Infant, Hear our prayers through thine.

Virgin all excelling, Mildest of the mild, Freed from guilt, preserve us, Pure and undefiled. Keep our life all spotless, Make our way secure, Till we find in Jesus Joy forever more.

Through the highest heaven To the Almighty Three, Father, Son and Spirit, One same glory be. **Amen.**

AVE MARIS STELLA

Ave, maris stella, Dei mater alma, atque semper
virgo, felix cœli porta.

Sumens illud "Ave" Gabriélis ore, funda nos in
pace, mutans Evœ nomen.

Solve vincla reis, profer lumen cœcis, mala nostra
pelle, bona cuncta posce.

Monstra te esse matrem: sumat per te precem qui
pro nobis natus tulit esse tuus.

Virgo singuláris, inter omnes mitis, nos culpis
solútos, mites fac et castos.

Vitam prœsta puram, iter para tutum, ut, vidéntes
Iesum semper collœtémur.

Sit laus Deo Patri, summo Christo decus, Spirítui
Sancto honor, tribus unus. Amen.

SINGS THE PRAISES OF
MARY EVERY DAY

Sing the praises of Mary every day O my soul; venerate her feasts and her wonderful mysteries.

O pure one, without the sign of a single stain, may I praise you with a pure and serene heart.

May I be chaste and modest, sweet, good, moderate, devout, honest, both shrewd and simple. May I draw knowledge and courage from the word of God, may I be attentive and shining with good deeds. Holy Virgin, look at how many dangers we must always face; sustain us so that we may remain steadfast and secure.

Protect and help all Christians, give us peace, so that evil times may not perturb us. **Amen.**

OMNI DIE

Omni die, Mariæ mea laudens anima; eius festa, eius gesta cole splendidissima.

Pulchra tota, sine nota cuiuscumque maculæ fac me mundum et incundum te laudare sedule.

Ut sim castus et modestus, dulcis, blandus, sobrius, pius,rectus, circumspectus, simultatim nescius. Eruditus et munitus divinis eloquiis, timoratus et ornatus sacris exercitiis.

Virgo sancta, cerne quanta perferamus iugiter tentamenta et sustenta nos ut stemus fortiter.

Esto tutrix et adiutrix christiani populi pacem presta ne molesta nos per cuncta sæcula. Amen.

Remember,
O Creator of the World

We could call this anthem a hymn to trust in Mary, a trust which will not be disappointed, as it is based on two foundations:
a) on Christ, who for love of us, assumed human nature in Mary's womb;
b) on Mary, who is mother of grace and mercy.
This hymn is sung at all "hours" in the Office of the Blessed Virgin Mary.

Remember, O Creator of the world, that being born of the womb of the Virgin Mary, you assumed the form of man.

O Mary, mother of grace and mother of mercy, protect us from the enemy, and welcome us at the hour of our death.

Glory be to the Father, and to the Son, born of the Virgin Mary, glory be to the Holy Spirit, Holy Trinity, one God. **Amen.**

Memento rerum conditor

Memento, rerum conditor, nostri quod olim corporis, sacrata ab alvo Virginis nascendo, formam sumpseris.

Maria, mater gratiæ, dulcis parens clementiæ, tu nos ab hoste protege, et mortis hora suscipe.

Iesu, tibi sit gloria, qui natus es de Virgine, cun Patre et almo Spiritu, in sempiterna sæcula. Amen.

THE GOD WHOM EARTH,
SEA AND SKY ADORE

The God whom earth, sea and sky adore, and laud, and magnify, who o'er their threefold fabric reigns, the Virgin's spotless womb contains.

The God whose will by moon and sun and all things in due course is done, is borne upon a Maiden's breast, by fullest heav'nly grace possessed. How blest that Mother, in whose shrine the great Artificer divine, whose hands contains the earth and sky, vouchsafed, as in his ark, to lie.

Blest, in the message Gabriel brought; Blest by the work the Spirit wrought; from whom the great desire of earth took human flesh and human birth.All honour, laud and glory be,

O Jesus, Virgin-born, to thee; all glory, as is ever meet, to Father and to Paraclete. **Amen.**

QUEM TERRA PONTUS SIDERA

Quem terra, pontus, sidera colunt, adorant, prædicant trinam regentem machinam, claustrum Mariæ baiulat. Cui luna, sol, et omnia deserviunt per tempora, perfusa cæli gratia, gestant puellæ viscera. Beata mater munere, cuius supemus Artifex, mundum pugillo continens, ventris sub arca clausus est. Beata cæli nuntio, fecunda Sancto Spiritu, desideratus gentibus cuius per alvum fusus est. Iesu, tibi sit gloria, qui natus es de Virgine, cum Patre et Almo Spiritu, in sempiterna sæcula. Amen.

COME TO THE AID OF THE MISERABLE

Holy Mary, come to the aid of the miserable, help the weak, comfort the afflicted, pray for all peoples, intervene on behalf of the clergy, intercede for all consecrated virgins: may all those who honour you feel your protection.

PRAYER OF ST. LOUIS GONZAGA

O most holy Mary, my Mistress and Mother, filled with trust in you, today and always, in life and at the hour of my death, I put myself under your singular protection, and as if in the bosom of your mercy, I commend into your hands my body and my soul; I place all my hope and consolation, my life and its end in you, so that through your intercession every action of mine may be guided and disposed of by your will and that of your most holy Son Jesus.

To Mary, Help of Christians
(St. John Bosco)

O Mary, powerful Virgin; you who are the great and most illustrious protection of the Church, you who are the wonderful help of Christians, you who are formidable as an army sent to battle, you who alone have destroyed every heresy in the entire world... in our distress, in our struggles, in our difficulties, defend us from the enemy; and at the hour of death, welcome our soul into Paradise. **Amen.**

5.
THE IMMACULATE HEART OF MARY

- Prayers
- Devotion of the Twelve Stars
- Chaplets
- Rosaries
- The Joys of Mary
- Devotion of the Three Hail Marys
- Miscellaneous Devotions

THE GREAT PROMISE OF THE IMMACULATE HEART OF MARY

The six apparitions of the Most Holy Virgin Mary to the three shepherds of Fatima (Blessed Francisco, Blessed Jacinta and Lucia) started at midday on the 13th of May, 1917, and continued on the 13th of every month at midday until the 13th of October, 1917; the Virgin Mary also promised to appear one more time in the future. At the third apparition, on the 13th of July, 1917, a great crowd of people accompanied the children. They were reciting the Rosary when the Virgin Mary appeared at midday. "What do you want from us?" *Lucia asked. Our Lady replied,* **"I wish you to come here on the thirteenth of next month and to continue to recite the Rosary every day in honour of Our Lady of the Rosary, in order to obtain peace for the world and the end of the war, because She alone can come to your assistance".**

Lucia said to the Virgin, "I would like to ask you who you are and would like you to work a miracle so that everyone can believe that you appear to us".

Our Lady replied, **"I have come to ask you to come here for six months in succession, on the 13th of each month, at the same hour. I will tell you, later on, who I am and what I want".**

Lucia asked for some graces to which Our Lady replied that she was to recite the Rosary and that the graces would thus be granted within a year. The Virgin rejoined, **"Make sacrifices for sinners and repeat often, especially every time you make a sacrifice, 'O Jesus, it is for love of you, for the conversion of sinners, and in reparation for sins committed against the Immaculate Heart of Mary' ".**

Lucia tells us that "saying these words, she opened her hands again as she did the previous month. The reflection (of the light) seemed to penetrate the earth and we saw a sea of fire. We saw demons and condemned souls immersed in this fire. They were like transparent embers, black and bronzed human forms which were floating and transported by the flames which issued forth from them, together with clouds of smoke, and which fell from everywhere just like the sparks of great fires, with neither weight nor balance, amid cries and groans of pain and despair which were horrifying and caused (us) to tremble with fear, (it must have been on seeing that vision that I let out that 'Ah!' which people say they have heard). The demons could be distinguished by their horrible and repulsive shapes (like those) of frightful and unknown animals; but the forms were transparent like black burning coals.

Terrified, and as if to ask for help, we raised our eyes to the Virgin Mary, who said to us with goodness and sadness: **'You have seen hell, where the souls of poor sinners eventually go. To save them, God wants to establish devotion to my Immaculate Heart in the world. If people do as I tell you, many souls will be saved and there will be peace. The war is going to end. But if people do not stop offending God, another war will start under the reign of (Pope) Pius XI that will be worse. When you see the night lit up by an unknown light, you shall know that it is the great sign that God is giving you, to show that he will punish the world for its crimes with war, hunger and persecutions of the Church and the Holy Father. To prevent this happening, I will come to ask for the consecration of Russia to my Immaculate Heart and for the Communion of reparation on the first saturdays.**

'If they heed my requests, Russia will be converted and there will be peace. If not, Russia will spread her errors throughout the world, causing wars and persecutions of the Church. The good people shall be martyred, the Holy Father will have much to suffer, various nations will be destroyed... In the end my Immaculate

Heart shall *t*riumph. The Holy Father will consecrate Russia to me which will be converted and a certain period of peace shall be granted to the world. In Portugal the dogma of the faith will be preserved; etc. (here it seems that the third part of the message which remains unknown was inserted). Do not tell this to anyone; you can only say it to Francesco' ".

The Virgin Mary, when appearing at Fatima on the 13th of June, 1917, said to Lucia among other things:
"Jesus wants to use you to make me known and loved. He wants to establish devotion to my Immaculate Heart in the world".

In that apparition, she showed the three visionaries her Heart which was crowned with thorns: it was the Immaculate Heart of Mary, offended deeply by the sins of humanity; the Virgin was asking in this way that reparation be made.
After the six apparitions to the three little shepherds Lucia had a further apparition on the 10th of December, 1925. "The Most Holy Virgin appeared in my bedroom," *Lucia tells us,* "with a child at her side, as if floating on a cloud.

The Virgin Mary had one hand on His shoulders and at the same time she held a Heart surrounded with thorns in the other hand.

"At that moment the Child said, **'Have compassion on the Heart of your most Holy Mother surrounded by thorns with which ungrateful people pierce it continously, while there is no one who makes acts of reparation to pull (the thorns) out".**

"And immediately the Holy Virgin said, **'Look, my daughter, at my Heart surrounded by thorns pierced continuously by the blasphemies and ingratitude of ungrateful people. May you, at least, comfort me and make this known. To all those who for five months on** the first saturday go to confession, receive Holy Communion, recite the Rosary, and keep me company while meditating on the mysteries for fifteen minutes with the intention of offering me reparation, I promise to assist them at the hour of their death with all the graces necessary for their salvation' ".

Jacinta also encouraged devotion to the Immaculate Heart of Mary, saying to Lucia on her death-bed, "Tell everyone that God gives us his graces through the Immaculate Heart of Mary; may they ask Her for them; the Heart of Jesus wishes that the Immaculate Heart of Mary be venerated with His Heart. May they ask the Immaculate Heart of Mary for peace, because the Lord has entrusted this (intention) to her".

The promise of assistance for our salvation associated with the First Five Saturdays is the great promise of the Heart of Mary which is linked to that of the Heart of Jesus. Mary promises to assist at the hour of death, with all the graces necessary for salvation, all those who do the following on the first Saturday of five consecutive months.

- *Receive the Sacrament of Confession with the intention of making reparation to Our Lady. (If one is unable to confess on the first Saturday, it is sufficient to confess within eight days either preceding or following that day as long as Holy Communion is received in a state of grace);*
- *Receive Holy Communion in a state of grace with the intention of making reparation to Mary;*
- *Recite the Holy Rosary, at least the third part, with the same intention;*
- *Meditate for a quarter of an hour on the mysteries of the Rosary with the intention of making amends for the offences committed against the Immaculate Heart of Mary.*

When Lucia was asked by her confessor the reason why Our Lady had specified five consecutive Saturdays, she replied that, through the devotion of the five first Saturdays, amends would be made for the five offences and blasphemies which offend the Immaculate Heart of Mary, to be precise: the blasphemies against Her Immaculate Conception; blasphemies against Her virginity; blasphemies against Her divine maternity, refusing at the same time to accept Her as Mother of all people those who seek publicly to instil into the heart of children indifference, contempt and even hatred towards this Immaculate Mother; those who insult Her directly in Her holy images.

PRAYERS

PRAYER FOR THE FIRST SATURDAY

Holy Virgin Mary, Mother of God, Queen of Angels and of all people, we thank the adorable and most Holy Trinity for the glorious privileges with which He has favoured you.

We believe that the Church teaches us about your greatness, your power, your goodness, your virtues; we believe in particular, O Mary, that your conception was immaculate; that your Maternity was united with your inviolate perpetual virginity; that through the fullness of the graces which you received and your faithfulness in responding to them, you raised yourself to the highest degree of holiness, above all heavenly and human creatures.

We believe, O Mary, that through the part you played in the redemption of the world, you merited the title of Co-redemptrix of humankind; that through the partnership that God gave you in dispensing his favours, you became the treasurer of such favours and the gate to heaven; that you, assumed into Heaven, body and soul, were given a universal kingdom and were proclaimed sovereign, Queen of Angels and of humankind.

We are glad to repeat, O Mary, that you are the

omnipotence of supplication, that you use this unlimited power for the salvation of souls and for the comfort of the afflicted, always helping anyone who invokes you, granting graces often to those who have not even invoked you!

O Mother of Divine Grace, Refuge of sinners and powerful help of Christians! Receive our humble thanksgiving for the great numbers of graces which you obtained for all the Church and for all your children; we offer you our thanks for your gifts!

Forgive us, O Queen, O Mother of Mercy, for all the unfaithful acts which we have committed against you! More than ever we promise to love you, O Mary; to honour you and to imitate you by the help of your divine grace.

Forgive, O Mother, all the blasphemies hurled at you. Forgive the violation of your images. Forgive the ingratitude and outrages which have pierced your motherly Heart. Forgive the many souls consecrated to you who are unfaithful to your grace.

We want to make amends for many insults, and we unite ourselves to the choirs of the angels and saints, to the Chosen Ones who praise you on this earth and in heaven... Accept the expression of our filial love, show yourself to be our Mother and make us worthy of being your true children and faithful servants, and grant that we may be worthy of being called as such. **Amen.**

DEVOTION TO THE
SACRED HEART OF MARY

Explicit devotion to the Sacred Heart of Mary originated in the seventeenth century through St. John Eudes (+ 1668) who was also the precursor of St. Margaret Mary in liturgical devotion to the Sacred Heart of Jesus. In 1668 he ob-tained permission for his congregation to celebrate the feast of the Sacred Heart of Mary. Fr. Pinamonti became his follower in Italy. Pope Pius VII gave his first formal approval in 1805, granting permission to the Regular Clerics of the Mother of God to celebrate the feast. The object, purpose and means of this devotion are similar to those of the Heart of Jesus.

*In the name of the Father, the Son,
and the Holy Spirit. Amen.*

O God come to my aid.
O Lord, make haste to help me.

Glory be
The Creed *(see page 26)*

Immaculate Heart of Mary, model of faithfulness for the fulfilment of all duties, may I too carry out my duties with promptness and constancy towards God, myself and my neighbour like yours.

Hail Mary

Sweet Heart of Mary, be the salvation of my soul
and the souls of all my family.

Immaculate Heart of Mary, full of grace, tabernacle of the Most High, may I too live a life of grace, may I consider myself to be the living temple of the Holy Spirit, may I flee from sin at all costs and make amends for my sins of the past by repenting and doing penance.

Hail Mary

Sweet Heart of Mary, be the salvation of my soul **and the souls of all my family.**

Immaculate Heart of Mary, blessed among all people for your trust in the Word of God, may I firmly and joyfully believe in all truths rev-ealed, and jealously keep the treasure of faith.

Hail Mary

Sweet Heart of Mary, be the salvation of my soul **and the souls of all my family.**

Immaculate Heart of Mary, always faithful to the will of God, may I not forget that my pur-pose on earth is to do the will of God, whatever it may be and at all costs.

Hail Mary

Sweet Heart of Mary, be the salvation of my soul **and the souls of all my family.**

Immaculate Heart of Mary, united continuously to God in a perfect interior life, may I also be raised up to God with all my soul in meditation and in prayer.

Hail Mary

Sweet Heart of Mary, be the salvation of my soul **and the souls of all my family.**

Immaculate Heart of Mary, profoundly humble despite the great dignity of being Mother of God, grant me the grace to recognise my nothingness, to accept the inevitable humiliations of life and never to seek human praise.

Hail Mary

Sweet Heart of Mary, be the salvation of my soul **and the souls of all my family.**

Immaculate Heart of Mary, grant me the grace to love that purity of heart which Jesus proclaimed as being a true beatitude on earth and an indispensable virtue in order to see God in Heaven.

Hail Mary

Sweet Heart of Mary, be the salvation of my soul **and the souls of all my family.**

Immaculate Heart of Mary, meek like that of your Divine Son, obtain for me the grace of being able to overcome every fit of temper, all resentment in the face of adversities, contradictions and offences.

Hail Mary

Sweet Heart of Mary, be the salvation of my soul **and the souls of all my family.**

Immaculate Heart of Mary, ever serene amid the most atrocious sufferings, grant me the grace to reiterate my resigned and Christian "Fiat" in the various difficulties of life.

Hail Mary

Sweet Heart of Mary, be the salvation of my soul **and the souls of all my family.**

Immaculate Heart of Mary, model of submission to domestic, religious and civil authority, grant that I may imitate you, always recognizing my legitimate superiors as being the representatives of God.

Hail Mary

Sweet Heart of Mary, be the salvation of my soul **and the souls of all my family.**

Immaculate Heart of Mary, all motherly goodness towards the needs of your children, grant that I too may love my neighbour as myself, never refusing to give advice, or help, or to pray for others.

Hail Mary

Sweet Heart of Mary, be the salvation of my soul **and the souls of all my family.**

Immaculate Heart of Mary, ardent for the salvation of souls, grant that I too may feel the spirit of apostolate for sinners and the unfaithful, and the spirit of compassion for the souls of Purgatory and may I work with all my strength to spread the kingdom of Jesus Christ in the world and to increase the number of saints in heaven.

Hail Mary

Sweet Heart of Mary, be the salvation of my soul **and the souls of all my family.**

PRAYER TO THE
IMMACULATE HEART OF MARY

O most pure Virgin Mary, I venerate Your most Holy Heart which was the delight and the resting-place of God. Heart filled with humility, purity and divine love, I, a poor sinner, come to You with my heart full of earth and wounds.

O Mother of mercy, do not reject me because of this, but rather have an even greater compassion for me and help me. Do not seek merits and virtues in me to help me, for I am lost and merit nothing.
I beg You to look only upon the trust I have in You and my desire to be purified. Consider what Jesus has done and suffered for me, and do not abandon me.

I offer to You all the sufferings of His life: the cold suffered in the stable, the journey to Egypt, the Blood poured out, the poverty, the hard work, the sadness He experienced, the death which He suffered for my sake in Your presence. For love of Jesus, strive to help me. O my Mother, I no longer fear that I will be rejected, now that I have come to You to ask Your help. If I doubted that You would help me, I would insult Your Mercy which searches for the afflicted in order to help them.

My Lady, do not deny mercy to those to whom Jesus did not deny his Blood. If You commend my soul to God, the benefits which I will receive, through the merits of His Blood, shall be greater.

My hope of salvation is in You! I seek neither riches, honours nor other earthly gains; I seek rather the Grace of God, love for Your Son, obedience to His will, and Paradise, so that I may love Jesus in eternity. Surely You will hear my prayer?

Yes, I am sure that You have already heard me, are already praying for me, are already granting me the graces I have requested, and already accept me under Your motherly protection. Mother, do not leave me! Continue to pray for me until you see me saved in Heaven at Your feet, blessing and thanking You for eternity. **Amen.**

DEVOTION OF
THE TWELVE STARS

The servant of God, Mother Mary Constance Zauli (1886-1954), foundress of the Adoring Handmaids of the Most Holy Sacrament in Bologna, Italy, was inspired, during a period of great physical and moral suffering, to practise and spread devotion to the Twelve Privileges of the Virgin Mary.

On the 30th of June, 1939, writing in her diary about her private revelations, she tells us, **"In that blessed visit the Most Holy Virgin taught me (about) the devotion of the Twelve Privileges and ordered me to make it known and to propagate it, because it delights her heart: to remember them, meditating on them mentally, and reciting for each one a Hail Mary and the following prayer of praise:**

May the Most Holy Trinity be blessed, praised and thanked for the graces granted to the Virgin Mary

In the name of the Father, the Son, and the Holy Spirit. Amen.

O God come to my aid.
O Lord, make haste to help me.

Glory be
The Creed *(see page 26)*

First privilege
PREDESTINATION OF MARY

"The deep was not, when I was born".

(Pr 8:24)

"When the deep was not, the Mother of God already exi-sted in the mind of the Creator". *(ref. Prv 8:24)*

Reflection

The Divine Father, planned His work of creation from eternity, admiring the perfection with which he was to imbue His creatures, and he delighted in his supreme masterpiece, His most precious jewel, when contemplating with admiration the Mother that He was to prepare for His Son.

Invocation

O Joy of the Most Holy Trinity, help me to welcome and to fulfil the design of love which the Father has for me.

Hail Mary

May the Most Holy Trinity be blessed, praised and thanked for the graces granted to the Virgin Mary.

THE IMMACULATE CONCEPTION OF MARY

"I shall put enmity between you and the woman".

(Gn 3:15)

In the garden of Eden, God announces the future Redeemer who, with the Mother, will crush the head of the snake under his feet".

(ref. Gn 3:15)

Reflection

The very first light of the dawn of Redemption, after the promise made in Eden, is found in the Immaculate Conception of Mary. With the first appearance of the morning star, humanity began to enjoy the first fruits of reconciliation with God, as the curtain of separation between us and Him was torn by the first heartbeat of His little chosen creature, thus allowing the mercy of the Most High to overflow from above.

Invocation

O full of Grace, be my strength to overcome sin and to grow in wisdom and grace.

Hail Mary

May the Most Holy Trinity be blessed, praised and thanked for the graces granted to the Virgin Mary.

THIRD PRIVILEGE

THE PERFECT CONFORMITY OF MARY
TO GOD'S WILL

"You see before you the Lord's servant, let it happen to me as you have said".   *(Lk 1:38)*

"Jacob's ladder, which unites unites heaven and earth, may be taken to represent the will of Mary, lovingly linked to that of the Lord".   *(ref. Gn 28: 12)*

Reflection

The soul of Mary was a true paradise of delight for her Son and the most beautiful ornament of glory for the most Holy Trinity. She could lift herself into the clear regions of faith where she was able to see her God and worship His most holy will, repeating her "fiat" with full and perfect dedication.

Invocation

Mother of the Faith, may I always be prompt and joyful in my daily "yes" to the holy will of the Father.

Hail Mary

May the Most Holy Trinity be blessed, praised and thanked for the graces granted to the Virgin Mary.

Fourth privilege
THE EMINENT HOLINESS OF MARY

"She would be glorious, with no speck or wrinkle... but holy and faultless". *(Ep 5:27b)*

"The house was founded on rock" *(ref. Mt 7:25)*

Reflection

The holiness of the Virgin Mary is a golden fabric woven with the simple pattern of perfect faithfulness to her duties and a simple and common state of life, which lends itself to imitation.

Invocation

O Model of holiness, save me from the hypocrisy of false virtue; teach me humility, love, and profound prayer.

Hail Mary

May the Most Holy Trinity be blessed, praised and thanked for the graces granted to the Virgin Mary.

THE ANNUNCIATION

"Rejoice, you who enjoy God's favour, the Lord is with you!". (Lk 1:28)

"The cloud is a sign of the presence of God".
(ref. 1 Kings 8:10)

Reflection

At the moment in which she was greeted by the Archangel, Mary was profoundly immersed in prayer. Her soul shone with three rays: adoration, love and dedication, all so perfect and elevated that they appealed greatly to God who, in that wonderful Creature, formed the Seat of Eternal Wisdom.

Invocation

O Chosen One from among women, give me the simplicity of your heart, your generosity, your never-ending trust in the Word of the Lord.

Hail Mary

May the Most Holy Trinity be blessed, praised and thanked for the graces granted to the Virgin Mary.

The divine maternity of Mary

"Look! You are to conceive in your womb and bear a son, and you must name him Jesus". (Lk 1:31)

"A shoot will spring from the stock of Jesse". (ref. Is 11:1)

Reflection

At the great moment in which the Word became flesh in Mary, her blessed soul and all her being remained overshadowed by the Holy Spirit who consecrated her as Mother of God. What ecstasy was hers! She was filled with the happiness of the Father and was enriched with the joy of being a mother.

Invocation

Mother of the Word, prepare me to accept the gifts of the Holy Spirit, so that I may become similar to Jesus and an obedient son (daughter) of the Church.

Hail Mary

May the Most Holy Trinity be blessed, praised and thanked for the graces granted to the Virgin Mary.

The perfect virginity of mary

"How can this come about, since I have no knowledge of man?".   *(Lk 1:34)*

"The lily among thistles".   *(ref. Ct 2:2)*

Reflection

The Blessed Virgin Mary is the shining glory of all creatures, who, in an extraordinary way, exalted the pure vessel of virginity. The souls who entrust themselves to her care can, in their turn, become living temples of God.

Invocation

You are Mother and Virgin, O Mary, nothing is impossible to God. Transfigure my body and soul with your pure and gentle light.

Hail Mary

May the Most Holy Trinity be blessed, praised and thanked for the graces granted to the Virgin Mary.

THE MARTYRDOM OF THE HEART

"Near the cross of Jesus stood his mother".   *(Jn 19:25)*

"The pierced heart of Mary".   *(ref. Lk 2:35)*

Reflection

Mary, preceded the steps of Jesus, with the strength and delicacy of motherly love while remaining totally dedicated to the wishes of the Father for the fulfillment of the work of Redemption, to the point of giving herself without reserve together with her Son, uniting herself with the beats of her Son's heart so as to form with Him a single victim of expiation.

Invocation

In time of sorrow you gave birth to me, O Queen of martyrs. Sustain my lack of constancy and perseverance and teach me to comfort those who suffer.

Hail Mary

May the Most Holy Trinity be blessed, praised and thanked for the graces granted to the Virgin Mary.

MARY REJOICES AT THE RESURRECTION AND ASCENSION OF JESUS

"My soul proclaims the greatness of the Lord and my spirit rejoices in God my Saviour". *(Lk 1:46-47)*

"The golden censer of the Angels (ref. Rev 8:3) symbolizes the following events among other things:
the Candle represents the resurrection and the Monogram of Christ on the cloud represents His ascension".

Meditation

At the moment of His Resurrection, Jesus poured forth his joy on Mary in abundance. For a Mother like her, it gave her great joy to see with her own eyes the exaltation of the Son whom she adored, and the happiness and treasures of the Kingdom of which He was coming into possession.

Invocation

Mother of Jesus, immolated Lamb, you are now rejoic-ing with Him in glory. Grant that I may adore the splendour of His holiness in the gift of the Eucharist.

Hail Mary

May the Most Holy Trinity be blessed, praised and thanked for the graces granted to the Virgin Mary.

TENTH PRIVILEGE
THE ASSUMPTION OF MARY INTO HEAVEN

"Today the sacred and living ark of the living God has found rest in the temple of the Lord".　　*(ref. 1Cr16)*

"The ark of the Lord brought to triumph is the symbol of the All Holy One being transported to heaven"

(ref. 1Cr 15:3)

Reflection

The Father, Son and Holy Spirit, filled with love for their daughter, mother and spouse when the course of her earthly life had ended, assumed her to heavenly glory in body and soul, accompanied by the angels singing "Hosanna!" unto the heights of the throne of God, from whom she received the greatest glorification.

Invocation

Woman robed with the sun, you are not far away; you are here acting with motherly tenderness, beside each one of us on our journey towards Heaven.

Hail Mary

May the Most Holy Trinity be blessed, praised and thanked for the graces granted to the Virgin Mary.

THE SOVEREIGNTY OF MARY

"The Lord God will give him the throne of his ancestor David and his reign will have no end".   *(Lk 1:32-33)*

"The sign of the woman robed with the sun".

(ref. Rev 12:1)

REFLECTION

In heaven Mary is the Paradise of the Holy Trinity, in which the Father, Son and Holy Spirit are well pleased. What power has been conferred on this Queen! It is all for our benefit. What an extraordinary gift God has bestowed on us in giving her to us as our Mother!

INVOCATION

You are Queen and you are Handmaid; for you and for Jesus, to reign means nothing other than to serve. Educate me, therefore O Mother, so that I may bear witness to truth and justice with the attitude of your queenship.

Hail Mary

May the Most Holy Trinity be blessed, praised and thanked for the graces granted to the Virgin Mary.

THE MEDIATION OF MARY AND
THE POWER OF HER INTERCESSION

"For whoever finds me finds life, and obtains the favour of the Lord".   *(Pr 8:35)*

"Mary receives the grace of Jesus and pours it out on all creatures".   *(ref. Jn 7:37-38)*

"The crown of the twelve stars reminds us of the twelve privileges of the Virgin Mary".   *(ref. Rev 12:1)*

Reflection

I see the Holy Virgin Mary interceding before the Most High for the salvation of all her sinful children. Mary, who receives graces emanating from the Primary Source and who has been rendered a true mediatrix by the Mediator, transmits graces to her children, and her generosity in giving increases her riches ever more.

Invocation

The Holy Trinity has given you the mission of a universal maternity: I welcome you as John did, with filial and spontaneous love, consecrating myself to your Immaculate Heart.

Hail Mary

May the Most Holy Trinity be blessed, praised and thanked for the graces granted to the Virgin Mary.

CHAPLET OF THE TWELVE STARS

Various chaplets have been composed in order to recall the twelve stars around the head of the Virgin Mary, which symbolize her queenship, her privileges and her virtues. St. Andrew Avellino recommended that recitation of this chaplet should not be neglected for the sake of any other occupation, and said that someone (who transpired to be St. Andrew himself), while reciting it, saw an Angel who offered every Hail Mary to the Virgin who, in her turn, appeared to be very contented. "Be sure," he added, "that through this you will obtain graces more easily and you will be greatly helped at the moment of your death". The chaplet in its most abbreviated form consists in reciting twelve Hail Marys, saying a brief prayer of one's own choice between each two Hail Marys. The chaplet in its common form is as given below.

In the name of the Father, the Son, and the Holy Spirit. Amen.

O God come to my aid.
O Lord, make haste to help me.

Glory be • The Creed *(see page 26)*

Eternal Divine Father, I adore you profoundly and I thank you with all my heart for that great power with which you preserved the Virgin Mary, your beloved Daughter, from original sin.

Our Father • Hail Mary *(4 times)*
O Mary, conceived without sin,
pray for us who recourse to Thee (You)
Glory Be

Eternal Divine Son, I adore you profoundly and I thank you with all my heart for that infinite wisdom with which you preserved the Virgin Mary, your true and sweet Mother, from original sin.

Our Father • Hail Mary *(4 times)*
O Mary, conceived without sin,
pray for us who recourse to Thee (You)
Glory Be

Eternal Divine Spirit, I adore you profoundly and I thank you with all my heart, for that great love with which you preserved the Virgin Mary, your most pure Spouse, from original sin.

Our Father • Hail Mary *(4 times)*
O Mary, conceived without sin,
pray for us who recourse to Thee (You)
Glory Be

Most Holy Trinity, I adore you profoundly and I thank you with all my heart, for that singular privilege granted to the blessed and glorious St. Anne, the only humanly fertile mother who gave birth to a child totally free from original sin.

Glory Be *(3 times)*

THE LITTLE CROWN OF
THE BLESSED VIRGIN

One of the exterior practices of the "true devotion to Mary", as taught by St. Louis De Montfort is the Little Crown of the Blessed Virgin. It is called the "little crown" (petite couronne) in order to distinguish it from the "great crown" of the Rosary (Indeed the saint was known as the Missionary of the Great Crown). St. Louis De Montfort recalls the fact that it is an ancient prayer to Mary; moreover he reminds us of its biblical foundation (Revelation 12: 1-18) and recommends that it be recited daily, giving some instructions so that it may be prayed well. The Little Crown of the Blessed Virgin used to be said frequently in the seventeenth century. In order to understand the division of the Little Crown of Virgin Mary, into three parts, suffice is to remember the three reasons for which Mary was crowned: firstly, for her unequalled greatness among all creatures; secondly for her unlimited power granted to her by Our Lord; thirdly, for her motherly goodness which attracts us most to her.

As God the Father is the Giver of all goodness, it is natural to think of Him while reciting the first Our Father, as we begin the Crown of Excellence. We address the second Our Father to the Son, who is the virtue of the Father, as an introduction to the Crown of Power. The third Our Father, recited before the prayers which exalt the goodness of Mary, is said in honour of the Holy Spirit, substance of the love between the Father and the Son.

**Accept our pleas, Holy Virgin Mary!
Make us strong to fight against our adversarie.**

In the name of the Father, the Son,
and the Holy Spirit. Amen.

O God come to my aid.
O Lord, make haste to help me.

Glory be
The Creed *(see page 26)*

I. Crown of Excellence
(To honour the divine maternity of the Blessed Virgin, her ineffable virginity, her purity without stain and her innumerable virtues).

Our Father
Hail Mary

Blessed are you, O Virgin Mary, who gave birth to the Lord, the Creator of the world; you gave birth to Him who made you, and remain a Virgin forever.

Rejoice, O Virgin Mary,
Rejoice a thousand times!
Hail Mary

O holy and immaculate Virgin, I do not know with what praise to extol you, since you bore in your womb the very one whom the heavens cannot contain.

Rejoice, O Virgin Mary,
Rejoice a thousand times!
Hail Mary

You are all fair, O Virgin Mary, and there is no stain in you.

Rejoice, O Virgin Mary,
Rejoice a thousand times!
Hail Mary

You virtues, O Virgin, surpass the stars in number

Rejoice, O Virgin Mary,
Rejoice a thousand times!
Glory Be

II. Crown of Power

(To honour the royalty of the Blessed Virgin, her magnificence, her universal mediation and the strength of her rule).

Our Father
Hail Mary

Glory be to you, O empress of the world! Bring us with you to the joys of heaven.

Rejoice, O Virgin Mary,
Rejoice a thousand times!
Hail Mary

Glory be to you, O treasure-house of the Lord's graces! Grant us a share in your riches.

Rejoice, O Virgin Mary,
Rejoice a thousand times!
Hail Mary

Glory be to you, O Mediatrix between God and humanity! Through you may the Almighty be favourable to us.

Rejoice, O Virgin Mary,
Rejoice a thousand times!
Hail Mary

Glory be to you who destroy heresies and demons! May you be our loving guide.

Rejoice, O Virgin Mary,
Rejoice a thousand times!
Glory Be

III. Crown of Goodness

Our Father
Hail Mary

Glory be to you, O refuge of sinners! Intercede for us with God.

Rejoice, O Virgin Mary,
Rejoice a thousand times!
Hail Mary

Glory be to you, O Mother of orphans! Render the Almighty favourable to us.

Rejoice, O Virgin Mary,
Rejoice a thousand times!
Hail Mary

Glory be to you, O joy of the just! Lead us with you to the joys of heaven!

Rejoice, O Virgin Mary,
Rejoice a thousand times!
Hail Mary

Glory be to you who are ever ready to assist us in life and in death! Lead us with you to the kingdom of heaven!

Rejoice, O Virgin Mary,
Rejoice a thousand times!
Glory Be

Let us pray.

Hail, Mary, Daughter of God the Father; Hail, Mary, Mother of God the Son; Hail, Mary, Spouse of the Holy Spirit; Hail, Mary, Temple of the most Holy Trinity; Hail, Mary, my Mistress, my treasure, my joy, Queen of my heart; my Mother, my life, my sweetness, my dearest hope, yes, my heart and my soul!

I am all yours and all that I have is yours, O Virgin blessed above all things! Let your soul be in me to magnify the Lord; let your spirit be in me to rejoice in God.

Set yourself, O faithful Virgin, as a seal upon my heart, that in you and through you I may be found faithful to God. Receive me, O gracious Virgin, among those whom you love and teach, whom you lead, nourish and protect as your children.

Grant that for love of you I may despise all earthly consolations and ever cling to those of heaven; until through the Holy Spirit, your faithful Spouse, and through you, His faithful Spouse, Jesus Christ your Son be formed in me for the glory of the Father.
Amen.

CHAPLET FOR THE GRACE
TO BECOME HOLY

This chaplet was composed by St. Cottoleng andit helps to dispel the erroneous idea that the path towards sanctity is too difficult and that holiness is something inaccessible; many people do not aspire to sanctity, on the contrary they believe that it would be a sin of pride to nurture a desire for holiness. St. Paul reminds us that it is the will of God that we become holy: "May the God of peace make you perfect and holy; and may your spirit, life and body be kept blameless for the coming of our Lord Jesus Christ. He who called you is trustworthy and will carry it out" (1 Ts 5:23-24). It we recite this chaplet with fervour, the desire to become holy and to practise what is necessary to attain this goal is enkindled in our hearts, and indeed the Queen of Saints will grant us the graces necessary to fulfil our desire. We recite it using the rosary beads.

In the name of the Father, and of the Son, and of the Holy Spirit. Amen.

O God, come to my aid.
O Lord, make haste to help me.
Glory Be
The Creed *(see page 26)*

On the beads of the Our Father we recite the:
Glory Be

On the beads of the Hail Mary we recite the following invocation:
Virgin Mary, Mother of Jesus, grant that we may become holy

At the end of the chaplet we pray as follows:
May the will of God, most righteous,
most high and most adorable,
be accomplished in all things and be praised
and exalted in eternity

We then recite the
Hail Holy Queen

CHAPLET IN HONOUR OF THE IMMACULATE HEART OF MARY

*In the name of the Father, and of the Son,
and of the Holy Spirit. Amen.*

O God, come to my aid.
O Lord, make haste to help me.

Glory Be
(To be said 5 times in honour of the five wounds of our Lord)

*On the beads of the Our Father,
we recite the following invocation:*
Immaculate and sorrowful Heart of Mary,
pray for us who trust in you!

*On the beads of the Hail Mary,
we recite the following words:*
Mother, save us with the flame of Love
of your Immaculate Heart!

To conclude the chaplet we pray as follows:
Glory Be *(3 times)*

*In honour of the eternal Father, to thank him
for the graces granted to Mary:*
**Our Father
Hail Mary** *(4 times)*

In honour of the Son:
Our Father

Hail Mary *(4 times)*

In honour of the Holy Spirit:
Our Father
Hail Mary *(4 times)*

After every four Hail Marys we recite the following prayer:

As a lily among thorns,
You, O Blessed Virgin Mary,
have been preserved from sin,
for you are the Mother of the Lord.

At the end, we say:
Pray for us, O Immaculate Virgin,
That we may be made worthy
of the promises of Christ.

Let us pray.
Grant, O Lord, the gift of your heavenly grace to us your children, so that the votive memory of the Immaculate Conception of the Blessed Virgin Mary, which gave rise to the beginning of our salvation, may increase your peace in our hearts. Through Christ Our Lord. **Amen.**

CHAPLET OF THE MOST
HOLY VIRGIN MARY

(Introductory prayers see page 872)

I venerate you with all my heart, most Holy Virgin Mary, to you I consecrate my soul with all its faculties. You whose intercession is powerful, help me in my present needs: you can come to my aid, do not abandon me; I ask this of you through the power that the Heavenly Father has given to you as his most beloved Daughter.

Hail Mary

I venerate you with all my heart, most Holy Virgin Mary, to you I consecrate my body with all its senses. You know my misery, you know what I carry in my heart, you know the need I have of your assistance: I commend myself entirely into your hands. I ask these graces of you through the incomparable wisdom which the Word, your Son, has communicated to you as his beloved Mother.

Hail Mary

I venerate you with all my heart, most Holy Virgin Mary, to you I consecrate my heart with all its affections. You, whose assistance no one has ever implored in vain, come to my aid. I ask these graces of you through the merciful goodness which the Holy Spirit has given to you as his beloved Spouse.

Hail Mary

CHAPLET OF THE IMMACULATE HEART OF MARY

(Introductory prayers see page 872)

Immaculate Heart of Mary, model of faithfulness in the fulfillment of all duties, grant that I too may fulfil my duties to God, to my neighbour and to myself with the same readiness and constancy .

O Mother of mine, hear and answer me.

Immaculate Heart of Mary, full of grace, tabernacle of the Most High, grant that I may live a life of grace; that I may consider myself as the living temple of the Holy Spirit; that I may avoid sin at all costs and make amends for my sins of the past by repenting and doing penance.

O Mother of mine, hear and answer me.

Immaculate Heart of Mary, blessed among all people for your faith in the Word of God, grant that I may firmly and joyously believe in all divine revelation, and jelously keep the treasure of my faith.

O Mother of mine, hear and answer me.

Immaculate Heart of Mary, who accomplish

the will of God in all things and at all times, grant that I may never forget that my purpose on earth is to do God's will, whatever it may be and whatever it may cost.

O Mother of mine, hear and answer me.

Immaculate Heart of Mary, united constantly to God by a perfect interior life, grant that I may lift up my soul to God in contemplation and prayer.

O Mother of mine, hear and answer me.

Immaculate Heart of Mary, profoundly humble, even though you are the Mother of God, grant me the grace to recognise my nothingness, to accept the inevitable humiliations of life and never to seek human praise.

O Mother of mine, hear and answer me.

Immaculate Heart of Mary, grant me the grace to love that purity of heart which Jesus proclaimed to be a true beatitude on earth, and an indispensable virtue in order to see God in heaven.

O Mother of mine, hear and answer me.

Immaculate Heart of Mary, meek like that of your Divine Son, grant me the grace to overcome every impulse of anger, and all resentment in the face of difficulties, contradictions and offences.

O Mother of mine, hear and answer me.

Immaculate Heart of Mary, ever serene in spite of the most atrocious sufferings, grant me the grace to accept always the various trials of life with Christian resignation.

O Mother of mine, hear and answer me.

Immaculate Heart of Mary, model of obedience to authority, domestic, and religious, civil, grant that I may imitate you, always recognizing my legitimate superiors as being representatives of God.

O Mother of mine, hear and answer me.

Immaculate Heart of Mary, ardent for the salvation of souls, grant that I, too, may feel the spirit of apostolate for sinners and for those who do not believe, and the spirit of compassion for the holy souls of purgatory, so that I may endeavour with all my strength to establish the kingdom of Jesus Christ in the world.

**Our Father
Hail Mary
Glory Be**

Chaplet to Our Lady of Fatima

In the name of the Father, and of the Son,
and of the Holy Spirit. Amen.

O God, come to my aid.
O Lord, make haste to help me.
Glory Be
The Creed *(see page 26)*

First day

O Virgin Mary, who deigned to appear on the lonely mountains of Fatima to three shepherds, teaching us that we must sometimes withdraw to be alone with God in prayer for the good of our souls; obtain for us a love of prayer and meditation, so that we may be able to listen to the voice of the Lord and fulfil his most holy Will with faithfulness.

Hail Mary
Our Lady of the Rosary of Fatima,
pray for us.

SECOND DAY

O most Pure Virgin Mary, who, clothed in purity white as snow, appeared to simple and innocent shepherds, teaching us how much we must love innocence of body and soul, help us to appreciate this heavenly gift, so much forgotten today, and do not let us offend our neighbour with words and actions, but rather allow us to help innocent souls to preserve this divine treasure.

Hail Mary
Our Lady of the Rosary of Fatima,
pray for us.

THIRD DAY

O Mary, Mother of sinners, who, appearing at Fatima, showed a slight shadow of sadness on your heavenly face, sign of the sorrow caused by the offences that we commit against your Divine Son, grant us the grace of perfect contrition of heart so that we may confess our sins with all sincerity in the holy sacrament of Confession.

Hail Mary
Our Lady of the Rosary of Fatima,
pray for us.

FOURTH DAY

O Queen of the Holy Rosary, who held white rosary beads in your hands and with great insistence asked that we recite the Holy Rosary in order to obtain the graces we need, awaken in us a great love for prayer, above all for the Rosary, model of vocal and mental prayer, so that we not allow one day to pass without reciting it with attention and devotion.

Hail Mary
Our Lady of the Rosary of Fatima,
pray for us.

FIFTH DAY

O Queen of peace and our compassionate Mother who, while the great tragedy of a worldly war threatened Europe, showed the three little shepherds the way to free ourselves from many calamities by the recitation of the Rosary and the practice of penance, intercede for us with God so that, through faith and Christian virtues, peace and prosperity may bloom in our midst, in honour of you and your Divine Son.

Hail Mary
Our Lady of the Rosary of Fatima,
pray for us.

O refuge of sinners, who encouraged the shepherds of Fatima to pray to God so that those poor unhappy people who reject the law of God would not go to hell, you who said to one of the shepherds that most souls who go to hell are lost because of sins of the flesh, grant us a great horror of sin, especially sins of impurity, as well as compassion and zeal for the salvation of souls who live in great danger of being lost in eternity.

Hail Mary
Our Lady of the Rosary of Fatima,
pray for us.

SEVENTH DAY

O Health of the sick, you replied to the shepherds when they asked you to heal some sick people that you would grant health to some and not to others, and thus taught us that illness is a precious gift of God and a means of salvation. Grant that we may accept the will of God in the difficulties of life which we encounter, so that we may not complain about our trials but rather bless the Lord, who offers us in this way a means of satisfying the temporal punishment merited by our sins.

Hail Mary
Our Lady of the Rosary of Fatima,
pray for us.

Eighth day

O most Holy Virgin Mary, who expressed to the shepherds your desire that a sanctuary be built in Fatima in honour of the most Holy Rosary, grant us a great love for the mysteries of our Redemption, which are remembered in the recitation of the Rosary, in order that we may live so as to enjoy its precious fruits, the greatest that the most Holy Trinity has granted to humanity.

Hail Mary
Our Lady of the Rosary of Fatima,
pray for us.

Ninth day

Our Lady of Sorrows, who, at Fatima revealed your heart as being surrounded by thorns, thus asking for consolation and promising as a reward the grace of a holy death, the conversion of Russia and the final triumph of your Immaculate Heart, grant, according the desire of the Heart of Jesus, that we may be faithful in offering you the gifts of reparation and love requested by you, on the first Saturday of the month, in order to share in your promised graces.

Hail Mary
Our Lady of the Rosary of Fatima,
pray for us.

THE ROSARY OF THE IMMACULATE VIRGIN MARY

When appearing at Marienfried, a village in Germany, in the year 1946, our Lady asked us to pray the Rosary of the Immaculate Virgin Mary. She said that it was the "rosary of graces". It may be said for individuals, for communities and for entire nations. The Rosary of the Immaculate Virgin Mary is a powerful prayer that takes away power from Satan through the intercession of Mary.

After the first part of each Hail Mary of the Rosary, we recite an invocation which differs for each mystery. The invocations are as follows:

FIRST MYSTERY
Through your Immaculate Conception,
save us.

SECOND MYSTERY
Through your Immaculate Conception,
protect us.

THIRD MYSTERY
Through your Immaculate Conception,
guide us.

FORTH MYSTERY
Through your Immaculate Conception,
sanctify us.

FIFTH MYSTERY
Through your Immaculate Conception,
govern us.

for example:

Hail Mary, full of grace,
the Lord is with thee;
blessed art thou among women
and blessed is the fruit of thy womb, Jesus.

Through your Immaculate Conception,
save us.

Holy Mary, Mother of God,
pray for us sinners,
now and at the hour of our death.
Amen.

After every ten Hail Marys, we recite the following words:

You, great Mediatrix,
You, faithful Mediatrix,
You, Mediatrix of all graces,
pray for us.

THE ROSARY OF THE HEART OF MARY

Before saying this Rosary we make the sign of the cross five times in honour of the five wounds of our Lord:

In the name of the Father, and of the Son, and of the Holy Spirit. Amen.

O God, come to my aid.
O Lord, make haste to help me.
Glory Be
The Creed *(see page 26)*

*On the beads of the Our Father
we recite the following invocation:*
Immaculate and sorrowful Heart of Mary,
pray for us who trust in you!

*On the beads of the Hail Mary
we recite the following words:*
Mother, save us through the flame of the Love
of your Immaculate Heart!

We conclude the Rosary by reciting the:
Glory Be *(3 times)*

THE JOYS OF THE
BLESSED VIRGIN MARY

Mary was not only Our Lady of Sorrows; she was first introduced to us as "the favoured One" in the words of the Angel Gabriel, "the Blessed One" in the greeting of St. Elizabeth, and she herself sang her heavenly joys in the "Magnificat". Mary's experience of human life was similar to that of Jesus, who, while being filled with joy in the depths of his soul because of his beatific vision, bore much sorrow and pain, not only in his body but also in his soul. Likewise, the life of Mary was an incomprehensible and closely woven fabric of joys and pains.

The joys of Mary have always attracted the attention of the faithful since the early days of Christianity, Initially they were remembered on the occasion of various feastdays of the Virgin, while later the joyous events of her life began to be associated with each other in the minds and hearts of the faithful, thus becoming the object of special devotion. The Virgin showed how pleased she was by such a devotion when appearing to St. Arnolf of Cornoboult and also to St. Thomas of Canterbury in order to rejoice at the celebration of her earthly joys by the faithful and to invite them to honour her heavenly joys as well, which she revealed to them (as found in the following chaplet). One of the great apostles of the Joys of Mary was St. Bernardine, a Franciscan, who professed that all the graces he received were granted to him through this particular devotion.

DEVOTION OF THE SEVEN JOYS OF MARY IN HEAVEN

In the name of the Father, and of the Son,
and of the Holy Spirit. Amen.

O God, come to my aid.
O Lord, make haste to help me.
Glory Be
The Creed *(see page 26)*

Rejoice, Spouse of the Holy Spirit, at the contentment which you now enjoy in Paradise for, you are exalted above the choirs of angels because of your purity and virginity.

Hail Mary

Rejoice, O true Mother of God, at the pleasure which you experience in Paradise because, like the sun which, here on earth, gives light to the whole world, so do you, with your splendour, adorn all Paradise and make it resplendent.

Hail Mary

Rejoice, O Daughter of God, at the happiness which you now enjoy in Paradise, because all the hosts of angels, archangels, thrones and ruling forces, and all blessed souls honour and acknowledge you as the Mother of their Creator and at the slightest indication of your wishes, obey you immediately.

Hail Mary

Rejoice, O Handmaid of the most Holy Trinity, at the greatest happiness which you experience and enjoy in Paradise, because all graces that you ask of your Son are granted to you immediately; and indeed, St. Bernard said that there is no grace granted here on earth that does not pass first through your most holy hands.

Hail Mary

Rejoice, O most serene Princess, because you alone deserved to sit at the right hand of your most holy Son who is seated on at right of the Eternal Father.

Hail Mary

Rejoice, O Hope of sinners and Refuge of the afflicted, at the immense happiness which you enjoy in Paradise because all those who praise and venerate you will be rewarded by the Eternal Father, with his most holy grace in this world, and with eternal glory in the world to come.

Hail Mary

Rejoice, O Mother, Daughter and Spouse of God, because all the graces, joys, happiness and favours which you enjoy in Paradise, will never diminish but on the contrary, will increase until the day of Judgement and will remain for all eternity.

Hail Mary
Glory Be

Let us pray.
O most shining mirror of sanctity, true image of God, glorious Virgin, who, as a fount of mercy, cannot deny any grace to those who implore your intercession with devotion, I humbly pray to you by virtue of these Seven Joys which I desired to recall devoutly in your honour; be kind enough to obtain from your Only Begotten Son, the remission of all my iniquities and sins, and may you protect my soul in a special way, especially at the hour of my death, so that I may be freed from all the snares which the devil habitually sets and may come one day to rejoice with you for ever in Paradise. **Amen.**

THE DEVOTION OF THE THREE HAIL MARYS

Why did God create us? God created us in order that we may know, love and serve Him in this life, and that we may rejoice with Him in Paradise. Jesus once asked, "What then will anyone gain by winning the whole world and forfeiting his life?" (Mt 16:26). Thus the most important concern in this life is eternal salvation.

If we wish to be saved, one sure way is to be devoted to the Blessed Virgin Mary. "The Salvation of the world began through her and through her it must be accomplished... she is the sure means, the direct and immaculate way to Jesus and the perfect guide to him, it is through her that souls who are to shine forth in sanctity must find him" (True Devotion to the Blessed Virgin, St. Louis De Montfort). *Let us therefore implore her protection by reciting three Hail Marys every day.*

This short and simple devotion was revealed by Mary, the Mother of God, to St. Matilda (ref. Liber Specialis Gratiae Chap.47). The latter feared the moment of death and therefore prayed to the Virgin Mary to assist her at that hour. Mary's reply was very reassuring. Moreover, it was addressed to all souls and can be summarized as follows: "Recite with devotion three Hail Marys every day:

the first one in order to thank the Eternal Father for having made me almighty in heaven and on earth; the second in order to honour the Son of God for having given me knowledge and wisdom which overcome that of all saints and angels, and for having bathed me with such splendour so as to light up the whole of Paradise like the shining sun; the third in order to honour the Holy Spirit for having enkindled in my heart the most ardent flames of his love, and for having made me so good and gracious

so as to be, after God, the most sweet and merciful (being)".

    The following is the special promise of the Virgin Mary for those who practise this devotion:
At the hour of your death:

- *I shall be with you, comforting you and keeping away from you every evil force;*
- *I shall fill you with the light of faith and knowledge, in order that your faith may not be tempted by ignorance;*
- *I shall assist you at the hour of your death, filling your soul with the holiness of Divine Love, in order that it may overpower you so much that every pain and bitterness related to death be transformed into great sweetness"* *(ref. Liber specialis gratiae, Chap. 47).*

    Many saints, including St. Alphonsus Liguori, St. John Bosco and Blessed Padre Pio of Pietrelcina, were propagators of this devotion. Moreover, the apostolate of the Three Hail Marys has been approved and encouraged by the Papacy. The Venerable Servant of God, Louis Marie Baudoin, wrote the following with regard to this devotion: "Recite the Three Hail Marys every day. If you are faithful to paying this tribute of homage to Mary, I promise you Paradise".

The devotion is prayed as follows:
In the name of the Father, and of the Son, and of the Holy Spirit. Amen.

Every morning and evening one says with fervour the words given below:

Mary, Mother of Jesus, and my Mother, defend me from the snares of the devil during this life, and in particular at the hour of death, through the power that has been granted to you by the Eternal Father.

Hail Mary

through the wisdom that has been granted to you by your Divine Son.

Hail Mary

through the love that has been granted to you by the Holy Spirit.

Hail Mary

DEVOTION OF
THE FIFTEEN SATURDAYS
in honour of the Blessed Virgin Mary

This devotion consists in going to Confession, assisting at Mass, receiving Holy Communion and reciting the Holy Rosary (preferably all fifteen mysteries) on fifteen consecutive Saturdays. Particularly suitable are the fifteen Saturdays before the feast of Our Lady of Pompei (8th of May) or the feast of the Holy Rosary (7th of October), but any other time of the year may also be chosen.

It is one of the practices most pleasing to the Blessed Virgin, as it includes the more essential acts of devotion in honour of Jesus and Mary, namely Confession, Holy Communion, and recitation of the Holy Rosary.

Now let us examine the reason for the number fifteen: The Holy Virgin asked St. Bernadette Soubirous to go to the grotto of Lourdes fifteen times to recite the Rosary together with Her.

It seems that the Virgin Mary was thus inviting us to honour and to remember the fifteen mysteries of the Rosary. Indeed, the Rosary itself is full of symbolism and meaning. It is one Great Crown, composed of three "crowns": Joyful, Sorrowful and Glorious, a sign of the unity of th Holy Trinity.

Each Rosary consists of fifty Hail Marys, the years of the Jewish jubilee year, in order to symbolize that recitation of the Holy Rosary helps us to obtain the remission of our sins, as in a Marian jubilee year.

The 150 Hail Marys of the entire Rosary recall the 150 Psalms of the Book of Psalms; for this reason the Rosary has been referred to as the Marian Book of Psalms. The five Our Fathers of every rosary recall the five wounds of Christ; the ten Hail Marys remind us of the ten commandments; finally, the fifteen mysteries are symbolic of the fifteen steps to the temple of Jerusalem, which in turn represent the virtues exemplified by the mysteries, through which we come closer to God.

THE PIOUS DEVOTION OF "THE THOUSAND HAIL MARYS"
As revealed to St. Catherine of Bologna

This devotion of the Thousand Hail Marys can be traced back to St. Catherine of Bologna who used to recite the Hail Mary a thousand times on Christmas night. On the night of the 25th of December, 1445, she was deep in contemplation of the ineffable mystery of the Nativity while practising this devotion when the Blessed Virgin Mary appeared and presented Baby Jesus to her. St. Catherine tells us that she held him in her arms for "the fifth part of an hour". In memory of such a wonderful event, the Daughters of St. Catherine in the Monastery of Corpus Domini repeat the Hail Mary either one thousand times on Christmas night, or throughout the entire year.

To make this pious exercise easier, the one thousand Hail Marys may be recited during the twenty-five days preceding Christmas, from the 29th November to the 23rd of December, praying forty Hail Marys each day.

It is hoped that this practice may spread once again among the faithful. The repetition of the angelic greeting to the most Holy Virgin Mary accompanied by meditation on the moving mystery of our Redemption is indeed a most suitable preparation for devoted souls to pray before Christmas.

In the name of the Father, and of the Son, and of the Holy Spirit. Amen.

O God, come to my aid.
O Lord, make haste to help me.
Glory Be
The Creed *(see page 26)*

In imitation of St. Catherine, we praise the great Mother of God for her Sacred Giving of Birth with these forty Angelic Salutations and the same number of blessings, in order to obtain from her protection in this life and assistance at the hour of death, so that from this land of pilgrimage we may reach the eternal joy of Paradise.

FIRST DECADE

Reciting the first decade of Hail Marys, which are accompanied by as many blessings, we consider the ineffable mystery of the Incarnation of the Word and the great dignity of the Virgin Mary in having been chosen to be the Mother of the Most High.

Hail Mary *(10 times)*
O Mary, blessed be the hour in which you were
chosen to be the Mother of God.

SECOND DECADE

Reciting the second decade of Hail Marys,
which are accompanied by as many blessings, we
meditate on the humility of the King of Heaven
who chose a humble dwelling for his Birth, as
well as on the joy which Mary experienced when
she beheld the Only Son of the Father, born of
her in the stable.

Hail Mary *(10 times)*
O Mary, blessed be the hour in which you became
Mother of the Son of God.

THIRD DECADE

Reciting the third decade of Hail Marys,
which are accompanied by as many blessings, we
bring to memory the perfect diligence of the Virgin Mary, who fulfilled to perfection the duties of
both Martha and Mary, by contemplating her Son
and our Redeemer, and serving and assisting him
while still a young child.

Hail Mary *(10 times)*
O Mary, blessed be the first heartbeat which you
felt for the Son of God.

FOURTH DECADE

Reciting the fourth decade of Hail Marys, which are accompanied by as many blessings, we consider the great reverence with which Mary embraced, hugged, kissed and adored her God and our God, made Flesh for love of us, closer to her heart than to her breast.

Hail Mary *(10 times)*
O Mary, blessed be the first kiss which you gave to your little Child who was the Son of God.

On the last evening, the 23rd of December, we recite the following prayer:

Blessed be God forever, for we have fulfilled this pious exercise in imitation of St. Catherine. We beseech the Queen of Angels, Mother of Jesus and our Mother, to deign to obtain for us, the special fruit of true repentance for our sins in this life and eternal salvation of our soul at the hour our death.

Let us pray.
O God, grant that we, your faithful, may be sustained through the intercession of the holy virgin Catherine, whose virtue attracted us by its perfume to rejoice in your holy mysteries.
Through Christ our Lord. **Amen.**

6.
ACTS OF CONSECRATION

• Prayers of Consecration

CONSECRATION TO THE IMMACULATE HEART OF MARY

A Reflection by Pope John Paul II

It is necessary to put all that we possess into the hands of Mary, even the very treasure of treasures, Jesus Christ, in order that she may preserve it.

We are like pots that are too fragile: let us not keep this precious treasure and heavenly manna to ourselves, for we have too many cunning and expert enemies: let us not rely on our own prudence and strength. We have had too many unhappy experiences of our own inconstancy and natural weakness; let us not rely on our own wisdom and fervour.

Mary is wise: let us put everything into Her hands; She will take care of us and of all that we have for the greater glory of God.

Mary is merciful: She loves us as her children and her servants. Let us offer everything to Her. We will lose nothing and she will change everything to our advantage.

Mary is generous: She gives to us in return more than what we have given to Her. Let us give to Her all that we have, without reserve, and we will receive all things in return in abundance.

Mary is powerful: no one can take away what has been given to Her. Let us place ourselves in Her hands. She will defend us and allow us to conquer all our enemies.

Mary is faithful: She neither loses nor damages what has been put into Her hands. She is the most faithful Virgin to God and to humanity. She has taken care of all that God has given Her, without losing anything, and continues today to guard with particular care all those who have entrusted themselves to Her protection.

Commend all things to Her faithfulness. Let us keep close to Her as we would (stay close) to a column which cannot be destroyed, an anchor which cannot be lifted, or rather to the mountain of Zion which cannot be moved.

We live in difficult, uncertain and troubled times. Today the infernal dragon dominates the world and has succeeded in constructing an atheist society.

Men and women, strengthened by technical and scientific progress, have put themselves in the place of God and have established a new secular society.

Such a radical refusal of God is the true punishment for this society.

As God is the Saviour and Jesus Christ is the only Redeemer of humankind, humanity can save itself only if it returns to the Lord. Otherwise it runs the risk of destroying itself by the work of its own hands.

How can it be saved, if it obstinately continues to reject God who is the only one can bring it to salvation?

This is where the function of Mary comes into play by virute of Her maternity.

Mary is the mother of Jesus and was appointed by Jesus to be true mother of all people.

Therefore, Mary is also Mother of all people of today, of this rebellious humanity which is so far from God.

Her maternal duty is that of saving (humanity). And Our Lady, in order to save it, wants to make of Herself a path for humanity to return to the Lord. This is the reason for her many extraordinary manifestations, which are so numerous today: she wishes to make us understand that the Heavenly Mother is present and working in the midst of her children.

She wishes to act in person, but not directly.

She can act through those children who consecrate themselves to her Immaculate Heart, who entrust themselves completely to Her care, so that in them, She Herself can live and manifest Herself (...).

The perfection of commending oneself to Our Lady develops through four successive steps:
• accustoming oneself to living with Mary;
• allowing oneself to be transformed interiorly by Her;
• entering into a communion of hearts with Her;
• finally, re-living Mary.

Therefore the aim of following the path of consecration (...) is to let Mary live and work in us. (...) Thus humanity of today may reach salvation by (following) the road of the maternal love of Mary, which becomes the channel through which the merciful love of Jesus can reach all people (...).

"And the act of personal consecration to Mary, repeated often with fervour and intimate joy of the soul, (though) often criticised by some people, is then highlighted with profound meaning (...).

"... How deeply we feel the need of consecration for humanity and the world: for the contemporary world!... How much are we hurt therefore by everything in the Church and in each one one of us that is opposed to holiness and consecration!... May all those souls who obey the call of Eternal Love be blessed. "Blessed be all those who, day after day, with inexhaustible generosity, accept your invitation, O Mother, to do all that your (Son) Jesus says, and are serene witnesses for the Church and for the world of a life inspired by the Gospel"
(Consecration to the Immaculate Heart of Mary made by John Paul II).

"It can ... be understood why Pope John Paul II considers the act of consecration or of commending oneself to the Immaculate Heart of Mary as being the most effective means of obtaining the gift of Divine Mercy for the Church and for all humanity"**(Dives in Misericordia, 15)**.

ACT OF CONSECRATION
TO CHRIST THROUGH MARY

With full knowledge of my Christian vocation,
I renew this day in your hands, O Mary,
the commitments of my Baptism.
I renounce Satan,
all his works and all his empty promises,
and I consecrate myself to Jesus Christ,
in order to carry my cross together with him
by fulfilling the duties of my daily life with faithfulness,
according to the will of the Father.
In the presence of the entire Church,
I acknowledge you as my Mother and Queen.
To you I offer and consecrate
my being, my life,
and the value of my good works,
those of the past, present and future.
Dispose of me and of all that belongs to me
for the greater glory of God,
in time and in eternity.
Amen.

CONSECRATION TO THE IMMACULATE HEART OF MARY

O Mary, Powerful Virgin and Mother of Mercy, Queen of Heaven and Refuge of Sinners, we consecrate ourselves to your Immaculate Heart. To you we consecrate our being and all of our life, all that we have, all that we love, all that we are. To you we offer our bodies, our hearts, our families, our country.

We want all that is in us and all that surrounds us to belong to you and to share in the benefits of your maternal blessings.

And so that this consecration may be truly efficacious and in order that we may persevere in our offering, we renew this day at your feet, O Mary, the promises of Holy Baptism and of our First Holy Communion.

We commit ourselves to the profession of the truths of our faith, with courage and in every circumstance, and to live as Catholics under the authority of the Pope and of the bishops in communion with him.

We commit ourselves to observe the commandments of God and of the Church, in particular, to keep the sabbath and feast-days holy.

We commit orselves to allow the consoling practices of our Christian religion enter into our lives, especially Holy Communion and the recitation of the Rosary.

Finally we promise, O glorious Mother of God and tender Mother of humankind, to dedicate ourselves with all our heart to the service of establishing devotion to you, in order to hasten and to ensure, through the reign of your Immaculate Heart, the coming of the kingdom of the Heart of your beloved Son in our souls and in all souls, on earth as in heaven. **Amen.**

ACT OF ABANDONMENT TO MARY

O Mary, Queen of the world,
Mother of Goodness,
with confidence in your intercession,
we entrust our souls to your care.
Accompany us every day
to the fount of joy.
Give us our Saviour.
We consecrate ourselves to you,
O Queen of Love. **Amen.**

CONSECRATION TO THE IMMACULATE HEART OF THE VIRGIN MARY

Thank you, O Mary, for your motherly invitations. O Mother of my Saviour and Mother of Peace, I offer my life to you with love this day.

As Jesus, when dying on the cross, entrusted me to your care, so do I now commend myself to you.

I want to love Jesus as you love him, O Mother. With you I want to learn how to listen to the Word of the Father and to fulfil his will.

O Mary, I want to learn with you how to love all people as my brothers and sisters, for all of them are yours.

I consecrate myself to you, so that my prayer may be prayer of the heart, in which I may find peace, love and the strength to be reconciled with myself, with God and with others.

I offer to you, O dear Mary, my past, my present and my future, all my abilities and my gifts.

I desire to grow by your side as Jesus did. From now on, may everything in me glorify my Lord together with you. From now on, may my soul exult in his love and mercy.

I also consecrate to you, O Mother, my family, all my friends, and all the people with whom I live and work.

O Mary, in union with you, I desire to be a

channel of the Holy Spirit. May my heart be obedient to his inspirations as yours was. O Mother of peace, I beseech you: through your intercession, may my words be irrevocable and may sin seduce me no more.
Amen.

Consecration to our lady

Mary, Mother of Jesus and my Mother, this day,
I, a little child of yours,
consecrate myself totally to you,
in order to live a holy life:
in order to be your little servant
so that you, sweet Mother,
may always be able rely on me,
and so that I may be able help you to fulfil in me
the plan of love
which the Father has for each one of us.
Give me, O Mother of Jesus and my Mother,
the grace to be always faithful
to the Church and to the Holy Father
and, in union with you, to love and worship
Jesus our Lord. **Amen.**

ACT OF CONSECRATION TO THE IMMACULATE HEART OF THE BLESSED VIRGIN

Virgin of Fatima, Mother of Mercy, Queen of Heaven and Earth, Refuge of Sinners, we consecrate ourselves in a very special way to your Immaculate Heart.

By this act of consecration we intend to fulfil with you and through you all commitments which we took upon ourselves with our baptismal consecration; we also commit ourselves to strive towards that interior conversion requested so much by the Gospel so that we may be freed from every attachment to ourselves and may not yield to compromises easily made for the sake of the world, in order that we may be, like you, always ready to do the will of the Father, and his will alone.

And while entrusting our life and our Christian vocation to you, O most Sweet and Merciful Mother, so that you may use us for your plan of salvation in this decisive hour which weighs upon the world, we promise to live that same calling in accordance with your desires, in particular to renew our spirit of prayer and penance, to participate with fervour in the celebration of the Eucharist and in the apostolate, to recite the Holy Rosary daily and to lead a simple way of life, in conformity with the Gospel, in order to be a good example for everyone of obedience to the Law of God, and of the practice of Christian virtue, especially purity.

We also promise you to be united to the Holy Father, to the bishops and to our priests, so as to impede the process of objection to the Magistery, which threatens the very foundations of the Church.

Indeed, under your protection, we want to be apostles of communion with the Pope in prayer and love, that unity which is so necessary today, and we ask you to protect him in a special way.

Finally, we promise you to encourage as much as we can those souls with whom we come into contact, to renew their devotion towards you.

Knowing that atheism has caused the faith of a great number of Christians to wane, knowing that desecration has entered into the Holy Temple of God, knowing that evil and sin are becoming ever more widespread in the world, we dare to raise our eyes towards you with confidence, O Mother of Jesus and our Merciful and Powerful Mother, to beg you to ensure the salvation of all your children, O clement, O loving, O sweet Virgin Mary. **Amen.**

Consecration to the Immaculate Heart of the Blessed Virgin Mary of Fatima

O Holy Virgin, Mother of Jesus and our Mother, who appeared at Fatima to the three little shepherds in order to give to the world a message of peace and salvation, I resolve to accept this message of yours. Today I consecrate myself to your Immaculate Heart, so that I may belong to Jesus in a more perfect way. Help me to fulfil my consecration faithfully, with a life dedicated to loving God and my brothers and sisters, following the example of your life. In particular, I offer you the prayers, actions, and sacrifices of this day, in reparation for my sins and for those of others, with the promise to fulfil my daily duties according to the will of the Lord. I promise you to recite the Holy Rosary every day, thus contemplating the mysteries of the life of Jesus, which are linked to the mysteries of your life. I want to live as a true child of yours always, and to offer you my life so that everyone may acknowledge and love you as Mother of Jesus who is the true God and our only Saviour. **Amen.**

Hail Mary *(7 times)*
Immaculate Heart of Mary,
pray for us.

ACT OF CONSECRATION TO THE IMMACULATE HEART OF OUR LADY OF FATIMA

O Virgin of Fatima, Mother of Mercy, Queen of heaven and of earth, refuge of sinners, we consecrate ourselves to your Immaculate Heart. To you we consecrate our hearts, our souls, our families and all that we possess.

And in order that this consecration may be efficacious and may last forever, we renew this day the promises of our Baptism and Confirmation, committing ourselves to live as good Christians and to remain faithful to God, to the Church and to the Pope. We wish to recite the Rosary, to take part in the Eucharist, to observe the importance of the first Saturday of the month, and to pray and work for the conversion of sinners.

We promise you also, Most Holy Virgin, to inflame our own heart and the hearts of others with devotion to you, in order to hasten, with our consecration to your Immaculate Heart and by means of your intercession, the coming of the kingdom of Jesus in the world. **Amen.**

PERPETUAL CONSECRATION TO THE IMMACULATE HEART OF THE VIRGIN MARY

Most Holy Virgin Mary, Mother of God and mother of humankind, we turn to your Immaculate Heart and implore graces help and defence in this hour of danger and sorrow. We entrust and consecrate ourselves to your Immaculate Heart, confident that we shall always be protected by you and hopeful that we shall be enriched by you with goodness and merits.

Mother of mercy, grant that we may obtain from God those graces which can convert our hearts, those graces which prepare, nurture and ensure the peace of our conscience. Queen of Peace, pray for us, and grant to all peoples the peace that they desire: peace in truth, justice, and in the love of Christ. Grant peace where there is war and give peace to souls, so that the kingdom of God may spread in the tranquillity of an ordered world. Mother of the Church, grant peace and complete freedom to the Holy Church of God.

Most pure Mother, arrest the overflowing flood of public and private immorality; fill the faithful with a love of purity, the desire to live a Christian life and with apostolic zeal, so that those who serve God may increase in number and in virtue.

We make a perpetual consecration of ourselves to your Immaculate Heart, O Mother and Queen of the world, so that your love and protection may hasten the coming of the kingdom of God among all people. Take us into your Immaculate Heart, O Mary, and offer us to the Divine Heart of Jesus, where we shall find truth, life and peace. **Amen.**

Hail Holy Queen

CONSECRATION TO THE IMMACULATE HEART OF THE BLESSED VIRGIN MARY

O Immaculate Heart of Mary, ardent with goodness, show Your love towards us. May the flame of Your heart, O Mary, descend on all humankind. We love You so.

Impress true love in our hearts so that we have a continuous desire for You. O Mary, humble and meek of heart, remember us when we are in sin. You know that all people sin.

Give us, by means of Your Immaculate Heart, spiritual health. Let us always see the goodness of Your Maternal Heart, and may we be converted by means of the flame of Your Heart. **Amen.**

CONSECRATION TO THE
IMMACULATE VIRGIN MARY

O Immaculate Virgin Mary, Queen of heaven and earth, Refuge of Sinners and our most loving Mother, to whom God desired to entrust the entire plan of His mercy, I, an unworthy sinner, prostrate myself at Your feet, humbly entreating you to accept my whole being as Your personal belonging and property, and to do as You please with me, with all the faculties of my body and soul and with my life, death and destiny in eternity. Use my entire being without any reservations, if You wish, in order to fulfil what has been said about you:

"The woman's off spring will bruise the serpent's head" (ref. Gn 3,15) and again:

"You alone have destroyed all the heresies of the entire world" (Lit.),

so that I may become a useful instrument in Your immaculate and merciful hands which may allow Your glory to shine through many lost and indifferent souls and be magnified in them, in order that the blessed kingdom of the Most Sacred Heart of Jesus may thus come to reign in as many hearts as possible. Indeed, where you enter, you obtain the grace of conversion and holiness, as every grace flows to us from the sweet Heart of Jesus through your hands.

Grant that I may praise you,
O most Holy Virgin Mary,
**Give me the courage I need in the face
of your enemies. Amen.**

ACT OF CONSECRATION TO THE IMMACULATE HEART OF MARY

O Mary, Powerful Virgin and Mother of mercy, Queen of Heaven and refuge of sinners, we consecrate ourselves to your Immaculate Heart. To you we consecrate our being and all of our life, all that we are, all that we possess and all that we love: our bodies, our hearts and our souls. To you we consecrate our families and our country.

We want all that is in us and all that surrounds us to belong to you and thus to have a share in the benefits of your maternal blessings.

We promise you to dedicate ourselves with all our hearts to the service of encouraging devotion to you in order to hasten and to ensure, through the establishment of the reign of your Immaculate Heart, the coming of the kingdom of the Heart of your beloved Son in our souls and in the souls of all men and women, in our dear country and in all the universe.
Amen.

CONSECRATION OF A CHILD
TO THE MOTHER OF GOD
(To be said in a sanctuary of Our Lady)

From the Gospel according to John:
"Near the Cross of Jesus stood his mother and his mother's sister, Mary the wife of Clopas, and Mary of Magdala. Seeing his mother and the disciple whom he loved standing near her, Jesus said to his mother, 'Woman, this is your son.' Then to the disciple he said, 'This is your mother.' And from that hour the disciple took her into his home" (Jn 19:25-27).

Let us turn to Mary, Mother of God and Mother of the Church, beseeching Her to accept, as Her own child, little (name) whom we are now consecrating to Her.

Let us pray.
O Mary, Mother of God and our Mother, in your goodness accept your children, pilgrims in this sanctuary, and present to the Lord the prayer which we say with confidence.

With you, we thank the Lord for the gift of this child who has brought joy to our family, and we consecrate him (her) to you and, through you, to your only Son, our Saviour.

We entrust this child to your protection, so that he (her) may grow to be healthy and may be preserved from all evil in the journey of life. We entrust this child to your protection, so that you may help him (her) to live according to his (her) Baptismal promises and to be faithful to them.

Together with him (her), we consecrate ourselves, our family, our freedom and our heart to you, so that we may be more faithful to Christ than in the past. Watch over this child consecrated to you, as you watched over the child Jesus! Guide him (her) along the path of faithfulness to the Gospel so that, inspired by the Holy Spirit, he (she) may be a witness to Christ in the world, may spread joy and fraternity and finally, may reach the glory of the Father in the kingdom of heaven. **Amen.**

Daily consecration to Mary

O Immaculate Virgin, my Mother, Mary, I renew this day and forever the consecration of all my being to You, so that You may dispose of me for the good of souls. My Queen and Mother of the Church, I only ask You to co-operate faithfully in Your mission for the coming of the kingdom of Jesus in the world. For the following intention, O Immaculate Heart of Mary I offer you, the prayers, actions and sacrifices of today:

(We express the particular intention of the month)

O Mary, conceived without sin, pray for us who have recourse to You, and also those for all who do not seek Your help, in particular for the enemies of the holy Church.

ACT OF CONSECRATION TO THE IMMACULATE HEART OF THE VIRGIN MARY

This consecration is recited by Sr. Lucia of Jesus, the Carmelite sister who is one of the three visionaries of Fatima.

O Virgin and Mother, with confidence in your Immaculate Heart, I consecrate myself entirely to you and, through you, to the Lord, with your own words:

Behold the handmaid of the Lord, be it done unto me according to your word, your will, and your glory.

ACT OF DEVOTION TO MARY

Mary, Mother of Jesus and my Mother, on this day, I, your little child, consecrate myself totally to you, in order that I may live a holy life and be your little servant, so that you, sweet Mother, may always be able to rely on me, and so that I may help you to fulfil in me the plan of love which the Father has for each one of us.

Give me, O Mother of Jesus and my Mother, the grace to be always faithful to the Church and to the Holy Father and, in union with you, to love and adore the Lord Jesus. **Amen.**

CONSECRATION TO JESUS CHRIST, INCARNATE WISDOM, THROUGH MARY
(Formula of St. Louis De Montfort)

Eternal and Incarnate Wisdom, most lovable and adorable Jesus, true God and true man, only Son of the eternal Father and of Mary always virgin, I adore you profoundly, dwelling in the splendour of your Father from all eternity and in the virginal womb of Mary, your most worthy Mother, at the time of your Incarnation.

I thank you for having emptied yourself in assuming the condition of a slave to set me free from the cruel slavery of the evil one.

I praise and glorify you for having willingly chosen to obey Mary, your holy Mother, in all things, so that through her I may be your faithful slave of love.

But I must confess that I have not kept the vows and promises which I made to you so solemnly at my baptism. I have not fulfilled my obligations, and I do not deserve to be called your child or even your loving slave.

Since I cannot lay claim to anything except what merits your rejection and displeasure, I dare no longer approach the holiness of your majesty on my own. That is why I turn to the intercession and the mercy of your holy Mother, whom you yourself have given me to mediate with you.

Through her I hope to obtain from you contrition and pardon for my sins, and that Wisdom whom I desire to dwell in me always.

I turn to you, then, Mary immaculate, living tabernacle of God. The eternal Wisdom, hidden in you, willed to receive the adoration of both men and angels.

I greet you as Queen of heaven and earth. All that is under God has been made subject to your sovereignty.

I call upon you as the unfailing refuge of sinners. In your mercy you have never forsaken anyone.

I... (*Here we mention our name*), an unfaithful sinner, renew and ratify today through you my baptismal promises. I renounce for ever Satan, his empty promises and his evil designs, and I give myself completely to Jesus Christ, the Incarnate Wisdom, to carry my cross after him for the rest of my life, and to be more faithful to him than I have been till now.

This day, with the whole court of heaven as witness, I choose you, Mary, as my Mother and Queen. I surrender and consecrate myself to you, body and soul, with all that I possess, both spiritual and material, even including the spiritual value of all my actions, past, present, and to come. I give you the full right to dispose of me and all that belongs to me, without any reservations, in whatever way you please, for the greater glory of God in time and throughout eternity.

FINAL PLEA

Accept, gracious Virgin, this little offering of my slavery to honour and imitate that obedience which the eternal Wisdom willingly chose to have towards you, his Mother. I wish to acknowledge the authority which both of you have over this little worm and pitiful sinner. By it I wish also to thank God for the privileges bestowed on you by the Blessed Trinity. I solemnly declare that for the future I will try to honour and obey you in all things as your true slave of love.

O admirable Mother, present me to your dear Son as his slave now and for always, so that he who redeemed me through you, will now receive me through you.

Mother of mercy, grant me the favour of obtaining the true Wisdom of God, and so make me one of those whom you love, teach and guide, whom you nourish and protect as our children and slaves.

Virgin most faithful, make me in everything so committed a disciple, imitator, and slave of Jesus, so that by your intercession and example, I may become fully mature with the fullness which Jesus possessed on earth, and with the fullness of his glory in heaven. **Amen.**

ACT OF CONSECRATION OF THE YOUTH TO THE VIRGIN MARY

O Virgin of Fatima,
Mother of mine whom I love so much,
I consecrate myself today in a special way
to your Immaculate Heart.
Through this solemn act
I offer you all my life,
my heart, my soul, my body,
and above all this period of my youth
that I am living.
Guide me along the path
that Jesus has shown us:
the path of love, goodness and holiness.
Help me to avoid sin, evil and
selfishness, and to reject all temptations
towards violence, impurity and drugs.
I promise you to go often to confession
and to receive Jesus into my heart
as the spiritual food of life,
to observe the commandments of God,
to walk along the road of love and purity,
and to recite the Holy Rosary every day.
I want to be a witness of unity
and to have a great love of
the Pope, the bishops and all priests.
I love you, my most sweet Mother,
and I offer you my youth for the triumph
of your Immaculate Heart in the world.

CONSECRATION TO THE "PILGRIM" VIRGIN MARY OF GRACES

Immaculate Virgin Mary, mother of God and Queen of the universe, consoler of the afflicted and comforter of the sick, you who crushed the head of the evil serpent, keep far from my soul every diabolic influence.

Free my family from every physical and moral evil; do not allow Satan to enter into my house to create confusion or to break up my family.

O Mary, you overcome infernal power; I take refuge under your motherly mantle; grant me the grace that I humbly ask of you ...

(Here we mention our specific request)

Immaculate Virgin, full of grace, help of Christians, never cease to protect and bless all those who ask your help in times of trial. Be sweet and gracious towards me, O Blessed Virgin Mary. **Amen.**

Hail Mary

PRAYER OF CONSECRATION TO OUR LADY AND ST. JOSEPH

As God the Father, in his infinite wisdom and abundant love, entrusted you, Mary, and you, St. Joseph, with the care of his only Son Jesus Christ while he lived here on earth, spouses of the Holy family of Nazareth, so do we, too, having become children of God through baptism, commend and consecrate ourselves to you with humble faith.

Look after us, our children and our families with the same care and tenderness with which you looked after Jesus.

Help us to know, love and serve Jesus as you knew, loved and served Him.

Grant that we may love you with the same love with which Jesus loved you here on earth.

Protect us.

Defend us from all danger and evil.

Help our faith to grow.

Keep us faithful to our vocation and our mission in the church. Make us holy.

At the end of this life, take us with you to Paradise where you already reign with Christ in eternal glory. **Amen.**

CONSECRATION OF THE FAMILY TO THE IMMACULATE HEART OF MARY

Mary, Mother of God and our Mother, our family gathered here today consecrates itself to you, so that we may pray together in our home in the presence of the sacred image of your Immaculate Heart, under your motherly protection, in times of joy and in times of sorrow, and with your spirit, which is the model of every virtue that should be found in the family.

May order and harmony reign in this family as in the Holy Family of Nazareth; may there be honesty in our hearts and in our social life, in accordance with the laws of God; may we all fulfil our duties with generous faithfulness; may our love for each other manifest itself ever more, even to the point of sacrificing our personal tastes and comforts; may we show Christian reverence in the practice of our faith and in the observance of the precepts of the Church.

May your motherly heart which mediates all graces, impart to us that heavenly life which allows us to enjoy peace here on earth and to be reunited with all members of our family in Paradise.

May our prayer unite us to that which gushes forth continuously from your most pure Heart, which is so close to that of Jesus Christ, your Son.

Through our consecration to your Immaculate Heart, we promise you to live in such a way that our family may never offend you, that it may make amends for the insults that many people hurl at you, and that it may always be faithful to its commitments.

Take possession of this family which desires become a little kingdom where your Heart and the Heart of Jesus reign.

ACT OF CONSECRATION OF OUR LIFE
TO CHRIST THROUGH MARY

*So that the church may become the fount
of new life for humankind.*

Mother, you are the Mother of Christ and the Mother of Holy Communion which your Son gives us as a gift always new and powerful; the taste of a new life. Through you, we consecrate ourselves and our lives entirely to Christ, along with all the sufferings that your Child permits us to encounter today, so that you may become the Mother of our life and Christ may give to all men and women the same taste of new life that he has given to us. **Amen.**

Consecration of the Sick
to Our Lady

O Virgin Mary, Mother of God and my Mother, who were present at the crucifixion and death of your Son Jesus on the hill of Calvary, have mercy on this poor suffering body of mine and, through the merits of your sorrows, grant me relief and comfort.

I consecrate myself to you, together with all my sorrows and sufferings.

Hail Mary

O Virgin Mary, Mother of God and my Mother, who witnessed many sick people being healed by the sacred hand of your Son Jesus, grant me faith in His merciful omnipotence, so that if it be His will, he may give me the gift of health and serenity.

I consecrate myself to you, together with all my sorrows and sufferings.

Hail Mary

O Virgin Mary, Mother of God and my Mother, who saw your innocent Son suffer great sorrow for my sins, help me to bear with patience these sufferings of mine: in atonement for my sins, for the purification and sanctification of my soul, for the conversion of sinners, for peace in the world and for the benefit of all the Church.

I consecrate myself to you, together with all my sorrows and sufferings.

Hail Mary

CONSECRATION TO THE IMMACULATE HEART OF MARY
by Pope John Paul II

Immaculate Virgin Mary, Mother of God and Mother of the Church, we consecrate to you, who try to come ever closer to us, all of our being and all our love. We also consecrate to you our life, our work, our joys and our sorrows. We entrust all that we have and all that we are to your care, Our Lady and Mother. Teach us to go continually to Jesus, and if we fall, help us to come back to Him by confessing our sins in the Sacrament of Reconciliation which gives peace to the soul. Hold us always lovingly by your hand.

7.
NOVENAS

# NOVENAS

From the 15th of January to the 2nd of March, 1933, the Virgin Mary appeared eight times to Marietta Becom in the little village of Banneux in Belgium. During the third ap-parition, the child, who was twelve years old, asked the Virgin Mary who she was, and Mary answered:
"I am the Virgin of the Poor".

In the spring of 1945, Cardinal Ildefonso Schuster, Archbishop of Milan, who came to visit the houses of the poor in the outskirts of the town, said to the faithful, "When the new parish church will be established here, it shall be dedicated to the Virgin Mary of the Poor".

This came to the knowledge of a humble Belgian miner who suggested to some Italian miners, who were his companions at work, to offer a statue of the Virgin Mary to the new church.

Cardinal Schuster blessed the first stone of the Temple of Our Lady of the Poor, and Archbishop Montini, who later became Pope Paul VI, blessed and opened the new Church on the 13th of May, 1955.

The "blessing of the sick" takes place twice a year in the Square of Our Lady of the Poor in Milan on the second Sunday of May and of October and is a sign of the Virgin's blessing of her needy children.

NOVENA TO OUR LADY OF THE POOR

(To be made from the 6th to the 14th of January)

*IIn the name of the Father, and of the Son,
and of the Holy Spirit. Amen.*

O God, come to my aid.
O Lord, make haste to help me.
Glory Be
The Creed *(see page 26)*

Our Lady of the Poor, fount of our joy, lead us to Jesus. Source of grace, grant that we may submit ourselves to the inspirations of the Holy Spirit so that the fire of love, which He came to bring to earth for the coming of the Kingdom, may burn in our hearts and in our world.

Hail Mary

Our Lady of the Poor, Queen of the world, save all nations: grant that we may have wise governors and grant that all peoples may be at peace and in harmony with each other, to form one sheepfold under one shepherd.

Hail Mary

Our Lady of the Poor, comforter of the afflicted, grant healing to all those who suffer; sustain all those who serve them out of love; grant us the grace of belonging only to Christ, and deliver us from all danger.

Hail Mary

Our Lady of the Poor, Health of the sick, with your presence, comfort those who are ill; teach us to carry our daily cross in union with Jesus, and grant that we may work faithfully to serve the poor and those who suffer.

Hail Mary

Our Lady of the Poor, help of Christians, intercede with your Son, and grant us all the graces necessary for our salvation and for the salvation of our families, of those who commend themselves to our prayers and of all humanity.

Hail Mary

Our Lady of the Poor, Mother of the Church, we believe in you, we trust in your motherly intercession and we abandon ourselves to your protection.

We entrust to you the journey of the Church in the third millenium, the moral and spiritual growth of the youth, the need for vocations to the priesthood, to religious and missionary life, and all the work of re-evangelization.

Hail Mary

Our Lady of the Poor, Queen of confessors of the faith, who said, "Believe in me and I will believe in you", we thank you because you trust in us. Render us capable of making choices which are in conformity with the Gospel, help us to use our freedom in the service of others and in the love of Christ, for the glory of the Father.

Hail Mary

Our Lady of the Poor, Glory of the Holy Spirit, fill us with graces, give us your blessing as you did to the young girl of Banneux by laying your hands on her head, and transform our lives. Grant that no one may allow himself to be a slave to sin but that we may be consecrated to Christ, the only Lord.

Hail Mary

Our Lady of the Poor, Mother of the Saviour, Mother of God, we thank you for your obedience to the will of God, the merit of which was the gift made to us of our Redeemer. We thank you because you listen to our invocations and present them to Jesus, the only mediator. Teach us to give thanks to the Father in all the circumstances of our lives and grant that the Eucharist, the food of eternal life, may bear fruit in our lives.

Hail Mary

PRAYER TO OUR LADY OF BANNEUX

Our Lady of Banneux,
Mother of the Saviour,
Mother of God,
Our Lady of the Poor,
you promised us:
"Believe in me, I will believe in you",
and therefore I place all my trust in you.

Listen to the prayers which we make to you,
have mercy on all our spiritual and material
poverty.
Give back to sinners the treasures of the faith
and give to the poor their daily bread.

Heal the sick,
attenuate all suffering,
intercede for us
so that the Kingdom of God
may extend to all nations.
Amen.

Novena to Our Lady of Lourdes
(To be made from the 2nd to the 10th of February).

Whatever the circumstances, even if they appear to be hopeless, this novena imparts particular graces of strength and peace, both for those who make it and those for whom we pray. It is suggested to recite the Litany to Our Lady of Lourdes before each prayer of the Novena (See Part Six, Chapter Two). The recitation of the Novena prayers is to be accompanied by resolutions to do a good deed or to demonstrate our devotion in some other concrete way, and therefore a proposal is given below for each particular day.

In the name of the Father, and of the Son, and of the Holy Spirit. Amen.

O God, come to my aid.
O Lord, make haste to help me.
Glory Be • The Creed *(see page 26)*

First Day

Our Lady of Lourdes, Immaculate Virgin, pray for us. Our Lady of Lourdes, here I am at your feet to ask for this grace... *(We express our intention)* My trust in your power of intercession is unshakable. You can obtain everything from your Divine Son.

LET US RESOLVE TO:
Make an act of reconciliation towards a hostile person or towards a person with whom we find communication difficult.

Hail Mary *(3 times)*
Our Lady of Lourdes,
pray for us.

**Blessed be the Holy and Immaculate Conception
of the most Blessed Virgin Mary, Mother of God.**

SECOND DAY

Our Lady of Lourdes, who chose a poor and
weak girl to be an interpreter for you, pray for us.
Our Lady of Lourdes, help me to use all means in
order to become more humble and to trust more
in God. I know that, in this way, I can please you
and obtain your assistance.

LET US RESOLVE TO:
*Choose a date to make our confession, and to keep to our
commitment.*

Hail Mary *(3 times)*

Our Lady of Lourdes,
pray for us.

**Blessed be the Holy and Immaculate Conception
of the most Blessed Virgin Mary, Mother of God.**

THIRD DAY

Our Lady of Lourdes, blessed eighteen times in
your apparitions, pray for us.
Our Lady of Lourdes, listen to my pleas. Grant
what I ask if it may give glory to God and serve
for the salvation of souls.

LET US RESOLVE TO:

Visit the Blessed Sacrament in a church.
Commend our relatives, friends and difficult relationships
to Christ in prayer, not forgetting those who are deceased.

Hail Mary *(3 times)*

Our Lady of Lourdes,
pray for us.

**Blessed be the Holy and Immaculate Conception
of the most Blessed Virgin Mary, Mother of God.**

FOURTH DAY

Our Lady of Lourdes, to whom Jesus can refuse nothing, pray for us. Our Lady of Lourdes, intercede for me with your Divine Son. Draw abundantly from the treasures of his Heart and give them to those who pray at your feet.

LET US RESOLVE TO:

Recite the Rosary today and to meditate upon it.
Hail Mary *(3 times)*

Our Lady of Lourdes,
pray for us.

**Blessed be the Holy and Immaculate Conception
of the most Blessed Virgin Mary, Mother of God.**

Fifth Day

Our Lady of Lourdes, whom no one has ever invoked in vain, pray for us. Our Lady of Lourdes, if it be your will, let no one who invokes you this day be left without having experienced the effect of your powerful intercession.

LET US RESOLVE TO:

Practise some fasting, denying ourselves of something at lunch or dinner, in reparation for our sins and also for the intentions of those who are making or will make this novena to Our Lady.

Hail Mary *(3 times)*

Our Lady of Lourdes,
pray for us.

Blessed be the Holy and Immaculate Conception of the most Blessed Virgin Mary, Mother of God.

Sixth Day

Our Lady of Lourdes, Health of the sick, pray for us. Our Lady of Lourdes, intercede for the health of the sick people whom we commend to you. Grant that their strength may increase and, if it be God's will, may they make a complete recovery.

LET US RESOLVE TO:

Recite with all our heart an act of consecration to the Virgin Mary. (See Part Six, Chapter Six).

Hail Mary *(3 times)*

Our Lady of Lourdes,
pray for us.

Blessed be the Holy and Immaculate Conception of the most Blessed Virgin Mary, Mother of God.

SEVENTH DAY

Our Lady of Lourdes, who pray ceaselessly for sinners, pray for us. Our Lady of Lourdes, who guided Bernadette to holiness, grant that I may be filled with that Christian zeal which does not wane in the face of danger, so that peace and love may reign ever more among all people.

LET US RESOLVE TO:
Visit a sick or lonely person.

Hail Mary *(3 times)*

Our Lady of Lourdes,
pray for us.

Blessed be the Holy and Immaculate Conception of the most Blessed Virgin Mary, Mother of God.

Eighth Day

Our Lady of Lourdes, motherly support of all the Church, pray for us. Our Lady of Lourdes, protect our Pope and our bishop. Bless all the clergy and in particular the priests who make you known and loved. Remember all the priests who have gone from this world, having passed on to us the life of the soul.

LET US RESOLVE TO:
Have Mass said for the holy souls of Purgatory and to receive Holy Communion with this intention.

Hail Mary *(3 times)*

Our Lady of Lourdes,
pray for us

Blessed be the Holy and Immaculate Conception of the most Blessed Virgin Mary, Mother of God.

NINTH DAY

Our Lady of Lourdes, hope and consolation of pilgrims, pray for us. Our Lady of Lourdes, having come to the end of this novena, I want to thank you already for the graces you have given me throughout these days, and for those which you will grant me. In order to accept them and to thank you in a more honourable way, I promise to pray to you as often as possible in one of your sanctuaries.

LET US RESOLVE TO:

Go on pilgrimage once a year to a Marian sanctuary, even to one very close to home, or to participate in a spiritual retreat.

Hail Mary *(3 times)*

Our Lady of Lourdes,
pray for us.

Blessed be the Holy and Immaculate Conception of the most Blessed Virgin Mary, Mother of God.

NOVENA TO THE BLESSED
VIRGIN MARY OF MIRACLES

(This novena is be made from the 28th of February to the 8th of March; ideally, the prayers are recited in a place of Marian devotion or pilgrimage).

In the name of the Father, and of the Son, and of the Holy Spirit. Amen.

O God, come to my aid.
O Lord, make haste to help me.
Glory Be
The Creed *(see page 26)*

Our Lady of Miracles and my Mother Mary, You revealed Yourself as being so good as to honour with your presence this place which You have chosen to be a centre of devoted pilgrimage and a source of graces and blessings. Grant that I, too, may enjoy these wonderful benefits and may obtain in particular that grace for which I pray to You this day with all my heart.

Hail Mary

Our Lady of Miracles and my Mother Mary, You have chosen a simple and honest people, to carry out your will, and thus teach me that humility is necessary to obtain your graces and favours. Grant that I, too, may render my heart simple and humble and therefore obtain from you that grace for which I pray to You today.

Hail Mary

Our Lady of Miracles and my Mother Mary, who accepted and rewarded the faith and love of our fathers who built this Church for You, and showed Yourself to be generous to them by granting every grace and benefit, look at my faith and my love for You and show your endless generosity by granting me the grace for which I now pray to You.

Hail Holy Queen

NOVENA TO THE BLESSED
VIRGIN MARY OF REVELATION
(To be made from the 3rd to the 11th of April).

It was a Saturday afternoon in Spring, the 12th of April, 1947, to be precise.

Bruno Cornacchiola, *a Roman tram driver of 34 years of age, a protestant, was making notes under the shadow of an eucalyptus tree in Via Lauretana, Rome, for a lecture which he was to give on the following day.*

He had been born of parents who lived in miserable conditions in one of the poorest and most disreputable districts of the capital.

During his stay in Spain, where he went to fight in the civil war (1936-1937), he had been persuaded by the words of a German protestant soldier to enter into the Adventist Church and became a great enemy of the Catholic Church, of the Virgin Mary and of the Pope.

While his three children, Gianfranco, Carlo and Isola, four, seven and ten years of age, respectively, were playing ball. Cornacchiola was searching a Protestant Bible for proofs which he was to use in a lecture that he was to give, part of which consisted in arguments against dogmas concerning the Virgin Mary. The Mother of God intervened, however, providing an answer for those who, for years, have wanted only to offend Her.

His children lost their ball and, unable to find it, they called on the help of their father.

Bruno stopped making his notes, put his notebook on the ground under the eucalyptus tree and ran to help his children. His notebook remained on the ground.

In fact, he was to need it no more; he never even gave his lecture, for the Virgin Mary was to convert him in a little grotto nearby and change him into a faithful servant, a precious instrument of evangelization.

It was about half-past three in the afternoon.

The "wonderful lady" appeared first to the children; she was standing upon a stone in a small grotto. Then, preceded by a great perfume of flowers, She appeared to Bruno, the man who, until that moment, was opposed to devotion to the Mother of our Redeemer.

The Virgin Mary was clothed in a long and splendid white dress, girded at the waist by a rose-coloured sash, and was wearing a white mantle which covered Her dark hair and extended to Her bare feet. The Holy Mother of God adressed Her persecutor with the following words:

"I am the One who is in the Divine Trinity - I am the Virgin of Revelation - you are persecuting me. Stop now! Enter into the holy sheepfold, the heavenly court on earth. Obey the authority of the Pope".

In her hands the Virgin Mary held a book with a grey cover; it was the book which contained Divine Revelation, the Holy Bible, and She proceeded to talk at length with Bruno on that eventful afternoon in April.

Then, having spoken among other things about her Assumption to Heaven **("My body could not decay and did not decay")**, She explained to the visionary in what way, in the future, he would be able to recognise the two priests who were to help him to reconcile himself with God and the Pope (whom he had previously wanted to kill with a dagger).

The following is one of the promises made by the Virgin Mary to Bruno:

"On this earth of sin I will do powerful miracles for the conversion of unbelievers".

And indeed, the earth of the Grotto of the Three Fountains, has been sanctified by the presence of Mary, as was the water of Lourdes and has become the means of many miracles.

Our intention for this novena:

That men and women may feel the desire for God, (or any other grace we wish to obtain)

*In the name of the Father, and of the Son,
and of the Holy Spirit. Amen.*

O God, come to my aid.
O Lord, make haste to help me.
Glory Be
The Creed *(see page 26)*

Most Holy Virgin of Revelation who dwell in
the Divine Trinity, graciously turn your eyes of
mercy and kindness towards us. Mary, who are
our powerful advocate with God, who, on this
sinful earth, obtain graces and cause miracles to
happen for the conversion of unbelievers and sinners, grant that we may obtain from your Son
Jesus, along with the salvation of our souls, perfect bodily health and the graces that we need.
Grant the Church and its Head, the Roman Pontiff, the joy of seeing the conversion of her enemies, the propagation of the kingdom of God on
all the earth, the unity of all believers in Christ
and peace among nations, so that we may love
you more and serve you better in this life, and
thus deserve to see and thank you eternally in
Heaven. **Amen.**

Hail Mary *(3 times)*
Hail Holy Queen

NOVENA TO THE BLESSED VIRGIN MARY OF POMPEII

(To be made from the 29th of April to the 7th of May).

In the name of the Father, and of the Son, and of the Holy Spirit. Amen.

Before beginning the novena, let us pray to St. Catherine of Siena so that she may recite it together with us; therefore, we say:

O Saint Catherine of Siena, my protector and teacher, assist me and unite yourself with me in this novena to the Queen of the Rosary, who placed the throne of Her graces in the Valley of Pompei; through your intercession, grant that I may obtain the grace I desire. Amen.

O God, come to my aid.
O Lord, make haste to help me.
Glory Be
The Creed *(see page 26)*

Immaculate Virgin, Queen of the Rosary, in these times of dying faith and the triumph of emptiness You wished to place your seat of Queen and Mother on the ancient land of Pompeii. From that place, where idols and demons were once worshipped, You, the Mother of Divine Grace, distribute today the treasures of heavenly mercy. From that throne where You reign with compassion, turn Your eyes upon me, O Mother, and have mercy: I have so much need of Your help. Show Yourself to be to me, as to many others, the true Mother of Mercy: "Mostra te esse Matrem"; while with all my heart I greet and invoke You as Sovereign and Queen.

Hail Holy Queen

At the foot of Your throne, glorious Lady, my soul, venerates You, while afflicted by sorrows and cares... In these troubles and worries, sadness and agitation in which I find myself, I raise my eyes with confidence to You, who chose as Your dwelling place the lands of poor and abandoned peasants. There, You, as Queen of Victories, raised your powerful voice to call Your devoted children from every part of Italy and from all the world to build a temple for You. Have mercy on them: You who are the help of Christians, free me from the trials in which I find myself, You who are our life, triumph over the death which menaces my soul in these dangers to which it is exposed; give me back peace, tranquillity, love and health.

Hail Holy Queen

Having heard that many have been blessed with benefits by You because they have appealed to You with faith, I have the courage to invoke

Your help. You promised St. Dominic that those who seek graces can obtain them through Your Rosary; and with the Rosary in my hands, I call upon You, Mother, to fulfil Your motherly promises. You Yourself continue to perform great wonders in order to call your children to honour You in the Temple of Pompeii. You wish to dry our tears, You want to calm our fears! With all my heart I call and invoke You: Mother, dear Mother, beautiful Mother, most sweet Mother, help me! Mother and Queen of the Holy Rosary of Pompeii, hasten to stretch out your hand to save me: any delay in Your help could bring me to ruin.

Hail Holy Queen

To whom should I turn, if not to You, who are the relief of the poor, comfort of the aban-doned, consolation of the afflicted? I confess that I am not worthy to receive graces, but You are the Hope of those who despair, the great Mediatrix between God and humankind, our powerful Advocate before the throne of the Most High, and Refuge of sinners! Say a word in my favour to Your Son, and He shall listen to You. Ask of Him, O Mother, this grace of which I am so much in need... You can obtain it for me: You, my Hope, my Consolation, my Sweetness, my Life. Thus, I hope that You shall grant it to me; let it be so.

Hail Holy Queen

Virgin and Queen of the Holy Rosary, Daughter of the Heavenly Father, Mother of the Divine Son, Spouse of the Holy Spirit, You who can obtain all things from the Holy Trinity, implore this grace which I need, but only if it is not an obstacle to my eternal salvation... I ask it for the sake of your Immaculate Conception, your Divine Maternity, your joys, your sorrows, and your triumphs: I ask for it through the Heart of Your Son Jesus, for the sake of those nine months that you carried him in Your womb, through His death on the cross, through His most Holy Name, and through His most precious Blood. I ask this grace of You through Your sweet Heart, in Your glorious Name, O Mary, Star of the Sea, powerful Lady, Mother of Sorrows, Gate of Heaven, Mother of every grace. I trust in You, I put all my hope in you. You must save me. **Amen.**

Hail Holy Queen

Novena to Our Lady, Help of Christians

As recited by St. John Bosco
(To be made from the 15th to the 23rd of May).

• *We recite the following prayers before the Blessed Sacrament for nine days:*
Our Father • Hail Mary • Glory Be *(3 times)*

O Sacrament most holy, O Sacrament divine,
All praise and all thanksgiving
Be every moment thine. *(3 times)*

Hail Holy Queen *(3 times)*

Mary, Help of Christians,
pray for us. *(3 times)*

• *During the Novena we go to Confession and receive Holy Communion.*
• *We give a donation or do some work in order to sustain a charity or apostolate, preferably one which supports the youth.*
• *We seek to renew our faith in the Blessed Eucharist and our devotion to Our Lady, Help of Christians.*

Let us pray.
O Mary, powerful Virgin: you, great and illustrious defence of the Church; you, wonderful help of Christians; you, terrible as those in line for battle; you, who alone destroyed all the heresies of the world; in our sorrows, conflicts and necessities defend us from the enemy, and at the hour of our death welcome us into Paradise. **Amen.**

NOVENA TO THE BLESSED
VIRGIN MARY OF CARAVAGGIO

(Caravaggio was an Italian painter of the nineteenth century, who depicted the Blessed Virgin Mary in many works of art. His novena is to be made from the 17th to the 25th of May).

In the name of the Father, and of the Son, and of the Holy Spirit. Amen.

O God come to my aid.
O Lord, make haste to help me.
Glory Be
The Creed *(see page 26)*

O Most Holy Virgin of Caravaggio, inexhaustible source of graces, honoured from ancient times, in these special days of the Novena, we pray to you so that the expectations of all those who approach you may not be disappointed and no one's plea may be made vain.

Our Lady of Caravaggio,
pray for us.
Hail Mary

O Most Holy Virgin of Caravaggio, in whose sanctuary and by whose patronage the blind return to the light of faith, grant that wavering and indolent souls may learn to walk swiftly along the path of the Divine Commandments, may ears that are deaf open to the teachings of God and may those who are dead because of their sins come back to true life to be enlight-ened and to find peace of heart.

Our Lady of Caravaggio,
pray for us.
Hail Mary

O Mary, our Heavenly Patron, grant that those who come to you imploring your assistance may grow stronger in faith and more steadfast in hope, and thus become so ardent with love that, no longer seeking the pleasures of this world, they may never stray from the path of goodness. O clement, O loving, O sweet Virgin Mary.

Our Lady of Caravaggio,
pray for us.
Hail Mary

(We pause for a moment of silence to express our special intention for this Novena).

Let us pray.
Lord Jesus Christ, who, to honour your Mother chose and sanctified this place in a particular way, look upon and listen to all those who pray to you here: the great love of your Mother and our Mother entrusts them to your care.
You who live and reign for ever and ever. **Amen.**

We fly to your patronage *(see pag. 818)*

FEAST OF OUR LADY OF MOUNT CARMEL

(16th of July)

On Sunday, the 17th of February, 1980, Pope John Paul II visited the Roman parish of St. Martin of the Mountains, entrusted to the Carmelites since 1299. During the meeting with the Pastoral Council, the Pope took into his hand the Scapular of the prioress of the Third Order of the Carmelites and with delight and pleasure on his face, put his hands on his breast and exclaimed, "I, too, have worn it for a long time!", emphasizing the last words "for a long time".

During the meeting with the Carmelites, the superior of the community greeted the Pope with a short complimentary address of thanksgiving, concluding with the following words: "May Our Lady of Mount Carmel, who is greatly loved also by your Holiness as we know, sustain you in guiding the Church in these times".

The Scapular of Our Lady of Mount Carmel

The Scapular of Our Lady of Mount Carmel is the "habit" of the Carmelites. By wearing the Scapular, we are permitted to belong to the Family of Carmel. The Scapular is also called "Little Habit" because it reproduces in small dimensions the habit of the Order. Wearing the Scapular of Carmel is one of the most beloved devotions among the people of God. To wear the "little habit" means to consecrate oneself to Mary; to be acknowledged as being one of her beloved children. By responding to the love of the Virgin Mary, her faithful live in the certainty of her protection amid the dangers of life, and are assured that even after death, "She will take care of the brothers and sisters of her Son with her maternal love, interceding for them.. until they reach the blessed homeland" (ref Lumen Gentium, 62). Indeed, Pope John Paul II tells us that Our Lady of Mount

Carmel can also guide souls who find themselves in Purgatory after death. The aggregate members of the Carmelite family become familiar with Mary, and this familiarity assumes a community and ecclesial character because Mary "helps all her children, wherever and in whatever way they may live, to find in Christ the way towards the house of the Father" (RM 47).

The Scapular is the little "sign" of the great ideal of Carmel: namely, friendship and intimacy with God. It consists of two pieces of brown fabric linked by a little cord or ribbon. It is normally worn around the neck. In many scapulars the image of the Virgin Mary is commonly found on the brown fabric, as is that of the Sacred Heart.

The Scapular and Christian commitment

Wearing the Scapular, which can be described as the synthesis of the Carmelite habit, is a sign of being associated to the Carmelite family and of enjoying its benefits, in particular the fruits of sharing the Carmelite spirituality (typically Marian) and enjoying the protection of Mary throughout our lives, at the hour of our death and even after death.

A decree was issued by Pope Paul V in 1613 stating the importance of wearing this scapular: "It is permitted to preach that the Blessed Virgin shall help, by her continued assistance and her merits, particularly on Saturdays, the souls of the members of the Scapular Confraternity who have died in the grace of God, if in life they have worn the scapular, observed chastity according to their state of life, and recited the Office of the Blessed Virgin Mary".

In daily life the commitment of those who associate themselves to the Carmelite family by wearing the scapular are as follows:

• They live as "brothers" or "sisters" of Mary in communion with Carmel, seeking to deepen their spiritual life and ideals;

- They give Mary ever more space in their lives, by trying to live in faithfulness to Christ with the spirit of Mary in whatever situation they may find themselves;
- They imitate the prayerful Virgin who "kept the word of God in her heart" (Lk 2: 19.51), dedicating time to meeting God in prayer;
- They practise chastity of body and soul, heart and senses, in accordance with their status and the evangelical requirements of their vocation, be it marital or celibate;
- Mary is invoked as the "Beauty of Carmel". All nature, esteemed and respected, thus sings with joy the praises of her Creator, following the path of Beauty, and devotion to Mary reveals itself once more as "a powerful help for the person who is on his way to the conquest of his fullness" (MC, 56).

Practical suggestions

The blessing and consignment of the Scapular may be carried out by all priests and deacons of the Carmelite family, or by any priest or deacon who has received permission from a superior of the Order. The Scapular can be substituted with the "Scapular Medal" which has the image of the Sacred Heart on one side and that of the Virgin Mary on the other. Both the Scapular and the Medal can be changed without a new blessing.

Those who wear it must always be devoted to Mary and bear witness by living a good Christian life. They must also dedicate some time every day to meeting God in prayer and, if possible, they should endeavour to receive Holy Communion frequently.

Requirements of this devotion are:
- To receive the imposition of the scapular and to wear it habitually. (The imposition is done with a scapular of wool. Afterwards a scapular medal may be worn).
- To guard one's chastity.

- To pray daily the Little Office of the Blessed Virgin. It may be substituted by:
- daily recitation of the Divine Office;

or:

- the recitation of the third part of the Rosary;

or:

- a brief period of "Lectio Divina" (meditation of Scripture);

or:

- the recitation of three Hail Marys;

or:

- the recitation of 7 Our Fathers, Hail Marys and Glory Bes.
- It is also suggested to pray to Mary in a particular way on Saturday, the day of the week specially dedicated to her.
- It is important to remember the annual solemn feast of Our Lady of Mount Carmel on the 16th of July.
- A certificate which reminds us of our consecration to Mary may be obtained and carried on our person.
- Commitment to the devotion of the Scapular may be communicated to:

OUR LADY OF MOUNT CARMEL
Viale Monte Oppio, 28 - 00184 ROME, Italy

• Finally, before going to sleep, one of the following prayers to Mary is to be recited:

Flower of Carmel, vine with blossom weighed, Shining light of heaven, bearing Child though maid, None like to thee. Mother most tender, whom no man didst know, On all Carmel's children thy favour bestow, Star of the sea.

Flos Carmeli (Traditional)

or:

We fly to your patronage *(see pag. 818)*

Rite for the blessing and presentation of the scapular of Mount Carmel

In the name of the Father, and of the Son, and of the Holy Spirit. Amen.

O God come to my aid.
O Lord, make haste to help me.
Glory Be
The Creed *(see page 26)*

The person who is to receive the scapular kneels, and the priest, vested in surplice and white stole, says:

V. Lord, show us your kindness and mercy.
R. And grant us your salvation.
V. Lord, hear my prayer.
R. And let my cry come to you.
V. The Lord be with you.
R. And also with you.

Let us pray.
O Lord Jesus Christ, Saviour of humankind, by your right hand sanctify this scapular, which your servant will devotedly wear for the love of you and of your mother, the Blessed Virgin Mary of Mount Carmel. By her intercession, may he (she) be protected from the wickedness of the enemy and persevere in your grace until death. You who live and reign for ever and ever.
R. Amen.

Then the priest sprinkles the scapular with holy water and imposes it upon the person (or upon each person), saying:

Receive this blessed scapular and ask the most holy Virgin that, by her merits, it may be worn with no stain of sin and may protect you from all harm and bring you into everlasting life.

R. Amen.

After this the priest adds:

By the power granted to me, I admit you to a share in all the spiritual works performed with the merciful help of Jesus Christ by the religious of Mount Carmel. In the name of the Father, and of the Son, and of the Holy Spirit.

R. Amen.

May almighty God, Creator of heaven and earth, bless you, whom he has been pleased to receive into the Confraternity of the Blessed Virgin Mary of Mount Carmel. We beg her to crush the head of the ancient serpent in the hour of your death and to obtain for you the palm and the crown of your everlasting inheritance.

Through Christ our Lord.

R. Amen.

The priest sprinkles the person with holy water. For several persons, the prayers are said in the plural.
If the scapular is to be blessed alone, then the blessing begins with "Lord, show us your kindness and mercy..." and concludes with the prayer "O Lord Jesus Christ...".

Novena to our Lady
of Mount Carmel

(To be made from the 7th to the 15th of July).

*In the name of the Father, and of the Son,
and of the Holy Spirit. Amen.*

O God, come to my aid.
O Lord, make haste to help me.

Glory Be
The Creed *(see page 26)*

O Virgin Mary, who, in thousands of ways reveal your mission as mediatrix of all graces, and through the Holy Scapular delight in manifesting to the faithful your special motherly protection grant that by wearing this sign of predilection we may show ourselves to be your true children.

Hail Mary

Queen of Mount Carmel, who, through the sign of protection of the Holy Scapular, call us to modesty, sacrifices, prayer and consecration to your Immaculate Heart, grant that we may understand this language, in order that we may be an example to our brothers and sisters and may experience your powerful help.

Hail Mary

Mother of Mount Carmel, who promised your help in the face of all danger to all those who wear the Holy Scapular, in addition to the grace of being saved from hell and freed quickly from Purgatory, grant that we, too, may be among those who merit such favours and graces, so that we may come to praise and thank you in heaven.

Hail Mary

Prayer:
Virgin Mary, Mother and Queen of Mount Carmel, united in a wonderful way to the mystery of Redemption, you accepted and kept in your heart the Word of God and persevered in prayer with the Apostles while awaiting the coming of the Holy Spirit. In you, as in a perfect image, we see the fulfilment of all that we desire and all that we hope shall be realized in the Church. O Virgin Mary, mystical star of Mount Carmel, enlighten us and guide us in the way of perfect love; encourage us to contemplate the face of the Lord. Lovingly watch over us your children who wear your Holy Scapular, sign of your protection, and light up our way, so that we may reach the peak of the mountain that is Jesus Christ, your Son and our Lord.

Hail Holy Queen

NOVENA TO SS. JOACHIM AND ANNE, PARENTS OF THE BLESSED VIRGIN MARY

(To be made from the 17th to the 25th of July).

The Venerable Marina d'Escobar asked Pope Gregory XV for a liturgical feast to be established in honour of St. Joachim. The Virgin Mary appeared to her and said, "I come to you to thank you for the pleasure you gave me by establishing a feast in honour of my father. Be sure that God will greatly reward you, and I, for my part, will be generous towards you".

In the name of the Father, and of the Son, and of the Holy Spirit. Amen.

O God, come to my aid.
O Lord, make haste to help me.
Glory Be
The Creed *(see page 26)*

PRAYER TO ST. ANNE

Blessed are you, St. Anne for having among all mothers, had the Immaculate Virgin Mary as your daughter, the delight of God the Father; I admire the greatness of your vocation and the graces with which the Lord, the God of our fathers, adorned you. I unite myself to your most holy protection and consecrate all my life to Jesus and to the Immaculate Virgin Mary. Grant that I may live as you did, actively awaiting the Lord Jesus in an attitude of humble openess and gratitude, so that by allowing myself to be loved by Him and by loving my brothers and sisters, I may come one day to praise and bless Him in eternity. **Amen.**

St. Anne, Glorious Mother of Mary, through the unfailing patience with which you bore the sorrow of your sterility, obtain also for us the grace of continuous acceptance in the face of all trials of this life.

Glory Be
St. Anne, mother of the Mother of God,
pray for us.

St. Anne, Glorious Mother of Mary, through the fervent and ceaseless prayer with which you asked God to console you with the gift of fert-ility, obtain for us the true spirit of prayer, in order to allow holy virtues to grow in our heart.

Glory Be
St. Anne, mother of the Mother of God,
pray for us.

St. Anne, Glorious mother of Mary, through a life of rigorous sacrifice which you united to your prayers in order that you be heard more rea-dily by God, grant that the fervour of our prayers may be accompanied the spirit of sacrifice, in order that we may be made worthy of heavenly graces.

Glory Be
St. Anne, mother of the Mother of God,
pray for us.

St. Anne, Glorious Mother of Mary, through the gentle violence with which you moved the heart of God through your almsgiving and works of charity, grant us a charity similar to yours, so that He may have mercy on us.

Glory Be
St. Anne, mother of the Mother of God,
pray for us.

St. Anne, Glorious Mother of Mary, through the holy confidence with which you hoped for the fulfilment of your desires, obtain for us a steadfast trust, with which we may be sure to obtain favours from heaven.

Glory Be
St. Anne, mother of the Mother of God,
pray for us.

St. Anne, Glorious Mother of Mary, through the marvellous gratitude which you showed to God when you perceived that you had become a mother through his grace, grant that we may be always grateful to God for the favours which we continuously receive from Him in order that we may be worthy to receive further graces.

Glory Be
St. Anne, mother of the Mother of God,
pray for us.

St. Anne, Glorious Mother of Mary, through that pure and holy love that you nurtured for Mary when you received the great grace of becoming her mother, grant that we may always love this Daughter of yours, who is our Mother, so dear to us and so holy, in order to merit her protection.

Glory Be
St. Anne, mother of the Mother of God,
pray for us.

St. Anne, Glorious Mother of Mary, through the great sacrifice of offering your daughter from such a young age to divine service in the temple, grant that we, with holy courage, may offer as a sacrifice to God anything he wishes to ask of us, in order to obey his Holy Will and to obtain his blessings.

Glory Be
St. Anne, mother of the Mother of God,
pray for us.

St. Anne, Glorious Mother of Mary, through that fervent holiness with which you served God all the days of your life, deign to pray to the Lord that we may live as righteous and holy people unto the end of our days.

Glory Be
St. Anne, mother of the Mother of God,
pray for us.

Prayer to St. Joachim

O Great and glorious patriarch, St. Joachim, how glad I am to think that you were chosen among all saints to co-operate in the divine mysteries and to enrich the world with the Mother of God, most holy! By virtue of this particular privilege, your intercession with the Mother and the Son become most powerful in order to obtain for us the graces we need. Therefore, with confidence, I appeal to your protection and commend to you all my spiritual and material needs, together with those of my family; moreover, I commend to you the particular grace I desire and which I seek from your paternal intercession *(Here we mention our specific request)* and as you were a perfect model of spiritual life, grant that I may feel called to pray and to detach myself from all earthly possessions and from the passing pleasures of this world; grant me also an ardent and constant love for Jesus and Mary. Implore the Eternal Father, I beseech you to grant that I may be faithful in my devotion and obedience to the Church and to the Holy Father who governs her, and I beg you to ask the Lord that I may live and die in perfect faith, hope and charity, invoking the most holy names of Jesus and Mary, and grant that my soul may thus be saved. **Amen.**

Glory Be
St. Joachim, blessed father of the Mother of God, **pray for us.**

NOVENA TO OUR LADY
OF THE ASSUMPTION

(To be made from the 6th to the 14th of August).

The solemnity of the Assumption of Mary derives from an old tradition.

In the Eastern Church, the feast of the "dormitio" or "falling asleep" of the Virgin probably dates from the fifth century. Indeed the church in the Garden of Gethsemane, Jerusalem, has celebrated the transition of the Mother of God ("dormitio sanctae Maria") as a solemnity for centuries.

The Feast of the Assumption was introduced in Rome towards the end of the seventh century and it immediately became one of the most important liturgical celebrations of the year.

The feast has been celebrated at Milan from at least the ninth century.

Christian art also confirms the antiquity of this devotion: in the mosaic at the Basilica of St. Mary Major, Rome, the Virgin is depicted as being assumed to her heavenly throne, where she is seated beside her Son, the King of kings, who is crowning her.

Recently, the Assumption of Mary has been defined as a dogma; in other words, it has been proposed by the infallible magistery of the Church as a truth revealed by God. (This was declared officially by Pope Pius XII in 1950). What Christians have felt to be true by intuition for many centuries, according to "sensum fidei" (the "sense of faith"), is now professed explicitly by all the Church; that which was formerly tradition has now become dogma.

In the name of the Father, and of the Son,
and of the Holy Spirit. Amen.

O God, come to my aid.
O Lord, make haste to help me.
Glory Be
The Creed *(see page 26)*

Immaculate Virgin, Mother of God and of humankind, we fervently believe in your triumphant Assumption, body and soul, into heaven, where you are honoured as Queen of all the choirs of Angels and the hosts of Saints; we unite ourselves with them in praising and blessing the Lord who exalted you above all creatures and in offering you our veneration and love.

Hail Mary
O Mary, assumed body and soul into heaven,
pray for us.

Immaculate Virgin, Mother of God and humankind, we know that your motherly gaze, with which you looked tenderly upon the humble and suffering humanity of Jesus Christ on earth, now delights at the sight of the glorious humanity of Incarnate Wisdom in heaven; we know that the happiness of your soul in contemplating the Holy Trinity face to face makes your heart leap with holy tenderness; we, poor sinners, whose body weighs down the flight of the soul, beseech you to purify our senses, so that we may learn in this earthly life of ours to be satisfied by God, God alone, in the wonder of creation.

Hail Mary
O Mary, assumed body and soul into heaven,
pray for us.

Immaculate Virgin, Mother of God and humankind, we trust that you may turn your merciful gaze upon our misery and suffering, on our struggles and weaknesses; may you smile at our joys and victories; may you hear the voice of Jesus say with regard to each one of us, as he did when referring to his beloved disciple: "Here is your Son"; we call you our Mother, we accept you, as John did, as our guide, strength and consolation in this mortal life of ours.

Hail Mary
O Mary, assumed body and soul into heaven,
pray for us.

Immaculate Virgin, Mother of God and humankind, we are certain that your eyes which shed tears on the earth, bathed in the Blood of Jesus, are now turned once more towards this world stricken by war, persecution, and oppression of the righteous and the weak; in the darkness of this vale of tears, we seek relief from your heavenly light and from your sweet mercy, to ease the pains of our hearts and to assist us in the trials of the Church and of our country.

Hail Mary
O Mary, assumed body and soul into heaven,
pray for us.

Immaculate Virgin, Mother of God and humankind, we believe that in the glory where you reign, clothed with the sun and crowned with stars, after Jesus, you are the joy and happiness of all the angels and saints; from this world, through which we pass as pilgrims, comforted by our faith in the resurrection, we look upon you, who are our life, our richness and our hope. Draw us to youself with the sweetness of your voice, so that you may show us one day, after this our exile, the blessed fruit of your womb, Jesus, O clement, O loving, O sweet Virgin Mary. **Amen.**

Hail Mary
O Mary, assumed body and soul into heaven,
pray for us.
Hail Holy Queen

NOVENA OF ROSARIES FOR FIFTY-FOUR DAYS FOR PEACE IN THE WORLD

(To be made from the 15th of August to the 7th of October).

In 1884, Our Lady herself asked for this novena during an apparition at Pompei: appearing to a sick child, Fortuna Agrelli, daughter of a commander of Naples, the Queen of the Rosary said, "Whoever desires to obtain graces from me must recite three novenas of supplication and three novenas of thanksgiving praying the Rosary", and after this, the Virgin Mary healed the child. Indeed, Pope Leo XIII was so moved by the miracle, accomplished through the Rosary, that he actively promoted this devotion.

The novena begins on the feast of the Assumption (15th of August) and ends on the feast of the Holy Rosary (7th of October).

Those who recite this novena should pray in the following words after each decade:

"Our Lady, Queen of Peace, pray for us".

All those who take part in the novena may consecrate themselves to the Sacred Heart of Jesus and to the Immaculate Heart of Mary through the Queen of Peace.

The devotion consists in the daily recitation of the Holy Rosary from the 15th of August to the 10th of September in supplication for peace in the world, and from the 11th of September to the 7th of October in thanksgiving.

The meditations vary each day, beginning on the first day with the Joyful Mysteries, then the Sorrowful Mysteries and finally the Glorious Mysteries, maintaining this order throughout the fifty-four days.

NOVENA TO THE CHILD MARY

*(To be made from the 29th of August
to the 7th of September).*

*A partial indulgence is granted once a day to those who
recite this novena with devotion.*

Holy Child of the Royal House of David, Queen of Angels, Mother of grace and love, I greet you with all the love of my heart.

Grant that I may love the Lord with generous faithfulness all the days of my life, and grant me fervent devotion towards You who are the First Born of Divine Love.

Hail Mary

O heavenly Child, who were born beautiful and Immaculate like a white dove, my soul exults before you, true prodigy of God's wisdom and goodness.

O creature chaste and pure, help me to live according to the heavenly virtue of purity at all costs, regardless of whatever sacrifice may be asked of me.

Hail Mary

Hail, gracious and holy Child, spiritual paradise of delights, in whom the true tree of life, the Saviour of the world, was planted on the day of the Incarnation. As you love me so much, help me to flee from the poisoned fruits of vanity and pleasures of this world and to detest them. Inspire my soul with the thoughts, sentiments and virtues of your Divine Son, which are the fruits of immortal life.

Hail Mary

Hail, O admirable little Child, closed garden that creatures cannot enter, open only to the heavenly Spouse who delights in resting among the flowers of your great virtues. O Lily of Paradise, marvellous example of humble and hidden life: grant that the heavenly Spouse may always find the door of my heart open to the loving visits of your graces and inspirations.

Hail Mary

O Holy Child, mystical dawn, happy door of Heaven, my soul trusts and hopes in you. How lukewarm I am in my service of God! How great is my danger of being lost! O powerful Advocate, graciously stretch out your hand from your little cradle, shake me out of my lethargy, sustain me in the journey of life... grant that I may devote myself to the service of the Lord with fervour and constancy unto my death and thus attain the eternal crown.

Hail Mary

NOVENA TO THE MOST
HOLY NAME OF MARY

(To be made from the 3rd to the 11th of September).

*In the name of the Father, and of the Son,
and of the Holy Spirit. Amen.*

O God, come to my aid.
O Lord, make haste to help me.

Glory Be
The Creed *(see page 26)*

Most Adorable Trinity, through the love with which you chose and delighted in the most Holy Name of Mary from eternity, through the power which you conferred on it, through the graces which you have reserved for your faithful, grant that this name may be a source of grace and of happiness also for me.

Hail Mary

May the Holy Name of Mary
be blessed forever.

May the beloved and powerful Name of Mary
be praised, honoured and invoked forever.

May the holy, sweet and powerful Name of Mary
be invoked by me throughout my whole life

and especially at the hour of my death.

Beloved Jesus, through the love with which you pronounced the Name of your dear Mother so many times, and through the comfort which you gave her in calling her by name, I ask you to commend me, a humble creature of yours and a servant of Mary, to her special care.

Hail Mary

May the Holy Name of Mary
be blessed forever.

May the beloved and powerful Name of Mary
be praised, honoured and invoked forever.

May the holy, sweet and powerful Name of Mary
**be invoked by me throughout my whole life
and especially at the hour of my death.**

Holy Angels, through the joy which the revelation of the Name of your Queen gave to you, and through the praises with which you celebrated it, reveal to me, too, all of its beauty, power and sweetness, and grant that I may invoke it in all my needs and especially at the hour of my death.

Hail Mary

May the Holy Name of Mary
be blessed forever.

May the beloved and powerful Name of Mary
be praised, honoured and invoked forever.

May the holy, sweet and powerful Name of Mary
**be invoked by me throughout my whole life
and especially at the hour of my death.**

Dear St. Anne, good mother of my Mother, through the joy experienced by you when you pronounced with great respect and on many occasions the Name of your little child Mary, or when you talked about her to your dear husband Joachim, grant that the sweet Name of Mary may always be on my lips.

Hail Mary

May the Holy Name of Mary
be blessed forever.

May the beloved and powerful Name of Mary
be praised, honoured and invoked forever.

May the holy, sweet and powerful Name of Mary
**be invoked by me throughout my whole life
and especially at the hour of my death.**

And you, most sweet Mary, through the favour which God granted you in giving you your Name, as his most beloved Daughter; through the love which you always showed for it by granting many graces to those who were devoted to it, grant that I, too, may respect, love and invoke this delightful Name. Grant that it may be my breath, my rest, my food, my defence, my refuge, my shield, my song, my music, my prayer, my tears, my all, together with the name of Jesus, so that having been the peace of my heart and the sweetness of my lips throughout this life, the same Name may be my joy in Heaven. **Amen.**

Hail Mary

May the Holy Name of Mary
be blessed forever.

May the beloved and powerful Name of Mary
be praised, honoured and invoked forever.

May the holy, sweet and powerful Name of Mary
**be invoked by me throughout my whole life
and especially at the hour of my death.**

Prayer to the holy name of Mary

O Mary, powerful Mother of God and Mother of mine, it is true that I am not even worthy of naming you, and yet you love me and desire my salvation. Grant that even though my tongue be unclean, I may always be allowed to call on your most holy and powerful Name in my defence, because your Name is the help of the living and the salvation the dying. Most Pure Mary, most sweet Mary, grant that your Name may be from now on the breath of my life.

Our Lady, do not delay in coming to my rescue every time I call on you, because in all temptations and in all my needs, I do not want to cease invoking you, repeating your name continually: Mary, Mary.

This I desire to do throughout my life and especially at the hour of my death, in order that I may come to praise your beloved Name eternally in Heaven:

"O clement, O loving, O sweet Virgin Mary".

Mary, most beloved Mary, what comfort, what sweetness, what trust, what tenderness my soul feels when pronouncing your Name or merely thinking of you! I thank my Lord and my God who gave you this amiable and powerful name for my benefit.

It is not sufficient for me to call on you only occasionally, I want rather to invoke you often and with all my love; I would like my love to prompt me to call upon you every hour, so that I could exclaim with St. Anselm:

"O Name of the Mother of God, you are my love!".

My dear Mary, my beloved Jesus, may your most sweet names live in my heart and in all hearts. May I invoke your adorable Names forever.

O Jesus, my Redeemer and Mary, my Mother, when the moment of my death approaches, when my soul is about to leave the body, grant, through your merits, that my last words may be, "Jesus and Mary, I love you; Jesus and Mary, I give you my heart and my soul".

Novena to Our Lady of Tears, (Our Lady of Syracuse)
In Order to Ask for Graces
(To be made from the 6th to the 14th of September).

In the name of the Father, and of the Son, and of the Holy Spirit. Amen.

O God, come to my aid.
O Lord, make haste to help me.

Glory Be
The Creed *(see page 26)*

Moved by the miracle of your tears, merciful Virgin Mary of Syracuse, I come today to prostrate myself at your feet and, inspired with fresh confidence by the many graces which you have granted, I come to you, O Mother of mercy, so that I may open my heart entirely to you and pour all my sufferings into your sweet motherly heart, uniting my tears to yours: tears of sorrow for my sins and tears for the sorrows which afflict me.

Look upon my tears with your gracious countenance, O dear Mother, and with merciful eyes and through your love for Jesus, I beseech you to comfort me and to hear my prayer.

Through your holy and innocent tears, I beseech your Divine Son to grant me the forgiveness of my sins, an active and deep faith, and also the grace that I humbly ask of you...

(Here we express our specific intention).

O Mary, my Mother and my Confidence, I place all my trust in your Immaculate and Sorrowful Heart.

Immaculate and sorrowful Heart of Mary,
have mercy on me.

Hail Holy Queen

O Mother of Jesus and merciful Mother of ours, how many tears you shed along the sorrowful path of your life! You, who are a mother, can understand so well the anguish of my heart which prompts me to appeal to your Mother's Heart with the trust of a child, even though I am not worthy of your kindness. Your Heart, rich in mercy, has opened for us a new source of grace in these times of great trials. From the depth of my misery I cry to you,

O good Mother; I come to you, O merciful Mother, and with my heart stricken by pain, I invoke the consoling solace of your holy Tears and your holy graces. Your motherly weeping permits me to hope that you will hear me graciously.

O Sorrowful Heart, entreat your Son Jesus to grant me the strength with which you bore the great sufferings of your life, so that I may always fulfil the will of God with Christlike obedience, even in times of sorrow. Grant, O sweet Mother, that I may grow in Christian hope and, if it be in accordance with the will of God, grant me, through your Immaculate Tears, the grace that I humbly ask of you with great faith and lively hope...

(Here we express our intention).

Our Lady of Tears, my life, my sweetness and my hope, I place all my hope in you today and forever.

Immaculate and sorrowful Heart of Mary,
have mercy on me

Hail Holy Queen

O Mediatrix of all graces, O healer of the sick, O comforter of the afflicted, O sweet and afflicted Virgin of Tears, do not abandon this child of yours in his (her) sorrow, but as a gracious Mother, come quickly to my assistance: help me, assist me! Accept the lamentations of my heart and, in your mercy, dry the tears which stream down my face.

Through the tears of mercy with which you accepted the body of your Son at the foot of the Cross, that same body which you had welcomed into your womb, accept me too, your poor child, and grant, through divine grace, that my love may increase towards God and towards my brothers and sisters who are also your children. Through your precious tears, O most beloved Virgin of Tears, grant me also the grace that I greatly desire and ask of you with confidence and loving insistence...

(Here we express our intention)

Our Lady of Syracuse, Mother of love and sorrow, to your Immaculate and Sorrowful Heart I consecrate my poor heart; accept it, guard it, save it with your holy, unfailing love.

Immaculate and sorrowful Heart of Mary,
have mercy on me

Hail Holy Queen

Let us pray.
Remember, O most compassionate Virgin Mary that never was it known that anyone who fled to your protection, implored your assistance or sought your intercession was left unaided.
Inspired with this confidence, we fly unto you, O Virgin of Virgins, our Mother. To you we come, before you we kneel, sinful and sorrowful.
O Mother of the Word Incarnate, despise not our petitions but in your clemency, hear and answer them.

Immaculate and sorrowful Heart of Mary,
have mercy on me

NOVENA TO OUR LADY OF FATIMA

(To be made from the 4th to the 12th of October).

In the name of the Father, and of the Son, and of the Holy Spirit. Amen.

O God, come to my aid.
O Lord, make haste to help me.

Glory Be
The Creed *(see page 26)*

O Most Holy Virgin, who, at Fatima revealed to the world the treasures of grace hidden in the recitation of the Holy Rosary, fill our hearts with a great love for this holy devotion, so that by meditating on the mysteries of the Rosary, we may obtain the graces and enjoy the fruits which we ask of you in this prayer, for the glory of God and for the good of our souls. **Amen.**

Immaculate Heart of Mary,
pray for us.

Hail Mary *(7 times)*

NOVENA TO THE VIRGIN MARY, HEALTH OF THE SICK

(To be made from the 12th to the 20th of November).

In the name of the Father, and of the Son, and of the Holy Spirit. Amen.

O God, come to my aid.
O Lord, make haste to help me.

Glory Be
The Creed *(see page 26)*

O Virgin Mary, who are invoked by the name of Health of the Sick, because You are the Mother of our Saviour Jesus, grant me the grace of health of my soul, thus allowing me to remain in the grace of God and to receive the holy sacraments.

Hail Mary

O Virgin Mary, who always listen with mercy to the lamentations of those who suffer, obtain from the Lord the grace for me to bear my sufferings with patience, allowing me to understand that a great treasure of wisdom and goodness is hidden within them.

Hail Mary

Virgin Mary, invoked as Health of the Sick because you are the comforter of the afflicted and health for those who are ill, grant me the grace of health,physical and mental, if it be in accordance with the holy will of God, healing me from present evils and giving me sufficient strength to carry out the duties of my state of life.

NOVENA OF THE MIRACULOUS MEDAL
(To be made from the 18th to the 26th of November).

*In the name of the Father, and of the Son,
and of the Holy Spirit. Amen.*

O God, come to my aid.
O Lord, make haste to help me.

Glory Be
The Creed *(see page 26)*

Immaculate Virgin Mary, may you be blessed for having wanted to choose a humble daughter of St. Vincent de Paul in order to manifest your motherly concern for humankind.

O merciful Advocate of ours, who, in your first apparition to St. Catherine Labouré deigned to show yourself to be crying over the miseries of your children and over all the disasters which were going to strike them, in particular over the persecutions which were going to break out against the clergy and the religious communities, and who promised your particular protection to those faithful to you, turn again your eyes of mercy towards your people, tormented by the same miseries, threatened by the same calamities and have mercy on us.

Defend and sanctify the clergy, protect the Church, exalt its gracious Head, and grant that by means of your medal, many of your children may be converted and saved.

Hail Mary
O Mary, conceived without sin,
pray for us who have recourse to Thee (you).

Immaculate Virgin, our powerful Queen, you showed yourself to your servant with your hands full of brilliant rings which coved the earth with their rays, symbols of the graces which you showered upon your faithful, and you said with sorrow that the rings from which light did not come forth represented those graces that we do not ask of you which you would like to grant. Mother of Mercy, look not on our unworthiness but through the love you have for us, let your power shine upon us in all its splendour, and grant all those graces which your goodness holds in reserve for those who ask you for them with trust.

Hail Mary
O Mary, conceived without sin,
pray for us who have recourse to Thee.

Immaculate Virgin, our sure refuge, may you always be praised, because by giving us your Medal as a powerful shield against our spiritual enemies and sure protection from every danger of the body, you taught us the petition which we must present to you in order to move your heart to mercy. Look therefore upon us, prostrated at your feet, O Mother, as we invoke you with the short prayer which you brought us from heaven and remind you of the glorious privilege of your Immaculate Conception, by virtue of which we ask you the graces of which we are in need.

Hail Mary
O Mary, conceived without sin,
pray for us who have recourse to Thee.

Immaculate Virgin, Comforter of the afflicted, may you always be blessed because you

wanted to render your Medal the instrument of your most marvellous acts of mercy in favour of all the afflicted, using it to convert sinners, to heal the sick, and to bring consolation in all kinds of misery. Do not allow, O merciful Mother, that the name which your grateful people wanted to give to your medal be ever said in vain, but rather pour forth your graces and miracles on us, too, and on all the people whom we commend to you, so that your Medal may be truly Miraculous also for us.

Hail Mary
O Mary, conceived without sin,
pray for us who have recourse to Thee.

Immaculate Virgin, you wished to be shown in the triumphant act of crushing the head of the infernal serpent, and in the devotion to your Medal you indicated to us the secret of victory. Turn then, O Mary, your eyes upon us, who, in order not to be victims of our enemy and

yours, have taken refuge under your protection. Grant that your Medal may be for us a secure shield and a powerful weapon, in order that after we too have conquered the evil one, we may praise your Immaculate Conception for ever.

Hail Mary
O Mary, conceived without sin,
pray for us who have recourse to Thee.

NOVENA IN HONOUR OF THE IMMACULATE CONCEPTION OF THE BLESSED VIRGIN MARY

(To be made from the 29th of November to the 7th of December).

In the name of the Father, and of the Son, and of the Holy Spirit. Amen.

O God, come to my aid.
O Lord, make haste to help me.

Glory Be
The Creed *(see page 26)*

FIRST DAY
MARY, WOMAN AMONG WOMEN OF HER TIME

From the letter of St. Paul to the Galatians.
"When the completion of time came, God sent his Son, born of a woman, born a subject of the Law, to redeem the subjects of the Law, so that we could receive adoptions as sons. As you are sons, God has sent into our hearts the Spirit of his Son crying, 'Abba, Father', and so you are no longer a slave, but a son; and if a son, then an heir, by God's own act" (Gal 4:4-7).

V. The Lord chose her,
    * He chose her before she was born.
R. The Lord chose her,
    * He chose her before she was born.
V. He made her live in his own dwelling place,
R. * He chose her before she was born.
V. Glory be to the Father, and to the Son,
    * and to the Holy Spirit.
R. The Lord chose her,
    *He chose her before she was born.

Brief text for meditation:

The Son of the Most High came into the world by being born of a woman, a woman who lived an ordinary life; if she had not been the mother of the Word, she would have been an unknown Hebrew housewife. She lived and worked, prayed and fulfilled her duties faithfully as did many other women of her era and country. If we look more closely at her life, however, there is one small particular which renders her "special":

She fully "expresses her feminine talent in service of others in the normality of everyday life" (Letter to Women, 12). Mary lived entirely according to the gift of her femininity, whether working or attending to the needs of others, because she placed God at the centre of her life, following the Divine Law (ref. Ex 20:2-6; Dt 5:6-10; 6:4-7). Her heart was and is lifted up to God constantly, and therefore she is full of grace, so that she "sees and reasons" with the heart (ref. Lk

2:19.51).

Mary's Heart, created immaculate by God, and kept immaculate by the Virgin herself, is a place which is pleasing to the Lord, a place where He dwells, and is thus destined to be a true tabernacle; a place where we can meet God our Father, who welcomes us as His children.

We pause for a moment of silent reflection.

Let us pray.

O Mary, Immaculate Mother of God, keep within me the heart of a child, pure and limpid like the water of a spring. Give me a simple heart, which neither dwells on, nor wallows in its own sadness; a heart generous in giving itself, easily moved to compassion, a faithful and generous heart, which neither forgets any good deed nor bears any grudges. Create in me a sweet and humble heart which loves without demanding to be loved in return, a heart which is content to disappear in other hearts, sacrificing itself for your Divine Son; a great heart that cannot be subdued, so that it may never be closed by ingratitude; a heart tormented by the glory of Christ, wounded by His love, with a wound that can only be healed in heaven. Give me your Heart, O Immaculate One. **Amen.**

Fr. Grandmaison S.J.

SECOND DAY

MARY, IN THE MYSTERY OF THE ANNUNCIATION OF THE LORD

From the Gospel according to Luke.

"In the sixth month the angel Gabriel was sent by God to a town in Galilee called Nazareth, to a virgin betrothed to a man named Joseph, of the House of David; and the virgin's name was Mary. He went in and said to her, 'Rejoice, you who enjoy God's favour! The Lord is with you.' She was deeply disturbed by these words and asked herself what this greeting could mean, but the angel said to her, 'Mary, do not be afraid; you have won God's favour. Look! You are to conceive in your womb and bear a son, and you must name him Jesus.

He will be great and will be called Son of the Most High. The Lord God will give him the throne of his ancestor David; he will rule over the, House of Jacob for ever and his reign will have no end. Mary said to the angel, 'But how can this come about, since I have no knowledge of man?'. The angel answered, 'The Holy Spirit will come upon you, and the power of the Most High will cover you with its shadow. And so the child will be holy and will be called Son of God. And I tell you this too: your cousin Elizabeth also, in her old age, has conceived a son, and she whom people called barren is now in her sixth month, for nothing is impossible to God. Mary said, 'You see before you the Lord's servant, let it happen to me as you have said.' And the angel left her" (Lk 1:26-38).

V. Hail Mary, full of grace,
   * the Lord is with you.
**R. Hail Mary, full of grace,
   * the Lord is with you.**
V. Blessed are you among women, and blessed is the fruit of your womb,
R. * the Lord is with you.
V. Glory be to the Father, and to the Son,
   *and to the Holy Spirit.
**R. Hail Mary, full of grace,
   * the Lord is with you.**

Brief text for meditation:

Mary served God perfectly in her everyday life because she wished to fulfil the will of God even in the most mundane occupations and in the matters of (apparently) little importance. She was therefore ready to accept unexpected events in her life, such as the message of the angel and to welcome God Himself into her very being in a unique manner. The angel greeted her with the words "full of grace", that is to say "full of the love of God". The fruit of this love is to be chosen to share in the life of God Himself; a gift which is offered to all people but which was accepted by Mary in a singular way, by her saying, "Yes" unconditionally to God. Thanks to this "Fiat", accompanied by the grace granted to Her by God, the Word of God became incarnate in her. The election of Mary as Mother of God was exceptional and unique. However, everyone of us is invited to say, "Yes" to God, that is to share in His plan of salvation for humanity and for each one of us.

We pause for a moment of silent reflection.

Let us pray.

Grant that I may praise you, O Immaculate Virgin! I adore you, O Heavenly Father, because You placed Your Only Begotten Son in Her womb that was most pure.

I adore You, O Son of God, because You deigned to enter Her womb and You truly became Her Son.

I adore You, O Holy Spirit, because You deigned to form the body of the Son of God in Her immaculate womb.

I adore You, O most Holy Trinity, One God in the Holy Trinity, for having dignified the Immaculate Virgin in such a divine way.

St. Maximilian Kolbe

THIRD DAY
MARY, VIRGIN AND MOTHER

From the Gospel according to Matthew.

"This is how Jesus Christ came to be born. His mother Mary was betrothed to Joseph; but before they came to live together she was found to be with child through the Holy Spirit. Her husband Joseph, being an upright man and wanting to spare her disgrace, decided to divorce her informally. He had made up his mind to do this when suddenly the angel of the Lord appeared to him in a dream and said, 'Joseph son of David, do not be afraid to take Mary home as your wife, because she has conceived what is in her by the Holy Spirit. She will give birth to a son and you must name him Jesus, because he is the one who is to save his people from their sins. Now all this took place to fulfil what the Lord had spoken through the prophet: Look! the virgin is which child and will give birth to a son whom they will call Immanuel, a name which means 'God-is-with-us'. When Joseph woke up he did what the angel of the Lord had told him to do: he took his wife to his home; he had not had intercourse with her when she gave birth to a son; and he named him Jesus" (Mt 1:18-25).

V. Grant us salvation,
  * O Virgin Mary.

R. **Grant us salvation,**
* O Virgin Mary.

V. Through the passion of Christ your Son,
R. *** O Virgin Mary.**

V. Glory be to the Father, and to the Son,
* and to the Holy Spirit.
R. **Grant us salvation,**
* O Virgin Mary.

Brief text for meditation:

What sublime love God poured into the Immaculate Heart of the holy Virgin!

*Indeed Her heart was so full of this love that she could dedicate herself fully to virginity, maternity and married life simultaneously. In Mary, virginity is the **expression** of Her giving herself totally to God and is also a prophetic sign of a new era which had already begun. Her virginity may be considered by some to be a state of sterility and passivity, whereas it is in fact a supreme manifestation of the highest activity: God Himself worked in Her and through Her! Her willingness to accomplish the will of God allowed Him to enter into the story of humankind and to work marvels therein.*

*In Mary, maternity is the **fruit** of having given Herself totally to God, and thus it is a maternity which cannot be confined only to one person, but through her, love extends to all humanity. It was*

Motherhood that brought her from Bethlehem to Nazareth, and from Golgotha to the Cenacle, where she was to manifest in a singular way her maternity within the Church which will last for all time.

*In Mary married life is the **means** by which she lives out the giving of Herself. She was and shall always remain the spouse of St. Joseph, guardian of our Redeemer, and in this way, sanctified married life. However, she is also the spouse of the Holy Spirit, who used His power in Her and continues to operate through Her in the Church. Moreover, through being an image of the Church, spouse of Christ, Mary's Martimony to God becomes fertile by Her willingness to co-operate with Him, thus showing the path which must be taken by the Church, and especially by Christian married couples, inviting them to be united to one another and to be open to life, to love and to the action of God in their lives.*

We pause for a moment of silent reflection.

Let us pray.

O holy Mother of God who, by accepting the message of the angel, conceived the Word, gave your consent by faith, gave birth by the flesh, were awed by the presence of God but trusting in the help of grace, accept the requests of your people, you who can listen to and hear in a perfect way the prayers of all people, grant that, by welcoming into your maternal womb all those who, being exiles in this journey of life, seek refuge in you with unwavering hope, they may reach salvation and be presented by you to our Lord Jesus Christ your Son.

Visigot Prayer

FOURTH DAY
MARY, THE MOTHER WHO HEARS
THE WORD OF GOD

From the Gospel according to Luke.
"It happened that as he was speaking, a woman in the crowd raised her voice and said, 'Blessed the womb that bore you and the breasts that fed you!' But he replied, 'More blessed still are those who hear the word of God and keep it!'." (Lk 11-27-28).

V. The Lord chose her,
  * He chose her before she was born.
R. The Lord chose her,
  * He chose her before she was born.
V. He made her live in his own dwelling place,
R. * He chose her before she was born.

V. Glory be to the Father, and to the Son,
   * and to the Holy Spirit.
R. The Lord chose her,
   *He chose her before she was born.

Brief text for meditation:

The proclamation of the law of God begins with the solemn announcement: "Hear, O Israel", almost as if to hear were the first of all the commandments. To hear means to "be all ears", and if we look at the ear we see that it is always open, and always ready to pick up and receive even the quietest sounds. Hearing is intimately related to knowing how to be silent, how to stop talking, being aware of the fact that God is speaking. And just as we had to remain silent when adults spoke to us as children, so now, as true children of God, must we take time to remain in silence in order to hear His Word.

The Immaculate Virgin not only stays quiet, but also has a heart free from all sin and harmful attachment. She is like a clean slate or an unused tape on which God can write or record His Word, and it is only through this Word that Mary and indeed, each one of us can truly accomplish works which are pleasing to God, works which are worthy of God, great works which bring forth fruit for eternity. Such is the attitude of those who "hear", an attitude which opens our hearts to the grace and light of God, and we know well that we can only give and pass on that which we have received. Thus we can learn from the Immaculate Virgin, who listens to the Word of God, how to live according to what hear, how to live in a way that is pleasing to God, so that we, too, can share in the life of the blessed of whom Jesus speaks. Through Mary, who was exalted in such a sublime way, we can receive all those graces which we need in order to reach the goal of our existence. The Immaculate Virgin, who teaches us to hear the Word of God, becomes the teacher of life and the way to reach heaven. May Mary, who was indirectly proclaimed blessed by the Son of God, help us to attain the bliss of Paradise.

We pause for a moment of silence and meditation.

Let us pray.
I greet you, O Immaculate Virgin Mary, Daughter of the Eternal Father, and beseech you to grant me purity in my thoughts. I greet you, O Immaculate Virgin Mary, Mother of the Eternal Word, and beseech you to grant me purity in my words.
I greet you, O Immaculate Virgin Mary, Spouse of the Holy Spirit, and beseech you to grant me purity in my actions. O Mary conceived without sin, pray for us who have recourse to you, and also for all those who do not turn to you, especially for the adversaries of the Holy Church and for those who commend themselves to your care.

FIFTH DAY
MARY, MOTHER OF LIFE

From the First Letter of St. John.
"Something which has existed
since the beginning,
which we have heard,
which we have seen with our own eyes,
which we have watched
and touched with our own hands,
the Word of life,
this is our theme.
That life was made visible;
we saw it and are giving our testimony,
declaring to you the eternal life,
which was present to the Father
and has been revealed to us.
We are declaring to you
what we have seen and heard,
so that you too may share our life.
Our life is shared with the Father
and with his Son Jesus Christ.
We are writing this to you
so that our joy may be complete" *(1 Jn 1:1-4).*

V. Hail Mary, full of grace,
   * The Lord is with you.
R. Hail Mary, full of grace,
   * The Lord is with you.

V. Blessed are you among women, and blessed is the fruit of your womb.

R. * The Lord is with you.

V. Glory be to the Father, and to the Son, *and to the Holy Spirit.

R. Hail Mary, full of grace,
**   * The Lord is with you.**

Brief text for meditation:

The consent of the Immaculate Virgin Mary at the Annunciation, together with her maternity, mark the beginning of a new life which manifests itself in Jesus Christ.

Through her, Life comes into our midst, life that will have the victory over eternal death.

Mary is the mother of all those who have been born to new life.

Through her acceptance and attentive care of the Word made flesh, the Immaculate Virgin became a perfect model of acceptance and of the concern for Life itself. In the Immaculate Virgin, God reveals to us that the life to which we are called is not only that of the body, but also, and indeed even more importantly, that of the soul. Thus to "live" really means to live in the grace of God. To dedicate oneself to life means, therefore, to commit oneself so that all people have life to the full: so that they may live, and live in dignity, so that they may live in God, purified and saved from sin, and live in the joy of being Children of

God. *"The glory of God is living man, but the life of men consists in seeing God" (St. Irenaeus).*

We pause for a moment of silent reflection.

Let us pray.
O Mary, dawn of the new world, Mother of the living, we entrust to you the action for life: look, O Mother, at the tremendous number of children who are impeded from being born, of the poor for whom survival becomes difficult, of men and women who are victims of inhuman violence, of the elderly and sick people killed out of indifference or out of presumed pity. May all those who believe in your Son be able to announce to the people of our time, the Gospel of life with frankness and love. Obtain for them the grace of welcoming life as a gift which is always new, the joy of extolling its merits with all their being in gratitude, and the courage to bear witness to it with active constancy, in order to construct, together with all people of good will, a society of truth and love for the praise and glory of God, creator and lover of life.

Pope John Paul II

SIXTH DAY
MARY, MOTHER MOST PURE

From the Gospel according to Luke.

"And when the day came for them to be puri-
fied in keeping with the Law of Moses, they took
him up to Jerusalem to present him to the Lord -
observing what is written in the Law of the Lord:
Every first-born male must be consecrated to the
Lord - and also to offer in sacrifice, in accord-
ance with what is prescribed in the Law of the
Lord, a pair of turtledoves or two young pigeons.
Now in Jerusalem there was a man named
Simeon. He was an upright and devout man; he
looked forward to the restoration of Israel and
the Holy Spirit rested on him. It had been revea-
led to him by the Holy Spirit that he would not
see death until he had set eyes on the Christ of
the Lord. Prompted by the Spirit he came to the
Temple; and when the parents brought in the
child Jesus to do for him what the Law required,
he took him into his arms and blessed God; and
he said: Now, Master, you are letting your ser-
vant go in peace as you promised; for my eyes
have seen the salvation which you have made
ready in the sight of the nations; a light of revela-
tion for the gentiles and glory for your people
Israel. As the child's father and mother were won-
dering at the things that were being said about
him, Simeon blessed them and said to Mary his

mother, 'Look, he is destined for the fall and for the rise of many in Israel, destined to be a sign that is opposed - and a sword will pierce your soul too - so that the secret thoughts of many may be laid bare'." (Lk 2:22-35).

V. Grant us salvation,
   * O Virgin Mary.
R. Grant us salvation,
   * O Virgin Mary.
V. Through the passion of Christ your Son,
R. * O Virgin Mary.
V. Glory be to the Father, and to the Son,
   * and to the Holy Spirit.
R. Grant us salvation,
   * O Virgin Mary.

Brief text for meditation:

Mary went to the Temple of Jerusalem with two purposes: Her purification and to present her Son as an offering to the Father. There, She met Simeon, an elderly man who lived under the guidance of the Holy Spirit and could see that She did not need purification but rather Her heart would be pierced by a sword of suffering and pain and by the sword of sacrifice which would consume Her by the cross of Her Son. Mary shared intimately in the expiatory act of her Son, co-operating in the work of Redemption, and thus helped to take away the sin of the world. Our Immaculate Mother has allowed Her most pure Heart to be opened in order to become a refuge for sinners who implore grace and forgiveness from the Father. With the sorrow of Her heart, Mary began, in a singular way, to make up for "all the hardships that still have to be undergone by Christ for the sake of his body, the Church" (ref. Col 1:24).

*The fact that Mary's **heart** was pierced by a sword indicates that the heart is the origin of sin, where evil hides itself in the human being and indeed the heart of each one of us needs to be redeemed:"It is from within, from the heart, that evil intentions emerge: fornication, theft, murder, adultery, avarice, malice, deceit, indecency, envy, slander, pride, folly" (Mk 7:21-22). Therefore, let us allow our hearts to be purified, permitting grace to enter and allowing ourselves to enter into the Immaculate Heart of Mary; the best way to accomplish such a purification is to go to confession regularly and to persevere in prayer.*
Let us ask Mary to impart Her purity to us.

We pause for a moment of silent reflection.

Let us pray.

O most pure maiden, calm the treacherous storm in my soul, you who showed yourself to be a haven on earth for those who sail amid the evils of life.

You who gave birth to the Light, enlighten, O

pure one, the eyes of my heart. You were given to us on earth to be our protection, our bulwark and our boast. You were given as a token and sure salvation, O maiden. Therefore, we, who lovingly praise you, fear our enemies no longer.

Giuseppe Studita.

SEVENTH DAY
MARY, ANTAGONIST OF SATAN

From the Book of Revelation.

"Now a great sign appeared in heaven: a woman, robed with the sun, standing on the moon, and on her head a crown of twelve stars. She was pregnant, and in labour, crying aloud in the pangs of childbirth. Then a second sign appeared in the sky: there was a huge red dragon with seven heads and ten horns, and each of the seven heads crowned with a coronet. Its tail swept a third of the stars from the sky and hurled them to the ground, and the dragon stopped in front of the woman as she was at the point of giving birth, so that it could eat the child as soon as it was born. The woman was delivered of a boy, the son who was to rule all the nations with an iron sceptre, and the child was taken straight up to God and to his throne, while the woman escaped into the desert, where God had prepared a place for her to be looked after for twelve hun-

dred and sixty days" (Rev 12:1-6).

V. Hail Mary, full of grace,
*the Lord is with you.
**R. Hail Mary, full of grace,
*the Lord is with you.**
V. Blessed are you among women, and blessed is the fruit of your womb.
R. * the Lord is with you.
V. Glory be to the Father, and to the Son,
*and to the Holy Spirit.
**R. Hail Mary, full of grace,
* the Lord is with you.**

Brief text for meditation:

At the dawn of Creation a battle began between the woman and the dragon, the ancient serpent: when original sin entered into the world, God said to the serpent, "I shall put enmity between you and the woman, and between your offspring and hers; it will bruise your head and you will strike its heel" (Gen 3:15). What St. John sees as a battle of cosmic dimensions is the ancient conflict between the woman, together with Her children, and the dragon with his children; between the people of Israel and Leviathan; between the Church and Satan; between Mary and Lucifer. Therefore, "who is this arising like the dawn, fair as the moon, resplendent as the sun, formidable as an amy" (Song of Songs 6:10) if not Mary, image and mother of the Church, who gathers her children together "as a hen gathers her chicks under her wings" (ref. Mt 23:37). Under her guidance we are called to fight for purity and holiness, against sin and immodesty. The Immaculate Virgin leads us to purity of heart if we allow ourselves to be among those whom she teaches and guides.

We attain purity only by means of a continuous and constant battle which consists in saying "Yes" to God numerous times and "No" to Satan as many times; it consists of prayer and vigil-ance, and many acts of love, both great and small; it consists in controlling our passions and dominating our faults. However, such a battle cannot be continued without the help of God which is given to us if we frequent the sacraments; nor can it be continued without commending ourselves to the Immaculate Virgin Mary who is the victorious woman; nor can we do without the assistance of a community of the faithful who are united with God and are all journeying towards the same destination: a community which gives support to those who stumble, courage to those of wavering faith and helps to their feet those who have fallen.

We pause for a moment of silent reflection.

Let us pray.
Grant that I may praise You, O Immaculate Virgin, with my commitment and personal sacrifice. Grant that I may live, work, suffer, consume myself and die for You, only for You. Grant that I may lead the entire world to You. Grant that I may contribute to Your greater glory, and Your utmost glorification. Grant that I may render You glory such as no one has ever given You unto this day. Grant that others may surpass me in their zeal for Your glorification, and that I may surpass them, so that, in noble emulation of each other, we may allow Your glory to grow ever more profoundly, ever more rapidly, ever more intensely, according to the desire of Him who exalted You in such an ineffable way above all beings.

St. Maximilian Kolbe

EIGHTH DAY
MARY, MEDIATRIX OF ALL GRACES

From the Gospel according to John.
"On the third day there was a wedding at Cana in Galilee. The mother of Jesus was there, and Jesus and his disciples had also been invited. And they ran out of wine, since the wine provided for the feast had all been used, and the mother of Jesus said to him, 'They have no wine.' Jesus said, 'Woman, what do you want from me? My hour

has not come yet.' His mother said to the servants, 'Do whatever he tells you.' There were six stone water jars standing there, meant for the ablutions that are customary among the Jews: each could hold twenty or thirty gallons. Jesus said to the servants, 'Fill the jars with water', and they filled them to the brim. Then he said to them, 'Draw some out now and take it to the president of the feast.' They did this; the president tasted the water, and it had turned into wine. Having no idea where it came from - though the servants who had drawn the water knew - the president of the feast called the bridegroom and said, 'Everyone serves good wine first and the worse wine when the guests are well wined; but you have kept the best wine till now.'

This was the first of Jesus' signs: it was at Cana in Galilee. He revealed his glory, and his disciples believed in him" (Jn 2:1-11).

V. Grant us salvation,
   * O Virgin Mary.
R. Grant us salvation,
   * O Virgin Mary.
V. Through the passion of Christ your Son,
R. * O Virgin Mary.
V Glory be to the Father, and to the Son,
   * and to the Holy Spirit.
R. Grant us salvation,
   * O Virgin Mary.

Brief text for meditation:

The Immaculate Virgin had a rôle *of the first order conferred on her by God Himself in the Annunciation, namely, to allow others to encounter God. Mary, as Mother of Jesus who is the Spouse of the Church, has the task of letting the bridegroom and bride get to know each other, allowing them to meet each other, and letting them love one another. At Cana Mary assumed this* rôle *and guided the first disciples of Jesus in their faith, making Him reveal His true identity of Messiah by means of a prophetic sign.*

Throughout the history of the Church, Mary has never ceased to carry out Her mission in this respect. God chose the Immaculate Virgin as a means of giving Himself to us in the Incarnate Word, in order to accomplish in this way the redemption and salvation of fallen humanity. As He gave the Grace of Graces to us through Mary, so does He continue to give us, through Her, all the graces which we need in order to reach our eternal home, and to sustain us in our journey in this valley of tears. And as a river of graces flows down to us by means of the Immaculate Virgin Mary, so too must the response of humanity, having arisen from the graces, follow the same way as that of the Immaculate Virgin, Spouse of the Holy Spirit, and of Her Son Jesus. The more we trust in Mary and entrust ourselves to Her care, the more we shall share in the glory of God *through Her, and Christ shall be **"everything and in everything. As the chosen of God, then, the holy people whom he loves, you are to be clothed in heartfelt compassion, in generosity and humility, gentleness and patience. Bear with one another; forgive each other if one of you has a complaint against another. The Lord has forgiven you; now you must do the same. Over all these clothes, put on love, the perfect bond"** (Col 3: 11-14).*

We pause for a moment of silent reflection.

Let us pray.

You who send forth the light and let the sun shine on the righteous and on the unjust, on those who are bad and on those who are good, You who light up the dawn and illumine the earth, O Lord of all, enlighten our hearts also. Grant, this day, that we may act in a way that is pleasing to You; defend us from the arrows which fly by day and from all the enemy powers. Mary, Our Lady, the Immaculate Mother of God, intercede for us. As it is in Your power to do so, O God, have mercy on us and save us. May we give glory to You: to the Father, to the Son and to the Holy Spirit, now and for ever until the end of time.

St. Basil the Great

From the Gospel according Luke.

"And Mary said: My soul proclaims the greatness of the Lord and my spirit rejoices in God my Saviour; because he has looked upon the humiliation of his servant. Yes, from now onwards all generations will call me blessed, for the Almighty has done great things for me. Holy is his name, and his faithful love extends age after age to those who fear him. He has used the power of his arm, he has routed the arrogant of heart. He has pulled down princes from their thrones and raised high the lowly. He has filled the starving with good things, sent the rich away empty. He has come to the help of Israel his servant, mindful of his faithful love - according to the promise he made to our ancestors - of his mercy to Abraham and to his descendants for ever" (Lk 1:46-55).

V. The Lord chose her,
   * He chose her before she was born.
R. The Lord chose her,
   * He chose her before she was born.
V He made her live in his own dwelling place,
R. * He chose her before she was born.
V. Glory be to the Father, and to the Son,
   * and to the Holy Spirit.
R. The Lord chose her,
   *He chose her before she was born.

Brief text for meditation:

*Jesus taught his disciples that **"if anyone wants to be first, he must make himself last of all and servant of all"** (Mk 9: 35). Mary allowed this Word to become flesh in Her from the beginning, by listening to the Word and obeying it, thus fulfilling Her vocation as spouse and mother. By placing Herself at the service of God, She let Herself be at the service of all humanity; Her service was one of love which She continues to this day. Indeed it was through serving others that Mary gained experience in Her life of "reigning" in a mysterious but authentic way. For Mary, to "reign" is to serve, and to serve is to "reign"! The Immaculate Virgin fulfils Her queenship by giving of Herself entirely, giving Herself to Her Son, and then to the whole of humankind, Her children. It is by serving others, with love and of our own free will, that we express the true "regality" of our being.*

The Almighty does great things for Mary and all generations call Her blessed, because She is a humble servant who does nothing but the will of God, and as thus been chosen by God to be Queen of heaven and earth.

We pause for a moment of silent reflection.

Let us pray.

Hail, song of the cherubims and praise of the angels.

Hail, peace and joy of the human race.

Hail, garden of delights; hail, O wood of life.

Hail, bulwark of the faithful, and haven of the shipwrecked.

Hail, rebuke of Adam; hail, ransom of Eve.

Hail, most holy temple; hail, throne of the Lord.

Hail, O Chaste one, who have crushed the head of the dragon and cast him into the abyss.

Hail, refuge of the afflicted; hail deliverance from the curse.

Hail, O Mother of Christ, Son of the Living God, to whom is owed glory, honour, adoration and praise, everywhere, now and for ever, until the end of time.

Ephrem of Syria

Tota pulchra *(see page 817)*

V. You were Immaculate, O Virgin, in your conception.

℟. **Pray for us to the Father whose Son you bore.**

Let us pray.
O God, through the Immaculate Conception of the Virgin, You prepared a worthy dwelling place for Your Son and, in anticipation of His death, You preserved her from every stain of sin; grant that we, too, by Her intercession, may come to be united with You in purity of spirit.
Through Christ Our Lord. **Amen.**

We may conclude the Novena by:
- *Consecrating ourselves to the Immaculate Heart of Mary. (For suitable prayers, see Chapter Six, Part Six). Consecrating oneself to Mary is like returning to the womb of the Mother to be reborn to a life of grace!...*
- *Obtaining a Miraculous Medal to be worn on our person.*

NOVENA TO OUR LADY OF LORETO
(To be made from the 1st to the 9th of December).

In the name of the Father, and of the Son, and of the Holy Spirit. Amen.

O God, come to my aid.
O Lord, make haste to help me.

Glory Be
The Creed *(see page 26)*

O Virgin Mary of Loreto, as I greet you with filial devotion, I love to repeat the words of the Archangel Gabriel together with your words:

"Hail Mary, full of grace, the Lord is with thee". "The Almighty has done marvels for me". Virgin Mary of Loreto, your House is the dwelling place of Light and Love: grant me true Light and perfect Love. Grant that peace may invade my spirit which is sometimes anxious and fearful. Grant that love may fill my life and shine upon all those around me. Prolong, O Mary, this moment of serene joy. Defend me from temptations and in all other difficult trials. I beseech you to help me, with your maternal protection, to reach the House of the Father, where you reside as Queen. **Amen.**

Hail Mary *(7 times)*

Prayer to Our Lady of Loreto

Immaculate Virgin Mary, with lively faith we contemplate the great mysteries which took place in Your humble House at Nazareth, which was then brought by the Angels to the pleasant hill of Loreto.

Within these sacred walls, where You were conceived without sin and lived your childhood in prayer and in sublime love, where the Angel called You FULL OF GRACE and You answered him with those wonderful words which opened the heavens and made it possible for the Saviour of the world to come down to earth.

Here, together with St. Joseph, You served the Lord, contemplating the Incarnate Word, in humility and in service, preparing your spirit for the great sacrifice that You were to offer on the hill of Calvary, in order to become the Mother of all humankind, redeemed by the Blood of Jesus.

Grant, O Mary, that after living in the grace of the Lord in our homes as You did in yours, we may keep far from sin and submit ourselves to the Law and Will of God, and thus come to live one day in the house of God in Paradise, together with You, for all eternity. **Amen.**

Virgin of Loreto,
pray for us.

NOVENA IN HONOUR OF
OUR LADY OF GUADALUPE
*(To be recited from the 3rd to the 11th of December
or at any other suitable time).*

*At dawn on the 9th of December, 1531, Juan Diego, a
Mexican Indian convert of fifty-seven years old, was going
to attend catechism class and hear the Mass. As he was
passing Tepeyac Hill, he saw a brilliant light on the summit
and heard the strains of celestial music. Then he heard a
feminine voice asking him to ascend. When he reached the
top he saw the Blessed Virgin Mary standing in the midst of
a glorious light. She spoke to him in his native language,
making known to him Her desire that a shrine be built there
where She could demonstrate Her love, compassion and
protection. "For I am your merciful Mother," She said, "to
you and to all mankind who love me and trust in me and
invoke my help. Therefore, go to the dwelling of the Bishop
in Mexico City and say that the Virgin Mary sent you to
make known to him her great desire."*

*The Bishop was reluctant to believe Juan Diego's story.
Juan thus returned to the hill where the Virgin had
appeared and behold, the beautiful Lady was waiting for
him. She bade him to return to the Bishop the next day and
repeat her wishes. Juan Diego obeyed and this time, the
Bishop asked for a sign. Two days later the Virgin satisfied
his request: She appeared to Juan on the road as he was
going to bring a priest to his dying uncle and told him to
climb to the top of Tepeyac Hill, where he would find many
flowers blooming. He was to cut them and bring them to
Her. "Do not fear for your uncle," said the Virgin," for he is
not going to die. Be assured... he is already well."*

*Juan Diego climbed the hill and found a marvellous
garden of dew-fresh blossoms which he cut and brought to
the Lady who rearranged them and told him to take them to*

the Bishop. When the latter arrived at the home of Bishop Fray Juan de Zumarraga, he opened his cloak and the flowers cascaded to the floor - but to the astonishment of the Bishop and Juan Diego, there appeared upon the coarse fabric of the Indian's mantle a marvellously wrought, beautifully coloured portrait of the Virgin Mary, just as Juan had previously described Her. Furthermore, earlier on that day She had also appeared to Juan's dying uncle and had healed him. The Blessed Virgin told Juan's uncle to tell the Bishop of his miraculous cure and said to him that her image was to be known as "Santa Maria de Guadalupe". Indeed, thus she has been venerated for more than four-and-a-half centuries.

The mantle bearing the Sacred Image of Our Lady has remained intact and may be viewed today at the Basilica of Our Lady of Guadalupe in Mexico City. Every detail which it contains is symbolic and yet, all who saw it after the apparitions were able to read and understand it. So it was in this manner that eight million natives were converted to Christianity in the short span of seven years. To commemorate the extraordinary events various chapels were built in the area and the first Basilica to venerate the original Sacred Image was completed in 1709. It was subsequently transferred to the new Basilica on the 12th of October, 1976, where thousands of pilgrims come each year.

On the 12th of October, 1945, Pope Pius XII proclaimed Our Lady of Guadalupe to be the Patroness of all the Americas. She is also widely invoked to protect unborn children. Her feast-day is the 12th of December and is a Holy Day of Obligation in Mexico.

*In the name of the Father, and of the Son,
and of the Holy Spirit. Amen.*

O God, come to my aid.
O Lord, make haste to help me.

Glory Be
The Creed *(see page 26)*

FIRST DAY

Dearest Lady of Guadalupe, fruitful Mother of holiness, teach me your ways of gentleness and strength. Hear my humble prayer offered with heartfelt confidence to beg this favour... *(Here we mention our request)*.

Our Father • Hail Mary • Glory Be

SECOND DAY

O Mary, conceived without sin, I come to your throne of grace to share the fervent devotion of your faithful Mexican children who call to you under the glorious Aztec title of Guadalupe. Obtain for me a lively faith to your Son's holy will always. May His will be done on earth as it is in heaven.

Our Father • Hail Mary • Glory Be

THIRD DAY

O Mary, whose Immaculate Heart was pierced by seven swords of grief, help me to walk valiantly amid the sharp thorns strewn across my pathway. Obtain for me the strength to be a true imitator of you. This I ask you, my dear Mother.

Our Father
Hail Mary
Glory Be

FOURTH DAY

Dearest Mother of Guadalupe, I beg you for a fortified will to imitate your divine Son's charity, to seek always the good of others in need. Grant me this, I humbly ask of you.

Our Father
Hail Mary
Glory Be

Fifth day

O most holy Mother, I beg you to obtain for me pardon of all my sins, abundant graces to serve your Son more faithfully from now on, and lastly, the grace to praise Him with you forever in heaven.

Our Father
Hail Mary
Glory Be

Sixth day

Mary, Mother of vocations, multiply priestly vocations and flll the earth with religious houses which will be light and warmth for the world, safety in stormy nights. Beg your Son to send us many priests and religious. This we ask of you, O Mother.

Our Father
Hail Mary
Glory Be

SEVENTH DAY

O Lady of Guadalupe, we beg you that parents live a holy life and educate their children in a Christian manner; that children obey and follow the directions of their parents; that all members of the family pray and worship together. This we ask of you, O Mother.

Our Father
Hail Mary
Glory Be

EIGHTH DAY

With my heart full of the most sincere veneration, I prostrate myself before you, O Mother, to ask you to obtain for me the grace to fulfil the duties of my state in life with faithfulness and constancy.

Our Father
Hail Mary
Glory Be

NINTH DAY

O God, You have been pleased to bestow upon us unceasing favours by having placed us under the special protection of the Most Blessed Virgin Mary. Grant us, your humble servants, who rejoice in honour in her today upon earth, the happiness of seeing her face to face in heaven.

Our Father
Hail Mary
Glory Be

The author would like to thank the Queen of Americas Guild for their kind contribution of the above Novena. Further information may be had by contacting:
Queen of the Americas Guild, P.O. Box 851, 345 Kautz Road, St. Charles, Illinois 60174, U.S.A.
Tel.: (630) 584-1822, Fax: (630) 587-2200

8.
PRAYERS OF PETITION

PRAYER OF PETITION TO THE QUEEN OF THE HOLY ROSARY OF POMPEII

It is customary to recite this prayer, which was composed by Blessed Bartolo Longo, not only at the Sanctuary of Pompeii but also in other churches at midday on the 8th of May and on the first Sunday of October.

In the name of the Father, and of the Son, and of the Holy Spirit. Amen.

O God, come to my aid.
O Lord, make haste to help me.

Glory Be
The Creed *(see page 26)*

O Great Queen of Victories, O Sovereign of heaven and earth, at whose name the heavens rejoice and darkness trembles, O glorious Queen of the Rosary, we, Your faithful children, reveal the sentiments of our hearts, and with childlike trust, we confide our troubles to You. From the throne of mercy, where You sit as Queen, turn, O Mary, Your merciful gaze on us, on our families, on Italy, on Europe, and on the world. Be compassionate towards us in the troubles and anxieties which sadden our lives. Look, O Mary, at how many dangers of body and soul, and at how many calamities and sufferings afflict us!

O Mother, implore mercy for us from Your Divine Son and win the hearts of sinners with

Your clemency. They are our brethren and Your children who continue to cost sweet Jesus His Blood and who sadden Your Heart that is so sensitive. Reveal Yourself to everyone as You really are, Queen of peace and forgiveness.

Hail Mary

It is true that although we are Your children, we are the first to crucify Jesus again in our hearts and to pierce Your Heart once more.

We admit that we are worthy of being chastised severely, but recall that You received at Golgotha, in association with the divine blood, the testament of the dying Redeemer, which declared You to be our Mother, Mother of all sinners. You, as our Mother, are thus our advocate and our hope. And, in our mourning, we stretch out our begging hands to you, crying, "Mercy! O good Mother, have mercy on us, on our souls, our families, relatives, and friends, on our dearly departed and especially on our enemies and on the many people who call themselves Christians, even though they offend the loving Heart of Your Son. We beg mercy for all corrupt nations, for all of Europe, and for all the world, so that having repented, it may return to Your Heart. Have mercy on us all, O Mother of Mercy.

Hail Mary

In Your kindness, graciously hear us, O Mary! Jesus has put into Your hands all the treasures of His grace and mercy. You sit at the right hand of Your Son, O crowned Queen, resplendent in immortal glory above all the hosts of Angels.

You spread Your dominion over heaven and earth, and all creatures are subject to you. You are omnipotent by grace, therefore You can help us. If You were unwilling to help us because of our ingratitude and unworthiness of Your protection, we would not know where to turn for assistance. However, Your motherly heart will not allow us, Your children, to be lost.

The Child whom we see on Your lap and the mystical crown which we admire in Your hand inspire us with confidence that we shall be heard. We trust in You completely; we let ourselves fall, as fragile children, into the arms of the most tender of all mothers, expecting to receive from You the graces which we desire this very day.

Hail Mary

And now we ask a final grace of You, O Queen, which you cannot deny us (on this most solemn day).

Grant us Your constant love and, most especially, Your motherly blessing. We will not leave You until you have blessed us. Bless also our Holy Father the Pope, at this time. O Mary, add the following grace to the ancient splendour of your crown and to the triumph of your Rosary in which you are invoked as Queen of Victories: grant that the Faith may triumph and Peace may reign in human society.

Bless our bishops, and priests, especially all those who are fervent in their devotion to your Sanctuary.

Finally, bless all those associated to your Sanctuary at Pompeii, and all those who cultivate and promote devotion to the Holy Rosary.

O Blessed Rosary of Mary, sweet chain which links us to God, bond of love which unites us to the Angels, tower of salvation in the assaults from hell, secure haven in the sinking of the ship of this world, we will never abandon You again.
You will be our comfort at the hour of our death; to You we shall give the last kiss of our life when it is coming to a close.

And the last word on our lips will be your sweet name, O Queen of the Rosary, our most dear Mother, O Refuge of sinners, O comforting Sovereign of the afflicted. May You always be blessed, this day and always, on earth and in heaven. **Amen.**

Hail Holy Queen

PRAYER OF PETITION TO OUR LADY
OF THE MIRACULOUS MEDAL

To be recited as near as possible to half-past five in the evening on the 27th of November which is the feast of the Medal, on the 27th day of each month, and at times of urgent need.

O Immaculate Virgin Mary, we know that You are willing at all times and everywhere, to hear the prayers of Your children in exile in this valley of tears, but we also know that there are days and hours in which You like to shower more abundantly upon us the treasures of your graces.

Therefore, O Mary, we turn to You and prostrate ourselves before You, on the same day and at the same blessed hour which you chose for the manifestation of Your Medal.

We come to You, full of gratitude and boundless trust, at this hour so dear to You, in order to thank You for the great gift which you have bestowed on us in giving us Your image so that it may remain a proof of Your love and a pledge of Your protection over us.

We promise, therefore, that the holy Medal shall be the sign of Your presence among us as You desire; may it be our book from which we will learn under Your guidance how much You love us and what we must do so that many of Your sacrifices along with those of your Divine Son may not be offered in vain.

Indeed, Your pierced Heart which is represented on the Medal shall always rest on our hearts and let them beat in unison with Yours.

Your heart will inflame our own hearts with love for Jesus and will strengthen them in order that we may carry our cross everyday, following Your Son Jesus.

This is Your hour, O Mary, the hour of Your infinite goodness and Your triumphant mercy; the hour at which You allowed that torrent of graces and prodigies which flooded the earth to gush forth by means of Your medal.

Grant, O Mother, that this hour which reminds you of the sweet compassion of Your Heart and which prompted You to come and visit us, bringing us the remedy of many evils, may also be our hour: the hour of our true conversion, and the hour at which You grant our prayers.

You, who promised in that blessed hour that great graces would be granted to those who asked for them with trust: turn your eyes graciously towards us who beseech You. We admit that we do not merit Your graces and yet, to whom can we turn, O Mary, if not to You who are our Mother, in whose hands God has placed all His graces? Therefore, have mercy on us.

We ask this through Your Immaculate Conception and for the sake of the love which urged you to give us Your precious medal. O Comforter of the afflicted, You who have already been moved to compassion by our sufferings, look upon the evils which oppress us.

Grant that Your Medal may spread Your blessed rays upon us and upon all our dear ones: may it heal our sick, may it bring peace to our families, and may it free us from every danger.

May Your Medal bring comfort to those who suffer, consolation to those who weep, and light and strength to everyone. In particular, grant, O Mary, that we may ask You for the conversion of sinners, at this solemn hour, especially the conversion of those who are dear to us.

Remember that they, too, are your children, and that it was also for them that You suffered, prayed and wept.

Save them, O Refuge of sinners, so that after having loved, invoked and served You on earth, we may come to thank and praise You eternally in heaven. **Amen.**

Hail Holy Queen

O Mary, conceived without sin, pray for us who recourse to Thee.

(3 times)

PRAYER TO OUR LADY
OF MOUNT CARMEL
*(To be recited on the 16th of July, the feast of
Our Lady of Mount Carmel).*

O Mary, Mother and Splendour of Mount Carmel, on this solemn day we raise our prayer to you and, with childlike trust, we ask for your protection.

You know, O Holy Virgin Mary, the difficulties of our life; turn your gaze towards us and give us the strength to overcome them.

The title of yours which we celebrate today recalls the place chosen by God where he wished to reconcile himself with his people who wanted to come back to him after having repented.

Indeed it was at Mount Carmel that the prophet Elijah said the prayer which obtained the gift of a shower of rain to restore the earth after a long drought. It was a sign of God's forgiveness which the holy prophet proclaimed with joy when he saw the little cloud rise from the sea which was soon to cover the sky.

In that little cloud, O Immaculate Virgin Mary, your children saw you, who rose in your purity from the sea of sinful humanity and, with Christ, generously poured out every blessing upon the earth. On this day, may you be once more the source of graces and blessings for us.

Hail Holy Queen

You recognize, O Mother, the Scapular that we wear in your honour, as a symbol of our filial devotion; in order to show us your affection, you consider it your habit and a sign of our consecration to you, according to the spirituality of Carmel.

We thank you, O Mary, for this Scapular that you gave us so that it would be our defence against the enemy of our soul.

In moments of temptation and danger may the thought of you and of your love call us back to the right path. O Mother of ours, on this day which reminds us of your continual kindness towards us, we repeat with emotion and trust, the prayer which the Order has adressed and consecrated to you for centuries:

**"Flower of Carmel,
vine with blossom weighed,
Shining light of heaven,
bearing child through maid,**

**None like to thee,
Mother most tender,
whom no man didst know,
On all Carmel's children
thy favour bestow,
Star of the sea".**

Flos Carmeli (Traditional)

May this day, which unites us at your feet mark a fresh desire for holiness in us all, in the Church and in Carmel. With your protection we want to renew the ancient committment of our fathers, because we too are convinced that "everyone must live in veneration of Jesus Christ and serve Him faithfully with a pure heart and good conscience".

Hail Holy Queen

O Mary, your love is great for those who are devoted to the Scapular of Mount Carmel. You are not content to help them only while on earth to live out their Christian vocation, but also ensure that their sufferings be mitigated in Purgatory, in order to hasten their entering into Paradise. You truly show yourself to be the mother of your children because you take care of them every time they are in need. Show then, O Queen of Purgatory, your power as Mother of God and of humankind, and come to the assistance of those souls who feel the purifying pain of the distance from God whom they have come, by now, to know and love.

We beseech you, O Virgin Mary, to take care of the souls of our dear ones and of all those who, during their life, wore your Scapular and sought to wear it with devotion and commitment. But we do not want to forget all those other souls who await the fullness of the beatific vision of God. Grant that all of them, having been purified by the redeeming blood of Christ, may be welcomed presently into everlasting happiness. We pray also for ourselves, in particular for the last moments of our life, when the supreme choice of our eternal destiny is decided. At that moment take us by the hand, O Mother, as a guarantee of the grace of salvation.

Hail Holy Queen

We would like to ask you many graces, O most Sweet Mother! On this day which our fathers have consecrated to you in gratitude for your blessings, we ask you to continue to show us your generosity. Grant us the grace to keep far from sin. Free us from the evils of body and soul. Grant us the graces which we ask you for ourselves and for our dear ones. You are able to answer our requests, and we trust that you will submit them to Jesus, your Son and our brother.

And now we ask you, O Mother of the Church, and splendour of Mount Carmel, to bless every-one: bless the Pope who, in the name of Jesus, guides his Church. Bless the bishops, priests, and all those whom the Lord asks to follow him in religious life. Bless all those who suffer aridity of the spirit and are afflicted by the difficulties of life. Enlighten unhappy souls and warm all hearts. Sustain all those who wear your Scapular and inspire other souls who have become tepid to wear your Scapular as a reminder to imitate your virtues. Bless and free the souls in Purgatory.

Bless all children, O Mother, our Consolation. Be with us at all times, in our joys and sorrows, in times of hope and sadness, now and at the moment of our coming into eternity. May this hymn of thanksgiving and praise become eternal in the happiness of heaven. **Amen.**

Hail Mary

Prayer to the
Virgin Mary of Loreto

To be recited at midday on the 15th of March, the 15th of August, the 8th of September and the 10th of December.

O Mary of Loreto, Glorious Virgin, we approach you with confidence: accept this humble prayer of ours today. Humanity is now greatly troubled by grave evils from which it would like to be freed itself. It needs peace, justice, truth and love, and illudes itself that it can find these realities far from your Son. O Mother! You carried the Divine Saviour in your most pure womb and lived with him in the Holy House which we venerate on this hill of Loreto; grant us the grace to seek him and to imitate his example which leads to salvation.

Through faith and filial love we come in a spiritual way to your blessed House. Because of the presence of your Family, it is the supreme holy home by which we want all Christian families to be inspired: from Jesus, may every son learn how to obey and to work; from you, O Mary, may all women, learn humilty and the spirit of sacrifice; from Joseph, who lived for you and for Jesus, may all men learn to believe in God and to live justly and faithfully in the family and in society.

Many families, O Mary, are not a sanctuary where God is loved and served: grant, therefore, we pray you, that each family may imitate yours, recognizing your Divine Son in their daily life and loving him above all things. Just one day, after years of prayer and work, he left this Holy House in order to proclaim his Word, which is Light and Life, in the same way the echo of his all-powerful word, which enlightens and converts, reach all people from the holy walls of this house which speak to us about faith and charity.

Hail Holy Queen

We pray to you, O Mary, for the universal Church, for Italy and for all peoples of the earth, for ecclesiastical and civil istitutions and for the suffering and for sinners, so that everyone may become a disciple of God. O Mary, on this day of grace, united to the faithful who are present in spirit and desire to venerate the Holy House where you were overshadowed by the Holy Spirit, with lively faith, we repeat to you the words of the Archangel Gabriel: Hail, O full of grace, the Lord is with you! We invoke you likewise: Hail, O Mary, Mother of Jesus and Mother of the Church, Refuge of sinners, Comfort of the afflicted, Help of Christians. Among difficulties and frequent temptations, we are in danger of being lost but we look to you and repeat: Hail, Gate of Paradise; Hail, Star of the Sea! May our petition rise to you, O Mary. May it tell you of our desires, our love for Jesus and our hope in you,

Mother. May our prayer come down on earth again accompanied by abundant heavenly graces.

Hail Holy Queen

INVOCATIONS OF OUR LADY OF LORETO

Our Lady of Loreto,

Pray for me.

Our Lady of Loreto,

Protect me.

Our Lady of Loreto,

Heal me.

Our Lady of Loreto,

Take care of my children.

Our Lady of Loreto,

Ease my sufferings.

Our Lady of Loreto,

Intercede for me.

Our Lady of Loreto,

Protect my dear ones.

Our Lady of Loreto,

Assist me at the hour of my death.

Amen.

PETITION TO OUR LADY OF GRACES

(who is venerated in the Church of the Cappuchin friars at San Giovanni Rotondo, sanctuary of Blessed Padre Pio)

O Heavenly Treasure of all graces, Mother of God and my Mother, Mary, as you are the First Born Daughter of the Eternal Father and have his Omnipotence at hand, have mercy on my soul, and grant me the grace which I ardently ask of you.

Hail Mary

O Merciful Bestower of divine graces, most Holy Mary, Mother of the Incarnate Word, who has crowned you with his great Wisdom, consider the greatness of my sorrow and grant me the grace of which I am so much in need.

Hail Mary

O Most Beloved Bestower of divine graces, Immaculate Bride of the Eternal Holy Spirit, Most Holy Mother, you who received from him a heart which is moved to compassion by human misfortunes and which cannot but help those who suffer, have mercy on my soul and grant me the grace which I seek with complete trust in your immense goodness.

Hail Mary

Yes, yes, O my Mother, Giver of all graces, Refuge of poor sinners, Comfort of the afflicted, Hope of those who despair and most powerful Help of Christians, I put all my trust in you and I am sure that you will obtain for me from Jesus the grace that I desire so much, if it be for the good of my soul.

Hail Holy Queen

PETITION TO OUR LADY OF SUFFRAGE

Most sweet Virgin Mary, to you, who, in your goodness, allow us to invoke you with the title of Our Lady of Suffrage, we ardently pray: turn your merciful gaze towards us, so that our lukewarm life may be transformed into fervour and holiness in order that we may love God immensely and may avoid ever being separated from you. Furthermore, we commend to you O tender Mother, the souls of all our dearly departed relatives and friends whom we still love today; may you watch over them. Graci-ously console them in their sufferings with your loving presence and grant them, through your interces-sion, divine forgiveness and the joy of eternal blessings.

Hail Mary

O most Holy Virgin of Suffrage, with firm trust we implore your help even now for the hour of our death. Give us at that moment the grace of being purified with sincere contrition from all stains of human fragility, so that we may come to enjoy the beatific vision of God. And grant, O Mary, you who are the Gate of Paradise, that the anxious time of the souls who suffer in Purgatory through our fault, while waiting to meet God, may be shortened, so that they may be welcomed presently with exultation into the heavenly family.

Hail Mary

Our Lady of Suffrage, through the ardent love which you bear for Jesus, we beseech you with all our heart to be a Mother to us forever, even if one day we find ourselves in Purgatory. Be our sweet hope and our powerful Advocate before the Lord; and do not allow those whom we leave on earth to forget us in their prayers.

Above all, we ask you, O loving Lady, to have a particular affection for all those souls in Purgatory who are most abandoned and forgotten by those who loved them during their lives on earth.

Compensate for the lack of intercession for them; inflame our hearts with their memory and with compassion towards them so that they may soon be united with God.

Listen to this ardent and humble prayer of ours, O intimate and beloved one of the heart of God, and grant that one day we may all love and praise God together, in union with you for all eternity. **Amen.**

Hail Mary
Eternal rest...

9.
OUR LADY OF SORROWS

- **Prayers**
  - **Rosaries**
- **Chaplets**

"There is a place in Jerusalem, on the Mount of Olives, where, according to tradition, Christ wept over the city of Jerusalem... The crying of Jesus over Jerusalem expresses his love for the Holy City, as well as his sorrow for its not so distant future which he foresees: the City will be taken over by force and the Temple destroyed, the young shall be submitted to the same torment (as Jesus), death on the cross... The Gospel tells us also about how Jesus was moved, when he exulted in the Holy Spirit... Jesus rejoices in Divine Paternity, he is glad because it has been asked of him to reveal this paternity, and in short, he rejoices because this paternity is spread out especially on little children.

"It is right, however, to remember also the tears of Peter. The Gospel of today tells us of the profession of faith of Peter in the vicinity of Caesarea Philippi. Let us listen to the words of Christ: 'Blessed are you, Simon, son of Jonah, for neither flesh nor blood has revealed this to you but my Father in heaven'. The other words (spoken by) the Redeemer to Peter are well known: 'In truth I tell you, before the cock crows, you will have disowned me three times'. And so it was. But when Jesus looked at Peter in the house of the high priest as the cock crowed, he 'recalled what the Lord had said to him... And he went outside and wept bitterly'. Tears of sorrow, tears of conversion to confirm the truth of his profession of faith.

"The evangelical accounts never speak of the crying of the Virgin Mary. We do not hear her crying on the night of Bethlehem when the time had come to give birth to Son of

God was born, nor at Golgotha, when she stood at the foot of the cross. We are not even told of her tears of joy when Christ rose from the dead. Even though the Scriptures do not mention (her tears), our faith speaks to us about them by intuition. Mary who cries out of sadness or for joy is the expression of the Church, which rejoices on the night of Christmas, suffers at the foot of the Cross on Holy Friday and rejoices once more at the dawn of the Resurrection. She is the Spouse of the Lamb, presented to us by the second reading taken from the book of Revelation (ref. Rev. 21:9).

"The tears of Mary appear in apparitions with which, from time to time, She accompanies the Church in its journey along the roads of the world. Mary cried at La Salette in the middle of the last century before the apparitions at Lourdes, in a period in which Christianity in France was experiencing growing hostility. She cried also here, at Syracuse, at the end of the second world war. One can understand this crying in view of these tragic events: the great massacre, caused by conflict, the slaughter of the sons and daughters of Israel; the threat of atheist communism against Europe coming from the East.

"The image of the Virgin Mary of Czestochowa at Lublin also cried during that period (in history), a fact which is scarcely known outside Poland while the story of Syracuse has reached many countries, and many pilgrims have come here. The tears of the Virgin Mary belong to the order of signs: they bear witness to the presence of the Mother in the Church and in the world.

"A mother cries when she sees her children threatened by some evil, be it spiritual or physical. Mary cries in order to share in the weeping of Christ over Jerusalem or (his tears) by the tomb of Lazzarus or finally on the way of the cross.

"Here today at Syracuse the Sanctuary is dedicated to

Our Lady of Tears. But now I come as Bishop of Rome, as the Successor of Peter, and it is with joy that I fulfil this service towards your community, and greet it with love in the person of its pastor, Mons. Giuseppe Costanzo, who, keeping the tradition of his predecessors, has prepared this day with great commitment. In a special way, I greet all priests, inviting them to be faithful imitators of the apostle Peter, who stayed in this wonderful town during his journey from Caesarea to Rome (ref. Ac 28:12). The mission which you have received, dear brothers, requires courage and constancy but the Lord will reward your generous service. I greet also all the religious and members of the secular institutes. I hope that consecrated life will shine as a witness to the values of the Spirit and will become the promoter of a "frontier" apostolate responding to the profound need of God in our times.

"I also greet with affection all the lay people, in particular all families, in this year which is dedicated to them: may they be the sign of a society which, instead of being often distracted and indifferent to self-sacrificing love, is rather rooted in the faith of the Church and open to life. I feel the words which Christ said to Peter resound in me today: 'You are Peter and on this rock I will build my church. And the gates of the underworld can never overpower it. I will give you the keys of the kingdom of heaven: whatever you bind on earth will be bound in heaven; whatever you loose on earth will be loosed in heaven' (Mt 16:18-19). These words of Christ express the supreme authority which He possesses as Redeemer: the power to forgive sins, acquired at the price of his blood shed at Golgotha; the power to absolve and to forgive."

PRAYERS

THE HAIL MARY OF ST. BONAVENTURE
*An indulgence was granted by Pope Pius IX
to those who recited this prayer.*

I greet you, O Mary, full of sorrows, the Crucified one is with you; sorrowful are you among all women and sorrowful is the fruit of your womb, Jesus.

Holy Mary, Mother of the Crucified one, obtain tears for us, who crucified your Son, now and at the hour of our death. **Amen.**

THE HAIL MARY OF
OUR LADY OF SORROWS

Hail Mary, full of sorrows,
Jesus Crucified is with you,
Worthy of compassion are you among all women,
and worthy of compassion,
is the fruit of your womb, Jesus.

Holy Mary, Mother of Jesus Crucified,
grant us, who crucified your Son,
tears of sincere repentance,
now and at the hour of our death. **Amen.**

PRAYER TO OUR LADY OF TEARS
Pope John Paul II, Syracuse

Sanctuary of Our Lady of Tears, you arose to remind the Church of the weeping of her Mother. Remind us also of the weeping of Peter, to whom Christ entrusted the keys of the kingdom of heaven for the benefit of all the faithful. May these keys be useful to bind and to loose, for redemption from all human misery. May many who are oppressed by the awareness of sin come here to be welcomed within these walls and may they experience here the richness of the mercy of God and his forgiveness! Here, may they be guided by the tears of the Mother!

They are the tears of sorrow for those who reject the love of God, for separated families or for those who are in difficulty, for the youth who are ensnared by the consumerist society and are often confused, for the violence which still causes much blood to be shed, for the misunderstandings and hate which dig profound ditches between people and nations. They are tears of prayer: prayer of the mother who gives strength to all prayers and humbly prays for all those who do not pray because they are distracted by a thousand other interests, or because their hearts are obstinately closed to the call of God. They are tears of hope which melt the hardness of hearts and open them to the encounter with Christ the Redeemer, source of light and peace for single people, for families, and for society as a whole. O Our Lady of tears, look with motherly goodness upon the sorrow of the world!

Dry the tears of those who suffer, those who are forgotten, those who despair and of the victims of every type of violence! Grant to everyone tears of repentance and new life so that all people may open their hearts to the life-giving gift of the love of God. Grant to everyone tears of joy, having seen the profound tenderness of your heart.

O SORROWFUL MOTHER

St. Bonaventure

O sorrowful Virgin Mary, what tongue can express and what mind can comprehend the immensity of your sorrow?

You, who were present at and shared in the passion of your son Jesus, and saw with your own eyes that blessed and most holy flesh which you had conceived without sin, nursed with much tenderness, had held so gently on your lap and kissed with love, saw the same flesh being torn away by each stroke of the whip, pierced by the pointed tips of the thorns, struck with the reed, and suffer slaps and blows .

You saw His flesh being pierced with nails and fastened to the cross, and while hanging there, become ever more lacerated. You saw it being exposed to mockery of every kind and finally, being wetted with gall and vinegar.

And you also saw the soul of your Son Jesus! With the eyes of your heart you saw that most divine soul being filled with the gall of every sorrow, sometimes being shaken by the trembling of the spirit, at other times afflicted by fright, in agony, disturbed, or deeply saddened, partly because of the most vivid sense of bodily suffering, partly because of the ardent zeal to make reparation to Divine Honour for having been wounded by sin, partly out of compassion towards you, Most Sweet Mother.

Looking with mercy upon you who stood by the cross, he bid you that sweet farewell: "Woman, here is your Son!". And in that way he comforted your sorrowful soul, knowing that you had been pierced by the sword of compassion more deeply than if your own body had been wounded. O Mary, Mother most merciful, turn your eyes upon the most sacred garment of your beloved Son, woven by the Holy Spirit in your most sacred womb, and implore forgiveness for us who turn to you so that we may be found worthy of being saved from eternal condemnation.

PETITION TO OUR LADY OF TEARS

Our Lady of Tears, we need You: we need the
light which radiates from Your goodness, the
comfort which comes forth from your heart,
the Peace of which You are Queen.
With confidence we entrust our needs to You:
our sorrows so that You may console us,
our bodies so that You may heal them,
our hearts so that they may be filled with contrition and love,
our souls so that they may be saved.
Remember, O Immaculate and Sorrowful Heart,
that Jesus refuses nothing
at the sight of Your Holy Tears
Grant, O good Mother,
that your tears may be linked to ours
so that your Divine Son
may grant us the grace of...
(Here we express our intention)
for which we ardently ask of You.
O Mother of Love, Sorrow and Mercy,
listen to us and have mercy on us!

Imprimatur:
Archbishop Joseph of Syracuse,
17th of October, 1969

Prayer to Mary,
Mother of the Sick

This prayer was found written on a piece of paper left under the statue of the Virgin Mary in the church of La Roche-Pozay in France.

Stay, O Mary at the bedside of all the sick of the world, of those who, at this moment, have lost consciousness and are going to die, of those who are going to enter into a long agony, of those who have lost all hope of being healed, of those who cannot look after themselves because they are poor, of those who would like to walk but are immobile.

Stay, O sorrowful Mother, by those who would like to rest and yet poverty compels them to continue to work, by those who by are looking for a less painful position in their beds and are unable to find it, by those who are tormented by the thought of the troubles of their family, by those who must renounce the plans which they had desired most for the future, and especially by those who do not believe in a better life, by those who revolt and swear against God; by those who do not know or do not remember that Christ suffered as they do.

Prayer to our lady of sorrows

O Immaculate Mary, who bore sorrow for our sake at the foot of the Cross, your Heart accepted the Blood which your Son shed and your Heart suffered the pain of the Cross, the thorns and the nails which tormented Him, and you accepted us as your children: grant that we may dwell in your Heart so sweet.

It is good to stay at the foot of the Cross with you, O Mary, Mother of God and our Mother, Advocate of sinners, Sovereign Mediatrix of the universe, Teacher of the truth...

O most sweet Mother, teach us to love Jesus, and to imitate his virtues, of which he revealed himself to be Master when hanging on the cross.

Inflame us with zeal to quench the thirst of our Saviour who yearns for souls.

Our Lady of Sorrows, help us to climb the hill of Calvary by the side of Jesus who carries the Cross and beside you who accompany him, so that we may reach the holy Mountain of God.

Mary, our Mother, grant that we may always embrace our cross and thus live united to your Heart forever...".

HELP US IN THESE DIFFICULT TIMES

by Pope John Paul II

Today we are looking at your sorrowful eyes, O Mother; we are looking at you who know everything that we lack, at you who know our sorrows and our hearts. You know, Mary, what we ardently desire. Speak about it to your Son, tell him about the difficult present times in which we live: speak about it to Him who is the guest of our future. Tomorrow begins today and it will be what we have made of it. O Mother of Christ, Mother of the Lord of the future, help us in these difficult times to listen your Son, to listen to him every day and at every moment of our life, even when he seems severe and demanding. To whom shall we go otherwise? He has the words of eternal life, the Gospel of joy and of commitment, of suffering and of salvation.

O Mother, with this Gospel in our hearts, help us to overcome the difficulties of today, in order to reach that "tomorrow" to which Christ has invited us.

THE SEQUENCE OF OUR
LADY OF SORROWS
(STABAT MATER DOLOROSA)

This prayer was probably composed by Jacopone da Todi who died in 1306. The main theme expressed by the se-quence is the desire on the part of the author to partake in the suffering of Our Lady of Sorrows. By contemplating the trials of Our Blessed Mother we console Her, and also grow in patience and perseverance so that our own sorrows become easier to bear. The sequence may be said or sung before the Gospel in the liturgy of the Feast of Our Lady of Sorrows (15th of September).

At the cross her station keeping,
stood the mournful Mother weeping,
close to Jesus to the last;

Through her heart, his sorrow sharing,
all his bitter anguish bearing,
now at length the sword has passed.

Oh how sad and sore distressed
was that Mother highly blessed
of the sole-begotten One.

Christ above in torments hangs;
she beneath beholds the pangs,
of her dying glorious Son.

Is there one who would not weep,
whelmed in miseries so deep,
Christ's dear Mother to behold?

Can the human heart refrain
from partaking in her pain,
in that mother's pain untold?

Bruised, derided, cursed, defiled,
she beheld her tender child,
all with bloody scourges rent;

For the sins of his own nation
saw him hang in desolation,
till his spirit forth he sent.

O you Mother! font of love,
touch my spirit from above,
make my heart with yours accord:

Make me feel as you have felt;
make my soul to glow and melt
with the love of Christ our Lord.

Holy Mother pierce me through;
in my heart each wound renew
of my Saviour crucified:

let me share with you his pain,
who for all my sins was slain,
who for me in torments died.

Let me mingle tears with you,
mourning him who mourned for me,
all the days that I may live:

by the cross with you to stay,
there with you to weep and pray,
is all I ask of you to give.

Virgins of all virgins best!
listen to my fond request:
let me share your grief divine;

let me, to my latest breath,
in my body bear the death
of that dying Son of yours.

Wounded with his every wound,
steep my soul till it has swooned
in his very blood away.

Be to me, O Virgin, nigh,
lest in flames I burn and die
in his awful judgement day.

Christ, when you shall call me hence,
be your Mother my defence, be your cross my
victory.

While my body here decays,
may my soul your goodness praise,
safe in paradise with you. **Amen.** (*Easter time: Alleluia.*)

V. Pray for us, Our Lady of Sorrows.
R. That we may be made worthy of the promises of Christ.

Let us pray.
O God, who wanted your Son to have his sorrowful Mother by his side, grant that your Holy Church, may share in the glory of the resurrection. Through Christ our Lord, who lives and reigns with you in the unity of the Holy Spirit, one God for ever and ever. **Amen.**

LATIN VERSION

Stabat mater dolórosa
iuxta crucem lacrimósa,
dum pendébat Fílius.

Cuius ánimam geméntem,
contristátam et doléntem
pertransívit gládius.

O quam tristis et afflícta
fuit illa benedicta
Mater Unigéniti!

Quæ moerébat, et dolébat,
pia mater, cum vidébat
nati pœnas íncliti.

Quis est homo qui non fleret,
Matrem Christi si vidéret
in tanto supplício?

Quis non posset contristári,
piam matrem contemplári
doléntem cum Fílio?

Pro peccátis suæ gentis
vidit Iesum in torméntis
et flagéllis súbditum.

Vidit suum dulcem natum
moriéntem desolátum,
dum emísit spíritum.

Eia, mater, fons amóris,
me sentíre vim dolóris
fac, ut tecum lúgeam.

Fac, ut árdeat cor meum
in amándo Christum Deum,
ut sibi compláceam.

Sancta mater, istud agas,
Crucifíxi fige plagas
cordi meo válide.

Tui nati vulneráti,
tam dignáti pro me pati,
pœnas mecum dívide.

Fac me tecum flere pie,
Crucifíxo condolére,
donec ego víxero.

Iuxta crucem tecum stare
et me tibi sociáre
in planctu desídero.

Virgo vírginum præclára,
mihi iam non sis amára;
fac me tecum plángere.

Fac, ut portem Christi mortem,
passiónis fac consórtem,
et plagas recólere.

Fac me plagis vulnerári,
fac me cruce hac inebriári,
et cruóre Fílii.

Flammis urar ne succénsus,
per te, Virgo, sim defénsus
in die iudícii.

Christe, cum sit hinc exíre,
da per matrem me veníre
ad palmam victóriæ.

Quando corpus moriétur,
fac ut ánimæ donétur
paradísi glória.
Amen. (T.P. Alleluia.)

DEVOTION TO THE
DESOLATE VIRGIN MARY

One of Our Lady's greatest sufferings, and one which is often forgotten, was the pain of being separated from her Son when his body was laid in the tomb, and the time which followed during her life on earth when she could no longer enjoy His presence in the same way as before. Although Mary suffered tremendously during his Passion, she had at least the consolation of suffering together with Jesus. Looking at her Son in his agony caused her overwhelming pain, and yet the sight of him gave her relief. However, while coming down from the hill of Calvary without her Son Jesus, she must have felt very much alone; what emptiness and solitude she must have experienced... Indeed, it would have been an even greater affliction had the Lord not provided for her: while hanging on the Cross, Jesus entrusted the care of his mother to St. John, the beloved disciple, who "took her into his home" from the hour of the death of Our Lord (ref. Jn 19:27). Let us thus console Mary in this sorrow of hers, so much forgotten, by keeping her company in her loneliness, partaking in her sorrows and reminding her of the Resurrection which was about to occur, compensating in a most unique way for all her sufferings.

A HOLY HOUR WITH THE
DESOLATE VIRGIN MARY

The reader is invited to find at least one hour which he or she can dedicate entirely to consoling the Virgin Mary in her desolation, which she still suffers today because many of her children are indifferent to her love and ignore her. This devotion is ideal for an hour of community or family prayer, or indeed, for a vigil of prayer whereby the faithful take turns to keep the Virgin Mary company, commencing on Friday evening and concluding on Saturday evening. In this hour we try to be close to Mary in her suffering, to read her Heart and to listen to her weeping. Let us comfort our dearest Mother while we consider the sorrow which she experienced:

1. When she saw the tomb of Christ being closed;
2. When she had to be taken away from it;
3. When on her return to the tomb, she had to pass nearby the hill of Calvary where the cross of her Son still stood;
4. When she walked again along the road to Calvary and was looked at with contempt by her people as the mother of him who had been condemned;
5. When she saw her empty house again, and while allowing St. John to embrace her, felt the loss of her own Son even more acutely;
6. During the long hours from Friday evening to Sunday, having constantly in mind the horrible scenes which she had witnessed;
7. Finally, we console Mary for the sorrow which she continues to experience, considering that much of her sorrow was suffered in vain for countless numbers of her children, not only those who do not believe in Christ but also many Christians.

What would you say to the Virgin Mary to comfort her? You should say what your heart inspires you to say to a mother such as Mary who has lost her son. Remind her of the Resurrection that is to come, of the glory that awaits Jesus, of the thousands of souls who will be saved through his Blood, and of the host of generous souls who throughout the centuries will recall his sufferings and be moved to tears by their memory.

Prayer in preparation for the Holy Hour:

O Sorrowful Mother of mine, grant that my poor soul may be united to those of St. John and of the holy women who stayed at the foot of the Cross, accompanying you in the deep sorrow which your motherly Heart felt when you no longer saw your beloved Son. It is only right that I partake in your sorrow and try to comfort you, because I, too, caused your tears by my sins. You cry for me, and thus it is right that I unite my tears to yours. O Mary, accept the desire I have to sympathize with you in your sorrow and to try to comfort your Heart.

I cry over my sins and resolve to be your consolation. Strengthen my desire, do not allow these tears to be shed in vain. Grant to me and to all sinners tears of true repentance so that having cried with you on earth, we may come to sing the eternal Alleluia with you in heaven. **Amen.**

Hail Holy Queen

ROSARY TO OUR LADY OF SORROWS
FIRST SCHEME

*In the name of the Father, and of the Son,
and of the Holy Spirit. Amen.*

O God, come to my aid.
O Lord, make haste to help me.

Glory Be
The Creed *(see page 26)*

INTRODUCTORY PRAYER

O dear Virgin Mary, Our Lady of Sorrows, I
want to pause in order to reflect on all those circumstances which caused you to suffer most. I
desire to remain a little time with you and to
recall with gratitude how much you suffered for
me. To your sufferings, which were present throughout your life, I unite my own sufferings and
furthermore, those of all fathers and mothers, of
all young sick people, of children and of the
elderly, so that every sorrow of theirs may be
accepted with love, and each cross may be borne
with hope in their hearts. **Amen.**

MARY HEARS THE PROPHECY OF SIMEON IN THE TEMPLE

O Mary, as you presented your Son to God the Father in the temple, the elderly prophet Simeon, foretold that Jesus was to be a sign that would be opposed and that your soul would be pierced with a sword of sorrow. These very words were already a sword to your soul: and yet you stored up all these things in your heart. Thank you, O Mary.

I offer this mystery for all parents who suffer because of their children.

Our Father
Hail Mary *(7 times)*

Blessed be the sufferings of the most Holy Virgin Mary, our Mother.

SECOND SORROW
MARY FLEES TO EGYPT IN ORDER TO SAVE JESUS

O Mary, you were forced to flee to Egypt with your Son because the great powers of the earth rose up against him to kill him. It is difficult to imagine how you felt when, at the invitation of your spouse, you had to rise in the middle of the night and help your Child to escape, that Child in whom you recognised and venerated the Messiah and the Son of God. You were left without the security which one's own country and home can offer. You fled to seek refuge, and thus united yourself to the sufferings of those who do not have a roof over their head and also of those who are emigrants or refugees, far from their homeland.

O Mary, I turn to you, who are my Mother and I pray to you for those who are forced to leave their homes. I pray to you for refugees, for the exiles; I pray for the poor who have not enough money to build a house and to provide for their families; I pray especially for those who have conflict in their families and have thus abandoned their homes to live on the streets; for the young people who disagree with their parents, for married couples who are separated, and for the rejected members of society. O Mary, lead them through their suffering to a new dwelling place.

Our Father
Hail Mary *(7 times)*

Blessed be the sufferings of the most Holy Virgin Mary, our Mother.

Third Sorrow
The finding of Jesus in the temple

O Mary, with great sorrow you searched for your Child for three days and finally, you were filled with joy on finding him in the temple. Your heart had suffered deeply. Your sorrow had been great because you were aware of your responsibility. You knew that the Heavenly Father had entrusted his Son to you and that he was the Messiah, the one who was to redeem humanity.

For this reason your sorrow was tremendous, but the joy at finding him was even greater.

O Mary, I pray to you for the youth who have left their homes and suffer greatly as a consequence. I pray to you for those who have had to leave their homes because of ill health and are now in hospital.

I pray to you for the young people who have been deprived of love and peace, and no longer understand the meaning of "home".

O Mary, search for them and grant that they let themselves be found so that the world may be renewed.

Our Father
Hail Mary *(7 times)*

Blessed be the sufferings of the most Holy Virgin Mary, our Mother.

Fourth Sorrow
MARY MEETS JESUS AS HE CARRIES HIS CROSS

O Mary, you met your Son while he was carrying his cross. Who could describe the sorrow which you felt at that moment? I am lost for words...

O most Holy Mother, I pray to you for those who have been left alone in their sorrow. Visit prisoners and comfort them; visit those who are sick; help those who are lost. Caress those who are afflicted by incurable illnesses, as you caressed your Son for the last time here on earth.

Help them to offer their suffering for the salvation of the world, just as you offered your sorrow to God the Father while accompanying him to Calvary.

Our Father
Hail Mary *(7 times)*

Blessed be the sufferings of the most Holy Virgin Mary, our Mother.

Fifth Sorrow
MARY WITNESSES THE CRUCIFIXION
AND DEATH OF JESUS

O Mary, I think of you as you stood by the cross of your dying Son. You followed him to Calvary in sorrow and finally reached the foot of the Cross where you experienced a sorrow that could not be humanly consoled. O Mary, you showed perseverance in your suffering. As your spirit was strong, sorrow did not allow you to shut your heart in the face of a new assignment: according to the desire of your Son, you became the Mother of us all.

I pray to you, Mary, for those who assist the sick. Help them to offer their help with love. Give strength and courage to those who feel unable to continue to care for their sick ones. In particular, bless mothers who have sick children; grant that they may grow through their experience of the Cross. Unite your sorrow as a mother to the sadness and exhaustion of those who are called to look after sick members of their family for months, years or perhaps throughout their entire life.

Our Father
Hail Mary *(7 times)*

Blessed be the sufferings of the most Holy Virgin Mary, our Mother.

Sixth Sorrow
Mary receives the body of Jesus as it is taken down from the cross.

I contemplate you, Mary, as you accept the body of your lifeless Son upon your lap, while your heart is stricken by overwhelming grief. Your suffering continues even when that of Jesus is over. For the last time you keep his body warm on your motherly lap, with the goodness and the love of your heart.

O Mother, I consecrate myself to you at this moment. To you I consecrate my sorrow together with the sorrow of all people. I consecrate to you those who are lonely, abandoned, rejected, or in conflict with others. To you I consecrate the entire world. May you keep everyone under your maternal protection. Grant that the world may become one united family where we are all brothers and sisters.

Our Father
Hail Mary *(7 times)*

Blessed be the sufferings of the most Holy Virgin Mary, our Mother.

SEVENTH SORROW
MARY ACCOMPANIES THE BODY
OF JESUS TO THE TOMB

O Mary, you accompanied Him to the tomb. You cried and sobbed for him, as a mother cries for an only child. Many people in the world mourn because they have lost their dear ones. Console them and let them be comforted by their faith. Many of the bereaved are lacking in faith and hope, and in strugging with the problems of the world, they lose their confidence and the joy of living.

O Mary, intercede for the bereaved, so that by growing in faith they may find the way to attain peace of heart. Let evil be destroyed and new life begin: life which is born from your suffering and from the burial of your Son. **Amen.**

Our Father
Hail Mary *(7 times)*

Blessed be the sufferings of the most Holy Virgin Mary, our Mother.

Let us pray.
O God, you wanted Our Lady of Sorrows to be present when your Son was raised up on the cross: grant that your Holy Church, united with Mary to the Passion of Christ, may share in the glory of the Resurrection. Through the same Christ our Lord, who lives and reigns with you, in the unity of the Holy Spirit, one God for ever and ever. **Amen.**

ROSARY TO OUR LADY OF SORROWS
SECOND SCHEME

In the name of the Father, and of the Son, and of the Holy Spirit. Amen.

O God, come to my aid.
O Lord, make haste to help me.

Glory Be
The Creed *(see page 26)*

FIRST SORROW
O Queen of Martyrs, what sorrow you felt when Simeon the prophet, advanced in years, foresaw that Jesus was to be a sign that would be opposed and that a sword would pierce your soul too. Through the merits of this prophecy, which cast the shadow of the cross on your divine maternity, show my sins clearly to me and help me to detest them with all my heart.

Hail Mary *(7 times)*

SECOND SORROW
O Queen of Martyrs, the persecution of Herod obliged you to flee unexpectedly to Egypt with your Child Jesus and your spouse Joseph and to affront the trials of being in exile. Through the merits of such long and painful suffering, free me from the seduction of Satan and of the world.

Hail Mary *(7 times)*

THIRD SORROW

O Queen of Martyrs, what sorrow you felt and shared with St. Joseph during the days in which Jesus remained in the temple of Jerusalem without your knowledge! Through the merits of this sorrow, do not allow me to spoil my friendship with Jesus through being "lukewarm" and half-hearted in my faith and through sin.

Hail Mary *(7 times)*

FOURTH SORROW

O Queen of Martyrs, what acute anxiety you suffered while you witnessed Jesus being misunderstood by many of his own people and being rejected and persecuted by the leaders of Israel! Through the merits of this sorrow, grant me the grace to follow Jesus resolutely, facing every misunderstanding and adversity courageously.

Hail Mary *(7 times)*

FIFTH SORROW

O Queen of Martyrs, what sorrow you felt when you saw Jesus being brought to the tribunal; while you watched him being insulted, scourged, crowned with thorns, compared to Barabbas and led in an exhausted state along the roads of Jerusalem under the weight of the cross! Through the merits of this sorrow, which goes beyond description, grant me the strength to give myself to Jesus without reservation.

Hail Mary *(7 times)*

SIXTH SORROW

O Queen of Martyrs, what torture your motherly heart had to endure while watching the fruit of your Immaculate Womb die on the cross, and his heart being pierced by the lance of a soldier! Through the merits of the piercing of your maternal heart, grant me the grace to live and die loving Christ crucified.

Hail Mary *(7 times)*

SEVENTH SORROW

O Queen of Martyrs, with what sorrow your heart beat when you received in your arms the lifeless body of your Son, torn by the tortures of his passion! Through the merits of such laceration of your maternal heart grant me the grace to detach myself from the vanities of this world and to seek to unite myself rather to Jesus, the Son of God, made man in your Immaculate womb.

Hail Mary *(7 times)*

ROSARY OF THE TEARS OF BLOOD OF THE VIRGIN MARY

*In the name of the Father, and of the Son,
and of the Holy Spirit. Amen.*

O God, come to my aid.
O Lord, make haste to help me.

Glory Be
The Creed *(see page 26)*

O Crucified Jesus, prostrate at Your feet, we offer you the sacrifice of the tears of the One who partook in Your passion and accompanied You with immense love along the road of Calvary.

Grant, O good Master, that we may treasure the teachings offered to us by the tears of blood of Your Most Holy Mother so that after having fulfilled Your Will here on earth, we may be worthy to praise You in heaven for all eternity.

*On the beads of the Our Father
we recite the following prayer:*

O Jesus, look at the tears of blood of the One who loved you most on earth...
and now loves You most especially in heaven.

*On the beads of the Hail Mary
we recite the following prayer:*

O Jesus, hear our prayers for the sake of the tears of blood of Your sweet Mother.

At the end of the Rosary we say three times:

**O Jesus, look at the tears of blood of the One who loved You most on earth...
and now loves You most especially in heaven.**

Final prayer:

O Mary, Mother of Love, Sorrow and Mercy, we pray to You: unite Your intercession to our petitions, so that Your Divine Son may hear them through the merits of Your tears of blood and may grant us, together with the graces which we ask, the crown of eternal life. May Your tears of blood, O Mother of Sorrows, destroy the power of evil, and save the world from the ruin which threatens it in these times. Amen.

DEVOTION TO THE TEARS
OF THE VIRGIN MARY

Many souls are moved to repentance when they consider all the tears which the Virgin Mary has shed because of the sins of humanity.

Besides the Lord Jesus himself, no one has shed as many painful tears as Mary, because no one has shared so intimately as she did in the mystery of Redemption.

"The thought of having caused a creature so innocent, so holy, and so good as the Mother of Jesus to cry in such a way is enough to cause those souls who have the grace of a deep sense of what Mary is, to burst into tears of pain" (Mons. Gay).

In pictures and apparitions of the Virgin Mary she has often shed tears. We recall in particular the miracle of Our Lady of Tears of Treviglio (Bolzano, Italy), the apparitions of the weeping Virgin Mary to St. Catherine Labouré in 1830 and to the little shepherds of La Salette, France, in 1846, the tears shed from the image of Our Lady in the picture of Syracuse (Sicily, Italy) in 1953, and the crying of the Immaculate Virgin on the night of the 18th of January, 1985 at Giheta (Burundi, Africa). However, the apparition which gave origin to special devotion to the tears of Our Lady is that which occurred at San Paolo, Brazil, in 1929, which we describe below.

ORIGIN OF THE CHAPLET OF THE TEARS
OF THE VIRGIN MARY

On the 8th of November, 1929, Sr. Amalia of Jesus Scourged was praying for the healing of one of her relatives whom the doctors had declared to be incurable. (Sr. Amalia was a member of the Missionaries of the Divine Crucifix, a congregation founded by Mons. Code D. Francisco del Campos Barreto, Bishop of Campinas, San Paolo, Brazil). While she prayed, offering herself in order to save the life of the poor mother who was dying, she heard a voice which said to her, "If you wish to obtain this grace, ask for it through the tears of my Mother. Everything that people ask of me through those tears, I am obliged to grant." The sister asked what formula she should use to pray to which Jesus replied that she was to use the invocation as presented below. Our Lord also promised her that his Mother would entrust the treasury of this devotion to Sr. Amalia's congregation.

On the 8th of March, 1930, while Sr. Amalia was kneeling before the altar, she felt as if she was lifted up from the ground and saw a lady of amazing beauty - the Blessed Virgin Mary. Her garments were of a violet colour. A blue mantle hung from her shoulders and she had a white veil. Our Lady was smiling lovingly and gave a rosary beads to Sr. Amalia which was made of beads which were as white as snow and as bright as the sun. The Virgin said to her, "Here is the crown of my tears. My Son entrusts it to you as an inheritance. He has already revealed my invocations to you. He wishes that I be honoured in a special way with this prayer and He will grant great graces to all those who recite this chaplet and pray it in the name of my tears.

"This crown will serve to obtain the conversion of many sinners and especially the conversion of followers of occultism. The great honour of bringing a great number of followers of this inauspicious sect back into the Church and

converting them shall be reserved for your institute. The evil one shall be conquered by this crown and his infernal rule shall be destroyed."

While leaving it to the Church to pronounce judgement on the supernatural origin of this prayer, we can nonetheless be assured that devotion to the tears of our Mother Mary, asking God for graces and forgiveness for their sake, is entirely in keeping with Christian tradition.

As regards the Chaplet, it has been approved by the Bishop of Campinas who has been given permission to celebrate the feast of Our Lady of Tears each year on the 20th of February in the Congregation of the Misionaries of the Divine Crucifix.

CHAPLET OF THE TEARS
OF THE VIRGIN MARY

This chaplet is composed of forty-nine beads, divided into seven groups which are separated by seven large beads; the concluding prayers are said on three small beads. If the chaplet is recited by a group of people, the first part of the invocations is said by a leader while the second part is recited by the assembly.

In the name of the Father, and of the Son, and of the Holy Spirit. Amen.

O God, come to my aid.
O Lord, make haste to help me.

Glory Be
The Creed *(see page 26)*

Introductory Prayer:
O Jesus, our Divine Crucified One! Prostrate at your feet, we offer you the tears of the One who accompanied you on your sorrowful road to Calvary with such ardent and compassionate love. O Good Master, hear our prayers and our requests for love of the tears of your most Holy Mother. Grant us the grace to understand the sorrowful teachings which are given to us by the tears of this good Mother, so that we may always fulfil your Holy Will on earth, and may be judged worthy of praising you and of glorifying you eternally in heaven. **Amen.**

On the beads of Our Father
we recite the following prayer:

O Jesus, remember the tears of the One who loved you most on earth!
And now loves you most ardently in heaven.

On the beads of Hail Mary
we recite the following invocation:

O Jesus, hear our prayers,
For the sake of the tears of your Holy Mother.

At the end of the chaplet we recite the following three times:

O Jesus, remember the tears of the One who loved you most on earth!
And now loves you most ardently in heaven.

Let us pray.
O Mary, Mother of divine love, Mother of sorrow and mercy, we ask you to unite your prayers to ours, so that your Divine Son, to whom we turn with confidence, may hear our prayers and grant us, as well as the graces which we ask of him, the crown of Glory in Eternity. **Amen.**

CHAPLET OF THE SEVEN SORROWS OF THE BLESSED VIRGIN MARY

The Virgin Mary spoke the following words to Marie Claire, one of the visionaries of Kibeho, Rwanda (Africa), who was chosen to spread devotion to chaplet:

"What I ask of you is repentance. If you meditate while reciting this chaplet, then you will have the courage to repent. Today many people do not know any longer how to ask forgiveness. They put the Son of God on the Cross again. Therefore, I wanted to come to remind you of this, especially here in Rwanda, because here there are still humble people who are not slaves of riches and money" (Message of the 31st of May, 1982).

"I ask you to teach it (the chaplet) to the entire world... even though you remain here, because my grace is all-powerful" (Message of the 15th of August, 1982).

In the apparition of the 9th of August, 1982, Our Lady cried and the visionaries cried with her, because they could see alarming images of the future: terrible wars, rivers of blood, abandoned bodies, and an abyss which was wide open. Let us, therefore, console Our Lady in her sorrow and pray this chaplet in order to obtain the grace of repentance for ourselves and for others.

In the name of the Father, and of the Son, and of the Holy Spirit. Amen.

O God, come to my aid.
O Lord, make haste to help me.

Glory Be
The Creed *(see page 26)*

INTRODUCTORY PRAYER

My God, I offer you this Chaplet of Sorrows for your greater glory, in honour of your most Holy Mother. I will meditate on her suffering and partake in it. I beseech you, through the tears which you shed at those moments, to grant me and all sinners, to be sorry for our sins.

**Grant to me and to all sinners
perfect sorrow for our sins.** *(3 times)*

**Act of contrition
(Act of sorrow)** *(see page 57)*

FIRST SORROW
THE PROPHET SIMEON ANNOUNCES TO MARY
THAT A SWORD OF SORROW
WILL PIERCE HER SOUL

"As the child's father and mother were wondering at the things that were being said about him, Simeon blessed them and said to Mary his mother, 'Look, he is destined for the fall and for the rise of many in Israel, destined to be a sign that is opposed - and a sword will pierce your soul too - so that the secret thoughts of many may be laid bare' " (Lk 2:33,35).
A deeper understanding of this event may be had by rea-

ding the entire description of the Presentation of Jesus at the Temple (Lk 2:22-35.)

We pause for a brief moment of personal reflection.

Our Father
Hail Mary *(7 times)*

**Mother full of mercy,
remind our heart of the sufferings
of Jesus during his Passion.**

Let us pray.
O Mary, humble daughter of Zion, who, on hearing the prophetic voice of Simeon, had the sorrowful road to be taken by your Son revealed to you, like a sharp sword which penetrated the depths of your heart, and experienced great sorrow because of his rejection by many, we ask you to obtain for us the gift of being able to comprehend the sacrifice of Christ, in order to follow his example as disciples, and to accept his gift of salvation. **Amen.**

A suitable hymn follows.

Second Sorrow
The Flight into Egypt

"After they had left, suddenly the angel of the Lord appeared to Joseph in a dream and said, 'Get up, take the child and his mother with you, and escape into Egypt, and stay there until I tell you, because Herod intends to search for the child and to do away with him. So Joseph got up and, taking the child and his mother with him, left that night for Egypt, where he stayed until Herod was dead. This was to fulfil what the Lord had spoken through the prophet: 'I called my son out of Egypt'." (Mt 2: 13-15).

We pause for a brief moment of personal reflection.

Our Father
Hail Mary *(7 times)*

**Mother full of mercy,
remind our heart of the sufferings
of Jesus during his Passion.**

Let us pray.
O Mary, young Virgin of Israel, who bore the trial of all mothers in defending every life from danger, grant the gifts of hope and courage to all those who, like you, care for and look after the birth and growth of future generations, as guardians of the design of God for the future of the world. **Amen.**

A suitable hymn follows.

Third Sorrow
JESUS IS LOST IN THE TEMPLE

"They were overcome when they saw him, and his mother said to him, 'My child, why have you done this to us? See how worried your father and I have been, looking for you'." (Lk 2: 48).
A deeper understanding of this mystery may be had by reading the entire account of the finding in the Temple (Lk 2: 41-52).

We pause for a brief moment of personal reflection.

Our Father
Hail Mary *(7 times)*

Mother full of mercy,
remind our heart of the sufferings
of Jesus during his Passion.

Let us pray.
O Mary, faithful woman, who rejoiced in having the strong presence of your Son at the celebration of Passover of your people and suffered for his unexpected "absence", grant to all those who have anxious doubts, the gift of searching constantly for your Son in faith, and grant us the joy of being found again when we get lost. **Amen.**

A suitable hymn follows.

Fourth Sorrow
MARY MEETS HER SON
WHILE HE IS WEIGHED DOWN BY THE ROSS

"Large numbers of people followed him, and women too, who mourned and lamented for him" (Lk 23: 27).

We pause for a brief moment of personal reflection.

Our Father
Hail Mary *(7 times)*

Mother full of mercy,
remind our heart of the sufferings
of Jesus during his Passion.

Let us pray.
O Mary, humble handmaid of the Lord, who allowed yourself be guided by the beatitude promised by your Son to all those who fulfilled the will of the Father, help us to be obedient to God's will for us and to embrace the cross on our path with the same love with which you accepted and carried it.

A suitable hymn follows.

Fifth Sorrow
MARY AT THE FOOT OF THE CROSS

"Near the cross of Jesus stood his mother and his mother's sister, Mary the wife of Cleopas, and Mary of Magdala. Seeing his mother and the disciple whom he loved standing near her, Jesus said to his mother, 'Woman, this is your Son.' Then to the disciple he said, 'This is your mother.' And from that hour the disciple took her into his home" (Jn 19:25-27).

We pause for a brief moment of personal reflection.

Our Father
Hail Mary *(7 times)*

**Mother full of mercy,
remind our heart of the sufferings
of Jesus during his Passion.**

Let us pray.
O Mary, sorrowful Mother of Jesus, who gave us such a great example of love and courage of the foot of the cross, teach us to show our love by being a generous presence for all our suffering brothers and sisters, and grant that we may welcome you in our homes as our Mother, so that through you, we may learn a new way of accepting the inevitable sorrows of life. **Amen.**

A suitable hymn follows.

MARY RECEIVES THE LIFELESS BODY OF HER SON

"After this, Joseph of Arimathaea, who was a disciple of Jesus - though a secret one because he was afraid of the Jews - asked Pilate to let him remove the body of Jesus. Pilate gave permission, so they came and took it away. Nicodemus came as well - the same one who had first come to Jesus at night-time - and he brought a mixture of myrrh and aloes, weighing about a hundred pounds. They took the body of Jesus and bound it in linen cloths with the spices, following the Jewish burial custom" (Jn 19:.38-40).

We pause for a brief moment of personal reflection.

Our Father
Hail Mary *(7 times)*

**Mother full of mercy,
remind our heart of the sufferings
of Jesus during his Passion.**

Let us pray.
O Mary, woman of unwavering hope, who believed in the announcement of glorious immortality made by your Son to the world, guide us at the hour of our death along the path which leads to the certainty and the joy of life everlasting.
Amen.

A suitable hymn follows.

SEVENTH SORROW
MARY AT THE TOMB OF JESUS

"At the place where he had been crucified there was a garden, and in this garden a new tomb in which no one had yet been buried. Since it was the Jewish Day of Preparation and the tomb was nearby, they laid Jesus there" (Jn 19: 41-42).

Brief personal meditation

Our Father
Hail Mary *(7 times)*

**Mother full of mercy,
remind our heart of the sorrows of Jesus
during his passion.**

Let us pray.
O Mary, faithful witness to the Resurrection, you too went to the tomb in tears, bringing an eternal seed of fertility, and "at the first sign of dawn after the Sabbath", came to know the joyful announcement of the resurrection, grant that we may always walk by your side, bearing with joy the fruits of a good life. **Amen.**

A suitable hymn follows.

At the end of the chaplet we recite the following:
Hail Mary *(3 times)*
Our Father *(3 times)*

**Mother full of mercy,
keep your sorrow alive in our heart.** *(3 times)*

or:
**Mother full of mercy,
remind our heart of the sufferings of Jesus
during his Passion.**
*(Maidron, as revealed at the apparitions
at Kibeho, Rwanda)*

Let us pray.
Hail Mary, full of sorrows, Jesus Crucified is with You, worthy of compassion are You among all women, and worthy of compassion is the fruit of Your womb, Jesus. Holy Mary, Mother of Jesus Crucified, obtain for us, crucifiers of your Son, tears of sincere repentance, now and at the hour of our death. **Amen.**

CHAPLET OF THE SORROWS OF MARY

In the name of the Father, and of the Son,
and of the Holy Spirit. Amen.

O God, come to my aid.
O Lord, make haste to help me.

Glory Be
The Creed *(see page 26)*

Mother of mine, grant that my heart may
accompany your sorrow at the death of Jesus.

FIRST SORROW

I sympathize with You, Mother of sorrows, for the first sword of sorrow which pierced You, when the words of Simeon in the temple, revealed to You the sufferings which humanity was to inflict on Your beloved Jesus.

You had a good knowledge of the Divine Scriptures, having meditated on them at length, and You knew that You would see your Son die before your eyes, hanging on an infamous cross, bleeding to death and abandoned by everyone, without Your being able either to defend or help Him.

Through that sorrowful memory which afflicted Your Heart for many years, I beg of you, my

Queen, to obtain for me the grace of always carrying in my heart the Passion of Jesus, together with Your Sorrows. throughout my life and at the hour of death.

Our Father,
Hail Mary
Glory Be
Mother of mine...

SECOND SORROW

I sympathize with You, Mother of Sorrows, for the second sword which pierced You, when the same people for whom Your innocent newly-born Son came on earth sought to kill him, forcing You to bring him to Egypt, secretly and at night.

How many trials You bore, gentle Handmaid, together with your exiled Son, in the wearisome and long journey through arid and hostile lands, and during Your stay in Egypt where, being unknown and foreigners, You lived in poverty for all those years, despised by the others! I beg You, my beloved Lady, to obtain for me through these sufferings of yours, the grace to bear the trials of this life with patience, together with You, until my death, so that in the life to come, I may be saved from eternal suffering.

Our Father,

Hail Mary
Glory Be
Mother of mine...

THIRD SORROW

I sympathize with You, Mother of sorrows, for the third sword which wounded you, when You lost your dear little Jesus, who remained for three days in Jerusalem far away from You. In those circumstances, when You did not have Your dear one beside You and did not know the reason of his absence, I imagine, my beloved Queen, that You did not sleep those nights but did nothing other than yearn for the One who was Your happiness in life. Therefore, my Lady, for the sake of the sighs of those three days which were so long and hard for You, grant me the grace to never lose my God, so that I may always live in His embrace and in the same way, leave this world when the moment of my death comes

Our Father,
Hail Mary
Glory Be
Mother of mine...

FOURTH SORROW

I sympathize with You, Mother of sorrows, for

the fourth sword which pierced You, when You witnessed your Son Jesus being condemned to death, bound with cords and chains, covered with blood and wounds, crowned with thorns and saw Him staggering along the road under the heavy cross which He had to bear on His wounded shoulders.

He went towards the place of His death like an innocent lamb, and all for love of us! When the eyes of Mother and Son met, You wounded each other's loving hearts through the sorrow manifest in each one's countenance. Through this great suffering, grant me, therefore, the grace to live in total abandonment to the will of God, carrying my cross with joy together with Jesus, until my last breath.

Our Father,
Hail Mary
Glory Be
Mother of mine...

Fifth sorrow

I sympathize with You, Mother of sorrows, for the fifth sword which pierced You, as You watched your beloved Son Jesus die on Calvary afflicted by physical torture and insults on the hard bed of the cross, without being able to give Him the least comfort such as we give even to the most embittered souls at the hour of death.

O most Holy Virgin Mary, how cruel that agony was which You felt, beloved Mother, together with your dying Son, and how greatly You were touched by his tenderness when he spoke to you for the last time from the cross, entrusted to Your maternal care all of us, together with St. John, to be your children, and then immediately afterwards, bowed his head and died! Mother, I beg you, for the sake of Your Crucified love, to grant me the grace to live and die crucified to all things that are earthly, in order to dedicate all of my life totally to God, and thus be able to enjoy seeing him face to face one day in Paradise.

Our Father,
Hail Mary
Glory Be
Mother of mine...

Sixth sorrow

I sympathize with You, Mother of Sorrows, for the sixth sword which pierced You, when you saw the sweet Heart of your Son being pierced right through although He was already dead, having died for those ungrateful souls who, even after His death, did not tire of tormenting him. For the sake of this sharp pain which was entirely Yours,

I beg You, therefore, to grant me the grace of making my home in the Heart of Jesus, wounded and opened for me, in that Heart which is a beautiful prison of love, the dwelling place of all souls who are devoted to God, and the place in which I desire to live, loving God above all things and having Him at the centre of my thoughts. Most holy Virgin Mary, You can accomplish this for me, I hope and trust that You shall grant me this favour.

**Our Father,
Hail Mary
Glory Be
Mother of mine...**

SEVENTH SORROW

I sympathize with you, my Mother of Sorrows, for the seventh sword which pierced You, when You held Your Son, who was already dead, in Your arms. He was no longer beautiful and radiant as You received him one day in the stable at Bethlehem, but rather blood-stained, bruised and covered with sores and wounds which were so deep as to reveal His bones. In that moment You could have said, "My Son, my Son, love has reduced You to this!".

Then, when the time came to bring Him to the tomb, You too wanted to accompany Him; You laid Him gently upon the shroud, and bidding Him farewell for the last time, allowed Your own Heart, that loved Him so much, be buried together with Jesus.

For the sake of the countless horrific sufferings which Your good soul experienced, I ask You to obtain for me, O Mother of Divine Love, forgiveness for the offences which I have committed against my beloved God.

I am heartily sorry for all my sins; may You defend me in times of temptation and assist me at the hour of my death so that I may obtain salvation through Your merits and through the merits of Jesus, so that with Your help I may thus come one day, after this exile on earth, to sing Your praises and those of Your Son in Paradise for all eternity. **Amen.**

Our Father
Hail Mary
Glory Be
Pray for us, O most sorrowful Virgin.
That we may be made worthy
of the promises of Christ.

Let us pray.
O God, whose Passion caused the sweet soul of the glorious Virgin and Mother Mary to be pierced by a sword, according to the prophecy of Simeon, in your mercy, grant that we, by recal-

ling her sorrow with devotion, may obtain the blessed fruits of the same Passion.

This we ask through Christ Our Lord, who lives and reigns with you for ever and ever. **Amen.**

Oremus:

Deus, in cuius Passione, secundum Simeonis prophetiam, dulcissimam animam gloriosae Virginis et matris Mariae doloris gladius pertransivit, concede propitius, ut qui dolores eius venerando recolimus, Passionis tuae effectum felicem consequamur.

Qui vivis, et regnas in saecula saeculorum.

Amen.

CHAPLET OF THE SEVEN SORROWS OF MARY

In the name of the Father, and of the Son, and of the Holy Spirit. Amen.

O God, come to my aid.
O Lord, make haste to help me.

Glory Be
The Creed *(see page 26)*

O Mary of Sorrows, I suffer with you the affliction which your tender heart experienced when you heard the prophecy of the elderly prophet Simeon. Dear Mother, through your afflicted heart, grant me the virtue of humility and the gift of wonder and awe in God's presence.

Hail Mary

O Mary of Sorrows, I suffer with you the sorrows borne by your most sensitive heart in the flight to Egypt and throughout your stay there. Dear Mother, through your most afflicted heart, grant me the virtue of generosity to the poor and the gift of holiness.

Hail Mary

O Mary of Sorrows, I suffer with you the worry which your anxious heart felt at the loss of your beloved Son Jesus. Dear Mother, through your troubled heart, grant me the virtue of patience and the gift of courage.

Hail Mary

O Mary of Sorrows, I suffer with you the dismay which your heart experienced in meeting Jesus as he carried the cross. Dear Mother, through your troubled heart, grant me the virtue of chastity and the gift of know-ledge.

Hail Mary

O Mary of Sorrows, I suffer with you the martyrdom borne by your generous heart in being present as Jesus was dying. Dear Mother, through your tormented heart, grant me the virtue of temperance and the gift of right judgement.

Hail Mary

O Mary of Sorrows, I suffer with you the wound with which your merciful heart was inflicted when the lance pierced the side of Jesus and wounded his heart. Dear Mother, through your pierced heart, grant me the virtue of charity and the gift of understanding.

Hail Mary

O Mary of Sorrows, I suffer with you, the pain which your most beloved heart suffered in watching the burial of Your Son Jesus. Dear Mother, through your heart which was so harshly afflicted, grant me the virtue of diligence and the gift of wisdom.

Hail Mary
Pray for us, O most sorrowful Virgin.
That we may be worthy of the promises of Christ.

Let us pray.
Our Lord Jesus Christ, grant that today and at the hour of our death the Blessed Virgin Mary, your Mother, whose most holy soul was pierced by a sword of sorrow during your Passion, may implore your mercy for us.

This we ask through you, O Saviour of the world, who live and reign with the Father and the Holy Spirit, one God for ever and ever. **Amen.**

LITANY OF OUR LADY OF SORROWS

Lord,	**Have mercy on us.**
Christ,	,,
Lord,	,,
God the Father of heaven,	,,
God the Son, Redeemer of the world,	,,
God, the Holy Spirit,	,,
Holy Trinity, One God,	,,
Holy Mary,	,,
Holy Mother of God,	,,
Holy Virgin of Virgins,	,,
Mother of Christ Crucified,	,,
Mother of Sorrows,	,,
Tearful Mother,	,,
Desolate Mother,	,,
Abandoned Mother,	,,
Mother deprived of her Son,	,,
Mother pierced by a sword of sorrow,	,,
Mother consumed by hardship,	,,
Mother filled with anguish,	,,
Mother whose heart was crucified,	,,
Mother, most melancholy,	,,
Mother of orphans,	,,
Fount of tears,	,,
Mass of sufferings,	,,
Mirror of patience,	,,

Model of penance,

Have mercy on us.

Rock of constancy, "
Anchor of trust, "
Refuge of the abandoned, "
Defence of the oppressed, "
Victory of unbelievers, "
Remedy for the sick, "
Strength of the weak, "
Haven for the shipwrecked, "
Navigator in storms, "
Relief of the dejected, "
Terror of the deceitful, "
Treasure of the faithful, "
Eye of the prophets, "
Strength of the apostles, "
Crown of martyrs, "
Guide of confessors, "
Pearl of virgins "
Comfort of widows, "
Joy of all saints, "

**Lamb of God, who take away the sins
of the world,**
Spare us, O Lord.

**Lamb of God, who take away the sins
of the world,**
Graciously hear us, O Lord.

**Lamb of God, who take away the sins
of the world,**
Have mercy on us.

Pray for us, O Holy Virgin of Sorrows
That we may be worthy of the promises of Christ.

Let us pray.
O Lord, we ask you to grant that, now and at the hour of our death, the Most Blessed Virgin Mary, your Mother, whose most sacred soul was pierced by a sword of sorrow at the hour of your Passion, may intercede with you, in your mercy, on our behalf. This we ask through you, who live and reign for ever and ever. **Amen.**
or
May we bear the Passion of our Lord Jesus Christ and the Compassion of the Blessed Virgin Mary in body and soul. **Amen.**
or
O God, you desired that the life of the Virgin be marked by the mystery of sorrow, grant, we pray, that she may accompany us on our journey of faith and that we may unite our sufferings to the Passion of Christ so that they may become an occasion of grace and an instrument of salvation. Through Christ our Lord. **Amen.**

LITANY OF REPARATION
TO THE VIRGIN MARY

O sweetest Mother of ours, grant that we, united by our desire to venerate and love you, may make reparation for the offences which have been committed against you by many who do not know the paradise of goodness and of mercy which is found in your motherly Heart. Let us promise to do so by reciting the following litany:

For the horrible offences committed against
your sweet Son Jesus,
> **We shall comfort you, O Mary.**

For the sword of sorrow with which corrupt
children once again pierce your
motherly Heart, "

For the abominable blasphemies uttered
against your most pure and holy Name, "

For intolerable denials of your most
wonderful privileges and glories, "

For all insults hurled at devotion to you, "

For the sacrilegious outrages which are
committed against your sacred images, "

For the defilement of your sanctuaries, "

For the sins committed against the angelic
virtue of purity, the virtue which
is most dear to you, "

For the offences committed through
 immodest fashion against the dignity of
 women, reclaimed and sanctified by you,
> **We shall comfort you, O Mary.**

For the horrendous crime with which even
 innocent children are torn away from
 your maternal womb,   „

For the incomprehension of many mothers
 of your divine maternity,   „

For the ingratitude of many children for
 your most precious graces,   „

For the coldness of many hearts in spite
 your motherly tenderness,   „

For the treatment of your loving invitations
 with disdain,   „

For the cruel indifference of many hearts,   „

For the bitter tears which you shed over
 the destiny of many of your unhappy
 prodigal children,   „

For the anguish of your sweet Heart, when
 you see your Son being betrayed and
 crucified once again by sinners,   „

For the agony of your most holy soul when
 you see Jesus being abandoned in so
 many tabernacles,   „

For the martyrdom which you experience for
the loss of many souls who had been
redeemed by the Blood of your Jesus
and by your tears,

We shall comfort you, O Mary.

For the horrible attacks which are made
against your Son Jesus, whose presence is
alive in his Vicar on earth and in his priests,   "

For the infernal conspiracy against the life
of your Son Jesus in his Church,   "

Let us pray.
O Holy and Sweet Mother, in your heroic
motherly love, you prayed at the foot of the Cross
for those who tortured your beloved Son Jesus
and broke your most tender Heart; have mercy on
those who offend you. Grant that they too may be
welcomed into your maternal heart, purified by
your blessed tears, and allowed to enjoy the wonderful fruits of your motherly mercy. **Amen.**

10.
THE MIRACULOUS MEDAL

- **Prayers**
  - **Chaplets**
- **Rosaries**

THE MIRACULOUS MEDAL
Introduction
"Carry it always with you, make it known!"

The miraculous medal is the most precious medal of the Virgin Mary because Our Lady herself expressed the desire for it to be struck, having given instructions as to how it was to be done when she appeared to St. Catherine Labouré (1806 - 1876), a religious sister of the Daughters of Charity, at her convent in Rue du Bac, Paris. On the night of the 19th of July, 1830, Our Lady appeared to St. Catherine for the first time and spoke to her in the following words: "My daughter, God wishes to entrust a mission to you. You shall have much to suffer, but you will suffer willingly, knowing that it serves for the glory of God. You will have the grace..." Subsequently, the Virgin Mary appeared to St. Catherine on the 27th of November of the same year, and specified the details of the mission which Our Lord desired of her; Mary gave the sister the task of having a medal struck which would resemble that which she showed her.

"Have a medal prepared according to this model,", Our Lady said to St. Catherine. "All those who wear it on their person will feel the protection of the Virgin. There shall be graces in abundance for those who wear it with confidence." Catherine affirmed that in the apparition Our Lady held the globe of the world in her hands... "like a compassionate mother, keeping it close to her heart, warming it with her tender love". It is from this ardent love of Our Lady for her children that her desire to assist them arises, showering upon humankind the graces which it asks of her, attending to our physical and needs alike. The Miraculous Medal is a manifestation of Mary's love and intercession for us, as well as being a symbol of Her graces and a

means of obtaining them; an instrument which God, in his great mercy, puts at our disposal.

The medal was propagated immediately in a prodigious way and by means of the same, countless graces of conversion, protection and healing have since been obtained.

Impressed on the medal is the image of the Immaculate Virgin Mary with open hands from which emanate rays of light. Around the Virgin are inscribed the following words: "O Mary conceived without sin, pray for us who have recourse to thee". On the other face of the medal we find the letter "M, surmounted by a cross. Beneath the letter "M" are two hearts: one is surrounded by thorns and the other is pierced by a sword. Surrounding the hearts are twelve stars.

One of the most famous miracles associated with this medal was the conversion of a Jewish person, Alphonsus Ratisbonne, who had put the medal around his neck only to please a friend. He entered by chance the church of St. Andrew of Fratte (Rome), and there Our Lady of the Miraculous Medal appeared to him. Alphonsus was greatly moved and overcome with emotion. Subsequently he became a Catholic and later, a priest and ardent apostle of Christ.

The saints have shown an unlimited trust in the Miraculous Medal. St. Catherine Labouré distributed it widely, especially to the sick and to those in particular need of conversion. As a little girl, St. Teresa of the Child Jesus used to put the medal into the pockets of the workers' jackets. St. Maximilian Kolbe referred to the medals as "ammunition". He obtained many graces from the medal and also witnessed miraculous conversions associated with it. Blessed Padre Pio of Pietrelcina always kept miraculous medals on his person in order to be able to distribute them to those whom he met, and indeed died with some medals still in his pocket.

Devotion to Our Lady of the Miraculous Medal can be expressed in the following ways:

- *Wearing the medal always around our neck in order to enjoy the protection of the Immaculate Virgin Mary and her assistance to help us to live in the grace of God.*

- *Reciting the invocation inscribed on the medal every day with which Our Lady wished to be greeted and invoked:*
"O Mary conceived without sin,
pray for us who have recourse to thee".

- *Distributing the medal to others, especially to those who are sick or suffering in other ways; this practice brings forth graces and heavenly comfort, both for those who distribute and those who receive it.*

Finally, let us recall the words of the prophet Isaiah which are so appropriate to the Virgin Mary as depicted on the Miraculous Medal:
"I will greatly rejoice in the Lord,
my soul shall exult in my God;
for he has clothed me with the garments of salvation,
he has wrapped me in a cloak of saving justice"
(Is 61:10).

PRAYERS

In the name of the Father, and of the Son,
and of the Holy Spirit. Amen.

O God, come to my aid.
O Lord, make haste to help me.

Glory Be
The Creed *(see page 26)*

PRAYER TO THE IMMACULATE VIRGIN MARY OF THE MIRACULOUS MEDAL

Immaculate Virgin Mary, beloved Daughter of the Father, dawn of peace promised to fallen humanity, who had the special privilege of being preserved from original sin, grant that we, too ,may always resist the seduction of the evil one and follow with loving faithfulness the inspirations of grace in the generous practice of the teachings of the Gospel.

Hail Mary

O Mary conceived without sin,
pray for us who have recourse to Thee (You).
Immaculate Virgin Mary, paradise of the

Incarnation, who were greeted with the words "full of grace" and who, in the fragrance of your virginal mystery, gave the Son of God to the world so that he might restore fallen humanity to its original state of innocence, enkindle in our hearts an ardent desire of chastity and purity and let a reflection of your heavenly purity shine on our souls.

Hail Mary

**O Mary conceived without sin,
pray for us who have recourse to Thee.**

Immaculate Virgin Mary, most pure Temple of the Holy Spirit, the joy which we feel in contemplating your triumphs is veiled by sadness because of the behaviour of many ungrateful children who offend your Son Jesus. Good and tender Mother, forgive them. With our affection as your children and our zeal offered in humble reparation, we want to prevent the diffusion of evil in the world. And you, Virgin, of Reparation grant us a greater fervour for our calling, and teach us to love and console the Heart of Jesus.

Hail Mary

**O Mary conceived without sin,
pray for us who have recourse to Thee.**

PRAYER

TO THE IMMACULATE VIRGIN MARY

Grant that I may give praise to You, O Immaculate Virgin, with my commitment and personal sacrifice. Grant that I may live, work, suffer, consume myself and die for You, only for You. Grant that I may lead the entire world to You. Grant that I may contribute to your greater glory, to Your utmost glorification. Grant that I may render You glory such as no one has ever given You unto this day. Grant that others may surpass me in their zeal for Your glorification, and that I may surpass them so that, in noble emulation of each other, we may allow Your glory to grow ever more profoundly, ever more rapidly, ever more intensely, according to the desire of Him who exalted You in such an ineff-able way above all beings.

St. Maximilian Kolbe

Prayer to Our Lady of the Miraculous Medal

O most powerful Queen of heaven and earth and Immaculate Mother of God and our Mother, most Holy Mary, through the merits of the manifestation of your Miraculous Medal, we beseech you to hear our petitions. To you, O Mother, we turn with confidence: send forth into the whole world the rays of God's grace of which you are treasurer and save us from sin. Through your intercession, may the Father of Mercy take pity on us and save us, so that we may be sure to enter into Paradise, where we shall be able to contemplate and honour you. **Amen.**

Hail Mary

**O Mary conceived without sin,
pray for us who have recourse to Thee.**

All holy are you, O Mary

In your conception, O Virgin Mary, you were blessed by the Lord and sanctified by God, your salvation.

Hail Mary

All holy and without shadow of sin, you became the Mother of the Lord.

Hail Mary

O Immaculate Virgin Mary, we follow you, attracted by your beauty and holiness.

Hail Mary

Lord Jesus, who appointed your Immaculate Mother to be a model and shining example for the Church, through her intercession, grant that we may be freed from our sins and may aspire to perfect holiness.
Amen.

# NOVENAS

PERPETUAL NOVENA PRAYER TO OUR LADY OF THE MIRACULOUS MEDAL

O Immaculate Virgin Mary, Mother of our Lord Jesus Christ and our Mother, penetrated with the most lively confidence in your all-powerful and never failing intercession, manifested so often through the Miraculous Medal, we your loving and trustful children implore you to obtain for us the graces and favours we ask during this Novena, if they be beneficial to our immortal souls and the souls for whom we pray.

(Pause)

Obtain for us, Mary, a deep hatred of sin, and that purity of heart which will attach us to God alone so that our every thought, word and deed may tend to His greater glory. Obtain for us also a spirit of prayer and self-denial so that we may recover by penance what we have lost by sin; and at length attain to that blessed abode where you are the Queen of angels and of men. **Amen.**

**O Mary conceived without sin,
pray for us who have recourse to thee.** *(3 times)*

Novena in honour of our lady of the miraculous medal

A Prayer of Saint Louise
Most Holy Virgin,
I believe and confess
Your holy and Immaculate
Conception.

Pure and without sin,
most pure Virgin,
through your virginal purity,
your Immaculate Conception,
your privilege of being the
Mother of God,

obtain for us from your
Divine Son,
humility,
charity,
great purity of mind and body,

the gift of prayer,
a holy life
and a happy death.

Memorare:
Remember O most
compassionate Virgin Mary

that never was it known
that anyone who fled
to your protection,
implored your assistance,
or sought your intercession
was left unaided.

Inspired with this confidence,
we fly unto you,
O Virgin of Virgins our Mother.

To you we come,
before you we kneel (stand),
sinful and sorrowful.

O Mother of the Word Incarnate,
despise not our petitions,
but in your clemency hear and
answer them.

Novena Prayer:
O Immaculate Virgin Mary,
Mother of Our Lord Jesus Christ,
with confidence we come
to implore your unfailing help.

Bearer of Life,
Mother of our Saviour,
give birth in our hearts

to Jesus your Son
who forgives our sins
and brings healing to our lives.

Mother of the Church on earth,
hear the cry of the lowly and the poor
who hunger for Jesus,
the Bread of Life,
and in your loving wisdom
make our prayers your own.

(We pause to make our needs known to our Immaculate Mother).

Virgin gentle in mercy,
Queen of the universe,
cover us with the veil of
your protection
and deliver us from the
darkness of evil.

Teach us by prayer and
self-control
the meaning of truth and
the beauty of love
so that with minds that are
healed and hearts that are pure
we may come in the end
to where you are
the Queen of Angels and of Saints. **Amen.**

Consecration to Our Lady of the Miraculous Medal

Our Lady of the Miraculous Medal and glorious Queen of the universe, we come before you, acknowledging your sovereignty and seeking to satisfy your maternal desire, in order to consecrate ourselves entirely, along with our families to your Sorrowful and Immaculate Heart, today and forever.

O good Mother, may you take us under your special protection and shower upon us ever more abundantly the rays of your graces according to your pro-mise.

Defend our bodies, heal those in our family who are sick, look after our temporal needs, but above all, we ask you to sanctify our souls, to keep our faith alive, to increase our trust in God, to give us the strength to observe his holy Law, and to grant that holiness of life and harmony of hearts may reign in our home, as in your Holy Family at Nazareth, so that, by virtue of your Medal, we may share one day in that eternal happiness which you have promised for those who are devoted to you. **Amen.**

Hail Holy Queen

Invocation of Mary Most Holy in Order to Obtain the Gift of the Holy Spirit

O most pure Virgin Mary, who, through your Immaculate Conception, became the chosen Tabernacle of Divinity by the power of the Holy Spirit, pray for us:

**That the Divine Paraclete may come soon
to renew the face of the earth:
Hail Mary**

O most pure Virgin Mary, who, in the mystery of the Incarnation, became the true Mother of God by the power of the Holy Spirit, pray for us:

That the Divine Paraclete...

O most pure Virgin Mary, who, while praying together with the apostles in the Cenacle, were filled with the Holy Spirit, pray for us:

That the Divine Paraclete...
Let us pray.
May your Spirit come upon us, O Lord, and transform us interiorly with his gifts: may he create in us a new heart, so that we may always please you and live according to your will.
Through Christ our Lord. **Amen.**

 **CHAPLET**

CHAPLET OF THE MIRACULOUS MEDAL

*In the name of the Father, and of the Son,
and of the Holy Spirit. Amen.*

O God, come to my aid.
O Lord, make haste to help me.

Glory Be
The Creed *(see page 26)*

Immaculate Mother of God and our Mother, Mary, through the manifestation of Your Miraculous Medal, we beseech You to hear our prayers and to grant us the favours we ask. O Mother, You know our troubles and the enemies that surround us. We can do nothing by ourselves: O Mary, have mercy on us and deliver us.

Hail Mary *(3 times)*

**O Mary conceived without sin,
pray for us who have recourse to Thee (You).**
(3 times)

Most powerful Queen of heaven and earth, through the manifestation of Your Miraculous Medal, work in us the same miracles used until now for the benefit of sinners. Through Your intercession, You have led many children who had gone astray back to the Father. We too are sinful children, O Mother: grant that the Father of Mercy may show us mercy for Your sake and save us.

Hail Mary *(3 times)*

**O Mary conceived without sin,
pray for us who have recourse to Thee (You).**
(3 times)

Mother of Divine Love, through the manifestation of Your Miraculous Medal, inflame our hearts with love for God. The world in which we live does not know that this heavenly fire is so precious. We turn to You, O Mother: You who are the treasurer of this fire of love, grant that we may be detached from earthly things and animated only by Divine Charity.

Hail Mary *(3 times)*

**O Mary conceived without sin,
pray for us who have recourse to Thee (You).**
(3 times)

Refuge of sinners, through the manifestation of Your Miraculous Medal, do not ever abandon us but rather show Yourself to be our Mother, especially at the hour of our death. Deliver us from evil spirits, free us from temptations, reveal Yourself to us, and with your presence, assure us that our death will be "precious" like that of the righteous.

Hail Mary *(3 times)*

**O Mary conceived without sin,
pray for us who have recourse to Thee (You).**
(3 times)

Mary, Gate of Paradise, through the manifestation of your Miraculous Medal, enrich us with Your graces, especially that of holy perseverance. Dear Mother, confident in your mercy, we desire to enjoy God's presence in heaven with you: open the gates of Paradise to us, as You have done for many of Your children, and save us.

Hail Mary *(3 times)*

**O Mary conceived without sin,
pray for us who have recourse to Thee (You).**
(3 times)

Prayer:

O Immaculate Mother of ours, we come before the throne of Your mercy to obtain from You the graces we need. Through a spiritual daughter of the great apostle St. Vincent de Paul, you revealed Your image radiant with light, symbol of your mercy for all people: O Mother, enlighten the children of darkness and let them become children of the Church, devoted to You. Spread out over all the world the rays of God's grace, of which You are the treasurer and save this poor humanity. May Your light shine upon the Church, the mystical Spouse of your Son and sanctify our priests, convert all sinners and grant perseverance to the righteous, and may this beautiful prayer resound on the lips of every one: "O Mary, conceived without sin, pray for us who have recourse to Thee".

Hail Holy Queen

CROWN OF THE SIXTY-THREE INVOCATIONS

In the name of the Father, and of the Son, and of the Holy Spirit. Amen.

O God, come to my aid.
O Lord, make haste to help me.

Glory Be
The Creed *(see page 26)*

Mystery or intention: in honour of the privilege of your Immaculate Conception.

We now recite the invocation of Our Lady of the Miraculous Medal ten times:
O Mary conceived without sin,
pray for us who have recourse to Thee (You).
(10 times)

Glory Be

Mystery or intention: in honour of the privilege of your Divine Maternity.

O Mary...

Mystery or intention: in honour of the privilege of your Perpetual Virginity.

O Mary..._(See page 1127)_

Mystery or intention: in honour of the privilege of your Assumption into heaven.

O Mary..._(See page 1127)_

Mystery or intention: in honour of the privilege of your Universal Intercession.

O Mary..._(See page 1127)_

Mystery or intention: in honour of the privilege of your Universal Queenship.

O Mary..._(See page 1127)_

The rosary concludes with the following prayer:

Remember O most
compassionate Virgin Mary
that never was it known
that anyone who fled
to your protection,

implored your assistance,
or sought your intercession
was left unaided.

Inspired with this confidence,
we fly unto you,
O Virgin of Virgins our Mother.

To you we come,
before you we kneel (stand),
sinful and sorrowful.

O Mother of the Word Incarnate,
despise not our petitions,
but in your clemency hear and
answer them.

Finally, we recite 3 times:
**O Mary conceived without sin,
pray for us that have recourse to Thee.**

## Part Seven

The Holy
Family

- **Prayers**
  - **Prayer of Consecration**
- **Rosary**
  - **Chaplet**

PRAYERS

PRAYER FOR THE FAMILY
by Pope John Paul II

God, from whom comes all paternity in heaven and on earth, Father, you who are Love and Life, grant that every human family on earth may become, through your Son Jesus Christ, "born of a woman", and through the Holy Spirit, source of divine mercy, a true sanctuary of life and love for the generations which continually renew themselves.

May your grace guide the thoughts and works of married couples towards the good of their families and of all families of the world. May the new generations find in the family a strong support for their humanity and for their growth in truth and love. May love, strengthened by the grace of the sacrament of matrimony, show itself to be stronger than every weakness and every crisis which our families experience at times.

Finally, we ask you, through the intercession of the Holy Family of Nazareth, to grant that the Church in the midst of all nations of the earth, may fruitfully fulfil her mission in the family and by means of the family. Through Christ Our Lord, the Way, the Truth and the Life for ever and ever. **Amen.**

PRAYER TO THE HOLY FAMILY

by Pope John Paul II

O Holy Family of Nazareth, community of love offered by Jesus, Mary and Joseph to one another, model and ideal for every Christian family, we entrust our families to you.

Open the heart of every home to the faith, to acceptance of the Word of God, to Christian witness, so that it may become a source of new and holy vocations.

Mould the minds of parents, so that they may guide children, with zealous charity, prudent care and loving mercy, to attain spiritual and eternal blessings.

Form a righteous conscience and a free will in the souls of young people, so that they may generously accept the gift of a divine calling, growing in "wisdom, stature and grace".

Holy Family of Nazareth, by contemplating and imitating your faithfulness in prayer, your dignified poverty and virginal purity, grant that we may all strive to fulfil the will of God and accompany with wisdom and discretion those among us who are called to follow more closely the Lord Jesus who "has given himself" to us.
Amen.

BLESSING OF OUR CHILDREN
before they go to sleep

Child: Bless me, Daddy (Mummy).

The mother or father says the following words, while placing his/her hand on the head of the child and making the sign of the cross on his/her forehead with holy water:

May the Lord bless you
and keep you *(ref. Nm 6,24-26)*.
Amen.

May he let his face shine upon you
and be gracious to you.
Amen.

May he show you his face
and bring you peace.

Amen.

> *All members of the family present
> make the sign of the cross, saying:*

> **In the name of the Father,
> and of the Son,
> and of the Holy Spirit.
> Amen.**

 **PRAYER OF CONSECRATION**

ACT OF CONSECRATION TO
THE HOLY FAMILY

*(Ideally, this prayer is recited every morning where
the circumstances allow).*

Holy Family of Nazareth,
I consecrate myself entirely to you forever,
so that I may follow the path towards
holiness under your guidance.
I take you, O Mary,
as my true mother,
and you, O Joseph,
as my guardian and master,
in order that I may live like Jesus
who submitted himself to your authority in all
things
and grew in wisdom, stature and grace
under your instruction.
Help me, O Holy Family,
to fulfil to perfection
God's plan of love for me
and grant that I may always live
in union with the Church and the Pope,
united to you and to your communion with the
Father. **Amen.**

Imprimatur Vicary of Rome, 5th of January, 1993, Remigio

CONSECRATION OF THE FAMILY TO JESUS, MARY AND JOSEPH

Holy Family of Nazareth, Jesus, Mary and Joseph, our family consecrates itself to you in this life and for eternity. Grant that our house and our heart may be a cenacle of prayer, peace, grace and communion. **Amen.**

CONSECRATION OF A CHILD TO THE BLESSED VIRGIN MARY

Blessed Virgin Mary, turn your maternal gaze on *(name of child)*. He (she) has been born to a new life through Baptism, and has become a child of God and an heir of heaven; but remember, Mary that he (she) is also a child of yours.
At this moment, Jesus repeats those memorable words to you: "Mother, here is your son...!"
Grant him (her) your special protection; now and for ever. Take care of him (her) and defend him (her) as one who belongs to you, and fulfil in him (her) your mission of Mother, so that, through you, he (she) may grow in goodness and holiness.
Defend him (her) also from all perils of body and soul and grant that he (she) may share one day in eternal life in the glory of heaven. **Amen.**

Hail Holy Queen

ROSARY

ROSARY OF THE HOLY FAMILY
OF NAZARETH

The example of the Holy Family's hidden life at Nazareth invites all people to be in communion with Jesus in the most ordinary situations of daily life: Nazareth is the school of the Gospel where we begin to understand the life of Jesus... Firstly it teaches us silence. Oh! if only we could appreciate once more the beauty of silence, that peaceful atmosphere so necessary to the soul! Secondly the House of Nazareth teaches us about the spirituality of work... Oh! Home of Nazareth, house of the "Son of the carpenter"!... How much we have to learn, understand and thus respect the redeeming value of human toil in spite of the difficulties which it poses!

In the name of the Father, and of the Son, and of the Holy Spirit. Amen.

O God, come to my aid.
O Lord, make haste to help me.

Glory Be
The Creed *(see page 26)*

FIRST MYSTERY
THE HOLY FAMILY, A WORK OF GOD

"When the completion of time came, God sent his Son, born of a woman, born a subject of the Law, to redeem the subjects of the Law, so that they could receive adoption as sons".

(Gal 4:4-5)

Here, at the threshold of the New Testament, as at the beginning of the Old Testament, there is a man and a woman. However, while Adam and Eve were the source of evil in the world, Mary and Joseph are the fount from which holiness spreads throughout the world. The Saviour began the work of salvation within this virginal and holy union, in which God manifests his divine will to purify and sanctify the family, the sanctuary of love and cradle of life.

Let us pray,
that the Holy Spirit may renew our families rendering them similar to the Holy Family of Nazareth.

Our Father

"HAIL, FAMILY OF NAZARETH" *(10 times)*
(A prayer modelled on the Hail Mary)

Hail, O Family of Nazareth,
Jesus, Mary and Joseph,
you are blessed by God,
and blessed is the Son of God, Jesus,
who was born in you.

Holy Family of Nazareth,
we consecrate ourselves to you:
guide and sustain our families,
and keep them faithful in love. **Amen.**

(With ecclesiastical approval, Milan, 1991)

Glory Be

Jesus, Mary and Joseph,
**enlighten us, come to our aid and save us.
Amen.**

Second Mystery
The holy family of bethlehem

"The angel said [to the shepherds]; 'Do not be afraid. Look, I bring you news of great joy, a joy to be shared by the whole people. Today in the town of David a Saviour has been born to you; he is Christ the Lord. And here is a sign for you; you will find a baby wrapped in swaddling clothes and lying in a manger.'... So they hurried away and found Mary and Joseph, and the baby lying in the manger".

(Lk 2:10-13,16-17)

The birth of Jesus in Bethlehem was the beginning of this unique and exceptional family in the history of humanity; in this family, the Son of God came into the world, grew and was educated, having been born of a Virgin Mother.

Let us pray,
to Mary and Joseph: through your intercession, may we be granted the grace to love and worship Jesus above all things.

Our Father
Hail, O Family of Nazareth *(10 times)*
Glory Be

Jesus, Mary and Joseph,
enlighten us, come to our aid and save us.
Amen.

Third Mystery
The Holy Family at the Temple

"As the child's father and mother were wondering at the things that were being said about him, Simeon blessed them and said to Mary his mother, 'Look, he is destined for the fall and for the rise of many in Israel, destined to be a sign that is opposed - and a sword will pierce your soul, too - so that the secret thoughts of many may be laid bare".

(Lk 2:33-35)

The ransom of the first-born is another duty of the father which is fulfilled by Joseph. The evangelist tells us that Jesus' father and mother wondered "at the things that were being said about him" and, in particular, at what Simeon said in his Canticle addressed to the Lord God, revealling Jesus as being the "salvation which God has made ready in the sight of the nations" and "a light of revelation for the gentiles and glory for his people".

Let us pray,
entrusting the Church and all families to the Holy Family.

Our Father
Hail, O Family of Nazareth *(10 times)*
Glory Be

Jesus, Mary and Joseph,
enlighten us, come to our aid and save us.
Amen.

FOURTH MYSTERY
THE FLIGHT OF THE HOLY FAMILY INTO EGYPT AND THE RETURN TO ISRAEL

"After they had left, suddenly the angel of the Lord appeared to Joseph in a dream and said, 'Get up, take the child and his mother with you, and escape into Egypt, and stay there until I tell you, because Herod intends to search for the child and do away with him.' So Joseph got up and, taking the child and his mother with him, left that night for Egypt. After Herod's death, suddenly the angel of the Lord appeared in a dream to Joseph and said, 'Get up, take the child and his mother with you and go back to the land of Israel, for those who wanted to kill the child are dead.' So Joseph got up and, taking the child and his mother with him, went back to the land of Israel". (Mt 2:13-14,19-21)

Just as Israel escaped "from the condition of slavery" in order to establish the Covenant at Sinai, so does Joseph, guardian and collaborator in the mystery of Divine Providence, help Jesus, who is to establish the New Covenant, to escape from Herod, and guards him while in exile.

Let us pray,
that we may listen to the Gospel and put it into practice with ever greater trust.

Our Father
Hail, O Family of Nazareth *(10 times)*
Glory Be

Jesus, Mary and Joseph,
enlighten us, come to our aid and save us.
Amen.

FIFTH MYSTERY
THE HOLY FAMILY IN THE HOUSE
OF NAZARETH

"He went down with them then and came to Nazareth and lived under their authority. His mother stored up all these things in her heart. And Jesus increased in wisdom, in stature, and in favour with God and with people". (Lk 2:51-52)

From the beginning of his earthly existence, Jesus received great love, care and tenderness from Mary and Joseph; he was their vocation; he was their inspiration; he was the great mystery, the centre of their lives. In the house of Nazareth Jesus lived under his parents' authority and was obedient, as all children should be. The years of his life spent in humble submission to Mary and Joseph account for most of his time on earth, and therefore constitute the longest period of that total and uninterrupted obedience which he rendered to the Heavenly Father. Thus the Holy Family is intimately involved in this divine mystery, and the fruit of his obedience is the redemption of the world.

Let us pray,
that the spiritual atmosphere of the house of Nazareth may be recreated in our families.

Our Father
Hail, O Family of Nazareth *(10 times)*
Glory Be

Jesus, Mary and Joseph,
enlighten us, come to our aid and save us.
Amen.

LITANY OF THE HOLY FAMILY

Lord, have mercy.	**Lord, have mercy.**
Christ, have mercy.	**Christ, have mercy.**
Lord, have mercy.	**Lord, have mercy.**
Christ, hear us.	**Christ, graciously hear us.**

God, the Father of Heaven,   **Have mercy on us.**
God the Son, Redeemer of the world,   "
God, the Holy Spirit,   "
Holy Trinity, one God,   "

Jesus, Son of the living God,
    who were made man for love of us,
    and have enriched and sanctified
    the bonds of love in all families,   "

Jesus, Mary and Joseph,
    whom the whole world
    honours by the name of the Holy Family,   "

Holy Family, image
    of the most Holy Trinity on earth,   "

Holy Family, perfect model of all virtues,   "

Holy Family, rejected by the people of
    Bethlehem, but glorified by the song
    of the angels,   "

Holy Family, that received the gifts of
    the shepherds and of the Magi,   "

Holy Family, exalted by the elderly and
holy Simeon, **Have mercy on us.**

Holy Family, persecuted and forced to take
refuge in a heathen land, "

Holy Family, hidden and unknown to the world, "

Holy Family, truly faithful to the Lord's
commandments, "

Holy Family, model of families renewed
in the Christian spirit, "

Holy Family, whose father is the model of
paternal love, "

Holy Family, whose mother is the model
of maternal love, "

Holy Family, whose son is the model of
obedience and filial love, "

Holy Family, patron and protector of all
Christian families, "

Holy Family, our refuge in life and hope
in the hour of death, "

O Holy Family, from all that can take away
our peace and unity of hearts, **spare us.**

From all despair, O Holy Family, "

O Holy Family, from attachment to earthly
possessions, "

O Holy Family, from worldly ambition and
vainglory, **spare us.**

From indifference towards the service of God,
O Holy Family, "

From an unholy death, O Holy Family "

O Holy Family, for the sake of the perfect
unity of your hearts,

hear us.

O Holy Family, for the sake of your poverty
and humility, "

O Holy Family, for the sake of your perfect
obedience, "

O Holy Family, for the sake of your trials
and sorrows, "

O Holy Family, for the sake of your daily toil
and your difficulties, "

O Holy Family, for the sake of your prayers
and silence, "

O Holy Family, for the sake of the integrity
of your actions, "

V. O venerable Holy Family, with hope and love,
we seek refuge in you.
**R. Grant us the benefits of your sound protec-
tion. Amen.**

CHAPLET

LITTLE CHAPLET IN HONOUR OF THE HOLY FAMILY OF JESUS, MARY AND JOSEPH

In the name of the Father, and of the Son, and of the Holy Spirit. Amen.

O God, come to my aid.
O Lord, make haste to help me.

Glory Be
The Creed *(see page 26)*

Blessed be the holy names of Jesus, Mary and Joseph forever.

O most lovable Holy Family, Jesus, Mary and Joseph, we humbly greet you, and for the sake of the great trials and sacrifices which you suffered in the stable of Bethlehem, we ask you to grant that our family may always live in communion with you in a spirit of humility, patience and acceptance of God's will.

Glory Be *(3 times)*
Blessed be the holy names of Jesus, Mary and Joseph forever.

O most merciful Holy Family, Jesus, Mary and Joseph, we humbly greet you and, for the sake of the ineffable goodness with which you welcomed the shepherds at the manger, we beseech you to protect our family and to help it in all its spiritual and temporal needs.

Glory Be *(3 times)*
Blessed be the holy names of Jesus, Mary and Joseph forever.

O beloved Holy Family, Jesus, Mary and Joseph, we humbly greet you and, for the sake of the great joy which you experienced at the visit of the Magi, pour out your blessings upon our family and grant that it may always walk in holiness and justice in the presence of God.

Glory Be *(3 times)*
Blessed be the holy names of Jesus, Mary and Joseph forever.

O most patient Holy Family, Jesus, Mary and Joseph, we humbly greet you and, for the sake of the great sufferings which you experienced in the flight to Egypt, grant that our family may always be preserved from all evil, and may bear the trials of life with calmness and serenity.

Glory Be *(3 times)*
**Blessed be the holy names of Jesus,
Mary and Joseph forever.**

O most gentle Holy Family, Jesus, Mary and Joseph, we humbly greet you and, for the sake of the sorrows that you suffered during your journey back from Egypt, and especially when you returned to Nazareth, for fear of Archelaus, defend our family from the assaults of all enemies and grant that we may live in safety and peace under your protection.

Glory Be *(3 times)*
**Blessed be the holy names of Jesus,
Mary and Joseph forever.**

O most compassionate Holy Family, Jesus, Mary and Joseph, we humbly greet you and, for the sake of the unique humility with which you made the journey to Jerusalem to celebrate the Pass-over, grant that our family may be be a good example for others by assisting at Holy Mass and receiving the Sacraments.

Glory Be *(3 times)*
Blessed be the holy names of Jesus, Mary and Joseph forever.
O most glorious Holy Family, Jesus, Mary and Joseph, we humbly greet you and, for the sake of your submission to the will of the Father in all things, grant that the members of our family may be obedient to God's will at all times, so that when their hour comes, they may have the grace to die in your embrace. **Amen.**

Glory Be *(3 times)*
Blessed be the holy names of Jesus, Mary and Joseph forever.

Let us pray,
O God our Father, who, by giving us the Holy Family, have provided us with a true model of life, grant that the same virtues and love may blossom in our families, so that one day, united in your house, we may enjoy everlasting happiness, Through Jesus Christ our Lord, your Son, who is God and lives and reigns with you for ever and ever. **Amen.**

## Part Eight

The Angels

1. Saint Michael the Archangel

2. The Guardian Angels

3. The Fallen Angels

1.
THE ARCHANGELS
GABRIEL, MICHAEL, RAPHAEL

- **Prayers**
  - **Act of Consecration**
- **Chaplet**
  - **Novena**
  - **Rosary**

THE ANGELS
WHO ARE THEY?

St. Augustine had the following to say about the angels: *"Angelus officii nomen est, non naturae. Quaeris nomen huius naturae, spiritus est; quaeris officium, angelus est: ex eo quod est, spiritus est, ex eo quod agit, angelus - 'Angel'* is the name of their office, not of their nature. If you seek the name of their nature, it is 'Spirit'; if you seek the name of their office, it is 'angel': from what they are, spirit', from what they do, 'angel'". Angels are servants and messengers of God with all of their being. "Continually in the presence of the Father... who is in heaven" (Mt 18:10), they are "mighty warriors who fulfil his commands, attentive to the sound of his words" (Ps 103:20). Insofar as the angels are purely spiritual creatures, they have intelligence and a will: they are individual and immortal creatures and surpass the perfection of all visible creatures, as proven by the splendour of their glory. Christ is the centre of the angelic world. They are **his** angels, as can be understood by the following words from the Gospel: "When the Son of man comes in his glory, escorted by all his angels, then he will take his seat on his throne of glory" (Mt 25:31). They are **his** because they are created through him and for him: "For in him were created all things in heaven and on earth: everything visible and invisible, thrones, ruling forces, sovereignties, powers - all things were created through him and for him" (Col 1:16). Furthermore, the angels belong to Christ because he chose them to be messengers of his plan of salvation: "Are they not all ministering spirits, sent to serve for the sake of those who are to inherit salvation?" (Heb 1:14).

From the beginning of Creation and throughout the history of salvation, the angels have announced salvation and have collaborated with their service in the realization of God's plan for the salvation of humanity: let us recall how they closed the earthly paradise, protected Lot, saved

Hagar and his child, and restrained the hand of Abraham; indeed, the Law itself was communicated by the angels (ref. Ac 7:53). In the Old Testament we learn how these heavenly spirits guided the chosen people of God along its journey of faith announced births and vocations, and assisted prophets. Finally, as we see in the New Testament, it was the angel Gabriel who announced the birth of John the Baptist and that of the Lord Jesus himself. After Mary, the Mother of God, the angels are the most noble creatures who exist, having come forth from the mind of God. They are extremely pure spirits, that is to say, beings with intelligence and will but without the burden of a material body although they are capable of assuming a visible nature. They are of such great beauty and majesty that St. John the evangelist was enraptured by the sight of an angel who came down from heaven and appeared to him as he himself describes in the Book of Revelation (ref. Rev. 18:1).

So great was the heavenly spirit's glory that St. John knelt at his feet to worship him, but the angel would not allow such adoration, saying, "Never do that: I am your fellow-servant and the fellow-servant of all your brothers who have in themselves the witness of Jesus. God alone you must worship" (Rev 19:10). And if this is the beauty of only one angel, who could ever express the overwhelming beauty of the hosts of these most noble creatures who pervade the universe?

We know that through a simple act of will, God created an immense varitey of angels even before creating human beings. Like the flowers of the earth, which resemble each other in their common nature but differ in their colour, shape and perfume, these sublime beings have the same spiritual nature, and yet differ in beauty and power.

There are nine categories or "choirs" of angels and they take their name from the different office that they perform for the Holy Trinity. Through divine revelation we know the names of these nine choirs: Angels, Archangels,

Sovereignties (Principalities), Authorities (Powers), Virtues, Ruling Forces (Dominions), Thrones, Cherubims and Seraphims. Thus, these heavenly spirits have been created to be faithful executors of God's commands. Some of the angels abused their office, however, and having rebelled against God, they became demons: Lucifer, who had received gifts of great beauty, intelligence and wisdom from the Father, responded to his Creator's generosity with pride and selfishness; being confident of his ability to act without the Father's help, he considered himself to be self-sufficient and thus seriously damaged his relationship with God in much the same way as humans do when they seek to be independent of their Creator; indeed, St. John of the Cross writes, "How much harm the delight in their beauty and in their own natural gifts brought to the angels and in the same way, how many ills come to man every day through this same vanity!".

St. Thomas tells us that Lucifer wished to be object of the adoration which he himself, a mere creature, refused to render to God. Our limited powers of imagination cannot conceive what subsequently took place. We know, however, that among the heavenly creatures one whom the Scripture calls Michael had been specially chosen to combat the rebellious angels and, placing himself at the head of the immense multitude who rejected the suggestions of Lucifer, he rose against him and his followers, reproached him for his folly ,and confronted him in rational and indisputable terms, as expressed in Scripture with the brief interrogative phrase from which his name "MICHAEL" derives, meaning "Who is God?". The opposing wills met in a conflict which, albeit brief, was harsh and violent.

The rebels, once having rejected God's Grace, changed their visible appearance and Lucifer, who had been known as "Daystar, son of Dawn" (ref. Is 14:12) took on a horrible aspect and fell "like lightning from heaven" (ref. Lk 10:18). The prophet Isaiah describes the events clearly and concisely: *"You who used to think to yourself: I shall scale the heavens; higher than the stars of God I shall set my throne. I shall sit on the Mount of Assembly far away to the north. I shall climb high above the clouds, I shall rival the Most High. Now you have been flung down to Sheol, into the depths of the abyss!"* (Is 14:13-15).

Nevertheless, the praiseworthy service of the "good angels" far outweighs the harmful activity of the "fallen angels". Indeed, God has entrusted to them the protection of the Church, of nations, of towns and of every soul. *"He has given his angels orders about you, and they carry you in their arms in case you trip over a stone"* (Mt 4:6); *"He has given his angels orders about you to guard you whenever you go. They will carry you in their arms in case you trip over a stone"* (Ps 91:11-12).

Moreover, these wonderful creatures acknowledge Christ as their King and Mary, Mother of God, as their Queen, are faithful and prompt executers of their orders, and defend and help their servants as well as all other souls. For our part, we have precise duties towards the angels: we must VENERATE them as our older brothers and future companions in heaven, we must IMITATE their obedience, purity and love of God, and we are called most especially to RESPECT their presence. We can be sure that, even when "alone" in the house, we are never truly alone because we have a sublime heavenly prince, our guardian angel, constantly at our side and therefore, we must avoid carrying out improper acts which would offend him. Finally, we should be FULL OF LOVE AND GRATITUDE for his kindness and full of TRUST in the prudent, attentive, patient and loving care that he has for us.

Let us conclude with those famous words sung by the angels who announced Christ's birth to the shepherds; the words which epitomize their main function, namely to give praise and honour to God: *"Glory to God in the highest, and on earth peace to those on whom his favour rests"* (Lk 2:14).

PRAYERS

PRAYER TO SAINT MICHAEL THE ARCHANGEL

Traditional version
Saint Michael the Archangel,
defend us in the hour of conflict;
be our safeguard against the wickedness
and snares of the devil;
may God restrain him,
we humbly pray;
and do thou, O Prince of the heavenly host,
by the power of God,
thrust Satan down to hell
and with him all the other wicked spirits
that wander through the world
for the ruin of souls. **Amen.**

Alternative version
Saint Michael the Archangel,
defend us in battle;
be our defence against the wickedness
and snares of the devil.
May God rebuke him, we humbly pray.
And do you, O prince of the heavenly host,
by the power of God
thrust into hell Satan and all the evil spirits

who prowl about the world
for the ruin of souls. **Amen.**

**O Saint Michael the Archangel,
enlighten us with your light,
protect us with your wings,
defend us with your sword.**

**O Saint Michael the Archangel,
defend our home from demons,
and from their wickedness,
and defend it from evil
committed by people of the earth.**

**O Saint Michael the Archangel,
defend us in battle,
so that we may not perish
in the last judgement.**

ACT OF CONSECRATION TO
ST. MICHAEL THE ARCHANGEL

Most noble prince of the angelic Hierarchy, courageous warrior of the Almighty, zealous lover of the glory of the Lord, terror of the rebellious angels, love and delight of all righteous angels, my beloved archangel St. Michael, since I wish to be counted among the ranks of your faithful servants, today I offer myself as such, I give and devote myself to you, and I put myself, my family, and everything that I possess, under your most powerful protection. The offering of my service is small, since I am a miserable sinner, but you delight in the love of my heart.

Furthermore remember, that if from this day I am under your protection, you must assist me throughout my life, obtaining forgiveness for the many sins I commit, some of them serious, and obtaining for me the grace of loving my God, my beloved saviour Jesus, and my sweet Mother Mary with all my heart. Grant me all the assistance I require to attain the crown of glory. Defend me at all times from the enemies of my soul especially at the hour of my death. Come to me at that moment, O most glorious Prince, and assist me in the final conflict. With your powerful armour keep far away from me that arrogant transgressor whom you once defeated in the conflict in heaven and send him back into the abyss of hell. **Amen.**

**St. Michael the Archangel,
defend us in the hour of conflict,
so that we may not perish
in the last judgement.**

CHAPLET

STRUCTURE OF THE CHAPLET OF THE ANGELS

The beads used to recite the Chaplet of the Angels are composed of nine parts, each of which contains a bead for the Our Father and three beads for the Hail Mary. The four beads which come before the medal bearing the image of St. Michael the Archangel, remind us that after invoking the Nine Choirs of Angels it is necessary to recite another four Our Fathers in honour of the Archangels Michael, Gabriel and Raphael and our Guardian Angels respectively.

ORIGIN OF THE CHAPLET OF THE ANGELS

This pious exercise was revealed by the Archangel Michael to Anthony De Astonac of Portugal, now venerated as Servant of God.

In his apparition to Anthony, St. Michael said that he wished to be venerated with nine invocations in honour of the Nine Choirs of Angels, and subsequently taught the following chaplet to the visionary.

Furthermore, the Archangel promised to obtain for those who honoured him with the recitation of this little chaplet before Holy Communion the grace of being accompanied by an angel from each one of the nine choirs, when receiving the Body of Christ. To those who recited the Chaplet everyday he promised his particular and constant help and that of all the angels throughout their lives, and also in Purgatory after their death.

Even though this revelation is not yet officially recognized by the Church, the recitation of the chaplet has spread among those particularly devoted to Michael the Archangel and all the angels.

The hope of receiving the graces promised by the Archangel has been raised and sustained by the fact that Pope Pius IX granted many indulgences in association with this pious and beneficial exercise.

CHAPLET OF THE ANGELS

In the name of the Father, and of the Son, and of the Holy Spirit. Amen.

O God, come to my aid.
O Lord, make haste to help me.

Glory Be
The Creed *(see page 26)*

FIRST INVOCATION

Through the intercession of Saint Michael and the Heavenly Choir of Seraphims, may the Lord render us worthy of the flame of perfect love. **Amen.**

Our Father
3 Hail Marys *(in honour of the first Angelic Choir)*

SECOND INVOCATION

Through the intercession of Saint Michael and the Heavenly Choir of Cherubims, may the Lord grant us the grace to abandon our life of sin and to proceed swiftly along the path of christian perfection. **Amen.**

Our Father
3 Hail Marys *(in honour of the second Angelic Choir)*

THIRD INVOCATION

Through the intercession of Saint Michael the Archangel and the sacred Choir of Thrones, may the Lord infuse in our hearts a spirit of true and sincere humility. **Amen.**

Our Father
3 Hail Marys *(in honour of the third Angelic Choir)*

FOURTH INVOCATION

Through the intercession of Saint Michael and the Heavenly Choir of Dominions, may the Lord grant us the grace to have control over our senses and to correct our disordered passions. **Amen.**

Our Father
3 Hail Marys *(in honour of he fourth Angelic Choir)*

FIFTH INVOCATION

Through the intercession of Saint Michael and the Heavenly Choir of Powers, may the Lord protect our souls from the snares and temptations of the devil. **Amen.**

Our Father

3 Hail Marys *(in honour of the fifth Angelic Choir)*

SIXTH INVOCATION

Through the intercession of Saint Michael and the choir of admirable Heavenly Virtues, may the Lord prevent us from falling into temptation, but deliver us from evil. **Amen.**

Our Father

3 Hail Marys *(in honour of the sixth Angelic Choir)*

SEVENTH INVOCATION

Through the intercession of Saint Michael and the heavenly Choir of Principalities, may the Lord fill our souls with the spirit of true and sincere obedience. **Amen.**

Our Father

3 Hail Marys *(Iin honour of the seventh Angelic Choir)*

EIGHTH INVOCATION

Through the intercession of Saint Michael and the Heavenly Choir of Archangels, may the Lord grant us the gift of perseverance in faith and good deeds, in order that we may reach the glory of Paradise. **Amen.**

Our Father

3 Hail Marys *(in honour of the eighth Angelic Choir)*

NINTH INVOCATION

Through the intercession of Saint Michael and the Heavenly Choir of all the Angels, may the Lord grant, in his mercy, that we may be guarded by them in our present life and then be led to the eternal glory of heaven. **Amen.**

Our Father
3 Hail Marys

(in honour of the ninth Angelic Choir)

Our Father *in honour of Saint Michael*

Our Father *in honour of Saint Gabriel*

Our Father *in honour of Saint Raphael*

Our Father *in honour of our Guardian Angels*

Let us pray.

Almighty and everlasting God, who, in your abundant goodness and mercy for the salvation of humanity, chose the glorious Archangel Saint Michael to be Prince of your Church, grant, through his beneficial protection, that we may be freed from all our spiritual enemies. May the ancient enemy not disturb us at the hour of our death, but let Archangel Michael lead us into the presence of Your divine Majesty. **Amen.**

LITANY OF ST. MICHAEL
THE ARCHANGEL

Lord, have mercy.

Lord, have mercy.

Christ, have mercy.

Christ, have mercy.

Christ, hear us.

Christ, graciously hear us.

God, the Father of heaven,

have mercy on us.

God the Son, Redeemer of the world,   "

God the Holy Spirit,   "

Holy Trinity, one God,   "

Holy Mary,   "

St. Michael the Archangel,   "

St. Michael, prince of the Seraphims,   "

St. Michael, messenger of the Lord,
 God of Israel,   "

St. Michael, councillor of the Most Holy Trinity, "

St. Michael, dean of Paradise, "

St. Michael, brightest star of the angelic order, "

St. Michael, mediator of divine graces, "

St. Michael, radiant sun of mercy, "

St. Michael, first model of humility, "

St. Michael, exemplar of meekness, "

St. Michael, first flame of most ardent zeal, "

St. Michael, worthy of admiration, **pray for us.**

St. Michael, worthy of veneration,   ,,

St. Michael, worthy of praise,   ,,

St. Michael, minister of Divine Mercy,   ,,

St. Michael, mighty leader,   ,,

St. Michael, dispenser of glory,   ,,

St. Michael, comforter of the downcast,   ,,

St. Michael, angel of peace,   ,,

St. Michael, comforter of the sick,   ,,

St. Michael, guide of the wandering,   ,,

St. Michael, stronghold of those who hope,   ,,

St. Michael, guardian of those who have faith,   ,,

St. Michael, protector of the Church,   ,,

St. Michael, generous dispenser,   ,,

St. Michael, refuge of the poor,   ,,

St. Michael, refuge of the oppressed,   ,,

St. Michael, conqueror of demons,   ,,

St. Michael, our courage,   ,,

St. Michael, our refuge,   ,,

St. Michael, our defender,   ,,

St. Michael, leader of angels,   ,,

St. Michael, comfort of patriarchs,   ,,

St. Michael, light of prophets,   ,,

St. Michael, guide of apostles,   ,,

St. Michael, relief of martyrs,   ,,

St. Michael, joy of confessors,   ,,

St. Michael, guardian of virgins,   ,,

St. Michael, honoured by all saints,   ,,

Lamb of God, who take away
the sins of the world,
Spare us, O Lord.

Lamb of God, who take away
the sins of the world,
Graciously hear us, O Lord.

Lamb of God, who take away
the sins of the world,
Have mercy on us.

Let us pray.
O Lord, may the powerful intercession of your Archangel Michael protect us always and everywhere; may he free us from all evil and lead us to eternal life. Through Christ our Lord.
Amen.

All you Holy Angels and Archangels,
defend us.
Amen.

INVOCATION OF THE NINE CHOIRS OF ANGELS

O Angels most holy, moved by a most ardent zeal for our salvation, who are our special guardians and protectors, do not tire of watching over us and of defending us always and everywhere.

Glory Be *(3 times)*

O Archangels most noble, guide us and direct our steps amid the dangers which surround us at all sides.

Glory Be *(3 times)*

O Principalities sublime, who govern empires and provinces, direct our souls so that they may never be dominated by our senses.

Glory Be *(3 times)*

O Powers invincible, defend us from the assaults of the devil who constantly prowls around us like a lion in order to devour us.

Glory Be *(3 times)*

O Virtues most powerful, have mercy on our weakness and obtain for us the strength and courage to bear the adversities and ills of this life with patience.

Glory Be *(3 times)*

O Dominions most high, reign over our spirits and our hearts, and help us to know and to fulfil faithfully the will of God.

Glory Be *(3 times)*

O supreme Thrones, on which the Almighty rests, obtain for us peace with God, with our neighbour and with ourselves.

Glory Be *(3 times)*

O Cherubims most wise, dispel the darkness of our souls and allow divine light to shine within us, so that we may clearly comprehend the truths of salvation.

Glory Be *(3 times)*

O Seraphims, ever ardent with love of God, enkindle in us the sacred fire which renders you blessed.

Glory Be *(3 times)*

Angels, Archangels, Thrones and Dominions, Principalities and Powers, Heavenly Virtues, Cherubims and Seraphims, bless the Lord for ever.

Glory Be *(3 times)*

NOVENA

NOVENA TO SAINT MICHAEL THE ARCHANGEL

(In association with this novena, a partial indulgence is granted daily and a plenary indulgence at the end of the nine days).

In the name of the Father, and of the Son, and of the Holy Spirit. Amen.

O God, come to my aid.
O Lord, make haste to help me.

Glory Be
The Creed *(see page 26)*

HYMN IN HONOUR OF ST. MICHAEL THE ARCHANGEL

You, O splendour and virtue of the Father,
You, O Jesus, life of our hearts,
we praise You among the angels
who hang on Your every word.

A mighty host of thousands
of leaders
combats under You,
and as a sign of salvation,
victorious Michael displays the Cross.

He pushes the proud head of the dragon
into the depths of hell
and strikes the chief with his rebels
off the heavenly rock.
In combat against the head of pride
we follow this Prince,
so that the crown of glory may be given to us
from the throne of the Lamb.

Glory be to God the Father,
for He who redeemed the Son
who was anointed by the Holy Spirit,
shall protect us by means of the angels.

At the presence of the angels
I shall sing to You, my God.
I shall adore You in your Holy Temple
and I give praise to Your name.

Let us pray.
Almighty God, grant that under the patronage of
Saint Michael the Archangel, we may always
aspire to heaven and may He whose glory we
proclaim on earth assist us by His prayers.
Through Christ our Lord. **Amen.**

First Grace

O Saint Michael the Archangel, we ask you together with the Prince of Seraphims of the First Choir of Angels to enkindle in our heart a fire of holy love and through your intercession, let us disdain the alluring deception of the pleasures of the world.

Our Father
Hail Mary *(3 times)*

Saint Michael the Archangel, defend us in battle so that we may not perish in the last judgement.

Second Grace

We humbly ask you, O Prince of the heavenly Jerusalem, together with the head of Cherubims of the Second Choir of Angels, to remember us especially when we are assaulted by temptations by the infernal enemy so that, with your assistance, we may gain victory over Satan and offer ourselves as a complete holocaust to the Lord God.

Our Father
Hail Mary *(3 times)*

Saint Michael the Archangel, defend us in battle so that we may not perish in the last judgement.

Third Grace

We earnestly beseech you, O invincible champion of Paradise, together with the Prince of the Third Choir of Angels, do not allow us who are devoted to you to be oppressed by evil spirits or by infirmities.

Our Father
Hail Mary *(3 times)*

Saint Michael the Archangel, defend us in battle so that we may not perish in the last judgement.

Fourth Grace

Humbly prostrate upon the ground, we ask you, our first minister in the Heavenly Court, to grant that together with the Prince of Dominions of the Fourth Choir of Angels, you may defend Christianity in all its necessities, and in particular our Holy Father the Pope, so that his happiness and grace in this life and his glory in the life to come may ever increase.

Our Father
Hail Mary *(3 times)*

Saint Michael the Archangel, defend us in battle so that we may not perish in the last judgement.

Fifth Grace

O Holy Archangel, we beseech you so that, together with the Prince of the Fifth Choir of Angels, you may free us, you servants, from the hands of our enemies, both hidden and manifest, spare us from false witness; free our country from discord and in particular deliver our home-town from hunger, pestilence and war; spare us also from thunder and lightning, earthquakes and storms, which the dragon of hell often causes to harm us.

Our Father
Hail Mary *(3 times)*

Saint Michael the Archangel, defend us in battle so that we may not perish in the last judgement.

Sixth Grace

O leader of the heavenly hosts, we implore you together with the Prince who holds the first place among the Powers which form the Sixth Choir of Angels, to provide for the needs of those who serve you in our country and in particular in our home-town, giving the earth its desired fertility and granting peace and harmony among Christian rulers.

Our Father
Hail Mary *(3 times)*

Saint Michael the Archangel, defend us in battle so that we may not perish in the last judgement.

SEVENTH GRACE

O Saint Michael, Prince of Angels, we ask you and the Head of Principalities of the Seventh Choir of Angels to spare us your servants, this nation and in particular our hometown from sickness, physical and most especially, spiritual.

Our Father
Hail Mary *(3 times)*

Saint Michael the Archangel, defend us in battle so that we may not perish in the last judgement.

EIGHTH GRACE

O Holy Archangel, we implore you together with the Prince of the Archangels of the Eighth Choir of Angels and all nine Choirs, to take care of us in this present life, to assist us in the pangs of death, and at the very moment of our passing from this life so that, under your protection, we may be victorious over Satan and thus come to enjoy Divine Goodness with you in Paradise.

Our Father
Hail Mary *(3 times)*

Saint Michael the Archangel, defend us in battle so that we may not perish in the last judgement.

Ninth Grace

We beseech you again, O most glorious Prince and Defender of the militant and triumphant Church, to grant, together with the Head of the Angels of the Ninth Choir your guardianship and patronage to us and all our families, to those who have asked us to pray for them and to all those who are devoted to you, so that under your protection, we may live a holy life and thus come to enjoy God's presence together with you and all the angels for ever and ever.
Amen.

Our Father
Hail Mary *(3 times)*

Saint Michael the Archangel, defend us in battle so that we may not perish in the last judgement.

At the end of the Novena we recite:

Our Father *in honour of Saint Michael*

Our Father *in honour of Saint Gabriel*

Our Father *in honour of Saint Raphael*

Our Father *in honour of our Guardian Angels*

Pray for us, most blessed Michael, Prince of God.
That we may be made worthy of the promises of Christ.

Let us pray.
Almighty and eternal God, who, in your great goodness, appointed the Archangel Michael as glorious Prince of the Church for the salvation of humankind, grant that, through his saving help, we may merit adequate defence from all our enemies so that, at the hour of our death, we may be freed from sin and may come before your most blessed Majesty.
Through Christ our Lord. **Amen.**

ROSARY

ROSARY IN HONOUR OF THE ANGELS

(To be recited especially on Tuesday of each week and on the 9th day of each month).

In the name of the Father, and of the Son, and of the Holy Spirit. Amen.

O God, come to my aid.
O Lord, make haste to help me.

Glory Be
The Creed *(see page 26)*

O sublime Seraphims, ardent with love, obtain for us the grace of holy chastity.

Our Father
Glory Be *(9 times)*
Hail Mary

O blessed Cherubims, visionaries of God, obtain for us a lively faith.

Our Father
Glory Be *(9 times)*
Hail Mary

O Thrones most high, bearers of Our Lord, grant us unwavering hope that one day we too may bear Him.

Our Father
Glory Be *(9 times)*
Hail Mary

O supreme Dominions of the Angels and of all things, obtain for us complete and rightful self-control.

Our Father
Glory Be *(9 times)*
Hail Mary

O Virtues who are most powerful and operate every marvellous deed, obtain for us the grace of overcoming all human opposition.

Our Father
Glory Be *(9 times)*
Hail Mary

O invincible Powers over demons, obtain victory for us over every diabolic temptation.

Our Father
Glory Be *(9 times)*
Hail Mary

O Principalities most wise, governors of the actions of the angels, obtain for us the grace of acting in perfect conformity with the will of God.

Our Father
Glory Be *(9 times)*
Hail Mary

O Archangels most noble, messengers of great events, grant that we may be obedient to the supreme commandments of God.

Our Father
Glory Be *(9 times)*
Hail Mary

O joyful Angels, ministers and messengers of the Most High, grant that we may always follow the inspirations of God.

Our Father
Glory Be *(9 times)*
Hail Mary

Queen of Angels,
pray for us. *(3 times)*

Pray for us, all you Orders of Angels.
That we may be made worthy of the promises of Christ.

Let us pray.
O God, who guide the activity of angels and of humankind with the utmost prudence, grant, in your mercy, that our life on earth may be sustained by your ministers, who constantly protect it from heaven.
Through Christ, our Lord and our God, who lives and reigns with you, in the unity of the Holy Spirit, one God for ever and ever. **Amen.**

2.

THE GUARDIAN ANGELS

- **Prayers**
  - **Act of Consecration**
- **Triduum**
  - **Chaplet**
- **Novena**

INTRODUCTION

From the time of the Incarnation until the Ascension, the life of the Word Incarnate was marked by adoration and service of the angels. As Scripture tells us, "when (God) brings the First-born into the world, he says: Let all the angels of God pay him homage" (Heb 1:6). Their hymn of praise at the birth of Christ has not ceased to resound in the song of praise of the Church, "Glory to God in the highest heaven, and on earth peace for those he favours..." (Lk 2:14).

The angels protected Jesus during his childhood, served him in the desert, comforted him during his agony when indeed, he could have been saved from the hands of the enemies by legions of angels as in the history of Israel. It is the angels who also "evangelize" or bring the Good News (ref. Lk 2;10), announcing both the Incarnation and the Resurrection of Christ. At the second coming of Christ, which shall likewise be announced by the angels, they shall be present to serve Christ in his judgement.

In the same way, the whole life of the Church benefits from the mysterious and powerful help of these heavenly ministers, as can be seen in the Liturgy.

The Church unites herself to the angels when pronouncing God three times holy before the Consecration: "And so, with all the choirs of angels in heaven we proclaim your glory and join in their unending hymn of praise: Holy, holy, holy..." (ref. Weekday Preface I). Similarly, in the "Supplices te rogamus" of the Roman Canon (Eucharistic Prayer I) we call on their assist-ance: "Almighty God, we pray that your angel may take this sacrifice to your altar in heaven". The angels are also invoked in the Liturgy of the Dead: "Come to meet him (her) angels of the Lord... May Christ, who called you take you to himself; may angels lead you to Abraham's side", while in the Byzantine Liturgy we find the

well-known hymn of the Cherubims. Furthermore, the enti-
re Church celebrates the feast-day of SS. Michael, Gabriel
and Raphael, Archangels, on the 29th of September and the
memorial of the Guardian Angels on the 2nd of October.

Thus, we can see that from childhood to the hour of
death, we are surrounded by the angels who protect us and
intercede for us. "Everyone of the faithful has an angel by
his side as protector and pastor, in order to bring him to
life" (St. Basil of Caeserea, Adversus Eunomium). Begin-
ning with the time we spend here on earth, our Christian
life partakes in faith in the blessed community of angels
and humankind, united in God.

THE GUARDIAN ANGELS

Our Guardian Angel is a friend whom we do not see but
nonetheless, his responsibility in our life is greater than we
can imagine.

Our Guardian Angel has the task of presenting to God
our acts of adoration, our proposals and our holy desires.

He watches attentively over us and being an envoy from
heaven, inspires us to good, according to God's desires for us.

He contemplates the face of God constantly and never
leaves the throne of the Lord although being at the service of
men and women, because the fire of love within him and the
obedience with which he fulfils his duties are inseparable.

Love is what renders our angels vigilant and allows
them to be in continuous adoration, while their service in
obedience to God makes them diligent and desirous of fulfil-
ling their mission. After this life, it shall be our Guardian
Angel who will lead us into the blessed Homelandof heaven.
Let us therefore love, invoke and respect our angels. When
it seems that we are alone, they watch over us.

Let us also respect him by behaving as in the presence
of someone with the duty of referring to the King all that
we do, because the sins unknown to others sadden our good
angel. May our behaviour be simple, dignified and full of

tenderness.

Even if we do not listen to the suggestions of others, let us always heed the inspirations of our Guardian Angel. Each good thought to which we pay no attention is an act of discourtesy towards him. Indeed, Jesus said, "They may listen but not understand" (Lk 8:9).

Let us therefore listen to our Guardian Angel! He speaks in the intimacy of our hearts; he speaks through other people; he even speaks through what we read. His voice is inspired by the Holy Spirit and, as such, mingles with the Spirit's voice, carrying out his desires.

When we feel sad let us invoke him so that he may bring us a ray of light, a spark of the purest joy of which angels are the bearers. Our recourse to him shall never be in vain.

True friends are considered by the Holy Spirit to be "treasure". In the world there are relatively few true friends. Many humans betray each other and abandon those who are in need. However, our Guardian Angel is a true friend who shares actively in our joys and sorrows, and while acting to protect us from all that damages our body and soul, he tries to help us to obtain all that is good for us.

We all encounter many occasions of sin in our lives, and though often unforeseeable, as are the countless risks to our health and life, our angel is like the light which illumines our path, showing us the dangers and helping us to avoid them with the aid of our will.

Therefore, let us not forget the one who remains at our side as our helper. Let us trust him and put our most difficult and important duties in his hands. Let us pray to him and thank him for the service that he renders us freely.

Our angels were victorious in the battle before Creation and have remained faithful to God, retaining that humility which distinguishes them from evil spirits.

Let us pray that we may imitate their faithfulness and meekness, and if we are ever asked to fight in order to defend the truth, may the cry of the good Angels, "Who is like our God?", be our cry and may the humility which they invoke for us become our principal virtue and the basis of our perfection. Furthermore, let us teach our children to pray to their Guardian Angels and let us commend the Church, our Holy Father the Pope, all families and institutions to their protection.

Even though the devil is astute and strong, the strength of the angels is by far superior because they fight in the name of the God of Hosts who has the whole universe in his hands. Moreover, our Guardian Angel is close to us day and night. Therefore, let us offer him a thought of affection or thanksgiving frequently throughout the day, as our hearts inspire us.

On Tuesday, the day consecrated to our Guardian Angels, let us attend Mass, receive Holy Communion and do any good deed in his honour, per-haps concluding the day with the recitation of the beautiful, efficacious and consoling Chaplet of the Angels (See page 00) which is like a hymn to the Nine Choirs of Angels. Furthermore, let us not forget to honour the Holy Angels during the year on their feast-days.

Thus, our holy Heavenly Friends and in particular, our Guardian Angels, shall rejoice with us and ensure that the Lord and the Blessed Virgin, their Queen, will multiply their favours and blessings upon our soul!

The writer knows of people who always find a parking place during rush hour thanks to a quick prayer to their Guardian Angels! He also knows some learned people who, before searching for a quotation in a book, call briefly on their Guardian Angel, close their eyes, stretch out their hand and find it.

Though these are matters of minor importance, the Gospel has taught us not to despise them. Indeed, our daily life is mainly composed of such minor episodes.

May we imitate the devotion of St. Francesca Romana

to her Guardian Angel, who honoured him at every moment, talked to him and never forgot to reserve a place for him at her side.

Let us be always thankful to the Heavenly Father who has given the Guardian Angels to humanity to protect our fragile nature from the snares of our enemies. May we place an ever-increasing trust in the angels who direct us on the paths of life and guide our steps towards heaven.

WHAT DO THE SAINTS AND SCHOLARS SAY ABOUT THE ANGELS?

"The desire of our Guardian Angel to come to our assistance is greater than ours to be helped".   (St. John Bosco)

"Angels show themselves only to those who love them and call on them".   (Card. Charles Journet)

"Remember that God is within us when we are in a state of grace, he is outside our body when we sin: but his Angel never leaves us. He is the most sincere and trustworthy friend, even when we cause him to suffer with our bad behaviour".   (Saint Pio)

(Saint Padre Pio trusted his Guardian Angel so much that he used to ask his angel to translate the letters which foreigners sent to him).

"When I have to visit an important person, I give my Guardian Angel the duty of coming to an agreement with that person's angel so that the latter may have an influence on his frame of mind. It is a little devotion which the Holy Father Pope Pius XI reminded me of and which I have found most fruitful".   (Pope John XXIII)

PRAYERS

*In the name of the Father, and of the Son,
and of the Holy Spirit. Amen.*

O God, come to my aid.
O Lord, make haste to help me.

Glory Be
The Creed *(see page 26)*

PRAYER TO ONE'S GUARDIAN ANGEL

Angel of God, my guardian dear,
to whom God's love commits me her,
ever this day (or night) be at my side,
to light and guard, to rule and guide. **Amen.**

PRAYER TO THE GUARDIAN ANGEL

Angel sent by God to guide me,
Be my light and walk beside me;
Be my guardian and protect me;
On the paths of life direct me.

PRAYER TO OUR GUARDIAN ANGEL

Most gracious angel, my guardian, tutor and master, my guide and defence, my wisest counsellor and most faithful friend, the Lord in his goodness, has entrusted me to your care, from the day of my birth to the last hour of my life.

How much respect I owe you, knowing that you are close to me at all times and wherever I am!

How much I need to thank you for the love which you cherish for me; what great confidence it gives me to know that you are my assistant and defender!

Holy Angel, instruct me, correct me, protect me, keep me safe and guide me along the right path which leads to the Holy City of God.

Let me not do things which would offend your holiness and purity.

Present my desires to the Lord, offer him my prayers, show him my weakness and obtain for me the purification of my soul through his infinite goodness and the motherly intercession of Mary most Holy, your Queen.

Watch over me when I sleep, revive me when I am tired, strengthen me when I am going to fall, raise me up when I have fallen, show me the way when I am lost, comfort me when I lose heart, enlighten me when I do not see, defend me when I am in trouble; now and especially on the last day of my life, be my shield against the devil.

With your defence and guidance, help me to enter into your light-filled dwelling place where I may express my gratitude to you and glorify Christ Our Lord and the Blessed Virgin Mary, our Queen, together with you for ever and ever. **Amen.**

PRAYER OF INVOCATION TO OUR GUARDIAN ANGEL

O holy Guardian Angel, may you be for me: a helper in my needs, a comforter in my difficulties, light in my darkness, protection when I am in danger, inspiration of good thoughts, a mediator with God, a shield to defend me from the evil one, a faithful companion, a true friend, a prudent counsellor, a model of obedience, a mirror of humility and purity.

Assist us, O Angels who watch over us, O Angels of our families, O Angels of our children, O Angels of our parishes, O Angels of our town, O Angels of our country, O Angels of the Church, O Angels of the Universe. **Amen.**

ACT OF CONSECRATION
TO THE GUARDIAN ANGEL

O holy Guardian Angel!

From the beginning of my life
you were chosen to be my Protector
and Companion.
Here, in the presence of
my Lord and my God,
my heavenly Mother Mary
and all the angels and saints,
I, a poor sinner, (N.   )
wish to consecrate myself to you.

I want to take your hand
and never let it go.
I promise to be always
faithful and obedient to God
and to our holy Mother the Church.
I promise to be always faithful to Our Lady, and
to take her
as the model of my life.

I promise to be devoted also to you,
my holy Protector,

and to propagate
devotion to the angels as best I can,
devotion to those who are given to us
in these times
as protection and help
in the spiritual war
for the victory of the Kingdom of God.

I pray to you, O holy Angel,
to grant me the strength of divine love
so that it may enkindle in me
a steadfast faith
so that I may fall into sin no more.

I ask that your hand may defend me
from the enemy.

I implore you to grant me the grace
of Mary's humility,
so that I may avoid
all dangers and,
through your guidance,
may reach the door
of the House of our Heavenly Father.
Amen.

TRIDUUM TO THE
GUARDIAN ANGEL

(To be recited from the 29th of September to the 1st of October or at any other time when we particularly desire to express our love for our Guardian Angel).

In the name of the Father, and of the Son, and of the Holy Spirit. Amen.

O God, come to my aid.
O Lord, make haste to help me.

Glory Be
The Creed *(see page 26)*

FIRST DAY

My Guardian Angel, you who have deigned to take care of me, a poor sinner, I beg you to revive my spirit with a lively faith, a steadfast hope and infinite mercy, so that I may think only of loving and serving my God.

Angel of God... *(3 times)*

SECOND DAY

Most noble Prince of the Heavenly Court, you who have been kind enough to take care of my poor soul, defend it from the snares and assaults of the devil, so that in the future, it may never offend my Lord.

Angel of God... *(3 times)*

THIRD DAY

Most merciful guardian of my soul, you who humiliated yourself greatly by descending from heaven to earth in order to fulfil your ministry to a poor creature like me, grant me the firm belief that I can do nothing without your powerful help and the grace of my Lord.

Angel of God... *(3 times)*

CHAPLET

CHAPLET TO OUR
GUARDIAN ANGEL

(To be recited from the 29th of September to the 1st of October, or at any other time when we desire to express our love for our Guardian Angel, or wish to invoke the help of the Guardian Angels for a particular grace).

In the name of the Father, and of the Son, and of the Holy Spirit. Amen.

O God, come to my aid.
O Lord, make haste to help me.

Glory Be
The Creed *(see page 26)*

FIRST DAY

My Guardian Angel, I thank you for having always taken special care of my spiritual and temporal needs and for continuing to do so: I beseech you to thank Divine Providence on my behalf for having been pleased to entrust me to the guardianship of a sublime Prince of Paradise.

Glory Be
Angel of God

SECOND DAY

My Guardian Angel, I humbly ask your forgiveness for the sorrow I have caused you by violating the law of God in your presence, ignoring your inspirations and warnings: I beseech you to grant me the grace of atoning for all the sins of my past with the required penance. I also ask you for the grace of assisting at Mass with ever-increasing fervour, and grant that I may always have great devotion to Our Lady who is the Mother of perseverance.

**Glory Be
Angel of God**

THIRD DAY

My Guardian Angel, I beseech you with insistence to increase your loving care of me, so that by overcoming all obstacles to virtue that are in my way, I may free myself from all the misery which oppresses my soul and by persevering in my respect for your presence, being ever fearful of your reproaches and following your holy counsel faithfully, I may deserve to enter one day into eternal happiness together with you.

**Glory Be
Angel of God**

NOVENA TO OUR GUARDIAN ANGEL

(To be recited from the 23rd of September to the 1st of October, or at any other time when we wish to express our love for our Guardian Angel, or to implore their intercession for a particular grace).

In the name of the Father, and of the Son, and of the Holy Spirit. Amen.

O God, come to my aid.
O Lord, make haste to help me.

Glory Be
The Creed *(see page 26)*

O Angel, whom Our Lord, in his goodness, chose to watch over me, I begin by thanking you with all my heart for the care and help which you have given to me until now, and I beseech you to guide my steps along the path of eternal salvation.

Angel of God...

O Angel most pure, I ask you forgiveness for the sins that I dared to commit in your presence, and I promise you that from now on, I shall never do anything that would displease you, for to you I owe my reverence and love.

Angel of God...

O Merciful Angel, who are my guide and defence, I love you and honour you; I implore you to watch over me in times of temptation, to deliver me from evil and to give me the courage I need to do good; I beg you to give me assistance in my needs, comfort in my difficulties, courage and strength in the sufferings of my soul. I beseech you to bring my prayers to the throne of God and to grant me the graces that I need for eternal salvation; I beg you, above all, to sustain, defend and comfort me at the hour of my death, so that I may be worthy of entering into heaven with you where I may bless the Lord for ever and ever.
Amen.

Angel of God...

Prayer of Thanksgiving.

O Angel of God, my true friend, my faithful companion and trustworthy guide, I thank you for the tireless mercy, watchfulness and patience with which you have always assisted and continue to assist me in my spiritual and temporal needs. I ask your forgiveness for having offended you so many times by disobeying your loving advice, opposing your prudent warnings and bearing such little fruit in spite of your holy instructions. Grant, I beseech you, that your most gracious protection may continue throughout my life, so that I may bless, thank and praise the Lord together with you for all eternity. **Amen.**

Angel of God...

3.

THE FALLEN ANGELS

• Prayers of liberation

INTRODUCTION

There was a seductive voice behind the disobedience of Adam and Eve, a voice which opposed itself to God and, out of envy, caused them to sin.

Scripture and the Church's Tradition regard this being as a fallen angel, known as "Satan" or the "devil". The Church teaches that he was initially a good angel, created by God. "Diabolus enim et alii daemones a Deo quidem natura creati sunt boni, sed ipsi per se facti sunt mali; the devil and the other demons were indeed created naturally good by God, but they became evil by their own doing" (Lateran Council IV [1215]: DS 800).

Scripture speaks of a sin of these angels. Their "fall" consists in the free choice of these created spirits who radically and irrevocably rejected *God and his reign. Their rebellion is reflected in the words addressed by the tempter to Adam and Eve: "You will be like God"(Gen 3:5). Indeed "the devil has been a sinner from the beginning" (1Jn 3:8), and is "the father of lies" (Jn 8:44).*

It is the irrevocable *character of their choice, and not a defect in the infinite mercy of God, that makes the angels' sin unforgivable (ref. Catechism of the Catholic Church, Part One).*

Scripture bears witness to the evil influence of the one whom Jesus calls "a murderer from the start" (Jn 8:44) and tells us that he even attempted to dissuade Jesus from the mission entrusted to Him by the Father. Indeed "the Son of God has appeared to undo the works of the devil" (ref. 1Jn 3:8). Among these works, that which had the worst consequences was the deceptive seduction which induced men and women to disobey God.

The power of Satan, however, is not infinite. He is but a creature, powerful because of being a pure spirit, but a creature all the same; he cannot prevent the building-up of the kingdom of God. Although Satan acts in the world out of hate for God and his kingdom, and although his works cause serious damage - of a spiritual nature and indirectly, also of a physical nature - for every man and woman and for society, these actions are allowed by Divine Providence, which guides the history of humankind and of the world with strength and tenderness. God's permission of the evil activity is a great mystery but "we are well aware that God works with those who love him, those who have been called in accordance with his purpose, and turns everything to their good" (Rm 8:28).

The victory over "the prince of this world" (Jn 14:30) is achieved once and for all in the hour at which Jesus gives himself freely unto death in order to give us his Life. Thus, the judgement of this world comes about and the prince of this world is "driven out" (Jn 12:31).

Scripture refers to Satan's battle against "the Woman" (ref. Gen. 3:15, Rev. 12:13). Many Fathers and Doctors of the Church have seen this woman as Mary, the mother of Christ, the "new Eve" who is "full of grace" imparted to her by the Holy Spirit, and free from sin and the corruption of death (as seen in the Immaculate Conception and Assumption of the Mary, Mother of God, Mary). As Mary has been "preserved from all stain of original sin and by a special grace of God [has] committed no sin of any kind during her earthly life" (ref. Catechism of the Catholich Church, Part One), Satan fails to capture her (ref. Rev. 12:16) and "enraged with the Woman", he goes away "to make war on the rest of her children" (Rev 12:17). Indeed, by our first parents' sin, the devil has acquired a certain domination over humanity even though we remain free: "the whole of man's history has been the story of dour combat with the powers of evil, stretching, as Our Lord tells us, from the very dawn of history until the last day. Finding himself in the midst of the battlefield, man has to struggle to do what is right, and it is at great cost to himself, and aided by God's grace, that he succeeds in achieving his own inner integrity" (GS 37§2).

It is for this reason that the Holy Spirit and the Church pray: "Come, Lord Jesus" (Rev 22:20); in fact, his final coming in glory shall deliver us from the evil one. Indeed, the so-called "Protoevangelium" or "first gospel" of Genesis tells us of the final victory of a descendant of "the Woman" over the serpent - and in the light of Divine Revelation, we know the victorious one to be Christ our Redeemer.

When asking to be freed from the devil, we are seeking to be freed from all ills, present, past and future, of which he is the author or instigator. Regarding this last issue, the Church brings be-fore the Father all the misery of the world. As well as asking to be liberated from the evils which crush humanity, the Church implores the precious gift of peace and the grace of perseverance in waiing for the return of Christ. Praying in this way, she anticipates in humble faith the final destiny of all people and of all things which shall be governed by the one who "holds the keys of Death and of Hades" (Rev 1:18), "the one who is, who was and who is to come, the Almighty" (Rev 1:8).

Thus, it is with fervour and insistency that the Church makes the following prayer in the Liturgy of the Eucharist: "Deliver us, Lord, from every evil, and grant us peace in our day. In your mercy keep us free from sin and protect us from all anxiety, while we wait in joyful hope for the coming of our Saviour Jesus Christ" (Communion Rite, Roman Missal).

All men and women are subject to the temptations of Satan, that is to his ordinary activity. However, we have the liberty to overcome them. Scripture assures us that God does not allow us to be tempted beyond our strength; that we can and indeed, must resist Satan, remaining "strong in *faith" (1Pt 5:2), St. James exhorts us with the following words: "Resist the devil, and he will "run away from you (Jm 4:7).*

Therefore, we must use all the means of grace which God provides for us, putting on "the full armour of God so as to be able to resist the devil's tactics" (Ep 6:11) and to respond to the words of admonishment spoken by the Lord himself in Gethsemane: "Watch and pray not to fall into temptation" (Mt 26:41).

*It is opportune at this point to refer to Sacramental exorcism. The latter can be administered **only by a bishop or by priest** who has been approved by the bishop to exercise this ministry.*

*It must be emphasized that a bishop can give permission to exorcize **only to priests**.*

The Gospel presents us with the most difficult case of liberation when it speaks to us of the young man over whom the apostles prayed in vain. This liberation requires three conditions: faith, prayer and fasting which are the most efficacious means of conquering evil. Undoubtedly, the power of prayer is even greater when more than one person supplicate God for the same intention, for the Gospel tells us: "If two of you agree to ask anything at all, it will be granted to you by my Father in heaven"(Mt 18:19) Prayer by more than one person, whatever our needs may be, is stronger; the Gospel also tells us this. Therefore, we must never tire of praying that we may be freed from evil and from the devil's temptations, for exorcisms without prayer are insufficient to combat the evil one. Let us pray, trusting that the Lord will give us all that we need, no matter how simple are words may be. Indeed, what could be more simple and effective than the words which Jesus himself tought us: "Lead us not into temptation, but deliver us from evil"?

With courage and an unwavering trust in God for whom

"nothing is impossible", let us thus persevere in our daily spiritual battle, using the powerful weapons against evil which God has given us:

1. *Living in the grace of God;*
2. *The Sacrament of Reconciliation;*
3. *The holy sacrifice of the Mass;*
4. *Holy Communion;*
5. *Eucharistic adoration;*
6. *Prayer in all its forms but especially the Psalms, biblical prayers and the Holy Rosary;*
7. *Blessings and sacramentals, such as exorcisms and the use of holy water.*

Let us conclude with the words of the Fathers and Doctors of the Church who seek to enlighten us as to why God permits evil in the world. St. Leo the Great tells us that "Christ's inexpressible grace gave us blessings better than those the denon's envy had taken away" (St. Leo the Great, Sermo 73), and St. Thomas Aquinas wrote, "There is nothing to prevent human nature's being raised up to something greater, even after sin; God permits evil in order to draw forth some greater good. Thus St. Paul says, 'Where sin increased, grace abounded all the more'; and the Exsultet sings, 'O happy fault,... which gained for us so great a Redeemer!'"

PRAYERS OF LIBERATION
FROM THE SPIRIT OF EVIL

PRAYER TO OUR LORD JESUS

O Jesus, my Saviour, my Lord and my God, my God and my all, who, through the sacrifice of the cross redeemed us and overcame the power of Satan, I beseech you to free me from every harmful presence and influence of evil.

I ask this in your name; I ask this for the sake of your wounds, I ask this through your blood, I ask this for the sake of your cross, I ask this through the intercession of Mary, Immaculate and Virgin, Our Lady of Sorrows. May the blood and water which gushed forth from your side flow down upon me to purify, free and heal me.
Amen.

PRAYER TO MARY

O venerable Queen of heaven and Sovereign of the Angels, who received the power and mission from God to crush the head of Satan, we humbly beseech you to send us heavenly hosts of angels, so that at your command, they may pursue the evil spirits, and go forth in combat against them in every place, suppress their audacity and drive them into the abyss of hell.
Amen.

Prayer to St. Michael *(see page 1160)*

Litany of the most Precious Blood *(see page 316)*

PRAYERS TO BLESS OUR HOME AND WORKPLACE

• Visit, Father, our home *(shop, office...)* and keep far from us the snares of the enemy; may your holy angels come to preserve our peace and may your blessing always remain upon us.
Through Christ our Lord.
Amen.

• Lord Jesus Christ, who have commanded your apostles to invoke peace on those living in the houses that they entered, we beseech you to sanctify our home through the prayer which we make to you with confidence.

Pour out your blessings and the abundance of your peace upon it.

May salvation come to our home, as it came to the house of Zaccheus when you entered it.

Command your angels to watch over it and to drive away from it all powers of evil.

May all those who live in this house please you with their virtuous works, so that when their hour shall come, they may be welcomed into your heavenly abode. This we ask you through Christ our Lord.
Amen.

Prayer Against Witchcraft

Lord our God, sovereign of the centuries, almighty and all-powerful; you who created all things and who transformed all things by the sheer power of your will; you who, in Babylon, transformed the heat of flame of the furnace, seven times hotter than usual, into the coolness of dew, and who thus protected and saved your three holy children; you who are physician and doctor of our souls; you who are the salvation of those who turn to you, we ask and beseech you to confound, drive away and put to flight every evil presence and malignant influence, every curse or evil eye of those who practise witchcraft and all evil deeds committed against your sevant.

Grant that wickedness and witchcraft may give way to goodness, blessings, strength, prosperity and charity.

O Lord, who love humankind, stretch out your powerful hands and your most high and powerful arms over us, visit us and come to the as-istance of this servant of yours, created in your image, by sending him (her) your angel of peace, stronghold and protector of body and soul, in order to dispel and keep far from him (her) any form of evil power, poisoning or witchcraft by which corrupt people may have tried to harm him (her), so that your servant may be protected and sing with gratitude: "The Lord is my light and salvation, whomshould I fear?" *(Ps 27).* Yes, Lord my God,

have mercy on me, your servant created in your image, ... and save me through the intercession of Mary, the Mother of God, your glorious archangels and all the saints.
Amen.

PRAYERS FROM THE ROMAN RITUAL

• Almighty Word of God the Father, Christ Jesus, Lord of all Creation, who gave to your apostles the power to tread on serpents and scorpions and the truly wonderful command of driving out demons; who, through the power of your arm, caused Satan to fall from heaven like lightning, to you I humbly address my plea: grant me, your most unworthy servant, firstly, forgiveness of my sins, and secondly, a steadfast faith and the ability to attack, in your name, and sustained by your power, this cruel demon, who disturbs your servant... This I ask through Our Lord Jesus Christ, who is to come to judge the living and the dead and this century in fire.
Amen.

• O God, Creator and Defender of humankind, you who created man in your own image and likeness, look upon this servant of yours... who is under attack by an unclean spirit, and troubled, shaken and terrified by the intrigues of the ancient adversary, the old enemy of the earth. Lord, guard us from his assaults, thwart his deceptive snares, drive away the tempter. Put your seal on your servant, and may he (she) be protected by your name in soul and body. Guard his chest, his organs and his hearts.

Dissipate the attempts of the opponent to penetrate his (her) heart of hearts. O Lord, grant that by invoking your most Holy Name, he who, until now, has been a source of terror, may be knocked to the ground and defeated; may he be gone, so that so that this servant of yours may duly serve you with a steadfast heart and sincere mind. Through Christ our Lord.
Amen.

PRAYERS FROM THE RITE OF CHRISTIAN INITIATION OF ADULTS

• With the breath of your mouth, send away, all evil spirits, Lord: command them to leave, because your "kingdom is close at hand".

Almighty and eternal God, who through your only Son, promised us the Holy Spirit, hear our prayer for this servant of yours who offers himself (herself) to you; keep far from him (her) every evil spirit, every work of error and of sin, so that he (she) may become a temple of the Holy Spirit. Through Christ our Lord.

We earnestly pray to you, Lord, for this servant of yours, who declares himself (herself) to be a sinner. Deign to suppress the inauspicious power of the enemy, and grant that, having experienced your mercy, he (she) may be healed from the wounds of sin and find peace of heart.
Amen.

• We earnestly pray to you, Lord, for this servant of yours, who adores you as the one true God: en-lighten and visit his (her) heart, keep far from him (her) every temptation and deception of the enemy, heal him (her) from all sin and infirmities so that, adhering to your loving will, he (she) may obey your Gospel with perseverance.
Amen.

## Part Nine

The
Saints

- **Prayer to St. Joseph**

  - **Novena to St. Joseph**

- **Prayers to St. Anthony**

  - **Blessed Padre Pio**

- **Novena to St. Teresa of the Child Jesus**

  - **Prayer to St. Rita**

- **The Plenary Indulgence of Assisi and the Prayer of St. Francis**

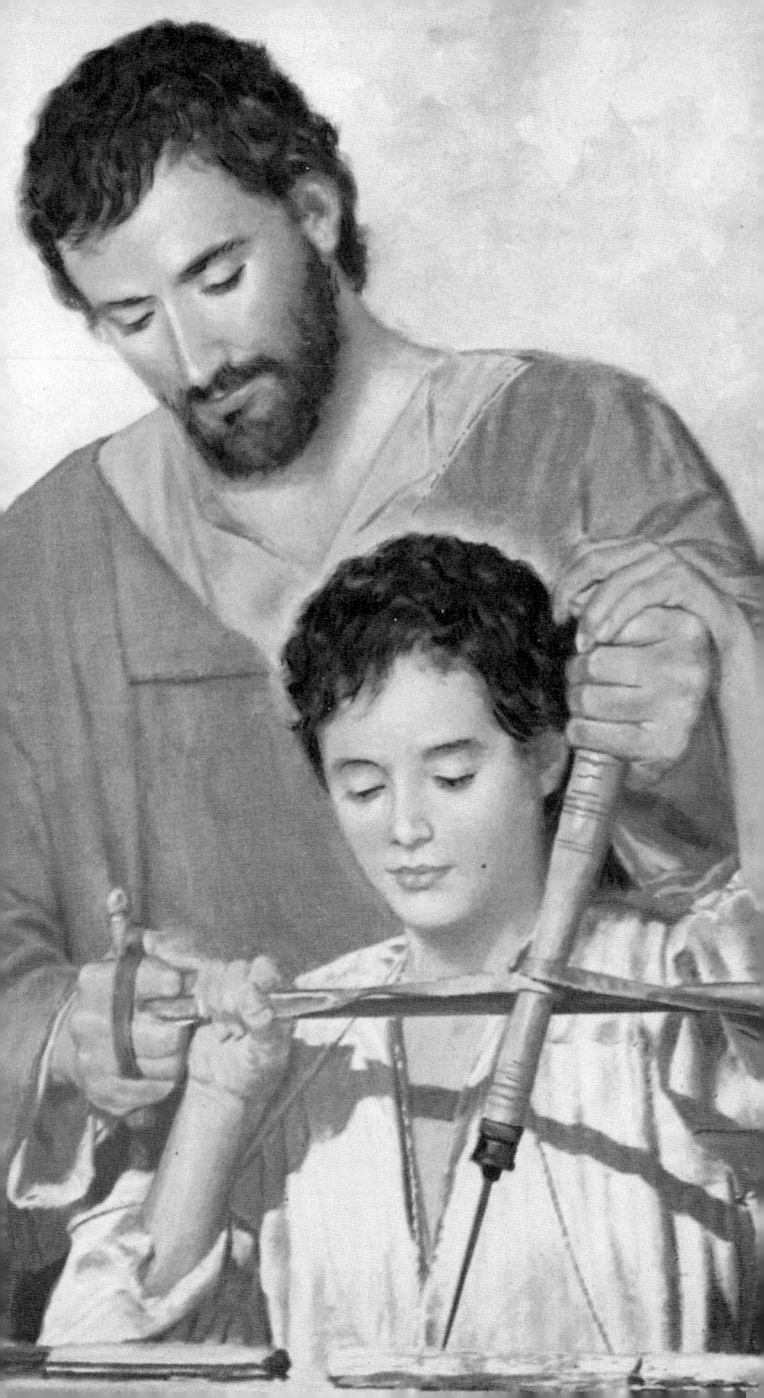

PRAYER TO ST. JOSEPH

Unto you, O blessed Joseph, do we fly in our tribulation and, having implored the help of your holy spouse, we now also confidently seek your protection. By that affection which united you to the Immaculate Virgin Mother of God, and by your fatherly love for the Child Jesus, we humbly beg you to look down with compassion on the inheritance which Jesus Christ purchased with his blood, and in our need to help us by your powerful intercession.

Do you, O prudent guardian of the Holy Family, watch over the chosen people of Jesus Christ. Keep us, O loving father, safe from all error and corruption. O great protector, from your safe place in heaven, graciously help us in our contest against the power of darkness. And as of old you did rescue the Child Jesus from the danger of death, so now defend God's holy Church from the snares of the enemy and from all adversity. Extend to each one of us your continual protection, that led on by your example and strengthened by your aid, we may live and die in holiness, and obtain everlasting happiness in heaven. **Amen.**

NOVENA TO ST. JOSEPH

*In the name of the Father, and of the Son,
and of the Holy Spirit. Amen.*

O God, come to my aid.
O Lord, make haste to help me.

Glory Be
The Creed *(see page 26)*

O St. Joseph, my patron and advocate, I come
to you, so that I may obtain the grace which I earnestly ask of you under your gaze. Even though I
am a sinner, must I lose hope in obtaining the
help of the Lord? "Oh! no!" would be the answer
of your devoted St. Teresa! "No indeed, O poor
sinners. In any need, however great, turn to the
efficacious intercession of St. Josph the Patriarch; abandon your needs to him in true faith and
all your requests will surely be granted." Therefore, I come to your glorious throne, imploring
your goodness: O St. Joseph, assist me as much
as you can in my tribulations.

Make up for my weakness and grant that
having obtained the grace that I ask through your

holy and powerful intercession, I may return to your altar to offer you my humble act of thanksgiving.

Our Father
Hail Mary
Glory Be

Do not forget, O most merciful St. Joseph that no-one who has come to you has ever been disappointed in the hope that he has placed in you. Countless are the graces and favours which you have obtained for the afflicted! The sick, oppressed, slandered, betrayed and abandoned souls who have had recourse to your royal protection have had their requests

granted. O Saint Joseph, do not allow that I may be the only one to be deprived of your comfort. Show your goodness and generosity also to me, a poor sinner, so that by thanking you, I may exalt the goodness and mercy of the Lord.

Our Father
Hail Mary
Glory Be

O Saint Joseph, head of the Holy Family, I venerate you profoundly. You have always granted comfort and graces to the afflicted souls who have prayed to you before me.

Therefore, in your mercy, console my sorrowful soul, too. O most wise saint, with God's help, you see all my necessities: you know how much I need the grace that I ask of you. Thus, I place all my hope in your intercession. If you grant me the grace that I ask of you with such insistence, I will strive to spread devotion to you everywhere, and to help and sustain the works which, in your name, bring relief to the suffering and the dying throughout the world. O Saint Joseph, consoler of the afflicted, have mercy on me in my sorrow!

Our Father
Hail Mary
Glory Be

Having said the novena prayers, we recite the following invocations to the most holy Trinity:

Eternal Divine Father, through your love that you have for Saint Joseph, chosen among all people to represent you on earth, have mercy on me.

Our Father
Hail Mary
Glory Be

Eternal Divine Son, through your love for Saint Joseph, your most faithful guardian on earth, have mercy on me.

Our Father
Hail Mary
Glory Be

Eternal Divine Spirit, through your love for Saint Joseph, who, with infinite care, watched over Mary most Holy, your beloved spouse, have mercy on me.

Our Father
Hail Mary
Glory Be

We conclude with the invocations below:

O most gracious spouse of Mary and virginal father of Jesus, for the sake of the treasure of your perfect obedience to God,
Have mercy on me.
For the sake of your life full of merits,
Hear my prayer.
For the sake of your most powerful Name,
Come to my aid
For the sake of your most merciful heart,
Graciously hear me

For the sake of your most holy tears,

> **Have mercy on me in my weeping.**

For the sake of your great sorrows,

> **Have mercy on me in my suffering**

For the sake of your joys,

> **Comfort my heart.**

O Saint Joseph,

> **Hear me.**

O Saint Joseph,

> **Graciously hear me.**

O Saint Joseph,

> **Have mercy on me.**

From all evil of body and soul,

> **Deliver me**

Come to my aid with your holy protection and, in your power and mercy, obtain from the Lord all that is necessary for me and, in particular, the grace that I need.

Our Father
Hail Mary
Glory Be

PRAYERS TO ST. ANTHONY

INVOCATION TO ST ANTHONY
OF PADUA

O dear St. Anthony, I turn my prayer to you, confident in your compassionate goodness which enables you to hear and to console every-one: intercede for me before God.

You, who led your life according to the Gospel, help me to live in faith and Christian hope; you, who preached the message of love, inspire all people with the desire for peace and fraternity; you, who helped with miracles those who were stricken by suffering and injustice, come to the aid of the poor and those who are forgotten in this world.

I ask you to bless in particular my family and my workplace, keeping far away from us all that may harm body and soul; may I always remain united to God in times of joy and in times of trial, may I have the faith and love of a child. **Amen.**

Prayer to St. Anthony

O God, good and merciful Father, who chose St. Anthony to be a witness of the Gospel and a messenger of peace among your people, hear the prayer which we address to you through his intercession.

May all families become holy; help them to grow in faith, conserve their unity, peace and serenity. Bless our children, protect the youth.

Come to the aid of all those who are afflicted by illness, suffering and loneliness.

Sustain us in our daily toil by giving us your love. Through Christ our Lord.

Amen.

SAINT PIO

Saint Pio (Francesco Forgione), now a saint, was born on the 25th of May, 1887, in a little town in southern Italy called Pietrelcina. His parents, though living in poverty, worked hard and educated their children in the faith from an early age. Indeed, when only five years old, Francesco had his first mystical experiences of suffering and ecstasy. at this age he already desired to consecrate himself entirely to God. At the age of fifteen he decided to become a Capuchin friar and by 1907, had taken his perpetual vows in that order. On the 10th of August, 1910, he was ordained a priest at Benevento, a town in southern Italy.

Saint Pio subjected himself to a life of austerity and rigorous penance. As a young priest he felt an ardent desire to offer himself to the Lord as a victim for the conversion and salvation of all sinners. He was continually afflicted by attacks from the devil, both physical and spiritual. However, he accepted these in perfect submission to the will of God, writing in one of his letters, "May it be as is desired; for me it is sufficient to know that all is wanted by God and I am happy just the same!" (Epistle 1, 206).

In the year 1909, saint Pio was forced to take a period of convalescence because of severe lung disease. His physical condition subsequently deteriorated to such an extent that his illness was said to have reached its terminal stage by the autumn of 1911. At this time he suffered from extremely high fevers and severe migraine and could take no food other than the consecrated host. In the summer of 1996 he moved to San Giovanni Rotondo, a hill-town in the south of Italy in order to take refuge from the intense heat.

The climate proved to be beneficial for his health and his superiors therefore decided to transfer him to the friary where he was to remain for the rest of his life.

It was here at San Giovanni Rotondo on Friday, the 20th of September, 1918, that he received the stigmata which he bore unto death and which were accompanied not only by physical suffering but also spiritual, for he did not consider himself worthy of resembling his Redeemer in such an evident manner. In one of his letters he wrote, "I will raise my voice with strength to the Lord and will not desist from entreating him so that His Mercy may take away from me not the pain and agony, because I feel as if I want to inebriate myself with pain, but these external signs, which confuse me and are an unbearable humiliation" (Epistle 1, 1094).

The isolated town where he lived, formerly unknown to the world, became a place of pilgrimage where many souls flocked to benefit from his help, counsel and spiritual direction, especially in the confessional.

Saint Pio had a tremendous love for Our Lady and always carried the Rosary beads in his hands. Indeed he recommended this prayer to his spiritual sons and daughters as an infallible weapon against evil. On the 22nd of September, 1968, having reached the age of 81, saint Pio fell ill at the end of the Mass which he had celebrated. In the early hours of the following morning, he gave up his spirit... and as if to give humanity a confirmation of resurrection, the stigmata and signs of Calvary which had accompanied him for fifty years miraculously disappeared.

Prayer to Saint Pio

O Jesus, full of grace and love, and a victim for our sins, who, inflamed with love for our souls, wanted to die on the cross, I humbly ask you to glorify, also on this earth, the servant of God, who, by generously partaking in your sufferings, loved you greatly and gave of himself without reserve for the glory of your Father and for the good of souls.

I beg you, therefore, to grant me, through his intercession, the grace of... *(Here we express our particular needs)* ... which I ardently desire.

Glory Be *(3 times)*

(See also the Chaplet to the Sacred Heart of Jesus which was recited by Saint Pio every day for all those who asked his prayers.............)

# NOVENA TO ST. TERESA OF THE CHILD JESUS (St. Thérèse of Lisieux)

(This prayer is recited for nine consecutive days for a special intention)

Dear Little Thérèse of the Child Jesus, the great saint of pure love for God, I come before you today to confide to you my ardent desire. Most humbly I come to implore your powerful intercession for the grace I ask...

(Here we pause to express our intention)

A short while before your death, you asked God if you could spend your heaven doing good on earth. You also promised to let a shower of roses fall upon us, little ones.

The Lord heard your prayer: thousands of pilgrims bear witness to the power of your intercession, at Lisieux and in all the world.

In my certainty that you never turn away the little ones who suffer, I come with confidence to implore your help. Intercede for me with your crucified and glorious Spouse. Let him know what I desire. He will listen to you, because you never refused him anything while on earth.

Little Thérèse, victim of love for the Lord, patron of the missions, model for simple and trusting souls, I turn to you as to an older sister, most powerful and most loving. Obtain for me the grace which I ask, if it be the will of God.

May you be blessed, little Thérèse, for all the good which you have done for us and which you wish to do for us until the end of the world.

May you be blessed and thanked a thousand times for allowing us to touch in this way the goodness and mercy of our God!

Amen.

 # PRAYER TO ST. RITA

O Saint Rita, saint who intercede for what seems impossible to change and advocate of hopeless cases, I turn to you, burdened by the weight of my trial.

Free my poor heart from the worry which oppresses it and give peace to my broken spirit.

You who were chosen by God to be the advocate of hopeless cases, obtain for me the grace which I ask of you...

(Here we express our intention)

Should I be the only one not to experience the efficacy of your powerful intercession?

If my sins be an obstacle to the granting of my dearest prayers, obtain for me the grace of sincere repentance and forgiveness by means of a good confession.

Whatever may happen, do not allow me to continue to live in such tremendous suffering. Take pity on me!

O Lord, look at the hope which I have placed in you!

Hear St. Rita who intercedes for us who are without hope because of our trials and tribulations. Hear her once again and in this way, manifest your mercy in us, your children.

THE PLENARY INDULGENCE OF ASSISI

THE PLENARY INDULGENCE OF ASSISI

One night, in the year 1216, St. Francis was immersed in prayer and contemplation in the little church of Porziuncola, Assisi, in central Italy, when suddenly, a dazzling light flooded the
church, and Christ appeared above the altar, clothed in light, and beside him, His most holy Mother, surrounded by a multitude of angels. Francis adored the Lord in silence, with his face to the ground!

Our Lord asked him what he deisred for the salvation of souls.

St. Francis' reply was immediate:

"Most Holy Father, although I am a miserable sinner, I beseech you to grant full and generous forgiveness to all who visit this church, having repented and confessed, with complete remission of all their sins".

"What you ask is great, O Brother Francis," answered the Lord, "but you are worthy of greater things, and greater things you shall have.

Therefore, I accept your prayer, but on condition that you ask this indulgence on my behalf of my vicar on earth."

Francis went immediately before his Holiness Pope Honorius III, who was staying at nearby Perugia at that time, and described the vision in with his characteristic sincerity and simplicity.

The Pope listened to him attentively and, after some hesitation, gave his approval. "For how many years do you want this indulgence?" Francis immediately replied, "Holy Father, I do not ask for years, but for souls", and happily made his way to the door. The Pontiff called him back, asking, *"Why do you require no document?"* *"Holy Father,"* Francis answered, *"for me your word is sufficient! If this indulgence is of God's making He shall take care of manifesting his work; I have no need of any document, the charter must be the Most Holy Virgin Mary, Christ shall be the solicitor and the Angels the witenesses."*

Some days later, Francis said to the assembly gathered at Porziuncola, with tears in his eyes, *"My brothers, I want to send you all to Para-dise!"*

From midnight of the 1st of August to midnight of the following day, or, with the consent of the Ordinary, on the preceding or the following Sunday (starting from midday on Saturday to midnight on Sunday), we can gain, once only, the plenary indulgence of Porziuncola or the "Pardon of Assisi".

In order to avail of this great manifestation of God's mercy, we should satisfy the following conditions:

1. A visit to a parish church or a Franciscan church (or to another church which can grant   the indulgence) within the prescribed time where the Our Father and the Creed are to be recited;
2. The Sacrament of Reconciliation should be received during this time;
3. One should receive Holy Communion.
4. One should pray for the intentions of our Holy Father the Pope (an Our Father, a Hail Mary and a Glory Be, or other suitable prayers);
5. The disposition of one's soul must be such as to exclude every attachment to sin, even venial.

The Indulgence may also be applied to the souls of the deceased.

Prayer of St. Francis of Assisi

We could not mention St. Francis without publishing this prayer for peace. It is a prayer which is known throughout the world and yet its popularity makes it no less meaningful. Indeed, its beautiful words are perhaps even more appropriate in these times when the world is so needful of peace than when it was first composed many centuries ago. May it continue to touch the hearts of all people now and in time to come.

Lord, make me an instrument of your peace:
where there is hatred let me sow love,
where there is injury let me sow pardon,
where there is doubt let me sow faith,
where there is despair let me give hope,
where there is darkness let me give light,
where there is sadness let me give joy.

O Divine Master, grant that I may
not try to be comforted but to comfort,
not try to be understood but to understand,
not try to be loved but to love;
Because it is in giving that we receive,
it is in forgiving that we are forgiven,
and it is in dying that we are born to eternal life.

LITANY OF THE SAINTS

The purpose of the following litany is to inoke Christ and the saints for our needs and requests. The literary expression of the Litany may vary however, not only from one region to another, but even within the community itself. For this reason several forms are suggested for various parts of the litany, which can be integrated either by introducing the name of the patron saint of a particular church, community or institute (for example, the saint to whom the Church is dedicated or the founder of a particular institute) or by adding the introduction of particular invocations, taking into account the various needs and circumstances of the assembly. Such an adaptation of the Litany may be used by a bishop who wishes to establish a common scheme for a particular diocese. It may also be adapted by a parish priest or by the priest presiding at the celebration in accordance with local tradition. The general scheme, however, must remain as follows, without omitting the general invocations.

Lord, have mercy.

Lord, have mercy.

Christ, have mercy.

Christ, have mercy.

Lord, have mercy

Lord, have mercy.

God the Father, our Creator,

Have mercy on us.

God the Son, our Redeemer,   ”

God the Holy Spirit, our Sanctifier,   ”

Holy Trinity, one God and Lord,   ”

2. INVOCATIONS OF THE SAINTS

Holy Mary,	**Pray for us.**
Holy Mother of God,	"
Holy Virgin of Virgins,	"
Saint Michael the Archangel,	"
Saint Gabriel,	"
Saint Raphael,	"
Holy angels of God,	"

PATRIARCHS AND PROPHETS

Abraham, our father in faith,	"
David, leader of God's people,	"
Saint John the Baptist,	"
All holy patriarchs and prophets,	"

APOSTLES AND DISCIPLES

Saint Peter and Saint Paul,	"
Saint Andrew,	"
Saint James and Saint John,	"
Saint Thomas,	"
Saint Philip and Saint James,	"
Saint Bartholomew,	"
Saint Matthew,	"

Saint Simon and Saint Jude,	**Pray for us.**
Saint Matthias,	,,
Saint Luke,	,,
Saint Mark,	,,
Saint Barnabas,	,,
Saint Mary Magdalene,	,,
All holy disciples of the Lord,	,,

MARTYRS

Saint Stephen,	,,
Saint Ignatius of Antioch,	,,
Saint Polycarp,	,,
Saint Justin,	,,
Saint Lawrence,	,,
Saint Cyprian,	,,
Saint Boniface,	,,
Saint Stanislaus,	,,
Saint Thomas à Becket,	,,
Saint John Fisher and Saint Thomas More,	,,
Saint Paul Miki,	,,
Saint John de Brébeuf and Saint Isaac Jogues,	,,
Saint Peter Chanel,	,,
Saint Charles Lwang,	,,

Saint Perpetua and Saint Felicity,	**Pray for us.**
Saint Agnes,	"
Saint Maria Goretti,	"
All holy martyrs of Christ,	"

BISHOPS AND DOCTORS OF THE CHURCH

Saint Leo and Saint Gregory,	"
Saint Ambrose,	"
Saint Jerome,	"
Saint Augustine,	"
Saint Athanasius,	"
Saint Basil and Saint Gregory Nazianzen,	"
Saint John Chrysostom,	"
Saint Martin,	"
Saint Patrick,	"
Saint Cyril and Saint Methodius,	"
Saint Charles of Borromeo,	"
Saint Francis de Sales,	"
Saint Pius X,	"

PRIESTS AND RELIGIOUS

Saint Anthony,	"
Saint Benedict,	"
Saint Bernard,	"

Saint Francis,	**Pray for us.**
Saint Dominic,	"
Saint Thomas of Aquinas,	"
Saint Ignatius of Loyola,	"
Saint Francis Xavier,	"
Saint Vincent de Paul,	"
Saint John Vianney,	"
Saint John Bosco,	"
Saint Catherine of Siena,	"
Saint Teresa of the Child Jesus,	"
Saint Rose of Lima,	"

LAY PEOPLE

Saint Louis,	"
Saint Monica,	"
Saint Elizabeth of Hungary,	"

(Other saints may be included here).

All holy men and women, "

3. INVOCATIONS TO CHRIST

Lord, be merciful,

Lord, save your people.

From all evil,   "

From every sin,   "

From Satan's power,   "

At the moment of death,   "

From everlasting death,   "

On the day of judgment,   "

By your coming as man,   "

By your suffering and cross,   "

By your death and rising to new life,   "

By your return in glory to the Father,   "

By your gift of the Holy Spirit,   "

By your coming again in glory,   "

By merciful to us sinners,   "

Christ, son of the living God,

Have mercy on us.

You who came into the world,   "

You who hung on the cross,   "

You who accepted death for us,   "

You who were laid in the sepulchre,   "

You who descended into hell,   "

You who rose from the dead,

Have mercy on us.

You who ascended into heaven,   "

You who sent your Spirit upon the Apostles,   "

You who sit at the right hand of God,   "

You who will come to judge the living
and the dead,   "

4. REQUESTS FOR VARIOUS NEEDS

Be merciful to us sinners;

Lord, hear our prayer.

Lead us to true conversion;   "

Bless this assembly consecrated to you;   "

Recompense those who have done good;   "

Give us the fruits of the earth and of our labour; "

Give us your mercy;   "

Raise our hearts to the desire of heaven;   "

Save us with all our brothers and sisters
from eternal death;   "

Grant eternal rest to the faithful departed;   "

Free humanity from hunger, from war
and from all disasters;   "

Grant justice and peace to the world;   "

Obligatory invocations:

Comfort and enlighten your holy Church;

Lord, hear our prayer.

Protect the Pope, the bishops, the clergy
and all ministers of the Gospel; ,,

Send new labourers into your harvest; ,,

Give unity in faith to all Christians; ,,

Lead all people to the truth of the Gospel; ,,

To be added on every occasion:

Protect our Church (N.) and our Bishop (N.); ,,

Be present in every home and family; ,,

Sustain and comfort the elderly with
the grace of your Spirit; ,,

Grant that the youth may grow
in your friendship; ,,

Enlighten rulers and governors with
your wisdom; ,,

Defend those who are persecuted
in the cause of right; ,,

Restore to the exiled their native land; ,,

Comfort our sick and suffering brothers
and sisters; ,,

Grant the joy of your kingdom
to all the deceased; ,,

5. CONCLUSION

Christ, hear us.

Christ, hear us.

Lord Jesus, hear our prayer.

Lord Jesus, hear our prayer.

Lamb of God, who take away the sins
of the world,

Have mercy on us.

Let us pray.
O God, our refuge and strength, accept the humble prayer of our Church; you, who fill us with filial trust in your Fatherly love, grant that we may obtain what we faithfully ask of you.
Through Christ, our Lord. **Amen.**

If the Litany is recited for a dying person, special mention may be made of his or her patron saints or those of the family and of the parish, and the following invocations may be added before the conclusion:

Bring N. to eternal life, first promised
to him (her) in Baptism,

Lord, hear our prayer.

Raise N. on the last day, for he (she) has
eaten the Bread of life,   ”

Let N. share in your glory, for he (she) has
shared in your suffering and death;   ”

INDEX

GENERAL
INDEX

Part One
EVERYDAY PRAYERS

Part Two
THE MOST HOLY TRINITY

Part Three
THE FATHER

Part Five
THE HOLY SPIRIT

Part Six
THE MOTHER OF GOD

Part Seven
THE HOLY FAMILY

Part Eight
THE ANGELS

Part Nine
THE SAINTS

SHALOM
p u b l i s h i n g

St. Joseph   Totus Totus   St. Michael the Archangel

The aim of this catalogue is to inform the reader of a considerable number of books, apart from those published by SHALOM publishing house (Catholic and Marian editors), which seek to deepen our knowledge of the Christian Faith, they are texts which have been selected under the guidance of religious people who are particularly competent in this field. Among these books, some of which are written by contemporary authors who discuss problems and issues of current interest, you will also find some writings of various saints and Fathers of the Church. As regards the books which are published by SHALOM editing house, it is important to note that they are intended to promote prayer among the largest volume of readers possible and to re-establish the devotion of the Eucharist, which must be central to our lives, as the first Christians taught: "they were devoted to the teachings of the apostles and the union of brotherhood, to the breaking of the bread and to prayer" (Acts of the apostles 2,42). In fact it is only on returning to a state of pureness and on looking at the roots of the first Christian teachings and in following the example and in the footsteps of the first Christian Communities, that each believer can have an important role in the modern world, it is only in this way that we can rediscover the courage within ourselves to "uplift the world" and become members of "the body of Christ": the church which imitates its leader, is: "the ruin and the resurrection of many, a sign of contradiction" (Luke 2,34). In order to fulfil this its aim, Shalom Editing House decided to become a non-profit organisation. This initiative was developed in order to partake in the triumph of the Immaculate Heart of Mary, with the certainty of being able to serve the Kingdom of God, participating in the faith and the obedience of Our Lady, Handmaid and Mother of the Lord. During these difficult times, when our faith in the one Church of Christ is constantly being put to the test, it is essential that we realise that part of our Christian experience is that we must live under the authority of Peter's successor (Pope John Paul II), in obedience to and in communion with him, encouraged and guided by Mary.

"Pray the Rosary every day: pray together

| Format cm. 12 x 19 |
| No of pages 256 |
| **Price € 4,00** |

Collana:
The Mother of God

A book by Father Slavko Barbaric OFM

code 8118

"Today I would like to propose to all Christian families to pray the rosary, so that they may experience the beauty of stopping for a moment in order to meditate together with Mary, the joyful, sorrowful and glorious mysteries of our redemption, and in this way sanctify the joyful moments and the difficult moments of our everyday lives. Praying together helps the family to be more united, peaceful and faithful to the gospel. Mary, Queen of the Holy Rosary, be our teacher, and guide all families in this prayer, which is particularly dear to me.

Reciting the Rosary, means learning from Mary how to live the needs of the Christian Faith in a deep and full way. When reciting the Rosary, we contemplate Christ from a privileged position, that is from the same position as Mary, His Mother. Let us meditate therefore on the mysteries of life, on the passion and the resurrection of the Lord with the eyes and with the heart of she who was nearest to her Son.

Pope John Paul II

The secret of Mary

Format cm. 10 x 14	
No of pages 128	
Price € 3,00	

Collana:
The Mother of God

A book by Saint Louis-Marie de Montfort

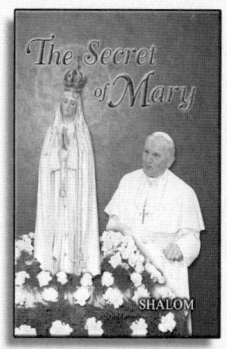

codice 8263

"For me, St. Louis Marie de Montfort is a significant person of reference, who has enlightened me at important moments of life… By relating the Mother of Christ to the Trinitarian mystery, Montfort helped me to understand that the Virgin belongs to the plan of salvation, by the Father's will, as Mother of the Incarnate Word, who was conceived by Her through the power of the Holy Spirit. In Grignion de Montfort's vision, in fact, Trinitarian faith totally permeates his prayers to Mary: (…) Mary is contemplated as "the mountain of God" (n. 25), the place of holiness that lifts us up to God and transforms us in Christ".

John Paul II

True Devotion to Mary

Formato cm. 12 x 19
Pagine 320
Prezzo € 5,00

Collana:
The Mother of God

I often remember a little book with the blue cover, dirty of soda.... When I used to work by the Solvay, I always brought that book with me, together with a piece of bread. For the afternoon and night-shifts. During the morning-shift it was difficult to read, while during the afternoon I could read that little book. Its title was "True devotion to Mary".

John Paul II

codice 8143

The secret of the Rosary

Formato cm. 12 x 19
Pagine 256
Prezzo € 5,00

Collana:
The Mother of God

After having been proclaimed the Year of the Rosary by John Paul II and after the Apostolic Letter, Rosarium Virginis Mariae, it acquires particular meaning to know this work of St. Louis Marie de Montfort, that the Pope defines "precious". The "Good Father of Montfort", missionary of the common people, narrates the miracles and the conversion obtained through the recitation of the Holy Rosary. He gives comments to the Our Father and the Hail Mary in a simple yet rich and profound way.

codice 8289

Jesus, I trust in You!

Format cm. 12 x 19

No of pages 256

Price € 4,00

Collana:
The Son

A book which is adapted from the diary of **St. Faustina Kowalska** and put together by the **congregation of the Sisters of the Blessed Virgin Mary of mercy**, it proposes the following:

- Forms of devotion of Divine Mercy
- The Feast of Divine Mercy
- Novena
- Rosary
- The hour of Mercy
- Via Crucis, Holy Rosary
- The diffusion of the devotion of Divine Mercy
- Prayers and various litanies

codice 8131

"Dearest Brothers and Sisters, I urge you to always confide in the merciful love of God, which revealed itself in Jesus Christ, dead and risen for our salvation. The personal experience of this love should make each of us, in turn, become witnesses of charity towards our Brothers. Say Sister Faustina's short yet beautiful prayer: "Jesus, I trust in you!"

(Pope John Paul II)

Besides its presentation of the content and the form of the message of devotion for Divine Mercy, this book has a particular and perhaps unique characteristic: that of supplying us with the prayers of Sister Faustina and therefore allowing us to turn towards God with the same warmth, intimacy and love as she had for Him, she whose heart was in love with God and spoke with Him.

The wonderful secret of the Souls in Purgatory

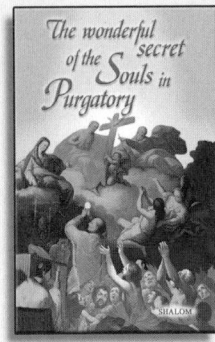

Format cm. 11 x 17
No of pages 256
Price € 4,00

Collana:
Souls of Purgatory

Maria Simma, who is 85 year of age, through a special gift of God, has been visited by souls in Purgatory for over 50 years. What do these souls tell her? The experiences reported in this book, collected by Sister Emmanuel directly from Maria Simma, give us much to ponder about; and perhaps they may help some people to change their attitudes and habits in life and start living in a different manner, according to God's desire...

codice 8153

A Rosary for the Souls of Priests suffering in Purgatory

Formato cm. 10 x 14
Pagine 32
Prezzo € 1,50

Collana:
Souls of Purgatory

"Everything that I was unable to obtain from the Saints, without fail, I obtained it by means of the intercession of the Holy Souls of Purgatory".
St. Teresa d'Avila
Not one of us has even the faintest idea of the extent of suffering endured in Purgatory. Among these souls however, souls who are condemned to the prison of Divine Justice, God as a special predilection for the souls of priests, whom he regards as the "pupil of his eyes".

codice 8260